RENEWALS 458-4574

DATE DUE

Locating Home

Locating Home

India's Hyderabadis Abroad

KAREN ISAKSEN LEONARD

Stanford University Press
Stanford, California
2007

Stanford University Press
Stanford, California

Printed in the United States of America on acid-free, archival-quality paper

Library of Congress Cataloging-in-Publication Data

Leonard, Karen Isaksen, 1939–
Locating home : India's Hyderabadis abroad / Karen Isaksen Leonard.
    p. cm.
Includes bibliographical references and index.
ISBN-13: 978-0-8047-5442-2 (alk. paper)
    1. East Indian diaspora.   2. East Indians—Foreign countries.
3. East Indians—India—Hyderabad.   I. Title.
    DS432.5.L46   2007
    304.80954'84—dc22
                                                    2006017977

Typeset by Newgen–Austin in 10.5/12.5 Bembo

Contents

List of Maps and Illustrations

My first acquaintance with Hyderabad city was not particularly auspicious. I spent my senior year at the University of Wisconsin, Madison, in India, as a "casual student" in Miranda House, a women's college at the University of Delhi. That was in 1961–1962, and after the Indian school year ended in April, I and the other two women students on the Wisconsin program set off for a month of travel in India before heading home. We took the train from Delhi to Madras, and it stopped midway in Hyderabad, on the high Deccan plateau. We got off for a night's sleep and there at the railway station was Nampally Serai, a Mughal-style inn for travelers evoking the old princely state of the Nizams (rulers) of Hyderabad. We booked a room for three rupees four annas (less than a dollar), and being young and thrifty, we refused to spend an extra eight annas for a fan. Little did we know how hot the night would be! Even pulling our beds out into the courtyard did not save us from the smothering, punishing heat. We were glad to get on the train to Madras the next morning.

Despite this unpromising introduction to the place, I returned five years later as a graduate student in history, doing my dissertation research on a particular caste associated with the Nizam of Hyderabad's provincial Mughal administration. The Kayasths of Hyderabad, high caste Hindus from North India and Rajasthan, worked at all levels of that administration, and, like the Kayasths, who were famous for their proficiency in the Persian and Urdu languages, I learned Persian and Urdu as I learned their history and that of Hyderabad State. My husband, also a history graduate student, had learned the Telugu language of coastal Andhra for his study of social reform movements in adjacent, formerly British, India. We liked living in Hyderabad city and made many friends there.

I have many, many people to thank, as the present study draws on over forty years of contact with the city and its residents. I start with other historians of Hyderabad, people from whom I have learned much in discussions and reading over the years. Drs. H. K. Sherwani, Sarojini Regani,

Muhammad Khalidi, Vasant Bawa, and Ziauddin Ahmed Shakeb were my earliest teachers, along with scholars among the Kayasths, particularly Roy Mahboob Narayan, Professor Mahender Raj Suxena, Gurucharan Das Saxena, Dharminder Pershad Srivastava, Kunj Behari Lal, and Hakim Vicerai. Other historians with whom I became acquainted, professional and amateur alike, include Rajendra Prasad, Narendra Luther, Rahimuddin Kemal, Asha Dua, and Bilkiz Alladin. S. A. Saleem selected and translated many articles from the Urdu newspaper *Siyasat* for me, and Digamber Rao also helped with translations. Dr. M. A. Muttalib helped me formulate, administer, and analyze a questionnaire at one point. I thank also the Hyderabadis who gave me Urdu and English articles and poems that they had written or found meaningful, people too numerous to list here.

Hyderabadis and others read drafts of chapters in which they were particularly expert or interested, although I am, of course, responsible for all errors of fact or interpretation. I thank the following for discussions and corrections: Dr. Omar Khalidi, Dr. Theodore Wright Jr., M. Farooq Ali Osmani, Moazzam Sheikh, Aziz Ahmed, Aziz and Habiba Razvi, Junaid Razvi, Prince Muffakham Jah, Jimmy Adams, Amina Ahmed, Mohamed Waseem, Christopher Robins, Dr. Riaz Hassan, Dr. Geoffrey Oddie, Dr. Ghaffar Mughal, Syed Zaidi, Dr. Samuel McCulloch, Dr. Raja Jayaraman, Dr. Supriya Singh, Kamala Rajah, Bruce Cox, Dennis Fallon, Betty Young, Emile Cox, Kerry Edwards, Ernest Adams, Dick Schoeffer, Joyce Corfield, Dr. Kenneth McPherson, Allaine Cerwonka, Madeline Coopsammy, Dr. Syed Ali, Dr. Syed Sirajuddin, Dr.Pnina Werbner, Drs. William and Helen Mulder, and Aziz Masood.

Lalitha and Chandrakant Gir hosted me several times in Hyderabad as I did research. I owe them special thanks for their generous assistance. Others who helped with hospitality and arrangements include Salim Beg in Lahore, Aziz Ahmed in London, Mirza Shamsher Ali Beg and Parveen and Shahid Ali Mirza in Kuwait, Anees and Maqsood Ali and Sharafat and Sultana Walajahi in Dubai, Zehra and Desh Bandhu in Toronto, and, in Australia, Geoffrey and Nola Oddie, Raja and Mythili Jayaraman, Supriya Singh, Rashmi and Judith Desai, Barney and Heather Devlin, Peter Reeves, and Kenneth McPherson.

Sources for multisite research projects are hard to find, and I am grateful to the Committee on American Overseas Research Centers, the Fulbright Foundation, the University of California, Irvine, and the Nizam's Charitable Trust for funding parts of the research. I thank also the Pemberley International Scholarly Centre of Sri Lanka for my brief stay as a resident scholar there. Special thanks to Narendra Luther, Shehbaz Safrani, Christopher Butt, Dilip Gir, and Syeda Khundkar for the photographs they supplied.

My editor at Stanford University Press, Kate Wahl, was extremely efficient and supportive throughout, and the comments of the outside readers of the manuscript proved insightful and useful. Kenneth Fox, computer consultant extraordinaire, provided indispensable help as I struggled to produce the book. Finally, I thank my children, Samuel Leonard and Sarah Olson, both of whom recently returned to Hyderabad as adults. Sam brought his spouse, Kimberly Wong, and Sarah her child, Evan Weiss, and all of them now share my affection for the city. Sarah's final incisive reading of the manuscript was absolutely invaluable.

TRANSLITERATION AND TRANSLATION PRACTICES

For Urdu, Persian, and Arabic words, I have generally followed John T. Platts, *A Dictionary of Urdu, Classical Hindi, and English* (London: Oxford University Press, 1960) but have chosen not to use diacritical marks. Those who know the words will not miss them and others will not care. Words are defined the first time they are used and there is a glossary. To save space in a long manuscript, I have translated Urdu article titles into English in the bibliography rather than give the Urdu original followed by an English translation.

Locating Home

CHAPTER 1

Starting Points

THIS STUDY BEGAN in 1990 in Los Angeles, when a notice in California's Indian ethnic newspaper, *India-West*, caught my eye: the Hyderabad Deccan Association of California was celebrating Hyderabad city's 400th anniversary. I attended that celebration at a local community center along with 1,000 Hyderabadis—I had had no idea there were that many Hyderabadis in the Los Angeles area. The evening of festive Hyderabadi food, Urdu speeches and poetry, and gorgeous Hyderabadi fashions made me long to return to my roots in Indian and Hyderabadi history after almost a decade of working on other topics, and I resolved to study Hyderabadis abroad to see why they were leaving their homeland and relocating elsewhere. I realized the members of my social network in Hyderabad would be good resources, as their children were among those emigrating.

When I first worked in Hyderabad in the 1960s, people from there rarely moved out. Hyderabadis used to fend off non-*mulkis* (noncountrymen or outsiders), people coming from Madras and North India. They themselves seldom left Hyderabad even for a short time, and when they did, people wept at the railway station; a daughter married off to Lucknow seemed to be going far, far away. By 1990, however, it was clear that many people from Hyderabad lived in the United States. People in their fifties still were not coming to this country, but their children were moving abroad for education, work, and, all too often from a parent's point of view, settlement. I had not really noticed these movements, nor had I thought of them as a collective phenomenon until the Los Angeles Hyderabadi celebration brought them home to me very dramatically.

Questions, Theories, and Themes

Studies of people in diaspora focus on processes of migration, resettlement, and continuing relationships with the place of origin. The word *diaspora* was traditionally used rather narrowly to designate the Jewish diaspora from Palestine, but current usage has expanded that model to cover other, larger dispersions, such as movements of Chinese and South Asian people beyond their homelands. Now almost any segment of a people living outside its homeland can be termed *diasporic*, and the Hyderabadi diaspora might best be thought of as a diaspora within the South Asian diaspora. Hyderabad was the only Mughal successor state left in India after 1858,[1] and Hyderabadis represent a kind of city-state: descendants and carriers within South Asia of the Indo-Muslim culture firmly established under India's medieval Mughal empire.

To follow emigrants from Hyderabad who settled in seven contrasting sites around the world, I had to look carefully at the special, local characteristics of their single point of origin and then at each site abroad. This also meant noticing, in each site, the numerous cross-references to people and events in other sites. What could one learn about diasporic processes and outcomes from the migrating Hyderabadis? What do their experiences contribute to the growing literature on diasporas, globalization, transnationalism, and cosmopolitanism?

Even though I am using the term *diaspora* and the literature on diasporas, one can argue even at the outset that Hyderabadis do not quite fit the definition of a diasporic community. If the six characteristics commonly proposed to define diasporic communities[2] are applied to them, Hyderabadis, like other South Asians, can clearly be seen to diverge from the definition in significant ways. The six characteristics are these: (1) members or their ancestors should have been dispersed from a center to two or more regions; (2) members retain a collective memory of the original homeland; (3) they believe that they are not and perhaps cannot be fully accepted by the host society; (4) they regard the homeland as the true home to which they or their descendants should eventually return; (5) they are committed to the maintenance or restoration of the homeland; and (6) they continue to relate to that homeland and to define their collective consciousness importantly by that relationship.

The experience of most Hyderabadi (and South Asian) immigrants was not one of being dispersed from their homelands but of leaving voluntarily. Perhaps Muslims were leaving India and *muhajirs* (Muslims who moved to Pakistan from India after partition in 1947, Hyderabadis among them) were leaving Pakistan disproportionately.[3] Although the Hyderabadi immigrants did retain collective memories of their homeland and sometimes organized themselves abroad on that basis, most recognized the "myth of return" as indeed a myth. Rather than commit themselves or their children to returning to Hyderabad, most Hyderabadi immigrants were settling into their new homes and finding various degrees of acceptance.

Three theoretical issues raised in the literature on diasporas are of particular interest: identity and the politics of identity; the politics and culture of citizenship; and the distinctions among globalization, cosmopolitanism, and transnationalism. As Stuart Hall remarked, we are no longer using the word *identity* to denote something relatively fixed by historical association or by ancestral and inherited position. Yet Hall hesitated to go to the opposite extreme, to consider identities so flexible, fluid, unpredictable, and performative as to be almost beyond constraints; he suggested the need for a third way of talking about identities.[4] Writing about Afro-Caribbean migrant identity and its mobilization in the United Kingdom (UK), he invoked the two perspectives commonly used by social scientists: the outside perspective, how people are seen by others, and the inside perspective, how people see themselves.

Identities may start with the past, with the way people give an account of who they are, but identities are just as importantly about where people are going.[5] This orientation to the future raises the issue of citizenship. Pnina Werbner argues that[6]

> [rather than being] an artificial construct of modernity, citizenship as a subjectivity is deeply dialogical, encapsulating specific, historically inflected, cultural and social assumptions about similarity and difference. The negotiation of these may generate at different times and places quite different sets of practices, institutional arrangements, modes of social interaction and future orientations. This is especially so because, unlike nationalism which grounds itself in a mythical past, citizenship raises its eyes towards the future. . . . [I]ts politics are aspirational. . . . [D]iscourses of citizenship constitute horizons of possibility. . . . [Citizenship is] always locally embedded in the particularities of culture, place and history.

Certainly emigrants from the former Hyderabad State carried with them clearly formulated ideas about citizenship in that state. They concerned themselves with orientations to the future that involved choices of citizenship. Citizenship, Werbner pointed out, involved matters of status in a community, matters of identity and difference. The countries to which Hyderabadis emigrated varied in terms of the accessibility and meaningfulness of citizenship and the mediations of citizenship by state projects of multiculturalism.

Finally, ideas about identity and citizenship interact with ideas about globalization, transnationalism, and cosmopolitanism in ways that illuminate the contrasting experiences of these emigrants. Narratives of transnationalism rest upon and often overlap with stories of globalization; it is

sometimes hard to separate the two. Many if not most scholars of transnational migrants view them as members of the proletariat,[7] even those
employing "romantic" definitions of transnationalism and transmigrants.
They talk easily about the development of social fields linking the countries of origin and settlement, connections that are on the whole viewed
positively as "maintained, reinforced, and . . . vital and growing" and
which enable the creation of "fluid and multiple identities grounded both
in their society of origin and in the host societies."[8] Even writers who draw
attention to the challenges and contradictions of the migrant experience
talk of "cultural bifocality, a capacity to see the world alternately through
quite different kinds of lenses" and of "multiple national loyalties."[9] Some
connect transnationalism firmly to postnationality, postulating that transmigrants will have "loyalty to a nonterritorial transnation first."[10] In these
discussions, immigrants seem to have considerable agency and are able to
maximize their resources in more than one society.

Darker views of transnationalism emphasize its rooting in global capitalism, in globalization. These scholars see the collapse of spatial and national barriers quite differently, as provoking "an increasing sense of nationalism and localism." This view maintains that the "small-scale and
finely graded differences between the qualities of places (their labor supply,
their infrastructures and political receptivity, their resource mixes, their
market niches, and so on) become more important because multinational
capital is in a better position to exploit them."[11] Here the immigrants are
granted little agency; they are used as resources in the international political economy.

Aihwa Ong's innovative concept of flexible citizenship usefully grants
immigrants agency. She proposes *transnationality* as a term that better captures the cultural specificities of global processes and the multiple uses and
conceptions of culture,[12] but her overriding emphasis on state powers and
cultural logics assumes rather more unified actors at both levels than my
ethnographic material suggests. However, her interest in non-Western actors is similar to mine. Most narratives of globalization are firmly anchored
in Western culture, implicitly assuming the ascendance of the liberal
nation-state. Positioning oneself outside the dominant theoretical constructions, viewing globalization and transnationalism from less familiar
standpoints—for example, those of Hyderabad's declining Indo-Muslim
state, Pakistan, or the Gulf states of the Middle East—should enable us to
see more diverse and complex patterns of interaction for individuals and
groups within and across the boundaries of nation-states.

I am also interested in an ongoing scholarly discussion distinguishing
between cosmopolitan and transnational behaviors and attitudes. In an

ongoing debate about class and global subjectivity, Werbner defines cosmopolitans as people who familiarize themselves with other cultures and know how to move easily between cultures; she defines transnationals as people who, while moving, build encapsulated cultural worlds around themselves—most typically, worlds circumscribed by religious or family ties.[13] These distinctions proved highly relevant to Hyderabadi identity politics and helped distinguish among Hyderabadi immigrants in different sites.

Whereas the question posed at the outset of the research concerned what one could learn about diasporas from the migrating Hyderabadis, another question arose in the course of the research. Hyderabadis abroad reflected so often and so seriously on the homeland left behind that it became essential to ask what one could learn about old Hyderabad from the diaspora. The novelist Raja Rao[14] said, "What links the overseas Indians is the idea of India,"[15] suggesting that diasporic communities retain collective memories of the homeland, continue to relate to the homeland, and define themselves primarily with reference to it. In fact, the Hyderabadis abroad had both more and less in common than ideas: I found that although their ideas of the homeland often diverged sharply, people participated together in both formal and informal networks. Just as memories of old Hyderabad differed according to placement in that past society, people's views of the past were used to place themselves in the new locations.

Issues of history and memory, a history always being remembered, rejected, or reconstituted by people removed from it in both time and space, are taken up in some detail throughout this book, albeit often in the endnotes. People change places, places change people, and competing visions of the past have important bearings on the future of both places and people. Whereas the economic forces of globalization strongly affect social and cultural domains, "anthropology has repeatedly focused not only on the pervasiveness of power, but on the power of culture."[16] These revisionings of the Hyderabadi homeland not only shape the futures of Hyderabadi immigrants but tell us something meaningful about the past.

This work of social history explores movement and memory, particularly the constitution and use of memories to claim old and new homelands. Social memory is a valuable source of knowledge, not to be devalued in favor of the textual paradigm of knowledge.[17] Collecting event narratives and life stories is not an exercise in "salvage ethnography" or nostalgia; rather, it evidences a painful, sometimes problematic, process of identity construction in new sites. People talked about the past and its meaningfulness in the present and wanted their names to be used, following not anthropological but historical convention.

James Clifford talks about people migrating, "changed by their travel but marked by places of origin, by peculiar allegiances and alienations."[18] These markings are various, individual, and historically contingent. Certainly migrants take with them "peculiar allegiances and alienations" associated with Hyderabad, their place of origin, but they are equally subject to changes brought about by travel. The markings of old Hyderabad are remembered, rejected, or reinvented to suit the migrants' new contexts, as their destinations significantly shape migrant identities.

Hyderabad city and the former Hyderabad State are my starting points for an exploration of migration, settlement, and social memories. A major historical theme in Hyderabadi history has been the relationship between indigenous people and immigrants, natives and newcomers. The definitions and occupants of these categories have changed over time. In the Deccan, that broad plateau in southern central India, the medieval terms were *Dakhni* and *afaqi*, more recently, *mulkis* and non-*mulkis*. The native-newcomer theme has shaped all of India's history:

> The Indian identity all through its recorded history has been shaped by the interaction of myriad immigrating cultures which readapted and integrated themselves with the new milieu without losing their respective individualities so that the end product was a colourful social mosaic rather than a dull homogenised mass.[19]

Furthermore, as the native-newcomer theme suggests, people have moved about for centuries in South Asia, leaving old homelands and finding new ones. I argue in the conclusion, following Sanjay Srivastava, that Hyderabadis like other South Asians attach "as much, if not greater, importance to the relationship between humans as an aspect of belonging and attachment rather than to fixed places, the ancestral village, or one's 'native place.'"[20] The native-newcomer theme has obvious relevance not only to Hyderabadi and Indian history but also to contemporary world patterns of migration and modern notions of citizenship.

The theme of "structures of feeling," following Raymond Williams,[21] proved highly relevant. Hyderabad persisted as a stronghold of Indo-Muslim culture and the Urdu language in an India increasingly influenced by British colonial culture and the English language. This aspect of Hyderabadi identity must be appreciated even as it passes from the contemporary scene, and it is clear in the interviews and emphasized in the conclusion. A. K. Ramanujan wrote, "Sanskrit is an urban-centered but non-regional language, as Urdu later was and English is now,"[22] and he postulated three successive hegemonic cultures in South Asia, ones that are, crucially, based not in linguistic regions but in cities. Some lamented the passing of the vital early Sanskritic Indian civilization,[23] whereas others welcomed the next phase of generative civilization, that begun by earlier Muslim rulers and solidly established by the Mughals. In the Indian context, this change is not loss but difference, with new migrations bringing Persian and eventually Urdu urban culture. Urdu is written in Perso-Arabic script and combines the grammatical structure of Sanskrit with a primarily Persian literary vocabulary. Just as Brahmanical and Buddhist civilization spread from the cities in ancient South Asia, Indo-Muslim civilization spread from the cities of medieval South Asia, and its strong links to Central Asia, Iran, the Middle East and East Africa added further layers to Indian civilization.

The East India Company came to India in the mid-eighteenth century and soon exercised control over both trade and territory, defeating European and Indian competitors. British colonialism constructed new trade and political connections and gradually shifted the subcontinent to the cultural hegemony of English. The period of English official use for administrative and educational purposes by the colonial rulers was relatively short, about one hundred years (the Company continued to use Persian until 1830). However, the impact of English proved decisive, although it was resisted in Hyderabad and other large native states; Hyderabad remained an outpost of Indo-Muslim civilization into the mid-twentieth century. Now English, as an urban-centered international language and "structure of feeling," engages Hyderabadis and other South Asians in an increasingly global economy and society.

Methods and Scope

This multisite ethnography involved seven national settings: Pakistan, the UK, Australia, Canada, the United States, and two Gulf states of the Middle East, Kuwait and the United Arab Emirates (UAE). I spent time in each of the major sites. The research took a decade. The research is also comparative in another way, as those who consider themselves Hyderabadi come from a wide range of class, caste, religious, and linguistic backgrounds and from different generations. In most cases this emigration dated from the late 1960s, so the first-generation immigrants were very much alive and dominated the interviews. The second generation was just coming of age, just embarking on careers and marriages. Whereas I had less unsupervised access to members of the second generation, their voices test some widely held notions about diasporas and transnationalism.

The research showed the limits of one of its founding assumptions, namely, that I was tracing a cohesive cultural formation. Although recognizing that the designation "Hyderabadi" inaccurately projected "a group of people as a unified actor," as Richard Handler puts it,[24] I nonetheless found it useful to follow self-identified "Hyderabadis" for this project. In tracing the movements of these subjects, I imputed to them "an initial, baseline conceptual identity that turns out to be contingent and malleable as one traces it."[25] This proved true, as no single sense of Hyderabadi citizenship and culture was being reproduced or produced in new locales. The revisionings of old Hyderabad from abroad shed light on the migrants' varied and fluid identities, highlighting the inadequacy of notions of fixed, inherited identities. These revisionings also provoked thought about the versions of the state's history being put forward by those working largely from written sources.

As George Marcus has remarked, one of the complications introduced by multisite ethnography is the increased importance of the researcher, who is a major source of connections and continuity in the work and a necessarily more prominent interpreter herself of the materials.[26] My location in this project was both more immediately accepted and more problematic than in my earlier projects. I have published on Hyderabadi history and culture since 1971 and my work was known to many of my informants, who discussed and disputed it with me. Much of the historical work on Hyderabad has been written by non-Hyderabadis, a fact much resented; also, as a native-born U.S. citizen I represented a nation in which many first-generation Hyderabadi immigrants found themselves uncomfortable to varying degrees. Thus I was no longer functioning as a historian and ethnographer but as an informant myself whose views on Hyderabadi and American societies could be solicited and challenged.

This project could not be based on firm quantitative grounds. I tried to get estimates of how many Hyderabadis were in each place of settlement, but they varied wildly. Hyderabadis number in the tens of thousands and reside all over the world, but no nation, state, or locality keeps records by the designation "Hyderabadi." There are statistical records for emigrants from India and Pakistan and for immigrants of Indian and Pakistani origin in the various countries I visited, but people from Hyderabad are not distinguished from others in those broad national-origin categories. I could not even attempt the closely contextualized examination that was possible in my previous work, studies of the Kayasths of Hyderabad city and the Punjabi Mexican population centered in California.[27] Instead, this more interpretive project rests on interviews, on the event narratives and life stories obtained from willing participants in the many sites under investigation.

The very term *Hyderabadi* was a contested term, and who was a Hyderabadi varied from speaker to speaker. There are Hyderabad associations established abroad, but they are not everywhere and all Hyderabadis do not join them. Although I included all emigrants who termed themselves Hyderabadis, I ended up interviewing a population dominated by those whose families were part of the former ruling class of Hyderabad State. Fifty years after the state's forced incorporation into India in 1948 and more than forty years after the reorganization of India's linguistic states broke the state into three parts in 1956, these families still thought of themselves as Hyderabadis. Hyderabad State had a majority Hindu population but was ruled by a Muslim dynasty, by the Nizam (governor, a Mughal title), and the majority of the ruling class was Muslim. So there were many Muslims among my interviewees, and fewer Hindus, Sikhs, Parsis, and Anglo-Indians. The language shared from the days of the Nizam was Urdu, but other mother tongues were represented, and English was well known to almost all. This highly literate group of emigrants produced Urdu and English prose and poetry, valuable sources for this project.

Because the study lacked a numerical baseline, to secure funding from traditional anthropological sources like the National Foundation of Science was difficult. What is the universe, the total population, they asked? How will you get a random sample? Can you replicate the research design in each national site? My answers were not satisfactory. Even funding sources that were friendly to "snowball sampling" techniques—methods in which one gets further sources from existing ones and tries to tap into many different networks—seldom were multinational in scope. One consequence of my inability to get one large, comprehensive grant was that the work took many years and involved many trips of short and uneven duration.[28]

The work began in 1990 and ended officially in 2000. It eventually included some 140 interviews in Hyderabad, 100 in Pakistan, 40 in the UK, 60 in the United States, and about 30 each in Canada, Kuwait, the UAE, and Australia. Some people were interviewed more than once and in different places. A very few were interviewed by telephone or e-mail. Because names are usually given in the text and I interviewed most people only once, interview references can be found in the bibliography rather than in cumbersome endnotes. Occasionally I merely describe interviewees or otherwise maintain confidentiality. The bibliography lists interviewees by name and location. Religious background is usually apparent from the names; it is obvious that I talked to Muslims, Hindus, Sikhs, Parsis, and Anglo-Indians—to any and all who claimed to be Hyderabadi.

The importance of religion, particularly Islam, in the lives of Hyderabadi immigrants in several of the destination countries was very clear. As the next chapter shows, in the former Hyderabad State people of diverse religions participated in a Mughlai or Indo-Muslim court culture, and religion mattered primarily at the personal, family level. Hyderabadis abroad, however, discussed religion and religious identities in both positive and negative ways, highlighting this aspect of their public identities.[29] Islamic beliefs and Muslim organizations proved particularly significant to many Hyderabadi immigrants in North America and Australia, but they were important to individuals elsewhere as well. Late twentieth-century scholarship on immigration underestimated the importance of religion, as this study makes clear.[30]

The interviews, usually conducted in a home, office, or social setting such as a restaurant, tea house, or wedding hall, focused on migration, the reasons for it and its consequences for family occupational, residential, and marriage patterns. I took notes on the spot and typed them immediately afterward into my laptop computer. Because there were usually several people present and noise levels were high, I did not tape-record these interviews (I also considered the time it takes to transcribe taped interviews). The research was overwhelmingly qualitative and reflects people's views of their experiences. Although I was interested primarily in people's interpretations of the past and present, initially I did use a brief questionnaire to elicit such facts as dates and places of birth, education, marriage, and migration for family members. I also experimented with longer questionnaires[31] and collected written materials from archives, libraries, books, and newspapers related to historical developments, national emigration and immigration policies and trends, and individual experiences.

Doing multisite ethnography presented problems of comparability. First, for historical reasons, the immigrants settling in different destinations had different demographic, religious, and linguistic profiles, so the Hyderabadi immigrant populations in these various sites were not directly comparable. Second, the material was gathered over a decade rather than a short time span. Third, different levels of funding meant that I spent varying periods of time in each location, so in some places I interviewed more people than in others, and I visited some places more than others. In other words, the sites were not investigated with "a uniform set of fieldwork practices of the same intensity."[32]

The methodology just described has strengths as well as weaknesses. Over the years, I was able to build on not just one but several kinds of networks, talking to people from various Hyderabad localities, schools, and occupational backgrounds. I followed people from different castes, religions, and social classes out of Hyderabad, meeting their relatives and friends all around the world. Return trips to major destinations allowed me to look up people referred to me by Hyderabadis settled elsewhere and enabled me to see how networks were built and maintained over time. I paid particular attention to the marriages of the second generation abroad. My notetaking captured people's own words as they spoke about their experiences and contrasted them with those of others, speculating about why they were similar or different. I am confident of the general outlines of Hyderabadi emigrant experiences in each country of destination. I am confident that most immigrants in each country will recognize these experiences as true for many others if not for themselves.

My interest throughout was to see how people perceived their lives to be changed by migration, how they placed themselves in old and new locations. Framing migration experiences in the new and differing national political, economic, and social contexts helped some to make sense of these perceptions, whereas others seemed to depend more on their family's previous status in the Hyderabadi homeland. To see the connections people maintained with their homeland and with each other, I looked closely at the ways Hyderabadi emigrants built associational, occupational, and marital networks across national boundaries and how they talked about these networks. These discussions with people from all walks of life were anchored by references to the particularities of old Hyderabad and its social landscape. Thus the speakers referred to relatives and friends, localities and schools, food and other aspects of Hyderabad's material culture. Their stories reproduce the structures and beliefs that underlie Hyderabadi diasporic networks.

The chapters follow a roughly chronological order. After an overview of Hyderabadi history and culture, there is a survey of the destination sites in the late twentieth century to set the contexts for the immigrants. Chapters follow on the Hyderabadi migrants to Pakistan, the UK, Australia, the United States, Canada, and the Gulf states of Kuwait and the United Arab Emirates, presenting individual stories followed by analysis of "the community" as a whole. Afterward is a chapter on the consequences of this diaspora for Hyderabad and those left behind. The final chapter reconsiders definitions of diaspora, transnationalism, globalization, and cosmopolitanism and what the experiences of Hyderabadis abroad tell us about these processes, with a close look at generational differences, the power of the nation-states, and an emergent global "structure of feeling."

CHAPTER 2

Necessary Orientations

HYDERABAD IS THE name of a city and a state that has undergone dramatic political transitions in India's recent history. In 1948, Hyderabad State became part of independent India and in 1956, as part of the reorganization of state boundaries along linguistic lines, it was divided among three new states. The city, formerly capital of Hyderabad State, became capital of the new Telugu-speaking state of Andhra Pradesh, producing major reorientations of language and culture. Hyderabad city was India's fifth largest city at the turn of the twenty-first century.

"Hyderabadi," or a person from Hyderabad, was an identity that linked one closely to the princely state on India's Deccan plateau ruled by the Nizam of Hyderabad. This involved citizenship not so much in the modern sense of participation in political decision making as in the sense of having a claim on the state for one's livelihood. *Mulki* (countryman) became a legal category with preference for state jobs in the late nineteenth century, and a process was established for non-mulkis (foreigners, outsiders, non-countrymen) to become mulkis. Being a mulki also implied closeness and loyalty to Hyderabad State. People's working definitions of mulki differ: some restrict membership in the mulki category to those resident in the Deccan by the mid-eighteenth century (consolidation of the Nizam's rule), whereas others include immigrants to Hyderabad up to the late nineteenth century but bar those coming in after that. Some think that people could become mulki Hyderabadis well into the twentieth century.

Hyderabadis were not only citizens of Hyderabad State but they also shared in and helped to constitute Hyderabadi culture, producing a sense of community particularly strong for members of the ruling elite. Hyderabadi culture was often termed Mughlai because its feudal overtones and elaborate courtesies derived from the Persian-based court culture of the

Mughal empire in Delhi. The first Nizam came to the Deccan as provincial governor for the Mughals in the early eighteenth century and only gradually established his independence. The Nizam's ruling class incorporated Marathi-, Telugu-, and Kannada-speaking nobles, officials, and local elites as well as Persian-, Urdu-, and Hindi-speakers who accompanied him from northern India. The nobility, the Mughlai bureaucracy, and the military included adherents of all religions, although Muslims were the majority of the urban, ruling elite and Hindus formed the bulk of the rural peasantry.[1]

Hyderabadi culture changed over time, responding to the colonial Indian culture developing under British rule all around it. English-educated officials were recruited from outside and English-medium educational institutions were established in Hyderabad. In fact, the non-mulki officials brought from British India from the time of the great nineteenth century Diwan (Prime Minister) Salar Jang I developed a modernizing bureaucracy on the Anglo-Indian model, yet Hyderabad continued its separate tack by shifting from Persian to Urdu as the state language in the 1880s, renewing and expanding its Indo-Muslim culture.

Writings about Hyderabad have been largely celebratory in nature, leaving the relationships between culture, power, and identity little investigated.[2] I have argued that Hyderabadi culture was not a cultural synthesis but the ruling class culture of a plural society, associated with the ruler and the state apparatus.[3] Although the Nizam and most leading state officials were Muslim, they ruled over a majority Hindu population, and the plural society of old Hyderabad included Hindus, Parsis, Anglo-Indians, and others. Members of the top families went to school together, socialized, and thought of themselves and their state as distinct from British India. Yet identity is a contested domain, an unstable, interactive, constitutive process,[4] and in the past, as now in the diverse diasporic settings, the Hyderabadi identity has been continually reconstituted.

Hyderabad's Deccani Cultural Roots

The history of the city and state given here highlights those features essential to understanding the emigrants' accounts of their experiences, such as foods and fashions, important political and social figures, major localities, and schools and other institutions. It introduces the chief elements of the social landscape or set of memories from which identities abroad are being reconstituted.

Some contemporary limericks[5] capture the ambience of old Hyderabad.

> Oh, Hyderabad is the land of *parsaun*,
> No hustle here of the northern *sarson*,

No flurry, no hurry,
Huzoor! Why worry?
Sab kuch kaam hoingaich—parsaun[6]

I love *kut, Shikampur* and *Biryani,*
Aloo-methi and *Ambada reshmani,*
Throw in *Dum-ka-kabab*
And *Murgh la-jawab!*
To enjoy these, first don your *sherwani.*[7]

These limericks locate old Hyderabad in the south, a city with its own version of Urdu, a leisurely sense of time, a distinctive cuisine and style of dress. Deccani Urdu drew from some of the surrounding languages, especially Marathi, and was considered nonstandard by northern Urdu-speakers. The customary salutation was *adab arz* (respects), offered with a low bow and a cupped hand raised toward one's forehead; this salutation had no religious connotations. Hyderabadi court dress drew on regional as well as Mughal styles. Hyderabadi men once wore distinctive *dastars* (turbans), now seen on grooms at weddings; later they wore the fez, called *rumi topi* (Turkish cap) in Hyderabad, and the sherwani, known elsewhere as the Nehru jacket after its most famous twentieth-century wearer. Many still wear sherwanis for formal occasions, often richly embroidered ones. Women wore the sari and often put *bindis,* red dots, on their foreheads for beauty; for weddings, the *kurti choli* and *khara dupatta,* an outfit with a distinctive brocaded bodice and head covering, was the Hyderabadi fashion.

Hyderabadi cuisine featured Mughlai dishes with a Deccani flavor, a touch of tamarind in the lentils (*khatti dal*) and sauces, a rich *biryani,* slow-roasted *kebabs,* delicious thick-sauced eggplant and green chili dishes (*bagara baigan* and *mirch ka salan*), and deserts like *double-ka mitha* (made from double *roti* or white bread) and *khubani ka mitha* (made with apricots). Persian teahouses and South Indian Brahmin vegetarian restaurants have long been established, and spicy coastal Andhra food has come recently. As in Central Asia and Mughal India, people sat on the floor and ate with their hands from dishes spread on a *dastarkhan* or tablecloth; this was called a *chowki* dinner (see figure 2.1). If South Indian, people ate with their hands from food served on banana leaves. Following a meal or at any time, many Hyderabadi men and women chewed *pan,* a concoction of paste and nuts wrapped in a betel leaf.[8]

The sherwani came into fashion in Hyderabad only in the late nineteenth century, but the foundations of Hyderabadi culture go back to Golconda Fort, a fort established under the Kakatiya Hindu Rajas of Warangal just north of the Musi River by the thirteenth century. In 1364, Golconda fell to the Bahmanis, a Shia Muslim dynasty of Iranian ancestry, and by 1530, the Bahmani kingdom had split into five Deccani sultanates, with the

FIGURE 2.1. *Chowki* dinner at Paigah noble Wali Uddaula's early twentieth century wedding party in the Nizam's Chou Mohalla palace. Courtesy of Syeda Khundkar, Huntington Beach, California.

Qutb Shahi dynasty ruling from Golconda. The new city of Hyderabad developed south of the river across from the fort and became capital of the Qutb Shahi dynasty in the sixteenth and seventeenth centuries. These medieval dynasties firmly established the Persian language and Shia Irani court rituals in the Deccan.

Although a bridge was built across the Musi River in 1578, Hyderabad city's traditional founding date is 1591, when the landmark Char Minar (a building with four minarets) was constructed during the reign of Muhammed Quli Qutb Shah. Popular belief credits Quli Qutb Shah's founding of the city to his love for a Hindu dancing girl, Bhagmati, who lived south of the river, and the city was first known as Bhagnagar (after her, or, in other versions, "city of gardens," *bagh*). After Quli Qutb Shah married her, Bhagmati was renamed Hyder Mahal and the city was renamed Hyderabad. Strategically situated on the road from Golconda to Machlipatnam, a seaport on the Telugu-speaking eastern coast of India, the city's gridiron layout divided it into four quarters and twelve *mohallas* or neighborhoods. The homes of the great nobles dominated one quarter, and the market at Char Kaman (four arches) was adjacent to the Char Minar. In this first phase, Hyderabad city was closely tied to Golconda Fort and adjacent Karvan and Begum Bazar, where the leading bankers so vital to the state lived.[9] Figure 2.2 shows the layout of the old and new cities, and figures 2.3 and 2.4 show Hyderabad's landmarks, the Qutb Shahi tombs near Golconda Fort and the Char Minar in the old city.

The Mughal emperor Aurangzeb conquered Golconda in 1687 and incorporated the Deccan into his empire. The Mughal provincial governor in the early eighteenth century, Nizam ul Mulk, made the Deccani province more or less independent of Delhi after 1724, but his capital city was Aurangabad, to the west. In the 1760s, the first Nizam's successors shifted the capital back to Hyderabad, and the great palaces of the Nizam and his nobles revitalized the city south of the Musi. Major gates in the city walls led to Machilipatnam and Delhi, while to the south lay the establishments of the Nizam's military officers, with weapons stored in their extensive gardens. Other gardens at the city's boundaries housed Hindu temples or Muslim graveyards.

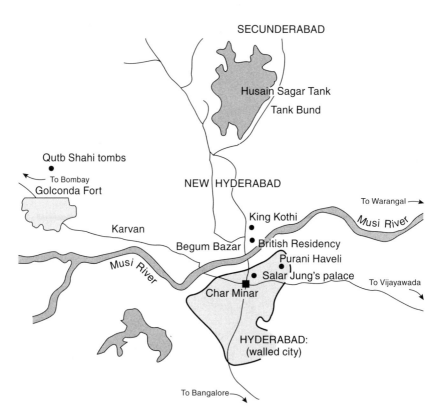

FIGURE 2.2. Golconda, Hyderabad, and Secunderabad.

FIGURE 2.3. The Qutb Shahi tombs. Courtesy of Narendra Luther, Hyderabad.

FIGURE 2.4. Char Minar, the heart of the old city. Courtesy of Christopher Butt, New York City.

The Shia Muslim Qutb Shahi ruling class culture was modeled on that of Persia[10] but included many Telugu-speakers, and, after 1687, Hyderabad's expanding culture incorporated Mughlai or Indo-Muslim elements and those who brought them. Muharram, the Shia commemoration of the martyrdom of the Prophet Muhammad's grandson Husain in 680,[11] continued as a major public observance, marked by ten days of mourning processions in the old city. Under the Sunni Muslim Nizams, many new men, speakers of Marathi, Kannada, Telugu, and Urdu, entered the ruling class. Leading noble families included the Sunni Muslim Paigah family of military men, the Shia Muslim family of Salar Jung (*diwan* in the mid-nineteenth century), the Hindu Khatri family of Maharaja Chandu Lal (*peshkar* or deputy minister in the early nineteenth century) and his descendant Kishen Pershad (*diwan* in the early twentieth century), and the two Hindu hereditary *daftardar* (keepers of the land revenue records) families, one of Maharashtrian Brahmans called the Rae Rayans, the other of North Indian Kayasths called the Malwalas. Hindu rulers of *samasthans*, small kingdoms in the Telugu-speaking countryside, continued to hold power and participated in court politics.[12]

Other new participants in Deccani politics were the French and British East India companies, contending with each other on Indian soil and giving European military training and arms to Indian soldiers. The Nizam eventually lost Machlipatnam, his eastern seaport, to the British East India Company, and the Company forced the Nizams to sign treaties of "subsidiary alliance" in the late eighteenth century. Hyderabad remained independent of direct British control, although it had to cede its rich Berar province to the Company in 1853.[13] The largest princely or native state in India, Hyderabad maintained a British-controlled military force and became known as Britain's "faithful ally." A British cantonment grew up in the hamlet of Secunderabad and a British Residency was built in Hyderabad north of the river.

Modernizing Hyderabad

The British cantonment and Residency reoriented Hyderabad city's expansion to the north. In this second phase of urban development, the twin cities became Hyderabad and Secunderabad rather than Golconda and Hyderabad. The British Residency's economic concessions attracted merchants and bankers to its adjacent Residency Bazar. In 1874 a railroad linked Hyderabad to Bombay and the British Indian economy. The Nizam built a palace near the Residency Bazar, and movement from the old walled city accelerated. The old Mughlai administration and its employees remained in the old city, while the new British-patterned administration and its high-ranking employees were based in the new city and Secunderabad.

The Diwan Salar Jung I, effective ruler from 1853 to 1883, carefully maintained the Mughlai bureaucracy and nobility and the mulki/non-mulki distinction as he initiated a modernizing administration. He recruited many outsiders after 1869, when the death of the fifth Nizam, Afzal-ud-daula, brought a very young sixth Nizam, Mahbub Ali Khan, to the throne. Salar Jung utilized British advice, administrative practices, and knowledgeable personnel as he carefully balanced old and new administrations in the state. Hyderabad's British-trained Indian administrators from outside the state were mostly English-educated men from British North India or the Madras Presidency. Again Muslims predominated, although Hindus, Parsis, and Europeans were also recruited. Syed Ahmed Khan's newly founded Aligarh Muslim University was a major source of recruitment in the late nineteenth century.

The newcomers were termed non-mulkis, although "Hindustani" was also used for those from North India. These men brought families, and other relatives followed them. As the years passed these newcomers claimed mulki status, but they were still labeled non-mulki and their dominance of the state administration, clear by the 1890s, was much resented and set in motion a kind of "affirmative action" plan for mulkis.[14] Non-mulki dominance was also reflected in the English-oriented society developing in new Hyderabad and Secunderabad, and Hyderabadi culture expanded in new directions. Non-mulkis looked down on the Deccani Urdu and old-fashioned ways of Hyderabadis, whereas mulkis valued their Mughlai court culture and insulation from British rule.[15]

The old walled city fell behind the modernizing new one, yet even in the newer city the pace of change was slower than in British India. Hyderabad was under a Kotwal (the Mughal equivalent of a police commissioner, city magistrate, and municipal commissioner) appointed by the Nizam until 1869, when a department of municipal and road maintenance was initiated under a municipal commissioner. A municipal corporation with elected representatives was initiated only in 1933, modeled on Bombay's late nineteenth-century incorporation.[16] In the 1870s, a modern Anglo-Indian legal system replaced the Mughlai judicial system, and, in the 1890s, a High Court on the British Indian model was established.

Hyderabad's educational system deserves close attention because schools loomed large in the memories and transnational networks of the emigrants. Education in Hyderabad officially began with an "oriental college," the Dar-ul-Ulum, and a small private Western education school, the Madras-i-Aliya, established by Salar Jung in 1856 and 1873, respectively. The Dar-ul-

Ulum was affiliated with British India's Punjab University. The Madras-i-Aliya met in Salar Jung's palace, enrolling his own sons and other young nobles, and shifted to the new city in 1877. The old city had no English-medium schools in the nineteenth century, and English was taught in only four private schools there (two Urdu- and two Marathi-medium).

The consolidation of Hyderabad's modern elite depended on its modern educational system. The non-mulki secretary of the education department, Syed Hossain Belgrami,[17] initiated the modern educational system in 1883–1884 with vernacular primary and secondary schools in the state's four major languages (Urdu, Telugu, Marathi, and Kannada). These fed into the small English-medium Nizam College, created by a merger in 1886 of the Hyderabad College[18] and the Madras-i-Aliya upper standards and affiliated with Madras University in British India in 1886–1887. For three generations the graduates of Madras-i-Aliya and Nizam College dominated the professions, services, and public life of Hyderabad State.[19] State scholarships were awarded to mulkis for study in England after 1897.[20] Western education became highly valued, and missionary and private schools like St. George's Grammar School[21] and the Hindu Anglo-Vernacular School[22] found students competing for admission. These and other English-medium schools were clustered above Abid's Circle in the new city and in Secunderabad, as figure 2.6 shows; figure 2.5 shows other localities and landmarks important to Hyderabadi emigrants abroad.

- Although the state initiated a modern educational system based on Western models in 1883, in that same year the state language was changed from Persian to Urdu, reinforcing its orientation to Mughlai rather than British Indian culture. By the early twentieth century, the use of Urdu in the administrative and educational system linked villages and towns to Hyderabad city. The inauguration of the Urdu-medium Osmania University in 1918 drew young, chiefly Hindu, speakers of Marathi, Telugu, and Kannada from the districts to the city, increasing the numbers of educated Hyderabadis and encouraging them to push for greater roles in the state. The innovative founding of Osmania as an Urdu-medium university was not only a modernizing project by the non-mulki administrators but was "symbolic of the age-long reaction against the continuance of English as the medium of university education in the country" and against "the subservience . . . to Madras University."[23] Even Osmania University's Indo-Saracenic architecture made a statement (figure 2.7). The university was intended to educate Hyderabad's youth and equip them for administrative service, using the state's official language and emphasizing its independence from British India. (Later, the choice of language would highlight the state's Muslim base and its difference from Hindu-majority India.)

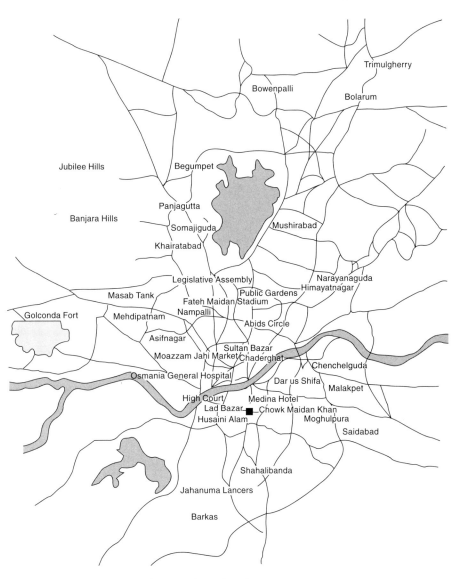

FIGURE 2.5. Major Localities and Landmarks.

Schools were established for girls too, although women's literacy rates varied greatly by family, caste, and community. Nampally Girls' School and the Stanley Girls' School opened in the new city in 1890 and 1895,[24] and Mahbubiyah Girls' School opened in the new city in 1907, a finishing school for upper-class girls with a British principal and mostly European staff.[25]

FIGURE 2.6. Higher Secondary Schools and Colleges.

Girls' schools developed in the old city only in the 1930s and 1940s. Purdah, or the seclusion of women, marked most higher educational institutions until 1948, when it was abolished in Osmania University and elsewhere.

The English- and Urdu-medium colleges and universities produced an indigenous, educated elite in Hyderabad in the early twentieth century.[26]

FIGURE 2.7. Osmania University. Courtesy of Narendra Luther, Hyderabad.

Bright young mulki men were being taken as sons-in-law to both non-mulki administrators and old Hyderabadi nobles. They were sometimes jokingly called sons-in-law of the state, meaning those close to power but not in the direct line of inheritance.[27] The city and district young men acquiring Western educations in local languages and Urdu were still ranked below those attending the English-medium intermediate schools and colleges in Hyderabad, but they felt empowered by the establishment of Osmania University. Yet English was a compulsory subject at Osmania, as its graduates "should not be inferior to those of the existing Indian Universities as regards their practical acquaintance with a language which has become essential in every department of life."[28]

Osmania offered mulkis a route to government service, but it also increased mulki–non-mulki conflict by setting North Indian Urdu as the standard. This was pushed by the non-mulki heads of the translation bureau and Persian department but opposed by the mulki heads of the Urdu and Arabic departments. The disputes over language fed into competing ideas of Deccani nationalism. Dr. Mohiuddin Qadri Zore, head of the Osmania Urdu department, and the institution he and other mulkis built, the Idara-i-Adabiyat-i-Urdu or Aiwan-i-Urdu, promulgated the idea of a Deccani cultural synthesis.[29] A populist mulki movement developed in the 1920s, urging the Nizam to initiate representative political institutions and empower indigenous Hyderabadis. The other theory of Deccani nationalism hailed Hyderabad as a Muslim state, an idea developed by a charismatic young nobleman, Bahadur Yar Jung, and the Muslim cultural organization he founded in 1927, the Ittehad ul Muslimeen.[30]

The mulki movement pulled together the local Osmania Graduates' Association and the London graduates and their Society of Union and Progress. Formalized in 1935 as the Nizam's Subjects' League or the Mulki League, it did have some genuinely Hyderabadi nationalist potential. As I was told in Karachi in 1993 by M. Farooq Ali Osmani, an Osmania graduate who migrated to Pakistan after 1948: "If not for the fall of Hyderabad, no one would have thought of going out, Osmania had produced a revolution, a multiclass society was developing and changing the state." The mulki movement might have broadened the base of the Nizam's rule and secured Hyderabad a more autonomous place in postcolonial India, but Hyderabad's ruling class failed to take advantage of it. Muslim nationalism was also growing in the state.[31]

The seventh and last Nizam, Osman Ali Khan, came to the throne in 1911 on the death of the popular Nizam Mahbub Ali Khan. Nizam Osman Ali Khan and others in leadership positions favored administrative but not political modernization of the state, and they were not attentive enough to political forces at home or in British India.[32] Family matters preoccupied some: in 1931, the Nizam's two sons, the Princes Azam Jah and Moazzam Jah, married two Turkish princesses, the daughter (Durru Shevar) and niece (Niloufer) of the last Caliph and former Sultan of Turkey. Moazzam Jah and the Princess Niloufer had no children, but the senior couple had two sons, Mukarram Jah and Muffakham Jah. Displeased with his sons in later years, the Nizam named his elder grandson, Mukarram Jah, his heir-apparent.

Turning Points: 1948 and 1956

Political forces new to the state grew in importance and ultimately decided its fate. The Arya Samaj, a militant Hindu nationalist organization based outside Hyderabad, held a massive *satyagraha* (peaceful demonstration) in Hyderabad in 1938. A Hyderabad State Congress developed from the overlooked Mulki League and worked with the Congress Party in British India for independence. The Muslim League, increasingly aiming for Muslim autonomy, had adherents in Hyderabad, and its leader, Mohamed Ali Jinnah, occasionally met or corresponded with the Nizam. Finally, a peasant uprising led by the Communist Party challenged the Nizam's rule in some Telingana districts. After Bahadur Yar Jung's death in 1944, the new leader of the Ittehad ul Muslimeen, Kasim Razvi, encouraged its militant wing, the Razakars. As negotiations with the British, the Indian and Pakistani nationalists, and then the Indian Union grew increasingly delicate, the Nizam gradually fell under the sway of the Ittehad ul Muslimeen and the Razakars and tried to remain independent of India. However, the state fell in 1948.[33] Major General Syed Ahmed El Edroos surrendered to the invading Indian Army without major military engagements, in what is known as the "Police Action."[34]

Hyderabadis experienced traumatic changes after 1948 as India imposed a new regime. Some Hyderabadis migrated to the new state of Pakistan, created along with India in 1947, but Indian rule in Hyderabad meant such major readjustments that it was almost as though those who stayed had moved to a new place. Some Hyderabadis found the American civil war novel, *Gone with the Wind*, evocative of the trauma.[35] They likened old Hyderabad to the American South, some of them with nostalgic approval, others with disapproval. Rereading the novel, I found certain analogies, ones I will sweepingly overstate (as Hyderabadis often do) for effect. In both cases, there was a hereditary aristocracy, a society marked by hierarchies of race, class, national origin, and gender. The men were concerned with horses, hunting, drinking, and the manners appropriate to their status; the women were sheltered and protected, concerned with dress, jewelry, food, and domestic arrangements. In both societies, arranged marriages, including cousin marriages, were common, and both men and women were heavily dependent on servants or slaves in the domestic sphere. Both cultures were said to be soft, indolent, and gallant, with family background valued more than education; there was contempt for commercial activities. Perhaps Hyderabadi men were better educated, on the whole, than American southerners, and they were certainly very fond of word-play, Urdu lending itself so beautifully to poetry and jokes. Both societies experienced conquest by powerful northerners, became part of larger nations, and underwent disruption and subjugation. Like the American southerners, Hyderabadi men were "too courteous, too polite" to compete aggressively in their new world. In both cases, one sees vanished worlds, diminished selves, and attempts to recapture those worlds in memory.

Ruptures outnumbered continuities. The Nizam became a figurehead *Rajpramukh* (Governor, a Sanskrit term) from 1948 to 1956, first under the military governor, Major General J. N. Chaudhuri, and then in 1949 under Chief Minister M. K. Vellodi of the Indian Civil Service.[36] At this point, the old Hyderabad Civil Service (HCS) ended and the Indian Civil Service, renamed the Indian Administrative Service or IAS, took over. After the rupture of 1948 came that of 1956, when India's reorganization of states along linguistic lines dismembered the old trilinguistic state.[37] Hyderabad city and the Nizam's Telingana (Telugu-speaking) districts were united

AFGHANISTAN

Northern Areas

Peshwar

Northwest Frontier Province

Islamabad

Baluchistan

PAKISTAN

Punjab

Lahore

Punjab

TIBET

Jammu and Kashmir

Himachal Pradesh

Punjab

Haryana

NEPAL

BHUTAN

Delhi

Rajasthan

Sind

Karachi

Gujarat

Uttar Pradesh

Bihar

INDIA

Madhya Pradesh

Bengal

Orissa

Calcutta

BANGLADESH

BURMA

Bombay

Maharashtra

Andhra Pradesh

Hyderabad

HYDERABAD STATE

Karnataka

6 Marathi-speaking districts

2 Kannada-speaking districts

8 Telugu-speaking districts

Madras

Tamilnadu

Kerala

FIGURE 2.8. Hyderabad State and Late Twentieth Century South Asia.

with the Telugu-speaking districts formerly under British rule and oriented toward Madras city, as shown in figure 2.8.[38] Hyderabad city became the capital of the new Telugu-speaking state of Andhra Pradesh.

Hindi became India's official national language, resolving the deliberate ambiguity of Mahatma Gandhi's 1920 designation of Hindustani (Urdu and Hindi, written in either Arabic or Sanskrit script) as the future national language. Accordingly, Hyderabad's languages of administration and education changed from Urdu and English to Hindi and English in 1948. Osmania chose Hindustani in 1949 as the medium of instruction (so that both Hindi and Urdu script could be used). English was used from 1951 in the arts and sciences faculties and in that same year Nizam College was affiliated to Osmania (rather than to Madras University).[39] Osmania offered English-medium medical training, awarding the increasingly popular M.B.B.S. or Bachelor of Medicine and Bachelor of Surgery degree (the acronym comes from the word order in Latin).[40] The languages changed again, to Telugu and Hindi and English in 1956 (India's three-language formula, where students learn the state language, the national language, and English). Shifting political boundaries and new political processes introduced Hyderabad to democracy—to competing political parties and hotly contested elections.

Some Hyderabadis rose to prominence on the national scene in the first decades after 1948, becoming part of India's national and international elite. It would have been too much to expect that the Nizam's successors would participate wholeheartedly in the new India, and both grandsons maintain homes abroad.[41] Several Hyderabadis served India as governors of states;[42] others became ambassadors.[43] Some joined universities outside Hyderabad and others joined the national government and lived chiefly outside Hyderabad.[44] Some of these Muslim men had Hindu wives, thus serving as personal examples of national integration. Much later, P.V. Narasimha Rao, a Telingana Telugu-speaker whose Urdu was excellent (he was educated in that medium), became India's prime minister in the 1990s.

These changes in the homeland in the decades after 1948 strongly influenced emigrants and the ways they reoriented themselves to their new settings. Most obviously, the state of origin has changed: the former Hyderabad State became Andhra Pradesh, with very different boundaries and constituent languages. Or was the real homeland Hyderabad city, standing more or less on its own all along? In fact, both the continued existence and the historical nature of this homeland, Hyderabad, whether city or state, proved to be matters of controversy. Most self-identified Hyderabadis abroad were first-generation migrants over the age of fifty who claimed some connection with the old Hyderabad State or its urban Mughlai culture, and many such people thought that their Hyderabad no longer existed.

Second, the meaning of "Hyderabadi" clearly changed, as people connected themselves to redefined state borders and cultures. Mulki status carried legal privileges in the old Hyderabad State and was always contested, and mulki status was still proudly claimed by many older emigrants. But political events sent some longtime Hyderabadis abroad and brought many newcomers from coastal Andhra into the city, producing people claiming to be Hyderabadis who may not have known the word *mulki*. The traditional greeting in Hyderabad was *adab* (respects), a nonreligious salutation uttered as one raised his or her right hand to the forehead, bowing slightly. Now many people say either *salam aleikum* or *namaste*, greetings many associate with Islam or Hinduism, respectively.

Late Twentieth-Century Life in Hyderabad City

After the first years of dramatic readjustment, we come to the recent past. The urban landscape has altered greatly over the last few decades. Those great hierarchies of language, class, and gender that marked the Nizam's kingdom have largely disappeared. One can no longer see the grand sweep of the cement roads, which were regularly washed and cleared for the passing of the Nizam and the great nobles. Also gone are the purdah cars and taxis parked before shops and schools, the purdah curtains held by servants as women and girls went from conveyance to entryway, and other aspects of gendered lives in the palaces and courtyards.[45] Telugu has replaced Urdu in schools and vies with it on the streets.

The late twentieth-century city is almost wholly changed in physical as well as cultural character, making it hard for longtime Hyderabadis to sustain their civic pride. A limerick[46] best evokes the pain of rapid urbanization, of growing from three-quarters of a million people (739,159 in 1941) to almost 5 million (a projected 4,273,498 in 1991).[47]

> In Hyderabad's traffic, the fumes
> engulf you in clouds as you zooms,
> Your temper will seethe,
> It's so hard to breathe,
> No wonder this town's full of tombs.

The most famous tombs, the Qutb Shahi, go back some four hundred years and bring us to a final limerick. This one highlights the dramatic ruptures in the city's history made obvious by largely abortive attempts to celebrate Hyderabad's 400th birthday in the city itself (it also highlights the diasporic dimension).[48]

> In London, L.A., Jeddah, and Kuwait,
> They've celebrated Hyderabad's anniversary fete.
> But here in A.P.,
> Not even a tea,
> Come on, politicians, let's set a date!

Why such delays in the celebration, why such controversy?[49] Lingering memories of the Police Action of 1948 and the Linguistic States Reorganization of 1956 marked contemporary politics at the end of the twentieth century, but the political boundaries have proved less significant than clashes of cultural orientation, clashes of the new and old languages of power and structures of feeling. The population of Hyderabad city is still heavily Muslim, particularly in the old city, and Urdu still has a hold on the city as a whole. Telugu regional culture and British Indian culture both threaten the Mughlai Persian and Urdu culture that ruled there for so long.[50] The Andhra peasant castes dominate the political arenas of city and state, causing the decline of specific communities and the rise of others.[51] Telugu-speakers, however, had looked south and east, to Madras city and coastal Andhra towns like Rajahmundry, and the abrupt reorientation to Hyderabad remains to be consolidated.

The defining features of the present city evoke competing versions of the past. The buildings from the Nizam's period, especially those so proudly constructed in the twentieth century just before the Police Action, remain much in evidence. The harmonious design imposed on the city by buildings like the High Court, Osmania General Hospital, and the Legislative Assembly has been broken by new buildings vying with them to represent the city. The new Telugu University, for example, has changed the landscape of the old Public Gardens, its bold Andhra architecture evocative of temples and contrasting with the graceful Indo-Saracenic lines of the older buildings.

Successive governments of Andhra Pradesh have been constructing a past that reaches back to the Buddha,[52] celebrates Buddhism and Hinduism, and tries to erase the Mughals and the Nizams. Andhra's chief minister in the early 1990s, the South Indian cinema star N. T. Rama Rao, installed a huge statue of the Buddha in Hussain Sagar lake.[53] On a high hill above the Buddha and the Tank Bund (the road running along Hussain Sagar that links Hyderabad to Secunderabad) stands a lovely white Hindu temple built recently by the Birlas (wealthy industrialists from western India). The temple overlooks the twin cities from the site on which the Mughal emperor Aurangzeb's victory drums were beaten in 1687. Statues erected by the state government now line the Tank Bund, most of them of cultural heroes from coastal Andhra. Only three statues are of Muslims and they do not include the last Nizam or Hyderabad's great nineteenth-century Diwan, Salar Jung. They are Tana Shah, the last of the Qutb Shahi rulers and the one who fought the emperor, Aurangzeb; the sixth Nizam Mahbub Ali Khan, a popular figure with all his citizens; and Makhdum Mohiuddin, communist leader of the Telingana rebellion against the Nizam in the state's last decades.[54] Then there is the sound and light show put on these days at Golconda Fort, again scripted by the state. It is an enthralling pageant, but ominous music plays when the Mughals come to the Deccan, and the show ends with that same music and a statement like "and darkness fell over Golconda." The cultural synthesis created under the Qutb Shahis, with its strong Telugu components, is valued whereas the more heterogeneous one created under the Nizams is not. In other ways, the Andhra government attacks the symbols of the Nizams' days,[55] and urban developers help remake the city by pulling down or drastically altering palaces and historic landmarks to erect shopping malls, apartments, hospitals, schools, and clubs.

The meaning of the city to its inhabitants depends very much upon which inhabitants one is talking about: there is no shared vision, no real urban community comparable to earlier times.[56] As one urban historian commented, "the cognitive geographies of different groups [do] not coincide," and the question posed by another historian, whether geography has power over political authority or political authority has power over geography, is very relevant here.[57] The Andhra politicians certainly are trying to assert control over Hyderabad, but they have not quite succeeded in vanquishing the city's strongly marked Indo-Muslim character.

The imposition of the Nizam's capital city on formerly British Telugu-speaking coastal Andhra is still being worked out. Hyderabad, especially the old city, appears to the Andhras much as Indian towns allegedly appeared to Englishmen, above all else "disorderly."[58] Yet to old Hyderabadis it is the Andhras who appear disorderly, uncivilized, barefoot; it is they who make the city dirty, crowded, and chaotic. The evolving sets of natives and newcomers have very different senses of architecture, decoration, and color, and the renaming of streets and localities emphasizes the disjunctions. Language is very much a matter of contention in the modern city, with Urdu still the language of the street in many localities. Some members of the old elite refuse to hire workers who cannot follow their directions in Urdu, and old Hyderabadi families make do with servants who do not know the old culture, cannot cook the old dishes, and cannot greet or serve guests properly.

From the 1950s to the turn of the twenty-first century, Hyderabad has been incorporated into greater India's developing urban culture, sharing trends evident elsewhere in the nation. In the 1960s, fancy gas stations with extensive grounds suddenly appeared to serve the new and privileged class of car and scooter owners; in the 1970s, palatial movie houses accommodated new audiences for India's expanding cinema industry. In the 1980s, family restaurants were opened and the city's exclusive clubs added family entertainments. In the early 1990s came the flashy pubs, following the fashion in Bangalore.[59] Now, former palaces transformed into marriage halls in the 1980s, bedecked with lights and with already-existing purdah arrangements, are being supplanted by banquet halls in modern hotels and huge new Telugu-style marriage halls with rooms common to both men and women. Osmania University is still there, with its striking Indo-Saracenic architecture, but the new federal University of Hyderabad has been built at some distance from the city, demonstrating the reach of the Indian nation-state centered in Delhi.

The educational system has students marching in step with those elsewhere in India, with ten years of primary and secondary school (to tenth class) followed by the first two years of college (to twelfth class) and the passing of the "intermediate" exams. The final years of college culminate in a B.A., B.Sc., engineering, or medical degree.[60] India's "three-language" policy requires students to know the state language (Telugu), the national language (Hindi), and English. All schools of higher education have "reservation" policies that reserve places for members of "scheduled castes and tribes," formerly disadvantaged groups for whom constitutional protection is now guaranteed. Osmania's days as an Urdu-medium institution are long past, and the university is supposed to be switching over to Telugu; in practice, English still prevails, as it does at the federal University of Hyderabad.

Some who live in the city are trying to bridge the historical ruptures and build a contemporary history together, and part of that effort is mutual education, through books, films, and symposia. Only in the last few years has the 1948 Police Action been discussed, chiefly through preparation and showing of a national television (Doodarshan) special one-hour documentary on the last days of the Nizam's state. A Hyderabadi Muslim who publicly protested against the Nizam's closeness to the Razakars and urged accession to independent India felt encouraged to publish another edition of his memoirs.[61] Historians of Hyderabad, both mulki and non-mulki in origin, are writing books at least partly intended to deepen the newcomers' appreciation of the city's past.

Citizens of diverse backgrounds work together to ameliorate the urban conditions that make everyday life in the city stressful. Water is available at certain hours only, so it is stored by the rich in tanks on roofs but stored by the poor in pots. New apartments and condos present impressive facades and interiors, but the lifts cannot work when the electricity is off and water often cannot make it to the upper floors, so small boys find employment carrying water to the top floors, much as the water carriers of old provided water to the great palaces.[62] Despite the best efforts at improvement of urban services and city beautification, cooperation breaks down when it comes to the old city, largely Muslim in population and increasingly deserted by the upwardly mobile. The official attitude toward the old city seems to be one of indifference and neglect, and the political will to remedy this seems lacking.[63]

Furthermore, the old Hyderabadi ruling class has lost power even where it had retained some degree of it. Members of landed Telugu-speaking families from the Nizam's former Telingana districts played major roles in city and regional politics, but in the 1990s, Telangana politicians lost decisively to Andhra interlopers in both municipal and district arenas. Development policies favoring the coastal areas of the state are resented; some mulkis point to the preferential treatment and others organize again for a Telingana, a state separate from Andhra Pradesh.[64] Even the spoken Telugu languages are different, speakers affirm, as they discuss these developments and their mounting frustration with the ongoing but uneven integration of the former Hyderabadis and the Andhras.

Hyderabad is now the center of a dynamic modern Telugu culture, one that will receive attention from other researchers in the future as the transformations underway gain still more momentum. Speaking in December of 2000 on the Hyderabadi diaspora at the University of Hyderabad's Centre for Study of Indian Diaspora, I found that the graduate students in the audience were largely from coastal Andhra and expected a talk about the recent exodus of software professionals from Hyderabad and Andhra. This project, following Hyderabad's former Indo-Muslim culture and its proponents as they moved abroad, was "history" to them.

This overview has shown that Hyderabad had always been a destination for migrants from both inside and outside South Asia, Hindus from the subcontinent, Persians from Iran, Turks and Uzbeks from Central Asia, and smaller increments of Arabs, Africans, Anglo-Indians, Frenchmen, Sikhs, and Parsis. Its boast was that those who came settled there and seldom ventured out. Now the flow of migrants is reversed. People from the city and former state of Hyderabad have migrated abroad in some numbers since the late 1940s and especially since the late 1960s, when push factors gave way to pull ones as Western democracies changed their immigration and citizenship policies and the Persian Gulf states began offering employment opportunities.

The timings and characteristics of the major migrations from Hyderabad since 1947 are examined in subsequent chapters. Some degree of initially shared identity related the immigrants to their homeland, locating them within it but carried abroad and reformulated in the new locations. Most emigrants tried to maintain some elements of Hyderabadi identity as they understood it, drawing upon many of the elements delineated above. They retained connections to their homeland, built networks across national boundaries, and tried to teach their children about Hyderabadi culture. They and their children, however, became participants in the national lives of the countries to which they migrated. The late twentieth-century environments in the destination countries outlined in the next chapter provided both constraints and opportunities for emigrants from Hyderabad. The new contexts offered different legal and political options with respect to migration, citizenship, and working conditions. They also offered different racial, religious, and class configurations, and, consequently, different possibilities for political and social alliances.

CHAPTER 3

Sites of Settlement

THE MAP IN FIGURE 3.1, from the Urdu newspaper, *Siyasat*, shows that people in Hyderabad were well aware of the wider world and where Hyderabadis were settling abroad. The policies and demographic and sociocultural profiles of these destination countries are reviewed here for two reasons. A review will allow us to do a better comparison of immigrant lives in the new locations, and we will learn about these destinations much as prospective immigrants learned about them (many references come from immigrant presses—friends and relatives exchanged information eagerly). The chapter highlights the strategic considerations that influenced Hyderabadis in the last decades of the twentieth century as they looked beyond Hyderabad to envision possible futures for themselves, considerations reflected in the interview material in subsequent chapters.

Hyderabadis moving abroad responded to the increasingly global political economy and to the changing immigration policies of receiving countries in the late twentieth century. The structure of international capitalism, wage differences between countries, political instability in South Asia, family reunification efforts—all these and other factors produced levels of international migration unprecedented in history. Hyderabadis of all classes managed to go abroad for education, employment, or settlement. In some cases, push factors were as important as pull factors. India and Pakistan did not restrict emigration: both had continuing problems of unemployment, particularly among the educated, and they welcomed the infusion of foreign currency remittances.[1] The "brain drain" issue, while of real concern, did not lead to significant restrictions on the emigration of highly skilled professionals.[2]

The contexts for Hyderabadi settlement abroad differed significantly. People's identities were shaped by their homelands, their new locations,

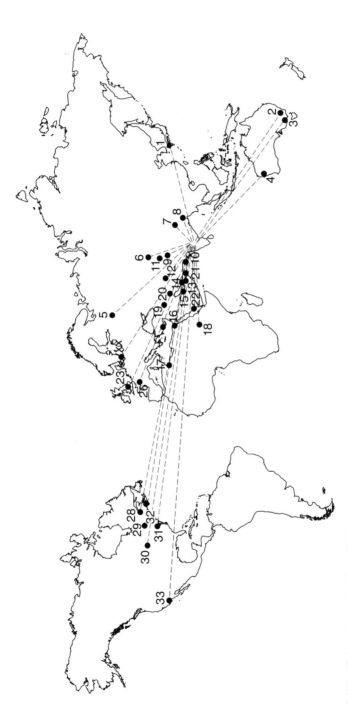

JAPAN: 1. Tokyo AUSTRALIA: 2. Sydney 3. Melbourne 4. Perth RUSSIA: 5. Moscow 6. Tashkent NEPAL: 7. Kathmandu BANGLADESH 8. Dacca PAKISTAN 9. Lahore 10. Karachi AFGHANISTAN 11. Kabul IRAN 12. Tehran UNITED ARAB EMIRATES 13. Doha (Qatar); Abu Dhabi; Dubai; Sharjah SAUDI ARABIA 14. Dhahran 15. Jeddah/Riyadh EGYPT 16. Cairo LIBYA 17. Sabah SUDAN 18. Khartoum IRAQ 19. Baghdad KUWAIT 20. Kuwait OMAN 21. Muscat LEBANON 22. Beirut UNITED KINGDOM 23. London; Birmingham; Bradford; Liverpool CANADA 28. Montreal 29. Toronto UNITED STATES OF AMERICA 30. Chicago 31. Washington 32. New York 33. Los Angeles, California

FIGURE 3.1. *Siyasat's* World. Redrawn. Courtesy of *Siyasat*, August 15, 1992.

and their relationships with people in other diasporic sites, making the concept of diaspora a resource for rethinking the nation-state system. Thus Khachig Tololyan writes of the "statelessness" of diasporas.[3] Yet the policies and projects of nation-states clearly shaped diasporic culture and politics, setting the parameters for migrant entry, citizenship, and participation. "All identity is constructed across difference,"[4] and the national configurations of sameness and difference with which immigrants interacted varied sharply in Pakistan, the United Kingdom, Australia, the United States, Canada, and the Gulf states of the Middle East.

Destinations Abroad

PAKISTAN

The last-minute partition of British India into India and Pakistan in 1947 produced massive movements of Hindus and Sikhs from Pakistan and Muslims from India as people fled from their homes, fearing violence or hoping for a brighter future. Some young Muslim activists and Hyderabadi Muslims in the Indian Civil Service and the British Indian military services opted for Pakistan in 1947, and when the Indian Army moved into Hyderabad State in 1948 and integrated it into India, more Hyderabadi Muslims went to Pakistan. Pakistan in 1947 had a western wing, with four regions dominated by speakers of Punjabi, Sindhi, Baluchi, and Pushtu, and an eastern wing dominated by speakers of Bengali. (In 1971, when the leaders of West Pakistan did not honor election results that would have empowered East Pakistan, the latter broke away and became Bangladesh.) Most of the migrants to West Pakistan from non-Punjabi-speaking parts of India settled in Karachi, Pakistan's first capital on the southern coast; others went to Hyderabad (in Sindh), Lahore, Peshawar, and Rawalpindi, or to the new, second capital of Islamabad after its building alongside Rawalpindi in the 1960s.

Despite their passionate commitment to the new nation of Pakistan, those moving from India found themselves labeled *muhajirs*. The *hijrat* or *hijra*, in Islamic history, refers to the escape or exile of the Prophet Muhammad from Mecca to Medina and was used to refer to the experience of Muslims displaced from India to Pakistan. Those who changed nations were called *muhajirs*, usually translated as refugees or exiles. Although an exchange of population occurred in the Punjab, with Punjabi refugees adapting relatively well in both the Indian and Pakistani Punjabs, it was the Urdu-speakers from UP (British India's United Provinces, now India's Uttar Pradesh), Bihar, and Hyderabad State who constituted most of the group. Their status was defined very strongly by language, as Urdu was not a regional language in Pakistan. Even though Urdu was designated Pakistan's official state language, its speakers, without a rural territorial base, were not "sons of the soil" and Urdu-speakers continued to be called muhajirs regardless of their place of birth.

In Pakistan's early days, muhajirs played foundational roles and muhajir had more than a tinge of valorization about it.[5] But a review of the situation of muhajirs in Pakistan since 1947 shows how their circumstances and the meaning of their name have changed. With the partition of India, some 7,200,000 Indian Muslims moved to Pakistan,[6] many of them bringing high qualifications and resources. Migrants continued to move from India to Pakistan, using permits until passports were introduced for Indians and Pakistanis in 1952 or 1953. Marriages arranged between citizens of the two countries continued to bring migrants, averaging about 40,000 a year in the 1950s and 1960s but falling to about 300 a year in the 1990s.[7]

The definition of "refugee" in international law excludes migrants from refugee status as soon as they acquire a new nationality,[8] yet Pakistan's first census (1951) enumerated the migrants from India as muhajirs.[9] This official practice can be partly blamed for the muhajir problem, just as the British Indian census practices can be blamed for strengthening communalism in colonial India.[10] Later censuses have not continued the category, but it can be ascertained by a "place of birth" entry for those born in India or by using the Urdu language as a proxy for those of Indian origin.[11] The muhajirs were particularly strong in Sind, where incoming Urdu-speakers immediately took over Karachi and Hyderabad, becoming the majority in both cities by the 1951 census.[12] No census was taken from 1981 to 1998, and the demand for one came partly from the MQM (the Muhajir Qaumi Movement, a political party), which wanted to set new quotas for education and employment based on current population percentages.[13] The quota groups were based on residency or domicile and "urban Sind" was used as a proxy for the muhajir category, but in popular conception this category is really based on place of origin (India), language (Urdu), and descent.[14]

At first, it was the non-muhajirs who were not well integrated into Pakistan's government, but the political core and periphery shifted over the years. Muhajirs were a powerful minority in administrative and educational positions and in the business community,[15] but they steadily lost political power after the 1951 death of Liaquat Ali Khan (a muhajir and the country's first prime minister). The shift of the capital from Karachi to Islamabad in the 1960s also worked against them, as Islamabad is not only more central, but it is also in the Punjab, home to Pakistan's largest population group (Punjabis constitute some 60 percent of the national population after 1971, the loss of Bangladesh). Despite the increased proportion of muhajirs after 1971 (they went from about 10 percent to 20 percent of Pakistan's population), their situation has worsened. Now Punjabis dominate Pakistan's administrative and military services.[16]

The muhajirs, citizens but not "natives," have no territorial base in a nation whose politics is still largely based on the mobilization of rural voters by "feudal" landlords.[17] The muhajir identity, persisting beyond the first generation of immigrants, was used to organize politically for urban jobs and resources, but identification as a muhajir or as a member of the MQM[18] made one conspicuous and vulnerable. Most muhajirs were concentrated in the Sindhi cities of Karachi and Hyderabad. Immigration, initially from India and then from within Pakistan, produced Sindhi/muhajir/Pathan conflicts and helped fuel the breakdown of urban civil society even as Pakistan experimented further with political democracy in the 1990s.[19] The trend toward Islamicization of the country, intensified under General Zia ul Haq (1977–1988) and reflected in legal, educational, and financial arenas, heightened tensions. Karachi, Pakistan's financial center, would take the brunt of the damage if the court-ordered "Islamicization" of the country's economy is ever implemented.[20]

In Pakistan, a debate has reopened about the meaning of independence and partition in 1947. The debate's strong anti-muhajir thrust repudiates the long history of Indo-Muslim culture and civilization in the subcontinent and questions the historical significance of the rest of South Asia to present-day Pakistan. The emerging consensus that the nation should celebrate the Indus Valley and the Punjabi origins of its civilization nicely justifies the loss of East Pakistan (an event almost entirely erased from public discourse). One writer argues passionately for the "Indus person" whose identity is distinct from the "India person"; another blames the muhajirs for emphasizing Islam and a centralized state at the expense of provincial autonomy, indigenous cultures, and local languages.[21]

Perceptions of Pakistan by outsiders have become harsher. The birth of Bangladesh showed that Pakistan had not served well as a Muslim homeland, and Indian Muslim migration to Pakistan slowed. Conditions in India were encouraging for Muslims in the 1970s, and during the same decade the Middle East emerged as a site of lucrative employment for many working class and professional people from India. Criticism of Pakistan has sharpened among India's Muslims, who see its continued policies of aggression in Kashmir and enmity to India as detrimental to their own position within India. One Indian Hyderabadi Muslim who settled in the United States even compared Pakistan unfavorably to the Zionist state of Israel, while some Pakistanis settled in southern California likened the muhajirs to Zionists, seeing them as religious zealots who came in and took over territory from the "sons of the soil."[22]

Political instability and socioeconomic problems have continued to plague Pakistan. It has seen five constitutions and four periods of rule without benefit of a written constitution, many distinct "constitutional systems" during its fifty-plus years. In addition, the superior judiciary has been significantly weakened since 1997.[23] General Pervez Musharraf reinstituted military rule on October 12, 1999, in a bloodless coup. The country was deeply in debt, its economy crippled by lack of family planning and failure to invest in health and education. It had the highest population growth rate among the seven most populous countries in the world, creating an alarming situation for its security, economy, social welfare, and environment.[24] Emigration, both temporary and permanent, was increasing. Thus Pakistan, initially a receiving country for emigrants from Hyderabad, became a sending country for Hyderabadi Pakistanis.

THE UNITED KINGDOM

The United Kingdom was an early destination for emigrants from Hyderabad, who joined other immigrants there from South Asia, East Africa, and the West Indies. As the British empire abroad collapsed from the 1940s, Commonwealth members could move to Britain from the Caribbean or South Asia not as immigrants but as British citizens resettling within the Commonwealth.[25] During World War II, troops from all over the British Empire were stationed in Britain, and workers, particularly from the West Indies, were recruited as factory workers. Most returned to their homes after the war but some subsequently came back to Britain as rising demand for labor in the 1950s drew immigrants from the Caribbean, India, and Pakistan.

Britain's policies have failed to stem the inflow. The Commonwealth Immigrants Act of 1962 that permitted dependents of persons already resident in Britain to enter freely but imposed controls on adults intending to work in Britain was meant to close the door to new entries, but instead it sharply increased immigration from India and Pakistan just before it took effect. In 1965 and 1968 regulatory controls were adjusted to Britain's need for labor, yet dependents, despite narrowings of the definition, have accounted for the bulk of the immigrants since 1962.[26]

Early South Asian settlers in the UK included Sikhs,[27] Gujaratis,[28] and Mirpuri, Campbellpuri, and Sylheti Pakistanis,[29] followed by East African Asians in the 1970s.[30] Most were self-employed or peasant and working-class people. Chain migration (the first immigrants bring relatives who bring more relatives) meant continued growth for these groups and they have dominated the South Asian immigrant category and the perceptions others have of it. Pakistanis, actually not the largest group, were nonetheless perceived to be so, and all South Asians were often glossed as "Pakistanis," or derogatorily as "Pakis."

Although Commonwealth rights to settlement and citizenship in Britain were cut with the 1971 Immigration Act and Commonwealth and other foreigners were put on the same footing in the 1981 British Nationality Act,[31] the model used when most immigrants were from the Commonwealth persisted, with immigrants treated as new citizens who required no special treatment. The goal was assimilation, achieved through schooling in Standard English and the adoption of British values, and foreigners could become citizens after five years of legal residence. But inner-city poverty and segregation and the workings of the police and criminal justice system showed the inadequacies of this model, and since 1965 a series of Race Relations Acts to protect ethnic and racial minorities has been passed. The racist violence and inner-city riots of the 1970s and 1980s[32] were followed by government measures to combat unemployment, make education more accessible, improve urban areas, and improve police practices.

By the late 1970s, assimilationist aims gave way to pluralist ones, particularly in education where multiculturalism was recognized in teaching and curriculum.[33] British policy became a mix of assimilationist and pluralist policies, concerned with social integration and management of intergroup relations.[34] In practice, the dominant conception of equality encourages assimilation to the majority culture in the public sphere and toleration of "difference" in the private sphere, while ethnic minorities press for the right to have "difference" recognized and supported in both public and private spheres. The introduction of an "ethnic group" question in the 1991 census was significant,[35] yet mobilization along ethnic, cultural, and even transnational or diasporic lines is clearly in tension with the older but continuing notion of assimilation into the "main body of the national community."[36]

Diversity among those labeled minorities was great. In 1990, the UK had some 1.9 million foreign-born citizens, 3.3 percent of the population. Those officially defined as ethnic minorities, the majority of them British-born people of Afro-Caribbean and Asian origin, were 2.7 million, or 4.6 percent of the population. Of these 2.7 million, 1.4 million came from South Asia and 455,000 from the Caribbean.[37] The Indians numbered 840,000, the Pakistanis 476,000, and the Bangladeshis 163,000. Measurements of class, household composition, and marital status showed Indians, Chinese, and African Asians doing better than the Pakistanis and Bangladeshis, who had higher levels of poverty and unemployment, larger households, and poorer housing. South Asians generally had high rates of marriage compared to all other groups and two-thirds of South Asian elderly people lived with their adult children compared to one in twelve of white elders.[38] In terms of intermarriage and cohabitation, Britain was far more integrated than the United States, although the Afro-Caribbeans outstripped the Asians in these measures.[39] Some Indian and Pakistani immigrants were becoming quite successful financially. The 1991 census showed 80 percent of the Indians owning their own homes, compared with 60 percent of the whites and Chinese and less than 50 percent of the blacks.[40]

In the 1970s and 1980s, political concepts of "blackness" were used to bring Afro-Caribbeans and Asians together.[41] British Asians, however, have increasingly defined themselves in terms of religion and culture rather than race, drawing attention to diversity within not only the "black" category but also the Asian category.[42] Religious issues engaged Muslims and Sikhs, as political events led them to mobilize the Muslim *umma* or the Sikh community internationally. Concepts of cultural hybridity have also engaged scholars and community members, especially younger ones, possibly drawing attention away from issues of class and discrimination to those of popular culture and its potential to erode racism.[43]

Britain's old elite of white males from public (that is, private) schools, particularly Oxford and Cambridge, still dominated top positions, with little change from 1972 to 1992.[44] However, the educational success and increasing numbers of Asians in the universities promised eventual mobility. In 1991, children of Asian background, although English is usually their second language, came ahead of all others in school English tests. A 1993 report showed young Britons of Indian, African-Asian, and Chinese origin more likely than whites to stay in education, and in 1994, Chinese, Indian, and even Pakistani and Bangladeshi students far outstripped white pupils in city schools' examinations. In 1997, 12 percent of British university students were from ethnic minorities, more than double their representation in the population.[45]

The educational system became a contested arena. Thousands of Christian, and some Jewish, schools in the UK received partial state funding,[46] but it took Muslim schools years of struggle to be accepted. There were at least forty Muslim schools in Britain, dependent on private donations, the fees paid by parents, and tax relief as charitable endeavors. In the mid-1990s, three Muslim schools were finally accepted for partial state funding (having been denied earlier despite recommendations from their local councils).[47] "The time to get to know others is at school, and Muslim schools would keep them separate," was a common justification for this reluctance to extend funding. The 1988 Education Act reflected public sentiment to uphold Christian values in schools by requiring a daily act of worship of a Christian nature in all schools.[48]

In a nation where, "partly because of its history of constitutional links between Church and State, there is a widespread attitude of tolerant in-

difference toward mainstream religion, but a lack of understanding of religious fervor,"[49] the vitality of the immigrant South Asian religions attracted attention.[50] Muslims have emerged as the second largest religious
community in Britain. Hindu, Muslim, and Sikh family laws were being
invoked in British courts, particularly when issues of arranged marriages,
dowries, and spousal migrations were involved.

British Muslims, some two-thirds of them South Asian, became active in the public arena. In 1989, when Salman Rushdie published *The Sa-
tanic Verses*, Muslims in Bradford burned copies of the book and wanted it
banned. In 1991, the Gulf War led to the inauguration of a Supreme Council of British Mosques to respond to Saddam Hussein's call for a holy war.
The council has taken up other issues, such as abolishing or reforming the
blasphemy law (it recognizes blasphemy only against Christianity and Judaism), having Islamic not British family law, and having special arrangements in schools (same-sex classes for adolescents, halal meals, special uni-
forms, and no art, music, or dance classes for Muslim children).[51] In 1992,
the destruction of the Babri Masjid (mosque) by Hindus in India aroused
Muslim fears of newly militant Hinduism and raised religious and political tensions further. Many young Muslims in the UK have become more
religiously orthodox than their parents.[52]

On the whole, however, the British South Asian second generation
was thought to be participating less in traditional religious and cultural
practices. More than half the married 16–34 year-old Pakistanis and Bangladeshis had their spouses chosen by their parents in a survey taken in
the 1990s, but, compared to their elders, younger South Asians are less
likely to speak to family members in a South Asian language, regularly
attend a place of worship, or have an arranged marriage.[53] They have been
termed "skilled cultural navigators,"[54] competently negotiating their way
in both South Asian community and British mainstream arenas. In fact,
the British South Asian younger generation was becoming celebrated for
its innovative, fusion products and activities. Young British South Asian
writers, musicians, and filmmakers played a key role in diasporic aesthetics
as they contributed to an international or transnational youth culture.[55]

AUSTRALIA

Australia, an island continent in the Pacific Ocean several thousands
of miles away from other major continents, with its nearest neighbors in
southeast Asia, Micronesia, and Melanesia, may seem an unlikely destination for emigrants from Hyderabad. Yet it was a place that Hyderabad's
Anglo-Indians sought early and, after changes in immigration policies, it
became a popular destination for other Hyderabadis as well. Australia had
aboriginal inhabitants, but its settlement by Britons and Europeans in the

late eighteenth century drew it into the world political economy. Its colonies were granted independence separately in the nineteenth century and formed a federation in 1901.[56] The federation set immigration restrictions in 1901 that envisioned an essentially "white" Australia, a country welcoming speakers of European languages, preferably those of British stock.[57] A prescribed dictation test had to be passed in a European language; after 1904, the test could be in "any prescribed language," but no non-European language was ever prescribed.[58] Some British Indian and Asian settlers had come as indentured or free laborers in the nineteenth century, before 1901, and Anglo-Indians with British passports were admitted after 1947.[59]

Australia gradually changed its immigration and citizenship policies to facilitate the settlement of non-Europeans, emphasizing those with special skills or relatives already in the country. Non-European spouses of Australian citizens were allowed from 1959, political parties removed "White Australia" from their platforms in 1965, and subsequent policy modifications led to an official declaration of a universal intake policy in 1973.[60] Economic recessions of the 1980s and 1990s generated periodic questioning of the new open immigration policies and sometimes a temporary reduction of the numbers admitted. In the late 1980s, many college-educated immigrants came from India and Pakistan,[61] but this large influx met with an economic recession soon after arrival. Australia's population growth declined slightly each year after 1989, when immigration began to be cut back for economic reasons. The Australian recession of 1990–1994 hit hard, with immigrants being underpaid according to their qualifications. Gaps between non-English-speaking workers and Australian-born workers widened.[62]

After the changes in its "whites only" immigration policy beginning in the 1960s,[63] national discourse shifted toward multiculturalism. Even more than in Canada and the United States, ideas of nationhood and society had been based on European settlement, but the new populations had an impact. Access to citizenship has become relatively easy. At first, children born in Australia were citizens and naturalization could be secured after five years, then the time to naturalization was shortened to three and finally to two years. Talk of multiculturalism began in the 1970s as politicians responded to new voters. Australia became committed to a multiculturalism model that envisioned individuals and groups being fully incorporated into society without losing their distinctiveness, a major change from the earlier expectation that newcomers should assimilate to the dominant Anglo-Celtic culture. Ethnic rights movements focusing on Australia's aboriginal population and non-English-speaking immigrants led to the 1978 declaration of multiculturalism as the official policy by the then-conservative government. The "Great Immigration Debate" begun in 1984 led to cuts of financial support for multiculturalism in 1986 (but many cuts were reinstated in 1987). In 1989, the National Agenda for a Multicultural Australia was proclaimed and the policy was extended to indigenous as well as immigrant populations. As in Canada, the initial emphasis on cultural preservation has shifted to issues of inequity and disadvantage.[64]

The federal government used its powers in the 1990s to promote multiculturalism strongly, with particular encouragement for education in both the national language and the mother tongue. Distinct divisions can be discerned between Anglo-Celts, non-English-speaking immigrants, and indigenous people, and multicultural policies were primarily focused on those from non-English-speaking backgrounds. Nonetheless, the popular perception was that "ethnics" were dying out and would assimilate to the dominant Anglo-Celtic ways. Their texts were seen as productions of nostalgia, their literary figures as writers in tension with and being absorbed into the Anglo-Celtic canon.[65]

By the 1990s, Australia had become one of the most urbanized countries in the world and presented a very different face from that of the 1950s. Sydney, Melbourne, Brisbane, Perth, and Adelaide, its five largest cities, had 10 million of the country's 17 million people in 1993, and workers continued to move away from agriculture and mining into urban occupations.[66] Australia has diversified its economy and expanded trade relationships within the Asian regional economy. Australia's trade with Indian Ocean countries in 1994 was 18.4 percent of its total trade, and Australia's foreign minister in 1997 supported the formation of the Indian Ocean Rim Association for Regional Cooperation.[67] In the 1991 census, Asian-born Australians were 4.3 percent of the total population. Since the 1970s, the percentage of immigrants who are Asian rose from 15 percent of the total in 1976–1977 to 34 percent in 1986–1987. Asian Aussies were, in 1997, 4.7 percent of the 18 million Australians, and of the 100,000 immigrants each year, about a third were Asians.[68] Recessions in the 1990s brought backlashes, political movements to resurrect and reinforce the old monocultural Anglo-Celtic Australia.[69]

India and Pakistan were important to Australia, sending tourists and students as well as immigrants. India was Australia's largest tourism growth market, sending some 18,000 visitors per year in 1995, and the numbers were rising.[70] Australian higher educational institutions have attracted a steadily increasing number of overseas fee-paying students. Australia advertised for students in India and Pakistan, arguing that the United States and Europe were not the only places to go for higher education. There were many advantages to studying in Australia, whether in colleges of technical education or leading universities. Admission procedures were simple, it was easy to secure student visas, and the cost was cheaper than in the UK or the states. Importantly, students were allowed to work up to twenty hours per week and full time during vacations. Finally, Australia was a safe, friendly, and tropical country. There were 700 students from India in Australia in 1993 and 3,000 in 1996.[71]

The Indian immigrant population profile has changed since the decades when most immigrants from India were Anglo-Indians. Since 1981 most Indian immigrants have been of ethnic Indian origin and they have done very well, earning more than the average Australian. Their numbers increased from 60,958 India-born people in 1991 to about 72,000 in 1993. Indian immigrants in the 1991 census had high incomes, their average earnings 31 percent higher than the average national earnings, and higher levels of postsecondary and education or trade qualifications in general. One-third of the Indian immigrants spoke languages other than English at home, but almost all of them had a good knowledge of English, which contributed to the figures above (and the second generation also valued education more highly than the total Australian population). Immigrants from India were a very urban group, only 8 percent of them settling outside of the major cities, compared to a national profile showing 31.2 percent of the Australian population outside the major cities.[72] Two-thirds of Australia's India-born immigrants lived in the three cities of Sydney, Melbourne, and Perth.[73]

Australia aggressively recruited immigrants from India and Pakistan. Like the students, South Asian immigrants had reasons to prefer Australia to the United States and Britain. Family values remained strong and crime rates were far lower than in the United States or the UK. Although some young Australians did cohabit before marrying, marriage and family remained important, and Australians looked to families for support, financial assistance, welfare, and care. An Australian Bureau of Statistics study showed that 88 percent of Australians lived in a family; 8 percent lived alone; and 3 percent lived in group households.[74] Signs of the South Asian presence were everywhere, in leading professional associations, new religious associations, the media, and popular culture. *India Today*, a national magazine like *Time* and *Newsweek*, started distribution in Australia in July 1994, and a Sydney Indian restaurant sponsored a beauty competition for Miss India Down Under in the same year.

THE UNITED STATES

The United States was a destination for small numbers of mostly male students and Punjabi farmers in the early twentieth century, and federal restrictions on Asian immigration kept the Indian immigrant population low.[75] Extensive lobbying by Indians in the United States was instrumental in the passage of the Luce-Celler Bill in 1946, finally allowing Indians access to naturalization and opportunities to sponsor relatives to immigrate. However, the quota was small, 105 per year each for India and Pakistan after 1947. The surge of new immigration came after 1965 when the U.S. Immigration and Naturalization Act reversed decades of discrimination, beginning preferential admission of Asian immigrants. Under the 1965 Act, visas were issued by national origin on the basis of preferred skills or family reunification, with annual quotas of 20,000 for each country. Highly educated professionals migrating in family units came from all over South Asia. By the late 1960s, their totals were rising dramatically and were still rising: Asian Indians (the census term adopted in 1980) numbered 8,746 in 1960, 815,447 in 1990, and 1,678,765 in 2000. Because so many were employed in industrial and service sectors of the economy as scientists, engineers, and health professionals, Asian Indians were heavily concentrated in metropolitan areas.[76]

The United States had the largest foreign-born population in world, 19.6 million, but this was only 8 percent of its total population (Canada's foreign-born percentage is double that). Asian Americans were a rapidly rising proportion of the total population: They will become 8 percent by 2020. Asian Indians became the third largest Asian American group (following Chinese and Filipinos) in the 1990s[77] and they stood out among Asian Americans for their balanced gender ratio. They made heavy use of occupational and investor categories of the 1965 immigration reforms to develop family networks and then utilize the family reunification provisions.[78] Family-based immigration continued to increase, particularly in the over-65 age group, and the U.S. Census Bureau expected immigration to outstrip births among Asian Americans for the next thirty or so years, so that the Asian American population will continue to be more than half foreign-born. The categories of relatives given preference and most frequently admitted were the siblings of U.S. citizens and their spouses and children and the spouses and unmarried sons and daughters of resident aliens and their children. This situation contrasted with the earlier-settled South Asian population in the UK, where fertility rather than immigration fueled population growth.

Indians and Pakistanis together were about 90 percent of America's South Asian immigrants and India's share was by far the largest, although a higher percentage of Pakistan's population was emigrating.[79] These recent immigrants came from all over South Asia, representing all the languages of the subcontinent. Among South Asians, most were Hindus, then came Muslims, and then Sikhs; the reverse was true in Canada, and in the

UK most were Muslims, then Sikhs, and then Hindus. But as in the UK and Canada, Islam was becoming the nation's second-largest religion, and about 25 percent of American Muslims were of South Asian descent.[80] In the United States, South Asians were emerging as the intellectual and political leaders of national and transnational Muslim political movements.[81]

The annual arrival numbers of South Asians fluctuated in response to the American economy and to specific immigration legislation and regulations. Students, workers entering illegally, and winners of a visa lottery program[82] also added to immigration. Students from India and Pakistan came in large numbers for higher education.[83] Many who came as students in the 1950s for training or degree study stayed on; more than half of all Indian immigrants who changed their status in the 1950s and 1960s to that of resident alien had come initially as students.[84] A 1990 Immigration Act made it easier to get nonimmigrant visas for religious workers; new federal regulations in 1995 made it harder to hire foreign workers as temporary professionals, but in 2000, these were changed to facilitate the hiring of computer software professionals. South Asian professionals scrutinized new visa allotments and changing employment regulations carefully. For example, South Asian doctors worried in the mid-1990s about policies setting quotas for foreign-born residents in hospitals.

The threats posed by anti-immigration sentiments in the mid-1990s and the cutoffs of some public benefits—Supplemental Security Income (SSI) and disability benefits even to legal immigrants—pushed South Asians to become U.S. citizens. Indian immigrants to the United States from 1970 to 1979 had a naturalization rate of 53.6 percent, and the rate has risen.[85] Legal permanent residents could become naturalized U.S. citizens after five years of residence if they could read, write, and speak English and had a basic knowledge of American history and government. Becoming a U.S. citizen gave one's relatives preference in the family reunification categories: the spouses and unmarried sons and daughters of citizens, for example, gained entry faster than those of permanent residents or green card holders. Thus immigrants often sponsored their parents, who became citizens and applied for their remaining unmarried children, a strategy that brought siblings to the United States faster.

These post-1965 Indian and Pakistani immigrants were very privileged, and in the United States, South Asians were often classified as white, giving them some claim to "model minority" status.[86] Those born in India (the population for which statistics were readily available) had the highest median household income, family income, and per capita income of any foreign-born group in the 1990 census, and a study of foreign-born professionals showed foreign-born Indians to be the highest paid among foreign-born professionals, with an annual median income of $40,625. The immigrants born in India also had the highest percentage with a bachelor's degree or higher and the highest percentage in managerial and professional fields.[87] Measures of family stability showed immigrants from India leading the foreign-born in percentage of population married and at the bottom in percentage of those separated and divorced, with four people the most common household size.[88]

Among the skilled South Asian professionals, many were doctors. A 1993 estimate put Indian doctors at more than 20,000, or nearly 4 percent of the nation's medical doctors, and the largest ethnic body of doctors in the United States is the American Association of Physicians from India. The Association of Pakistani Physicians of North America overlapped somewhat with the Islamic Medical Association of Canada, and there were associations of Indian pharmacists and Indo-American physicians and dentists. Other large groups were of Indian computer professionals and engineers, and Indian business students outnumbered any other international group.[89] Occupational patterns for Asian Indian men and women in the United States showed many Asian Indian women working in professional positions. Frequently both spouses were working, and savings rates were high.[90]

Well placed in the American economy and founders of their own networks of new immigrants, the post-1965 immigrants from South Asia appeared to be successfully maintaining South Asian culture in the United States. Their position was strong in academia and mainstream cultural arenas like literature, film, and music. The first wave of post-1965 South Asian immigrants was responsible for these high standards, but those arriving since the mid-1980s had a much lower percentage in managerial and professional jobs, much lower median incomes, and a much higher unemployment rate. Later arrivals coming in under the Family Reunification Act were not so well qualified, and many also came during recessions.[91]

In presenting themselves to the wider society, people from the Indian subcontinent found that Americans often knew little about their countries and did not know what "South Asia" denoted. And despite their relatively high socioeconomic profile, South Asians experienced prejudice and discrimination, leading them to become active in political funding and campaigning. They have made their numbers and influence felt at the state level, and they are also forming national federations, both Indian and Pakistani, in the United States.

Although the state played no major role in recognizing and supporting ethnic cultures, unlike the situation in Canada, and a strong emphasis on individualism set the parameters for racial and ethnic identity politics, South Asians explored identifications with larger racial and/or ethnic categories in the population. Asian Americans or Muslim Americans were the preferred choices, with both Indians and Pakistanis making such moves. Among South Asian second-generation students on American campuses, Asian American and Muslim American organizations were popular. "Progressive" political people called for an alliance with African Americans and other racial minorities in the United States,[92] but as in the UK, this alliance was more often avoided and never was historically strong. Many young people are achieving prominence in fusion activities, unlike members of the first generation who more often invest in "authentic" national origin activities.

CANADA

Canada, reflecting its long historical connection with the British Empire, was a popular destination for Indian and Pakistani immigrants, including Hyderabadis. Like the United States, Canada began getting immigrants from India around the turn of the twentieth century, almost all Sikhs from the Punjab who settled in British Columbia.[93] Canada had no formal immigration policy until 1952, although in practice the emphasis was on economic needs; "social undesirables," especially Asians, were excluded by administrative discretion. In 1962, Canada amended its evolving immigration regulations to provide for universal admission according to skills, family unification, and humanitarian considerations. Given the continuing decline in fertility of the Canadian population, subsequent legislative changes affirmed principles of nondiscrimination and provided for refugee status determination. Immigration control problems were minor and Canada remained relatively open to immigrants and refugees.[94]

At the turn of the twenty-first century, migrating to Canada was easier than entering the United States, and a striking 17 percent of Canada's population was foreign born. The percentage of foreign born was higher in cities: 35 percent of Vancouver's population and 40–42 percent of Toronto's.[95] Because one could not apply for immigration from within the country, fewer students came to Canada. Some new Canadians came by way of the UK, Australia, or the Gulf states of the Middle East[96] where British influence remained strong. One could get permanent residence in Canada without first having a job offer or labor certification and there was no country quota to limit admissions. In 1967, a point system began evaluating applicants in business or skilled worker/professional categories, with bonus points given for relatives who were already Canadian citizens or permanent residents. An immigrant could become a citizen after three years of residency. Canada claimed to be "kinder and gentler" than the United States, a North American country without America's "three Gs": guns, ghettoes, and gated communities. Earnings might be lower and taxes higher than in the United States, but state schools were generally good, tuition was low, and health care was publicly funded and universal. Canada was rated the safest place to live in the industrialized world. However, unemployment was double that in the United States and after-tax income was one-third lower.[97] Also, the number of immigrants allowed in annually was cut in 1994, and fees were increased on newcomers in 1995; family-sponsored immigrants are hit hardest by these measures.[98]

Canada adopted an official policy of multiculturalism in 1971, replacing the earlier bicultural policy based on long-established British and French populations. The Canadian state extended equal rights to immigrants as citizens and to ethnic communities, its multicultural policies explicitly supporting the maintenance of ethnic cultures. Policy emphasis, initially on the right to preservation of one's culture and ethnicity, shifted to issues of equality, social participation, and national unity.[99] The phrase "visible minority" was often used in public discourse for immigrants from Asia, Africa, and other non-European places.

Recent immigrants have had a major impact on national demography, given the high proportion of immigrants in the national population. Most immigrants came from Asia. In 1998, the list of the top ten senders of immigrants to Canada started with eight Asian countries (including Iran) and ended with the United States and Russia.[100] Of Canada's 1.5 million Asians, the Chinese were the largest group, followed by South Asians. More than half of the country's Asians were in Ontario, particularly Toronto.[101] In fact, chewing *pan* was common on the streets of Toronto, but the Department of Health and Welfare classified all forms of betel-nut a health hazard and banned it.[102]

Because Canada determined its multicultural categories by nation of origin, the operative categories for South Asians were India and Pakistan. Not only Sikhs but also Indian Muslims, both somewhat dissatisfied minorities in India, were forced into the India box to secure state funding and influence policy decisions. Although religious institutions benefited from certain taxation and incorporation policies, ethnic institutions benefited from multicultural funding programs.[103] Resisting these rules emphasized religious identities and Sikhs, just 2 percent of India's population, were still the largest group among Canada's South Asians; Muslims came next, and then Hindus.[104] There was pressure from both Canadian Sikhs and Muslims to organize along religious lines, in the first case as a subnational group and in the second as a transnational one in terms of Canadian notions of ethnicity.

Islam is the second largest religion in Canada, mainly due to the rapid influx of immigrants and refugees from many nations and a relatively high birthrate in those groups.[105] As in the UK, this Muslim minority has had an impact, although in Canada the issues were posed more in terms of the delivery of appropriate social services.[106] There were tensions: the Canadian branch of the Islamic Society of North America joined the Evangelical Fellowship of Canada in opposing spousal pensions to homosexual partners.[107] There were also accommodations. In Ontario, where more than half of Canada's Muslims resided (146,000 of 250,000, according to the 1991 census), the election of *shari'a* or Islamic law for domestic family issues was being discussed as an option for Muslims. Most academics and journalists have emphasized the positive thrust of Canadian Muslim identity. A reporter quoted the board chairman of the Cambridge, Ontario, Islamic center and mosque: "The mezzanine for the ladies, the social gatherings, a gym for the boys and girls would not have been found in mosques 'back home' he pointed out. But there is nothing un-Islamic about adapting to North American culture."[108]

While many of the post-1960s Indian and Pakistani immigrants were middle- and upper-class, as in the United States, the higher rate of acceptance of refugees in Canada has meant an almost equally large number of immigrants with low socioeconomic status.[109] Although immigrants were calculated to contribute more to the public purse, earning and saving more than Canadian-born households, the proportion of those coming for family reunification, typically relatives with lower levels of education and skills than their sponsors, has been rising and may change that calculation.[110]

Canada's "visible minority" label sometimes disadvantaged Indians and Pakistanis as "non-whites," as in Britain. However, there were many success stories, particularly in British Columbia where Punjabi Sikh descendants have attained political positions. Authors, filmmakers, comedians, playwrights, models, activists, and professionals of South Asian ancestry have achieved recognition. South Asians in Canada might rail against the "multicultural boxes," but they also used them to gain resources for heritage languages and cultures.

THE GULF STATES OF THE MIDDLE EAST

For South Asian and other expatriates in the Gulf, postwar capitalism produced opportunities to use their skills for higher pay and in better working conditions than at home. Businessmen, professionals, service workers, and laborers left their homes to become part of a flexible international labor force, yet the Arab rulers set rigorous conditions for expatriate work and family life.[111] South Asian expatriates benefited slightly from the long-standing historical ties between South Asia and some of the Gulf states, particularly Oman and the United Arab Emirates (UAE).[112] British dominance in the Gulf continued to be oriented to India but Britain conducted separate relations with each state, leading to separate flags, travel documents or passports, and ultimately national anthems.[113] The states, whose boundaries and relations with each other had been historically fluid, developed distinct identities, yet British dominance produced important commonalities. The Indian rupee was the principal currency in the Gulf, Indian stamps were used (overlaid with state names), political officers applied British Indian regulations, and Hindustani (Urdu and Hindi) words infiltrated the Arabic coastal dialect.[114] Yemeni and other Gulf Arabs worked as soldiers in Indian native states, including Hyderabad. Other links to India included those developed through the pearl diving industry, the mainstay of most Gulf economies before the oil discoveries commencing in the 1930s. For decades, Gulf merchants sent pearls to Hyderabad for stringing and setting into jewelry. The 1929 Wall Street crash, the resultant world economic depression, and the Japanese introduction of cultured pearls brought about the collapse of the pearl industry, plunging the Gulf economies into crisis.[115] But it was just at that time that foreign oil companies began arriving in search of concessions, and the oil concessions established a pattern of reliance on foreign expertise and manpower that has persisted beyond the termination of the foreign oil concessions in the late 1970s.

The Gulf to South Asians meant the six monarchies of Saudi Arabia, Kuwait, Bahrain, Oman, Qatar, and the United Arab Emirates. These six formed the Gulf Cooperation Council, or GCC, in 1981, primarily for security reasons. There were only two categories of residents in the Gulf states, citizens and noncitizens, and the limitation of citizenship to "nationals" or "locals" rested on a "genealogical" conception of nationalism.[116] The ruling families conceived of the states as theirs, of their fellow tribesmen as their subjects and citizens, and of the large numbers of expatriate workers of all classes and national origins as perpetual outsiders. Like the other Gulf rulers, the Arab rulers of Kuwait and the seven emirates that made up the federation of the UAE[117] delegated few political rights even to their own citizens. Their citizens, did, however, receive many economic benefits. Home ownership was nearly universal for citizens, and water, power, and telephones were heavily subsidized; sanitation services were free. Free education often included education abroad, and free or nearly free health care could include care abroad. The expatriate workers also benefited from some state subsidies.

Workers came to the Gulf from all over the world, providing an international and flexible work force. Of the total population of these six GCC countries in the 1990s, estimated at 23 million, some 10 million were foreigners, one million of them maids.[118] At first, expatriate workers were drawn from Persia and from neighboring Arab countries, but workers from Asia steadily increased. Pakistanis moved into the Gulf in the early 1970s, followed and surpassed by Indians in the 1980s, with strong representation from Bangladesh and Sri Lanka by the 1990s. The Philippines, Thailand, and South Korea increasingly sent workers to the Gulf, and the "better trained and disciplined" Southeast Asians intensified the competition for jobs and contributed to the lowering of wages and salaries.[119]

This globalization of the labor market did not erase difference; as Michael Watt remarked, such globalization "revalidates and reconstitutes place, locality, and difference."[120] Foreign workers were ranked by places of origin, receiving differential payment and treatment.[121] The ranks roughly reflected salary differences, with non-GCC or "other Arabs" ranked above Asians, and gradations within the groups as well. Thus the other Arabs of Lebanese, Palestinian, and Syrian origin commanded the highest wages and salaries, Egyptians and Sudanese received half as much, and South and Southeast Asians received one-third as much. Among laborers, Indians ranked above Pakistanis, who ranked above Bangladeshis and Chinese. There were also strong gender differences within and across citizen and noncitizen categories. Political participation, if any, had been extended chiefly to male citizens, and although expatriate male laborers were covered by state labor codes, domestic workers, predominantly female, were not. Expatriate women came as maids, but also as doctors, teachers, nurses, and wives. In Kuwait, most maids were from the Philippines, and in the UAE most were from Sri Lanka; other maids came from Bangladesh, India, and Indonesia.[122]

India and Pakistan were major suppliers of labor to the Gulf. Although the percentage of India's export earnings from remittances was not very significant, remittances from abroad, 75 percent of them from the Middle East, constituted the single largest source of export earnings for Pakistan.[123] Thus the declining numbers of Indian and Pakistani workers in the Gulf in the late 1980s and especially after the Gulf War of 1990–1991 proved disruptive. In 1995, Pakistan reported that its manpower exports to the Gulf had dropped by more than 50 percent since 1985 because of increased competition and a shift from unskilled to skilled workers and professionals. India also saw a decrease in the annual outflow of manpower.[124]

South Asians were the largest expatriate group in both Kuwait and the UAE at the end of the twentieth century, but Asians constituted 85 percent of expatriates in the UAE and only 57 percent in Kuwait. Indians were approximately double the number of Pakistanis in each, with more Bangladeshis and Sri Lankans than Pakistanis in Kuwait and the reverse in the UAE. The population of Kuwait was about two-thirds noncitizens, and most foreign workers in Kuwait were male (only 31% were female) and bachelors. In the UAE, 75 percent of the population was said to be expatriate, and in Dubai that proportion was said to be 80 percent. The sex ratio among expatriates in the UAE was 70 percent male and 30 percent female, almost identical to that in Kuwait.[125]

The Gulf states regulated expatriate labor heavily, requiring visas, sponsors, work permits, residence permits, and medical checkups. Recruitment started in the home countries, involving brokers and manpower recruiting agencies at both ends; costs were high and some were unofficial.[126] The state regulations were quite similar in Kuwait and Dubai. Citizen sponsors were needed even for visitors' visas (save for GCC citizens), and residence visas were of three types: work, dependent, and servant. Whether businessmen, professionals, or workers, expatriates over the age of sixty were not permitted. A noncitizen could do private business in the Gulf in many closely regulated ways, most of them involving a local agent, sponsor, or partner (in Kuwait this had to be a man, but it could be a woman in the UAE). These working relationships were typically quite nominal, with sponsors taking commissions from many foreigners annually but not participating in the businesses.[127]

Family life for expatriates depended on their class. A man who made a certain amount of money monthly and had secured a residence visa could sponsor his wife and children to live with him; the amount was high (slightly less in the UAE than in Kuwait) to discourage workers from bringing their families. If both spouses were working, their salaries could be added together. Wives could not sponsor husbands in Kuwait, but women doctors and teachers could sponsor husbands in the UAE. In both sites, adult (over eighteen) unmarried daughters could be sponsored but not adult sons, and no dependents could work without their own sponsors and work visas. Parents could visit for one to three months (since 1995 in Kuwait, they could stay longer for a high annual fee).[128] Foreigners (except GCC citizens) could not own land or real estate and had to rent accommodations, customarily unfurnished ones.

Expatriates could employ other expatriates. They could sponsor one full-time household servant (again there was a minimum salary requirement).[129] If a man sponsored a female servant he had to be married and have his wife living with him. Maids had to be between twenty and fifty years old, and family members could not be brought as servants. Maids and other domestic workers lived in their employers' households, whereas male laborers and service workers usually grouped together in rooms or dormitories and contracted for two or three meals a day at dining halls.

South Asian expatriates working in the Gulf benefited from salaries many times those at home, and their incomes were tax-free. Working conditions were excellent, with modern facilities and technology, and living conditions were also good, with cheap and dependable water, electricity, air conditioning, and other amenities. In Kuwait, expatriates and their dependents got free health care until 1994, after which they have paid low fees for nonemergency procedures. Food in both places was government subsidized. Because of the extremely hot summer, government workers got one month's leave and private workers got at least that every year, plenty of time to holiday in Europe, have a long visit home, or drop in on relatives elsewhere. Although residences had to be rented, leases could be arranged for five-year stretches.

The Gulf cities compared very favorably to cities in the Western world, and yet they were culturally non-Western, an important consideration for those who viewed Western culture as threatening to personal safety or to family and religious values. Professional and businesspeople believed that they were still in an Asian context—in South Asia, the Gulf is also called West Asia.[130] Law and order were strictly maintained, and in Kuwait and Dubai, unlike Saudi Arabia, one could freely practice one's religion. Those who worked in Dubai had additional incentives. Dubai was fun, although people saved less because enjoyable diversions were plentiful and more of them brought families.

The one certainty was that expatriates could not stay in the Gulf permanently and they were psychologically prepared for this, retaining strongly positive relationships with India or Pakistan and seeing themselves as overseas citizens of those states. South Asians working in the Gulf invested in consumer durables back home, building and repairing houses, celebrating family occasions, and schooling their children well.[131] Middle-class expatriates often held multiple citizenship or immigration rights, an Indian citizen securing a U.S. and/or Canadian green card, and Pakistanis obtaining dual citizenship with the UK, United States, or Canada (those countries, but not India, allowed it). The laborers typically had fewer options but were just as prepared to return home or go elsewhere to work.

Assessing Destinations

The voices of the Hyderabadi emigrants in the following chapters show that the policies and demographic and cultural configurations of the various nation-states reviewed here set important parameters for their evolving identities as individuals and as members of communities abroad. They bring alive the power relations embedded in the "politics of location," the local, regional, and national dimensions of "situatedness," the ways in which cultural location produces new ethnicities and new political identities.[132] The government proved a more significant player in some countries than in others, as we will see through the words and experiences of ordinary immigrants in the various destinations.

The different contexts for immigrants encouraged different kinds of sociocultural and political organizations and coalitions. The Hyderabadi immigrants formed Hyderabad associations in some sites but not in others. They created or joined associations based on language, religion, educational affiliation, and profession or occupation, associations that also evoked homeland loyalties. Immigrants sometimes joined associations grounded in the new sites like national associations of lawyers, doctors, or business-people, and some associations cut across national boundaries and raised theoretical issues related to transnationalism and cosmopolitanism.

Transnational considerations complicated family life for the emigrants from Hyderabad. Those who went abroad for education or work often stayed on and raised children in the new sites, children whose marriages they tried to arrange later on; there was also a growing tendency to bring their parents from Hyderabad. The relative merits of medical facilities, health insurance and other government benefits, and paths to permanent residency or citizenship in different destinations were compared and debated as immigrants planned how best to care for their elderly parents. There was the fact that Hyderabadi women abroad often made desirable, even necessary, contributions to family earnings, empowering them within the family.

Transnationalism became more complicated as members of Hyderabadi families ended up in more than two nations. As we will see in subsequent chapters, siblings commonly scattered, some migrating to the United States while others went to the UK, Canada, and Australia, or worked for periods in the Middle East. Some became twice- or thrice-migrants, moving on from one destination to another; Pakistan in particular stopped receiving Hyderabadis and began sending them abroad. Such dispersion of family members produced complex patterns as parents and children traveled back and forth. Some families or communities had a preference for cousin marriage, but when cousins were raised in different countries, unforeseen problems could arise in the marriages arranged between them. In fact, marriages of any type challenged scattered relatives to select the most convenient and desirable places for weddings to be held and couples to be settled. But let us turn to the destinations and see how Hyderabadis have fared in the diverse sites.

CHAPTER 4

Pakistan: Changing Nations

JUST A YEAR BEFORE Partition, anticipating it, her father sent a young woman raised in Hyderabad to Kinnaird College in the British Indian city of Lahore, foreseeing it would be in Pakistan. Bushra Waheed recalled her youthful impressions:

> Had I not gone to Lahore, to Kinnaird, my perspective on the world would have been entirely different. In Hyderabad I thought the world belonged to the Muslims, the Hindus were the riffraff, the Dravidians. The elite, the fair, good-looking people were Iranians, Turks. . . . [W]e moved in high circles in Hyderabad. . . . All the top students were Muslims. Then I went to Kinnaird and got a great surprise. I saw the lists of the best scholars, the best athletes, and all the names were Hindu. How little we knew of British India! In our country, even X's daughters [X was a very high-ranking Hindu noble], in my class, were at the bottom, they didn't have that confidence. In Lahore, all the smart, top, good-looking people were Hindus. . . . And those Hindu girls threw their *dupattas* [long scarfs] around and even wore shorts, some of them; we Muslims were shy and wrapped modestly. I and my friend were astonished.

Her vivid statement not only reminds one that worlds were turned upside down in 1947 and 1948 but illustrates how quickly the young are socialized into new environments, how strongly their identities are shaped by the intersections of power, culture, and place. Although she spoke as a Hyderabadi, this young woman had spent only ten or eleven years there, after Osmania University recruited her father, Dr. Anwar Iqbal Qureshi, to be professor of economics.[1] From Jullundur, east Punjab, he was a non-mulki Hyderabadi whose daughter attended Hyderabad's elite institutions, St. George's Grammar School and Mahbubiyah Girls' School.

Strong relationships among culture, power, and place have framed the Hyderabadi experiences in Pakistan from their beginnings. The most strongly committed and concentrated in time of all Hyderabadi emigrations, the movement to Pakistan nevertheless included people of exceedingly diverse backgrounds and ideologies. The emigrants experienced conflicts at many levels in their new nation, conflicts with each other, with other immigrants and indigenous Pakistanis, and, not least, conflicts between Pakistan and India. Having made a sudden and irreversible commitment to the new nation, Hyderabadis, like others from India, disconcertingly found themselves labeled *muhajirs*. "How could we be refugees, coming to our homeland?" one man asked, and his dismay was echoed by others. A "return to the homeland" was for most an imaginative exercise, based on idealistic notions of Islam (a few did have recent roots in the Punjab or the northwest frontier). While some Hyderabadi immigrants successfully distanced themselves from the muhajir label and were accepted as "unmarked" Pakistanis, others remained identified as Hyderabadis.

By the mid-1960s, the Hyderabadi migration to Pakistan was essentially over, and by the 1980s another move was under way. Despite their strong self-identities as native Pakistanis, many members of the second generation were moving out, going abroad for education, jobs, and marriages. This second move shows that Hyderabadis were doing well enough in Pakistan to send their children abroad but also that they were losing confidence in their children's futures in Pakistan, or, at least, that they wanted their children to have options.

Leaving Hyderabad

PATTERNS OF MIGRATION

Muslims from Hyderabad who chose to go to Pakistan rather than remain in what became India were mostly newcomers to East or West Pakistan, bringing their visions of what Pakistan should be. Members of the Razakar paramilitary movement of Hyderabad State's last years, Hyderabadi Muslims from the Indian Army, and Urdu journalists were among those who immediately opted for Pakistan. Some leading educators and officials were quickly recruited by Pakistan, and other Hyderabadis moved after the 1956 creation of Andhra Pradesh. Most immigrants settled in Karachi, with outposts in Lahore, Peshawar, and the twin cities of Islamabad and Rawalpindi.[2] Pakistan's first capital, Karachi, was a port city little developed in comparison to other cities in British India. Peshawar, on the Afghan frontier at the end of the Grand Trunk Road across northern India from Calcutta, had once been an important trade link to Central Asia, Iran, and China. Rawalpindi was a British Indian Army cantonment town. Only Lahore was a major urban center, the former capital city for both Mughals and Sikhs with its own university. West Pakistan was a new landscape to Hyderabadi immigrants, and even more so the monsoon-soaked rice fields of East Pakistan and its Bengali language. Some Hyderabadis did go to East Pakistan as government officials, but after the 1971 birth of Bangladesh, they moved to Pakistan or elsewhere.

Until the introduction of passports for Indians and Pakistanis in 1952 or 1953, migration from India could be carefully planned and affairs in Hyderabad comfortably wound up. Conditions thereafter became more difficult, although in 1953 the government in Hyderabad and the Pakistan government agreed to apply Hyderabad service (of more than five years) to Pakistan service, benefiting those who transferred mid-career. But parents who followed their adult children to Pakistan later had to forfeit their Indian citizenship and often their pensions from the Nizam's government; once these steps were taken there was no going back.

Early Hyderabadi immigrants to Pakistan were young men below the age of twenty, some of them participants in the Razakar paramilitary movement.[3] When the Indian Army took over in 1948, these young men had no future in India; many were wanted men. Other young Muslims struck out for Pakistan feeling they would have greater career opportunities there. Bachelors from lower-middle-class and middle-class families, they tended to marry Punjabis, Kashmiris, or Sindhis in Pakistan.[4]

Some emigrants had found the new Indian Hyderabad humiliating. Khwaja Masihuddin, a schoolboy in 1948, was carrying his books home when an Indian Army soldier ordered him to take off his fez and asked him if he was a Razakar. He complained to an Indian Army officer nearby, who restrained the soldier but told him "Now look, your days are over in Hyderabad."[5] Syed Shah Baleequddin, president of the Muslim Student Federation and an Osmania student in 1948, spoke for many like him: "All of my generation, educated or not, realized that there was no future for us in India. Victimization had begun. In Pakistan, we Muslims would be of one culture."[6] A. A. Jabbar of the Hyderabad Civil Service (HCS) stayed in Hyderabad initially but found that "the Indian government was insulting, the policy was insulting; when Aurangzeb conquered Golconda, he was courteous and good to the former rulers, not like that."[7] "Of course we had good Hindu friends in Hyderabad," Mrs. Barkatullah said, "but other Hindus came, and we feared differences with them."

Hyderabadi immigrants brought needed skills and, sometimes, financial resources. They filled crucial military, administrative, educational, medical, and entrepreneurial positions. The Nizam himself forwarded funds, at least 20 crores rupees or 200 million rupees[8] (in 1948, at 3.31 rupees to the dollar, that was $60,422,961) that enabled the young nation to pay initial salaries and other expenses.

Hyderabadis who opted for Pakistan were explicit about why they had come and what they contributed to the new nation. Military men saw it as "a straightforward decision: I was Muslim, therefore I went to Pakistan."[9] Educators left Osmania to help form the government[10] and build universities in Pakistan.[11] In Sind, the educational level was very low and muhajirs quickly took control of the new country's banking system, with Hyderabadis reportedly dominating the State Bank of Pakistan.[12] Osmania graduates were the leading doctors in Karachi for many years. People from Hyderabad's Deccan Airways founded Pakistan International Airlines (PIA), and the PIA air hostess uniform copied the Hyderabadi style pajama and *kamiz*. The Industrial Exhibition started in Hyderabad by the Osmania University Graduates was duplicated in Pakistan. The former owners of Hyderabad's Liberty Theatre developed Lahore's new Liberty shopping area. These and other achievements were eagerly listed, in ways revealing that the Hyderabadis saw themselves as coming to a tabula rasa, a place without talent, education, or institutions.

Hyderabadis who migrated were very differently equipped for life in the new nation. Students and professors, scientists and engineers, and bureaucrats and businessmen sought jobs and resources from the Hyderabad Trust and their new government, and India and Pakistan vied with each other for the best of them. Class divisions and internal tensions marked the first-generation "Hyderabadi community" in Pakistan. Men who were not used to competing in the marketplace had to do so, often against other Hyderabadis. Those who moved mid-career or some years after 1948 sometimes experienced downward mobility. Some people "without family background" forged dynamic careers and considered 1948 a blessing, while others from aristocratic families languished in the new setting.

COMING IN AT THE TOP

Several important Hyderabadis found themselves in Pakistan almost by accident, their presence commanded by others. These men were crucial to building the new nation and to supporting other Hyderabadis. At center stage in the early days was Nawab Mushtaq Ahmed Khan, whom the Nizam appointed as his agent general in Karachi from April of 1948.[13] Mushtaq Ahmed Khan, born in 1903 in the eastern Punjab, had moved to Hyderabad in 1912 when his father Fakhr Yar Jung became finance minister. Educated at Aligarh, then abroad at Cambridge, the London School of Economics, the Middle Temple, and finally in France, Ahmed Khan joined the Hyderabad Railways and was to become general manager in

1948. Instead, he found himself packing his suitcase at the Nizam's request for what he thought would be a three-month stay in Pakistan. Stranded in Karachi by the Police Action, he had with him 20 million rupees of Hyderabad State's money.[14] He deposited this in the State Bank of Pakistan, stipulating that nothing was to be spent without his knowledge and consent.[15]

This money caused continuing conflict among Hyderabadi immigrants. The governor general of Pakistan then was Ghulam Mohamed, who had been Hyderabad's finance minister from 1942 to 1945; he was one of the men of Punjabi origin who found it easy to "return" and get a good position.[16] Mohamed wanted to form a Hyderabad Trust to use the money for Hyderabadi immigrants, but Mushtaq Ahmed Khan would not agree. He was instructed not to let India get the money, nor let it be used to support individuals or start industries; the money was for the freedom struggle of Hyderabad. In 1950, Ghulam Mohamed sent Mushtaq Ahmed Khan to Lahore,[17] and the State Bank of Pakistan turned the money over to a Hyderabad Trust without Mustaq Ahmed Khan's authorization.[18] The trustees[19] included Ghulam Mohamed, Liaquat Ali Khan (prime minister of Pakistan from its founding to his assassination in 1951), and Mir Laik Ali (president of the Nizam's Executive Council in its final year). The Indian Army had put Mir Laik Ali under house arrest when Hyderabad surrendered on September 17, 1948,[20] and he was held until March of 1950 when he escaped to Karachi.[21] Laik Ali became chair of the Hyderabad Trust, and his background in engineering and business helped it set up industries.

The Hyderabad Trust provided support for Hyderabadi immigrants, allotting housing, land, and stipends. The Trust facilitated pension and insurance transfers from India. The initial issue the Trust faced was defining who was and was not a Hyderabadi. Those Hyderabadis charged with constituting the list for charities from the Trust occasionally refused to validate the names of non-mulkis who had been in Hyderabad for "only a few decades" before 1948, denying them housing or allowances.[22] Dissension also arose over other aspects of the management, or mismanagement, of the Trust. The Trust established a factory to make matches and factories to make fired bricks and ceramics.[23] Most successfully, the Trust established the Bahadur Yar Jung Academy (named after the Ittehad ul Muslimeen's charismatic leader) and the much-needed Liaquat National Hospital in Karachi.[24]

Leading educators were recruited by Pakistan, sometimes coming for what they thought would be a short consultation but being almost forcibly detained. In 1947, Pakistan had only two universities, in Dhaka and Lahore, and it needed more.[25] In the new universities, 95 percent of the faculty members were muhajirs, with Peshawar dominated by Osmania people and Karachi by Aligarhians. Even Lahore's university had to be rebuilt as most faculty and students had been Hindus. Professor M. Raziuddin Siddiqi, vice-chancellor of Osmania University in 1948, became a key figure, although he had not intended to go to Pakistan. Raziuddin had a Ph.D. from Cambridge and had done a postdoctorate in France, and the government of India valued him. While attending a science conference at Aligarh, he met Pakistanis who asked him to come and advise them. India's Prime Minister Nehru personally gave him a fifteen-day leave to go to Pakistan. Once there, Prime Minister Liaqat Ali Khan asked him to be president of the University of the Punjab or to establish and head a university in Karachi. Then the chief minister of the Northwest Province[26] abruptly appointed him head of a new university in Peshawar and sent Nehru a telegram, "we've retained your man, please send his family." Nehru finally let the family go.[27] After heading the University of Peshawar, Siddiqi served as vice-chancellor of Sind University and then Islamabad University. An internationally distinguished scientist, he spent time at American universities, and three of his children settled in the United States. The Siddiqis had left a daughter behind to be adopted by an aunt, and although she stayed just over a decade she had trouble later adjusting to Pakistan in one important respect. She had stood second in Hindi at Osmania (the official national language, Hindi replaced Urdu in most Hyderabad schools), and then she married into Pakistan and had to master Urdu.

Young Hyderabadi women also went to Pakistan and contributed to its educational and cultural arenas, sometimes forfeiting marriage by moving when they did. Waheeda Naseem, educator, historian, novelist, and poetess, moved to Pakistan in 1952 and retired as principal of the Government Girls Science College, Nazimabad, in 1987.[28] Fatima Suraiya, or Bajjia, rose to become one of Pakistan's most famous TV drama writers.[29] Known as a muhajir, she was not marked out as a Hyderabadi. Her grandfather had gone to Hyderabad from the United Provinces (UP), so they were, she said, "*ghair-mulkis* [non-mulkis] there and *ghair-mulkis* here." When the Indian Army began moving against Hyderabad, her grandfather put together a group of 101 people (mostly relatives) and started for Pakistan via Bombay. K. M. Munshi, India's agent general in Hyderabad, phoned him and said, "Why are you leaving? If you leave, other lesser Muslims will leave." "But I have young girls, can you guarantee their safety?" her grandfather asked, and Munshi had no answer.[30] Bajjia, eighteen then, was the oldest of several daughters. She never married, but her seven sisters and four brothers all married non-Hyderabadis. Bajjia modeled the plural society she celebrates in her serials on old Hyderabad, working toward harmony,

"a larger canvas." Members of the family's younger generation, although
some have been schooled abroad or are working there temporarily, are not
Westernizing or settling overseas. "Going to the Gulf is better than going to the West, and moving again would be a bad business, because my
grandfather and father had such a hard time in Pakistan, because muhajirs
are not accepted."[31]

Leading Hyderabadi military men who migrated to Pakistan included
Admiral Sayed Mohamed Ahsan, commander of the Pakistan Navy and
then governor of East Pakistan,[32] Colonel Mustafa Khan, an Aurangabadi
who married the elder sister of Zulfiqar Ali Bhutto, and Brigadier Masoud
Ali "Hesky" Baig, a world-class polo player and friend of Britain's Prince
Philip. Baig, formerly of the Bengal Lancers, faced Rommel in Cairo in
World War II and ended up in Hiroshima guarding MacArthur. He played
polo all over the world; Santa Barbara, California, gave him a key to
the city.[33]

STARTING OVER AND STARTING OUT

Ordinary Hyderabadis migrating to Pakistan came from a wide range
of backgrounds but all of them faced starting over or starting out in Pakistan. Members of the Hyderabad Civil Service moved mid-career. Ahmed
Faruq Baig ranked high in the HCS as deputy collector in Nizamabad and
kept the peace there during the handover to India. He was commended
by a Sikh colonel and Hindu major from the Indian Army and could have
stayed and been promoted. But the new Hyderabad government offered
pensions with early retirement, an incentive for HCS men to leave. An-
guished at Hyderabad's defeat and worried about the future, his family
members conferred and chose Pakistan. Ahmed Baig did not expect the
same kind of position and he did not get it, starting with the bank but
moving to the foreign office as a passport officer where he eventually became deputy director. There was an effort to accommodate Bengalis, more
than muhajirs, he said. His friend A. A. Jabbar, moving later, found that
too, and Jabbar's HCS juniors who had migrated earlier outranked him in
Pakistan's civil service.[34]

Mohamed Yousuf, from the first Nizam College batch affiliated to Osmania (1951), moved to Pakistan without even trying for a job in Hyderabad, although an older brother was well placed. "Our generation was
heavily influenced by ideological movements, we felt that the future for
Muslims was in Pakistan. We dreamed of a model Islamic state, not a
theocratic one but one with progressive moral values." He joined the civil
service in Pakistan and held a series of important jobs, being sent to the

prestigious American universities Berkeley and Harvard for training in development and administration.[35]

M. Farooq Ali Osmani left Hyderabad regretfully: I quoted him earlier saying that, if not for the fall of Hyderabad, no one would have thought of leaving because Osmania had produced a multiclass society. However, Osmani felt no regrets about his subsequent career in Pakistan. An educator with an M.A. in sociology, he migrated because Muslims had been the rulers, and he felt marked as a "second class citizen" because he wore a sherwani. An only child, he struck out against family advice in 1951, brought a bride from Hyderabad in 1956, and encouraged relatives to follow him, including his parents in 1968. Osmani went into educational and rural welfare work, becoming regional director of Allama Iqbal Open University in Karachi in 1976. He benefited from a UN training course in social welfare, an international study tour, a Fulbright to the University of Wisconsin, and Open University training in the UK, and he undertook community development work all over Pakistan and the world.

Hyderabadi businessmen in Pakistan included men from business backgrounds and also men new to business. Khwaja Azeemuddin, Hyderabad's chief engineer and builder of the Nizam Sagar dam, founded the Associated Construction Company, providing employment to many in East Pakistan, the Middle East, and Africa.[36] Mushtaq Hussein moved with his wife and uncle in 1948, leaving relatives in the ancestral jewelry business in the old city of Hyderabad but establishing a Karachi branch of Mushtaq Hussein Jewellers; according to his son, Naseem Mushtaq, there had been a ready clientele.

Men new to business had harder times. Maseeh uz Zaman had been in the army, and his commanding officer gave him leave to visit Pakistan but encouraged him to come back to India; Zaman stayed in Pakistan as he had intended and he and his wife worked hard to establish themselves.[37] He was one of many who told me that coming to Pakistan had benefited people because "no one is idle here." Masood Ali, from Warangal College and Hyderabad City College, had been a military contractor during World War II. He stayed in Hyderabad and saw that "the Indians didn't know who was who, or even how to drink water, it was a cultural encroachment," so he went to Pakistan with his wife and baby in 1949 and "hungered to take on any business." He wasted time in Karachi trying to start a dairy farm (the climate was wrong, there was no grass) and then moved to Lahore and inaugurated Industrial Exhibitions and other businesses.[38]

Urdu and English journalists left Hyderabad for Pakistan, many of them having advocated Hyderabad's independence. As editor of *Meezan*,

Habibulla Auj had supported the Razakars, so he was arrested in 1948; when released in 1956, he went to Lahore.[39] Two others, Sayeed Khan Qamar and Farhad Zaidi, had been Razakars. Qamar, who became an executive editor of Pakistan Press International in Islamabad, left Hyderabad in early 1949. He migrated alone at age fifteen, preceded by an older brother in Pakistan's Air Force, and finished his education in Karachi. Qamar moved with the capital to Islamabad and married a Punjabi woman in 1959, leaving Karachi and marrying a non-Hyderabadi because he "did not want to be a refugee."[40] Zaidi, editor of Islamabad's *The Muslim*, was from Aurangabad, where his father had been an official in Hyderabad's final days. After 1948 his father was charged (wrongly, Farhad thought) with the murder of Hindus, so he had rushed to Delhi, to Dacca, to Karachi by ship, and finally to Lahore, where he got permits for his family to migrate. Farhad was nineteen at the time, studying at Osmania, and in Pakistan he married a Kashmiri. His seven siblings also married non-Hyderabadis (Punjabis, Kashmiris, other muhajirs).[41] Mehmood Ali Khan, a journalist running *Payam* with his brother-in-law until they ran afoul of Hyderabad's martial law administrator in 1951, got into the movie business in Lahore. He had not been back to Hyderabad since 1958, but kept in touch through *Siyasat*'s editor, Abid Ali Khan.[42]

MIGRATION THROUGH MARRIAGE

Parsi women from the Nizam's state ended up in Pakistan, the forerunners of many women who migrated through marriage. Parsis were long established in what became Pakistan, especially in Karachi.[43] Two Parsi women from Secunderabad who married into Lahore exemplify the far-flung marriage networks of this prosperous community. Mehera Chenoy of Secunderabad had married Feroz Cooper, a Cambridge-trained barrister, in 1924, and her visits to her home in Secunderabad stopped after her father's death. In 1992, she was ninety years old and her husband had been dead for many years; without local relatives, she was living with a Muslim family.[44] Mrs. Jal Pestonjee, nee Kedarwala, married into Lahore in 1951, and her husband, Jal, still worked as a successful businessman at age seventy-five. "The Parsis have always been a cosmopolitan community," Jal said, "and we of the Parsi community always have been dedicated and loyal to the place where we live. Where you get your bread and butter, that's your country." The three Pestonjee sons, all electronic engineers, married Parsis of their own choice from Pakistan. One son was in the Pakistan Air Force, but the other two had migrated to Australia.[45]

Hyderabadi parents willingly sent brides to Pakistan in its early decades. A daughter settled in Pakistan provided, if not a definite commitment, at least a future option for older parents evaluating the environment for Muslims in India and the evolving society in Pakistan. Nayyar Ehsan Rashid's father, Nawab Ehsan Yar Jung, brought her to Karachi in 1950 and left her with her older married sister to study, a plan foiled by the prime minister, Liaquat Ali Khan, who advised, "get her married; you cannot leave her." Nayyar was quickly married to a man in Pakistan's foreign service, and he and she opened the Pakistani mission in Australia, one of their many foreign postings.[46] Mehrukh Yousuf finished Mahbubiyah School and attended the opening ceremony of her marriage on the same day, marrying a Hyderabadi already in Pakistan. She too traveled after marriage, chiefly within Pakistan but also abroad. Sultana Basith, India's women's table tennis champion for six years (1950 to 1956), married and migrated in 1957. She reigned for the next three years as Pakistan's women's table tennis champion, and her son later was a championship player at Louisiana State University in the United States.

Some Hyderabadi women developed political careers in Pakistan. With family in both Hyderabad and Pakistan's Punjab, Begum Afsar Riza Qizilbash grew up in Hyderabad but married her Punjabi cousin and became a social worker, a Muslim League politician, and eventually a minister in the federal government. She saw many old classmates when she traveled abroad but said she knew few Hyderabadis in Lahore.[47] Another political figure was Mrs. Munawar Ali of Karachi, who migrated with her husband and became vice-president of the All Pakistan Women's Association and a leader of its family planning efforts.[48]

Hyderabadis, Muhajirs, or Pakistanis?

BECOMING NON-MULKIS

It is ironic that those Hyderabadis migrating to Pakistan were immediately categorized as muhajirs, in effect non-mulkis, a categorization about which they were quite ambivalent. They often disclaimed the label, yet its derivation from *hijra* and the muhajir role in the formation of the state (see chapter 2) gave it prestige in earlier years. Like other muhajirs, most Hyderabadis were concentrated in the cities of Karachi and Hyderabad. The Hyderabadis who settled elsewhere in Pakistan had a much easier time escaping this label.

In Karachi, muhajirs organized politically to seek jobs and resources, but the Hyderabadi immigrants were not active in the Muhajir Qaumi Movement (the MQM, the muhajir political party). Some did say they were MQM sympathizers, but there seemed to be no Hyderabadi members, much less leaders, of that organization. "The MQM is for UPites and Biharis," I was told; "it's their clique," and "we agree with the demands but not the name." Some Hyderabadi military men stated that as military men they hated politics, but they knew the role they could play if they chose. Hesky Baig, the famous polo player, said that agents of Altaf Hussain (leader of the MQM) had approached him, saying that if Baig joined the MQM, "the whole of the Hyderabadis would follow" (but he refused). Recognizing that economic opportunities had narrowed for them and their children, people criticized the MQM's failure to put economic priorities ahead of political ones. An idealistic way of avoiding the issue was by asserting that "in Islam, there is no 'son of the soil,' all Muslims have the same culture, and there should be no ethnic or regional barriers or markers."

HYDERABADI CULTURE IN PAKISTAN

Despite internal divisions and the frequent failure of outsiders to distinguish among the various groups of muhajirs,[49] Hyderabadis did remain distinctive. Hyderabadi culture was both a prized asset to its upholders and a liability in the eyes of many outside the community. Marked by their distinctive Urdu and elegant manners, some Hyderabadis felt they were more appreciated than muhajirs from UP or Bihar, but others remarked on the prejudices against them. Styles of dress and jewelry marked both women and men.[50] And Hyderabadis in Karachi remained largely endogamous (like other true diasporics), marrying other Hyderabadis. They formed a community of nostalgia, much like that of the muhajirs from Lucknow so beautifully written about by Joginder Paul in *Sleepwalkers*.[51]

Many Pakistanis viewed Hyderabadis somewhat negatively. They said the Nizams were "traitors to the Muslim cause," first because Hyderabad State fell so fast to India in 1948, and second, because Hyderabad State fought against Tipu Sultan and with the British in the eighteenth and nineteenth centuries, thus betraying the "Muslim Liberation Movement" of those times. Bahadur Yar Jung, the Ittehad ul Muslimeen's leader linked to Jinnah, was far more widely known and admired in Pakistan than the last Nizam, despite Jung's premature death in 1944 and the Nizam's substantial financial support.

Unfavorable stereotypes of Hyderabadis were also related to their coming from a princely state (remarks on their intriguing, scheming nature, their proneness to exaggeration and rumor) and to their "different" public enactment of male/female roles. Hyderabadi women were thought to be more educated and progressive than other women, and, like Hyderabadi men, "they did more when they got out of Hyderabad," contributing to images of Hyderabadi wives as aggressive and Hyderabadi husbands as henpecked. The women's reputation as strong and domineering perhaps derived from their speech: women speaking Hyderabadi Urdu sometimes used masculine verb forms, producing a more assertive presentation of self; and certainly, the men's gentle demeanor contrasted with that of other Pakistani men. Hyderabadis defended their women's higher educational levels and conversational abilities and their men's considerate treatment of women, while insisting that Hyderabadi culture's outward courtesies had little to do with power relations within marriages.

First-generation immigrants always stated that they were Muslim first, Pakistani second, and Hyderabadi last.[52] "Many Hyderabadis do not want to call themselves Hyderabadi, 99 percent will say Pakistani," one non-Hyderabadi man said, a view affirmed by many. "Hyderabadis have changed a great deal in Pakistan," Captain Massoud Baig opined, "not so much in Canada or the United States. Here it was not necessary to keep that identity; in fact, most are afraid to say that they are Hyderabadi, and non-mulki Hyderabadis from northern and central India gave out that they were not Hyderabadi."[53] "Hyderabadis fit in nowhere," said one critic, himself a Hyderabadi (but a non-mulki one). Even those proudly retaining Hyderabadi identity showed an awareness of its dangers: one man said that of course he still spoke Hyderabadi Urdu, "since I am of high status, who can object?" Others tried to deemphasize or change their dialect in public discourse.

In the Hyderabadi Colony (sometimes called the Mecca of Deccanis) in Karachi, people continued many practices from the former homeland. As most early migrants had settled in Karachi, their relatives and friends continued to settle there; the numbers of Karachi Hyderabadis were in the tens of thousands.[54] In the 1990s, only half the Hyderabad Colony residents were Hyderabadis, and the Hyderabadis' major institutional base was the Bahadur Yar Jung Academy. Marriages in Karachi continued to be arranged with other Hyderabadi families for the most part, and the traditional wedding rituals were followed, with costumes and jewelry either supplied locally or brought from Hyderabad itself. Hyderabadi pickles and other special foods could be obtained in shops and restaurants (and were exported to Australia and the United States). Rashid Turabi, the leading Shia *zakir* (preacher) in Karachi, was a Hyderabadi with a son in Los Angeles. Hyderabadi bankers, doctors, engineers, writers, and bureaucrats loomed large in Karachi society.

The social hierarachy governing relationships in old Hyderabad was upset in Karachi. Family reputations from Hyderabad no longer garnered automatic respect, although in earlier decades children were taught to "*adab*" well-known men of high lineage, men who sometimes fell into poverty in Pakistan. Traditionally rich people, without defense mechanisms, gave away their money and possessions and ended up penniless, while upwardly mobile young businessmen imported heirlooms like chandeliers, jewelry, domestic items, and even food for weddings from Hyderabad to establish themselves as "Nawabs" in Pakistan. Given the clustering of families in Karachi and their endogamous practices, however, family and community reputations from old Hyderabad still served as a frame of reference.

The situation was very different in Pakistan's other cities, where Hyderabadi Pakistanis were few. Brigadier Mustafa Anwer explained:

> There is no collective Hyderabadi identity, and a good thing too. We have been able to merge here, adopt the local culture, while those in Karachi who have not changed have had trouble. . . . I am careful not to associate myself with Hyderabadis that way, the typical Hyderabadi with no outside connections I don't trust. . . . I do not want to be seen as an outsider, when people ask where I am from I always say Lahore. You can't be a refugee all your life.

Reasons for the lack of emphasis on being Hyderabadi in Lahore included the Punjabi background of many non-mulki Hyderabadis settled there, the class differences among them, and the fact that many had intermarried with non-Hyderabadis.[55]

In Peshawar, many faculty members from Osmania University took up positions at the new University of Peshawar. They were professors, often department chairs, of engineering, law, English, Urdu, math, chemistry, zoology, and home economics.[56] Some were recruited by Professor Raziuddin Siddiqi, first vice-chancellor of the university, but most seem to have arrived on their own. Many of these families were Shias and some were "Madrasis," from the British Indian Andhra districts but educated in Hyderabad.[57] As in Lahore, there were marriages with non-Hyderabadis and some strong connections to local society, in particular through Obaidullah Durrani, an engineering professor and a "Madrasi" Shia who was also a Hindu-taught homeopath with a large following near Swat. "He was like a pir," I was told, and he had been made an MP (member of parliament) by Zia ul Haq.

"After the wives came," these ten to twenty Hyderabadi families in Peshawar began having "one-dish potlucks" once a month. But Hyderabadi food, although a focal point for the group, evoked both nostalgia and ambivalence about the homeland. A first-generation immigrant said, "Muslims in Hyderabad were so busy eating and cooking and observing their customs, their leisure, that India took over," and the younger people no longer liked Hyderabadi food. "Relatives in Karachi prepare those *khatti* (sour) things, I can't eat them"; "Hyderabadi dishes are painful to make and painful to eat, so spicy," were typical remarks.

Justice Samdani, one of Pakistan's leading jurists, came from this Peshawar group, although, migrating at age eighteen, he finished his B.A. at Punjab University in 1951 after three years at Osmania. The family was South Indian, "Andhra or Madrasi, not really Hyderabadi," and it "came straight there [Rawalpindi]; luckily we were not hooked into the Karachi Hyderabad scene."[58] After completing his B.A., Samdani became a lecturer in physics in Islamia College, Peshawar, where he fell in love with the martial Pathans and the Northwest Frontier Province and married a local girl from Kohat. Although he praised his Hyderabad education, saying that because of its high standard, "Hyderabadis own me," he learned Pushtu (his wife's mother tongue was Hindko, their home language was Urdu) and, according to his daughters, claimed to be Pathan! A High Court judge in Lahore, he resigned and went to London after a dispute with General Zia ul Haq. His daughters said that only in London did they have contact with Hyderabadis: "there we were sucked into it, that was the first time we heard our father speak Hyderabadi Urdu, and mother made a point of joining the Hyderabad Association."[59]

In Islamabad, Hyderabadis were few and tended to be officials in the central government, highly placed educators, or businessmen with international connections. There were no "one-dish potlucks" or other regular meetings. Turnover was a feature of life, and many of the Hyderabadis posted there had homes elsewhere; their connections outside Islamabad, through their children, for example, tended to be with places other than Karachi. In contrast, many of the Peshawar academics retired to Karachi, while Lahoris stayed in Lahore.

Despite their regional differences and uniform public stance as Muslims and Pakistanis first, Hyderabadi immigrants to Pakistan often privately expressed great affection for old Hyderabad and its culture. Most felt that their culture was superior to that of other Pakistanis. They boasted that Hyderabad had the first cement roads in all of India and they were washed every morning, that Hyderabad had double-decker buses in 1945 whereas Karachi got them only in 1951, and so on. Hyderabadi food was preferred for its reliance on rice rather than breads and its characteristic use of tamarind for that sour taste. Differences in table manners reportedly persisted, although the *chowki* dinners had vanished (as they had almost done in Hyderabad). A man recalled that his mother's maidservant, one of the few brought along to Pakistan, found the pushing and shoving at a Punjabi buffet dinner "disgusting." Remembering the courteous behavior at Hyderabadi dinners, the servant remarked that "any servant in Hyderabad knows much better how to behave." But people recognized that Hyderabadi culture "as a whole" could not be maintained. Part of the reason was the lack of servants trained to support it. A few Hyderabadis had brought servants with them, but they usually returned to India where their families remained or were lured away by higher pay from other Hyderabadis.[60]

Changes in Hyderabadi culture in Pakistan were not always welcomed. Initially, hosts received guests as in Hyderabad, only in formal sherwani (long suit coat) and with elaborate courtesies. When informal dress began to be worn, it was resisted. The first time a host received a friend on Id (the day commemorating the end of the month-long fast of Ramadan) wearing a *kurta* (loose overshirt) instead of a sherwani, his friend protested and refused to come inside; in five years, however, that friend was doing the same. At weddings, the dowry was delivered on the traditional painted trays rather than in the Samsonite luggage favored by Punjabis, and eating "never used to be done on the street or in roadside cafes." Muslim families kept purdah, as did many Hindus, in Hyderabad,[61] but Pakistan's Westernizing upper classes did not adhere to this rigorously. Depending upon a family's religiosity, weddings and parties might or might not feature gender separation and avoidance of alcohol.[62] I never saw a Hyderabadi woman in Pakistan wearing a *hijab* (headscarf), although perhaps some did.

Wedding fashions were a key not only to changing Hyderabadi identities but to the consumerism of Pakistan's upper classes. In the 1950s and 1960s, Hyderabadi brides in Pakistan sometimes chose not to wear Hyderabadi finery, even when their grooms were also Hyderabadi (the groom's family traditionally furnishes the bride's dresses). Mrs. Khwaja Masihuddin did not wear the Hyderabadi *kurti choli* and *khara dupatta* (distinctive short-sleeved sari blouse and long scarf) or jewelry but a *gharara* (flowing full pants with overblouse) and a diamond set, since she wanted to be Pakistani in her new country.[63] Her three daughters, however, all wore full Hyderabadi dress and jewelry, not because they wanted to be Hyderabadi, but because Hyderabadi wedding finery, lavish and glittering, was emulated throughout Pakistani society in the late 1960s and early 1970s. Hyderabadi jewelry was definitely preferred for weddings, whether obtained in Hyderabad or Karachi. The Hyderabadi silver *pandan* remained an essential gift to daughters upon marriage (although not all daughters valued it, and a few Punjabis also had *pandans*). Very significantly, most Hyderabadi wives continued to wear the *kalipot*, a black wedding necklace probably South Indian and Hindu in origin.[64] Mrs. Parvaiz resisted her husband's insistence that she wear it, saying "It tells people, people you don't care to know, that you're from Hyderabad." Servants in Pakistan did not understand the value placed on this necklace. One older woman, a first-generation migrant from Hyderabad, broke her *kalipot*, and in great distress gave it to a servant for immediate repair, sitting down on a white sheet to abstain from food until its return; that, unfortunately, was not until the next day, because the servant forgot to do it until she found her mistress still sitting on the sheet, not eating.

Even those who remembered minute details of Hyderabadi dress, jewelry, makeup, food preparation, and rituals might not practice them. Grandmothers who wanted a grandchild's *bismillah* (initiation to reading the Qur'an) to be performed "traditionally" could be blocked by non-Hyderabadi daughters-in-law or sons-in-law. In other cases, the senior women who supervised these customs had died. The younger women, particularly those who spent time in boarding schools because their fathers were in the army and who attended Hyderabadi events irregularly, never learned how to do the rituals. "Now that *we're* the seniors, forget it," Tami Alam told me.

In fact, the trend among Pakistan's middle and upper classes was perhaps less to form or follow a "national" Pakistani culture than to formulate an international or Westernized Pakistani culture. As one of the earliest Hyderabadis in Pakistan stated, "Pakistani culture is still forming and the influence of the West is dominant." This was increasingly reflected in the choices being made by the second generation about where to go for education, jobs, and perhaps settlement.

HYDERABADI ORGANIZATIONS IN PAKISTAN

Initial Hyderabadi-based organizations and institutions were all in Karachi and stressed economic readjustment and residential settlement (the Hyderabad Colony and its Welfare Society; the Hyderabad Cooperative Housing Society). Another early institution was the Bahadur Yar Jung Academy, of which some Karachi Hyderabadis were members from the beginning, whereas others just knew each other and met informally. In the 1980s, the latter began joining the Academy, talking about the old days in Hyderabad, and the Academy's president began publishing an Urdu journal in 1979 with the same title as the Urdu monthly published in Hyderabad, India, by the Idara-e-Adabiyat-e-Urdu.[65] Some Hyderabadi school-based associations were formed (Osmania University, Mahbubiyah Girls Society),[66] along with other school-based associations (Aligarh Muslim University,[67] Karachi University, and the Doon School of Dehra Dun, India). Bushra Waheed and five or six women friends in Lahore who had been non-mulkis together in Hyderabad met regularly, the women likening it to the way their parents had met informally in Hyderabad. In Lahore, a few men started a Hyderabad association but quickly disbanded it.

In all of Pakistan, there was no named Hyderabad association, no social or community organization with Hyderabad in the name, such as I found in other Hyderabadi diasporic settings. People put their Pakistani identity ahead of their Hyderabadi one, uneasily recognizing that too strong an identity as Hyderabadi worked against acceptance in Pakistani society.[68] And there was no 400th anniversary of the founding of Hyderabad city celebrated in the early 1990s in Karachi, again in contrast to most other sites abroad. Such a celebration might have been inappropriate, given the immigrants' decisive repudiation of their birthplace.

In the late 1990s, some senior retired men founded what was, in effect, a Hyderabad association in Karachi. They began with a Platinum Jubilee for Osmania University to celebrate its innovative Urdu curriculum, but tentative plans to invite the Princess Durru Shevar and Prince Muffakham Jah aroused controversy. Some were enthusiastic, some thought the surviving members of the royal family quite irrelevant to Pakistan, and others advocated giving funds to Bosnia instead.[69] In 1992, in preparation for the Jubilee, an Osmania Old Boys Association was reactivated in Karachi, with emotions running high over the elections to the executive committee.[70]

But how could organizations based on schools in Hyderabad continue recruitment in Pakistan? The Osmania Old Boys Association had some 350 members in the mid-1990s, but, as Majid Baig said:

> How to get new members? No one from Pakistan is going to Osmania any more, so they are changing the bylaws. Just as people from Hyderabad could all enter Osmania, now people from Hyderabad and their children can all enter the Association.

Thus Osmania stood for Hyderabad, and a variation on the old mulki rules allowed access to Hyderabadis and their children in Pakistan.

Not only "old boys'" associations but "old girls'" ones had been organized, a Mahbubiyah Old Girls' Society reviving an earlier one. The Society started with only fifteen members and had sixty-three in the early 1990s, some five or ten of whom were not Mahbubiyans but "only Hyderabadis";[71] this society also used the mulki rules to gain new members. The "old Mahbubiyans" had an uneasy relationship with the Bahadur Yar Jung Academy that gave them premises; they were pressured to open a "Mahbubiyah type of school," but instead they opened a Literacy Center in the Club building for poor children in the neighborhood, mostly Pushtu-speakers and the children of cleaning women and servants.[72] The Society had an annual function or *milad*, "as was done in Hyderabad under Miss Linnell," but so many of its members had children abroad whom they visited regularly that meetings had to be scheduled with these "migratory birds" in mind. A 1993 visit to Karachi by a Hindu "old Mahbubiyan" from India, Lakshmi Devi Raj, had occasioned great enthusiasm. In Hyderabad, Lakshmi told me how hard it had been to get the visa. The Pakistani official said, "but you have no relatives there," but she replied, "I have so many sisters," and began naming old Mahbubiyans. She got the visa.

A final, spectacular example of the strength of old school ties comes from the reproduction in Pakistan of the Doon School, an effort led by a Hyderabadi. Arguably the preeminent British public school in India, the Doon School's scientific and secular principles were designed to produce modern citizens, and its Old Boys had begun meeting in Lahore just before the school's Golden Jubilee in 1985. Many of the fifty or so Old Boys in Pakistan went to India for the Jubilee at the personal invitation of Rajiv Gandhi, then prime minister of India and himself a Doon School Old Boy. "We were amazed to find it still a good school, while in other places, standards have deteriorated so much," Brigadier General Mustafa Anwer said. He and other Pakistani alumni founded a Doon School Society and called for donations upon their return. They received 25.5 million rupees, "too much just to hold an annual dinner," so they bought land and planned to construct a boys' college, a girls' college, and a university.[73]

RE-VIEWING HYDERABAD

A representative Hyderabadi Pakistani view of Hyderabad as a Muslim state was well captured by the account below:[74]

> The fall of Hyderabad is a major catastrophe in the history of Muslims [in the subcontinent]. . . . Its loss as an important centre of revival of Islamic studies and survival of Muslim culture, in the background of the wailing vale of Kashmir . . . [was in line with] the 'supposed' wishes of Hyderabad's Hindu majority. . . . the Hindu Government of India ordered its armed forces to overrun this Muslim State. . . . [this] Muslim rule, which was not only tolerant but patriarchial, had, in fact, infused a Deccani synthesis even among the Hindu cultivators. The Nizam was revered as a religious dignitary by Muslims throughout India and beyond, and as a ruler by the millions of his Hindu subjects. . . . A large proportion of these Hindus belonged to the "Depressed" classes who were happier under Muslim rule than under that of their own higher castes elsewhere. The Christians, being followers of a Judaic religion, were also a happy community. . . . After its fall, the erudite class (which migrated to Pakistan) helped build Pakistan, in their [sic] own humble way, particularly in the field of education and learning.

Very few reevaluated old Hyderabad negatively. However, Syed Hussein El-Edroos, a grandson of General El Edroos who had surrendered to the Indian Army on behalf of Hyderabad in 1948, said, "My own thinking was that it was a very good deal for the people who were Muslims, but for the Hindus, Hyderabad was a bad deal."[75]

Publicly, many Hyderabadi immigrants maintained not only that Hyderabadi identity was now irrelevant to them but that Hyderabad itself had ceased to exist in any meaningful way. When I said I had been to Hyderabad, one man replied angrily, "Madame, you certainly have not;

you have been to Andhra Pradesh; there is no longer a Hyderabad." The public stance was to disavow Hyderabadi identity in favor of an unmarked Pakistani one. Also, many Hyderabadis like other Pakistanis "refuse to believe that a Muslim can live with any kind of dignity in India."[76]

Most Hyderabadi Pakistanis had severed links with the Nizam's descendants, links maintained at least in memory elsewhere in the diaspora. "The Nizam's family is history," one couple told me, and others were unsure who its members were. People got the two grandsons of the Nizam mixed up and were not sure if their mother, the Princess Durru Shevar, was alive or dead; one second-generation Hyderabadi asked if she was Ayub Khan's daughter-in-law. A Lahori woman was sure Hyderabadi Pakistani youth would rather see Michael Jackson than any relatives of the late Nizam. The Nizam's descendants had been on the social horizon in the 1980s, when one person wrote a letter to the elder grandson asking him to come and straighten out the Hyderabad Trust funds,[77] but by the 1990s they had faded from the picture.

Close connections between Pakistani and Indian Hyderabadis have been officially discouraged. Both governments gave or denied visas according to the state of political relations over the years, and both censored or "took notice of" letters between the two countries. Hyderabadi Pakistanis complained of getting only overnight visas or no visas at all to visit Hyderabad,[78] and families connected to Pakistan's armed forces were particularly wary of maintaining communication or contact with people in India. During the wars between India and Pakistan in 1965 and 1971, people sent letters through relatives and friends in the UK. Widows living with their children in Canada or the United States got their widows' pensions far more easily than widows living with their children in Pakistan. As relations between the two nations worsened, relatives ceased writing to each other.

In Pakistan, people had lost knowledge of India or been taught inaccurate and negative things about it. A young person of Hyderabadi background confidently asserted that Hyderabad city was the capital of Maharashtra. An older Hyderabadi Pakistani hosted a young Indian Hindu visitor who had come for a cricket match, and "to make him feel at home, I put up pictures on the wall for him to worship, but he laughed and said they were *bharata natyam*[79] dancers." A young Hyderabadi Pakistani visitor to Hyderabad for a wedding in the early 1990s shocked longtime friends of her family by saying, as she introduced herself, "I come from your enemy country," a remark indignantly recalled and criticized for months afterward.

Hyderabadis in Pakistan held strong, mostly negative, views about modern Hyderabad and India. They stressed poverty, dirt, and deterioration, citing their own or others' visits back to the city. Cases of relatives who married into Hyderabad but preferred to return to Pakistan were also cited. Hyderabad was "no longer pleasant; it used to be fabulous and well-organized"; visitors came away "very upset and depressed." One Islamabad family, descended from the leading nineteenth-century educator Moulvi Cheragh Ali, told me that Telugus were calling the lane near the ancestral home, Cheragh Ali Gully, Chera Gully (narrow gully), thus erasing the family history (but this proved untrue). Another woman spoke of her visit in 1959, when a Hindu minister invited her to see her old family home in Banjara Hills, in which he was living. The home had featured a marble hallway and pantry near the entry, and she said the pantry had been plastered over with cowdung to purify it for cooking. People thought there were "only two sorts of Muslims left in Hyderabad, those not doing well and those doing well but sending their children overseas." Tami Alam, who had fifty-two first cousins in Hyderabad whom she used to visit, said that most had emigrated because of depressing conditions in the city and discrimination against Muslims. However, they had gone "anywhere in the world save Pakistan, as young people in India have turned against us."

People voiced conspiracy theories and outdated ideas, one man putting forward Katherine Mayo's *Mother India* (1932) as the best authority on modern India. Many stated that Muslims were in a uniformly bad position in India, restricted to pulling rickshaws or making *bidis* (hand-rolled cigarettes). Habibullah Auj was sure that India's press was more controlled, that he and emigrants had had better careers in Pakistan. He believed that educated Muslims in Hyderabad were in a pitiable condition and that, after the Police Action, some 35,000 teachers were given ninety days to study Telugu and qualify in it. Most failed, he said, were expelled from their teaching jobs, and ended up pulling rickshaws.[80]

Others had more balanced views. Farooq Ali Osmani went back in 1988 and found his relatives doing well. But the city was dirty, and the Osmania University library was noisy, crowded with students in "underwear and shorts, not *rumi topi* and sherwani." Then he criticized Pakistan, where Hyderabadis no longer knew each other by family reputation and had changed for the worse. People who had been satisfied, self-contained, almost simple people had become materialistic and status-conscious, competing in a new society and relying on consumer goods to establish identities.

Commodore K. M. Hussain who returned in 1954 found it so changed he would not go again. He said, "Hyderabad today is not the same. When I was a boy, everyone knew one another. As children playing on the streets, we experienced this. Even the beggars knew our families. Once we tried to give the few coins we had to a beggar, but he refused, saying, 'but you are the children of so and so, you must give more.'" His wife returned in 1980, however, and while the old family residences were demolished or buried inside new lanes and buildings, the shopping was still good, and she very much enjoyed visits with her mother's old servants, family retainers whose loyalty was of such a high standard "they cannot be found here, in Pakistan."

Changing Nations

ASSESSING THEIR MOVE

For members of the first generation, thoughts about their migration depended to some extent upon their age and status at the time they moved. Those who moved as young men and women built their lives and careers in Pakistan and most of these Hyderabadi Pakistanis remain convinced of Pakistan's bright future and that of their children there. They expressed satisfaction that when they moved, Hyderabad had been more modern than Pakistan, but the situation had been reversed. Those who had settled and worked outside of Karachi seemed particularly satisfied with their contributions to the new nation. Conspicuously successful immigrants included some non-mulkis in Hyderabad now resettled in Lahore or Rawalpindi, and educators who had established new institutions throughout the country. Also, many Shias, accustomed to being a minority, seemed to have adjusted easily to the new context. Although recognizing their country's problems, a representative of these optimistic citizens said, "Pakistan is still forming its character; fifty years is nothing in the life of a nation." Another said, "Non-mulkis, that's what they still call us here, muhajirs. But it can't last forever."

Many of these Hyderabadi immigrants had deliberately intermarried, wanting to put down local roots. Lieutenant Colonel Ali Bin Ahmed, a Hyderabadi of Arab ancestry, commented that he had consciously transformed himself, taking up a military career, marrying a Kashmiri muhajir and removing the "bin" from his sons' names to prevent their misidentification as Arabs. Farhad Zaidi, a Shia who had intermarried, commented "But we don't want to stay differentiated from the mainstream—Hyderabadis should not have a collective future here." Yet the contradictions involved in retaining or disavowing Hyderabadi identity remained when it came to arranging the marriages of the second generation, even for those parents who themselves had married out of the Hyderabadi community. Many of the young Razakars, without relatives in the new nation, had made alliances with those around them, yet they had trouble securing spouses for their children. After his non-Hyderabadi wife's death, one man was left to arrange his children's marriages himself, and, without female relatives of his own, looked to other Hyderabadis in Karachi for potential spouses. Those trying to marry their children to non-Hyderabadis found prejudice against Hyderabadis. Paradoxically, this was strongest in places where muhajirs were rare. Thus in Lahore, the Hyderabadi wife of a Punjabi found her children penalized when prospective in-laws heard that she was a Hyderabadi. "They ask, *'Begum kahan ki?'* [where is the wife from?], and when they hear Hyderabad, they fall silent. It's not a problem in Karachi, they're used to Urdu-speakers."

Men who had been older and from high status families were somewhat ambivalent about their move. "Those of us who knew the old Hyderabad miss it; those who are nouveau riche here don't miss it," said A. A. Jabbar, who had been a high-ranking HCS man in 1948. He missed not only Hyderabad but the rest of India, and, having gotten to know and love East Pakistan, he missed it too.[81] HCS men who experienced downward mobility in Pakistan were aware that many of their Muslim HCS colleagues who stayed in India got selected for the Indian Administrative Service (IAS) and did well. Ahmet Baig had not revisited Hyderabad (his wife had), because he felt he could not show his face there. His career in India had been promising, but he went to Pakistan for his "peace of mind" only to find "limited scope for muhajirs." When his old friends from Hyderabad visited him in Pakistan and asked, "Why did you leave? No harm would have come to you, you were at the top," he had no real answer. "I was a *ghair-mulki* there and I'm a *ghair-mulki* here, but I'm still a Hyderabadi," this man said.[82] Some were bitter about the prejudice against Hyderabadis. They contended that the Nizam's money was Pakistan's lifeline in the chaotic first years, yet not even a road had been named after the Nizam. "Hyderabad was sacrificed for Pakistan," one said, "our blood was the foundation of Pakistan, and now it's no good."

Nostalgic contrasts were made between Hyderabadi and Pakistani cultural values and styles. Often the contrast was with Punjabis, said to be materialistic and getting more so, while Hyderabadis were soft and cultured, interested in ideas and ideologies rather than things. Mehrukh Yousuf believed that Indians were better human beings, more helpful, gentle, and better to one another, while Pakistanis were often cruel. "No," her husband said, "people here are very open, they just express themselves without inhibitions, although it's true that Hyderabadis are more soft-spoken and cultured. They're still not affected as much by materialism as those here, and the old hospitality is there."[83]

Some Hyderabadis expressed disillusionment with their new nation. One woman, struck by a poignant 1993 TV drama about the Partition (*Rahim ki Talash*, by Hyderabadi Fatima Suraiya), said:

> In the beginning, we chose Pakistan, but now the myth is over; we came thinking Pakistan had everything, but it failed. The conditions are the same for poor people here as there, in India. It's very sad, what the muhajirs dreamed, aspired to—and then the disappointment. It was the muhajirs who struggled and gave their strength.

Others despaired of the country's mounting problems and foresaw that their children too would be immigrants, elsewhere.

Even the successful first-generation migrants feared that their own adaptation had not necessarily been institutionalized. One worried about prospects in Peshawar, where Hyderabadis had contributed so much: "The only thing in Peshawar was academics, and the locals have come up and taken the places now." Another man commented, "Karachi was a stronghold of Hyderabadis, doctors and engineers, but now the locals too are educated and Hyderabadis are not to be found in good administrative positions." Mr. and Mrs. Syed Sabir Parvaiz feared for their young daughter. He said:

> We became the underdogs here, not being sons of the soil we had to strive twice as hard. Our hope was that this identity crisis would end with the second generation, but it continues. . . . [S]he is enthused about Hyderabad and uses Hyderabadi Urdu even though we tell her not to. We tried to overcome this; I talk and behave just like the Punjabis.

Khwaja Masihuddin spoke Hyderabadi Urdu proudly and said it did him no harm, as Hyderabadis had made major contributions to Pakistan and were held in high regard. His daughter, however, deliberately spoke a Punjabi style of Urdu—she did not say "*ji han*" but "*han ji*" (yes).

THE SECOND GENERATION DISAPPEARS

Second-generation Hyderabadis in Pakistan identified fully with the new nation.[84] In fact, there were no second-generation Hyderabadis in Pakistan, at least according to those who might be so categorized. There were Pakistanis, the children of the Hyderabadi immigrants, who also claimed to be Punjabis, Sindhis, Karachiites, even Pathans. Those who went abroad, the better to secure their futures, sometimes identified themselves as Pakistani Hyderabadis in their diasporic locations to distinguish themselves from the Indian Hyderabadis. Although their parents said they were Muslim, Pakistani, and Hyderabadi, in that order, the members of the second generation omitted the Muslim, taking it for granted, and put

Pakistani first, followed by a regional label such as Sindhi, Punjabi, Karachiite, or Lahori.

Those of the second generation staying in Pakistan were strong in their affirmations of non-Hyderabadi identity. Asadullah Shah said:

> I'm a Pakistani, we don't think in terms of origin, we don't talk about Hyderabad things. . . . I'm from Lahore, the muhajirs here speak Punjabi, the muhajirs in Karachi are influenced by the MQM . . . but [for me] Karachi's like New York, we're out there to make a buck, it's a dog eat dog world; there's no Hyderabadi network there for my work or play, it's not useful for me in any way.

The half-Pathan daughters of Justice Samdani reported that "He claims to be Pathan, but we ourselves claim only to be Pakistani." Daughters of an Islamabad couple had been married in full Hyderabadi dress only because it was the most fashionable. "Hyderabadi is a category used by others," one of them said, although she felt she could identify with the "Islamic past" of Hyderabad but not the "Hyderabadi culture past." Naseem Mushtaq, born in Karachi, said that his children were definitely Pakistanis and his Hyderabadi identity was limited to wedding customs and language. "Why think of yourself as Hyderabadi; what's the sense in that?" he said, referring to his brothers-in-law from Hyderabad as "men who ran here after marriage, B grade citizens, from India."

Mrs. Barkatullah's son, an engineer in Karachi, said there was "no way" he would speak Hyderabadi Urdu in his future home; he did not speak it much in his mother's house even, since "We identify as Karachi people, Sindhis, Pakistanis, not as Hyderabadis." Another young "Karachiite" (his term), a son of Aziz ur Rehman, said:

> Lahore had an old culture, but Karachi is a cocktail, all different kinds of people and no history, no culture of its own. . . . [W]e have become Pakistani here. And that's OK with our parents, there's no big difference between Hyderabadi and Pakistani culture, it's not like the West, where there is a big difference and parents find it very objectionable to think their children will take up UK or U.S. culture.

The speaker worked in Saudi Arabia and loved traveling in Italy, France, and the United States. He had no desire to see Hyderabad, which, he opined, was "a poor place."[85] Other young people brought up in Pakistan were not very interested in going to Hyderabad, telling me they preferred Agra, Aurangabad, Ajanta, and Ellora as tourist destinations. Mr. and Mrs. M. A. Rashid Khan said, "Our children have completely changed, they don't want Hyderabadi spices in their food, they prefer *tikka* (barbecue) and fast food, and they don't speak Hyderabadi Urdu. Their college friends form their culture, in college the differences of accent have been dropped, you cannot tell them apart, the Hyderabadis, Punjabis, and so forth."[86] "Almost none of my close friends are from Hyderabad," Mrs. Barkatullah's son said; "I met them in college and only later got to know where they came from."[87] Major Aslam Bin Nasir's daughter complained that she was tired of *bagara mirch* (Hyderabadi-style chilies), "the older people always want that."[88]

The most extreme statement of identity was made with a four-wheel drive vehicle in a Karachi driveway by the son of a "typical, very Hyderabadi" mother and a Pathan father from Pakistan's Kaghan valley. A. R. Khan had worked in Hyderabad for only fourteen years before the Police Action sent him back to Pakistan.[89] His son proudly showed me a huge black jeep labeled "Conqueror" (he said this referred to Genghis Khan) and studded with brass shields (like those on gates to defend against war elephants). It had a Kohistan (Kaghan valley) license plate and a bumper sticker proclaiming "swift silent deadly hunter." The parents had deliberately arranged their children's marriages to two Pathans, a Punjabi, a Baloch, and a Pakistani Hyderabadi, and the children strongly identified as Pakistani.

The stance of the second generation was exemplified by the passionate testimony of a self-identified Lahori. One of six sons of a Hyderabadi immigrant, Mahboob Ali Asim, unlike his brothers who married before him, had married a girl from a Punjabi, not Hyderabadi, family. As he drove me back from the joint family home in Lahore, his tiny son in the back ("very smart, a cross-breed"), he recounted disagreements with his father. His parents had always advised him to

> keep away from those Punjabis, avoid the problems we faced here. . . . But when my mother died, who came to her funeral? It was my Punjabi friends and my brothers' Punjabi friends, all crying, saying "meri ma mar gai" (my mother has died). Where was my father's brother, his sister? To hell with them, they're in India; we live here. . . . We need relations who can stand with us, be here for us. . . . We are Muslims, Muslims have no particular land, what is this village, what is that city Hyderabad, what is that Char Minar, to us?

Here, answering the immigrant generation and doing so partly by turning its own primary identity as Muslim against it, spoke a self-made son of the soil. The soil he claimed was that of Lahore and the Punjab, not Hyderabad.

BEYOND PAKISTAN

Many young Pakistanis are emigrating these days, among them second-generation Hyderabadi Pakistanis with strong regional or metropolitan

Pakistani identities. In 1997, a survey of students from English medium schools in Islamabad showed that a majority preferred settling abroad after their education (43% of these in a Western country and 56% in a Muslim country).[90] Mrs. Barkatullah said that in Pakistan, only doctors and engineers were valued, so if young people could not get admission for those courses, they went to the United States for those or other degrees. "Once there, they can stay for jobs, and they can do any old jobs there, which cannot be done here." That their children might be leaving permanently was certainly a possibility in the minds of parents, and some thought was given to where health benefits for the aged were said to be best.

The children of many of Pakistan's leading Hyderabadis had settled abroad, and Hyderabadi immigrants in general seemed to have grandchildren being brought up in the United States, the UK, Canada, Turkey, the Middle East, and Australia almost as frequently as in Pakistan. The United States was a popular destination, at least partly because of the U.S.-Pakistan political alliance in the decades following Pakistan's independence. Many of the first-generation immigrants whom I interviewed had held Fulbright or other educational grants to the United States. Three of Professor Raziuddin Siddiqi's children were American citizens. His son was an energy and environmental scientist, and his daughter Shirin served at the National Security Council and was chosen by President George H. W. Bush to be a U.S. ambassador to the UN.[91] Mushtaq Ahmad Khan's son Mahmood Mushtaq was also a U.S. citizen,[92] and many descendants of Mir Laik Ali lived in the United States. One of Hesky Baig's granddaughters lived in New York and was an investment banker with Morgan Stanley.

There were strong push factors from within Pakistan. In 1971 the birth of Bangladesh disappointed some who had believed Pakistan to be a Muslim homeland. Moves toward "Islamization" in Pakistan, on the other hand, had sent out both Muslims and non-Muslims who had a more secular vision of the nation. Two sons of a Parsi family in Lahore left because, their father explained, "We tolerate things, but the younger people cannot put up with this, they cannot dance or anything; they don't want to live with *mullahs* [Muslim clerics], and opportunities are lacking." The muhajir status that once afforded Hyderabadis close connections with Pakistan's political leaders ultimately worked against them.

Then there were Pakistan's continuing economic and political problems, particularly the lack of law and order in Karachi. Dr. Muneer Uddin explained that when he received offers from Britain and the United States after a postdoctoral fellowship in anesthesiology in the UK (1956–1962), he chose to return and serve Pakistan. In Ayub Khan's time, conditions in Karachi were appealing, he said; it was a peaceful and attractive place.

But increasing troubles were evident in his hospital—for example, in the numbers of stabbings that were treated there. Young people might have stable jobs (one of his sons-in-law was with a bank) but the urban situation was not stable. His other two daughters lived in the United States—one in Houston and one in southern California—and his son studied at Southern Methodist University. Other parents regretfully reported that their own children and nieces and nephews were settling abroad, because, as one said, "the opportunities and money are simply better outside."

The younger relatives of Hyderabadi Pakistanis were almost all settled overseas in Western countries. Mr. and Mrs. Parvaiz testified that on the husband's side, his mother's older sister (a former president of the All Pakistan Women's Association) and his own seven brothers and sister were in the United States, and, on the wife's side, her sister's eight children from Karachi were all in the United States (as were her brother's seven children from Hyderabad, India, so the emigration was not just from Pakistan). The couple also had cousins in the UK, and some of those in the United States and the UK worked in the Middle East from time to time. He and she stayed in Pakistan because "someone has to have a house for those guys to drop in on here. But we feel that the children being raised in the United States and the UK are totally alien, more so in the United States; their values are quite different and their parents are helpless. I cannot relate to them at all, or vice versa; they're like people from outer space."[93] Their twelve-year-old daughter, however, did not agree with her parents' views of youth in Western countries, although they were echoed by a grandmother in Karachi who called her Los Angeles granddaughter "an alien with loose hair listening to wild music."

Another dramatic example of the outmigration came from the family of Karachi businessman Majid Baig. His sister's children lived in Karachi, Dubai, Istanbul, and Los Angeles, and every summer those abroad came back to Karachi with their children to "keep the family, the cousins, together." The two daughters living in Los Angeles complained that they were not recognized as Hyderabadis by Indians in the southern California Hyderabad Association but just as Pakistanis, while in Pakistan they were recognized just as Hyderabadis.[94]

To take better advantage of opportunities elsewhere, some Pakistanis held multiple citizenships or green cards. Azra Hussein in Lahore, brought up in Pakistan and married to a Hyderabadi in the UK in 1970 when she was seventeen, held British and Pakistani citizenships as well as, via her British citizenship, U.S. and Canadian green cards. After her husband's death and the downfall of the bank for which she worked, she came back from London to Pakistan in 1992 and married again, because "here, one has to have an identity through a man," she said. She was giving her young daughter a different identity by marrying her to a cousin settled in the United States.[95]

Transnational marriages could be a strategy to maximize people's options, but they could also involve heavy costs. Sometimes marriages made in Pakistan broke up when men went to work in the United States or Canada. Because the quickest way to get a green card was by marrying a citizen, they divorced the wives left behind and married North Americans. The protection afforded Muslim women by *mehr* (a financial settlement given to brides) was also under threat, its amount and very existence problematized as immigrants from Pakistan came under the marriage and divorce laws of other nations.

The current emigration from Pakistan could be seen as draining the country or as placing it on a larger, transnational map. According to Dr. A. A. Qadeer,

> This second or third migration is disastrous. Karachi was the hub of my family, three to four hundred family members were here, and now they are all in America. When we hold a marriage here, only forty-five to one hundred people can be invited now, while for my elder daughter's wedding I had invited one thousand four hundred. Such large groups are now in Chicago, Los Angeles, or Miami.

But Karachi was still a preferred location for some transnational weddings, particularly if the bride's family lived in the Middle East, where visas for visitors could be difficult to obtain. It was also cheaper to hold weddings there than in the UK or the United States, and cosmopolitan Karachi could supply Hyderabadi wedding supplies almost as easily as Hyderabad itself.

Changing nations, done after 1947 by some Muslim Hyderabadis in response to dramatic events in India, Pakistan, and Hyderabad, was not the decisive and final move most had anticipated. Instead, changing nations became an ongoing process for many Pakistani Hyderabadis, and the outcomes of these moves were not settled matters. The unsettled identity of Pakistan itself contributed greatly to this process. There was no longer a single destination, and both parents and young people strategized about where to obtain an education, where to work, and where to establish family residences for the next generation. Even members of the second generation, committed to a Pakistani identity, often carried it abroad.

CHAPTER 5

The United Kingdom: An Early Outpost

ZULFIQAR GHOSE wrote about leaving his native Punjab in 1942 (the town of Sialkot, later located in Pakistan) for Bombay, India, and then leaving India for England in 1952:[1]

> We were leaving two countries, for in some way we were alien to both and our emigration to a country to which we were not native only emphasized our alienation from the country in which we had been born. This distinction between the two countries of my early life has been the schizophrenic theme of much of my thinking: it created a psychological conflict and a pressing need to know that I do belong somewhere and neither the conflict nor the need has ever been resolved. I know that many other Indians and Pakistanis suffer from this conflict and I think that this is one unconscious motive why so many Indians and Pakistanis have come to live in England—the immediate motive, of course, being an economic one; for the English, when ruling India, gave us the last chance in our history to live together. If I wanted a nationalist label, I would call myself an Indo-Pakistani.

The United Kingdom held a special place in the diasporic Hyderabadi world. As the quotation above suggests, it was a third option, neither India nor Pakistan, but postcolonial Britain. Here, drawing on the Nizam's former status as "faithful ally" just beyond the reach of British imperialism,[2] Hyderabadis could retreat to a society that historically encompassed the Nizam's former kingdom but did not rule it directly.

The United Kingdom could be seen, especially in the 1950s and 1960s, as the headquarters of Hyderabadi networks around the world. Young Hyderabadis went to Britain for education from the late nineteenth century, and members of well-known families settled there, including many from the former nobility. The Nizam's younger grandson, Muffakham Jah, maintained a London residence and headed an important international network.

Many Hyderabadis involved in international business ventures or careers were based in London. Some Anglo-Indian Hyderabadis immediately moved "home" and Hyderabadis from Pakistan moved as twice-migrants. Thus Hyderabadis of different backgrounds converged in the UK, and most associations in which Hyderabadis abroad are active (Hyderabadi associations, Urdu associations, or Old Boys' or Old Girls' school associations) had their earliest incarnations in the UK. Yet after the 1960s, Britain drew few immigrants from Hyderabad, and in some ways it became a backwater, bypassed by streams of migration to other destinations.

Hyderabadis had a hard time establishing a unique and positively valued identity in Britain. They were often lumped with Britain's working-class, residentially clustered South Asian or "Paki" population, lost in a sea of Punjabis, Gujaratis, and Pakistanis and perceived as "black" or "Asian" by others in Britain. The general knowledge of India and even of Hyderabad by the British public did gain them some recognition, and the presence of members of the last Nizam's family, some of them prominent in London society, helped as well. They established a Hyderabad Deccan Association. This relatively small association was less active than the Urdu associations and Islamic associations that could draw on broader constituencies, and it relied upon the cultural ties and nostalgia felt by members of the first generation.

Given their early vantage point, Hyderabadis in Britain have watched the newer migrations from both India and Pakistan with some interest. Their interest was in one sense "above it all," but many became personally involved in the transnational networks through their relatives and, sometimes, their own children. Acknowledging that the more recent and usually less well-born immigrants to the United States and elsewhere were doing well in both economic and social terms, even some of those who fiercely defended their own move to Britain began sending their children to the newer Western destinations for education or marriage.

Paths to Britain

STUDENTS, WORKERS, AND ROYALTY

Hyderabadi students were studying in Britain long before the collapse of Hyderabad State. Hyderabadis appeared in a historical study of Indian Muslim students and their organizing efforts in London,[3] but settlers were few until after 1948. Many leading professionals and administrators of modern Hyderabad obtained their training and degrees in the UK, and the Nizam provided generous scholarships to outstanding students of all backgrounds.[4] After 1948, a few Hyderabadi students stayed on; others continued to come, and some of those stayed as well. In the 1960s, when Pakistan had become less attractive because of changing conditions there, young men from Hyderabad migrated primarily to the UK.

The Hyderabadi men settling in Britain ranged from clerks and chartered accountants to architects and physicians. Many were from modest backgrounds, had been educated at least partly in Urdu-medium schools, and had a passion for Urdu literature and poetry. Others came from high-status families, had been educated in English-medium schools, had family traditions of going abroad for higher education, and valued Western culture. They were not, as a group, driven out by a conviction that India was discriminating against Muslims; rather, they thought that opportunities for qualified men were better abroad. They stayed on in Britain after their schooling or returned after initial work experience in Hyderabad, persevering despite the racial prejudice they often experienced in the 1960s.

Many members of the first group of upwardly mobile Urdu enthusiasts had been members of the Orient Hotel coffee house circle in Hyderabad in the 1950s, where aspiring poets, writers, trade union leaders, and politicians gathered for hours of serious and pleasurable talk.[5] Abbas Zaidi, an Osmania degreeholder and member of the Orient Hotel circle, left for Britain in 1959 and brought his wife in 1962.[6] Viqar Lateef, a writer and engineer with degrees from Nizam College and Osmania, followed in 1964 after one year in Pakistan. Lateef was a talented writer who published Urdu short stories and poems in both India and Pakistan. Once in London, he married an Italian/English woman and worked as an engineer.[7] Syed Masud Ali, another Nizam College graduate, moved to London in 1965 and worked in social services; his father was a poet in the old city of Hyderabad and Masud Ali also became very active in Urdu-promoting activities in the UK. All of these men were avid readers of and contributors to *Siyasat*, Hyderabad's leading Urdu journal founded in 1949, whose founder and editor Abid Ali Khan proved especially interested in stories about Hyderabadis abroad.

Members of the second group, well-educated professionals from families grounded in English as well as in Urdu culture, continued to study and settle in Britain. These doctors, bankers, lawyers, architects, and educators settled not only in London but in Manchester, Glasgow, and other places. Majid Ali Khan, instrumental in revitalizing the Hyderabad Deccan Association, did a course of hotel management in London after earning his M.A. at Osmania and meant to settle in Britain. He went back to Hyderabad to help set up packaging industries there, but then he married, moved to London, and became an economic analyst, while his wife worked in the British civil service.[8] Mustafa Ali Khan moved in 1964 for cost accountancy, accompanied by his wife, and their child was born in Britain.[9] Wajih Dad Khan Mandozai, from a leading Afghan family in the Deccan, studied in St. George's Grammar School and Nizam College and chose Britain to study architecture in 1960, where he practices it today.[10] Dr. Hamid Hussain, a medical doctor from Hyderabad, moved in the 1960s, married an Englishwoman, and became politically prominent and closely associated with the British Medical Association. Dr. Sideshwar Raj Saxena was a distinguished doctor in Hyderabad for decades following his 1957 Osmania M.B.B.S.; he came to Britain in 1979 and achieved further honors (heading the Hyderabad Deccan Association in 1991). Dr. Yusuf Ali Khan, Saxena's colleague earlier in Hyderabad, had already established himself in London and they worked together again.[11]

The pattern was for the men to come first and then bring their wives, some of them highly educated professional women following careers and some of them women who chose to stay at home. For a few couples, intercommunity marriages (Muslim and Christian, or Muslim and Hindu) that marked them out in Hyderabad seemed easier for others to accept in Britain. These Hyderabadi families working in Britain did not necessarily intend to relocate permanently, but the years went by. Their children grew up in the UK, were well educated there, and were entering professions. As their own parents died in Hyderabad, the first-generation migrants went there less and it became increasingly difficult to think of returning permanently. Some lost ancestral properties because of being away, and others thought of selling ancestral properties and buying small flats in Hyderabad for stays of six months or less. Decisions about where to marry their sons and daughters entered into their retirement considerations.

Finally, London was home not only to Britain's royal family but to many displaced rulers and descendants of formerly royal families, among them leading members of the Nizam's lineage. The last Nizam's two grandsons studied in the UK, at Cambridge and Oxford, in the 1950s and 1960s, and their mother, the Turkish-born Princess Durru Shehvar, eventually settled in London. Her younger son, Muffakham Jah, and his Turkish-born wife lived there about half the year.[12] Nawab Mir Mohsin Ali Khan, descended from another line of Hyderabad's royal family, also studied in the UK, just after 1948. Married to a Swiss citizen and with a home in Geneva, he nonetheless conducted a public life in the UK, where he was socially prominent as a "prince of Hyderabad" and exemplified its tradition of courtly manners and cultural synthesis.[13] These members of the royal family maintained a certain distance from others (and, indeed, from each other), but London was a special place for many Hyderabadis around the world because of their presence and leadership activities.

"RETURNING HOME"

Anglo-Indians constituted a major group of Hyderabadis settling in the UK after 1948, "returning home" as many put it, in an imaginative move similar to that of Muslims going to Pakistan. Some of the British or Anglo-Indians settled in Hyderabad were British citizens. If one was born abroad of a British father, then one was a British citizen with the right of abode in Britain. This right, however, extended for only one generation, so not all Hyderabadi Anglo-Indians were able to establish British citizenship despite British ancestry.[14] And it transpired that not all who "returned home" elected to stay there (many moved on to Australia).

Military officers in the Nizam's army moved to the UK right after 1948, some of them doctors and others soldiers, men whose careers were jeopardized by the Police Action. Dr. Dennis P. Gay's closeness to Hyderabad's royal family gave him vivid memories of old Hyderabad.[15] His father was chief medical officer of the Nizam's military service, and had, at the end of his career, been doctor to the nobleman Sir Salar Jung II and his family. After medical training in the UK and service in World War I,[16] Dennis Gay returned to India and joined the Nizam's military, passing an Urdu exam to do so. He also served as doctor to the Nizam's younger son, Moazzam Jah, and his wife, the Princess Niloufer. Dr. Gay took his wife and daughter to the UK on study leave in 1939 and left them there when World War II broke out and he was called back to Hyderabad. He served in the Punjab and Italy and returned to Hyderabad. Just before the Police Action, Dr. Gay tried to resign, because "Hyderabad was being overcome by all the rest of India." To persuade him to stay on, he was promoted to principal medical officer in charge of Osmania Hospital (and his rival, "a non-mulki Madrasi," left the service). But in 1947, "the state was surrounded, everything was finished, it was a very sad time." He retired in 1950 and joined his family in Britain but continued to serve the Nizam, supervising the education and living arrangements of Prince Mukarram Jah (the elder grandson) at Cambridge.[17] He drew a pension from the Nizam for many years and then his official connections with Hyderabad ended.[18]

Lieutenant Colonel A. J. M. (Jack) Hudson, an Englishman born in Trimulgherry (near the Secunderabad British cantonment) in 1908, also "came home." A self-professed Hyderabadi who moved to the UK in 1948,[19] he too was in the Nizam's army, a cavalryman in the 1st Hyderabad Imperial Service Lancers. As Hudson remembered it, life in Hyderabad had offered many advantages: big houses and compounds, good servants, door-to-door shopping, a low cost of living, excellent postal and telegraph service, railroads, and banks. There were nearby hill stations and many enjoyable social activities, including dances, picnics, shoots, and dinner parties. True, there was a rigid social hierarchy of long-established communities based on status, wealth, and religion, but events always included British, Anglo-Indian, and Indian colleagues.[20] There were divisions among the British and Anglo-Indians too, based on race but also on occupation. The military officers and the engineers lived in the Cantonment and Hyderabad, respectively.[21] Hyderabad had been, Hudson thought, the most stable area in all of India, a kind of self-contained capsule immune from political upheavals. But "the Nizam was ill-advised, he didn't know how much better the Indian Army was than his army; he thought India would never be partitioned and that the treaty with the British would protect his sovereignty." After the Indian takeover, the Hudsons headed for England.[22]

Jimmy Adams moved to the UK after 1948 at age eighteen with his parents.[23] It was a "terrible uproot" for his parents, who remembered Hyderabad as the best place to live in; their memories of the Police Action and the Indian Army were not good.[24] They lived by Masab Tank, across the street from General El Edroos (who surrendered Hyderabad) in a house they called "Eden." Some family members were "thorough Europeans," others had married "Indian ladies." His grandfather was the mint master and his father, a mechanical engineer, was in charge of the electricity department.[25] Deciding to follow relatives to Britain, Mr. Adams had to prove his British nationality, so "he went to cemeteries and wrote to Somerset House to prepare the family history." It was a tricky situation: proving his British nationality endangered his pension from the Nizam. Therefore, his son recalled, he first got an Indian passport and "swore something," then he got his gratuity payment, a one-time final payment, and then the family moved to Britain and obtained citizenship. Sentimentally, Jimmy's father named his house in Middlesex "Osman Sicca" (the state's currency, actually Osmania *sicca*) because the money for it came from "the good old Nizam." Jimmy's father had to start over, working in the Dunlop tennis racquet factory, but as he established his family in the UK, his relatives the Corfields left for Australia. As Jimmy explained, those who had been soldiers in Hyderabad had no qualifications that would help them in an industrial nation like the UK, and the climate did not suit them either.[26]

Jimmy was a schoolboy during those last difficult years, at Bishop Cotton's School in Bangalore and then at the Hyderabad Public School (Jagirdars' College) for his Senior Cambridge.[27] In Britain, Jimmy worked for a bank; he and his sisters all worked for banks, and he met his wife through her brother who worked in a bank with him in London (she was from a Lahore Anglo-Indian family, from British India). "All the Anglo-Indians in Hyderabad used to be interconnected," he said, "and perhaps they still are, in Perth, but not in the northern hemisphere."

SECONDARY MIGRATIONS

Other Hyderabadis were "twice-migrants,"[28] moving to Britain by way of Pakistan or the Gulf states of the Middle East. After the partition of British India, some Hyderabadi Muslim students in the UK "returned" to Pakistan instead of Hyderabad. Within a decade, however, some of those who went to Pakistan from Britain moved back to the UK. Others joined them in a secondary migration from Pakistan, finding conditions there difficult. In the late 1950s, the UK was welcoming Indians and Pakistanis. Hyderabadis also moved on to Britain from the Middle East, where Indians and Pakistanis found good jobs from the 1960s.

Perhaps best known of those who passed through Pakistan is Abdul Qader Habib Hyderabadi, one of the upwardly mobile Urdu enthusiasts, who wrote an Urdu autobiography entitled *Inglistan Me* (In England). Of modest background, he took a Nizam College degree in commerce and was associated with the Razakars; he married in 1952 and his brother-in-law Mughni Tabassam brought him into the progressive movement. He migrated to Pakistan in 1954, but, wanting to study further, he and his wife moved to Nottingham, UK, in 1957. He worked as a laborer, a bus conductor, and a taxi driver in the difficult early years, sometimes dealing with racial discrimination. He, his wife and two children, and his younger brother shared a single room, and his wife worked also. Then a British firm offered him a chief accountant post, and "when economic conditions improved, I began taking part in social activities." His wife Siddiqa was in civil service, and together he and she became active promoters of Urdu.[29]

Amina Ahmed and her husband also moved to Britain after trying to settle in Pakistan. She had migrated to Pakistan with her parents in 1962 when she was eighteen, following her grandfather (an Osmania University professor whose books were largely ruined in the course of the move, a story of loss, like Hudson's) and a sister. The family had built a house in Karachi and Amina trained as a teacher. Then she married, and her Hyderabadi husband had studied in Britain. He took her there in the late 1960s because of "the mess, Pakistan was not stable, not a good place to be," and there was prejudice against them as muhajirs. Both sets of parents had settled in Pakistan, "but the next generation moved, for their jobs and their futures." Amina's teaching credentials were accepted in the UK and she worked, first as a full-time teacher and then two days a week.[30]

Ghulam Yazdani was another twice-migrant, moving from Hyderabad to Pakistan to the UK. He studied in Urdu-medium schools and earned an M.A. in sociology at Osmania but felt that Hyderabad presented declining opportunities for Muslims, so he went to Pakistan. As Pakistan had no sociology programs, he earned an LL.B., still in Urdu. Urdu was made Pakistan's official language, but the policy was slow to be implemented and Yazdani found the atmosphere there "unsuitable, quite different; Pakistan was not a democracy." Unhappy, he left for London, brought a bride from Hyderabad, and became a barrister. He and his wife tried Pakistan once more in 1966–1967 but returned to the UK, where their children were born and brought up. His specialties included immigration law and discrimination cases.

Another twice-migrant via Pakistan was Adeel Yousuf Siddiqui, whose father died shortly after the Police Action, leaving his widow with nine children and a small pension. The family moved to Pakistan in several stages, Adeel at age eighteen migrating last with his mother and two younger brothers in 1954. Except for one sister who stayed in India with her husband, they all settled in Karachi, where they found themselves "second-class citizens." They had been non-mulkis in Hyderabad, the grandfather and father both moving down from the United Provinces (UP), and they were "like that in Pakistan." Siddiqui married in Pakistan (his wife is from Poona, not Hyderabad) and had two daughters, but the family moved to the UK in 1972. He worked for Pakistani and Islamic banks, jobs that took him frequently to the Middle East. He and his wife and two daughters took British nationality.[31]

The Gulf states—the UAE, Qatar, Bahrain, Oman, and Kuwait— were, like Pakistan, staging posts for onward migration to Britain. Aziz Ahmed, son of Hyderabad's chief of police (Deen Yar Jung) at the time of the Police Action, worked first in banking in the Middle East, in Qatar, before trying India for a year and then moving on to the UK. Ahmed chose to stay in Britain, preferring it because of the scholarly and artistic resources in London and because his old friends had almost all left Hyderabad and settled elsewhere. He had a brother in Hyderabad and sisters in Boston, Hyderabad, and Madras; another (widowed) sister lived with him in London between visits to her children in Bedford, Geneva, and New York.

Hyderabadi entrepreneurs went back and forth as opportunities presented themselves between Pakistan, London, and the Middle East, or India, London, and the Middle East. They included Sharafat Walajah, head of Britain's Hyderabad Association in 1990, whom I met in Dubai in 1993, and Secunder Zaman Khan, who had lived in London but shifted to Kuwait in the late 1980s. It was even possible to travel from London to the Gulf states for weekend excursions to family or cultural events.

Some Hyderabadis who participated in international business and professional networks used London as a base. One posh block of flats had at least three Hyderabadi tenants: a Muslim doctor working in Riyadh, Saudi

Arabia, whose children were being educated at Harrow; a Muslim UN official whose job was in Geneva; and a Hindu businessman whose wide-ranging activities were conducted from London. The third man, V. Keshav Reddy,[32] was schooled largely outside Hyderabad, partly in the UK, and he had been a pilot in the Indian Air Force from 1939 to 1946. He left that to become traffic manager for the Nizam's Deccan Airways, an excellent airline,[33] but he quit the day before the government of India nationalized it in 1950. "I'm a Hyderabadi, we had latitude; the Indians were all tied up in ribbons, too many rules," he explained. Pan Am and Westinghouse International vied for his talents, and after supervising Middle East and Iranian operations for Westinghouse (he showed off his Persian and his Hyderabadi manners when he met the Shah of Iran), he worked for the American military (the Gulf Corps of Engineers) and had personal flats in Cairo, Teheran, and Beirut. That job ended in 1962,[34] and after a brief stint in Baghdad, his father's death took him back to Hyderabad. After the division of the family property, he went into the jewelry and real estate business in Geneva, Switzerland, where he met and married his second, Italian, wife. Although a job in Los Angeles beckoned, a friend in the UK needed help with a factory he had bought, so Reddy ended up there, but briefly. Next, he built a factory to make razor blades in Nigeria, but the Biafran war sent him back to London, where he bought a hotel with an Indian friend from Nigeria. He went from there to managing a tea estate in the Cameroons and again returned to London to manage Veeraswami's Restaurant.[35] In 1978, Reddy used his expertise again in the Middle East, air freighting building materials to Dubai and Sharjah with English and American partners, men he knew from Air Cargo and Deccan Airways. Men like Reddy and the others in his block of flats represented a new transglobal elite with jobs and homes everywhere and nowhere.

Hyderabadi, Asian, or British?

HYDERABADI CULTURE IN THE UK

Hyderabadis in the UK held strongly positive views of both British and Hyderabadi culture and thought the two had much in common. Hyderabadis had been "allies" of the British, and despite feelings of betrayal over treaty obligations unfulfilled,[36] the stance was one of equality and pride. Hyderabadis had a strong consciousness of ancestry and status and felt that Britain's class society was congenial to them. The British and the old Hyderabadis both valued privacy, formal manners, and literary pursuits, as well as refined, polished language and conservative cultural values. People identified with "indirect assertiveness, the British, not the American, way."

Both Muslim and Hindu descendants of the old Hyderabadi ruling class were numerous in Britain, most of them highly educated professionals. People in this class voiced regret and guilt: they, the bearers of the distinctive culture of the former state of the Nizam, were destroying it by leaving Hyderabad. Nawab Mir Mohsin Ali Khan recited a poignant Urdu poem to me, a rough translation of the last two lines being: "now the remaining remnants of the culture are few, we are the scattered history of the Deccan." Stories published in *Siyasat* illustrated the lasting attachment of expatriates in London to their homeland. One story was that of an old Hyderabadi man, someone's chauffeur, standing at Charing Cross, the center of the British world with its signposts saying so many miles to here, so many miles to there. Recognizing him as a fellow Hyderabadi, a second man asked him, as they looked at the signposts together, "How many miles to Hyderabad, I wonder?" "Oh, Hyderabad is here, *janab* (sir)," the old man said, placing his hand on his heart. Another *Siyasat* story by a Londoner was entitled, "The Body in London, the Heart in Hyderabad."[37]

Those in the UK of aristocratic lineages, high levels of education, and a deep appreciation of Hyderabadi history and culture often did not understand that I was interested in contemporary migration and settlement abroad. They kept referring me to people of noble descent in London or Hyderabad who could inform me about, instead, the history and culture of the former Hyderabad State. Quite often when a name was mentioned or when I was introduced to someone, the names of fathers and grandfathers and their positions in old Hyderabad were discreetly mentioned. I was encouraged to seek out informants from certain families, avoiding "the clerks" and "semiliterate Hyderabadis."

Other Hyderabadis in London resented this elitist view and claimed that the virtue of Hyderabadi culture was its inclusiveness. Jack Hudson, for example, had liked Hyderabad very much for its "open house civilization, open house hospitality," although he felt he was "on the Muslim side of it." The international entrepreneur Keshav Reddy also talked about old Hyderabad's inclusive friendship networks. When asked by an outsider how Hyderabadi Hindus, Muslims, Parsis, and others could be so close to each other, Reddy told him, "we knew each others' secrets, we had to be nice to each other." He then told an anecdote from the last days of the Nizam, when Reddy was doing secret work for the Indian government. Hyderabad's chief minister got a note from the man who at that time was commissioner of police telling him to arrest Keshav Reddy. Captain Alex Norton,[38] an old family friend of Reddy's, was aide-de-camp to the chief minister and warned the chief minister (successfully) against the arrest: "But think of all the trouble we'll have from the Muslims, don't touch him." "Not from the Hindus, but from the Muslims, notice," Reddy emphasized, "we sent food and presents, we were so close." His best friend, with whom he stayed when visiting Hyderabad (where he no longer had property), was from the Chenoy Parsi family.[39]

Many Hyderabadis in London felt they had moved well beyond the cultural boundaries of their homeland. In a few cases of intercommunity marriage, the couples had eloped or moved to London at a time when such marriages entailed severe social sanctions in Hyderabad (Yusuf and Mary Ali Khan, Jayakumari and Humayun Yar Khan, Feroze and Laura Khan). Other immigrants simply felt they had become more liberal and secular in cosmopolitan London. Adeel Yousuf Siddiqui eloquently quoted Iqbal's Urdu verse that "the only thing durable is change" and stated that Hyderabadis in London, in contrast to those he met in the Middle East, had broadened their outlooks in their thirty to forty years in Britain. The children of such pioneers in Britain were broadening not only their outlooks but sometimes also their range of marriage partners.

HYDERABADI ORGANIZATIONS IN BRITAIN

Social divisions in Hyderabad were certainly reproduced in Britain. Differences of both class and ideology were reflected in Hyderabadi support of key organizations in Britain. A Hyderabad association was long established in London, although it had lapsed and been restarted, and the membership base had changed over the years. The students from Hyderabad initiated the first Hyderabad Majlis (association) in London in the years between 1908 and 1912 under the leadership of Latif Sayeed, in England for medical training. This organization lapsed[40] and was revived in 1929 by Ataur Rahman, Baqar Ali Mirza, and Dilsukh Ram, and revived again in 1946 by Ataur Rahman when he returned to London as the state's offical adviser to Hyderabadi students.[41] (The Nizam's scholars to the UK in the 1940s and 1950s were so numerous that the Nizam appointed an adviser for them, a practice continued well after 1948.)

Hyderabadis restarted an association yet again in the late 1960s, calling it the *Bazm-i-Ehbab*, or Society of Friends, as some spouses were not from Hyderabad. But when an English name proved necessary to register the organization as a working-man's or Friendly Society in 1974, the name "Hyderabad Deccan Association" was chosen and some members dropped out, feeling that they and their non-mulki spouses were no longer fully welcome. The first printed constitution, around 1976,[42] specified membership by birth, naturalization, marriage, or parental links—qualifications repeated on the application form of the 1990s. "Naturalization" meant the process by which non-mulkis became mulkis, and membership by marriage was explicitly recognized.[43]

In the 1960s and early 1970s, some fifty or sixty families were involved in the Hyderabad Deccan Association. There were, at first, no Hindu members, and Shia Muslims too were underrepresented (in Hyderabad, the Shia were 20% or 30% of all Muslims). Most meetings occurred in homes and were family gatherings for birthday celebrations, Muslim religious events, or musical or poetry evenings. Gender segregation was observed, and babies and children were brought along.[44] In the shift from a student to family base, association activities reflected a primarily Muslim membership of young professional people who were close friends and often related by blood or marriage.

In its most recent incarnation, from the 1970s on, the Hyderabad Deccan Association has employed the image of the Char Minar on newsletters and an official tie.[45] The association's most important event, the Ramadan Id dinner marking the end of the month of fasting, featured a feast included in the dues[46] and prepared by some of the members. A potluck was held on the other Id (marking the end of the annual hajj or pilgrimage to Mecca) and *mushairas* (poetry readings) were sponsored; there were about six functions per year. The association fielded a cricket team, Hyden (Hyderabad, Deccan) and experimented with events for youth. But at least 150 families were involved (six to ten of them non-Muslim), so gatherings could run to 600 or 700 people. As one man told me, "with more wives working, the preparation of Hyderabadi food has become difficult—but mulkis oppose commercialization, so this tradition must be kept!" "Tradition" also involved last-minute confusion over the numbers attending events. In 1990, 350 guests had registered for the Annual Dinner by the stated deadline, but the number rose to 425 on the morning of the dinner, and 533 people actually turned up.[47]

Association activities at the turn of the twenty-first century continued to focus on the Id potluck, mushairas, and group excursions (to Istanbul, the Isle of Wight, and the Netherlands).[48] A fund-raising dinner for Hyderabad Flood Relief (summer of 2000) and a talk by an Egyptian scholar on the relationships of Muslims with non-Muslims were also sponsored. A new subheading appeared under the association's name on its newsletters: "The premier Association of Hyderabadis in the world."

People from Hyderabad had a range of opinions about the association. Some chose not to join, saying it prevented assimilation into Britain—but most Hyderabadis maintained that they could continue to support Hyderabadi culture and assimilate into British culture at the same time. Others had conflicts with leaders at one time or another, or they preferred to associate only with old family friends, or they no longer celebrated old Hyderabad and its ruling class. One man's analysis split Hyderabadis into two contending parties, those who vehemently opposed efforts to laud the old

Nizam and those, "the jagirdars," he termed them, who remained loyal to the Nizam's descendants. Another man said he joined the London Hyderabad Association because friends urged him to do so. Although he saw it as a social and cultural effort worth supporting, he had reservations about trying to impose the old culture on the children being raised in Britain. And a third person asserted that even the smallest gathering of Hyderabadis was never split into less than half a dozen parties.

The Hyderabad Deccan Association suffered from class and ideological tensions in the 1990s, as nonmembers accused the leadership of being "very elitist, self-promoting, money-making people," and within the leadership there was a struggle over how best to define, maintain, and, possibly, expand the membership. The Urdu language was central to many association events (not just the *mushairas*), and two of the annual meetings were held to commemorate the Muslim Ids, yet the second generation was losing command of Urdu and non-Muslim Hyderabadis were not attracted by Islamic religious occasions. Disagreements about qualification for membership lingered, as some told me that among the members were people who were "not really Hyderabadis." This could mean, depending on the speaker, that they were not known to the speaker, were non-mulkis, or had come via Pakistan.

Certainly the involvement of Pakistani Hyderabadi immigrants in the association was an additional complication. Some such people have become not just members but leaders of the association. However, reclaiming their Hyderabadi identity did not mean reclaiming an Indian identity, so the association could be strongly affected by the recurrent political problems between India and Pakistan. It was also stated that the Hyderabadis from Pakistan were go-getters, while the Indian mulkis were not. One man claimed that making money was against the mulki character, whereas those from Pakistan were "keeping up with the Joneses." Thus the resentment against "successful people" was perhaps directed against the allegedly more conspicuous consumption patterns of Pakistani Hyderabadis.

In London, too, Prince Muffakham Jah was spearheading an effort to build an international Hyderabad association. The prince felt that Hyderabadi culture was being best maintained abroad and lent his support to various efforts to reinforce it.[49] Inevitably, among his closest contacts were members or descendants of the former nobility or high-ranking state officials and persons close to the Nizam's household, yet he was keenly interested in all Hyderabadis. He tried to take a survey of Hyderabadis around the world, he spurred the formation of several Hyderabad Associations (notably in Chicago, California, and Toronto), and he tried to start an International Hyderabad Club. The club would have offered an attractive club building in Banjara Hills with accommodations for visiting members, dining and recreational facilities, conference and party rooms, a business center and car rental office, a resource center for networking, and an "entertainer" for visiting young persons who found family obligations "boring." This ambitious effort was faltering, probably because the initial fee was high, the members had to be elected, and overseas members (about half of the projected 500) would derive little benefit as they made such short visits to Hyderabad. There were also old and new clubs in Hyderabad to which some overseas Hyderabadis already belonged, and most of those visiting from overseas stayed with relatives in the city.[50]

URDU-PROMOTING AND OTHER ACTIVITIES

Urdu literary associations in the UK were so ubiquitous that there was sometimes confusion about which association was organizing which activity, and Hyderabadis were very much involved in them. The successful Durbar Dinner held in 1990 organized by the Hyderabad Deccan Association was thought by some to have been organized by the Urdu Majlis (Urdu Society) to commemorate the 400th year of the foundation of the city of Hyderabad (these were two separate events). The Princess Durru Shehvar and Prince Muffakham Jah and Princess Esin attended the Durbar Dinner, along with the Indian and Pakistani High Commissioners in London and those Hyderabadis who could get tickets (it was sold out).[51] The 400th birthday commemoration event seems to have been inaugurated back in Hyderabad by Abbas Zaidi (of the Hyderabad Association and Urdu Majlis) on a visit home and Abid Ali Khan (editor of *Siyasat*).[52] Ironically, the commemoration to be held concurrently in Hyderabad did not take place, and scholars, poets, and journalists from Hyderabad attended the London event.[53] Relations between Hyderabadis and Indian government representatives in London, however, have generally been very good. There was a slight strain in 1992, when the tearing down of the Babri Masjid (mosque) by militant Hindus led Indian officials to call Indian Muslims reassuringly, arousing indignation because many felt it unnecessary. Confident citizens of India, they did not, in Britain, want special attention as a minority.

London was said to be the world's third largest center of Urdu activities, with a professor of Urdu established at the School of Oriental and African Studies. It had supported more than one organization to promote Urdu over the years.[54] An Urdu Majlis leader stated proudly that Queen Victoria had had two Hyderabadi tutors to teach her Urdu, thus reading Urdu back into English history (perhaps inaccurately, as others said that the Queen's one Urdu tutor was from Agra). He listed the many Urdu magazines published and the many Urdu-promoting functions held in London. The Urdu

Majlis had had an earlier incarnation and Hyderabadis led its revival in 1978.[55] An Urdu Markaz (Urdu Center) event in 1984 named the wife of the writer Habib Hyderabadi, Sidiqqa Shabnam, as a Markaz member and current president of the Hyderabad Deccan Association. A meeting was held in honor of Sidiqqa's brother, Hyderabadi poet Dr. Mughni Tabassam.[56] A London branch of the Amir Khusro Society hosted a concert by the world-famous sitarist Ravi Shankar, and *mushairas* included one attended by the Pakistani Urdu poet Faiz Ahmed Faiz and presided over by the poetess Zehra Nigah.[57]

Organizational activities to promote Urdu and Hyderabad in London often overlapped. In 1984, Hyderabadi participants in the Anjuman-i-Taraqi-Pasand Musanafin (Progressive Writers' Association) helped sponsor an evening with Ali Sardar Jaferi, a visiting poet from northern India, and in 1985 the same association held an international conference in which Hyderabadis were active. In 1985, the Hyderabad Association's annual Ramadan Id program was held in conjunction with the annual *mushaira* of the Urdu Markaz,[58] with Prince Muffakham Jah as chief guest. The program featured the Hyderabadi comedian Mushtaba Hussain and musicians Mustafa Ali Beg and Vithal Rao. "Sometimes," the article said, "we think that we are not in London, but it is three decades earlier, and we are in Moghulpura, Ghazipura, and Dar us Shifa."[59] Another overlap occurred with the Iqbal Academy of Britain, which joined the Hyderabad Deccan Association in 1990 to sponsor a *mushaira* honoring Muhammad Iqbal, the poet and philosopher whose vision was drawn upon to create Pakistan.[60]

Hyderabadis were members of both the Hyderabad Association and the Urdu Majlis,[61] but the latter was sponsored by the Greater London Arts Council and drew membership from first-generation migrants of Indian, Pakistani, and other backgrounds. Punjabis were particularly enthusiastic.[62] The Urdu Majlis was preferred by some to the Hyderabad Association, as it had a wider base of support, was free (in contrast to the high membership and function fees of the latter), and reached out to the youngsters through regular meetings and a quarterly journal, *Hayat-i-Nau*. The journal tried to publish second-generation writers, and a story in 1989 focused poignantly on "the problem of the second generation" in the UK.[63]

Significant linkages to British culture occurred through the British Broadcasting Corporation (BBC), an important early source of employment for immigrants. This strengthened London's centrality in Urdu literary circles and linked the BBC to Hyderabad's newspapers, writers, and performing artists. Amjad Ali, once a magistrate in Hyderabad, was put in charge of BBC's Urdu programming. Akbar Hyderabadi came to the UK to study architecture in 1955, married an Italian woman working in England, and also did some work for the BBC in Oxford.[64] Their connections with the BBC allowed Hyderabadis employed there to arrange programs that hosted Urdu poets, journalists, and other visitors from Pakistan and India. When the Hyderabad Deccan Association brought the poet Sayeed Shaheedi from Hyderabad in 1990, the BBC featured him. The Urdu Majlis and the Hyderabad Deccan Association also held *mushairas*, one of them a particularly memorable function. It was remarkable partly because Zehra Nigah, herself an Urdu poet, presided over it (it was unheard of, in Hyderabad, for a woman to preside over a mushaira) and partly because the Hyderabad Deccan Association made a point of inviting anyone from India or Pakistan, whether connected with Hyderabad or not, on this occasion.[65]

Akbar Hyderabadi's career working for the BBC in Oxford demonstrated the wide audience for Urdu in the Hyderabadi diasporic world. He went on to be feted in Karachi, London, Los Angeles, and Copenhagen for his five books of poetry. In Los Angeles in 1994 he won the International Urdu Markaz prize for the best book of Urdu verse published in the West; six critics, one based in Pakistan, one based in India, and four based in the West, selected him. The selection was rather remarkable, given that Akbar lived a somewhat isolated life in Oxford, teaching Urdu to police and social workers, and working on the local commission on community relations.[66] He was never a prominent participant in Hyderabadi or Urdu associational activities in London or Birmingham, although he was one of the small number of artists and poets who met at Oxford's Randolph Hotel for some time. Akbar's reputation as a poet grew steadily as he published his fourth and fifth books in 1993 and 2000 and they circulated in India, Pakistan, and other countries where Urdu-speakers had settled. A friend maintained that Akbar's selection for the Urdu Markaz honor was the exception to the lower standards for Urdu poetry particularly evident in modern *mushairas* in the diaspora, and he quoted Saib's stanza, "Two things devalue a poem, the praise of those who know nothing and the silence of those who know."

A few Hyderabadis won recognition in Britain as experts on Indian history, art, and culture. Museums, auction houses, and the language and student counseling departments of universities consulted these scholars on a range of subjects. One cultural expert, Mrs. Shehzad Hussain, wrote cookbooks and was a food consultant at Marks and Spencer. Another, Ziauddin Ahmed Shakeb, earned his Ph.D. in medieval Deccani history but left the Andhra Pradesh State Archives in 1980 to teach and consult in London. Shakeb was a consultant for Christie's and numerous academic institutions and departments and also a frequent speaker on Hyderabadi history and culture at Hyderabad Association events.[67]

Another Hyderabadi intersection with British culture came through cricket, a game avidly followed by British, Indians, and Pakistanis alike. Strongly associated with British colonial rule, cricket was also taken up in princely India.[68] In earlier decades, Hyderabadis S. M. Hadi and Nawab Mohammed Hussain had been Oxford Blues, and Hyderabad State's Deccan Blues was a famous team in the subcontinent. After Britain's Indian empire ended, teams from the former colonies overtook Britain—the West Indies, Pakistan, and India became world forces in international cricket. Asif Iqbal Rizvi, having played for Madras-i-Aliya, Nizam College, Hyderabad, and South Zone in India, went on to lead Pakistan's cricket team, moved to Britain and played for Kent in the 1970s, and in the early 1990s was organizing matches in Sharjah and Dubai in the UAE.[69] Dr. Afzal Ali Khan, Habib Ahmed, and Govind Raj, Hyderabadis who played for Hyderabad or India, also resided in Britain,[70] and Hyderabad's own Mohammed Azharuddin, India's flamboyant captain in the international test series in the 1990s, spent 1991 in Britain playing for Derbyshire County.[71]

The first-generation Hyderabadi immigrants in Britain had not taken leadership positions in British Islamic associations, although the Nizam of Hyderabad contributed money, along with the Nawab of Bhopal, to Britain's first mosque, in Woking, and was the major funder of the second mosque, in Regents Park.[72] Yet "it is not in the Hyderabadi mind to sing the song of Islam," as one person put it, referring to people in both Hyderabad and the UK.[73] There was an Indian Muslim Association in London and some Hyderabadis were active in it, but this was primarily secular rather than religious in its emphasis.[74] The Hyderabadis thus contrasted greatly with the very different Pakistani Muslim community in Manchester, where the Mosque Association was the central arena for internal politics and the business community was the dominant one.[75] Furthermore, despite tales of racial and national origin discrimination, no Hyderabadis seem to have been active in the "Black British" politics of the 1980s. Instead, first-generation Hyderabadi immigrants were leaders of a variety of other associations, particularly Urdu and "old boy" ones like the Aligarh Association. Salim Quraishi reported that when he attended a meeting of the Aligarh Association in November 1992, all the leaders were from Hyderabad, although only five or six of the 100 to 120 attendees at the meeting were Hyderabadis.

With respect to taking British citizenship, Hyderabadis from India and Pakistan had different constraints. India did not permit dual citizenship, but Pakistan and Britain did. Although British citizenship was fairly easy to obtain (basically, it took five years of residence), because so many Indian Hyderabadis still had property in Hyderabad and were ambivalent about whether to return, most of the men from India had not become naturalized British citizens.[76] Their children, however, were usually citizens, and sometimes the wife (the non-property-holder) had become a British citizen. Pakistani Hyderabadis, on the other hand, eagerly obtained British citizenship without relinquishing that of Pakistan and could then obtain "green cards" for Canada and the United States more easily. The Pakistan High Commission in the UK negotiated visa exemptions and air travel concessions for Pakistanis with dual nationality in the UK after 1995.

Friends back in Hyderabad observed that British Hyderabadis began visiting frequently as they grew older, becoming increasingly obsessed with their homeland and whether to return to it. One man said that as people overseas aged, their identity crises seemed to become more acute, particularly for those who had gone first to Pakistan and not visited Hyderabad for many decades. "They come and revisit old friends, the old school networks," he said. Viqar Lateef, whose wife (and thus his two children) were English, phoned M. Narsing Rao, an old friend from Orient Hotel coffee house days in Hyderabad and said he was flying home in two days and needed to be met with an oxygen chamber upon arrival. He arrived but died three days later.

An Early Outpost

VIEWING THE DIASPORA FROM LONDON

Hyderabadi migration to the UK followed close upon the Police Action, as did the moves of some young Hyderabadi Muslims from the UK to Pakistan but then back again to the UK. Hyderabadis based in Britain have since seen relatives from both India and Pakistan migrating elsewhere, to Canada, the United States, and Australia, many of them by way of sojourns in the Middle East. The view from the UK of the ongoing diaspora reflects the early, often privileged, position of the onlookers.

Speakers from this early outpost usually maintained that the UK was still preferred by Hyderabadis in both the UK and Hyderabad. The Poetry Society, a leading group of intellectuals back in Hyderabad city, was proud to be affiliated with the London Poetry Society. A graduate of St. George's School (arguably the best in Hyderabad) assured me that St. Georgians prefer London to other overseas destinations, and a high-ranking judge in Hyderabad was confident that being a Hyderabadi was the key to acceptability in the UK. Britain was also advantageous as a site because it was a fairly neutral ground, where migrants from India and Pakistan could meet and invoke, under British auspices, a pre-1948 shared past. Like Britain, some Middle Eastern countries (Saudi Arabia, the UAE, Qatar, Bahrain, Oman, and Yemen) were neutral grounds and people from Britain worked for short periods in the Middle East. Thus overseas Hyderabadis moved and mingled in Britain and the Middle East, but those who had opted for Pakistan, however briefly, seldom visited Hyderabad again.[77]

One Hyderabadi scholar in London distinguished between early and late migrations from Hyderabad and between "economic pull" emigrants and "deprived of opportunities push" emigrants.[78] Earlier, he said, it had been an honor to go abroad, and only very influential, intellectual, and capable people had gone abroad, and usually on scholarship. Then, as education increased in India, more people went abroad for study and work, and, since 1965, he discerned two groups. The first consisted of people of all class backgrounds going to the Gulf for temporary stays and strictly economic returns, whereas the second consisted of highly educated and skilled people going to the Western countries to utilize their training better and be appreciated. "Britain has a particular appeal, people from America and Europe also want to settle here; all the culture of the world is gathered in London," this writer said. He stressed the respect shown for India's culture by Britain's higher educational institutions, the development of Urdu literary culture in Britain, and the Government Translation Bureau, which was open twenty-four hours a day and covered 124 languages. He counseled immigrants to adjust themselves to this receptive setting by giving up some Asian habits and assuming new, individualistic identities so that they could be "happy, not critical."

Like this speaker, many people assured me that the "really cultured" Hyderabadis and the "real" Hyderabadi culture were to be found in London, not America. But this view appeared to be under challenge: remember the slogan "premier Association of Hyderabadis in the world" the Hyderabad Deccan Association based in London added to its newsletter in the 1990s. This challenge was particularly galling because several people reported, after visiting the United States, that Hyderabadis there reflected a very much wider range of backgrounds. One such visitor, who had held a green card for the United States for many years but said he would never use it, said "The background of those settling in the United States is different, the majority are alien to us and would be even if we were all living back in Hyderabad." Another said:

> Hyderabadis in Chicago are a different class—mechanics, petrol pump workers, lower class and uneducated but well paid. College dropouts are brought by relatives, they're more materialistic, they want TVs, cars, things like that. Those who go to the United States go for money; it's even better for that than Saudi Arabia, better accommodations and better education for the children.

Despite such contrasts between themselves and the immigrants to the United States and elsewhere, the Hyderabadis in London recognized that those emigrants often did quite well. There was some resentment that while the class structure of Britain had failed to admit *them* fully at the level they deserved, less deserving immigrants in the newer destinations were benefiting from more open (or less knowledgeable) societies. Jokes captured their feelings.

> One young fellow in an ill-fitting suit was being seen off at Nampally railway station by many members of his family, taking the train to Bombay. His grandmother hugged him and sobbed, "Oh son, if only you'd passed your Andhra matric [the matriculation exam for which pupils appear who cannot pass any other exam], you wouldn't have to go to America!"

> An old Hyderabadi man was telling about his three grandsons and how they'd turned out. "The first one is very bright, he's doing well here as a bus conductor. The second one is doing fine, he's in the Forest Department and has a big family. And the third one, a good-for-nothing, has gone to the USA."

Yet it was precisely because of such successes in the United States that some of those who had migrated so deliberately to Britain were planning to send their children to the newer Western destinations and would perhaps join them later on. One reason was that "the children in the United States are becoming Americanized faster than our children are becoming British." Another reason, voiced especially by Hyderabadi women in Britain, was that American neighbors seemed friendlier than British neighbors.

THE SECOND GENERATION

If being Hyderabadi means loving the food, the jokes, the company, a certain kind of Urdu, and distinctive dress, then many members of the second generation in Britain were still Hyderabadi. There was a continuing sense, among Indians, that Hyderabadis were different from Delhi people, Baroda people, and so on. A lot of this depended on their use of the Urdu language, however, and even the children of those most active in the Urdu activities were losing the language. They might speak it, but at home English was usually spoken between parents and children, and many of the second generation could not read Urdu. Hyderabadi jokes, heavily dependent on the language, could no longer be appreciated.

In contrast to the high value placed on Hyderabadi culture by members of the first generation and their efforts to transmit it to their children, the young people whom I met were not committed to it. I met many parents who made extra efforts to speak Urdu at home with their children and furnished their homes with beautiful keepsakes from Hyderabad, hoping to inculcate respect for the old culture. People with many relatives in Hyderabad still visited there frequently. Yet one husband and wife, visiting

Hyderabad many times with their children, recognized that Hyderabad could not have the same meaning for their children that it did for them. Another parent said his daughters were "going their own way." A father said his daughters wanted to visit Australia and the United States, not Hyderabad (but another man's daughter, traveling around the world adventurously, did include Hyderabad in her lengthy itinerary). One young man going into business, son of a leading proponent of Hyderabadi culture, told me, "Hyderabadis, they're lousy, at least for business. Of course the 'culture' is fine, but those Nawabi Hyderabadis are lazy and undependable; you can't do business with them; there's no guarantee they'll come through."

The Hyderabad Deccan Association tried to attract members of the second generation, holding events especially for them and occasionally recruiting officers from among them, but a general pattern of declining participation on the part of young people seemed clear. The association sponsored a disco once, but "only the more Westernized came, that is not our custom." It also tried doing sports for the youngsters and formed a separate youth association. The Hyden Cricket Club competed regularly in the early 1990s but then died. One association leader speculated that age and gender patterns among the leadership hindered wider participation:

> The men are more aggressive; they take the leadership; wives and youngsters are fairly quiet. We older men are the leaders, and we don't want to sponsor the kinds of activities that we know the youngsters would like; we don't want to put on coeducational parties with music and dancing.

These same first-generation leaders were also reluctant to give up use of the Urdu language at meetings, although they admitted it was a barrier to the young people's understanding of the programs. Urdu was still the dominant language in association activities, and the young people had particular difficulty understanding poetry. When "the current set of young adults was growing up, unlike now, there were no Urdu/Hindi/Punjabi classes; maybe the younger people will recover the language," one man said. In the 1990s, in schools with high proportions of Asian children, the students could elect to take Urdu, and the association had successfully shown videos about Hyderabad city and culture to the young people.[79] Once, when a scholar known for his excellent English and his knowledge of old Hyderabad came from Hyderabad, he was asked to speak about Hyderabad in English so that the young people could follow his talk.[80]

Hyderabadis in the UK, like those elsewhere in the Western world, had fears about the second generation, and not only fears that their children were losing the Urdu language and Hyderabadi culture. They feared they were acquiring unwanted features of Western culture such as dating, lack of respect for elders and relatives, and extreme individualism. A story in the 1989 *Hayat-e-Nau* annual issue presented a father's worst nightmare. His uneducated wife had wanted to move back to India before the children "become strangers," but the narrator had decided to stay in Britain because of India's poverty, increasing population, and the possibility that the children would not like it there. The story took place on an evening when his daughter had been picked up by an English girlfriend, a girl who had left home and taken her own apartment, and focuses on the father waiting helplessly for his daughter to come home. When she finally did so, at 3 A.M., dazed and drunk and with her blouse torn, she berated her father for waiting up for her and announced that she should get her own apartment; it would be better to live alone.[81]

There was ambivalence about religion, particularly among the Muslims. Many Hyderabadis felt that their children were "better" Muslims than they themselves were growing up in Hyderabad, or, perhaps, that the children found it easier to turn to religion as an identity than to turn to Hyderabadi culture and Urdu literature. Furthermore, in the British context where assertive religiosity was becoming the basis of identity for some young Muslims, Hyderabadi manners marked those who maintained them as "cowards," one couple commented, seeing a conflict between culture and religion. Sharp differences in religious observance were developing in a population where such differences had been uncommon. Among the Hindus too, there was more conspicuous practice of religion. One Muslim told me that some of his Hindu friends were "putting gods in a cupboard for their kids to worship (a common practice, given house designs in the West)."

There was also some parental fear of Muslim fundamentalism in the UK. At least one second-generation son had become involved in fundamentalist activities in college, and parents were refusing proposals for their daughters from "otherwise nice boys who only wear sherwanis and Afghan caps and say they'll never wear suits because suits are un-Islamic." The extent of one's religious observance was a new index for assessing marriage proposals, as prospective brides and grooms had clear ideas about their religious identities. Some grooms expected their brides to wear the *hijab*, not a custom among these Hyderabadis. Conversely, a young British Muslim woman had divorced her Hyderabadi British husband because he was not religious enough; she found his brand of "Hyderabadi secularism" unsatisfactory.

Patterns of friendships, careers, and marriages for the second generation of Hyderabadis in the UK were not yet clear. One man spoke movingly of his hopes for his children. Himself without close English friends, he used to be optimistic about the Hyderabadi children being raised in Britain, but friendships had not materialized for them either, he thought, whereas in the United States it seemed to be different. He rationalized that his daughter, although less shy than his son and very active, probably did not really want to date or be close to English friends anyway. But some of the young people were making British friends. With respect to careers, many of the younger generation were qualifying as doctors, dentists, and solicitors; a few were becoming newscasters, artists, and scholars. The course of study most frequently chosen was medicine, according to recent Hyderabad Association newsletters.

There were several patterns among young Hyderabadis with respect to marriage. The Anglo-Indian young people did not identify as Hyderabadis, and all of them seemed to be marrying Britishers. One such daughter and her fiancee planned to be married abroad without parental attendance at a Florida amusement park in the United States (she worked for Virgin Atlantic). As Jimmy Adams said, "The weddings are for them and their friends; why should the kids invite people they haven't seen in thirty to fifty years—people who are, in any case, their parents' friends?" Dr. Dennis Gay's only child, a daughter, married a distinguished British scholar of art and architecture, and all three of Lieutenant Colonel Hudson's children married Britons.

For most young British Hyderabadis of Muslim and Hindu background, however, marriages were still largely a matter of parental arrangement. Some of the first-generation immigrants who came for education or work said they still intended to go back to Hyderabad, and a few married their daughters into Hyderabad in preparation for their retirement there. In one instance, the daughter of a UK Urdu Majlis leader visited relatives, and when she was in Hyderabad a family asked for her. Thinking that they would return to Hyderabad, the parents agreed, and the marriage took place. According to the daughter, her Hyderabad in-laws were quite old-fashioned. Her mother-in-law objected to her short haircut and she had to grow her hair long and learn to speak Urdu better.[82] But her parents probably will not return to Hyderabad.[83] Settling a child in Hyderabad through marriage from Britain has become rare.

The parents not only chose or strongly directed the choice of the spouse, but the entire wedding was also theirs to plan. Marriages with cousins were still preferred among many of the Hyderabadi Muslims. They sometimes brought young women from Hyderabad and Pakistan as brides for their sons but preferred young women from the UK, ideally aged twenty-two to twenty-four. Many gave their daughters to grooms in Canada or the United States, the directions of movement of young women indicating relative rankings in the marriage system (daughters generally marry up). Marriages more often took place in the UK but could be held in Pakistan, Hyderabad, or the Middle East.[84] The location was determined not only by considerations of cost but by seeing where most of the parents' friends and relatives resided. Weddings seemed to be more and more often held in Hyderabad and were celebrated more and more lavishly, with English friends and employers attending as guests. Another feature of weddings was the display of eligible young women. One wedding in Hyderabad with 1,200 guests from all over the world led to twelve marriage proposals for a young British Hyderabadi woman, proposals that gave her a choice of husbands in several different countries.

The young people getting married and their parents might not even talk in detail about wedding arrangements, as parents simply assumed it was their responsibility to handle all the planning and invitations. As I sat at a kitchen table in London asking a father and son about plans for the son's wedding (not yet arranged), the son said it would be better not to hold the wedding in Hyderabad, even if lots of relatives were there and it cost less money. His friends were in Britain, he said; "I've grown up here and want to have my wedding here, so my friends can attend at least the reception." His statement caused his father consternation. "But," the father replied, "We have at least 300 people we have to invite, all Hyderabadis, all family and friends." He was startled at the suggestion that his son's friends, rather than his own and his wife's relatives and friends, should be given places on the invitation list.

A few young British Hyderabadis were marrying beyond the communities of their birth. Parents settled in Britain who did not believe arranged marriages were appropriate have seen their children marry Britons and even other Europeans.[85] People thought it was better for Hyderabadi girls to marry English men than the other way round. Those men become good Muslims, it was said, whereas with some of the English wives there have been divorces (although a couple of recent divorces of such couples, in which the husband was English, have perhaps unsettled this stated preference). Divorces, said one man with an international perspective, were happening among Hyderabadis first in the UK, and then in the eastern United States, with a half-generation lag for the latter.

In this early outpost of Hyderabadi immigrants, the integration of both the first and second generations into British society was occurring only gradually. Evidently most Hyderabadis came to Britain not only because of economic opportunities but also because of idealistic notions about British culture and its "fit" with Hyderabadi culture. By and large, their expectations about economic opportunity seem to have been met. Many women were working and taking leadership positions in Urdu-promoting and other organizations. Their children, too, were benefiting from good educations and occupational opportunities. However, the "boundedness" of British culture seems to have prevented much interaction between Hyderabadis and Britons, and therefore there had been little "unsettling" of the cultural notions brought from Hyderabad by first-generation immigrants. Another contributor to the cultural continuity may have been that many of those who came first were unclear about whether they were immigrants or sojourners. However, as the decades passed and young Hyderabadis grew up as British citizens, the cultural worlds of parents and children have diverged in some obvious ways. Despite that, this early outpost of Hyderabadi emigrants was arguably the one in which Hyderabadi culture retained the highest degree of stability and cultural continuity.

First-generation Hyderabadi immigrants drew on ancestral and inherited positions and invoked historical associations, puzzled perhaps that these were not gaining fuller acknowledgment and acceptance for them in the UK but unwilling to divest themselves of the status and memories provided by the past. There was no pressure to give up the old Hyderabadi identity, as in Pakistan, but tradition was not used as a resource to produce itself anew but seemingly as a defense, a retreat.

The directions being taken by the second generation were far less clear, although it seemed poised for educational and occupational success in the UK. My lack of clarity might be partly because I had little private access to the young people. British urban transport systems were so good that young Hyderabadis were seldom delegated to drive me home or anywhere else (as happened often in places like Australia or the United States). Thus I always spoke with young people in the presence of their parents or other elders. Given British and Hyderabadi cultural consensus that relationships between parents and children should be governed by respect and a degree of formality, particularly when an outsider is present, I heard few expressions of personal preferences different from those of their parents from the young Hyderabadis I did meet in Britain.

CHAPTER 6

Australia: Things Fall Apart

MY FIRST CONTACT with a Hyderabadi settled in Australia was intriguing and predictive. When in Hyderabad,[1] I encountered Lyn Edwards, the adult son of J. W. and Marjory Edwards. Visiting his parents from Australia, this confident, athletic man was dressed in unusual attire for Hyderabad—bright Bermuda shorts, short-sleeved knit shirt, and rubber thongs. Lyn split a Kingfisher beer with me and talked about his Hyderabadi mates in Sydney, particularly those on the Deccan Blues cricket team. He recalled one of the first events he attended in Australia:

> It was a twenty-first birthday party, given by my teammate, Killer Khan, for his daughter. The party had disco and everything. When I entered, I said, 'What the hell's all this,' and Dr. Khan said, 'Well, that's the way here.' . . . Australia's changed a lot since the old White Australia days; now it's 'spot the Aussie' contests.

Anglo-Indian migrants, cricket, and Australian mateship rituals[2] were key elements in his story, and they proved central to the Hyderabadi experience in Australia.

Australia's national culture and its efforts to integrate new immigrants were brought to bear on three sets of Hyderabadis that immigrated at different time periods. The first two consisted of Anglo-Indians, and their recollections and experiences highlight that minority culture in old Hyderabad. For Anglo-Indian Hyderabadis around the world, Australia, not the UK, became the center of their networks, the major destination for the first wave of British or Anglo-Indian emigrants from Hyderabad after 1948. The second wave of Britons and Anglo-Indians migrated to Australia in the 1960s and 1970s, the later timing because some did not qualify under the pre-1960s discriminatory policies, or tried the UK first, or finished out their careers in India. Their growing children were also affected by India's "three-language formula" (requiring students to learn Hindi, English, and Telugu) and the increasing shortage of "desirable" marriage partners. For the later immigrants, North American and other transnational connections played a noticeably more active role. The Anglo-Indians were clearly the most significant group of ex-Hyderabadis in Australia. Anglo-Indians who were British citizens and whites (the older definition of Anglo-Indian) from all over India and Pakistan were allowed into Australia in the first decades after 1947. Some 100,000 Anglo-Indians emigrated from India at the end of the British Raj, mostly to Britain but with a remigration from Britain to Australia.[3] As late as 1981, some 75 percent of India-born Australian residents were probably of Anglo-Indian origin.[4]

The Australian change of immigration policy in the 1960s attracted a third group of transnational economic migrants of diverse backgrounds— Muslim, Hindu, and Parsi as well as Anglo-Indian. Most of these economic migrants were well-qualified professionals with experience elsewhere who could choose where to settle. In the 1980s and 1990s, Australia's aggressive pursuit of qualified students and professionals drew Indian and Pakistani Hyderabadi young people born well after the traumatic events of 1948 and 1956.

Hyderabad and Australia: Possible Attractions

Special attractions for Hyderabadis in Australia included the enduring reputations of individual Australians who were educators in Hyderabad, most notably the Reverend C. E. W. Bellingham and others at St. George's Grammar School. Then, in the last days before the Police Action, a daring Australian pilot, Sidney Cotton, flew missions between Hyderabad and Pakistan for the last Nizam.[5] Finally there was the last Nizam's heir, his grandson Mukarram Jah, who lived near Perth for more than two decades. For many Hyderabadis outside Australia, it was often these figures who placed Australia on the Hyderabadi world map, at least initially.

St. George's Grammar School had many Australian teachers and missionary connections through the Anglican Church because the Anglican Church in Australia had begun under the diocese of Calcutta. Founded in 1834 by the Church of England for expatriate children in Hyderabad, St. George's began admitting local children in 1865.[6] Whenever I mentioned my visit to Australia to Hyderabadis elsewhere, St. George's alumni immediately inquired about their old principal, the Reverend Bellingham.[7] The Reverend Bellingham went from Sydney to Hyderabad in 1933 to be a teacher and later principal at St. George's Grammar School. His Australian wife-to-be, Dorothy, arrived in Hyderabad to teach in 1946; they married, had four children in Hyderabad, and retired to Australia in 1961.

The Bellinghams' recollections of their days in Hyderabad started with fond memories of Muslim, Christian, and Hindu friends, Mughlai cuisine in their home, and Urdu lessons. As principal, the Reverend Bellingham said, he needed to know just how bad a boy's language was so he could mete out appropriate punishment. They dwelt on the pleasant, easy relations they had had with the Nizam's Muslim officials[8] and proudly asserted that no St. George's "old boys" were Razakars, Muslims they termed "fanatical." They praised St. George's "old boy" General El Edroos, commander of the Nizam's army in 1948 who advised the Nizam not to fight. The general surrendered to the Indian Army forces outside the city to spare Hyderabadi lives, according to the Reverend Bellingham. The Bellinghams spent two days during the Police Action under British protection in Begumpet. After the Police Action, they felt that anti-white feelings developed, and that Hindu officials became more prevalent and were less courteous.

When the Bellinghams retired and their ship landed in Australia in 1961, their children were amazed at all the white faces on the dock. The children had liked India; they could speak Urdu and Telugu well, and the eldest daughter returned twice for visits. The Bellinghams themselves returned for a visit in 1980 and were feted by many friends and former students. Over the years, at least twelve "old boys" have visited them in Australia, too. The son-in-law of one of these visitors, settled in Sydney, was amused to see his dignified father-in-law reduced to boyhood, bowing low to the reverend and calling him "Sir."

Another special attraction might have been Prince Mukarram Jah. Elder grandson of the last Nizam, he was installed in 1967 as the eighth Nizam, a title no longer recognized in India but one recognized informally by many Hyderabadis.[9] Educated at Harrow, Sandhurst, and Cambridge, Mukarram Jah lived outside India. In 1993 he had been settled in Australia for over two decades. A visit to friends from Cambridge had brought him to Australia in 1970, and he bought a 500,000-acre sheep ranch near Perth. He married an Australian woman in 1974, after his first, Turkish, wife divorced him. His Australian wife divorced him in 1981. He took a Turkish third wife, and in 1993 he brought a fourth wife, a young woman from Morocco, to Australia briefly; his third wife then divorced him. He divorced his fourth wife and he married a fifth wife in 1995. Financial problems plagued him.[10] In fact, few if any Hyderabadis followed or accompanied Mukarram Jah to Australia, and Hyderabadis in Australia had little or no contact with him. Some Anglo-Indian Hyderabadis recalled family connections to the royal family back in Hyderabad, but these have almost entirely lapsed.

Leaving Hyderabad

THE EARLY ANGLO-INDIAN EXODUS

Long before the retirement of the Reverend and Mrs. Bellingham to Australia in 1961 or the arrival of the eighth Nizam there in 1970, many British and Anglo-Indian families from Hyderabad had chosen Australia. Some of them settled in Sydney, more in Melbourne, and even more in Perth. As they moved, the meaning of the term *Anglo-Indian* was changing. Before 1948 in Hyderabad, there were the "true" Anglo-Indians, those of British blood, such people told me, and afterward, "those others—we had no name for them, perhaps 'half-caste,'" came to be called Anglo-Indian too.[11] The Australian government knew the difference and enforced it until the 1960s, accepting only immigrants who could establish their British or European blood and citizenship. Later, government restrictions eased and the meaning of Anglo-Indian expanded to include those of mixed background.

The patterns that united or divided these families were based on kinship and marriage, occupations back in Hyderabad (army, railway, police, customs, or private business), church membership (Protestant or Catholic),[12] residential localities, school affiliations, and sports teams. Distinctions brought from Hyderabad still held to some extent in Australia, although there were unexpected developments, as some "true" Anglo-Indians found they really disliked "English-English, pompous people" and some of the "new" young Anglo-Indians discarded their parents' emphasis on Anglo descent and claimed to be only Indian. Children born or brought up in Australia were marrying a variety of other Australians and some were reclaiming a broader Indian heritage through cultural activities and travel in India.

Anglo-Indians in the Nizam's military service and the British Indian Army were immediately affected by World War II, Indian and Pakistani independence in 1947, and the Police Action in 1948. Those "of British blood" in the Indian and Hyderabad armies moved first to Australia. Henry Luschwitz, director of music (bandmaster) for the Nizam's military forces, and Brigadier Garnett Chamarette applied for Australian migration immediately after 1948 and went to Sydney and Perth, respectively.[13] Luschwitz had been one of two liaisons with Sidney Cotton, the Australian gunrunner for Hyderabad in its last days,[14] and he advised his nephews and nieces to leave India, as an English name would ruin their prospects.

One of those nephews was Alex Norton; he was only twenty-five in 1948, a captain in the Indian Army with a prestigious appointment. He too feared for his future in India.[15] Appointed aide-de-camp to Hyderabad's new civilian chief minister, M. K. Vellodi of the Indian Administrative Service, he accompanied Vellodi to Delhi and secretly saw the Australian High Commissioner McKay, whom he had met in Hyderabad. McKay encouraged him to migrate, so Norton again used connections he had made as aide-de-camp, this time to India's Foreign Secretary Pillai, and managed to get passports for himself, his wife, and child. Put under house arrest just as he planned to leave the country (some suspected he was going to Pakistan), he again got help, this time from an uncle who was superintendent of the railway, to get to Bombay and board a ship to Australia in 1950.[16] After ten years as an Aboriginal welfare officer, Norton settled in Sydney with his wife and four children and went into real estate, building a nursing home and private hospital business.[17] His children all married "Aussies" and knew little of Hyderabad. His son confirmed that none of them spoke Urdu or felt that they were Hyderabadi; they knew Hyderabad only through relatives and their parents' Hyderabadi friends in Australia.[18]

Many Hyderabadi Anglo-Indian men who saw action in World War II or Partition ended up in Australia. Stamford Chamarette's experience led him to state that he had chosen to leave "not Hyderabad, but India." Taken prisoner of war by the Japanese during World War II, he was guarded in Singapore's Changi Prison by Sikh regiments that had joined the Japanese, embittering him against both Japan and India. Released by an Australian regiment, he made many friends among its members and migrated to Australia at his own expense as a result. Dennis Fallon, member of an old Hyderabadi military family, was one of six young men selected in 1936 at age eleven for a Nizam's scholarship to the Royal Indian Military College in Dehra Dun. The six boys were permitted by the Nizam to join the Indian Armed Forces upon reaching eighteen, and Fallon joined the 5th Probyns Horse, like five generations of Fallons before him. In 1947, four of the six youths opted for Pakistan, and Fallon and another opted for India.[19] Fallon was fighting Pakistanis in Kashmir at the time of the Police Action, and he stayed in the Indian Army until 1968. Then, at age forty-three, he retired prematurely and migrated to Australia; three older siblings preceded him there but two younger sisters remained in India.[20]

Fallon saw continuity and progress in Hyderabad after 1948 rather than disruption, and he attributed this to the victorious Indian major general who accepted the Nizam's September 18 surrender, J. N. Chaudhuri, military governor of Hyderabad. Fallon's father had met Chaudhuri in Bolarum when both were junior military officers, and Fallon viewed Chaudhuri as a competent man who liked Hyderabad. Thus, military training and service traditions bridged the rupture of the Police Action and made Hyderabad's transition to India, like Fallon's own, quite comfortable. Fallon's view, however, was not widely shared by those who stayed in Hyderabad and especially those in the Hyderabad Army.

In Hyderabad, the consequences of the 1948 Police Action more often spurred Anglo-Indian military people to leave immediately. "Very Indian it became in the 1950s, the army was our profession and it was broken up; there were no jobs, so all of us Europeans left," as Bruce Cox put it. George Cox, a retired commander of the Hyderabad Lancers, advised his sons to leave Hyderabad. George, with many relatives in the Nizam's service, had gone off to Bombay as a young man to do something different, but the Nizam found out and asked him to "come back and join my army." That kind of personal connection vanished in 1948. With British passports, family members were able to migrate to Australia, so Billy, Emile, and Philip Cox, followed by their sister, Betty, did so from 1950 to 1952, and their brother, Bruce, moved in 1957. In 1949, when his father urged his sons to give up on jobs in India and go to Britain, Emile and his brothers suspected Britain would be "a terrible place" and chose Australia instead.[21] Emile and Philip took a ship from Bombay to Perth, each with thirty-two pounds in travelers' checks and seven pounds and ten shillings in cash. After sixteen months in Perth, Emile moved to Melbourne, married an Australian, and settled down.[22]

Emile Cox jokingly called himself the 'Nawab of Saifabad,' for the family had lived in that pleasant suburb as neighbors of Brigadier Taufiq Ali, a legendary horseman in the Nizam's cavalry. Brigadier Taufiq had given Emile his first pony, a wonderful memory, and Emile referred to his childhood as "Victorian, a world of our own, with servants and all." In Australia, Emile still identified himself as a Hyderabadi and told about going back and being mistaken for an outsider. Buying a pot in the old city, a man in the back of the shop shouted in Urdu to the woman serving him to overcharge him. When Emile protested, in Urdu, that he was a mulki Hyderabadi, she apologized and insisted on giving him the pot.[23]

Emile Cox's sister, Betty Cox Oates Young, and brother, Bruce, were reputed to be enthusiastic Hyderabadis. Betty's first husband was in the Hyderabad Army and unwilling to start over in the Indian Army, so he and she moved to Perth in 1952, where his (Oates's) sisters had preceded them. It had been hard at first.[24] Betty missed Hyderabad, where she had attended Mahbubiyah Girls' School and then a boarding school in Poona. She had been back for visits, her family ate curry and rice almost every day, and her Urdu was good. Her children had been born in Hyderabad and proudly said so, although they had never gone back and both married

Australians (but one grandson was named Jai; her son found the name in a book and liked it). A key figure among Hyderabadi Anglo-Indians, Betty organized one-dish potlucks in Melbourne and frequently visited "all the army people" in Perth.

Bruce Cox stayed in Hyderabad until 1957 and kept in touch with old friends there and in Pakistan and Canada. The family history included five generations in India from the Palmer side (his great-grandmother was descended from the famous banker, William Palmer, and his "Indian Devi") and two generations on the father's side (some Portuguese ancestors). The Coxes were Protestants and in the army, and Bruce remembered that in the 1940s society was very class-minded; one mixed only with certain people, through school (St. George's, for him) and then through families. The Anglo-Indians in the army did not mix with those in the railways,[25] and Bruce and his siblings were never allowed out of the house without shoes. (The image of barefoot Andhras coming to Hyderabad after 1948 occurred again and again; here, it implied class differences among Anglo-Indians.)

"We were more with the Muslim side," Bruce Cox stated, recalling the exchange of sweets marking the Muslim Ids. Paradoxically, the person he recalled bringing sweets to the Cox family on Id was Chandrakant Gir's father, a Goswami Hindu banker, with one tray especially for Bruce.[26] In fact, the Coxes were related to Hyderabadi Muslims through a Fallon woman married into a Muslim family (Bruce's mother was a Fallon). As children, the Coxes and their Muslim cousins did not know they were related.[27] Now they knew, and a relative, Fehmida Khan from Montreal, Canada, on a visit to Australia, asked Bruce to help organize a Hyderabad Association branch in Australia, a task Bruce cordially refused.

Bruce had visited Hyderabad last in 1980 and was dismayed by the changes. "One hears Telugu now, not Hyderabadi Urdu, and the Indians seem to resent the Muslims, that is, the Hyderabadis." He himself saw more of people from Lucknow than from Hyderabad,[28] did not socialize much with the Anglo-Indians save at his sister's potlucks, and had become "quite Australian." Nonetheless, Bruce Cox had his own story about being Hyderabadi. On a visit back, he was buying shoes, and the shopkeeper tried to sell him two left shoes. Bruce lambasted him in fine colloquial Urdu, invoking the family's long history as customers. The owner's father, who had known Bruce's father well, came out to apologize and served him Coca-Cola and sweets.

Many Hyderabadi Anglo-Indians settled in Perth right after the Police Action, people from the army but also those in private business in Secunderabad. From different occupations, residential localities, and church affiliations back in the twin cities, they knew each other well in Perth and shared a nostalgia for the homeland. Barney and Heather Devlin convened a large gathering of people of British backgrounds,[29] all of them among the earliest Hyderabadis in Australia.[30] Heather's father was a British manufacturer's representative working in Secunderabad, where Heather grew up and attended St. Anne's Convent. Secunderabad, she said, was "the upmarket place, cleaner by far, better, with European theaters." Her family had connections to the Nizam's nobles and was especially close to Salar Jung III, who sent a station wagon to deliver toys for the children every Christmas.[31] In 1946, even before India gained independence, business began declining and Heather's family considered emigrating. One son was on a Nizam's scholarship studying architecture in Britain, so Heather and her mother first went there, but they hated the climate. In 1948, when Heather was sixteen, the family moved to Australia, her father sponsored by the Freemasons. Heather's mother hated it there too (she and Heather wanted to go back to India), but she was happier when her sisters and their families followed. Heather's brother Jeff Howlett, trained at the Nizam's expense, became a prominent architect in Perth.

Barney's family was based in Hyderabad, not Secunderabad, and he and Heather met only in Australia. His father, son of parents who came out from Ireland, was deputy commissioner of excise in the Nizam's service, so he brought up his eight sons in the Hyderabad districts and his work was all in Urdu. Barney considered that the best part of his life, but "when India took over, we were respected but we got no jobs, the opportunities were gone." Barney's older brothers set out for the UK but were not happy there, so Barney picked Australia over Canada, figuring Australia was less developed and would offer more. After attending Bishop's High School,[32] he traveled with his friend David Burton, son of the owner of Secunderabad's well-known John Burton Tailors, and landed in Perth on ANZAC day, Australia's most important holiday (commemorating the landing in 1915 near Gallipoli on the Turkish Aegean coast by the Australian and New Zealand Army Corps, ending in the loss of 10,000 lives after an eight-month siege). Barney said that Hyderabadis had no trouble establishing themselves in Perth, as it was quite backward in those days and Hyderabadis were well-educated people with fine manners.[33]

Brigadier Garnett and Kathleen Chamarette also came very early, in 1948. Kathleen was born in Aurangabad, in the Duke of Wellington's bungalow (later the Engineer's bungalow). She attended St. George's primary school and then Mahbubiyah Girls' School and later taught at Mahbubiyah; these were the schools attended by members of the nobility and those who, like Kathleen, spoke excellent English. She proudly showed me a 1938 photo of the seventh Nizam's elder son, the Prince of Berar Azam Jah, standing with the polo team: General El Edroos, Colonel Yusuf

Ali Baig, Brigadier Taufiq Ali, and Brigadier Chamarette, all names well known in Hyderabadi military history.[34] Kathleen believed that to stay on in India after 1948 would have meant giving up their British passports and taking Indian citizenship. "The generation that knew us we trusted, they looked after us; but the new people, we couldn't be sure." Feeling that India would not reward those with English names, the Chamarettes took their four children aged five to eleven to Perth. Some friends in Hyderabad had been bitter. "There was a bar here, we could go and they couldn't; we had to prove our British citizenship then, that's why I have all these papers," Kathleen recalled.[35]

Jean Luschwitz had been in Perth almost as long as Kathleen, and, both widowed, Kathleen and Jean still enjoyed watching Indian movies on Australian television. An Englishwoman, Jean had met her first Hyderabadi husband, Dr. Hastings Adams, when he came to the UK for medical studies. After his death in a Japanese prison camp in World War II, she had married Wolfgang Luschwitz (the Luschwitzes lived across Public Gardens Road from the Adamses).[36] She and Wolfe and the children migrated to Australia in 1951; Wolfe had cried for six months, he was so homesick.

Initially, life in Australia proved difficult for these immigrant families. The women had never done household tasks in Hyderabad and were too busy to meet each other in Perth at first. "Talk about culture shock," they said; they themselves had never cooked. The families ate lots of tinned spaghetti and baked beans. The women had never handled raw meat, could not buy enough rice or onions because of rationing, and looked fruitlessly for mangoes. Two of the women prepared their own Hyderabadi cookbooks and they all had pressure cookers for *dal* curries. Meals mixed Western and Indian food, and at Christmas, Anglo-Indian families made *kalkals* and *doldols* (deep-fried dough pieces and black rice flour candies), along with traditional Christmas cakes. Dinner timing in Australia was disconcertingly early: "Dad wanted a late dinner for years, but people dropped over after their dinners, and we wouldn't have eaten yet." They remembered "the Mohamedans" as being very hospitable, more so than most Australians—for example, Muslims welcomed children at weddings, as did these Anglo-Indian families and Italian Australians (several of the next generation married Italian Australians).

More stories of the "true Hyderabadi" genre came from Barney Devlin, whose nostalgia had led him to plant banyan and peepul trees in his yard so he could hear the leaves rustling. When visiting Hyderabad in 1974, he had gone into Abdul Qadeer's Secunderabad shoe shop, and an old chap there asked him in English where he was from. He said "Australia," but the man persisted, saying he had seen him before, wasn't he from Hyderabad? Yes,

Barney said, his family name was Dualin, giving it the local pronuncia-
tion, and the man switched to Urdu, recalling Barney's mother who had
died in 1938, his many brothers, and his aunt, Winnie Evans.[37] He took
Barney back to meet the shopowner, saying, "This man's parents made
your shop a success." Even more touching was Barney's experience visiting
the districts with an old friend, Bobby Reddy.[38] In Nirmal, Barney said he
wanted to meet someone who had worked for his father, and Reddy sent
out word. Next day, as the men drank coffee, an Arab in a *lungi* (loincloth)
came toward them down an avenue of trees, and Barney said, "I know
him." "Impossible," said Reddy, but when the man arrived Barney found
himself saying his name, "Sheikh Ahmed," and both men cried. "After
forty years, there was still loyalty and love, that's the way it was there,"
Barney said.

These stories elicited further testimony about the old days when there
had not been differences between people, between Hindus and Muslims
or upper and lower classes. Some said the good old days stemmed from
the British influence, the Resident's presence serving as a safety umbrella.
Most disagreed, arguing that differences had come in from British India.
"We were very happy with the Nizam. He supported our churches, he
paid the salary of the Anglican minister; the Nizam's rule catered to every
community without favoritism." But there were cliques in the good old
days, they acknowledged. The British Anglo-Indians stuck together yet
were close to "the Mohammedans, who spoke English so well, as well as
we did, yet they went home and spoke another language." Barney Devlin began quoting Urdu poetry and jokes,[39] leading people to recall Bryan
Oates. Bryan had stood first in the Hyderabad Civil Service exam, competing with the Muslims in Urdu, and he also had known Marathi and
Telugu. People recalled other old friends, a Parsi, a Muslim Mahbubiyah
classmate, and the Muslim sisters related through the Fallons to the Coxes
(Kathleen Chamarette's mother played mahjong with their mother, while
the men played polo together).

The children of these Devlin, Chamarette, and Luschwitz families had
adjusted well to Australia. One of the children had felt ashamed of eating
curry in earlier years, and another had said to his mother "You're a Paki,
I'm an Aussie," but he was "just joking." Most of them had had "traditional
Australian" twenty-first birthday party celebrations,[40] when one is given
a half-yard- or one-yard-long beer glass from which one has to drink as
much and as fast as possible and a big wooden key to the house symbolizing
adulthood and independence. (This interview and others confirmed that
immigrants observed the twenty-first year celebration to some extent or
were made to feel they were not conforming to an important Australian

ritual.) Kathleen had four children, Jean had six, and the Devlins had two; these twelve had all married Australians save two whose partners were English.[41]

One of Jean Luschwitz's sons, Ernest, had been eighteen, just out of Loyola College in Madras, when he preceded the family to Perth. "After, what was it, Police Action, we decided to migrate, talked of UK but chose Perth." He would have had to repeat some schooling in Australia to go into medicine, so he ended up in the wholesale drapery business and then worked his way up to deputy chief executive of the Western Australia Turf Club. He married an Australian he met on a blind date when he was in the National Service and, after retirement, he became extremely active in the Masons, which included many people of Indian and Chinese background. He used to read and write Urdu but had forgotten it, and he had lost track of many former friends in India; he and his family had "no interest" in Hyderabad.[42] But "we do cook curries, ball curries, *vindaloos* [Goanese curries], *gulab jamuns* [sweets], pickles, and lots of hot stuff nibblies." He remembers his youngest son "on Wolfe's knee, eating his curry and rice, and green chilies, too, without any trouble," and he is glad that they can get guavas, mangoes, and Hyderabadi pickles (from Pakistan) in Australia now. Recalling his skill in Urdu, Ernest said that he had also known Telugu and Tamil, and he thought that Australia should have a second language policy because it had been good to know other languages.

THE SECOND ANGLO-INDIAN EXODUS

Other Hyderabadi Anglo-Indians had at first not wanted to leave Hyderabad. But as their children grew up, reaching their intermediate and college years, they worried about their futures in India. The three-language policy presented difficulties—the children needed to pass exams in Hindi and Telugu even if they did brilliantly in the other subjects. By 1970, Canada and Australia were readily accepting immigrants, and as relatives in Australia could sponsor newcomers, all that was required was $100 Australian and the guarantee of a week's accommodation.

Men, women, and older children all found jobs. The wives had the hardest time, as in Hyderabad they had had servants, familiar foods had been readily available, and the shops were all open late. Initially some families were without cars, but things got easier as they earned the means to buy land, houses, and cars. Back in Hyderabad, some of the Anglo-Indians had not owned homes because railway and police jobs included accommodations; in Australia, all or most soon owned homes. "A humanitarian country," Australia even offered plans for aging people: "the government would buy your home and buy another one for you." Some laws seemed excessive—for example, those against noise pollution: Anne and Bernie D'Costa missed the ringing of church bells but not the killing of goats on Bakr Id, also prohibited in Australia. (The Id of sacrifice ends the time of the hajj, the annual pilgrimage to Mecca.)

Henry and Joyce Corfield wanted to stay on in Hyderabad after 1948 but soon felt that their white skins and English names barred their children from opportunities. They left for England in 1951. But England just after World War II proved difficult. There was rationing, they knew no Hyderabadis in London,[43] and they disliked the climate. When Australia "opened up" twelve years later, in 1962, they migrated to Sydney, sponsored by the Church of England. "Everything fell into place straightaway," Joyce said, whereas in England, "you struggled and nothing fell into place." In Australia they liked the climate, the spaciousness, and the job opportunities, and this time they had a bank balance to bring along. They found others from Hyderabad already settled in Sydney, and four families—the Henry Luschwitzes and their six children, the Hugo Luschwitzes and their seven children, the Alex Nortons and their four children, and she and Henry with their two children—got together often for "a lovely time."

Although Joyce Corfield felt "somewhat Hyderabadi," she did not know any Muslims or Hindus from Hyderabad in Sydney. She knew only "pidgin Urdu" for use with servants, but she did like curries and her husband "would eat curry every day of the week." She and Henry made one trip back to Hyderabad, in 1984, and found it "very sad"; they never wanted to go again. Widowed, Joyce attended a monthly "potluck curry meeting" of other widows with Hyderabadi connections.[44] Before Henry's death, the Corfields went to Perth in 1987 and met with others from Hyderabad, the Devlins (Henry had gone to St. Patrick's school in Secunderabad with Barney), Jean Luschwitz, and others, and Joyce knew where members of other Hyderabadi Anglo-Indian families were living in Australia. However, her children, like those of others she knew, did not feel Hyderabadi at all and married "dinkumdie Aussies," "real" Australians.[45]

Dick Schoeffer moved to Australia in 1968 after retirement in India (mandatory at age 55). Retiring as assistant commissioner of police, he was able to work ten more years in Australia, where his two brothers had also moved. He cooked *bagara baigan* himself but "it needs that vital scented ingredient, in the muslin bag; it doesn't taste Hyderabadi without it." Dick spoke Urdu but his children did not and they married Australians. Dick's brother Donald and wife Winifred Schoeffer, both in their early eighties in 1993, had also migrated in 1968, to Perth where they lived in a rented state-owned house. There had been no need to move earlier, they said, since theirs were not army people; Donald had worked for the railway and she for the sports department of Nizam College.

Like Barney Devlin, Donald Schoeffer felt that the best years of his life had been spent in Hyderabad. "Oh, those years," he said; "we were British-administered. Yes, the Nizam was there, but the British Resident was it. Only when the British pushed out and the Nizam and his lot took over, that's when it all broke down. All India took over."[46] The Schoeffers recalled the Nizam's regard for her father, Dr. Barrett, and the Nizam's ordering a pension for her mother upon the doctor's death. They had a framed photo of St. Joseph's cathedral where Don and Winifred had married in 1938 and they told stories of Dr. Barrett's lovely rented house and its mango trees. By 1968, "when all that went, good old Hyderabad, we drifted here." They explained, "there were two sorts of people, the Telinganas and the Andhras, and the Andhras were lowering the tone of the country." Telugu became the first language, Hindi the second, and English only the third. There were no longer any eligible boys in Hyderabad, and their two girls "kept going to dances and picnics with Sikhs, Muslims, and Hindus." The Schoeffers moved with their daughters to Australia and "left Hyderabadi culture behind."[47]

The family of Bryan and Norma Oates, well remembered back in Hyderabad, had migrated only in 1972.[48] Bryan had stood first in the Hyderabad Civil Service exams, served in the Nizam's Hyderabad Civil Service (HCS),[49] and continued with the Indian Administrative Service (IAS) after 1948. His widow convened a luncheon group for me in her Perth home. She displayed a 1947 photo of Bryan in fez and sherwani with his colleagues, along with a painting of Christ presented to him by the people of Mahbubnagar District in 1965 and other service momentos.[50] People reminisced about the Nizam's family. Norma's sister Iris had met the Nizam's Turkish daughters-in-law when she was a teacher in Hyderabad, and Norma and Bryan had attended Mukarram Jah's 1967 installation as Nizam, a "gorgeous celebration, with fifteen or twenty dwarf acrobats performing." They knew Mukarram Jah was settled near Perth but had no contact with him.

Norma Oates summed up their reasons for staying on in India. "We loved the Indian culture, *bharata natyam, ghazals, ragas,* and Indian weddings, partly because of Bryan's fluent Urdu. We had so many Indian friends, and so few Anglo-Indian ones—of course, most of them had left. A certain group of Anglo-Indians doesn't want to mix, but we did."[51] When Bryan and Norma's son Tim was born, the *hijras* (transvestites) came and danced at their house (most Indian families give money to *hijras* for this celebratory custom).[52] Norma talked of the old servants to whom she still wrote and sent money and of the many old friends in India to whom she wrote. After Bryan's death in 1988, Norma got a letter from one of his best friends in Delhi that showed the affection people had for him: "Aunty, I thought about Uncle and my new glasses fell off and broke, and I came to know that was the day he died."

Norma Oates and Kathleen Chamarette and their daughters and grand-children discussed India and their identity as Anglo-Indians. Some families had not intermarried with Indians while others had; some wanted this to be clarified and others did not, but none wanted to disavow the Indian heritage. The older women were proud of their Hyderabadi identity whereas the youngsters defined themselves more broadly as Indian. Norma's children had married Australians (two of them Italian Australians) and an American, and whether these spouses liked spices or India was an issue in some of the marriages. India was a constant point of reference,[53] and most of the young people had revisited India or were planning trips in the near future. Hyderabad was a major destination, but one daughter referred to it as Andhra Pradesh, and the trips included other tourist places like Kashmir. One of Norma's daughters had learned *bharata natyam* (Hindu temple) dance, as people in Melbourne had told me.

The latest Anglo-Indian arrivals came as parents or grandparents, older people following their children and moving at least partly because of the growing marginalization of, even discrimination against, Christians in India.[54] The Malvern Balms came to Perth from Secunderabad's Indian Catholic community. These eleven children and their parents shifted to Perth throughout the 1980s; the first to move was an older daughter marrying into a Hyderabadi family already in Perth. Malvern had held many jobs, ranging from the Indian Army to social work and Christian missionary activities, jobs that had taken the family from the Aurangabad districts of Hyderabad State to a recent stint in Japan with an American missionary institute. He retired in 1980, and the family's gradual shift to Australia began after that, fueled by growing disillusionment with the situation of Christians in India.[55]

The Balm parents had survived well until the 1960s, "because the Nizam held Anglo-Indians in high regard," employing them in the customs, police, railway, and other departments, and "employing only Anglo-Indian women as teachers to the women in his family." The senior Balms "treasured the days of Hyderabad, but not of India," saying that the Indians "turned on us, we lost all that," after 1948 and 1956. The Anglo-Indians were "thrown out, and we had to sell whatever we owned to get the kids through school. The English-sounding names gave us away." The Balms felt that "Hinduism was rising." Although he and his wife both came from families established in Hyderabad since the nineteenth century and Malvern had fought alongside leading Anglo-Indian politician Frank Anthony to define an Anglo-Indian identity in India, the Balms decided Australia offered more to their children.

Each Balm family member became a citizen two years after arrival so that he or she could sponsor relatives and get a public service job. Of the family's twelve children, eleven were settled in Australia; nine of them were married, seven to Hyderabadis of various backgrounds ("true blue" Anglo-Indian, "other" Anglo Indian, Telugu Christian, and Parsi). One married a Goanese Indian and the youngest son married an Australian. The eldest daughter was well settled in Madras but had sent one of her sons to Australia to study. The Balms said that India and Hyderabad were still very much on their minds. They valued the excellent educations they had received in Hyderabad and felt that crime was not a problem there; however, overpopulation and lack of jobs were problems for them, so they emigrated. Anglo-Indians related to them by marriage had settled in Melbourne and Perth; those left in Hyderabad could not meet Australia's criteria, being overage or without qualifications. The Balms were raising money in Perth to repair the roof of St. Joseph's Church in Secunderabad.[56] Malvern Balm was involved in many organizations, including the Australian India League.

The Balm family was very conscious of being part of a diaspora in process, a movement of Christian families out of India.[57] Yet at the same time, the youngest Balm daughter, Marian, reported that "we youngsters identify as Indian, both there and here; Dad worked hard to define Anglo-Indian, but we see them as Indian, our parents, they and we are clearly more Indian." Anglo-Indian might be defined as British blood on the male side, but how many generations back, she asked, and asserted that Balm was actually a Maharashtrian name. In Australia, the young people were comfortable with their Indian side; they thought the Australians less concerned about race than were the British, in India or the UK.

Combining old and new Anglo-Indian histories in Australia, Charles and Blossom Corfield finally arrived in Melbourne in 1993 after three decades of trying to migrate.[58] Over the years, they had seen their six children scatter around the world, three settling in Australia and three taking Irish or British citizenship. Charles, an officer in the British and then the Indian Army, had been held captive by the Japanese during the war. His wife came from a respected Hyderabadi Anglo-Indian family; her Urdu was excellent, and she cooked Hyderabad's distinctive eggplant dish, *bagara baigan*, well.[59] However, after 1948, Hyderabad had felt less like home. "We were under British rule; of course it was the Nizam's state but the British were there, and afterward conditions deteriorated." The family residence back in Secunderabad, named Tiger Hall by the last Nizam,[60] was up for sale in 1993 as all of the children had emigrated, but the sale and the importation of its numerous decorative tiger skins into Australia (one relative had shot thirty-two tigers) apparently posed problems.[61] The Corfield children, like other Catholics from India, including those of Goanese, Tamil, and Telugu ancestry, were marrying partners of Italian, Greek, Sri Lankan, and Australian backgrounds whom they met through church, cricket, or dance clubs. The youngest son, Joe, had just arrived with his parents and told of attending an Anglo-Indian dance and playing "spot the Aussie," difficult because there were so many Indians in attendance.

NEW ECONOMIC MIGRANTS

The newest Hyderabadis in Australia were economic migrants who began arriving about 1970, well-qualified professionals who typically had worked or could have worked in other countries. In the 1980s and 1990s, Australia recruited qualified students and professionals from South Asia, including Hyderabadi young people of Hindu, Muslim, Christian, and Parsi backgrounds. While their ties to Australia were initially tentative, these younger people of Hyderabadi ancestry were developing new professional, cultural, and religious associations. In Australia, unlike most other sites, the Urdu-promoting activities seemed confined to Muslims. Many Muslim Hyderabadi newcomers from India or Pakistan related to Australia's growing Muslim community through support for Islamic institutions and activities and Urdu literary associations.

Muslim Australians. Muslim history in Australia dates back to Afghan camel drivers and farmers who pioneered development of the interior in the late nineteenth century.[62] This population declined from 1900 to 1940, but after World War II European Muslim refugees were admitted, followed by migrants from Turkey and Lebanon. Australia's Muslim population grew in numbers and diversity, with 200,000 Muslim Australians in 1990, 80 percent of them in Melbourne and Sydney. Sydney's Muslim population was the largest and the majority was of Lebanese origin. Muslim organizations began in 1957 with the Islamic Society of Victoria that included Albanians, Yugoslavs, Turks, Turkish Cypriots, Arabs, Lebanese, Egyptians, Indonesians, and Malays; in the 1990s it boasted sixty-five different ethnic and sectarian groups. An Australian Federation of Islamic Councils (AFIC) formed in 1976 to lobby the federal government, network within the Muslim community, and provide representation internationally. One in three Australian Muslims was Australian-born, and educational institutions for Muslim children were being developed; the first Islamic school opened in Melbourne in 1982.[63]

The Hyderabadi Muslims taking the Islamic or Muslim path included many twice-migrants who had gone to Pakistan or held long-term jobs in Africa or the Gulf states. Dr. S. Bader Qadri, a medical doctor, left Hyderabad in 1953 as a young man and did his medical training in Karachi, Pakistan. Signing on as chief surgeon on a British ship from 1967 to 1969, he liked Australia when his ship stopped in Sydney, so he disembarked, brought his Kashmiri wife from Pakistan, and raised three children. His children said they were Pakistanis but have gone back for visits to both Karachi and Hyderabad and prefer Hyderabad. Qadri thought he was the first Pakistani Hyderabadi in Sydney; he was soon joined by Indian Hyderabadis, graduates of Osmania Medical School. Pakistanis, some 5,000, outnumbered Indians in Sydney, he said, and most Hyderabadis in Australia were in Sydney and were extremely active in various cultural and religious organizations. Qadri helped start the Anjuman Taraqqi Urdu, an Urdu language association, where Indians and Pakistanis mixed easily.[64] There was no Hyderabad Association in Sydney, but there were other organizations. G. Q. Siddiqui, a Muslim chemist from Hyderabad unhappy with politics there, was the founding president of the Aligarh Old Boys' Alumni of Australia in 1992 and was also a member of the Islamic Association and the Anjuman Taraqqi Urdu.[65]

Mr. and Mrs. Kazim Hussain, Indian Hyderabadis, migrated to Australia after a decade in Africa, where Kazim Hussain headed science departments in boys' schools in Nigeria and Zambia. When they visited India with their growing children in 1972, the three-language policy was discouraging; they felt India offered obstacles rather than opportunities for the children, the eldest of whom was ready for higher education. Hussain picked Australia over Canada and the United States because the job prospects and the weather were best. The family felt very pleased about becoming Australian. The Australian government did much to faciliate their move. An official met them when they landed in Sydney, and a van took them and their luggage to a migrant hostel. A welfare officer took the children to a school for admission, and another official took Mr. Hussain by car to the education department. He was posted within a month, bought a house within a year, and became a citizen in two years. The Hussains had been able to travel back to India eight times in twenty years and had also visited Pakistan and Saudi Arabia.[66] Initial hardships had included lack of servants (they had had them in Africa, as in India) and the lack of other Hyderabadis in the early 1970s. After a while they found a few other

Indian families from Hyderabad—it was an important day for the Hussains when these families first met each other at a Muslim gathering in Sydney Town Hall.[67]

Hussain and other Hyderabadi Muslims were instrumental in forming the Islamic Council of New South Wales (NSW) in 1975, the Australian Federation of Islamic Councils in 1976, and the Muslim Youth Association in 1977. The Anjuman Taraqqi Urdu was formed in 1986, "culture after religion," and then the Forum for Australian—or, as it was immediately renamed, Australasian—Muslim Professionals. The Muslim Youth Association held youth camps for eleven years, from 1979 to 1990, involving 150 young people of both sexes each year. Dozens of marriages resulted from the camps. The Hussains had a Lebanese daughter-in-law whom their son met in the Muslim youth camp, and they favored the camps and such marriages. However, radical Muslims wanted single-sex camps, and conflict over this ended the youth camps.

Kazim Hussain's son, Fahmi Hussain, grew up in Africa and Australia and reclaimed his Hyderabadi heritage by bringing a wife from there. He bridged the diverging Muslim and "old Hyderabadi" worlds by playing on Sydney's Deccan Blues cricket team. Recognizing that Muslims were a growing constituency in Australia, this ambitious young lawyer in his early thirties was, he thought, the first Indian-ancestry person to stand for public office in Australia.[68] In 1993, Fahmi was the attorney for twenty Islamic organizations and secretary of the Islamic Council of NSW;[69] he was also on the NSW Commission for Ethnic Affairs and the NSW Water Board Waste Watch Committee. Defining his community as both Islamic and Indian, he gained public attention as a media spokesman for Australian Muslims during the Gulf War of 1990–1991.[70]

The drift toward a more Islamic identity was evident among Hyderabadi Muslims in Melbourne who wanted to start a Hyderabad Association.[71] These families were from India, and the two men who organized a dinner meeting for me were medical doctors, classmates from Osmania.[72] Dr. Mateen ul Jabbar had migrated to Australia in 1969 but had been recruited to work for the Saudi Arabian military for seven years;[73] his classmate Dr. Farhat Ali Khan had followed him to Australia in 1971. Asked why they wanted to form an association, they said, "Because you called; because it's always good to see each other; because we want to maintain our culture. And we are all settled here, we have nothing to go back for, we are citizens here now." They talked about the second generation, teenagers and children who did not read and write Urdu. The youngsters went back every two or three years for visits, but the parents thought a Hyderabad Association would reinforce Hyderabadi culture in Australia.

There was an emphasis on orthodox Islam among these Melbourne Hyderabadis. A few of the women wore the hijab and the men all prayed when the time came for evening prayer.[74] In the 1990s, there was some anti-India feeling, anger about the 1992 Babri Masjid incident (Hindu militants tore down the mosque). Not only did these families belong to the Melbourne UMMA, or United Migrant Muslim Association, but many also had joined the Pakistan Australia Association rather than the Australian India League. When they asked me about Hyderabad associations, they were thinking of a Muslim membership focused on the Nizam and the largely Muslim nobility rather than the broader cultural synthesis that inspired most Hyderabad associations in the diaspora (although they mentioned one Hindu from Vizagapatnam in coastal Andhra as a possible member).

The earliest Hyderabadi Muslim to come to Melbourne, in 1964, had married an Australian, and his daughter had recently married a Hindu from India. I learned this from an "American Hyderabadi" present that night from Ames, Iowa, in Melbourne to visit his brother, and their uncle was the man who had come in 1964. This American Hyderabadi had played for the Deccan Blues back in Hyderabad, as had one of the evening's organizers, so they all knew Lyn Edwards, then captain of the Sydney Deccan Blues, but they knew him from cricket in Hyderabad. The people present did not know any of the Anglo-Indians in Melbourne whom I was meeting. Nor did they know a young Hyderabadi Muslim woman and her Hindu husband, also residents of Melbourne and about to give a Diwali party. (Diwali, the festival of lights, is a national holiday in India, commemorating the harvest season and, for many, a new year.) This group was dumbfounded to hear of the party, apparently considering Diwali a purely Hindu holiday.

The young people from these Melbourne families, however, had their own ideas, as I learned when driven home by a daughter. Staunchly Muslim, she criticized Australians for their ignorance of Islam and prejudice against it. She reported that identifying herself as a Muslim often brought the response, "Then why are you being educated?" She always answered, "Come again? My family stresses education, Islam stresses education; women are highly valued in Islam." She went on to criticize Saudi Arabia for its un-Islamic discrimination against women and then recounted an argument she and her girlfriends were having with their mothers about wearing tank tops. "Why not a tank top, when you wear a sari, which is just as un-Islamic and bares the midriff too?" She saw the Hyderabadi customs at weddings (such as wearing the *kalipot* or marriage necklace) as "not Hindu, just cultural, not harmful." She was doubtful that the youth would value a Hyderabad association, as they already thought it unnecessary to restrict the one-dish potluck group to just Hyderabadis; they wanted to include friends from Bombay and other places in India. Her orientation was to India, although she had visited and enjoyed both India and Pakistan.

Cricketeers and Other New Migrants. New economic migrants included Muslims, Hindus, Parsis, and Anglo-Indians coming directly from Hyderabad. Among them were Lyn Edwards (a quotation from him opened the chapter) and his younger brother, Kerry. Lyn migrated in 1971 and Kerry followed in 1974. Although related to many of the earlier Anglo-Indian immigrants, the brothers were actually part of the new migration of professional people, spurred by economic rather than political factors.[75] Kerry was twelve years junior to Lyn, and his memories of his childhood in Hyderabad showed that integration into India did not dramatically change the culture of the city, at least for some people. Kerry, born in 1955, testified:

> The best part of life growing up in Hyderabad was the many different cultures I mixed with. As a boy I had Hindu, Muslim, and Parsi friends, some of whom would be friends with me from nursery school in 1959 to my graduation in Class 12 in 1972. The best part of having these friends was the times we had at school as well as inviting them to and being invited to birthday parties. . . . Another part of life in Hyderabad which springs to mind was the endless variety of food that was available. The local restaurants, and there were many including Bombay Bakery, Azizia Hotel, would serve up the best Moglai food peculiar to Muslim Hyderabad cuisine. . . . The Parsis were also delightful in their preparation of huge Jelabis on Parsi New Year's Day. The Hindus always supplied the ghee sweet-meats. . . . My mother being principal of the school was showered with these gifts regularly at the various festivals. . . .[76]

Lyn sponsored Kerry's migration to Australia, and Kerry said, "I had the opportunity to play cricket with Lyn . . . for the first time." The Edwardses and other new immigrants played for the Deccan Blues Cricket Club in Sydney, an incarnation of that famous and still thriving Hyderabadi team. In 1993, Lyn Edwards captained the over-thirties team, and it linked many "old Hyderabadis" among the new migrants. Attending a game between the Deccan Blues and a Pakistani team, I found Hyderabadis on both teams.[77]

Cricket was a major bond between South Asia and Australia. Some eight "Indians Down Under" teams were started after 1985 in Sydney.[78] Three classmates from Osmania Medical School founded the Deccan Blues team in Sydney: Dr. Obeidullah Khan, Dr. K. Hemchander Rao, and Dr. Harinath, who migrated in the late 1970s and represented Urdu-, Telugu-, and Marathi-speakers from the old Hyderabad State, nicely illustrating significant intersections between cricket, medical school, and old Hyderabadi culture. Lyn Edwards played for Nizam College and Hyderabad State before migrating to Australia, and, before 1948, Alex Norton, Krishna Reddy, Dr. Bader Qadri, and two Hyderabadi Muslims in Melbourne had played for the Deccan Blues in Hyderabad. The "Indians Down Under" teams were, however, essentially cosmopolitan rather than simply transnational. The Deccan Blues included Hyderabadi players who had worked in the Middle East, non-Hyderabadi players from Pakistan, and players who, migrating as bachelors, had married Australians and New Zealanders.[79] Fahmi Hussain, central to Muslim Australian activities, and Hindu Hyderabadis recruited by the Australian government (who came slightly later than Muslims from Pakistan and India) were also active cricketeers.[80]

One of the three founders of the Deccan Blues was Dr. K. Hemchander Rao, a medical doctor who left India in 1965 for the UK, where he was recruited for migration to Australia in 1978. Central to several important Hyderabadi networks in Australia, Dr. Rao and his wife were Telugu-speakers, but Telingana mulki ones noted for their proficiency in Urdu. They estimated there were some 250 Telugu-speaking families in Sydney, but the Raos had a preference for Hyderabadis, for cosmopolitan Urdu-speakers whether of Muslim or Hindu background. Dr. and Mrs. Rao both had wide-ranging and overlapping networks of schoolmates, fellow doctors, relatives, and friends, easily listing the Osmania Medical Graduates in Sydney (distinguishing the mulkis from the non-mulkis), his Osmania classmates in New York, Los Angeles, Chicago, Pittsburgh, and London, and their many relatives in India and the United States. They also had close friends in the local Tamil Association,[81] the Telugu Association, and the very new Telugu Vanita Mandali Ladies' Association. Dr. Rao was quite active in the Australia-wide Overseas Foreign Medical Graduates Association and the Australian India League.[82] With close political connections to India's prime minister at the time,[83] Dr. Rao and his wife also followed Pakistani affairs closely because of Hyderabadi friends there.

Yet this central figure in Hyderabadi Australian circles talked about wanting to be in the United States and his wife talked about wanting to be in India; they were undecided about their future residence. Dr. Rao had many classmates and younger relatives settled in the United States, and he viewed American society as more rewarding. Mrs. Rao had many beloved family members in India, and she viewed life there, based in part on the family's wealth, reputation, and servants, as richer and more varied.[84] The Raos had not become Australian citizens, and they thought their children were only "half-Australian." In fact, they were considering retirement to Hyderabad, partly because of his involvement with the U.S.-based Mediciti Hospital project run by many of his old classmates. Both husband and wife spoke of close family and personal friendships with Muslims in

Hyderabad, Pakistan, London, and various American locations. Both also spoke of the feeling of warmth and closeness with other mulkis at mushairas or Hyderabadi weddings. They saw food, music, and language as the basic ingredients of Hyderabadi culture. Dr. Rao requested the names of Hyderabadi Anglo-Indians in Australia, saying "we've lost them, they don't belong to any of our associations, we need them."[85]

Other Indian emigrants who were "lost," at least partly because they were deliberately moving away from their Hyderabad and Indian roots, were members of a very diverse group of young Indians who had arrived in Australia around 1989, just in time for a major recession. I met them in Melbourne at a Diwali party, and, compared to the long-established Hyderabadi Anglo-Indians and newer but well-established Muslim and Hindu professionals, the young people attending the party seemed extraordinarily vulnerable and courageous. These young couples with small children had come in the late 1980s and many were still struggling to find adequate jobs.

The hosts were Farha and Ajit Bangera, a Hyderabadi Muslim woman married to a Bombay Hindu man, who had met and trained in the hospitality industry. Both Ajit and Farha had had good jobs in India and Nepal, moving from Hyderabad to Madras, Kathmandu, and Agra, where he had been executive chef at Agra's Sheraton Hotel. However, conditions in India had disheartened them: the communal riots, the rising population, the bribes, and above all, the pressure on their very young children to carry heavy bookbags, do excessive homework, and get into certain schools. She was particularly distressed about heightened religious distinctions in Hyderabad, as the old respectful *adab arz* was being replaced by *salam aleikum* among Muslims, and the older generation of Hindu family friends was dying out (she referred to these friends as "half-Muslim" in culture, meant as a compliment). She and her husband applied for permanent residence permits to Australia and got them almost immediately; indecisive, they finally migrated a day before their visas lapsed.

Her Muslim family had always celebrated Diwali in Hyderabad with Hindu friends, and the friends the Bangeras invited to celebrate Diwali in Melbourne included people from Mussoorie, Kerala, Punjab, and Bombay. Many of the men were working as chefs and had known each other in hotel school or hotels in India, but others were working as chauffeurs, in the shipping business, and at miscellaneous jobs. The women were also working, full- or part-time, in banks, restaurants, and private businesses. Recruited from India but not placed in positions appropriate to their qualifications, some of these migrants were questioning the wisdom of their move.[86] The women had trouble arranging for child care, and some had given up their own careers. They felt that Indians were an unknown factor to most Australians, and they had met with discrimination. Most employers did not accept their Indian qualifications and experience, and even the government that recruited them seemed insensitive to their problems. Inevitably, some made comparisons with friends who had gone to other countries. These young people were keenly aware of conditions elsewhere in the diaspora, and only the hope that the move would pay off for their children kept them going.

The last Hyderabadi I met in Australia fit an entirely cosmopolitan pattern. Although living in Perth in close proximity to many Hyderabadi Anglo-Indians and the eighth Nizam, Mukarram Jah, Kamala Rajah said she knew no one there from Hyderabad except two nephews she had sponsored. She and her two children and Malaysian husband lived there because of his work with the United Nations. A talented writer, she had studied in the UK, been a Fulbright scholar in the United States, and taught English as a second language in Perth. A Hindu from the Reddy landowning caste by birth but a Buddhist by spiritual inclination, Kamala was a mulki Hyderabadi from the King Kothi area whose brothers had attended All Saints. Her six siblings were all in Hyderabad. She missed the city and had written poems about it that had been published in the *Deccan Chronicle*, Hyderabad's leading English language newspaper.[87]

Things Fall Apart

DIVERGING IDENTITIES

Hyderabadi immigrants in Australia fell into three time periods and several distinct networks based on race, religion, occupation, and, more recently, national origin. These networks were increasingly divergent. The British and Anglo-Indian families moved to Australia first, propelled abroad by political events in Hyderabad and India. Many, especially army and business people, left immediately, whereas others followed later. They experienced economic hardship and cultural shock initially, but most Anglo-Indian families had settled well in Australia and could afford to look to the past with fond nostalgia.

Many of the older people expressed a deep sense of loss with respect to Hyderabad, several offering stories of Urdu proficiency and former patron-client relationships to validate their mulki status. Their views of the old state, however, differed. Most credited the Nizam for the tolerance and security they had experienced and some, chiefly those from Secunderabad, credited the British presence. A shared perception of closeness to Muslims and Mughlai culture and of distance from Hindus had produced anger or ambivalence with respect to India's takeover of Hyderabad. But particularly among the younger Anglo-Indians, positive attitudes toward India were quite evident.

The Anglo-Indians told stories demonstrating their historical place in Hyderabadi society and testifying to deep affections across religious and linguistic boundaries. They claimed their status as mulki Hyderabadis when they revisited the city and more easily relinquished an identity as Anglo-Indian (an internally divided category in Hyderabad) than as Hyderabadi. Emile Cox called himself a Nawab, albeit jokingly. Kerry Edwards, whose letterhead showed his house name as "Purani Haveli" (old palace, after one of the Nizam's city palaces), wrote: "Now after 24 years, I am grateful to God for my success in this new country. But I might hastily add that the richness of the people of Hyderabad, their culture, manners, humour and hospitality can never be equalled by any of life here in Australia. . . . I am proud to be a Hyderabadi Mulki first and an Anglo Indian second."[88] In Australia, the appropriation of names that invoked high status in old Hyderabad and the still-told poems, jokes, and stories about the Nizam, the army, and the old neighborhoods symbolized the confidence and pride of Hyderabadi Anglo-Indians in their old and new homelands.

Just as old names and titles were put to new use, other aspects of Hyderabadi identity were adapted to the new setting and others in it. The Urdu language had been effectively dropped by the Anglo-Indians, whose English language helped them assimilate quickly. The old urban court culture of Hyderabad was known only among the older Anglo-Indian immigrants and offered no bridges to others in Australia, and their closeness to Muslims and Mughlai culture in Hyderabad had not brought these Anglo-Indians close to Muslims in Australia.

The organizational expressions of identity among the Hyderabadi immigrants to Australia were diverse, and, more like the immigrants to Pakistan and unlike those in Britain, collective expressions of a distinctively Hyderabad identity were few and tentative. The Reverend and Mrs. Bellingham were recalled more by those overseas than those in Australia, and the presence of the eighth Nizam in Perth provided no rallying point.[89] First-generation immigrants to Australia retained Hyderabadi identities privately to varying degrees, but what struck one was the existence of several strong but poorly connected networks of Hyderabadis. Among the Anglo-Indians, city-bridging networks kept former neighbors and relatives in close touch. Among the Muslims, there were Islamic institutions and Urdu literary associations, the former bringing Hyderabadis and many other Muslims together, the latter bringing Indian and Pakistani Muslims together. The Parsis had an Australian Zoroastrian Association with some 400 to 500 members, about 100 of them from Pakistan according to the Pestonjees. Among the recent professional immigrants, networks and associations based on cricket, occupations, religions, and languages brought Hyderabadis together but always with non-Hyderabadis too. Anglo-Indians were represented among the cricketers but were overlooked when Urdu literary events were planned.

The Anglo-Indian immigrants to Australia recalled details of a very distinctive subculture in old Hyderabad and yet quickly became Australian. Most left the Anglo-Indian identity behind, blending quickly into Australia's Anglo-Celtic majority. Although there was a large Anglo-Indian association[90] in Australia, most Hyderabadis did not belong to it. Perhaps, like Hyderabadi muhajirs in Pakistan, they felt it was an identity disadvantageous to them in the new setting. Because of residential dispersion or easy movement into existing churches, Anglo-Indians in Australia made no effort to attend particular churches patronized by other Christians from Hyderabad or Secunderabad. In Melbourne, for example, there was no one church that Hyderabadi Catholics all attended. Nor did the Anglo-Indians reproduce cricket teams like the Lallaguda and Bohiguda ones among railway workers back in Secunderabad and Hyderabad; a few upper-class players were on the Sydney Deccan Blues, as they had been on Hyderabad's parent team.

The newer Hyderabadi Australians could also be categorized into diverging groups, although some people clearly bridged them and all involved people from both India and Pakistan. Hyderabadi Muslims were generally unaware of the earlier movement of Anglo-Indians to Australia and were building Islamic institutions and Urdu-based cultural associations in Australia. Other new professionals of diverse backgrounds continued to draw on old Hyderabadi ideas and networks, their activities focused on cricket and professional associations. These boundaries were flexible, including Hyderabadis but also many others and sometimes confusing the lines of recruitment as in Sydney's cricket teams. All these associations were rooted in the new site, not necessarily and only sometimes drawing on other Hyderabadis or received understandings of old Hyderabad.

Professional and educational networks related people to colleagues and classmates not only in Australia but beyond it. People invoked the "old boy" networks, but only an Aligarh Muslim University association existed in Australia in 1993.[91] With no established Hyderabad Association, immigrants in Australia could not be challenged by a hegemonic group defining Hyderabadi status. However, the Hyderabadi identity had little utility in Australia and immigrants were pushed toward the Pakistani or Indian associations, institutionalizing highly politicized identities that separated ex-Hyderabadis from each other in the diaspora.

In Australia, the nature of the immigration laws and the different timings of the Anglo-Indian, Indian, and Pakistani migrations helped prevent the rebuilding of friendships across lines of race and religion, links that many believed characteristic of old Hyderabad. Food remained central and culturally significant but had become a private marker of identity. Anglo-Indian women learned to make the foods that symbolized Hyderabadi culture and most made all the specialities: *bagara baigan, biryani, khatti dal*, even *dam ka kebab* and their own mango pickles.[92] In other countries, Hyderabadi associations and weddings showcased Hyderabadi food in large public gatherings, but in Australia the "one-dish potluck" remained the favorite format. Both Anglo-Indians and Muslims mentioned potluck groups, but the groups met separately.

LOOKING AHEAD

The older immigrants and their children looked confidently to their futures in Australia. Older immigrants had gone back to Hyderabad for visits, but, as one put it, "We felt like strangers in India, not part of the changes that had occurred there at all, and so many friends had died or migrated." The weak tendency to build "old boy" associations, the permeable boundaries of the cricket teams, and the new religious and professional coalitions were all strongly driven by new identities as Australians and by Australian identity politics. A few families were actively connected to transnational networks beyond Australia.

Australia's "mateship" concept helped build bridges to the new dominant culture, through sports competitions and the twenty-first birthday party tradition. In private life, Australia's twenty-first birthday party was added to the round of family rituals, a ritual that had not been observed in Hyderabad. Its adoption represented a conscious incorporation of the host country's culture, although orthodox Muslims did not incorporate the drinking of alcohol so characteristic of the ritual.

Most Hyderabadis viewed integration into Australian society very positively, although a Hyderabadi Muslim critic saw it as a danger. From his cricket club contacts, Fahmi Hussain felt that Hindus were "having more problems" with the younger generation; he saw more young Hindus taking anglicized names and making mixed marriages, "breaking the line of cultural transmission." He thought the Hindus had changed more, as individuals, and that one reason for the difference was Hindu use of alcohol, making them vulnerable to "Australian mateship ideas." Islam was a more demanding or rigid religion, he said, actually a positive thing because it helped people maintain their traditions.[93] But the role of Islam in the lives of Hyderabadi Australian Muslims differed markedly from its role back in Hyderabad, tending toward greater orthodoxy and defensively opposing "hybridity." Employment in the Middle East or years spent in Pakistan contributed to these changes, but the Australian context and contact with Middle Eastern Muslims were the primary catalysts. Many Muslims and their children were moving from an identification with Hyderabad to one with Pakistan or other Muslim Australians.

In Australia, marriage networks reflected a growing integration into Australian society. The Anglo-Indians were most obviously "marrying out," and some of the Indian and Pakistani professionals who came as bachelors were doing so as well. This was not so true of Hyderabadi Muslims, although the broadening of their marriage networks to Muslims of other national origins seemed likely and would create an Australian Muslim identity.

The younger people of all backgrounds were much changed by the movement to Australia. Redefining their heritage to feature Kashmir, the Taj Mahal, *bharata natyam* dancing, and perhaps even Saudi Arabia more prominently than the Char Minar, they became "Indian" or "Pakistani" or "Muslim" rather than Hyderabadi. But most often the younger people, especially the Anglo-Indians, were moving to an identity as Australians and were finding it confirmed by Australian society. The contrast was great with the Hyderabadi immigrants in Pakistan, where even in the first generation and certainly in the second the tendency was to claim a Pakistani identity fiercely but at the same time, finding it contested, to look beyond Pakistan. Young Hyderabadis in the Australian second generation were simultaneously redefining their place of origin and their future community, moving beyond the familiar and often interconnected parental networks back in Hyderabad.

CHAPTER 7

The United States: New Frontiers

RAM MOHAN ROY, from a Hindu family in Hyderabad's old city that had long served the Nizams, explained his youthful orientation to the United States and migration there before 1965:

> When in high school, I became a patriot, I turned away from thoughts of going to Oxford or Cambridge and turned toward the United States; I wanted to move ahead, be different from my family, caste, old city people. But I went to Chaderghat College and then Osmania, where there were Muslims, where the dress and language was familiar (Nizam College was too different); then I taught at colleges in the city and Warangal district. I applied for a Fulbright scholarship to do my Ph.D. in America; I got one in 1962 and headed for Los Angeles, to Claremont Graduate School. There were only three or four others from India. . . . I ate ice cream and potato chips and what I thought was Hyderabad-style ground lamb (it turned out to be beef). I spoke about India at churches, labor unions, the Democratic Party, for small fees, and I founded the International Club at Claremont; I went to teach at Memphis State University and did these things all over again and met my Greek-American wife there. I managed to send money home all those years for my eight younger siblings.[1]

The pre-1965, immediate post-1965, and 1980s United States-bound immigrants contrasted with respect to their backgrounds, activities in the United States, and views of themselves. Roy and many early students in the states, most of them from elite or well-connected families, saw themselves as being different, as pioneers choosing not to tread the well-worn path to the UK. Their earliest anchors in the United States were not other Hyderabadis, but other international students or Americans. They spoke out as authorities on their home countries, and they learned to cook and fend for themselves. Many of them struck out in new directions with respect to marriage as well.

After the 1965 Immigration and Naturalization Act redressed the historic discrimination against Asians, professionally qualified Hyderabadis began coming to the United States. Doctors, engineers, and other professionals were drawn by the new immigration preferences. The American Association of Physicians from India became the largest ethnic body of doctors in the United States, supplying 4 percent of America's doctors.[2] Indian engineers were the second largest foreign-born group of engineers, and Indian business students outnumbered any other international group. The post-1965 Hyderabadis came not just from India, but as twice- or thrice-migrants from other countries. They settled throughout the country and moved around a great deal within the United States.[3] Finally, a third wave of immigrants began arriving—aging parents and newcomers of all social classes—at the end of the twentieth century.

Three Waves of Immigrants

STUDENTS STAYING ON

Most Hyderabadis who came to the United States before the 1965 opening up of migration from Asia were students, individuals scattered across a very large country. Hyderabad's Education Department gave scholarships to students in areas the state thought it would need to develop: just before World War II, mulki scholars were sent abroad for degrees in electrical engineering, agricultural economics, and other such subjects. The Nizam's Trust also funded students before and after 1948 for study overseas and sent many to the United States. Typically, these scholars were young men, and many of them married American women, but women from Hyderabad, most of them marrying first to gain family support for their studies and careers, were among the pioneers.

In Hyderabad, several American influences directed students to certain places. The vigorous U.S. Agency for International Development (USAID) program, with its high-profile professors from Kansas State University at Osmania University in the 1960s, encouraged students to head for Kansas State. William Mulder, a popular University of Utah professor, taught at Osmania in 1957–1958 and helped initiate the American Studies Research Center affiliated to Osmania in 1964; he headed the Center from 1965 to 1968, returned briefly in 1974, and headed it again from 1979 to 1982. He and his family made many friends in Hyderabad and drew students to Salt Lake City.[4] The Peace Corps was active from 1962 for about a decade in India, its young, enthusiastic teachers in Hyderabad inspiring students to choose the United States for higher education. The U.S. Information

Service (USIS) library and information center in Hyderabad from 1952 to 1971 actively helped students gain admission and scholarships in American colleges and universities.

Washington, D.C., New York, and regions adjacent to those cities drew early Hyderabadis. K. D. Mathur, like R. M. Roy from an old city Hindu family with close connections to the Nizam's regime, won a scholarship from the Nizam's Trust to study medicine in the United States in 1947, but shortly after his arrival in the Washington, D.C., area, Hyderabad State fell to India. The scholarship vanished in the confusion, and Mathur took a clerical job with the Indian Embassy. He left his medical studies, earned a Ph.D. in public administration, and began a teaching career at the University of Maine. He was an unofficial ambassador of India and briefly served as Nepal's representative to the United Nations. He first lived in the International House in Washington, D.C., and spoke at functions with Chester Bowles, former U.S. Ambassador to India. Mathur married an American woman and his two children later married Americans.[5]

Habeeb Ghatala, whose grandfather had supervised the Nizam's Public Gardens, sailed aboard the Queen Elizabeth in 1960 and took his master's degree at Kansas State, then went to the University of Wisconsin, where he met other Hyderabadis and married an American woman. His Hyderabadi friends there also "married out": V. Krishna Kumar and Riyaz Mahdi married women from Japan and S. M. Shahed married a Hindu from Lucknow.[6] Habeeb took jobs in Utah, Texas, Saudi Arabia, and finally Philadelphia. Divorced and remarried to a Hyderabadi widow from London, he recalled how hard he and others worked in the early decades. He had worked as a dishwasher and at other menial jobs in the summers. He felt that the post-1965 immigrants "had no idea how we earned our way in America."

Given the changes over the decades, Habeeb thought it unreasonable to expect the second generation to be Hyderabadi in any meaningful way. Religion was becoming more central than it had been in Hyderabad, with some Muslim Hyderabadi daughters adopting the hijab and some older Hyderabadi women adopting it and trying to persuade their American-raised daughters to do so. Marriages among the young people were a source of anxiety. Habeeb's own son, in college, expected to choose his own spouse; the daughter of Habeeb's Shia Muslim friends in Philadelphia was about to marry a Jewish American. Among Hyderabadi couples long-settled in the area, many second-generation children were marrying Americans, only some of whom converted to the relevant Indian religion.

Chicago, another early destination, had the largest population of Hyderabadis in the United States and vied with London and Toronto as center of the Hyderabadi diasporic world. Hyderabadis generally called the city Chicago Shareef, likening it to cities in India dominated by Indo-Muslim culture or known for the tombs of saints like Gulbarga Shareef or Ajmer Shareef.[7] In the Chicago area, Hyderabadis were residentially dispersed, some in the city and more in the surrounding suburbs. Hyderabadis were an important group in Chicago, especially among Muslims, and reportedly the International House at the University of Chicago was known informally as Hyderabadi House for years. Devon Avenue, the northside center of Indo-Pakistani businesses, had at least two Hyderabadi restaurants in the early 1990s,[8] and several downtown Muslim institutions were led by Hyderabadis. People talked about Hindu Muslim polarization and about prejudices, prejudices sometimes racial and sometimes based on national origin: Chicago had many immigrants and many African Americans.[9]

Dr. Shakeela Hassan arrived in Chicago as an intern in 1957 with a medical degree from Osmania and joined the University of Chicago in 1961 as an anesthesiologist. Although Shakeela was the oldest of several siblings, a brother had preceded her to study engineering at Purdue; he married an American woman. A sister studied journalism at Northwestern and married an American. Another brother studied architecture at Oberlin and married an Australian artist. In the United States, Shakeela married a Pakistani Punjabi Muslim, an Engineering Ph.D. from the Illinois Institute of Technology (IIT) who became dean of the Stuart School of Business at IIT. The Hassans had three daughters: a doctor, a lawyer, and an international business and finance major.[10] Shakeela spoke of her early, hectic days in Chicago as an intern; when her brothers came to visit her, she got one day off to show them the city and that was the first time she had seen it herself. There were very few Hyderabadis then, one from India and one from Pakistan at the IIT, but later more came and they held an annual picnic. Although her husband "is an American at heart, he doesn't even speak Urdu," Shakeela continues to value Hyderabadi culture, which she defined as "understanding different people and having a common value system."[11] She was also proud of Hyderabadi women in America, whom she saw as determined and career-oriented, with stronger personalities than women in Hyderabad. Dr. Hassan was instrumental in organizing both Hyderabadi cultural and Muslim religious activities in Chicago. Because of her father's job, Shakeela and her brothers were close to the Nizam's grandsons (a brother played polo with them), and when Chicago Hyderabadis and Prince Muffakham Jah in London began planning a Hyderabad Foundation in Chicago in the 1980s, the prince called on her for leadership.[12]

Syed Asif Ali Hashmy, another leader of Chicago's Hyderabadis, went to Kansas State University in 1960, personally recruited in Hyderabad by

Dr. James McCain, president of the university. Asif became the first foreign student to be elected to Kansas State's student senate and served as president of the India Association, the Islamic Association, and the Coordinating Council of Foreign Student Organizations. Hashmy's job with International Minerals and Chemicals (IMC), Coromandel Fertilizer's parent company, took him to Chicago in 1965 (but he left for Amoco, the American Oil Corporation, when IMC wanted him to go to Vishakapatnam in coastal Andhra). Only ten or fifteen other Hyderabadis were in Chicago at that time, he said, students living in rented rooms or the YMCA, and they all stayed on, finding wives or bringing wives; only one returned to Hyderabad after a divorce late in life. Hashmy married Khatija, an architect, in 1964 and brought her from Hyderabad to the United States in 1965; she worked for a Chicago architectural firm. Hashmy came from a family closely associated with the Nizam and headed the Hyderabad Foundation in Chicago.[13]

Meher Ali, a young woman who wanted to get out of Hyderabad and study in the United States, also ended up in Chicago. She and her first cousins summered in their Vikarabad home outside the city, where they rode their bikes, sang "American" songs, and went to the hospital for "American vitamins." By semi-arrangement in Hyderabad, she met a graduate student studying at Harvard, liked him, and married him.[14] She was nineteen, it was 1963, and there was an immigration quota, so she had to wait a year or two to join him in Chicago, where he worked for General Motors. The new bride bargained with her husband and in-laws to let her study psychology and teacher training at Elmhurst College before having a child. When she graduated, she was pregnant, and she combined career and motherhood from then on.

Meher Ali owned and directed two Montessori schools. Her husband, mother-in-law, and mother supported her in this career; the latter two each sending her a maid from Hyderabad, young girls, every year. Her parents came to visit in 1970, when her second daughter was born, but her mother hated the United States. "You work like a slave here, babies, teaching, and homemaking too," she said, and returned to Hyderabad, never to visit again. But Meher's father liked it and stayed almost two years, helping them move from an apartment into their first home in Downer's Grove, seeing the children off to school, meeting the neighbors, attending garage sales, and studying the Bible and Christian Science.[15]

Meher and her husband paid little attention to whether there were other Hyderabadis nearby in earlier years. "We are Americans, we function in the world as Americans, and our children are Americans too." Meher's brother and his Hyderabadi wife lived nearby, but Meher and Mansoor socialized primarily with his friends from Harvard. Their three daughters had the very best that America had to offer, from strollers to food to schools. The oldest daughter attended Sarah Lawrence and the middle one attended Boston College. For religious education, Meher once checked out an Islamic School in the suburbs but was completely turned off when the Arab *imam* spoke about American neighbors as enemies who must be converted. The Alis taught their daughters about Islam themselves; orthodoxy did not appeal to them. Meher's paternal grandmother had ridden horses English style, sidesaddle, and had spoken English; Meher's mother and her grandmothers never covered their heads. But as the Ali girls grew up, Meher realized they knew little of Hyderabad and its culture, despite occasional visits there. When the leaders of the Hyderabad Foundation contacted them in the 1980s, Meher and Mansoor agreed to join the board. The girls were already American, and now the Foundation promised to give them their ancestral heritage; it was a providential opportunity.[16]

Pre-1965 Hyderabadi students chose schools in both northern and southern California. Noel de Souza was seventeen in 1948 and chose the University of California, Berkeley, to study architecture because Berkeley's liberal reputation seemed to accord with Hyderabad's cosmopolitanism. His family was of Goan (Portuguese Catholic) ancestry, and its well-known store in Secunderabad sold imported beer, wine, pork, cheeses, and other items catering to European tastes. Noel's sister was one of the early lady doctors in the city, and he too was a pioneer. His mother, Noel said, often told him he had been born in the wrong country: he was too friendly with poor people, with everyone; he did not maintain "proper relations." To prove to his father that he was a practical person, Noel took a business degree, but his real love was acting and he made his way to southern California through friends in Berkeley's international student community. He returned to India and took a company job in Calcutta, but, with family approval, he soon returned to southern California's Pasadena Playhouse and worked in Hollywood for many years. Once married but divorced, he planned to retire to Kodaikanal in Kerala, because the Hyderabad he knew was lost. He lost faith in the United States as well, having liked it best in the 1960s, and he was critical of the new post-1965 immigrants from India for not giving to their own community. He thought of himself as a citizen of the world.[17]

Other Hyderabadis were sent to UC Berkeley in the 1940s by Hyderabad's Education Department. Dr. Talib-ul Haq's elder brother arrived on scholarship in 1946 and Talib followed on his own funds in 1949, earning a doctorate in forensic science. Dr. Haq found some 130 Indian students at Berkeley, among them at least thirty-five from Hyderabad. Most of these, young Muslim men, went back to Pakistan instead of India, but some stayed in the United States. Dr. Haq's elder brother tried to find a position in Hyderabad but ended up in Pakistan; Dr. Haq tried for a job in Hyderabad too but forensic science was not well established. He returned to the United States in the 1950s and worked in private industry and then higher education.[18]

After 1948, some Hyderabadis who chose Berkeley came by way of Pakistan. K. M. Hussain arrived at Berkeley in 1956, having moved as a teenager with his widowed mother to Pakistan in 1947–1948. He met Donna, an American, in Europe, chose Berkeley for his Ph.D., and married Donna in Berkeley in 1957. She was the third "outsider" to marry into his large Karachi-based family (earlier, there had been one Swedish and one English bride).[19] He taught in New Mexico and Donna was a technical writer; they co-authored books on computing and information systems. K. M. and Donna adopted two children and raised them as "just Americans" (not Muslim, Hyderabadi, Indian, or Pakistani). Retired to Sacramento, California, they joked that K. M. had more relatives in the United States than Donna did, as all eight children of Hussein's Karachi relatives have moved to the states.[20]

Southern California also attracted pioneer Hyderabadis, and those who did well tended to build mansions. Shafi Babu Khan, from one of Secunderabad's leading business families, left a promising career in the family's Nizam Sugar Factory in 1956 for Chapman College (where he was on the varsity tennis team). Shafi wanted exposure to other cultures; he had always felt different from his conservative family and its adherence to tradition. He married a Greek American artist named Calliope in 1958, and they tried India from 1961 to 1963 but returned to the United States. Shafi went into electronics and then real estate; he has been president of Babu-Khan Enterprises since 1975. Calliope's paintings and prints blended with antiques in their Pacific Palisades home. Their daughter, a doctor, did not consider herself a Hyderabadi and married an American doctor. Shafi liked the United States because "here, nobody can touch you; you can be what you want to be."[21]

Other early Hyderabadi immigrants striking out in new directions in Los Angeles included Ahmed Lateef and Akbar and Rehana Hasan. Ahmed Lateef's father, a Gandhian schooled at Cambridge and Edinburgh, was the principal of Jagirdar's College. Ahmed came for a master's degree to UCLA in 1951 and went back to be wed, bringing his bride (from the Paigah noble family) to Los Angeles where their daughter was born. The marriage broke up, and he remarried an American and settled into a Hollywood career, writing hundreds of screenplays and commercials. Akbar Hasan, Ahmed's best friend (they were in kindergarten together at Mahbubiyah), first imagined himself as an American when he was in the American School in Paris as a child during his father's posting there. He came in 1951 to do auto design in Detroit but came first to California, where he stayed and went into real estate. Akbar brought his bride, Rehana, from Hyderabad (her mother was German, her father a Hyderabadi Muslim). Rehana owned and supervised a preschool in Los Angeles. The couple's westside home had a pool in the backyard and an American flag hanging outside the front door. Akbar and Rehana brought their son and daughter up with no particular religion, celebrating Christmas and other holidays. They formed a network of Hyderabadis, but most of these Los Angelenos had not been back to Hyderabad for decades.[22]

Like Rehana (and Meher Ali in Chicago), other Hyderabadi women became educators in the United States. Niloufer "Nilu" Ulla, successful entrepreneur in the preschool business in northern California, came as the bride of a pre-1965 Hyderabadi student. Her husband studied engineering in Kansas in 1960 and returned to wed in Hyderabad, bringing her to California in 1967 where he had a job with IBM. Unhappy at first, having left a teaching career and many relatives and friends to come to a place with few Indians and fewer Hyderabadis, Nilu had her husband's encouragement after the birth of their first daughter to go night school for her California teaching credentials. In 1972, Nilu bought her first preschool. The family held meetings of Indian Muslims in its home in earlier days and she was a leader in the Hyderabad association based in San Jose, but Nilu viewed herself as a bridging person, one whose friends, teachers, and students were of all backgrounds. "You live in a country with great opportunities, you should take advantage of them," she said.[23]

The Ullas were educating their daughters well. The older daughter, Shahana, earned a marketing degree at San Jose State and was thinking about a graduate degree in education; her parents bought another preschool for her to run. The younger sister studied biochemistry at UC Davis. Shahana was pressed into service as a board member of the Hyderabad Association of Northern California, as the leaders were anxious to attract the second generation. She was, in 1992, concerned about how her marriage would be decided. Hyderabadi Muslims seemed to be marrying within their own circles, but many of Shahana's girlfriends were making their own choices, marrying outside their communities and even living with boyfriends. A San Jose Hyderabadi Muslim girlfriend had just had a traditional seven-day wedding. Shahana would not mind her parents finding a good boy, she said, but she wanted an educated and ambitious one, not necessarily a Hyderabadi.

Another educator who migrated as a bride just before 1965, Faizi Akbar Ali was the first girl in her family on her mother's side to go outside the home for schooling. Faizi saw herself as a rebel supported by cousins and brothers who encouraged her to study (her father died when she was one year old). She attended Residency Women's College and successfully agitated for a psychology coeducational class at Osmania; she then earned a master of arts in psychology in Bangalore. She won a Nizam's Trust grant for graduate study in the United States in the early 1960s, possibly the first woman to get such a grant she said. Her mother required that she marry first, so Faizi looked for a California groom and married a student at UCLA, a friend of her best friend's brother. Arriving in Los Angeles in 1965 in time for summer school, she earned master's degrees at UCLA in psychology and education and headed for Ph.D. work at Northwestern (her husband got a job in the Chicago area after acquiring his Ph.D. in Engineering). A psychologist in Los Angeles, Faizi loved living in the United States and found she could easily retain her Islamic value system; she encouraged her son to join the Muslim Students Association at UCLA instead of the India Association because of its broader, international scope.[24]

San Diegans Junaid and Anjum Razvi (he a nuclear engineer, she an architect) had backgrounds that not only linked India and Pakistan but drew on relatives' pre-1965 student experiences in the United States. Aziz and Habiba Razvi, Junaid's parents, went to Pakistan in 1950, leaving their youngest son Junaid behind with her parents. Aziz and Habiba had studied in the United States, he doing journalism at Stanford in 1956 and Habiba earning a master of arts in literature at the University of Chicago, but they went back to Karachi. Junaid grew up in Hyderabad with his grandparents, Aisha and Habib ur-Rahman (ur-Rahman was the founder of Urdu College and Urdu Hall in Hyderabad). Encouraged by an uncle and aunt who had migrated to the United States in 1957 to work at Argonne National Laboratory, Junaid proceeded at age seventeen in 1966 to Wabash College in Indiana. One of only three foreign students in his class, Junaid stayed on and prospered.[25] Junaid's parents, visiting him and other relatives, saw their two grandchildren as "very American" but somehow did not expect their son to be so despite his long residence in the United States. Having met Aziz and Habiba in Karachi, I met them again in San Diego when they visited Junaid. We sat at first in the living room but had to move, as it was Super Bowl Sunday and the young people wanted to watch the Super Bowl. "Our son has forgotten his Hyderabadi manners," the parents said.[26]

POST-1965 CAREER-BUILDERS

The new immigration law encouraged professionals from a wider range of backgrounds to come to the United States. Members of elite families continued to arrive. Shehbaz Safrani was among the first of the post-1965 immigrants to the east coast, moving to New York in 1968 following stays in Damascus, Syria, and Rome, Italy (his adopted father was Indian ambassador to Iraq and Syria). Safrani pursued his own studies in fine arts throughout and settled in a Manhattan penthouse apartment in 1970. "I had a dream, as a boy, about living on top of a skyscraper," he said. From a family with Indian nationalist connections, Shehbaz was a painter, writer, and art appraiser; his American wife was a freelance photographer and editor. An agnostic fiercely committed to a secular India and to Hyderabad's past cultural synthesis, Shehbaz proudly called his Shia tradition in Islam "the Qutb Shahi faith." An articulate writer and speaker, he was occasionally engaged for Hyderabadi events like a St. George's Grammar School reunion in Montreal. He passionately protested the increasing religiosity of many Muslim Hyderabadis and held his Hindu friends very dear. He was especially upset by criticism of his chapter on Golconda *picchwais* (cloth paintings of Lord Krishna as Sri Nathji) in his book on Golconda and Hyderabad, criticism offered by some Muslims who saw Hyderabadi culture as essentially Islamic.[27]

Medical doctors, however, were the more typical post-1965 Hyderabadi immigrants, people who came for professional, not personal, reasons. Dr. Syed N. Asad, who graduated with an M.D. from Osmania in 1968, arrived in New York to do a residency in medicine and postgraduate education in 1969. Asad's brother did a medical residency in 1962–1964 in the United States, and Asad's wife was a pathologist (they were classmates). Not only he, but ten or fifteen other classmates came in 1969; only a few stayed in Hyderabad. Dr. Asad had experienced no discrimination, he said; he was a member of the local Rotary Club. Concerned about his two daughters' religious education, he helped start an Islamic Association of Long Island in about 1983 but was alarmed by the increasing religiosity of many Indian Muslim immigrants. He preferred the Hyderabadi music and poetry evenings held by a psychiatrist in Queens. A member of the Osmania Graduates Association (part of the American Association of Physicians from India) and the Islamic Medical Association of North America, Asad was in private practice after years of teaching and administration. He felt his Hyderabadi background had prepared him well for multicultural America.[28]

Dr. Madhu Mohan, a medical doctor and officer of the Osmania Graduates Association in the United States, migrated in the 1970s with his wife, an Osmania classmate. His first "memories" of the states came from Peace Corps teachers at the Methodist High School and the bishop who came to the high school in a Chevy Impala. Born in 1950, Madhu came from "the feudal class; my grandfather was Raja of Kolhapur, but I missed the historic days." Nonetheless his experience at Osmania had committed him to Hyderabadi culture. In the United States, Mohan had become American, which he defined as "going into debt, working too hard, not a perfect way of life but the best I've found so far. Philosophically, there's nothing wrong with Hyderabadi ways, but, as Khalil Gibran said, to accomplish anything one needs money, and, unless one is born a prince, a professional must move to a free market economy and practice time management." Mohan had taken American citizenship, but that was "only paper," and with globalization he could maintain his dual identity. In his heart he was both Hyderabadi and American.[29]

Dr. Mohan joined a group of Osmania graduates at the University of Pennsylvania, professionals who wanted to do something that made a difference back home. They had worked to prove themselves as immigrants and been rewarded well by the system. The six wondered, if Hyderabadis overseas could be so successful, why not those in Hyderabad, no longer rising at 9:30 in the morning as in the Nizam's days, no longer handicapped by government and caste systems that held back productivity? Instead of giving equipment (if a CAT scan machine was sent, it soon stopped working), Hyderabadis in the United States should export the entire American system, they decided. They founded the nonprofit Science Health Allied Research Education (SHARE) and placed an ad in *India Abroad*. Thus the ambitious Mediciti project in Hyderabad began.

Religious and cultural issues concerned more of the post-1965 than the pre-1965 immigrants. Ahsan Syed came to the United States in 1967 to earn a civil engineering degree at Mississippi State University; worked in Pennsylvania, Ohio, and Saudi Arabia; and finally settled in Palo Alto, California. An engineer, he taught in an Islamic school on Sundays. When an American consul attended a 1967 reception in Hyderabad for the students going abroad, Syed had asked him how he should change to be acceptable in America. The consul told him, "Don't change; give what you are to our society," and Syed has been exemplifying Hyderabadi culture and explaining it to American colleagues ever since.[30] He grew up in the old city by Purana Pul, near Dr. Digamber Singh, a well-known Rajput doctor whose courtesy and Urdu were both enviably impeccable. "Only one thing was not done properly; when culture clashed with religion, culture won out," he said. "*Adab arz* was really Persian, not an Islamic greeting at all." However, Syed had just used it when visiting his old professor of hydraulic engineering settled in Pennsylvania, Dr. Venkatadri, who "still cries over the loss of Hyderabadi culture."

Syed felt that in America many Hyderabadis were learning Islam for the first time. The Nizams had been Muslim in name only, he asserted, and in many ways Hindu customs had crept into the city's culture. He said, however, that Hyderabadi Muslims had not avoided beef out of respect for Hindu sensibilities but because it was cheap, poor in quality, and eaten by the lower classes. He mentioned ladies' rituals at weddings, such as songs about grinding wheat, and stated that these were silly, ignorant, and not Islamic; they had been done only because the ladies seldom got together and needed entertainment. In the United States such rituals should be discarded as unnecessary, as ladies got together here more often. "Yes," Mrs. Syed chimed in (she was a radiology technician), "here we all drive, we just get in the car and go." Her husband cautioned, "Some are getting too ahead here," and said that free mixing of men and women was not permitted in Islam and that in some circles—for example the Hyderabad Association—Indianized culture, not Islamic culture, prevailed.

Ahsan Syed's feelings about culture, religion, and politics were complicated. The Syeds were concerned about preserving their values for their three children. Fond as he was of Urdu and Urdu poetry,[31] Syed knew that Urdu had to go, because religious education was the first priority and the children knew English and not Urdu. Islam could certainly be transmitted in English in the United States. He had "faced discrimination as a Muslim" when he graduated and competed for jobs in India, and "to come to the United States directly is like a heaven; there is no choice but to come here." He had not seen Pakistan as an option, despite its embrace of Islam and Urdu. His father, the rest of whose family had gone to Pakistan, had said, "When people leave for Pakistan, remove their names from the human race; they change, they act in inhuman ways." Ahsan added to his father's comments,

> They are too materialistic. When they visit Hyderabad, it's like they're seeing animals in a zoo, they tell success stories only, of cars, money, servants, vacations in Rome. They have a superiority complex, and it's just those in Pakistan, not Hyderabadis who go elsewhere. After thirty, thirty-five years in the United States, I still feel the pain, but it's they who cut off the relationship, who felt no pain, who gave no help. Now we're meeting here but [I have] no forgiveness.

Hindus Leela and Anand Mamidi attended activities of the India Association in Davis, California, and the Indian Cultural Association in Sacramento, "since Hyderabadi culture prepared us to relate to people from both north and south India." The couple owed its settlement in the United States to the Nizam's Trust. Anand Mamidi came to Southern Illinois University in 1971, his airfare paid by the Trust because he was a mulki. His father and grandfather were in the forest service; his uncle studied at Berkeley in the 1950s and went back, his older brother studied in Boulder, Colorado, in 1962 and went back. Anand, the fifth child, earned an environmental engineering degree and stayed, making an arranged intercaste marriage with Leela (both families were "old Hyderabadis"). Two of Leela's female relatives married Hyderabadi Muslims and lived in Canada and Iowa.[32] The Mamidis knew there was a Hyderabad association somewhere nearby and would have loved to attend a *mushaira* or *qawwali* (Sufi Muslim devotional singing) or see the prince (Muffakham Jah) if he came. They felt that they had known more Muslims back in Hyderabad than in Davis, where the local Islamic Center advocated orthodox practices; Leela mentioned a Hyderabadi Muslim wife who wore skirts when she first came to the United States but now had her three young daughters "cover up" (wear the hijab, something not done by that family in Hyderabad). Their own two children had been back to Hyderabad once, when they were seven and ten, and had asked to "go home," which for them was the United States.

Leela and Anand still felt they had two homes, and they were ambivalent about where to retire. Anand talked about retirement to Hyderabad, because it was kinder to old people and six of his eight siblings were there. But the Mamidis found Hyderabad so changed it was no longer fun to return, the biggest change being the loss of Urdu. Leela and her siblings reflected the linguistic changes: she and her next two siblings could read and write Urdu, while the last four knew only Hindi. The Mamidis even missed the old courtesies: "Back then things took forever, it was so polite it killed you, but now there is no time for manners, there or here."

Many post-1965 immigrants to the United States had moved from country to country and city to city in quest of both professional and personal satisfaction. Dr. Suraiya Rasheed was a thrice-migrant whose career brought her to California in 1970. Her father followed the rest of his family to Pakistan but waited until 1958, after Suraiya's Osmania Ph.D. in pathology and her marriage. Then, her father soon followed her older brother to the United States and Suraiya won scholarships for study abroad in 1960–1961. She chose the Commonwealth scholarship to the UK, not the Fulbright to the United States, and took another Ph.D. from the external examiner on her Osmania Ph.D. at his home institution, the School of Hygiene and Tropical Medicine in London. She did cancer research at a hospital west of London, tracking the characteristics of a particular sarcomavirus, and her colleagues advised her to go to the United States where better research facilities were available. Suraiya found her niche at USC, developing a viral oncology research unit and becoming head of it in 1980. She discovered the gene causing cancer in rats, now called the Rasheed Rat Sarcoma virus, and pioneered the isolation of the HIV virus. Her older daughter was a pediatrician with a USC degree, and her son had a USC drama degree.[33]

A twice-migrant and social activist in southern California, Shamim Ibrahim founded and helped lead NISWA (*niswa* is the Arabic plural of women, and later they decided to call it also the National Islamic Society of Women of America). Her brother, Dr. Nazir Khaja, a medical doctor, initiated and hosted an Islamic TV show from Los Angeles. Shamim and her husband (a *sahibzada*, member of the Nizam's family) went to Pakistan, he in 1951 and she in 1952 (finishing her Osmania B.A. after her marriage). They were in East Pakistan (now Bangladesh) and enjoyed it; after the 1970–1971 Bangladeshi conflict with Pakistan erupted, the Ibrahims moved to Karachi but, not liking life there, came to the United States in 1971. Having advised many later immigrants, Shamim commented that those moving from Pakistan and India should stop first in New York or Chicago, cities with good transport systems. "Those of us in California cannot drive them about all the time looking for jobs; one needs cars and driving skills in California," she said. Her husband was an accountant and she was a psychologist with the Los Angeles School District; they supported the public school system and valued pluralism, likening old Hyderabad to the United States in some respects. Shamim thought of herself as a Pakistani American with Hyderabadi cultural values, but she recognized that the Hyderabadi identity was not a useful one in the United States and that the second generation would not be Hyderabadi.[34] "We respond to the environment in which we live," she said, "while maintaining the basic Hyderabadi values of tolerance, love, and active interaction with others."

Although Shamim was on the board of the Hyderabad Deccan Association of southern California, she put her energy into NISWA, running a thrift shop and a home for battered women and encouraging Muslim families to sign up to care for foster children. NISWA worked with all women but explicitly targeted Muslim women, including African American Muslims. Shamim and other NISWA leaders broke the Ramadan fast every year at an African American mosque in downtown Los Angeles. Shamim, in 1993, opened a preschool with an Islamic curriculum, Sunshine School, in her neighborhood. The first eleven students to sign up were all non-Muslims. When Shamim asked one mother, probably a Chicana by her name, if the study of Arabic and other subjects would be a problem, she replied "No, it's great if my child learns Arabic, why not?" Shamim hoped, however, that word of her school would get around to Muslims.[35]

A twice-migrant who was sure his true home was California, Noshir Khan left Hyderabad in 1959 for higher education in the UK. His bride, a doctor, joined him in 1967 and they worked hard but "to no avail." Unhappy in Britain, they moved to the United States, to Florida in 1975 and to California in 1979. Noshir felt contemptuous of those with nostalgia for old Hyderabad, "a feudal society reserving most of its privileges for Muslims." As a little boy, he had accompanied his father, a government official, to the districts, staying in *dak* bungalows (for travelers on government business) where big cloth fans, *pankahs*, were pulled to cool them. Noshir had pitied the man whose job it was to stand and pull a *pankah* all day, and he recalled others whose menial jobs supported the privileged class. Remarking that Hyderabadis who had gone to Pakistan were still treated as refugees and those who went to the UK were still treated as foreigners, he indicted Pakistanis in general for arrogance and hatred of India. He called those Hyderabadis who had gone to Pakistan "our cousins from Hyderabad. We know nothing of their life in Pakistan; we don't really call them anything, there is a distance." He loved southern California (the family home was on the beach in Malibu) and felt it had been best for his two children, named Ashley (after a park in the UK) and Oona (after Charlie Chaplin's wife). The children, in college, had been to Hyderabad but were not being pushed to be Hyderabadi or "marry Hyderabadi."

Dr. Syed Samee, another post-1965 immigrant, left Hyderabad in 1973 for two years in London, spent seven years in Chicago, and moved to practice medicine in southern California in 1982. Dr. Samee loved Urdu poetry and literature more than medicine and he valued Hyderabadi history and culture. However, he thoughtfully observed that now, as a minority person in the United States, he could understand how much Hyderabadi Hindus, Parsis, and Christians had given up to join in the Indo-Muslim Hyderabadi culture; he lauded them for that. Dr. Samee headed the southern California Hyderabad Deccan Association at one point, but after the Babri Masjid crisis of 1992 in India, when Hindu fanatics pulled down a medieval mosque in northern India, he and other Hyderabadi Muslims put their energies into a Coalition for a Pluralistic and Egalitarian India. The Hyderabad association annual dinners seemed less important than working with others to improve Hindu/Muslim relations. An observant Muslim, Dr. Samee had two living rooms in his first house in southern California, one for men and one for women, but his second and larger home had just one splendid living room, suitable for holding *mushairas*.[36]

Post-1965 Hyderabadi professionals were drawn to Texas by the oil business in the 1970s and 1980s, most of them twice- or thrice-migrants within the United States. Those settling in Houston promptly nicknamed it Domalguda after a humid and mosquito-ridden locality in Hyderabad. Probably the greatest success story was that of Sanjiv Sidhu, whose net worth in 1996 was $415 million, according to *Forbes 400*, the annual list of the 400 richest Americans published by *Forbes* magazine. Another success story, of Dr. Abdul Ali who worked with the famous heart surgeon, Dr. Denton Cooley, attracted Hyderabadis to Houston for heart operations.[37] Houston had an Osmania Graduates Association, a Hyderabad House sponsored by a doctor in a shopping mall, an Aligarh association dominated by Hyderabadis, and an Urdu association. Houston initiated a Hyderabad Day in 1984, as Khalid Razvi convinced the mayor that Hyderabad not only had the best diamonds in the world but had also sent some 250 illustrious families to the city, including seven Ph.D.s, twenty-seven doctors, and seventy engineers.[38]

The stories of three sets of Hyderabadi migrants to Texas illustrate the diverse backgrounds of the post-1965 immigrants and their increasing concerns about religion—about Islam in these cases—over the course of their lives abroad. Sara Ghafoor grew up speaking and reading English so fluently that her uncle called her Bernie, after Sarah Bernhardt. He encouraged her to marry a young man employed in the United States whom she first saw at the United States Information Service (USIS) library in Hyderabad. She knew Peace Corps teachers in Hyderabad too and wanted to study abroad, so, after graduating from Women's College and earning an M.A. in English Literature at Osmania University, she combined that goal with marriage. On her way to join her husband in St. Louis, Missouri, in 1966, Sara studied for a summer in Edinburgh, Scotland. She had already been admitted to Radcliffe and two other American universities and had the promise of a Nizam's Trust grant when she arrived in the United States. But she started graduate work at Washington University, and after having the first of her three children and surveying the job market in English literature, she began to think of law or teaching instead. Then her husband was killed in a plane crash, leaving her with three children under thirteen and a pension from the airline. She could have lived in Hyderabad or joined her husband's relatives in Karachi, but her children were American and her brother and sister were settled in Houston, so she moved there in 1982. The children attended the University of Texas, Austin, and went into pharmacy, law, and Middle Eastern studies. The young people had become more religious in the United States, Sara and other relatives said, so, although being Hyderabadi and having a good Urdu accent was what parents wanted in potential spouses for their children, being a good Muslim and speaking English without an accent were what the youngsters wanted.[39]

Syed and Shahnaz Rizvi, who were related to the Salar Jung Shia Muslim noble family (the photographs of well-placed ancestors adorned their walls), moved to Houston from Chicago in 1978. Syed's older brother earned an M.B.S. in the United States, returned to Hyderabad, then came back to the states where all four brothers and their mother eventually settled.

Syed earned a B.S. in chemistry at New Mexico State University in 1969 and wanted to stay in the United States "to avoid discrimination against Muslims in India." To gain his mother's approval for this, he married within the family (Shahnaz and he were fourth cousins), with the *nikah* (signing of the marriage contract) in Hyderabad in 1970 and the *rukhsati* (the bride's homecoming), along with an American-style ceremony for his co-workers, in Chicago in 1972. Classmates invited the Rizvis to Houston for a vacation and they moved there in 1978. Their daughters, when I met them in 1995, were taking pre-med and pre-law courses; their son was in ninth grade.

Syed and Shahnaz wanted to move back to Hyderabad after his retirement. They missed having servants, she said,[40] and they returned for three-month periods every three or four years. Shahnaz had worked in the United States, giving up her sari to wear dresses as a salesperson in a department store and then starting her own daycare center. After she ran that for about four years, their son was born and she stayed home. She taught classes at the Islamic Education Center and learned that Lebanese, Iranians, Arabs, and South Asian Muslims understood Islam in different ways. She also felt that the Muslim clerics who came to teach Islam needed to respect the situation of Muslims in America. She started wearing the hijab (in Hyderabad, her relatives did not wear it). Although the Iranian revolution in 1979 had been a wake-up call and her pilgrimage to Iraq in 1982 had also made her think about it, Shahnaz actually adopted the hijab in 1989 when her daughters prodded her "to practice what you preach" and the older daughter, at thirteen, needed a role model. Both parents believed strongly that American society presented dangers to women. Explaining his fear of women walking about, sometimes in the dark, and dating, Syed asked me, "Don't you think that a woman is by nature delicate, a flower, not to be opened to the public?" The Rizvis' fear of feminism and their fear that there were no suitable partners for their daughters in the United States reinforced their desire to return to Hyderabad.

The third family, of doctors Shakila and Basheer Ahmed, settled in Arlington, Texas, in 1978. Basheer had frequented the USIS library and had always wanted to go to the United States, but he journeyed first to Karachi for a medical degree, then to Glasgow, Scotland, for another one, and finally to London for a degree in psychiatry. He married Dr. Shakila Ahmed, who had an Osmania medical degree, in Hyderabad in 1967 and they moved to St. Louis in 1968. After living in New York City and Dayton, Ohio, they moved to the Dallas–Fort Worth area of Texas, where they were both active professionally and in Hyderabadi and, increasingly, Islamic activities. Their daughter and son, university students exploring options in psychology, literature, medicine, and law, were "American, not Hyderabadi," the son said.

Dr. Basheer Ahmed told me of meeting other Hyderabadis when a student in Glasgow and later in New Zealand and Australia. "Down under" he had met with a classmate unseen since 1952, and he had met many of his wife's Osmania medical school classmates too. (Dr. Basheer was a classmate of Dr. Asad in New York and Dr. Shakila had been to school with Dr. Suraiya Rasheed in Los Angeles.) One of the fifty to seventy-five Hyderabadi families[41] in the Dallas–Fort Worth area joined the Ahmeds to break the Ramadan fast while I was there. The two couples broke their daily fast with dates, figs, and other fruit, along with a Black Forest cake from a nearby Swiss bakery. There was also what I took to be *dahi* or yogurt but turned out to be French onion dip, served with chips and salsa.

THE LATEST ARRIVALS

Those who came before 1965 as students tended to be from high-ranking families with scholarships from the Nizam's Trust or the Hyderabad government, and those who came immediately after 1965 qualified through their professional credentials; those arriving in the 1980s and 1990s, however, came from an even broader range of backgrounds and included older people following their children, people coming for family rather than personal or professional reasons.

Higher education continued to draw young Hyderabadis to the United States. Irshad Ahmed was an outstanding Gold Medalist in chemical engineering at Osmania whose family business near Char Minar in the old city was cleaning and polishing the gold and silver on valuable saris; he was the first in his family to earn a modern higher educational degree. He traveled to Cornell in 1984 for a Ph.D. in biochemical engineering. His parents in Hyderabad were trying to find a literate young woman for him, a search complicated by his extreme upward mobility: Irshad had his own private company and seven employees in Washington, D.C. His parents had visited him in Washington but they did not know English and were unhappy there. Washington was unlike Chicago, he said, where areas of many Urdu-speaking settlers made parents like his feel comfortable.

Javeed and Mahjabeen Mirza, two young teachers, arrived in New York City about 1982. Javeed was a Telingana Muslim who knew Telugu and Urdu, an atheist, socialist activist, high school teacher, and Ph.D. candidate. His wife followed him and was attending community college classes even as she worked as a translator in a public school. They invited me to their apartment for an occasion that not only broke the daily Ramadan fasting but celebrated the *ameen* (first complete reading of the Qur'an) by the second of their three sons. The Bangladeshi *alim* (scholar) teaching him was there, along with fifteen to twenty other people, in the small apartment. Husband and wife considered this a cultural rather than religious event, one that helped maintain Hyderabadi culture. The couple was determined to return to Hyderabad, where she had taken the children for months at a time. Mahjabeen's brother and cousins had worked in Saudi Arabia but her brother was back in Hyderabad, so her family was still based there.[42]

Another young couple, Ashfaq and Ayesha Saeed from Karachi, Pakistan, tried to adjust to Los Angeles in the early 1990s. Ashfaq, son of Mohammed Syedullah, secretary of the Bahadur Yar Jung Academy in Karachi, arrived in 1988 for a master's degree in engineering at Northrop University; he went home to marry in 1992 and brought his bride in 1993. They were both Hyderabadis, since "the muhajirs, including Hyderabadis, came from a higher culture than other Pakistanis, but here in the United States all Pakistanis are mixed up and also with people from India." They had relatives in both Pakistan and India but did not know those in or from India well (and their cousins in India read and wrote Hindi and Telugu, they said). Both had relatives in the United States—in Houston, Pasadena, San Francisco, and Los Angeles. Ayesha said that she was more religious in the United States because "I don't have anything else to do," although she was taking classes to become a preschool teacher. They made friends through Pakistani grocery stores and the mosque in Inglewood. They intended to return to Pakistan after Ashfaq got more engineering experience, but that was proving difficult during the recession.

A unique story was that of Mumtaz Patel, once the third wife of a Gujarati Hindu millionaire in Hyderabad, who arrived in Chicago in the 1990s as a fashion designer for Louis Farrakhan's Nation of Islam. Three of her sisters preceded her to the United States, but her own path there came through the boutique in Abu Dhabi (the United Arab Emirates) that Mumtaz established after her husband's death. Louis Farrakhan and his son Leonard, traveling in the Gulf, visited her boutique and were so impressed with her designs that they sponsored her to come and design clothes for members of the Nation, including bow ties for the men. One of the few "born Muslims" as opposed to converts in the Nation, Mumtaz was often consulted about details of Islamic belief and practice, but she could not necessarily provide answers.

Some young Hyderabadi immigrants earning Ph.D.s in business, marketing, and information systems have joined social activist, not religious, movements. On the east coast, prominent examples were Ali Mir and Raza

Mir, brothers active in the New York-based SAMAR (South Asian Magazine for Action and Reflection) who frequently spoke about the Progressive Movement in Urdu poetry at academic meetings (although their degrees and jobs were in business management), and Biju Mathew, also part of the SAMAR editorial collective and chief organizer of NYTWA (New York Taxi Workers Alliance).

Many of the latest Hyderabadi arrivals in the United States were the aging parents of those who came earlier. Retired, some of them took the lead in Urdu-language cultural activities. Hasan Chishti, a founder and joiner of several Urdu associations in Chicago, came with his wife in 1986 following two sons and two daughters.[43] In southern California, a senior academic from Hyderabad, Dr. M. A. Muttalib, and his wife spent more and more time with their sons. The oldest son, Dr. Azhar Muttalib, migrated first and married an American-born Hyderabadi, yet Muttalib senior characterized himself and other parents joining their children as first generation because "we are older, we are the parents." In contrast, some of the young people born in the United States considered themselves first generation, because they were the first to be born in the states and the first to be "really American."

Cosmopolitan elders on the move, Feroze and Laura Khan, joined most of their children in Dallas, Texas, in 1990. Their son Jeffrey Khan went to Dallas in 1973 for higher education and taught at the University of Dallas. He was eventually joined by two sisters and two brothers and their families as well as his parents.[44] Laura was the daughter of Theodore La Touche, noted Anglo-Indian journalist (author of books and a regular column for the *Deccan Chronicle*), and Feroze was from the Afsar ul Mulk family. Feroze became a pilot for Deccan Airways after 1945, where Laura was working as secretary to Keshav Reddy (see the UK chapter), and, as Feroze put it, "India gained freedom in 1947 and I lost mine in 1948." The La Touches were Catholic, so Feroze and Laura had three weddings in 1948: a Valentine's Day registrar wedding, a Catholic church wedding, and a *nikah*—"three weddings but only one wife," he said. Feroze worked with his father-in-law as a sports reporter and *Time/Life* correspondent and Laura worked with USIS until it began closing down in 1969. Laura's American Embassy connections took them to Delhi but they soon moved to the UK, where Laura continued working for the U.S. Embassy and Feroze and the children had greater opportunities.

Feroze and Laura considered themselves to be Hyderabadi first, then British; they had had many British friends among Hyderabad's military people and felt they knew Trafalgar Square as well as the Char Minar and the Lad Bazar in Hyderabad's old city. In Britain, they had gone to Stratford-on-Avon; to Dickens festivals; to theater, cricket, tennis, and horse-racing events. "When Hyderabad ceased to exist as we knew it, the next best place to go was Britain; India is not a place for Muslims or Christians," Feroze said. They had returned to India only once in twenty-three years, preferring to travel widely in Europe. But Britain changed over the years, as new Pakistani and Indian immigrants decreased British respect for South Asians. The Khans visited their son Jeff in Texas, liked it, and moved (Laura was still working, this time at the University of Dallas). Being in America, they said, was like being in a totally new country, nothing was familiar.

Despite their long separation from Hyderabad, the Khans had become members of the local Hyderabad Association and took me along to a potluck meeting when I visited them in 1995. There I met relatives of people I had interviewed in London and Perth. Less pleasantly, I witnessed a young second-generation hijab-wearing woman telling Laura, "My family were Nawabs; who are you to criticize this *tomater ka kut* (tamarind-spiced tomato sauce) as badly prepared?" Laura replied in excellent Urdu that she was a Hyderabadi, and from a family more eminent than the speaker's.

Identities: Competing or Complementary?

Hyderabadis were active in many organizations and activities, most notably Hyderabad associations, "old boys'" associations, Urdu literature associations, and religious and professional associations. In most centers of Hyderabadi residence in the United States, these groups waxed and waned and their memberships overlapped.[45] Nonetheless, Hyderabadis in one place could tell me who the leaders were in other places and that the daughter of one society leader was being married to the son of another.

HYDERABADI ASSOCIATIONS

The Hyderabad associations founded in the United States always invoked the Deccani synthesis of old Hyderabad and their stated focus was on cultural activities. Prince Muffakham Jah in London asked certain people close to him in Chicago, Los Angeles, and San Jose to initiate such associations in the 1980s. At that time, the prince wanted to publish a directory of overseas Hyderabadis for mutual information and assistance. When in Chicago to help start the Chicago Hyderabad Foundation in 1984, the prince called people on the west coast and they set up receptions for him and founded associations; some eighty people came to a reception at the Hilton Hotel hosted by USC in Los Angeles in 1986, Shamim Ibrahim said, and a somewhat smaller number initiated the one in San Jose in 1988. Professor Mir Mohiuddin Ali, in Washington, D.C., told me that when he met the prince in London in 1991, the prince urged him to start an association; he and others did.[46] Other associations sprang up in Houston, north Texas, Iowa, Atlanta, and Florida. Some of those invited the prince to be chief guest at their annual dinners.

In Chicago, Prince Muffakham Jah, Princess Esin, and a handful of elite Chicagoans inaugurated the Hyderabad Foundation on September 19, 1984. Its quarterly publication, *The Letter*, set a high standard in the quality of its writing and production. The first issue stressed that Hyderabad was a symbol of an indigenous "Dakhni" (Deccani) cultural synthesis, and that the new association did not spring from "an emotional outburst of nostalgia" but "an urge to make this country rich by making a distinct and distinguished contribution in the fields of business, industry, trade, commerce and education."[47] The foundation was a registered nonprofit organization and tried to serve both the first and second generations. From 1985 to 1987 the foundation sponsored two youth tours to Hyderabad, and in the 1990s, one board member was a younger person. Chicago's mayor proclaimed a Hyderabad Day in 1987. Projects proposed could not always be undertaken because there was no dues-paying membership, but the most conspicuous and popular activity was the annual fund-raising dinner.[48] The foundation sponsored sports and picnic days, Urdu classes for young people, and workshops on career counseling, marriage counseling, and the welfare of the elderly.

The Chicago Hyderabad Foundation was central to other Hyderabadi associations in the United States. It reported news from other Hyderabadi associations[49] and sent *The Letter* free to anyone who requested it. It initiated invitations to the prince and princess from London and then other associations invited them to annual gala evenings (thus Houston had "the best gathering of Hyderabadis this city has ever seen" in 1987 when the prince visited). It published stories from leaders of other Hyderabadi associations and was the first to announce the prince's 1992 initiative to found a Hyderabad International Club. In contrast to some other associations, it made a conscientious effort to avoid programming focused primarily on Muslim Hyderabadis. Despite this, the association's youth excellence awards, obituaries, and marriage announcements featured almost entirely Muslim names. While *qawwali* programs (Sufi devotional music) were popular earlier, by the late 1990s they had become controversial. The Chicago Hyderabad Foundation's banquet in 1996, when I was a speaker, also featured the Warisi Brothers, a *qawwali* group from Hyderabad. Some Hyderabadi Muslims refused to attend, saying Sufism was not orthodox Islam.

Most Hyderabad associations in the United States could not depend on dues-paying members and simply put out newsletters and held annual dinners, picnics, and Id functions. The annual dinners tried to take reservations ahead of time but always had to deal with last-minute guests. In Hayward, California, in 1996, the northern California association's Hyderabad Durbar evening had gotten reservations from 350 people but 550 showed up for dinner and entertainment. More food was sent for, people were fed from 8:10 to 10:10 P.M., and then the entertainment began. Small Hindu girls danced in front of a "Nawab" seated on a red velvet sofa, followed by skits, jokes, music, and poetry. One man had borrowed a sherwani to attend; another family had flown up from San Diego but had to leave before dinner was served and feared the children would never again attend such a function.[50]

In the Washington, D.C., metropolitan area, the Hyderabad Association of the Greater Washington Area held an annual Sham-e-Deccan (Deccani Evening), featuring Hyderabadi cuisine and recognizing community leaders. Of the 300 to 400 families in the area, chiefly Muslims attended the annual event. However, when Syed Hashim Ali, former vice-chancellor of Osmania University and Aligarh Muslim University, visited in 1995 and recalled that his old Hindu classmate K. D. Mathur was in the area, Mathur told me he was promptly contacted by association leaders and asked to attend and write a poem. In 2000, the association inaugurated a lecture series in memory of the seventh Nizam and Dr. Suraiya Rasheed from USC in Los Angeles was the first speaker. In 2002, Moazzam Siddiqi was master of ceremonies and the speeches "were in the most chaste Deccani Urdu or King's English," whereas the audience displayed "the best of the erstwhile Mughal Muslim Tahzeeb [culture]." There was a pause for Islam's evening prayer, followed by vocal and instrumental music.[51]

The Hyderabad Deccan Association of California (southern California) went through several stages after its 1986 inception. With a mailing list but no membership dues, it held splendid banquets in 1990, 1991, and 1992, the last attended by Prince Muffakham Jah.[52] It was criticized for not attracting enough non-Muslims. One man, from a leading Muslim noble family, said that when he asked a leader why so few Hindus were at a dinner, the man replied, "Well, we asked them." A few Hindus, usually Kayasths, were in fact always present. The main problem came with the Babri Masjid incident in 1992. This created such a feeling of crisis that many association leaders put their energy into a secular coalition instead. Hyderabadi Muslims helped form the Coalition for a Pluralistic and Egalitarian India, and the Hyderabad Deccan Association lapsed.

There were other Hyderabad associations in the United States. The Hyderabad Cultural Association in Houston[53] was started on local initiative in 1979 and the one in north Texas began in 1992; others were started in Florida, Atlanta, and Iowa in the late 1980s. They shared certain characteristics. Journals were published in both Urdu and English and highlighted photos of the Char Minar, Osmania, and other favored historical sites. Short biographies of adult achievers and lists of young graduates (almost all in medicine or law) sometimes appeared, along with advertisements from Hyderabadi local businessmen and professionals. Despite a stated emphasis on the preservation of the Hyderabadi cultural synthesis, programs and participants usually reflected overwhelmingly Muslim events and memberships. This sort of slippage into an increasingly Muslim version of the "cultural synthesis" seldom became an explicit concern for association members, although outsiders commented on it. When asked, Muslim leaders claimed that Hindus had fallen away, attracted by other associations based on language, religion, or caste.

ISLAMIC ACTIVITIES

Religion clearly played an increasing role in the lives of many Muslim Hyderabadi immigrants. Interestingly, the seventh Nizam was the first Hyderabadi to contribute to an Islamic cause in the United States, helping to build Washington's Islamic Center in 1948.[54] At least two Hyderabadis were founding members of the Muslim Student Association in 1963, the campus organization that developed into the Islamic Society of North America, the nation's largest Muslim religious organization.[55] Those who came as pre-1965 immigrants tended to work with Arab Americans to build Muslim organizations; the post-1965 Hyderabadis were more directly involved with other South Asians and could be seen as challenging Arab organizations and leadership.[56] Hyderabadis were prominent leaders in many of the thirty or forty Muslim organizations in the Chicago area. Notably, Hyderabadi Muslim leaders in the United States were nonspecialists in religion—that is, they were professional, Western-educated men and women who had become religiously active (or more active) in the United States. Other Muslim Hyderabadis, of course, remained secular people, proud of the "old Hyderabadi synthesis" and its congruence with American pluralism.

In Chicago, the biochemist Dr. Amir Ali became a leader of the Muslim Community Center (MCC) and later the Institute of Islamic Information and Education (IIIE). He left Pakistan in 1962 to earn a master's degree from the University of Iowa and moved to Chicago in 1967 for a Ph.D. He was stunned on his first visit to the Chicago Shriners Temple for Id prayers, because of the 500 Muslims there, 450 were Hyderabadis! In 1967 he married Mary, an Iowan who converted to Islam and became his helpmate. Although Ali had meant to go back to Pakistan, the Bangladesh

War of 1970–1971 and the election of Zulfiqar Ali Bhutto and Mujibur Rahman who were "traitors, not real Muslims or Pakistanis" made him decide to stay in the United States where he felt a duty to publicize Islam. Dr. Amir Ali joined the MCC in 1972, and the core members were Hyderabadis. After working as a biochemist, starting his own businesses, and working in Saudi Arabia from 1980 to 1985 (where his wife and four children joined him), Ali returned to Chicago and started the IIIE with the goal of educating all Americans about Islam in twenty-five years. Part of his educational program has involved sharp disavowals of the Ahmadiyas or Qadianis (a Muslim sect declared non-Muslim by the government of Pakistan in 1974) and the Nation of Islam, groups well represented in the Chicago area.[57] When Ali's children married, the first consideration was Islam, and in 1990, the older son married a Hyderabadi woman and the older daughter married an American Muslim convert. Although Amir Ali knew Hyderabadi leaders of cultural organizations in Chicago and once attended an Amir Khusro Society function, he considered these diversions from religion.[58] His wife, who wore hijab, worked with him and as registrar of the American Islamic College in Chicago.[59]

Dr. Mohammed M. Farooqui of the Consulting Committee of Indian Muslims (CCIM) in the Chicago area focused his interest less on Islam than on Muslims.[60] Also a biochemist, Dr. Farooqui came to the United States in 1967 to Akron, Ohio, to earn his Ph.D. and moved to Chicago in 1969. He was also active in Aligarh "old boy" activities and Urdu poetry associations. Although the family had only one uncle's daughter in Pakistan and Farooqui led Indian Muslim organizations in the United States, he published his Urdu fiction and poetry in Pakistan, because Urdu was not flourishing in India and his work dealt with topics like Kashmir and communal riots.

Farooqui's four children grew up in Chicago, and his wife, Bilquees, was a high school graduate in India and had been in purdah there before her engagement at thirteen and marriage at seventeen. In the United States, she worked in a laboratory for thirteen years and liked it but left when her mother came from India and her husband said, "Money isn't everything; be with your mother." The Farooquis' older son attended medical school in Hyderabad and married his father's sister's daughter there when he finished the course (Farooqui and his wife were also first cousins).[61] The Farooquis' other son, Zubair, and one daughter flew over as a surprise to attend this traditional five-day wedding in Hyderabad. There were 1,200 guests. Zubair Farooqui described his experience as "weird." Because he looked so American, a taxi driver tried to cheat him and was surprised when he spoke Urdu. He took the advice of his many cousins (about thirty, whom he met for the first time and found "overwhelming") and put on Indian dress and felt more comfortable. When he saw his brother for the first time in three years, Zubair was horrified and told him to shave off his full beard as "friends here would be taken aback; he looked like a terrorist" when they saw his wedding photos in the United States. The brother did shave, appearing bearded in the first day wedding photos and beardless after that.

Local contexts were important determinants of immigrant practices and attitudes, with nearby Islamic centers or mosques encouraging more orthodox practices and attracting or sometimes discouraging Islamic religiosity. Of the many women running preschools and schools, some catered to the general population and some to Muslims. Some interviewees debated issues of culture and religion: was the hijab or headscarf religiously mandated or a cultural custom? Was an *ameen* ceremony commemorating a child's first reading of the Quran a way of retaining one's culture or emphasizing religiosity? Did the Nizam's state favor culture over religion? Did other Muslims, particularly Arabs, welcome or challenge South Asian Islamic beliefs and practices? Most of these questions concerned South Asian Muslims in general, not just Hyderabadis, but they came sharply into focus when Indian and Pakistani Hyderabadis met, with the verdict usually being that Pakistani Hyderabadis were less religious than those from India.

I interviewed no Hyderabadi *imams* in the course of my research, only one Sufi *pir* from Karachi whom I met at a Chicago Hyderabad Foundation banquet. But a Hyderabadi *halal* (the Islamic equivalent of kosher) grocer and butcher was central to the Los Angeles Islamic and Hyderabadi communities. When Professor Syed Sirajuddin from Hyderabad came to Los Angeles, we went to Mecca Meats (a *halal* grocery and restaurant) to pick up some *bagara baigan*. The Pakistani Hyderabadi owner, Abdus Sattar, and his wife chatted with Sirajuddin, who was astounded to recognize her as the daughter of a well-known scholar in Hyderabad who had gone to Pakistan. Now the scholar's daughter was in Los Angeles, cooking food and selling meat to customers. The husband, blood-spattered from butchering chickens, had attended All Saints High School in Hyderabad before going to Pakistan. This was clearly downward mobility, yet the couple was doing well: Mecca Meats was across from the Islamic Center of southern California and Abdus Sattar catered most Hyderabadi functions in the 1990s.

A major debate centered on the roles of Arabic, Urdu, and English when it came to the transmission of Islam. Could Islam be transmitted and practiced in English? Yes, said some; the reality was that people had a new American identity and must get rid of non-English languages. Another view was that all Muslims should turn to Arabic for religious purposes, and a third view was that all languages must be continued, including Urdu and others in which Islam was taught in the homelands. That third view was difficult to implement, as Urdu language classes were needed for the second generation. Yet the conviction that Islam was "not a regional culture" sustained most people in their faith that the religion could be adequately transmitted in English.

Religious activities and ceremonies showed the mix of culture and religion and the changing practices in the United States. Usama Khalidi and his family[62] took me along to the Reston Community Center in Virginia, outside Washington, D.C., for a potluck dinner, an Id celebration. Arabs, Pakistanis, Indians, and African American Muslims all crowded together while leaders of the Islamic Center tried to get "the brothers and sisters" to sit on separate sides of the big room; more people, however, eschewed gender segregation and sat family style. Then a leader tried to get brothers to help the sisters in the kitchen, but it was mainly women who set out the ethnic potluck dishes on separate women's and men's tables and fifty takeout pizzas on a separate children's table.

Weddings highlighted changing religious and social practices. The invitation to one Hyderabadi Muslim wedding in Los Angeles stated the *nikah* ceremony would be promptly at 6 P.M., and when I arrived (the first guest to do so) at 7 P.M., I was shown to a designated "ladies' section" of the hotel hall, a boxed-in area at the left rear. More ladies arrived and immediately redefined the ladies' section as the very front row, seating themselves (and reseating me) just left of the center stage. Following the *nikah* at 9 P.M., we were ushered into the dining room for the wedding dinner. Mexican waiters had been instructed to enforce separate seating for men and women. But the first party in (led by an American-born daughter-in-law with me in tow) insisted on taking a center table and sitting all together, family style, and many families followed this example. At this wedding, the bride wore traditional Hyderabadi attire and the groom wore a sherwani, but there were no flower garlands and the bride's brother wore a tuxedo with a beautiful red cummerbund. At another wedding, that of a Hyderabadi woman with an American groom who converted to Islam, the groom wore a sherwani and his female relatives wore Hyderabadi dress brought for them from Hyderabad. The *imam* who conducted the latter ceremony translated and explained the proceedings in English to the audience.[63]

URDU LITERARY ACTIVITIES

"There are many Hyderabadis in Chicago and because they come from the Nizam's independent kingdom, they have had the experience of ruling, so they do more than their share," several people stated. Hyderabadis were indeed conspicuous among those engaged in Urdu literary activities everywhere. Voluntary associations promoting Urdu across the United States included the Urdu Markaz International (Urdu Center), Bazm-i-Urdu (Urdu Society), the Pakistani American Arts Council, and the Federation of Indian Muslims in North America. Some associations were branches of national or international ones, but local officers showed high levels of commitment, and women were prominent among them.[64] These Urdu associations could be exclusively Pakistani or Indian, but more often the memberships, poets, and audiences bridged political boundaries back in South Asia. There was overlap with other activities, and the local contexts and patterns of activity varied across the country. In Chicago, Hyderabadis active in the Bazm-i-Urdu and the Bazm-i-Deccan earnestly believed that Urdu was vital to the survival of Hyderabadi culture, and they mentioned the Amir Khusro Society, the Bahadur Yar Jung International Research organization, the Coordinating Committee on Indian Muslims, and Urdu Markaz as complementary, not competing, organizations. Urdu literary activities seemed to be an avenue for social mobility for women and for men not quite successful in the United States or seeking to establish themselves by touring and performing. There were linkages nationally and also internationally among poets and literary societies.

Members of the first generation of Hyderabadi immigrants did not all attend *mushairas* and few were poets, but they were generally reluctant to give up Urdu. Zulfiqar Ali Khan felt so discomfited being addressed, in English, as "You," that he requested his son to speak in Urdu and use the polite "ap," as "you" seemed like the impolite, less respectful "tum." Parents did want their children to retain proficiency in Urdu, and many told me that their children could both speak and read Urdu but were not interested in attending *mushairas*. When I asked the children about this, they usually said they could not read the language and found spoken poetry difficult.

WOMEN'S ACTIVITIES

The leadership of the preceding activities was largely male and the goals were directed toward a vanished nation, a religion based abroad, or a homeland language. Although some Hyderabadi women were conspicuously active in those activities, more typically women's activities focused on their location in the United States and the problems caused by being there, such as career and marital problems, the welfare of older family members, and the care and education of children. Caring for parents, in the homelands or in America, concerned many. Aging parents were brought to the United States, either coming permanently or simply visiting often enough to maintain their eligibility for citizenship and then to sponsor others. In Chicago, professional women worked with older Hyderabadis, getting them together to meet and trade phone numbers and explaining the Social Security and medical insurance systems. Sometimes the younger people brought their parents to the Hyderabad Foundation functions, but with rising admittance fees, the old parents might no longer be automatically included in the evening gatherings.

Women from Hyderabad often worked in the United States, sometimes giving up their jobs when an aging parent was brought from India or Pakistan and needed attention, but just as often pressing the parent into service as babysitter, message-taker, or cook. Some Hyderabadi women were divorced and had independent careers in the United States but still felt a special responsibility to a parent remaining in India or Pakistan. Such women saved their money for vacations in the homeland with the parent. For one successful career woman in Chicago, going home meant additional problems as her husband had verbally divorced her in Pakistan but had not registered his action, so although she lived as a divorcee in the United States, when she returned to Pakistan she was considered still married.

As we have seen, Hyderabadi women often successfully combined migration with marriage and education, or combined marriage, childbearing, and careers once in the United States. With family support, many did very well, achieving a wide range of career goals. Professional women were active beyond Hyderabadi, Islamic, and Urdu-promoting activities. For example, Mrs. Khatija Hashmy, the architect in Chicago whose husband was a pre-1965 immigrant, was active in professional women's groups, including the Indian Club of Women and the South Asian Women's Association. Bilquees Farooqui, a more traditional, less-educated Hyderabadi Muslim woman who came as the wife of a post-1965 immigrant, also reported being a member of several women's groups: a neighborhood mothers' group, mosque-based groups, and auxiliary groups for women. For these groups, the most popular topic of conversation was what to do about the young people's cultural orientations and marriages.

New Frontiers

The Hyderabadis who came earliest to the United States saw themselves as venturing beyond familiar frontiers, and their children often undertook careers and marriages beyond familiar frontiers as well. The post-1965 Hyderabadi immigrants, far more numerous, represented a narrower range of careers and featured more endogamous marriages with respect to religion and community, so their children experienced more constraints although they were growing up in a context that encouraged boundary-breaking in many respects. As this newer, second generation of young Hyderabadis

came of age in the 1990s and the early twenty-first century, the first generation attempted to reach out to the homeland and its culture for the sake
of their children.

SECOND-GENERATION CAREERS AND MARRIAGES

The young people of Hyderabadi background, according to Suraya
Hasan, an employment counselor in Chicago, were expected to be as their
parents wanted them, "not changing." But the children were away from
home eight hours a day, leading two lives, in effect. Suraya herself had
come to the United States from Pakistan as a student for a two-year educational degree, and everyone considered her unchanged upon return. She
had changed, however, although no one asked questions about her life in
the United States, just as people never asked questions of their own children about their social lives or about boyfriends or girlfriends. "They are
our children, they won't change," was the attitude. But they did change,
although the evidence was clearer for the children of the earlier immigrants (many children of the later immigrants were still making marriage
and career decisions). The children of the early immigrants, like their parents, have entered a wide range of professions and married a diverse set of
spouses, whereas both the careers and marriages of the second generation
of the post-1965 Hyderabadi immigrants seemed, so far, more narrowly
bounded.

One son of a post-1965 immigrant, whom I've given the pseudonym
Mahdi, gave striking testimony about the careers and marriages expected
of his generation. Attempting to survey Hyderabadis in the United States,
I sent out packets of surveys. The surveys, developed with a senior Hyderabadi academic, were different for men, women, and youngsters, and the
packets were given to the head of the household, the father. This young
man did not return the survey for two years, delaying because his father
wanted to collect it from him and send it back. Mahdi waited until he went
away to school to fill it out and sent it back himself. "Personally, I think
Hyderabadis are unbelievable," he wrote, "close-minded people who have
and will continue to have a hard time adjusting to life here. I have many
thoughts on this matter that I cannot do justice to on this paper. Call me
for additional comments." When I called, Mahdi said he thought of himself as a Pakistani American or Muslim American, not a Hyderabadi (his
father had gone to Pakistan after 1948). Moving to the United States, his
father thought assimilation would be slow and take several generations,
but Mahdi was sure it would be rapid. Hyderabadis had two qualities, he
stated: they valued education and they valued the family. Yet their focus
was narrow: of his sixteen cousins on his mother's side, thirteen were going

into medicine. He was one of the three who was not, as he was in law school (the other two were young women married to doctors). Mahdi felt this pattern was insane, yet his own sister was in medical school and he himself was ready to marry a doctor to make his mother happy (having dated despite his parents' prohibition of it, he felt he could handle an arranged marriage). Endogamy with respect to religion and place of origin was taken for granted and now extended to occupation, he said. Mahdi felt he was deviating from the norm by going into law, yet this seemed to be the second most popular choice for a young Hyderabadi. The Hyderabad association newsletters contained many references to the educational achievements and ambitions of the young people, and the preferred occupations were medicine and law, followed by engineering and computer science. The careers of the children of pre-1965 immigrants also reflected these preferences but to a far lesser extent. Given the hefty percentage of Hyderabadi doctors among the post-1965 foreign-born doctors and their success in the United States, the pattern was hardly surprising.

Marriages for the children of the post-1965 immigrants continued to be more or less arranged, with a preference for spouses who would settle in the United States if not there already. Parents were concerned about "intellectual compatibility," and young people often met each other before agreeing to marry. There were strongly enforced age preferences for marriage, at least for young women, and deviation on the part of one sibling endangered the marriages of others. Parents willing to let their children make choices became impatient when no choice was made by "the age to marry," and they might then step in. But they acknowledged that they did not have the hold on their children that their parents had on them; they could not demand obedience.

While young people of Hyderabadi background were generally going along with arranged marriages and many immigrant parents arranged transnational marriages with other Hyderabadis, the evidence was mounting that arranged marriages entailed risks. Young people brought up in different countries, even if they were cousins, turned out to have very different expectations about marriage, sex roles, and many other things; divorce had become not only a distinct possibility but an option increasingly exercised. Many arranged marriages among Hyderabadi youth did not work out, as Habeeb Ghatala's friend, a producer of wedding videos in Chicago, has learned: he waits to edit them, because a newly married couple might decide within two to three weeks to call off the marriage.

As for marriages, the "general Muslim point of view" was that first preference was for a Hyderabadi Muslim, and second preference was for any

Muslim from the United States, perhaps a white convert or an Arab. The India-Pakistan rift among Hyderabadis was reflected in opinions about marriage-making. Many Hyderabadis from India with close relatives in Pakistan pronounced the cultures too different for successful marriages. "The vision of a plural, composite society has gone in Pakistan, and Pakistani Hyderabadis are more assertive, very different now," people said, and "the Pakistanis judge Hyderabad harshly when visiting it now; they look at it with Western eyes; they see economic deprivation first and may not look further." Other people argued that "the family is more important than the country" and continued to arrange marriages across the India-Pakistan boundary.

But everyone agreed that, generally, bringing young men from Hyderabad was not good. Mirza Ahmed Baig and other members of the northern California Hyderabad association knew of three grooms recently brought from Hyderabad. "All three marriages ended in divorce, in two cases with the brides' families even going after the boys' green cards in court. The girls in the United States expect too much, the boys from Hyderabad are unused to such demands and unprepared for life here. Also, Hyderabadi boys have different ideals of beauty. Divorce is rising and remarriages are occurring more often." One could bring girls from Hyderabad and even send a daughter there, they said, although the more educated "the children" were the less this second option appealed. Most Hyderabadis were not marrying their children back into India or Pakistan. As Asif Ali Hashmy said, "dislocating myself was enough; no need to dislocate them [the children]. Their life style is from here now."

Some young Hyderabadi women in the United States made love marriages, and more often these young women were Hindus, not Muslims. Young men of Hyderabadi background, including young Muslims, did marry outside their own communities.[65] But young women of Hyderabadi Muslim background were under strong constraints. Muslim women were prohibited from marrying non-Muslims (Muslim men may marry Christians and Jews), so ideally a potential husband should convert to Islam. A few marriages of Hyderabadi Muslim young women to non-Muslim men took place in the United States. Usually the men converted to Islam, but sometimes these marriages were kept secret from the parents.[66]

TAKING THE DIASPORA HOME

Hyderabadis in the United States who were doing well wanted to use their resources to stay connected to Hyderabad and assist the homeland. They were concerned about their children's knowledge of Hyderabadi culture and about certain constituencies back in Hyderabad. Some of these efforts to stay connected were pursued through Hyderabad associations and others through professional or religious associations.

In the 1980s, with Hyderabad associations springing up abroad and in Hyderabad, the Chicago Hyderabad Foundation thought of sending the children growing up overseas on an organized trip to Hyderabad. The local host would be the Hyderabad Deccan Society, presided over by Bilkiz Alladin, chairwoman and writer of plays and other works about Hyderabad,[67] and Prince Muffakham Jah, patron of many overseas associations. The plan to take young Hyderabadis "home" took shape in 1986 and again in 1987, when groups of Chicago Hyderabadi children went over, some ten to twelve young people aged fourteen to eighteen who had never been to Hyderabad. They stayed in their own relatives' homes, but there were problems. The young visitors proved reluctant to venture far: they would not go to Gulbarga or to Ajanta and Ellora, just to the local Golconda Fort and the Nizam's old palaces. "One girl saw bugs in everything, and sure enough, at the final banquet there was an ant in her kebab." They would not sit on the floor at the prince's residence, so their older hosts and hostesses had to do that, a reversal of the usual hierarchy. The youngsters were also notably less polite to their elders than children raised in Hyderabad. A Hyderabadi youth, when asked how he had liked the visitors he had hosted, said, "Auntie, you want the truth? They treated us like dirt." One Hyderabad resident, remembering this visit, said, "Ah, yes, when Muffakham Jah wanted to bring the children back, to be here and learn Hyderabadi culture, and my own relatives came along. But there were no proper arrangements, and they liked Delhi and Bangalore much better, better than Hyderabad." Some who were involved with the trips hoped for better results from young visitors from the UK and others wanted reciprocal trips, taking Hyderabadi young people or Hyderabadi cultural shows abroad. No more organized trips have taken place.

Another venture was the International Hyderabad Association initiated by Prince Muffakham Jah in the early 1990s. The prince spoke in Los Angeles in 1992 at the Hyderabad association dinner, invoking familiar themes and urging adoption of this ambitious project. An eloquent speaker in both Urdu and English, he urged flexibility to keep Hyderabadi culture alive. "We of the older generation feel the language is the backbone of the culture," he said, "but the younger ones may let the language go and keep the food."[68] Then he described the proposed International Hyderabad Club, to be based in Hyderabad. Fifty percent or more of the members would be overseas Hyderabadis, who, when they visited the city needed facilities that matched those in the West. Because local relatives were not in their former spacious homes, visitors could stay at the club, where the food would be safe and varied ("multicuisine"). Recreation like tennis and swimming would be available, and the staff would run errands (to the Medina Building in the old city for *biryani* and *mirch ka salan*, to *pan* shops for *pan*, to sweets shops for sweets). Receptions for weddings or family reunions could be held at the club, and there would be a resource center with a computerized database (for which the Hyderabad Association of Northern California had offered to take responsibility). Membership applications were being received, with a one-time fee for joining and an annual subscription. A Hyderabadi, for membership purposes, was defined as a person born within the boundaries of the old Hyderabad state or a descendant or spouse of such a person. The prince urged people to apply at once because a house and garden had been found that would be perfect and he wanted to go ahead with the project. They had confused the owner, he said, by offering the full price, so he was negotiating for more; there would be no false economies in this venture, like the Hyderabadi who went on his honeymoon alone. "Don't be left behind on this honeymoon," the prince said. But the venture never got off the ground.

Efforts to assist poor Muslims in Hyderabad city and the former Hyderabad districts were mounted by U.S.-based Hyderabadis. The Coordinating Committee of Indian Muslims raised money for Muslim students and targeted some in districts formerly in the Nizam's dominions but now part of Karnataka and Maharashtra. The United Economic Forum, based in Hyderabad but reaching out especially to diasporic Muslims in the U.S., raised money for Muslim projects in Hyderabad city and for rural Muslim primary schools, adult education centers, and craft centers in Andhra Pradesh.[69] The American Federation of Muslims from India and other groups mounted similar efforts sporadically, with Hyderabadis being among the beneficiaries of education and health projects aimed at India's Muslims.

The most successful outreach was probably that mounted by doctors from Hyderabad. As Dr. Madhu Mohan recounted, a group of Osmania graduates, primarily medical professionals, wanted to make a difference back home and decided to "export the American system" by establishing a hospital and medical research facility in Hyderabad. In 1983, SHARE secured $250,000 in donations and started trying to work with the Andhra Pradesh government. Frustrated by government instability and red tape, when an Indian Administrative Service official advised them to "just go private," they did. They bought 200 acres outside of Secunderabad and started Mediciti, backed by three entities, the original SHARE, SHARE Medical Care, and the Osmania Graduates Association.[70] The modern hospital would be staffed with doctors from India but supervised by the three U.S.-based organizations, and doctors from the United States would rotate in and out. The U.S. doctors would work there by choice, the American way, and although 70 percent of the patients would pay for treatment, 30 percent would be treated free. An office was operating in Secunderabad with thirty staff in 1992 and the hospital, designed by a Boston firm, opened in December of 1992. Dr. Mohan mentioned other former Osmania classmates, Dr. Masud Faruqi in Middlesex, UK, and Dr. Hemchander in Sydney, Australia, anticipating a transnational support base for Mediciti.

Hyderabadi immigrants to the United States fell into three main groups by timing. Members of the pre-1965 group generally saw themselves as pioneers, drawn to a new country by personal connections or a sense of adventure. They pursued an array of livelihoods and many married non-Hyderabadi spouses. The immediate post-1965 immigrants from Hyderabad were typically professional people, primarily doctors, moving as nuclear families and eventually staying and becoming citizens. Their advent sparked the initiation of collective activities in which Hyderabadis were leaders or major participants. Hyderabad associations arose in several cities, with some connections to those in Canada and the UK. Urdu literary associations claimed international leadership by awarding prizes to diasporic writers of Urdu in Europe and America. Religious activities became increasingly important to some Muslims, linking them to American Muslim organizations and uplift efforts in India. Doctors from Hyderabad developed Mediciti, a modern hospital in Hyderabad. The later post-1965 immigrants included not only students and professionals from increasingly diverse backgrounds but also older parents who reinforced interest in cultural and religious activities. The motives for immigration shifted from personal to professional to extended family unification. At the same time, the growth of the second generation highlighted generational differences and the difficulties of transmitting Hyderabadi culture in the new setting.

CHAPTER 8

Canada: Mixing In

COLONEL M. ASMATULLAH, a retired military man brought by his son in 1988, described the generations of Hyderabadis in Canada as he saw them.

> The first generation, the very few older people, are still wearing the sherwani and perhaps the *rumi topi* still, but they are without any place to go, and there are so few of them; they only dream and go to the mosque. Members of the second generation, those who actually came first and as young people, have discarded the old culture, changed their clothes and ways. When they visit Hyderabad, they only feel comfortable in the homes of relatives but not outside, to them Hyderabadi culture is just wearing a *salvar kamiz* and speaking Urdu. They don't really know the old culture and their friends are all in Canada. Then the third generation, the youngsters brought up in Canada, they know only that Hyderabad was their parents' place. They may never have gone there themselves or gone very young, or sometimes their parents make them dress in Hyderabadi style or go to a prayer meeting. The fourth generation will be lost, like the West Indians in Canada. They will be Canadians but they will still be thought of as "ethnics," not totally accepted; color counts a lot, in Canada.

Referring to himself and others like himself as the first generation and to the initial migrants as the second generation, Asmatullah saw the generations raised in Canada as new kinds of persons, persons formed by the Canadian context. Important aspects of this context were the high proportion of other immigrants, especially Muslims, and the state's multicultural policies.

Those Hyderabadis who pioneered in Canada were often students, both men and women, and their numbers were small. After Canada changed its immigration rules in 1962 and its relative openness and flexibility became apparent, it became an increasingly common destination for Hyderabadis from Hyderabad, Pakistan, and the Middle East, many of them twice- or thrice-migrants.

Canada's blustery winter weather was new to Hyderabadi immigrants, but the summers were temperate. Hyderabadis were scattered across the country's vast expanse (it is the second largest country in the world, after Russia). A few lived in the mountains in the west or on the plains and more plains in the center, but most clustered in the lowlands in the east. The Toronto region, with its high proportions of immigrants from many backgrounds, drew the most, but Hyderabadis were outnumbered there by incoming Chinese, Jamaicans, and even Somalis. The impressive high-rise city center employed many of the immigrants and the suburbs stretching for miles around the city housed them. In terms of the Hyderabadi diaspora, Toronto and Chicago were rivals. Each claimed to have the most Hyderabadis in North America and, therefore, to be second only to London as an overseas center.

Students who came to study managed to become Canadian citizens and brought their siblings and parents; economic migrants also became citizens and brought their siblings and parents. The numbers continued to rise, although recessions in 1975 and 1981 sent some Hyderabadis back to India and Pakistan or on to other diasporic sites. In the 1990s, migration to Canada was a popular option. Immigration consultancy firms advertised in India and abroad, even in California, citing their successful services to clients.

Anxious parents of the early migrants tried to ensure their return to Hyderabad by arranging marriages for them, yet many parents ended up following their children to Canada. A very few students married Canadians, but even those whose spouses were Hyderabadis found that the Canadian cultural environment easily permitted separation and divorce. Certainly among the younger generation, with its diverse friendship networks, non-Hyderabadi spouses and divorces could be found, along with proud records of educational and career achievements.

Students, Professionals, Workers

THE EARLY BIRDS

Hyderabadis came to Canada before the 1970s as students and for career opportunities. One young man, Kamran Mirza, was descended from Maharajah Kishen Pershad, Hyderabad's famous Hindu prime minister of the early twentieth century, through one of his Muslim wives. Mirza came to McDonald College to study civil engineering in 1957, then switched to agricultural engineering and took a master's degree at Guelph University. Why Canada? Kamran's father, a civil aviator in Delhi, had an aviator Sikh friend who had migrated to Canada, and Kamran stayed with the Sikh family when he came as a student. Also, a cousin had visited Canada when he was twelve with the Boy Scouts and liked it. Kamran was married in 1963 by proxy (via telephone) to his first cousin Rashida in Karachi, daughter of his father's sister.[1]

Rashida called her life in Canada an adventure and Canadians very friendly. She had met Kamram briefly when he stopped in Karachi on his way to Canada but did not really know him before journeying alone to become the second Hyderabadi at Guelph (her husband was the first). Rashida came with a bachelor of science in home economics, and after having two children—a daughter born in the United States while Kamran earned his Ph.D. in soil mechanics at the University of Illinois and a son born in Pakistan—she earned a Canadian elementary school teaching certificate and began teaching.

Rashida Mirza felt she had been a Hyderabadi when she left Karachi, but she has become far more interested in her Urdu language heritage. She was one of five writers producing an Urdu text as part of Canada's elementary school "heritage language" project. The state-sponsored text focused on Canada, not India or Pakistan, with short stories, poems, pictures, and a teacher's manual in English. Rashida felt the text was very important, as it would be used in evening or Saturday schools, in challenging "off-hour" courses like the ones she has taught.

Rashida knew immigrant scholars, writers, and enthusiasts who led Urdu and Islamic societies in Toronto and Montreal but was not herself involved in any societies. She did volunteer as a teacher in an Islamic school, explaining, "In Pakistan, religion is there; here, we have to make it happen." She and her mother, the latter now a sponsored immigrant after three or four earlier visits, were engaged in local debates about Islam. The two women argued that Indo-Muslim culture was just as authentically Muslim as Arab culture or Iranian culture, insisting strongly that contemporary Saudi Arabia, with its royalty, was not "the original or the appropriate model for Islam."

Rashida said that her son and daughter felt closer to Pakistani culture than to Hyderabadi culture, that Pakistani Hyderabadis were exposed to other cultures such as Punjabi and Sindhi while "pure Hyderabadis" tried to stick together. She also said that her daughter, born in the United States, sometimes felt American. The daughter was a marketing assistant in a big company, and her parents had sought a husband from Hyderabad for her and provided visa, house, car, and schooling for him. The Mirzas had felt that they had to turn to Hyderabad for their daughter's spouse; they had migrated so early that there were only fourteen or fifteen other Hyderabadi families in their cohort and few potential spouses for their children. Their son was in Malaysia on his job with the ministry of resources of

British Columbia, a job he had secured in competition with candidates from all over Canada.

Rashida had no regrets about coming to Canada. Life had its ups and downs, she said, and divorce was everywhere anyway (their daughter was single again). Her friends were from all over India (the Punjab, Delhi, Hyderabad, Aligarh, Bombay) and from Canada; her children's friends were Chinese, Jewish, Greek, Anglo-Canadian, South Asian, Indonesian, and Estonian. Her daughter's wedding photos included the Sikh couple with whom Kamran had stayed when a student, an American woman from Illinois where the daughter was born, and many of the daughter's Canadian friends, including her best—Estonian—girlfriend and her parents.

Others who came in the 1960s were young men in search of better careers. Haroon Siddiqui ended up at Canada's largest national daily newspaper, *The Toronto Star*, retiring as editor of its editorial page.[2] Haroon's father had gone to Hyderabad from North India, where he "became a Hyderabadi." Haroon graduated from Nizam College, earned a journalism degree at Osmania in 1963, and then worked in Bombay as a reporter. He covered the Canadian High Commission, and the commissioner told him, "Go to Canada, young man." He obtained his immigration visa in 1965 and used it in 1967 because "that was an exciting time in Canada, Expo 1967, and not a good time for Muslims in India."[3]

Despite his journalistic work in Bombay, people told Siddiqui he needed Canadian experience, and for a short time he sold men's clothing at a Toronto department store. Meeting Canadians at the grassroots level and interacting with them as a salesman was good, he said, and he linked it back to Hyderabad, where people had come to his home to sell things; one had to learn how to hustle in life. Siddiqui moved to *The Brandon Sun* in Manitoba, where his then-wife, Shaila, had been admitted to college,[4] and became managing editor in ten years. Wooed by both the *Globe and Mail* and *The Toronto Star*, he picked the *Star* and moved to Toronto in 1978. He rose steadily, being the "first South Asian," "first Muslim," and "first visible minority" to do many things. He was awarded the Order of Ontario in early 2001 and the Order of Canada in late 2001, the highest civilian honors of the province and the nation, for his advocacy of diversity in the media and his stance against the stereotyping of minorities. He, along with Prince Muffakham Jah from London, helped start a Hyderabad Foundation in Toronto in the 1980s.[5]

Another early arrival was a Hindu, Desh Bandhu, who left India in 1962 and took jobs in the paper industry in Germany, Switzerland, and Sweden before coming to Canada in 1965. His father had been from Dera Ghazi Khan (now in Pakistan), and participation in a Hindi/Urdu mushaira in

Aurangabad[6] led him to a professorship of Hindi and Sanskrit in Hyderabad. A pioneer in the Hindi and Arya Samaj movements, the professor worked to keep Urdu and Hindi together in "the upheaval of the freedom struggle." Desh grew up in a new city Hindu neighborhood, Hardikar Bagh, attended All Saints High School (his sister was in Rosary Convent), and had no contacts with Muslims. "They were more well-to-do, they played cards, were fun-loving, and had no goals," he said, "I only came to know and love Hyderabadi culture in Toronto."

Desh went home from Europe in 1964 to marry a bride from a Hindi-speaking background, a marriage arranged through his father the professor's scholarly contacts. She stayed in Hyderabad, completed a master of arts degree, and joined him in Toronto in 1967. Before his wife's arrival Desh had been living with two Hyderabadi Muslims who introduced him to Hyderabadi food, Urdu poetry, and "all of Hyderabadi culture." He briefly sold men's clothing at the same department store where Siddiqui had worked and then became an insurance agent with the Allstate insurance company, only to leave that and build his own successful business with a clientele of Hyderabadi Muslims. "I moved with Hyderabadi people, 99 percent Muslims, the *ghazals*, the meat, the sweets, I learned it all," he said.

Moving in the same circles was an Urdu poetess from Karachi, a Hyderabadi Muslim who had been taken to Pakistan at the age of three. Zehra did full-time staff work at a local college, and she, like Desh, had had an arranged marriage and had two sons. In Canada, Zehra had come to appreciate Indian and Hindu culture, taking an interest in temples, the Holi festival, and wearing the *bindi* (red dot on the forehead). She and Desh became friends, often attended the same *mushairas*, and gradually fell in love. As a younger relative of Zehra's observed to me later in Hyderabad, "Being in Canada, they thought they could do that, divorce and remarry; they would never have tried it here." They did divorce and remarry each other and have suffered heavy penalties; Muslim women are not supposed to marry non-Muslim men.[7] Zehra, a Shi'a Muslim, had always enjoyed *majlises* (congregational mourning sessions) during Muharram but was no longer welcome at them. Desh lost his clients and his business and had to start over again, building on a different client base.[8]

Older men in search of better careers also migrated to Canada in the 1960s. I met Ather Hussein only because someone urged him to overlook the form letter I had sent in advance. He had thrown away my photocopied "Dear Hyderabadi" letter because "I am a Canadian now, no longer a mulki or an Indian, and also because it was not addressed to me by name—Hyderabadis are formal people; you did not do it right." From a distinguished family, he had migrated to Canada at the age of fifty. Hussein was a Sufi, "really just a Muslim by accident of birth; there were so many fine Hindus in Hyderabad, and they could stay, while we had to get out." After 1948 no one would employ him, he said; "no one would give me a damn thing." Just before 1948, the Nizam had proposed sending him as agent general to Canada, but then Hyderabad was incorporated into India. The idea, however, had stuck in Ather Hussein's mind, and he migrated to Canada in 1966. Like Siddiqui and Bandhu, he tried department store work, but he could not fold shirts, a task done for him at home, and eventually he became projects manager for Scarborough College, University of Toronto, until 1981. He had come alone, but his twenty-one-year-old son followed to attend college and settled down to work for the Bank of Montreal. Hussein's two daughters and their husbands were also nearby, each couple with its own house. Hussein's wife had also migrated but was ill and stayed with a daughter.[9]

Ather Hussein felt out of touch with Hyderabad: "Once out of Hyderabad, one can be anywhere." He felt that "Canadians also move and do not keep in touch; only the British keep in touch, only the British know the value of writing letters." He remembered Aziz Ahmad, a distinguished Hyderabadi scholar who had been professor of English at McGill University.[10] But Canada was changing, he lamented, accepting too many new immigrants from China and Jamaica, "people who do not uphold the nation's former standards of honesty and public order."

LATER ARRIVALS

Canada's increasing numbers of immigrants in the 1970s included more Hyderabadis, many of them sponsored by relatives already settled in the country. Nawab Asif Alikhan, like Ather Hussein a member of Hyderabad's former nobility, was, unlike Ather, still very much in touch with Hyderabad although his family was no longer based there. Author of recent coffee table books on Hyderabad and friend of *Siyasat*'s editor Abid Ali Khan, he had migrated in 1972.[11]

> I'm the oldest of eight siblings, and all but I were sent to the United States or Canada for education; all eight of us are now settled in Toronto. I have sixty-one first cousins, and fifty-three are in Canada and the United States; only seven or eight are in Hyderabad, in Mushirabad. My grandfather's house, built in 1892, is still there, administered by lawyers and lived in by old servants. . . . Of course I have regrets; it was my beloved country, and any vacation there is, I go to Hyderabad. . . . But tomorrow I'll fly off for a wedding, the *nikah* is in Winnipeg and the *valima* in Chicago.

In Toronto, Alikhan was an insurance agent and broker; in Hyderabad, he had been a personal assistant to high-ranking Andhra Pradesh and government of India officials (including Narasimha Rao, who became prime minister of India, and Nilam Sanjiva Reddy, who became governor of Andhra Pradesh). He kept track of his old friends and classmates and informed me that in Springfield, Ohio, alone, there were nine doctors from Hyderabad.[12]

Alikhan loved old Hyderabad, fondly remembering Mukarram Jah's coronation and the colorful Maiseram (Irregular) Regiment headed by Brigadier Taufiq, but he also had a critical view of it. Like others, he had been involved in court cases over ancestral property. One case lasted for twenty years, but when he finally won it and went back to claim his land, he found he could not do it.

> The fellow shook my hand and said, "All this land, my grandfather and father paid you so much all these years, what have you done to deserve it? I won't turn it over." I shook his hand and said, "You're right, never mind, keep it." I didn't want to get shot trying to possess it. Yes, that *jagirdar* business was bogus. Now, here, we're rewarded for the things we're doing; the *jagirdars* just sat and ate. My grandfather was there; then my father, with a tenth-grade education, was made collector of customs and later commissioner of customs; and my wife's sister's husband, with only a fourth grade education, was made a commissioner of something. . . . [A]t the funerals of their fathers, unqualified sons of good family were given positions by the Nizam.

Asif Alikhan's daughter Husna contrasted her generation to her father's. She had twenty-five first cousins in Mississauga and many second cousins in Toronto: "Our roots are here." Of her first cousins, three men had taken brides from Hyderabad and one's bride had come from Canada, a young woman of mixed Hyderabadi and Madrasi heritage. Husna's sister had married a second cousin, her brother a first cousin; her own marriage had been to a Hyderabadi Canadian. She and others of her generation understood but did not speak Urdu; she knew Arabic and wanted to learn Urdu because she planned to be an immigration lawyer.

Farooq Mirza, first in his family to migrate to Canada in 1974, had been preceded by his wife's sister. She had gone to Ottawa as a student and married a Canadian a year after arrival. Her husband became a Muslim, learned Urdu, and took an active interest in her family history (the sisters are distantly related to the Paigah noble family). The sister and her husband both served in Canada's diplomatic service and the couple's two daughters were studying law and government. This couple sponsored Farooq Mirza's move to Toronto when, working for his father in Hyderabad, he wanted to strike out on his own. Farooq, his wife Shehnaz, and their two oldest children made the move, and they had three more children in Canada.[13]

Mirza had had a rough start, working with his hands—something he had never done. However, after one year he bought a freehold town home with government assistance, and he became production supervisor in a factory making household goods. Shehnaz had also had a hard time. One of ten children, she suffered from homesickness and depression and had been going to Dr. Ganga Ram Devi, a Telingana Hyderabadi Hindu woman doctor from Gandhi Medical College with clinics in Ottawa and Toronto, since she first came to Canada. Shehnaz had three more children after moving to Canada and worked intermittently. She had two sisters in Canada and two more in the United States.[14] In 1974, the Mirzas remembered, there were only four or five of his classmates there, one or two Indian shops, and 500—perhaps 1,000—Indians; in 1994, there were countless Indian shops and South Asian immigrants. Although many of their friends had moved to the United States because of Canada's 1975 and 1981 recessions, the Mirzas were well settled in Canada.

Farooq and Shehnaz Mirza initially participated in small gatherings of friends from Hyderabad, India, and Pakistan—weekly potlucks—but as more people came the parties began clustering by people's place of origin, class, and sometimes school (Farooq was an All Saints boy). The Mirza children had attended Hyderabad Foundation functions when it was active, but only to see the other youngsters, "not for the speeches or the old customs." The children did go to a mosque and worked to have Muslim religious activities recognized in their school. Farooq himself was not actively religious, although his brother in Hyderabad was in the Tabligh-i-Jamat and had recently visited them as part of a touring Jamat missionary group.[15] Since the demise of the Hyderabad Foundation, the Mirzas had attended activities like the Pakistani Mela (fair) that was being held then at the Bramford Community Center. However, their relationships with Pakistani Hyderabadis were somewhat awkward. They did not think it useful to take me to the Mela since "those Pakistani Hyderabadis will prefer not to be singled out."

In fact, the family was uncertain about how to identity itself, Farooq said.

In the beginning, we told people, we're Hyderabad *Deccan*, we're *not* Pakistani, we're *Indian*. Now we're disappointed; we're not proud of India. Muslims are being killed there; the way the government is handling things is not good. I've lost my homeland, lost my ground . . . there are riots, not so much in Hyderabad but in Bombay, in Kashmir. . . . The BJP [the Hindu nationalist Bharatiya Janata Party] said things I didn't like; I don't watch the India TV programs anymore. Back in old Hyderabad, there was never a difference with the Hindus. We went to Dusserah, Diwali, we never thought about the differences. Here, there are some Hindus, from Ahmedabad; we left our children [with them] for babysitting; we trusted them. But some feelings are there on the part of Pakistanis. They call themselves Hyderabadis when they see us; otherwise they call themselves Pakistanis. That kind, they talk like Pakistanis, they are completely Pakistani, they hate India, feel different, want to fight; they are muhajirs, however. Those who come directly from Hyderabad to here are different; they don't have that same feeling. . . . My wife now insists that we say Pakistani, not Hyderabadi, but I think the reverse. We have nothing left, only Hyderabad, but they have Pakistan, and Islam too.

The five Mirza children were not very interested in Hyderabad, according to their parents. They understood Urdu and spoke some, except for the fourteen-year-old, but they always spoke English with their Jamaican, Canadian, and Chinese friends. They had completely given up the everyday dress, as even the first generation had generally done. The first generation had even given up Hyderabadi Urdu in front of Pakistanis, who felt it was not really Muslim to talk Hyderabadi Urdu. Hyderabadi wedding clothes and jewelry were copied by Pakistanis, and of course Hyderabadi weddings were still done by Hyderabadis in Canada.

The Mirza parents hoped their children would marry Muslims, but the children said they would marry only partners from Canada. The point was illustrated by a horror story. A friend from Hyderabad in Canada found a young woman in Hyderabad for his son but sent a distant relative to inquire about a dowry, and this shameful incident caused the young woman's family to break the engagement. The son was devastated when he found out about this much later, because, being born in Canada, he was "totally opposed to dowry." The Mirza children did not even want Hyderabadis for their future spouses, thinking them old-fashioned and referring to arranged marriages as an instance of parental backwardness.

The Mirza children moved in and out of the living room as we talked. The oldest child, a daughter, was studying accounting at the University of Toronto and wanted an M.A. in sociology. The twenty-year-old son, a student and a musician who mixed English and Urdu in fusion music, paused as his parents showed me an album photo of the Nizam at her father's wedding to ask, "Who's the Nizam?" "The King of Hyderabad," his father answered. "Well, if he came tomorrow, I'd just say, 'Hey, how you doing,'" the young man said. Later he said he would not join the Hyderabad Foundation but might consider working in the Middle East. His younger brother, eighteen, stopped to tell me in a Jamaican accent, "I kind of treat everyone the same. I can't read or write Urdu; I'm more into English." The red plush sofa, mirrored wall, and embroidered pillows in the house recalled some homes in Hyderabad, but at lunch we ate hamburgers and macaroni and cheese. I was offered a white bread sandwich.

Less satisfied with Canada was another family that had arrived in 1974, that of Qaisar and Sabiha Beig. A Hyderabadi woman married into Pakistan, Sabiha and her husband had lived in Karachi for ten years and then moved to Canada. They too followed a sibling, her brother, who left an unstable Pakistan to study in Canada in 1971. Qaisar and Sabiha were seeking better educational opportunities for their three daughters. Qaisar was an accountant, and Sabiha, with a home economics degree from Osmania Women's College, took a degree in early childhood education in Canada and had a teaching and daycare job at York University (she had held a similar job in Karachi).

Sabiha had been caught up in Islamic Society of North America (ISNA) activities in Toronto and had just decided to wear the hijab, or headscarf. It was a smooth, informal transition for her, she said, and it stemmed from reading and learning about Islam in an ISNA women's group. This monthly Quran study group followed an ISNA course outline and included Pakistani Hyderabadis and "direct migrants" of mixed ages, women linked by concern for their children. The leader was a Hyderabadi woman; Sabiha thought that about 20 percent of Toronto's Hyderabadi Muslims were religiously active. "In Hyderabad, people were brought up Muslim but had little formal training, so they need to move from culture to religion." She knew about the Hyderabad Foundation and its decline but had not been interested in it; she did participate in Urdu-promoting activities.

Being in Canada had sharpened Sabiha's sense of cultural values.[16] She deplored the patterns of family breakup that she saw around her, like divorce, unmarried couples living together, and disrespect for elders. Visiting Pakistan just a month before my visit, she had found that Pakistan too was losing its values and she wanted to go back to found a school there. She had convinced her husband to semi-retire and go with her, but their three daughters would probably stay in Canada. The three were college students, all working part-time in banks; they were enrolled in women's studies and English literature, aesthetician/beautician studies, and international business, respectively. The young women spoke Urdu but did not read or write it. "The girls claim to have our values, but perhaps their religion needs to be revived," their mother said. She went on to talk about their identities, "as Hyderabadis, yes, but more importantly as Muslims and Pakistanis." Although her eldest daughter was born in India and calls herself Indian Canadian, when Sabiha and this daughter went to Hyderabad in 1988 they did not like it, because, she said, "the people were great but not the place, and girls didn't wear the hijab."

Sabiha's mother lived with them. "Since her husband's death in 1979 in Toronto, she's lived in turn with my brother and me," Sabiha said. "As a country, of course, she prefers her own, India, but it's all the same to her; she has nothing to do, no preferences. The hijab is not necessary at her age, she just needs a *dupatta*, and she respects my studies and my decision." Sabiha's mother told me that Hyderabad had become very different: "It's dirty, the people are South Indian now. Our culture was different. The grandchildren think our accounts of the old days, when it was peaceful, neat, and clean, are fairy tales." She hoped to help her granddaughters choose Muslim spouses, "not Hyderabadis, but Muslims, but probably they will not want my help."

The most conspicuous group of "later arrivals" was that of parents joining their adult children settled in Canada. In three instances above, widowed mothers were living with their daughters, but the older men tended to live alone. Ghulam Mohammed Khan Lodhi had been brought to Canada by his son in 1977, upon Lodhi's retirement at age sixty-five as a special metropolitan magistrate in Hyderabad. He lived with his son and then moved to a government-run senior citizens' apartment complex when his application to it was granted in 1986. He thought Canada was the best destination for senior citizens: "the facilities are better than in the UK or the United States." Lodhi's second son, the one who had brought him to Canada after consultation with another son in the UK, died in 1980, but yet another son had migrated to Toronto and was in hotel management. Lodhi occupied himself with Urdu literary meetings. He was secretary of the Urdu Society (four or five Hyderabadis attend the monthly gathering of fifteen to thirty people) and also attended meetings of a split-off from that: the Pakistani Writers' Forum. He had written a memoir of Hyderabad in Urdu for his grandchildren, but none can read Urdu. About the Hyderabadi youth in Canada, he said, "They have lost their culture; they are socializing with everyone, speaking in English, with Chinese, Italians, and so on. . . . [T]hey have adjusted and concentrate on their studies. They don't want to go back. One grandson went to Hyderabad and hated it, because of the mosquitos."

Another retiree brought to Canada by a son was Colonel Azmatullah, the ex-Indian Army officer quoted at the beginning of the chapter. His father had been chief engineer and secretary of the power and water department in the Nizam's Hyderabad, his grandfather a justice of the High Court there.[17] After retirement from the army, Azmatullah had served as chief security officer for industries and hotels and then as secretary and executive officer on Prince Mukarram Jah's staff. His eldest daughter and her husband had migrated to Canada in about 1974 and his youngest daughter and her family were in Indiana, in the United States. The son who had moved to Toronto had been cricket captain at Public School, then top cricketer of India, winning the Ranjit trophy, but in Canada there was no cricket and he had taken up golf. In Canada, the colonel continued to hold security and other positions. He lived in a senior citizens government-run apartment complex, the same one in which Lodhi resided, and, somewhat to his surprise, attended a local mosque in Toronto regularly. Although he had followed two of his children to Canada, the colonel considered himself the first-generation immigrant and his children second-generation immigrants.

Colonel Asmatullah felt Hyderabadi culture was lost, its adherents scattered all over the world.[18] On his last visit to Hyderabad in 1993, he had found the old culture but rarely represented (for example, by his Parsi friends), and "the city was full of outsiders, Punjabis and Andhras." His widowed elder sister had recently returned to Hyderabad after thirty-five years in Glasgow, a mistake, he felt, since the city had so changed. He himself was thinking of moving to Los Angeles, where he had good friends.

Seeking people of diverse backgrounds, I tried to track down members of Hyderabadi Anglo-Indian families who had reportedly put down roots in Canada in the 1970s, but they were not in touch with the numerous Muslim Hyderabadis. I finally reached Enid Isaacs, from the Gunfoundry locality in new Hyderabad and niece of a man I had met in Perth, Australia, by phone. She had come to Canada on her own in 1970 because a friend who had gone ahead, a classmate in Rosary Convent, had asked "Why not you?" So Enid applied, got the visa, and migrated. Never married, she was active in Christian activities and worked as a secretary. She knew some of the people I was looking for but said she should have gone to Australia where there were more Anglo-Indians.

A few of the Hyderabadis in Canada were settled in Montreal, Ottawa, and Calgary. In Montreal, people estimated that there were fifty to sixty Hyderabadi families. A pioneer Montreal couple, Fehmida and Aftab Khan, had moved to Montreal in the late 1960s. Aftab, one of eleven children, had gone to Pakistan with his family but stayed only a few months and proceeded to London to study. After going into the textile business in Montreal, his display at a 1967 Pakistan exposition earned him the title of honorary Pakistan consul, and the mayor of Montreal asked him to open a Pakistani restaurant. Fehmida joined him in 1969 but went back to Hyderabad to have their two children (Aftab and Fehmida were related but the family had split at partition). Fehmida had become interested in Islam and spoke of a 1998 controversy in a Montreal French school concerning the wearing of the hijab; in the end, a young Muslim woman was permitted to wear her hijab.

Shahbaz Ashraf, an energetic businessman in Montreal, had moved with his parents to Pakistan in 1960 and set out for Montreal in 1977. He followed a sister, who had moved to Canada in the late 1960s and worked for the Canadian government and then for UNESCO. Shahbaz started out in

Canada in textiles and then went back to the shipping business, where he had worked before. Shahbaz traveled frequently and far, and his knowledge of Hyderabadi networks around the world was vast. He joked that he was called Liaquat in school, Shahbaz at home, Ashraf in Pakistan, Ash in the textile business, and now Lee in Canada and in shipping circles.

Shahbaz's wife Shaheen worked too, and she was active in the Canadian Council of Muslim Women. The couple's four children grew up in Montreal, although the son was a tennis coach in Atlanta, Georgia, and had married an American. Shahbaz's wife had put on the hijab after making a pilgrimage to Mecca in 1998, and another daughter also wore it and worked in a medical technician job. Two other daughters did not wear the hijab, and one of them played football, a challenging activity for any young woman. Devout Muslims, the parents were enthusiastic Hyderabadis and their home was filled with memorabilia.

Shahbaz took it upon himself and his family to host a reunion of St. George's Grammar School graduates in the summer of 2000, following successful reunions in 1997 in St. Louis and 1999 in Chicago. I attended and gave a talk, as did Shehbaz Safrani from New York and the Reverend Donald Hood from New South Wales, Australia. Hood had taught long ago in Hyderabad and he and his wife had attended the St. Louis and Chicago reunions. People talked of a St. George's group in Karachi, and one in London. Many of the one hundred or so attendees were from the United States, with a few from the UK and Dubai.

The reunion had one feature that undercut its cosmopolitan theme. The attendees, old classmates from an elite school in Hyderabad affiliated with an Australian Christian denomination, listened while the Reverend Donald Hood stressed his own Christian missionary motives and Safrani and I highlighted the "Deccani synthesis" theme in our remarks. Most of those attending were Muslim, but Hindus, Parsis, and Christians were present.[19] The host, however, insisted on announcing and personally observing the Islamic prayer times throughout the reunion, even at the informal picnic in a park. No one commented on this publicly, but privately there was surprise and discomfort among some of the guests.

Hyderabadi Social and Cultural Activities

Hyderabadis in Canada participated in a range of activities. Early migrants had helped to form literary and cultural organizations. Ather Hussein had started an arts and letters organization for cultural and literary purposes in 1972 but left when it turned into a singles organization; others mentioned one or another of the Urdu-promoting associations. More recently, Islamic institutions and organizations, along with a Pakistani association,[20] had engaged many immigrants. Activities or organizations focusing on Hyderabadi ancestry and culture had not been very important, although some people had gathered for potluck dinners when their numbers were small.

In Toronto, a Hyderabad Foundation started out promisingly in the 1980s, its leaders well placed in both Hyderabadi and Canadian society. It started with a very successful mushaira held by the Canadian Urdu Society, of which the journalist Haroon Siddiqui was Secretary. Siddiqui had invited Prince Muffakham Jah from London to be chief guest, and the audience had doubled, from 500 the previous year to 1,000. "Many, many Hyderabadis were eager to see the prince, talk to him—it was a touching and historic event," said Siddiqui. So Shahid Malik Khan,[21] Haroon Siddiqui, and others formed a Hyderabad Foundation in 1986 (then the Prince and Siddiqui flew to Chicago, where they met those who led the Chicago Hyderabad Foundation). Malik Khan published a commemorative booklet, the *Hyderabad Times of Canada*, with the Char Minar on its cover and eighteen articles, along with jokes and poems, in English and Urdu. The booklet promised a World Congress of Hyderabadis in Toronto in July of 1987 but this was not held.[22]

The association formed to celebrate Hyderabadi culture; Haroon Siddiqui explained carefully that Hyderabadis took pride not in nobility but in the refinement of interpersonal relationships. He saw Hyderabadi culture as a code of ethics and an assumption of collective responsibility that was opposed to or different from the pursuit of individuality. He and others realized that the old Hyderabad society could never recreate itself but could perhaps achieve the goal of upholding family, extended family, and community values. Messages from Prince Muffakham Jah and Princess Fatima Esin reproduced in the inaugural *Hyderabad Times* booklet set the tone. The prince spoke of Hyderabad's composite culture and turning that harmony to "compassionate, coordinated mutual asssistance." He ended with "Can our 'dal' be anything but 'khatti'? Can the evening shadow of Golconda be anything but long? Can we fail to succeed?" The princess wrote memorably about her perception of a distinctive Hyderabadi culture and her appreciation of it because she too was an expatriate, as "you all are today."

After several successful functions the Hyderabad Foundation of Toronto declined. Some talked about changing leadership, some about the typical ethnic organizational pattern of initial enthusiasm followed by decline, and others about limited resources. Haroon Siddiqui said there was no particular reason for the decline, that the Chicago Foundation had done a good thing by sending some young people to Hyderabad, and that the international organization, to which the Toronto one should have been linked, had not gotten under way. Colonel Asmatullah stressed the lack of a meeting place. Asif Alikhan said the Hyderabad Association flourished for two or three years and that the high commissioners of both India and Pakistan had come to its second function. According to Ghulam Mohammed Khan Lodhi, after good first and second meetings, the leaders "failed to arrange a meeting properly to receive Princess Durru Shevar when she came from London and they had to take her to Chicago where the Hyderabad Association does well." Mrs. Laila Kamal, a businesswoman and the last president of the Hyderabad Foundation of Toronto, stated, "Because there was never a quorum, in about 1991 I gave the remaining money to the mosque, to the Islamic Center in Scarborough, and it ended." This confirmed a comment that the group was "too Muslim" and suggested that many Hyderabadis were members of the Scarborough Islamic Foundation.

At the start of the twenty-first century, new leaders with somewhat different goals founded a new Hyderabad association in Toronto. A nonprofit charitable organization, the Deccan Hyderabad Community Services Center targeted immigrants from Hyderabad and Hyderabadis from the Middle East in its website statement.[23] The four men on the board of directors—a staff sergeant in the Toronto police, an engineer with the Toronto Housing Authority, a realtor, and a business manager—came to Toronto in the 1970s. The staff sergeant was the leader. Jamal Khan arrived in 1970 with a degree in commerce from Anwar-ul-Ulum College and experience as a chartered accountant. He joined the Toronto Police Service and his years working homicide, fraud, intelligence, family and youth services, and community services acquainted him well with the Canadian environment. A founding member of the South Asian section of the police ethnic relations unit in 1977, Khan helped implement policies to prosecute hate crimes and handle South Asian family disputes. He also wrote for the Urdu newspaper, *Awaz*, and for the police chaplain's newsletter (giving a Muslim officer's view). On trips back to Hyderabad, he addressed the National Police Academy on community-based policing and participated in a *Siyasat*-organized seminar on migration to Canada.[24]

The new organization was launched September 23, 2000, with a Jashan-e-Hyderabad, an evening of songs, music, speeches, and fund-raising for a community services center.[25] Its message emphasized not only preservation of Hyderabadi culture but service to people in need, people of all races, colors, religions, and ethnic origins. The new organization's focus was firmly on Canada and problems for Hyderabadis in the new context, including youth involvement in drug use and gangs. Its emphasis was also on Hyderabadis from India, and it had good connections with the *Siyasat* newspaper in Hyderabad.[26] On the website, the Center's logo featured the Nizam's *dastar* (turban), with the colors red for the Canadian flag, green for the Indian flag, and saffron for old Hyderabad's flag. A globe stood for the global status of the Hyderabadi community and the home page pictured Char Minar, the Canadian flag, and the Toronto skyline. Unconnected to other Hyderabadi associations in the diaspora and without famous patrons, the group hoped to put down strong local roots and purchase a building. If successful, it would be a first among Hyderabadi diasporic organizational efforts.

Urdu literary activities also engaged many Hyderabadis in Canada. Pakistani Hyderabadi men who had migrated to Toronto in the 1970s and 1980s constituted one group of Urdu enthusiasts. As children, they had accompanied their parents to Pakistan, and four of the seven had non-Hyderabadi wives, Punjabis and other muhajirs from Pakistan. All had left Pakistan for political and economic reasons. Some had siblings in Australia or the United States, and they were in touch with Urdu literary people like themselves all over the world.[27] These men wanted to restart a Hyderabad association but in conjunction with an Urdu literary association (the Anjuman Taraqqi Urdu, Anjuman-i-Urdu-i-Canada, and Writers Forum were all active in Toronto). One reason for starting yet another association was because the Pakistani Association was "so big." Furthermore, their Hyderabadi identity had been a source of "some ambivalence" in Pakistan and now their Pakistani identity was something of a problem in Canada. They talked about the pressures to discard the Hyderabadi identity, especially in Karachi. With both Pakistani and Canadian passports, they found the Canadian ones much better for going to India. They felt their identities were in crisis in Canada, partly because of an increasing emphasis on an Islamic identity. They loved Hyderabad and wanted to preserve its culture but "had no time." Some of them spoke chaste Hindi and also attended Hindi literary meetings in Canada. Toronto's numerous Hyderabadis, these Urdu enthusiasts said, were active in all the organizations.

Pakistani Hyderabadis like these Urdu enthusiasts were meeting people, even family members, in Canada with whom they had lost touch years ago. One man had met his parents' cousins and his own cousins from India only in Canada. A cousin had called him from the Middle East and said, "My mother and your mother are sisters, but our families haven't met or written for so many years. I don't know anyone in Canada, and now there is a proposal for my daughter from there. Can you find out about this guy?" Another had met old friends unseen for forty-two years. Most of these men had never gone back to Hyderabad, either for political reasons or because all their close relatives had left the city.

Mixing In

Hyderabadis in Canada mentioned a range of interests, organizations, and reference groups, but there was no "core community," even in Toronto. People's activities often reflected conflicting interests. Explicitly Islamic activities were a major focus for many and, just as explicitly, others preferred Urdu-promoting activities. An effort to build a Hyderabad Foundation in the 1980s proved short-lived, and another effort, with a different set of goals and leaders, was under way in 2000. Relationships between Indian and Pakistani Hyderabadis seemed uneasy. There were few Hindus or Anglo-Indians from Hyderabad and connections among Hyderabadis of different class and religious backgrounds seemed nonexistent or weak.

People in Canada talked frequently about relatives and events in other diasporic sites. One wide-ranging dinner discussion concerned Hyderabadis in Toronto, Karachi, and Hyderabad. Hosted by Desh and Zehra Bandhu, the group included Hyderabadi neighbors long-settled in Canada (in whose home two doors down the young people gathered separately to play video games), relatives visiting from Karachi, and a Punjabi couple long resident in Canada. Most of the guests had worked in the Middle East and some had relatives in London. Those from Pakistan confirmed that it was not good in Karachi to be from Hyderabad; the language was ridiculed and Hyderabadis were resented. "Let's face it, the Hyderabadi standard of living was just higher, the *shikar* (hunting), the Nawabi style." In Toronto, too, Hyderabadis had a distinct reputation: they were likened to Newfies, or people from Newfoundland, whom others thought of as simple people. However, the meaning was not quite the same, as Hyderabadis were thought to be not only simple but easygoing, laid back, perhaps even lazy. Certainly in Canada real Hyderabadis and Pakistani Muslims did not get along well, in the opinion of people at the dinner party.

The young people of Hyderabadi parentage identified most strongly as Canadians, according to their own comments and those of others about them. Few felt a need to be hyphenated Canadians, and some maintained that there really were no categories like those in the United States, categories like Asian Canadian or any other kind of Canadian. Two daughters, however, reportedly designated themselves Indian Canadian or Indian American because one had been born in India and one in the United States (in the former case, the daughter's preference was for India and her mother's was for Pakistan). The youngsters who had been to Hyderabad, Karachi, or London felt they had gone as tourists and they had no special feelings for the places of ancestors or relatives. The few young people to whom I spoke maintained that there were no racial problems in Canada and that most of their friends were Anglos or other non-Hyderabadis. They professed disinterest in a Hyderabad association.

Muslim grandmothers from Hyderabad who visited Canada occasionally, speaking as outsiders, generalized that religion had assumed greater importance in the lives of their children and grandchildren there. In Canada, Miriam Bilgrami and Khatija Mehdi saw resentment expressed against Indian immigrants and reported an increase in religious orthodoxy that, in their view, created problems for the grandchildren. One spoke of a granddaughter in Canada who went to an Islamic Sunday School wearing shorts. The *moulvi* (Muslim cleric) terrified her, telling her she would burn in hell, and the girl developed a 105 degree fever; her parents removed her from the school. "Those clerics should pay attention to where they are," protested the loyal grandmother. The other, visiting in Toronto at the time of Muharram, said, "Every school was taken over for twelve days for *majlises* and the children had to be there with you every day. One had to have religion, like it or not, more than here [Hyderabad]."

The young Canadians of Hyderabadi background were quite different from their parents. They seemed relatively unhindered by national boundaries in making career and marriage choices. The trend was toward professional training and careers. Law school was the most popular choice, with several young people planning to concentrate on immigration law. Educational horizons included graduate and professional schools in the United States as well as Canada. Despite strong identities as Canadians, the youngsters seemed prepared to study and perhaps to settle elsewhere in North America. While many young people continued to accept marriages arranged by their parents and other relatives, others found their own spouses, both within and outside the family-defined community. Young men growing up in Canada had more freedom than their sisters when it came to dating and several Hyderabadi youths had American or Canadian girlfriends. Two young Muslim men going to school or working in the United States married American non-Muslim women (one marriage ended in divorce and subsequent remarriage to an Iranian woman resident in India, but the couple is settling in the United States). One young Hindu man married an Italian Canadian, whereas his brother brought a Hindu bride from Australia. Such relationships involved movements between Canada and other English-speaking diasporic sites.

The young women confidently displayed a readiness to divorce if an initial marriage did not work out. Well-educated and undertaking careers, they felt they would be better off without a spouse who was "not working out." Two young women, having agreed to marriages advocated by their parents, pronounced those marriages unsuccessful and asked for parental support in seeking divorces; the parents gave them that support and they will probably make their own decisions about their next grooms.

One Hyderabadi daughter had been married in the last decade of the twentieth century to a Hyderabadi Indian recommended by a Karachi relative working in the Gulf with the young man. That recommendation, plus the excellent reputation of the groom's family in Hyderabad, had persuaded the young woman's parents to go ahead, but the marriage failed. The husband proved unable to study although the wife's parents paid his tuition, unable to drive despite private lessons from his mother-in-law, and unable to work. His mother-in-law said, "My daughter learned Hyderabadi cooking and really tried, but finally she said it was like living with a fourteen-year-old and gave it up. He once commented, when she did well at something, 'leave something for me'; my daughter was just too competent, too confident, for his taste."

As the number of immigrants from South Asia kept rising, young people were finding their own matches in the universities. This seemed more promising than parental arrangements, and especially more promising than bringing young men from Hyderabad. "Bringing boys is more risky than bringing girls. But boys from Karachi and the UK are better prospects than those from Hyderabad, because the lifestyles there are closer to the Canadian lifestyle," said Rashida Mirza.

In Canada, first-generation Hyderabadis moved between identities as Indians or Pakistanis, the nation of origin categories employed by the state, or, resisting those categories, between identities as Muslims or scholars of Urdu literature. These tended to be oppositional more often than overlapping identities, and the India-Pakistan division seemed sharp. Anglo-Indian and Hindu Hyderabadis were few and they were relatively unconnected to Hyderabadi Muslims in Canada. A Hyderabad Foundation thrived briefly among the elite immigrants but was transformed in its next incarnation by new leadership into a social welfare association closely linked to Canadian policies and institutions. The children of the Hyderabadi immigrants from India and Pakistan interacted primarily with the children of immigrants from other nations in Toronto. They comfortably claimed Canadian identities but could also see themselves as more broadly North American. Among both old and young people of Hyderabadi background, commitment to Hyderabad or Hyderabadi culture was eclipsed by other commitments.

CHAPTER 9

Kuwait and the United Arab Emirates:
Futures Reconfigured

WORDS LIKE *cosmopolitan* and *transnational* cannot be applied so easily to the Hyderabadi migrants to the Gulf states as to those elsewhere. Rather, "expatriate" best captures their sense of being away from their native lands, albeit voluntarily. In both Kuwait and the United Arab Emirates (UAE),[1] expatriate workers and professionals had temporary and similarly circumscribed economic roles, yet their experiences in the two sites were qualitatively different. Mohammed Hoshdar Khan, in Kuwait, saw separation from the host society.

> We mix with Kuwaiti men but a wall is there. . . . There's no question of adopting Kuwaiti culture, no temptation anyway, we prefer Indian and Hyderabadi culture, our ways of public behavior, our relations with elders. Our youngest used to say, "I was born here, I am Kuwaiti," but he was only six in 1990. Now he understands, "I am an Indian."

In contrast, Hasan Bozai, in the UAE, felt close to local people and made claims on the host society.

> We do socialize with the locals, we meet on Id and other occasions; with the men only of course, that reservation is always there. This is better than Kuwait, and these locals have been educated in Karachi or Bombay often; they are much exposed to South Asians. . . . Who has built the UAE, running the banks and everything? And now a generation [of locals] is coming up, and we say [to them], don't make life miserable for those who built it up. But medical fees are doubling, and visa fees. . . . It's still a place to earn, compared to there, but we're working harder than the pay, really.

The two Gulf environments (Kuwait and the UAE; see figure 9.1) differed significantly, despite having roughly similar populations of two million with expatriates constituting some 75 percent of them. In Kuwait,

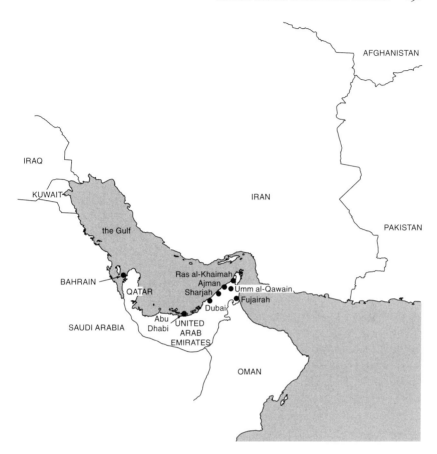

FIGURE 9.1. Gulf states of the Middle East.

distinctions of class, place of origin in Andhra, religion, and gender were important to the competing definitions of "Hyderabadi" being developed there in the context of a basically Arabic language Islamic environment. In the UAE, religious and gender practices differed significantly from those in Kuwait; class was important too, but language proved even more important as many Arabs as well as the Indian and Pakistani expatriates readily spoke and understood Urdu or Hindustani. Urdu and English, not Arabic, were the languages one heard on the streets of Dubai and Sharjah; Arabic did prevail in Abu Dhabi. The South Asians felt closer to the Arabs than in Kuwait, calling them "locals" rather than "nationals," and the "locals" were generally liked rather than disliked. Both states, of course, were very hot, and when I did my research there in August the daytime temperatures hovered around 120 degrees. Most Hyderabadi women and children were back in Hyderabad or Karachi, in fact, for the hot season. An accepted feature of life for families in the Gulf, these annual returns ensured a close and continuing engagement with the homelands.

Kuwait: Many Workers, Few Professionals

WORKERS AND THEIR LIVES

The workers in Kuwait came from various places of origin in Hyderabad city and Andhra and embodied competing definitions of "Hyderabadi." Mirza Shamsher Ali Beg, a young air conditioner repairman, was an old friend, a recent migrant there, and my chief guide.[2] A Telugu-speaking Muslim from Secunderabad whose mother taught Telugu in Centenary School and whose three sisters were all graduates with good jobs in Hyderabad, Mirza took a technical course in Madras and responded to a Kuwaiti air conditioning firm's advertisement placed in 1990. With his earnings, he bought a lot in a new suburb of Secunderabad and built a house for his family. Among his friends and neighbors in Secunderabad, overseas connections were numerous.[3]

Mirza was pleased with his experience in Kuwait. When Iraq invaded Kuwait in 1990 (known as the Invasion), he had been abruptly sent back to India but returned quickly. He planned to secure another work permit when his current one ended. He lived in a company dorm at the edge of the city with six or seven other workers, and four other Hyderabadis, plus one from Pakistan, worked in his firm. He met all kinds of people on the job, working for Arabs, Americans, and Indians. Like other workers from old Hyderabad, Mirza enjoyed hanging out in the Murgab area by Kuwait's impressive Communication Tower on Fridays and Sundays.[4] On those holidays, workers from all over Kuwait congregated by place of origin, people from Karimnagar, Andhra Pradesh (AP), to the left of the Watin Complex and people from Cuddapah, AP, around the Sheraton Hotel, including many maidservants in colorful *saris* or Western clothes.

In Murgab, workers bought cassettes to record messages home, as many could not read and write readily. The Sagar Restaurant there was a favorite with Hyderabadis; other favorites included the Mann-o-Salwa, the Mubarakiah, and the Paradise for the south Indian snacks *idli* and *dosa*. But the workers could not enjoy themselves too much, as their employers (particularly of maids) often picked them up at the end of the day, as they had dropped them off there at the beginning. In addition, the Kuwait Police force was unfriendly to expatriate workers. Mirza said, "If we're in a group and a friend gets stopped for something, arrested, the rest of us have to run away and leave him, otherwise we too might be detained and deported."

Workers enjoyed these respites from work, where pressures to produce were intense and where "nationals," especially women and children, posed dangers to them. Workers were afraid of Kuwaiti children. "They are nuisances and dangers to us," said Mirza; a colleague once gently pushed a child away while working, and the child complained to his father who complained to the job supervisor. Workers also had to be cautious about women in Kuwaiti houses, as "sometimes a Filipino wife or another woman who is 'a bit ahead' comes out in jeans and T-shirt to point out the problems, leading to misunderstandings if her husband walks in. It's better to deal only with men."[5]

Some workers were in Kuwait because they felt insecure back home. Hamad Nazmuddin from Hyderabad's old city had come to Kuwait in 1977 and ran a luggage shop in the Watin Complex shopping mall. Mrs. Nazmuddin joined her husband in 1979,[6] and their children were born and raised in Kuwait. Hamad worried about the security of Muslims in India and throughout the world. Despite almost all family members being in Hyderabad, the couple had determined to go to Canada, which "is giving nationality" more easily than the United States and where Hamad had a brother. They had to move soon, too, because the children were in intermediate level at school and could not continue their studies in Kuwait. Another reason for not going back to Hyderabad was that as NRIs (nonresident Indians) or non-mulkis, they would need to give double the donations of locals to get school seats for their children.[7] But most important, "We are seeing the dark future for Muslims; in Hyderabad particularly, there are riots, businesses are burned, small percentages of jobs only go to Muslims and they are dismissed without cause. . . . N. T. Rama Rao[8] is trying to kill Muslim culture, there is Telugu in the offices, idols and *puja* [Hindu worship] in the offices, and we have to sign in Telugu now." His children, Hamad said, were "thinking like Kuwaitis, asking if they are Indian or Kuwaiti," and they knew Arabic, which is compulsory in the schools, but could not read or write Urdu well. It was time to leave Kuwait, the parents concluded. Hamad's assistant Khaja Idris Ahmed, a younger cousin from Mehdipatnam and one of six or seven cousins in Kuwait, directed me to jewelry stores nearby where he said many workers were Hyderabadis.

These "Hyderabadis" in the jewelry stores, I discovered, were all from coastal Andhra, the formerly British colonial districts. A. G. Prasad, owner of the Atlas Store, proved to be a Telugu-speaking Hindu from Cuddapah, and he and his clerk sent me to see the "first jeweler from Hyderabad," a man who had come from Tirupati in coastal Andhra in 1980.[9] Cuddapah people in Kuwait called themselves Hyderabadis, I found, and are called that by others. "We 'real' Hyderabadis ask them," one Hyderabadi from the city reported, "why do you call yourselves that, you're spoiling our name? But they keep on; people can't place them otherwise." Another city man said, "The Cuddapah people, they call themselves Hyderabadis because no one here knows of Cuddapah; it is not recognized; but now, when we say we are Hyderabadis, we are taken to be from Cuddapah!" Many of those from coastal Andhra were Muslims, like Hidayat Khan, who told me about Hyderabad (helped by a co-worker from Gujarat who knew as much about Hyderabad as Khan did).[10]

Khan's story differed greatly from narratives given by former citizens of the state.

> Hyderabad is a well-known city of the Nawabs, mainly known from Quli Qutb Shahi times. Char Minar is famous, and Hyderabad city is now the capital city of Andhra Pradesh. Some of the main people are Mukarram Jah, who is there now and is a very nice man. One thing about Hyderabad is that there are many Muslims there, and Hindus too, and they are in unity; they will not have disputes. And Hyderabad and Secunderabad are there, two cities together, with the language of Urdu which is spreading throughout Andhra. They take *pan*, another major thing, and they are very fluent and very dignified and have no quarrels. And the main thing of Hyderabad is business, there are more improvements in that than in other cities. Another main person is Sultan Salahuddin Owaisi, a daring person, taking care of Muslims [Muslim politician from the revived Ittehd ul Muslimeen]. The Nawabs before did some good things, like the Osmania hospital; there were were some drawbacks too.

I got a more familiar "insider" narrative from members of the Hyderabad Muslim Welfare Organization.[11] Its president, Abdul Karim, and other lower-middle-class Hyderabadis met me for tea and an interview, and ascertaining whom I had been meeting, pronounced them "the wealthy people—we, now, are also the post-independence generation, we can tell you different things." A narrative in Urdu opened our meeting, for the speaker, Mr. Ehtashamuddin, could be more eloquent in that.

> Old Hyderabad was a paradise on the Indian map, one whose blessings were all cut, lost in cold blood after 1948; the culture of the Muslims was cut into pieces then and in 1956.[12] In my childhood, capable people mingled and got the jobs they deserved, but afterward, people from other states came and brought their cultures and the style of life was adversely affected. Urdu went down, Telugu came up, and the linguistic policies have taken their toll on the new generations. Jobs and opportunities are less, competition is greater and conditions are difficult, we [Muslims] have become backward. For the sake of our children, we began to go out for employment, and, reaching here, we have become even more distant from our culture. How special that culture was in the world we can see even more here, where there are people from all over the world.

The friends present agreed with this view and agreed also that Kuwaiti culture was completely strange, had no common points with their own, and held no attractions for them. Even though the Hyderabadis held responsible jobs, they worked for the Kuwaitis, and, in Kuwaiti houses, the maids, drivers, and cooks were from South Asia. The Arabs did not want to mix and saw all Indians as servants. "Our culture is one of mixing, but not with Kuwaitis," they said, and few had attended any Kuwaiti wedding, much less a *diwaniyeh* (men's gathering).

All these men had come since 1970 and most held jobs that enabled them to have their wives and children with them, although they generally did not want their wives "taking activities outside" so the women were "nonproductive." They wanted their children to learn Urdu but some sent their children to English-medium schools and to an Islamic Presentation Committee for Urdu lessons ("but Urdu cannot give the bread"). They wondered why Indians stayed in the United States, apparently thinking it both a physical and cultural danger zone; diplomatically, they did not pursue this subject further with me. Men in this group did have some connections with the Cuddapah workers but declined to call them Hyderabadis, designating them as Andhras or "neighbors." These men also had connections with Muslims from Karnataka, Kerala, and Tamilnadu. There was an Aligarh "old boys'" association but, despite many Osmanians, no association in Kuwait.

A follow-up visit to the home of one of these Hyderabad Muslim Welfare Association members, Mohammed Habib-al-Deen, gave a lively impression of family life in the locality of Farwaniyah, where wives and children were numerous. Habib-al-Deen had spent eighteen years in Kuwait and regarded it as "the cream of his life," surrounded by his family and the friends he had made there. Pakistani neighbors and others trooped through the home to meet us on their way to games at a sports center, and Habib and others gave me addresses in the UAE, my next stop.

Although they did not agree on the definition of Hyderabadi or the story of old Hyderabad, the coastal Andhra shopkeepers and the members of the Hyderabad Muslim Welfare Organization both told me about the "biggest Hyderabadi" they knew of in Kuwait, Hoshdar Khan. This big businessman from Hyderabad had sponsored the 400th birthday celebration of Hyderabad and major cricket tournaments in the city. The members of the welfare organization advised me to meet Khan, saying "Mr. Hoshdar Khan is our head, or our member; sometimes he helps us. Some say he is a showboy, but we disagree; he calls many people, scholars, doctors, and others, he has brought 300, no, 1,000 people here [including half the men at the table]. . . . Many are big people, but only he mixes with us."

I tried to meet Hoshdar Khan, walking about in the heat to find his office. Khan was in Hyderabad, I was told, but his brother-in-law was expected momentarily, so I went next door to a watch repair shop. The shopworker turned out to be from Hyderabad and told me that his shop's owner was a very big man, such a big man that he could not even send my card over to him and he would certainly never appear before him. This big man had been in Kuwait since the 1970s and had sponsored many Hyderabadis: his name was Hoshdar Khan, and his office was just around the corner. Several other onlookers, Hindu and Muslim, came forward and introduced themselves as Hyderabadis from Cuddapah. All these men owed their presence in Kuwait to Hoshdar Khan, who had secured their visas and put them up for a year in one big building.[13]

Back in Hoshdar Khan's office, Akbar Khan arrived and gave me a picture of the big man's activities.[14] A Mehdvi Pathan of Afghan ancestry, Khan became prominent due to his sponsorship of Hyderabad's 400th birthday celebration (held in May, 1990, before the Iraqi invasion, in an ice-skating rink), and his sponsorship of two Asia Gold Cup cricket matches in the 1990s. The 400th celebration was free and held after 7 P.M. so that workers could attend. Ninety percent of the attendees were Hyderabadis. Soon after that, when the 1990 Invasion occurred, Khan stood on the border with Jordan offering help to people returning to India.[15] Khan headed the Indian Muslim Welfare Association in Kuwait that met the first Sunday of every month in his office, his brother-in-law said, and he was considered a "mini-consul, always serving others and a good friend of the current Indian ambassador."[16]

The American presence added another complication to life in Kuwait after 1991. Kola Shankar, a driver for the American Embassy whom I met at Hamad Nazmuddin's shop, had gotten his position in a convoluted way. First recruited to Kuwait in 1980 by Mrs. Rizwana Qadri, a well-known recruiting agent in Hyderabad's Banjara Hills, he had worked for Kuwait Transport Corporation for two years as a bus driver. The conditions were bad, the promised eight-hour job stretching to over ten as the driver had to report one hour early and then stay and account carefully for the cash afterward. Returning to Hyderabad, Kola lived on his savings for three years and then secured a job through the same agent in Saudi Arabia as a driver from 1985 to 1988; the conditions and hours were better but the pay was low. Again he lived on his savings and was able to marry off four of his seven sisters. He returned to Kuwait in February 1990 when a Bombay recruiter pursued him, knowing he had a Kuwaiti driver's license, which is extremely hard to get. On the night of the Invasion, he had bought a Billy Ocean cassette and was playing it over and over, "Suddenly, life had new meaning for me," he said, "when I heard there were Iraqis in the streets." Because people were leaving, the U.S. Embassy needed drivers: "I went over there and got this good job." He married in 1992 on a visit home, brought his wife, and had two children born in Kuwait. His attitude and general demeanor differed from those of many whom I interviewed in Kuwait[17] and perhaps signaled a shift in the environment.

BUSINESSMEN, PROFESSIONALS, AND FAMILY LIVES

Hoshdar Khan was a relative newcomer to the upper-middle and higher-class Hyderabadi world in Kuwait, but two of the first Hyderabadis to do business in Kuwait, pioneers who had done very well, traced the evolving class structure. Aqueel Azimuddin, an electrical engineer, grew up in the old city.[18] His elder brother, an architect, went to Kuwait in 1956, and another brother and Aqueel followed shortly. In 1961, Kuwait had "about 150 Indian nationals and very few Hyderabadis"; Aqueel estimated that by 1995 there were almost 13,000 Hyderabadis and 200,000 Indians, most of them working class.[19] Aqueel supervised electrical and air conditioning work (and was among the first brought back to Kuwait after Liberation, to put the emir's Bayan Palace in order). He married Rizwana, from Bombay but with a mother from Hyderabad, and brought her to Kuwait in 1970; Rizwana was disappointed to find Kuwait "not modern then." However, she adjusted, taught English in a Pakistani school, and then worked with the UN Development Program.[20] Their daughter studied in Bombay University and returned to Kuwait to work as a lab technician, the only woman and non-Kuwaiti in her lab. The family socialized with many people, not especially with Hyderabadis. At the 400th birthday celebration, the daughter met many Hyderabadis in Kuwait for the first time. At that event, Aqueel captained the Golconda cricket team and was named best batsman, although the Char Minar team, captained by Dr. Riaz Khan, my young friend Mirza's doctor, won the match.[21]

Syed M. Bilgrami, from Hyderabad's Bilgrami clan, had been established in Kuwait since 1964. His career started in Iraq in 1962, where his uncle had been India's ambassador[22] and where Syed worked for an import company. Bilgrami's marriage (the *nikah*) took place in 1960, but he waited for the *rukhsati* (the bringing home of the bride) until 1968 when he had become self-sufficient. He was proud to be in business, stating that very few Hyderabadis were businesspeople.[23] Invited to Kuwait in 1964 by a Mercedes car agent, he worked in insurance for twenty-three years and was a partner in a firefighting equipment firm.[24] He and his children stayed in Kuwait right through the Invasion and the American Liberation; they felt patriotic about Kuwait.[25] Bilgrami employed a maid from Hyderabad and a cook from Bangladesh whom his wife had taught to prepare Hyderabadi dishes. Only big businessmen and some doctors could manage to have servants in Kuwait, he said, but the workers did very well. His peon got almost ten thousand rupees a month (about $250); "what's his name, Narasimha Rao [India's then-prime minister, from Hyderabad], gets some $400 a month and an ordinary foreman here gets $2,000 a month!"

There had been a big 400th birthday celebration for Hyderabad in Kuwait, and there was a Hyderabad association in Kuwait, Bilgrami said, but he was not active in it. One needed official permission for such associations and he did not think the Hyderabadis really had that; he feared to jeopardize his business. His social life "as a market man" did not depend on Hyderabadis, and he mixed as much or more with Punjabis and Gujeratis as he did with Hyderabadis. Also, he had family in Kuwait—two of his sisters and their families, perhaps twenty people in all. Although there was no Sunni/Shia problem in Kuwait, he said, he thought some of the other big Hyderabadi businessmen were Muslim fundamentalists; he himself was a humanist and mixing with them would be bad for business.[26]

Until 1966, only three Hyderabadi families had been in Kuwait,[27] and Bilgrami said that most Hyderabadis there in 1995 were workers. Also, very few were Shias. When he thought about marriage partners for his children, he realized that most Indian Shias in Kuwait were married already or were uneducated. He had not visited Hyderabad much in the past, but since taking up golf, because Hyderabad had a green, not brown (unwatered, as in Kuwait) golf course, he was going every year. When there, he got offers for his daughters, but rather than give a dowry as many requested, he wanted the groom to come work in Kuwait.[28]

When I asked about another Shia Hyderabadi businessman there, Shahid Ali Mirza, Bilgrami pronounced him a friend, telephoned him, and soon we were lunching at Caesar's Chinese Restaurant. Shahid, best friend of Jeff Khan in Texas, had been in Kuwait since 1978. Like Bilgrami, he did contracting work, but he felt Kuwait was reaching the saturation point for business. He promised to bring his wife, Parveen, to meet me and reported that she was less happy in Kuwait than he; an educated Bombay woman, she was not able to use her education.

That very evening at 9:30 P.M. Shahid and Parveen and their daughters, seven and two, came to my hotel. She was in an *abayah* (full-length covering) as he had not told her with whom they would be dining and she had assumed it would be men. We ate out at a Chicken Tikka place (the Hyderabadi-owned Indian restaurant we tried first was closed), took a walk on the beach after midnight when it was cool, and then drove home (stopped briefly by a police security check, a frequent occurrence, they said). Asked if she had come to Kuwait after marriage, she replied, "Of course, what other possible reason would one have for coming?" Parveen had done a course in hotel management, but, because of her young children and the culture in Kuwait, she was not working. She and Shahid were thinking of the future, of going to Australia or the United States. She preferred Australia because the United States was clearly too dangerous, not so good for children. The elder daughter was in a very good Indian school and had learned English well from TV (*Sesame Street, The Simpsons,* and Donald Duck).[29]

I visited Parveen in her home a few days later and learned more about women's lives in Kuwait. Because women should not take buses or orange taxis alone, I journeyed there in the private taxi owned and operated by Parveen's Egyptian neighbor, calling ahead on her building watchman's illegal phone as they had just moved and her phone had not yet been put in. Such watchmen in Kuwait were always expatriate Arabs, and all Arabs referred to Parveen as "Zainab's mother" rather than by name. The children had Barbie dolls and watched carefully chosen American TV programs, and Parveen had a part-time maid, a Sri Lankan Catholic who had converted to Islam during stints in Saudi Arabia and the UAE. We lunched, talked, and, after 7 P.M. when the day was cooling down, went to McDonalds on the beachfront, where the girls played on swings and we all had strawberry milkshakes. We called the same Egyptian taxi driver for the ride home. The night before, the family had attended a *majlis* (it was Muharram, the Shia month of mourning) and then gone to the beach at 3 A.M.

Another longtime businessman in Kuwait, Mujeebulla Mukarram,[30] had started in 1967 as a chemist in an American company and moved into business for himself, supplying chemicals to companies. "I was taking a chance; I was the first in my family to go east, not west," he said. The Gulf offered, he said, the best of both worlds, Western amenities and Eastern culture and values. His wife taught English for the Kuwaiti government, and his children grew up in Kuwait with all good things available to them, including holidays in Europe. Hyderabad itself had become spoiled, with "rotten" conditions, and his children would not consider settling there, declaring it "fit for shopping and for marriages but not for living." The Mukarrams established their children as students in Canada (and, having become Canadian citizens themselves as business investors, they had been flown out of Kuwait by the Canadian government in 1990).[31] Most of Mukarram's friends, St. Georgians, were in London, Canada, and elsewhere. Hyderabad society was being best preserved in London, in his opinion.[32]

Mohamed Yousufuddin, another "senior Hyderabadi" in Kuwait, was from a less cosmopolitan background but his children too seemed to be heading west. He had been there since 1975, and, as deputy manager of strategic purchasing for "the biggest food company in the Gulf," he had many responsibilities. An extremely busy man, Yousufuddin was annoyed that a parking problem made him two minutes late for our appointment. His ancestral home was in the old city, and he had attended City High School and double majored in commerce and physical education at Osmania. Osmania's fine education had sent him and other Hyderabadis abroad, he said, and in his case it was the "sports side" that had brought him to Kuwait; he had come for a sports conference and been offered a job. His wife and children returned to Hyderabad after the children reached the tenth class, and the children had all earned higher education degrees there. Of Yousufuddin's three daughters, who had degrees but were not working, two were married with children in Medina and one was in New Jersey expecting his "first American grandchild; her husband's an American, from Hyderabad of course." Of his five sons, four (an engineer, a doctor, an MBA, and a future civil servant) were in Hyderabad and one (an engineer) was in Kuwait. The sons were just beginning to marry, the first to a Hyderabadi in India, the next to a Hyderabadi in the United States.[33]

Professionals from Hyderabad who enjoyed high salaries and other benefits reported that the Gulf lifestyle and the contrast with life in Hyderabad, brought home to them starkly during forced stays there during the Gulf War, were prompting reconsiderations of their future plans. Mohammed Hoshdar Khan and Mir Ibrahim Ali Khan, a company manager and an architect, had both gone back to India during the Invasion. Mohammed Hoshdar Khan reported that the communal riots in Hyderabad in 1990 had meant sleepless nights and had upset his children. "We pacified them, said it was normal routine there, just a political problem, not really a religious thing." Then it struck him that in his twelve years in Kuwait there had been no communal riots. His children had also been uneasy walking to school in Hyderabad with open drains running onto the road. The second man, Mir Ibrahim Ali Khan, had worked as an architect in Iran and Saudi Arabia before Kuwait. Three of his wife's brothers were in the United States and he was deciding to send his children there for higher education. They were being educated in Hyderabad, although they "cried for years when sent back, found it difficult to adapt . . . and ask to come for vacations to Kuwait." Ali Khan regretted that he was probably too senior to start over in the United States himself.[34]

Taqi Hyder and his wife,[35] an engineer and a teacher in a Kuwait school for physically and mentally handicapped children, respectively, had done well in Kuwait but "lost everything" to looters in 1990. Their son, Zulfiqar, sent back to Hyderabad during the Invasion, had initially had difficulties but came to appreciate the greater freedom there, the freedom to move about easily, taking buses, walking, and so on. Zulfiqar had gone to Cyprus for college, choosing an option that would allow transfer to the

United States after two years, but the family was building a new home in Banjara Hills and had planned to return to Hyderabad. Yet they felt the city was "an urban disaster, with so many problems, like water, electricity, the population . . . urban services were impossible, even Banjara is a mess." But they could not become Kuwaiti citizens, starting fresh overseas would be very difficult, and their families were still based in Hyderabad.

Doctors, prominent members of the expatriate professional class, had been pressed to stay in Kuwait during the Invasion. Because jobs in India were less lucrative, Dr. Syed Mehmood ur Rahman[36] had spent "a terrible year" in Libya and then moved to Kuwait in 1983. He had Kuwaiti friends, sheikhs who came to him for treatment, and he introduced the business-man Hoshdar Khan to them. He himself had been "too busy" to attend the 400th birthday celebration or the Gold Cup games.[37] Their social life in Kuwait revolved around their four children and they missed their relatives; she had many working in the emirates but none nearby. When the Invasion came, like other doctors, Dr. Rahman was called on to prioritize people for medical evacuation, but he and his wife could not leave themselves because their small daughter had just had a heart operation. Life was far from normal; they could not take their four children out to McDonalds, Hardees, Baskin Robbins, and the beach, nor could their four children watch their regular carefully screened TV programs. His wife kept music playing in the home so the children would not hear the bombs dropping. During the seven months Occupation, Rahman and his wife helped some one hundred Bangladeshi workers who had been abandoned by their employers, left without food, money, or places to sleep. Some Kuwaitis had also "left their maids in the road." Rahman and other doctors who stayed and "helped so many Kuwaitis" had been promised on the radio and in the press that they would be paid for their wartime services, but that had not happened.[38] The Rahmans intended to go back and had bought property in Hyderabad.

Family life for upper-middle-class and upper-class Hyderabadis in Kuwait was vividly evoked by Hoshdar Khan's brother-in-law Akbar Khan as he spoke about his own family. His wife, like so many other wives, had gone back to Hyderabad during the hot season. He had arrived in 1978, started as a lab technician,[39] and became a plant manager. He came for the money and got hooked, he said; the money was so good. His eldest child, a daughter, was in twelfth grade at the American School and next had to be sent to India or the United States. The family planned to return to India, "even though there might be discrimination against Muslims—the richer Muslims had to stay and help the poor ones." However, Akbar feared his children would not be happy in Hyderabad. They no longer liked Hyder-abadi food, finding it too spicy and preferring sandwiches, hamburgers,

and other junk food. When sent back after the Invasion, even though Akbar provided a car, a maid, and good schools for them, the children "could
not adjust." They had had a hard time in Hyderabad's schools, with forty
to fifty students per class and no cold water available. They said, "Daddy,
call us back to Kuwait as soon as you can!" They had also had a bad experience visiting Hyderabad after the 1992 Babri Masjid incident. They could
not sleep for several nights for fear of communal riots, and Akbar stayed
up with a rifle listening to news. The children asked what the danger
was, who was after them, and why? "What to say, we cannot poison their
minds," Akbar said. He went on to contrast his children's experiences in
Kuwait, where they knew no Hindus, with his father's and his own experiences with Hindu friends since childhood.[40]

Social life for Hyderabadi men and women in Kuwait, Akbar reported,
was overwhelmingly with fellow country people as the Kuwaiti government allowed only "nationalities," country-based categories, to form associations. Activities that drew South Asians together centered on "national"
events, sports (cricket), *mushairas*, and religious prayer or educational groups.
In Kuwait, women's associations did not exist and were not thought desirable, so women's lives were quite restricted.

Akbar Khan vividly portrayed the situation for Hyderabadi women in
Kuwait:

> My wife wore a burqah years ago at home, before it went out of fashion, but
> here she put on the *abayah*, like other highly educated women, and my daugh-
> ter donned the hijab at age ten or eleven. Purdah, in fact, is observed more in
> Kuwait than in India, because the country is a more religious one. Everything
> is more religious, from prayers at work to family activities. Here, my wife and
> children are more dependent on me; I must do everything for them, drop them
> and pick them up in groups of women and children. If it is just my own wife
> and children who want to go somewhere, I must accompany them; it does not
> look good for them to go on their own. There is no danger to them in Ku-
> wait; this is just for appearances. Kuwaiti women are different from the Indian
> women; the Kuwaiti women work, they leave their houses and children, they
> depend totally on servants. But Indian women do not work; they stay in the
> home, taking care of the children. They may have maids but they also like
> housework. Just a few Indian women work, like [X's] wife (but don't tell him
> I said so). When I alone can support my family, why should my wife be bur-
> dened? But my daughter wants to go for an MBA, she wants to go for a pilot
> training course in the United States; she goes to the American School.

He emphasized the widely shared preference in Kuwait that women not
work outside the home but his views about traditional gender roles did not
extend to his daughter.

Another Hyderabadi couple discussed family life in Kuwait. Abu Turab
Mujeebuddin worked for the Kuwaiti government and Mrs. Mujeebuddin

wore the burqah in Kuwait and in Hyderabad and enjoyed many things in Kuwait, especially the food and the medical facilities. He was active not in Hoshdar Khan's Indian Muslim Welfare Organization but in the Hyderabad Muslim Welfare Association, which guided students and helped people. But Mujeebuddin faced sending his wife and children back soon, as the eldest was reaching tenth class. His wife enjoyed being with her husband and having the use of a car in the Gulf, and she was resisting going back, although if the daughter stayed through twelfth class or intermediate, the family would be considered NRIs and the daughter would find it harder to get one of the limited seats.[41]

Evacuated to Hyderabad during the Invasion, the Mujeebuddins had had a horrible experience—traveling with four young children and lots of luggage and staying in the desert in tents for ten days in Iraq and Jordan. Back in Hyderabad, the children had not liked the bad roads and other features of life there. When he returned to work, including six months while oil was still burning (the retreating Iraqi army set fire to Kuwait's oil wells, spreading heavy oily smoke throughout the area), he found their furnished flat had been completely looted. Other things had worsened, too, after the Gulf War. As a government employee on a year-to-year contract, he was vulnerable to increased Kuwaiti government efforts to employ more Kuwaitis and fewer expatriates, and the government had stopped giving children's allowances to expatriates.

Indian Hyderabadis seemed not to socialize with Hyderabadis from Pakistan in Kuwait. Tahar Affandi, general manager of a trading and contracting firm, was one of the few Hyderabadis I met who had close Pakistani friends. His background was unusual, but he considered himself "pure Hyderabadi, in language, food, and other domestic things." Tahar's father was born in Saudi Arabia but married a Hyderabadi, as did Tahar and all of his siblings except one sister who married a Pakistani Hyderabadi.[42] Tahar had "gone outside" (of India) to work, partly because Indira Gandhi's land ceiling measures drastically subdivided the family's farmland and partly because of the politicization of religion. "The Hindus who are doing well in the Gulf, as a minority, should understand the position of Muslims in India and prefer to keep them as they are, not crush them. . . . Segregation has become worse; we feel it when traveling; people ask the name at once, before going on talking. Before, it was not like that." However, he and his other relatives working abroad intended to retire to Hyderabad, where they were buying property.

At a luncheon held by Tahar and his wife Husna, the guests shared a preference for careers in Kuwait above all other places. One older man had gone to Pakistan in 1969 but left for Kuwait because of bad conditions in the 1970s. A young man had left Chicago for Kuwait because he "did not like to sacrifice his values by marrying an immigrant girl [he meant a Hyderabadi girl born in the United States]." Another man had worked in Iraq but moved to Kuwait in 1975, sending his children to India and the United States for higher education. A Karachi-born wife who was present, a woman who had visited Hyderabad, told us all she had found it "untidy"; perhaps in retaliation, the Hyderabadis present decried Pakistani habits like dancing at weddings and wearing a *ghararah* (a woman's dress different from Hyderabad's distinctive wedding dress, the *khara dupatta*). All the Hyderabadis except Tahar's sister (based in Karachi) planned to return to Hyderabad after staying in Kuwait as long as possible. "This is a peaceful country," they said, overlooking the recent Gulf War. The consensus among the guests favored large families and disapproved of women working outside the home. "This is the way of the best people (*sharif log*), women should come in the bridal chair and leave in the coffin (*doli me jae, dola niklae*).

A final portrait of family life, or the lack of it, came from a professional and a self-professed Hyderabadi, Dr. Naidu Venkat Rao,[43] who planned to stay just one more year in Kuwait. After twenty-two years teaching at Osmania and the Agricultural University, ending as professor and head of pharmacology, in 1979 he looked abroad. He had decided to head the Kuwait Ministry of Health's Drug Control section in Kuwait[44] rather than teach in Nigeria. He moved abroad to finance his children's education, since caste politics and low pay in Hyderabad meant that an ordinary businessman on the street did better than a professor; furthermore, Indian education was getting more and more commercialized. His daughter had completed Gandhi Medical College in Hyderabad, married a Hyderabadi structural engineer in New Jersey, and was doing her residency in the United States; Rao's wife was there with her, looking after the couple's baby girl.[45] Dr. Rao managed the Hyderabad Cricket Club in Kuwait, one of sixteen teams regularly engaged in tournaments,[46] and he had been convenor of sports for the 400th birthday celebration. He recommended Mujeebulla's restaurant for *biryani*, and he had often hired the Mann-o-Salwa's cook for private parties before his wife went back to Hyderabad. She had not returned after the Occupation, although most of the cricket team members, the guests at his parties, had. Dr. Rao was very lonely in Kuwait.

HYDERABADI COMMUNITY LIFE IN KUWAIT

Hyderabadi society in Kuwait was quite separate from Kuwaiti society. Few Hyderabadis socialized with Kuwaitis or mentioned them favorably, and most felt that the separation became more marked after the war. One person compared the situation of children being raised in Kuwait and America: "Our kids can never become Kuwaitis, unlike the situation of those living in America; our children here go to Indian British style schools, apart from Kuwaitis."

Hyderabadi society in Kuwait was stratified by class, religion, and gender, as one perceptive expatriate observed:

> Many people here are clawing their way up; they are from the old city, from humble backgrounds, and they are going right back, trying to make a place for themselves back there. But there are others, more educated, more supportive of working wives. The class structure determines the options and restrictions here.

Views about women were closely connected to class and religion, with the "decadent, dangerous West" standing in implicit contrast to the safe, Islamic environment of Kuwait. The wearing of the hijab was generally adopted in Kuwait, even by Hyderabadi women who did not wear it elsewhere, to "fit in" and for protection in an environment where few women moved about alone or uncovered. In some circles—for example, that developing around the big businessman, Hoshdar Khan—pressure to wear the hijab was growing. One woman told me, "there is pressure to wear it, in that group, even his own wife didn't wear it before. I do generally wear it when moving about, but at the cricket match at the 400th birthday celebration I went without it; I didn't want to be grouped with those others."

Hyderabadis in Kuwait acknowledged the religious atmosphere and its effects on their daily life. The traditional nonreligious salutation, *adab arz*, was giving way to the Islamic salutation, *salam aleikum*, although some Hyderabadis meeting other Hyderabadis raised their hands to their foreheads as is done with *adab*, while saying *salam aleikum*. One person commented that religious meetings inaugurated in the 1990s by the businessman Hoshdar Khan meant the "replacement of family fun outings by those religious meetings every Friday, and about 100 people go now; one must take food; it requires work. This has become social climbing." A man named as a rival leader of an Indian Muslim society in Kuwait, significantly, was a green card holder in the United States and had children in the local American School.

A Hyderabad Association had been organized to put on the 400th celebration in 1990, people said. The celebration had been outstanding, "the best of all the 400ths, we spent lots of money, we had the 'must' guests, all were here," as Mohamed Yousufuddin put it. And the celebration was "not just the big people, we all did it together."[47] But afterward, although there were about the same numbers of Indians and Hyderabadis in Kuwait, they were not the same people as before 1990. "Many are new, the old people were not called back," and the association had not continued. People explained that, also, it was expensive to rent halls in Kuwait and that everyone was very busy. (This was certainly true; people constantly changed my appointments with them, citing new business appointments that took priority.) The Hyderabad Muslim Welfare Organization was rather small and aimed at economic and social problems in Hyderabad as much as in Kuwait, and there were no women's organizations among the Hyderabadis in Kuwait.

There were broader organizations in Kuwait, for example, an Aligarh "old boys'" association and similar school associations from Kerala. An Urdu association, the Bazm-i-Urdu, bridged national divisions, and there were Urdu enthusiasts in Kuwait, albeit busy ones. The businessman Yousufuddin was one of them, convinced that teaching Urdu to the children overseas was all that was needed to preserve the treasure of Hyderabadi culture.[48]

> Hyderabadi culture was a mixed thing of both Muslims and Hindus: even the Hindus had the clothing and daily behaviors, and Islam, in Hyderabad, had as a courtesy accepted some Hindu things to create good relations. Urdu is, therefore, necessary for both Hyderabadi culture and for Islam, which must be known through Urdu or Arabic; Urdu is the third language of the world.

Most officially favored of the broader associations was the Indian Muslim Welfare Association, formed in 1995 with a push from the Indian Embassy. The embassy reportedly wanted a registered Muslim association to hold functions similar to those being held by "the Hindu associations." The relationship with the embassy was generally good, but this association was viewed somewhat cynically by at least one important businessman. Another told me that he wanted to be called Indian first, then Muslim, then Hyderabadi, and that the Babri Masjid incident in India had shaken the Indian Muslims in Kuwait badly.[49]

Although a leading businessman who employed many people likened the Gulf to prepartition India and said that Indians, Pakistanis, and Bangladeshis mingled easily, others pointed to tensions, and most informants clearly drew boundaries based on national origin as well as class.[50] Tellingly, when people spoke of arranging their children's marriages, most Indian Hyderabadis would not consider Pakistani Hyderabadis. One emphatic naysayer said that he "would not consider a Pakistani Hyderabadi because of their consumer culture, their materialism, and the fact that in Pakistan there's no control, no check; everything from culture to the economy to politics is out of control there." Other Indian Hyderabadis said: "We cannot depend on them, in business or anything; business relationships are very negligible and not at all do we want family relationships"; "they are not trustworthy for any business, even tailoring prices can be changed to their advantage"; and "No, certainly not, political differences are there and the second generation Hyderabadis there are definitely Pakistanis and not at all like Hyderabadis."

The UAE: Expatriates "Closer To Home"

WORKING THEIR WAY UP IN THE UAE

The United Arab Emirates (UAE) business environment was as competitive as Kuwait's, probably even more so because of the UAE's vigorous efforts to diversify and attract foreign investors. Hyderabadis took personal pride in the UAE's achievements, particularly those of Dubai.[51] Of the seven emirates, Abu Dhabi, Dubai, and Sharjah were the leading ones and most Hyderabadis worked in them.[52] Sindhis (from Sind) dominated the business classes, especially in the gold and jewelry bazaars, and Keralites (from Kerala) dominated the service classes in the UAE. In fact, Keralites were said to be the most numerous group from India, and local sayings about them abounded—for example, "even a sheikh cannot survive without a Kerala man." People argued about whether Sindhis or Hyderabadis came second, but everyone knew that the late Sheikh Rashid (1958 to 1986), the ruler of Dubai credited with its innovative development, had had a Hyderabadi driver of whom he was very fond. Sayings about Hyderabadis emphasized their feudal heritage and their Nawabi culture: "Hyderabadis cannot make money, they have no dash; in front of Keralites they cannot shine. They stick away, at a distance, doing *adab*." (Note that they were still saying *adab* in Dubai.)

Hyderabadi businessmen and workers began coming to the UAE more than thirty years ago. Many came by launch, a trip of about three days from Bombay to Dubai, and sometimes they swam ashore. Taxis waited on the beaches, but many swimmers had no passports at all, and people sometime shot at them. All the early shopkeepers were from Kerala or Barkas, Hyderabad's Arab locality. There were many marriages back then between local Arabs and women from Barkas or other parts of Hyderabad State, so South Asian culture was part of the home life as well as the work life of many UAE Arabs.

Those Hyderabadis who arrived in the 1950s and 1960s have seen dramatic changes in Dubai and the other emirates. In the early decades, some migrants were given emirate passports, nearly impossible to obtain after the formation of the UAE in 1971. Mohammed Abdul Jabbar, who ran a popular Hyderabadi restaurant in Sharjah, came as an illiterate worker in 1973, following a brother-in-law already working there. When his launch from India landed, a queue of three or four taxis was waiting on the beach. It was summer and "blazingly hot, but one would work in the flames of hell to get out of Hyderabad then." He shared a taxi with a Chaous, an Arab from Hyderabad who had come in 1952 and gotten a local passport; Mir Miraj Ali and Ahmed Hassan remembered that same Chaous as an early contact of theirs.

Jabbar began as a messenger, then did some cooking for co-workers, and, finding his culinary skills in demand, became cook for a Pakistani *Begum* (married woman) in Ajman. With that family's sponsorship, he brought his wife and two children from Yaqutpura and started his own restaurant in 1977, at a time when the city did not inspect or license restaurants, when "all was desert and people walked everywhere." The city "came up so fast," his business grew, and his brother came and helped him and his wife, catering for weddings and developing a lunchbox or tiffin carrier service. Jabbar and his wife had another ten children and sent them all to good schools. His money went for those schools and the taxis to transport the children to them; they were his biggest expenses, along with rent, sponsor fees, and air conditioners for the house and restaurant. If he had educated his children in India, he could have built one or two houses for each of them there, the savings would have been so great, he said. He seldom cooked time-consuming Hyderabadi specialties anymore, as the volume of his take-out business was so large. Also, he became disillusioned with Hyderabadis over the years, as some took advantage of his generosity.

Mir Miraj Ali and Ahmed Hassan, from Abu Dhabi, talked about the early days and what had changed. They had come in 1968 and 1975, when the Indian rupee was the local currency and everything came by sea from India and Pakistan: "food, newspapers, people, everything." They tried to remember the name of another mulki old-timer, a Hindu Telugu-speaker from St. George's Grammar School, a Nissan salesman married to a Lebanese woman. Most Telugu-speakers in the Gulf in 1995, they said, were not mulkis but had been coming for only ten or fifteen years and had their own association. The new Telugu-speakers had not joined the Hyderabad Association formed in 1978 in Abu Dhabi and led by Hyderabadi businessmen.[53] Hassan, the earlier arrival, had an Osmania science degree but had studied Arabic; when visiting cousins in Bombay, he served as interpreter for Yemeni businessmen from Qatar making a deal with the Tatas (one of India's largest family businesses). The Tatas immediately employed him to open a branch in Abu Dhabi. He then worked for Phillips Oil, exploring the desert with caravans and growing to like it despite the heat. Eventually he became a journalist for the *Khaleej Times*, an expatriate English-language newspaper based in Dubai. He married a Hyderabadi in 1972 and brought her to the Gulf, where they had four children. His wife had many relatives in the United States, but he was sure it would be hard to settle there—the religious atmosphere in Abu Dhabi was preferable. Hassan was one of many Hyderabadi Muslims who termed Islam in the UAE more "real" or authentic than that in India or Pakistan.[54]

Miraj Ali was also a religious man, his red-dyed beard showing that he had made the pilgrimage to Mecca. An architect with an Abu Dhabi firm, he too had brought his wife and children to the Gulf, although those still in school were back in India studying (his wife, supervising them there, came every six months to keep her resident permit valid). Ali's firm was a private one with two locals as partners, and he had joined it in 1983.[55] He noted changes in the Gulf culture after the death of Sheikh Rashid in 1986. For example, Indian *mujra* (North Indian dance, associated with dancing girls at the Mughal court) was being performed in hotels, and other "Western/tourist stuff" was coming in; the Sheikh's sons were young men, Ali explained. He noted another change: the locals used to go to India or Pakistan for education, and now they were going to the UK, and people from South Asia used to go to the UK for education, but now they were going to the United States. Thus the locals and South Asians were diverging, no longer sharing educational institutions.

Other Hyderabadis worked for the *Khaleej Times*, including the photographer Hasan Bozai. A member of the Ittehad ul Muslimeen as a student in Hyderabad, he went to Pakistan in 1948, following his sister and her husband.[56] Recruited in 1978 from the Karachi newspaper, *Dawn*, to work for the *Gulf News*, he switched to the rival *Khaleej Times*.[57] Bozai did not plan to return to Pakistan;[58] two of his four sons were settled in Toronto, both married to Canadian Hyderabadis.[59] Hyderabad was still important to him, and he was a member of an informal group that contributed fees for Muslim schoolboys and schoolgirls, most of them in Hyderabad but some in Pakistan.[60] Another *Khaleej Times* journalist,[61] Ali Ishrati, and his family had come to the UAE in 1978, but because of some initial problems, his wife had taken their two daughters back to India until 1982. That had been good; the children liked India, where "life was unpredictable, a struggle, and the children learned to do things themselves; in Dubai, they just board a designated school bus; all is boring and routine."[62]

Hyderabadi businessmen, big and small, formed a significant group in the UAE and some had been harmed by the Gulf War, although its impact was less in the UAE that in Kuwait.[63] Sharafat Walajahi, a Hyderabadi from Pakistan,[64] moved from London right after the war as manager and then

owner of a clothing factory. Walajahi grew up in Kachiguda and graduated from Osmania at age seventeen in 1947. His father had been treasurer
of the militant Muslim organization, the Ittehad ul Muslimeen, and the
young Sharafat had addressed a gathering of 50,000 Ittehad followers when
only thirteen. He went to Pakistan in 1948, the youngest in his family and
the first to go, because "there was no future for us in India." With dual
citizenship in Pakistan and the UK, he spent a decade in the UK and was
president of London's Hyderabad Deccan Association before taking up the
challenge of running a factory in the UAE.[65]

Walajahi and his wife lived in Dubai and arranged a dinner party for me
in 1995. His wife Sultana, an "old Mahbubiyan," had moved from Hyderabad to Pakistan as his bride and retained many Hyderabadi connections.[66]
They took care to invite, he said, "all three types of Hyderabadis in the
Gulf: those prominent businessmen who are from Hyderabad and are going back there, pure Hyderabadis; those who migrated to Pakistan but still
associate closely with some Hyderabadis from India; and those who have
become pure Pakistanis." He put himself in the second category.

Although Sharafat had not been to Hyderabad for thirty years,[67] he displayed an impressive grasp of its social landscape, remarking on the people
he had invited and their family histories.[68] Most of the older couples present had been in Dubai since the 1970s, coming from both India and Pakistan, some via the UK. Because it was the hot season, several wives were
in the United States, the UK, Canada, and Pakistan visiting adult children.
Absent wives included those of M. A. Saleem, in the roofing and floor-
ing business, and Shoukatullah, an architect, both from my old locality,
Himayatnagar; Surender Singh, a tire tycoon whose cousin was building a house next to the Girs in Banjara Hills; Hasan Bozai, photographer
with the *Khaleej Times*; and Taufiq Baig, brother of Majid Baig in Karachi.
Some of the younger couples had never been to Hyderabad but were attached to it; they felt they shared its values, loved the food, and still spoke
Urdu. Others qualified their commitment to Hyderabad, mentioning the
UK, Pakistan, and even Saudi Arabia or Dubai as places with which they
identified more closely. Many were uncertain about where they would
eventually settle.[69]

As in Kuwait, Hyderabadi doctors were a significant set of expatriates.
Dr. Ashfaq and Dr. Razia Khan, husband and wife, practiced in one of
the smaller emirates.[70] He had "gone out" to Iran in 1982, and then, after
their 1984 marriage, the couple settled in the UAE, living in Umm al-
Qawain and working for a private clinic and the ministry of health hospital
there. Other Hyderabadis in Umm al-Qawain were either the wives of locals or workers. The Khans had a servant from Hyderabad, and his mother

lived with them unhindered by regulations (doctors got such privileges from the emirates, along with very high salaries). For the time being, they were happily employed and their children attended an excellent school in Sharjah. Other relatives were in the Gulf, Hyderabad, Pakistan, and the United States.

The doctors Khan were reconsidering their plans to return to their new house in Banjara Hills. When they visited Hyderabad, their children found it a shock and always became ill from the food and air pollution. Dr. Ashfaq Khan said:

> Muslims are a neglected lot, and the government favors uneducated and sched-uled caste groups. We have become alien to our own place. . . . Osmania uni-versity was so fine, the sherwani was the uniform, Urdu the language; now, even on my diploma, some Telugu script is there. But I still enjoy going to look at the University, it is so grand. . . . At heart, we are Hyderabadis, but the changes make us feel dejected and hurt, and we cannot properly confront them; still, our forefathers are buried there.

The children's futures were the family's chief consideration, and India offered advantages. Khan continued:

> The children must get used to their native place; schooling is good and reason-able in India, and the children are more competent in India; they don't need all these things we have here, to get along; here, they are spoiled. . . . Later on, after their schooling, the children can go to any part of the world for their betterment. This is a new world; they will have their own wishes; we don't want to pressure them, even for marriage; the life partner will be his or her choice. . . . I prefer my relatives, of course; the customs will be too different, but it is a modern world now.

They were "even prepared to settle in America," Dr. Ashfaq said, where Razia's siblings were obtaining a green card for her, but they were ap-prehensive about the culture. They knew doctors were treated well but feared, for example, the tolerance of homosexuality.[71]

Another cluster of Hyderabadis in Dubai came from Secunderabad[72] and several were friends of Mirza Shamsher Ali Baig, my guide in Kuwait. Anthony David, Mirza's neighbor back in Marredpalli, came in 1979, fol-lowing his older brother Charles who came in 1975. Using their Gulf earn-ings, Tony and Charles built a big bungalow back in Secunderabad and married off two sisters and a brother. Tony married in 1992 and brought his wife Elizabeth to Dubai. She worked as a computer operator until a baby came and getting babysitters proved a problem. Because Elizabeth no longer worked, they were saving little, and she planned to go back soon to Hyderabad (partly to continue her government job there). Tony was a Tamil-speaker, but he and his wife spoke mostly English at home. He loved languages, he said, and could speak Telugu, Konkani, Urdu, Hindi, Gujarati, Sindhi, Arabic, and even Pushtu, the last learned from a Pakistani watchman in Dubai. Anthony and Elizabeth David enjoyed Dubai, where they attended St. Mary's Catholic Church. Tony knew no "locals" except his own sponsor and he knew no Hyderabadi or Pakistani Muslims in Dubai. "We feel we are staying in our own country," he said; "we do not relate to others but only to those we know."[73]

Mahesh Jetty Maheshwar Rao, a Telugu-speaker, had followed Tony David, his best friend and classmate, to Dubai in about 1985. Both men worked in a Cosmos showroom, in the Hyatt Regency Galleria, perhaps Dubai's top luxury hotel complex in the mid-1990s, and like Tony he had married and brought his wife. Neither Mahesh nor his wife had ever been out of Hyderabad before, nor had they been to Golconda or the famous Salar Jung Museum in Hyderabad's old city. Mahesh's work schedule was heavy, from 9 to 1 and then 4 to 9, with half-days off on Fridays only. He had two younger brothers still at home and advised them to stay in India.

Another cluster of Secunderabad men in Dubai worked for the Melromass Company, selling encyclopedias and school texts on commission. Six of the nine salesmen in the Melromass Company were from Hyderabad (Hindus, Muslims, and Christians); the other three were from Kerala. The salesmen traveled throughout the seven emirates, although most orders came from Abu Dhabi, El Ain, and Dubai. Arun De Souza, a Tamil-speaking Christian, was still known primarily as Mr. Ganesh, his pre-conversion and passport name. He had come through the "famous lady for visas," Rizwana Qadri, in Banjara Hills, who "sold" him to a man in Bombay who made him and other workers wait there almost a month while he tried to get more commission from Rizwana before sending them on to Dubai. Arun grew up near the Secunderabad Club and was its squash marker; he got his Melromass job in Dubai through a Secunderabad man to whom he had taught squash at the Club.[74] Arun had his wife and two daughters in Dubai, where they attended St. Mary's Catholic Church. His wife liked it in the Gulf, as there were no elders in the home or nearby; she also worked, and they had built a house in Secunderabad to which they would return in about two years, when the girls needed higher schooling.[75] She did cook Hyderabadi food, *bagara baigan, biryani,* and *khatti dal;* and he was asking her to learn Chinese cooking as well.

Vinaya Shekhar, another Melromass salesman from Secunderabad, was a recently arrived (1993) bachelor who was really struggling in the Gulf. A Telugu-speaker whose mother had taught school to support the family after his father, a captain in the army, died, Vinaya had insisted on coming to Dubai when offered a job there after graduation. He worked very hard but the market for encyclopedias was dwindling, and he was not sure he had made the right decision. He shared a flat in Deira, near the office, with three men from Bangalore; Sharjah would have been cheaper but involved transportation costs. Because his irregular hours meant sometimes going without food, he had a tiffin carrier supply him with meals. His company, at least, "belongs to the Hyderabadis," so he felt secure in Dubai, but his efforts far outstripped his earnings. With no salary, he was dependent on 10 percent commission on his sales.

He spoke vividly of his struggles.[76]

> In the Gulf, one has to deal with illiterate people, people with no manners; people who started as tea boys become receptionists, and higher. Reception- ists say "No" to us, a hundred times over, and we cannot sell costly encyclo- pedia sets to people who have come here to earn, not spend. . . . Taxis are a big expense; we try to share them; the company takes four of us salesmen to Abu Dhabi with a car and driver, and then I walk in the sun for hours, taking Electrolyte and trying to make a sale. . . . There are so many different na- tionalities here, and they talk funny in Urdu, the Filipinos, Thais, Egyptians, Palestinians, and Iranis. The Filipinos buy best, almost 100 percent of my business is with them, for their kids and the kids' education, and some schools give encyclopedias as rewards. Those Egyptians, Palestinians, Jordanians, and Lebanese, they never buy, they just waste your time. . . . Also, people can can- cel within twenty-four hours, and some pay monthly installments (others do the collections but we reps have some responsibilities for that); the job is hard, frustrating. . . . [T]his month, I've made no sale yet. But, having seen Dubai, the style of life here, the facilities, the communications, the roads, to go back is to go down. And if you go back to India, somebody catches you and says, "have coffee, do you think because you've been to the Gulf you're too good to have coffee with me?" So you do have coffee, and there's ten minutes wasted, time wasted. . . . Here, one cannot waste time, and I read biographies, and I watch Star TV, about how someone rose, how he came up in life, how he became rich . . . and at night I go to the boats, to Abra Creek, having tea after 9 or 10 P.M., talking to anyone, Germans, anyone.

Vinaya stated that either suffering or good luck awaited one in Dubai, and one Anglo-Indian family from Secunderabad had met with very good luck. Fred Ellis was in banking back in Hyderabad and three of his sons followed banking careers. The first Ellis in the Gulf was Eugene, Fred and Mavis Ellis's second son, in 1975. Another son, Ambrose, followed, and then the fourth child, Elizabeth, went in 1982 and was joined by her parents. The youngest of the six Ellis children, Joan, also worked in the Gulf.[77]

Elizabeth Ellis had done very well in the Gulf. She had been a sports person, not too good at school (St. George's), a swimming coach at the Secunderabad Club.[78] In Dubai, she held a man's job, supervising construc- tion workers (mostly Pathans from Pakistan). "I wish my teachers could see me now," she said; "I can shout at the Pathans, I really get respect." Her mother kept house for her, as Elizabeth always came late and the job was stressful, and her father, although over sixty, was still working.[79] Fred, Mavis, and Elizabeth all felt that they were Hyderabadi because they knew Urdu well and ate only Hyderabadi, not European, food. They told friends coming from home to bring them "that *bhojanam masala*" (the first a Telugu word for meals, the second a Hindustani one for seasoning). Liz asked also for a hymn book and a St. George's school tie. They followed Andhra politics, watching the BBC news and Star TV.[80] Life in the Gulf had become increasingly difficult, with the tightening of rules and renewals of her parents' residence permits coming up annually. But, Liz said, "I owe this country a lot; from nothing I became something; I can afford it all here, and I've seen other parts of the world. Dad had a personal audience with the Pope in 1988."

WOMEN AS WIVES AND WORKERS IN THE UAE

For Hyderabadi women, life in the UAE was qualitatively different from that in Kuwait. They moved about freely and met women from many countries on the job and in everyday life, especially in Dubai. A visit to a beauty salon, *Zenana*, with Anees Ali illustrated this. The owner was a Kenyan woman, whereas the hair cutters, colorists, and threaders came from Goa, Bombay, and Delhi, and the manicurist was a Filipina. A Sudanese woman customer bargained vigorously for a bridal special beauty package, and most of the women in the salon knew each other from previous visits.

Hyderabadi women saw the UAE as a middle ground, a place that required neither rigid preservation nor drastic alteration of family and community traditions.[81] A *bindi*-wearing Muslim woman (*bindis* were more typically worn by Hindus) from Hyderabad city, Sarosh, told me of her effort to teach her husband, a Muslim from coastal Andhra schooled in Hyderabad, to be a Hyderabadi; she had given up but in the course of the effort had reflected on Hyderabadi culture. Cultural things had long ago replaced religious ones in Hyderabad, she thought, things like "how one did *adab*, how one prepared *pan*, what one ate with what—it was decadent, really. I rebelled, served something to someone wrong, just handed it to him on a plate, and my mother was horrified." Yet she, like other women in her family, continued to wear a *bindi* and decried what she saw as increasing religious orthodoxy among Hyderabadis in Western countries. She commented on Hyderabadi weddings held in Canada and the United States, where she could see on videos that

> people are doing all the things we no longer do in Hyderabad, washing feet with milk, putting on *haldi* [turmeric], and so on. Things are changing at home, but people are becoming more religious outside, giving up birthday celebra-

tions, not taking prawns, becoming totally conservative after going on hajj, and so on.

Sarosh was teaching English at a local college of technology, and, like her, most Hyderabadi women in Dubai were working and needed household help and childcare. Bringing servants (maids, cooks, ayahs) from Hyderabad was the favored solution, and Sarosh had brought her mother's cook from Hyderabad. He came to her three times a week (and to Ayesha, another working wife I met, and to others too, including some non-Hyderabadi Pakistanis).[82]

One young professional couple brought a maid from home, the endeavor showing the problems Hyderabadis encountered trying to recreate a homeland atmosphere in the Gulf. Given the expatriate sex ratio in the UAE, the couple did not want a young maid, as men would be courting her; they wanted an older woman who spoke Urdu, could prepare Hyderabadi food, and would reinforce Hyderabadi culture for the children.[83] As a maid already in the Gulf would be a risk (she might be illegal, and a maid's original sponsor had the most control over her), the couple sponsored an older woman recommended by relatives. The salary offered was 3,000 rupees (almost $100) a month, far above Indian salaries. The husband stood in lines to get the maid's visa and pay the UAE "maid tax," paid the maid's full airfare from India and met her at the airport, and got her a health check (another fee). All this accomplished, he was given an annual registration card for that maid, good only for her.

This maid, an impoverished Muslim woman of about sixty away from home for the first time and unable to read or write, did not work out. Her employers did not allow her to go out of the apartment, feeling that she would not be comfortable in the extreme heat or capable of negotiating the big city. The children could not go outside either, partly because of the heat and partly because there was nothing to do, no cricket, no outdoor sports; they played video games and watched TV. The maid was miserable, confined to a second floor apartment with her young charges. She slept on the floor of the children's room, and her bathroom was private only because others would not use it. The children looked down on her, speaking English to each other, pretending not to understand her Urdu, and sometimes refusing to eat the food she prepared. She retaliated by washing the children roughly, pinching them hard to discipline them, preparing foods they did not like, and breaking their favorite toys. Unable to answer the phone correctly and told not to answer it, she persisted and sabotaged the message machine. She stood in the corner of the room every day and cried, begging to be sent back to India. Eventually, she had to be sent back. For her employers, hard-working career people, she had been a bad investment; like her, they had lost time, money, and emotional serenity. Such relationships caught and constrained women of both classes; professionals trying to make the Gulf a liberating yet familiar place by importing domestic servants and maids trying to benefit economically yet finding exile from home too oppressive to bear.

Finally, there were Hyderabadi Muslim women who had been brought to the UAE as the wives of Arabs.[84] Most of these wives were from Hyderabad's old city Barkas locality and were descended from Yemeni and Saudi Arab immigrants to the Deccan. They spoke some Arabic and their parents were willing to give them in marriage to a Gulf Arab for much less than a Gulf bride would cost. Bridegrooms in the Gulf traditionally paid a high brideprice and provided the wedding jewelry and a fully equipped household. Non-local brides (Indian Muslims, maids of various nationalities) were much less expensive. A Hyderabadi bride could be had for some 10,000 rupees ($286) plus twenty to thirty grams of gold ($500 to $700), whereas a Dubai bride cost 200,000 to 300,000 UAE dirham ($54,500 to $81,745), the taxi driver Aijaz declared. Typically, these women became the second, third, or fourth wives of much older husbands. Dr. Ashfaq Khan, who treated many such women, believed that such marriages provided economic security for the wife and her family back home. The women and their children blended into the indigenous Arab population, and when they became widows, they could inherit real estate and businesses and sponsor nonlocals.[85]

HYDERABADI COMMUNITY LIFE IN THE UAE

The pecking order in the UAE put the British rather than "other Arabs" at the top as in Kuwait. South Asians ranked higher than in Kuwait but had their own pecking order (when I left one meeting with Hyderabadi businessmen, they sent their Bangladeshi servant down, making him put on shoes, to get me a taxi driven by a Pathan from Peshawar). Hyderabadis were perceived to be a large and distinctive (if loosely defined) group. As in Kuwait, Hyderabadis did not socialize much with local Arabs, but there was a general appreciation of UAE Arabs as congenial people familiar with Hindustani culture. Hyderabadis stood back and contrasted the UAE favorably with places like Saudi Arabia and Kuwait. The UAE was itself a federation of seven emirates, and Hyderabadis enjoyed comparing all the Gulf states and emirates.[86]

Mir Miraj Ali of Abu Dhabi ranked the Gulf states thus: first was the UAE, but Abu Dhabi in particular; second was Saudi Arabia, third was Qatar, then Oman, Kuwait, and finally Bahrain. His was later termed an "orthodox Islamic ranking" by Hyderabadis at Sharafat Walajahi's party in Dubai, who came up with a different scale: first was the UAE, but Dubai in particular; then came Bahrain, Oman, Muscat, Qatar, Kuwait, and, last, Saudi Arabia. Their criterion was the style of life, and they eschewed places where they could not have dinner parties freely and people could not stand about on balconies in groups. They also valued the accessibility and amiability of the locals.

At Ali Ishrati's dinner party in Dubai, people compared sites within and across the Gulf states. Abu Dhabi was dismissed, its people labeled as inhospitable and arrogant, its rents so high that some people who worked there drove daily from Dubai. Another drawback of Abu Dhabi was its police force, whose members, though they may have known English or Urdu, spoke only Arabic to expatriates. As Junaid Adil explained, "They were out to get you. Here in Dubai, they speak Urdu, they have 'cordiality lessons,' they will listen to your explanation. One stopped me and told me, *meherbani-se* (please), to put on my seat belt."[87] Of the Gulf states, Oman was pronounced "the greatest" by Arsalan Mirza, who had spent ten years there before coming to Dubai in 1991. A Hyderabadi was personal physician to the Oman ruler, he said, and Oman had been associated with Hyderabad longer than other Gulf states.[88]

The two-tier class structure so strong among expatriate Hyderabadis in Kuwait was more muted in the UAE, with more families present and greater mixing across class lines. Hyderabadis of lower class origins who were upwardly mobile in the Gulf, "people with no manners," might be part of the everyday social worlds of Hyderabadis from "noble clans," crossing a gulf in the UAE that was harder to cross in Kuwait, with more mixing across national boundaries as well. Big businessmen were important in Dubai as in Kuwait, but there seemed to be more middle-level businessmen moving in and out of the UAE, rather than a few big men settling in for years of dogged endeavor.[89] Lower middle-class professionals did most of their business with other expatriates—for example, the encyclopedia salesmen who dealt, in Urdu, chiefly with Filipinos, Thais, Egyptians, Palestinians, and Iranis.

"Hyderabadis from India and Pakistan meet in business circles but rarely elsewhere, and they always avoid political discussions," one man told me. Rivalry and distance between Hyderabadi Indian and Pakistani businessmen and professionals was somewhat less than in the case of the service workers and laborers, partly because of historical and marital connections among elite Hyderabadis and partly because relationships were mediated through mutual connections in other places, like the UK. Hyderabadi Indian and Pakistani children could attend the same elite schools in the UAE, although most attended Embassy-affiliated schools, thereby confirming the national boundaries. Some Hyderabadi Muslims from both countries resented the prominence of Hindus among the big Indian businessmen in the UAE, men who reportedly did as well as or better than South Asian Muslims there.

Indian and Pakistani workers interacted minimally. Baluch and Pathan tribesmen migrated to the UAE from Pakistan's remoter areas to work on the roads, serve as drivers, and do construction work. Most taxi drivers in the UAE were Pushtu-speakers from Peshawar and its hinterland, and many construction workers in El Ain, near Abu Dhabi, came from the same background. Employers tended to prefer one or the other national category of workers. Dilip Gir, manager of an auto repair shop, told me (in Hyderabad) of the unsuccessful introduction of a Pakistani into his largely Indian work force and the eruption of serious friction.

Hyderabadis and others met in particular localities on Fridays, but national and regional differences divided them even in these informal gatherings. In Dubai's Deira Bazar, Pakistanis were on one side, Bangladeshis on another. Construction people coming in from the desert work sites even divided according to villages. Indian Hyderabadis tended to go to Abra Creek, especially those from Guntur and Godavari and other coastal Andhra places working on big construction jobs, and the Sikhs had another favorite gathering spot. Even among Indian and Pakistani Christians, people kept to their own groups. St. Mary's Church, so important to Catholics from Hyderabad, held a separate Pakistani Urdu mass.

Relationships among Hyderabadis in the UAE reflected events in India and Pakistan, as political conflicts were extended abroad rather than attenuated in a neutral setting. The Indian and Pakistani consulates were both active in the UAE, most often dealing not with each other but with the UAE government to settle disputes over wages, working conditions, or the abuse of maids. Before the communal riots in Hyderabad following the Gulf War of 1990–1991 and the Babri Masjid incident of 1992, the most serious displays of Indian and Pakistani patriotism arose whenever the Sharjah-hosted cricket competition, the Australasia Cup, pitted the two nations against one another. People recounted the fierce vocal and even physical attacks mounted then, attacks in which Hyderabadis of both national backgrounds participated.[90]

The Babri Masjid incident of 1992 provoked demonstrations such as had never been seen in the UAE. Ironically, it was chiefly Pakistani, not Indian, Muslims who protested at the Indian consulate in Abu Dhabi, but the police controlled the crowds without firing shots or mounting charges against the public. In Dubai, riot police in full gear with armored vehicles restored order in the Hindu-dominated Sona Bazar or Gold Souk. In Abu Dhabi and Sharjah, Indian shops were closed down. In Al Ain, the Indian School was closed and buses were burned; Pathan Pakistani laborers there staged illegal demonstrations and consequently were deported. People in the UAE were impressed by the government's maintenance of law and order: "When Babri Masjid happened, gangsters in Sharjah came out to beat Hindu shops and their owners, the police stopped them in five minutes"; "the police here stopped it, stopped them breaking up the Indian shops here, and said 'Go to your own country if you want to do that'"; "the police in Dubai told them, 'stop, this is not your country, and if you don't stop, we'll deport you all, everyone.' So they stopped."

Hyderabadi associations in the UAE owed their demise at least partly to these communal conflicts of the early 1990s. Hyderabadi associations were linked historically to Sharjah. Ramachandran placed Hyderabadis in Sharjah by the 1950s and lumped them together over time.

> The sheikh gave them a colony, some forty years ago, and gave some passports. . . . All are working-class people, and also handicraft people who do sewing and embroidering, and there are lots of Hyderabadi ladies married to Arabs. . . . [Now] all the construction workers and technical people, lift and crane operators, petroleum people, all are Hyderabadis, from Telingana, then Rayalseema, then Rajahmundry and Visakhapatnam.

I had names, from *Siyasat* articles of the 1980s and early 1990s, of Hyderabadi leaders and associations, the Bazm-i-Adab, Deccan Humor Society, Bazm-i-Deccan, but most people I met in 1995 knew nothing about them. Earlier associations had been formed by bachelor workers with patronage from leading businessmen, men no longer active or, perhaps, eclipsed by wealthier businessmen. Indeed, the numbers of Hyderabadis in the UAE had declined, down from 5,000 to 500 in the "businessman/professional category," I was told. Since 1990, many had left for the United States or elsewhere. As for workers, an estimated 10,000 were still in the UAE, plus another 5,000 men and women from a Barkas or Chaous background.

I finally located a Bazm-i-Deccan officer named in *Siyasat*, Mohamed Hussain Arif. Arif worked in an electronics showroom and had been in the UAE since about 1980. Although brought up as a very orthodox Muslim in Mehdipatnam, he had married a Mangalore Christian woman whose family had been in the UAE since 1970.[91] Arif mentioned his cricket team, the Hyderabad Blues (90% of the players were Hyderabadis), then doing well in the B League, the biggest tournament in the UAE, and then he turned to history. There were 15,000 Hyderabadis in the UAE in 1987, when a "kind of census or count" was taken, he said. A small Hyderabadi group in the 1980s of bachelors and close friends got leading businessmen as sponsors and started the Bazm-i-Deccan, with 1,000 members from all over the UAE, holding seminars and feting expatriate scholars.[92] It celebrated Id and the Prophet's Birthday and held functions featuring the Andhra

Pradesh Small-Scale Industries and an Islamic investment group from the United States. It also sponsored an Urdu comedy presentation in 1991 in the Dubai Folklore Theatre.[93]

But the Bazm-i-Deccan voted to close down in 1991. One problem was the enforcement of the UAE's policy against registration of any but national associations. The group had been registered in Sharjah, but UAE registration was refused. Internal problems stemmed from the 1990–1991 communal riots back in Hyderabad after the Gulf War. Muslims banded together in the UAE; the association opened its arms to all comers and two representatives "from the labor class, semi-skilled men," joined the leadership. Membership expanded as dues were cut from ten dirham to one dirham. But the newcomers, "who cannot talk to you in English, only Urdu," acted too aggressively, and there was trouble over funds. Muslim multi-class membership grew, whereas the earlier association included all Hyderabadis and was middle- and upper-class. The association leaders called for a secret ballot, and then, no longer a small clique of friends, voted to disband.[94]

There was no 400th anniversary celebration for Hyderabad in the UAE, although the Deccan Humor Society of Sharjah or the Bazm-i-Deccan had meant to hold one. The Bazm-i-Deccan wanted to put on a *chowki* dinner with the elder prince, Mukarram Jah, but the dissolution of the association ended that.[95] A Hyderabadi Pakistani said there had not been a celebration because there was little interest in the prince, but it was not clear which one he meant. Another person (formerly of London), had tried to get the younger prince, Muffakham Jah, to come to Dubai to promote the International Hyderabad Association, and he had lined up twenty to thirty people in the Gulf to join it. But then came 1992 and the Babri Masjid incident, causing "problems" in the UAE.

Hyderabadis in the UAE did not view what they nonetheless termed "the Hyderabadi community" as a "close, tight, and helpful one, like other communities." Some explained that was because it was a *tejari* (trading) lot; others pointed to its internal diversity and transient nature. The situation was hard to assess without comparative data on other "communities," especially when a man who stated emphatically that Hyderabadis did not help each other later mentioned casually that he, an Indian Hyderabadi, had gotten his job through a Pakistani Hyderabadi by playing "the Hyderabadi card."

Futures Reconfigured

In both Kuwait and the UAE, Hyderabadis maintained strong connections to their homelands and had planned to return. Workers and professionals alike invested heavily in building residences in the homelands. Isolated from the politics of the host countries, they had also become distanced from homeland politics. Yet political events in the Gulf and in India, the Gulf War of 1990–1991 and the Babri Masjid destruction of 1992, sharply impacted their lives and, for many, unexpectedly altered plans for the future.

Hyderabadis in Kuwait and the UAE generally took one of two stances about their expatriate status and their futures. Those who took the first stance were resigned to their inability to control the timing of their stay in the Gulf but did try to control its meaning, cherishing the notion that they were in an Asian cultural context, living much as they did in India or Pakistan but better and protecting their children from the disruptive effects of Western culture. They trusted that their sojourn abroad would not disrupt their attachment to the homeland. Arsalan Mirza said, "One becomes defensive. One has to inwardly accept the terms and be prepared to leave tomorrow, and then it's OK." Mir Miraj Ali put it almost identically: "You should always be ready to go back; if you have that readiness, you can enjoy life here." These people intended to return and many intended to educate and settle their children in Hyderabad or Pakistan as well, despite indications that resettlement in South Asia would not be easy for the children.

Others took a second, more proactive stance, looking to new sites and anticipating that their children's futures might even require their own movement elsewhere. These Hyderabadis were more open to changes in cultural, occupational, and even marital patterns, changes that they themselves might find uncomfortable but that they could envision for their children. Two men in the UAE illustrated the propensity on the part of some expatriates in the Gulf for flexible, shifting identities and global citizenship. One was Ramachandran, director of the NRI Trading Establishment and Super Market in Sharjah. His import/export business featured "the Nizam's special rice," a product that rated a story in the *Khaleej Times*.[96] A Malayali-speaking Hindu born in Singapore who moved to Madras, Rajahmundry (coastal Andhra), and then Hyderabad, he said, "my complete life and attachments are to Hyderabad."[97] He went on to say that "20 percent of those who claim to be Hyderabadis really are not; nowadays anyone can be a Hyderabadi." His definition of a Hyderabadi was akin to that developing in Kuwait as workers from coastal Andhra identified themselves as Hyderabadis.

Ramachandran's views of his family's future were wide ranging. He had a wife, a Madrasi, and two teenage sons. The boys went to St. Paul's in Hyderabad and to the Indian School in Sharjah. The first boy was "a man of American culture; he will go to America"; the second son "will go back to India; he's best suited for the IAS." The sons "can marry European ladies, Muslims, all are OK." Ramachandran's wife wanted to return to Madras to go to temples, but he planned to stay in Sharjah and expand his operations to Africa or Canada, where he saw marketing opportunities.

Finally, Vipin Singh, a certified public accountant (CPA) at Emirates Airline, mused about the Hyderabadi identity and Hyderabadi futures in the UAE. His Punjab-born parents had moved around India a great deal. Vipin had attended Hyderabad Public School for six years as a youth, and then, after moves to Bangalore and Bombay, had returned for one year's CPA training in Hyderabad. He had been introduced to me as one, but was he a Hyderabadi? No, he said; perhaps his sister and brother were; they had gone to university there, but he had not, and all his friends had moved away.[98] His Hyderabadi Urdu was adequate, but it was not his usual Hindi, and English had always been his first language. Of course he loved the food, but he had no special attachment to the place, and if a Hyderabad association formed in the UAE he would probably not join it. Vipin called himself a world citizen and was considering graduate work in the United States.[99] About future prospects, he voiced the thoughts of many: "What with the economic liberalizations in India, people are thinking, why are we here? Why not go back, or go West?"

CHAPTER 10

Hyderabad: Reorientations

TWO SISTERS, MIRIAM BILGRAMI and Khadija Mehdi, talked to me in a Banjara Hills home in Hyderabad; most of their grandchildren were in the United States and Canada. One sister said:

> All my children are abroad, all my grandchildren are abroad; we didn't want it this way, we could never think it would be like this. But providence . . . My eldest sister is in Lucknow; she married there, and my mother was so upset, sending her all that way out of Hyderabad. But look at us.

The other sister reported that all her grandchildren dislike India and hate to come to it. She has visited them in Los Angeles, but she tells them, "India is my home; you must respect it, you must visit me here." A third grandmother, Pushpa Umapathi, talked unhappily about her visits to Texas, where her daughter and son-in-law had just bought a house although "of course they are planning to return to Hyderabad." There, her granddaughter anxiously asked her not to wear a sari when walking her to school. When I asked if her grandchildren identified as Hyderabadi in any way, she burst out: "Hyderabadi? They're not even Indian."

Life for the residents of Hyderabad city has changed in ways that go far beyond new architecture and road names, rising population density, and new administrative and street languages. The changes after the Police Action in 1948 and the creation of Andhra Pradesh in 1956 were overwhelming enough, as Hyderabadis struggled to find places in independent India and the new Telugu-speaking state. Families moved from the old city to the new and young men took up new careers. More women began to work and have careers. Globalization, however, has meant another level of change altogether.

Since the 1960s, Hyderabadis have participated in an increasingly global economy and society. Almost every family has members overseas. For aging parents, once-welcomed opportunities abroad for their children have led to painful and possibly permanent separations. Family histories rooted in Hyderabad and India have been swept aside and replaced by new narratives grounded in new places. Family members try hard to see continuities or relinquish the past. As the grandmothers' laments above indicated, it was those left behind in Hyderabad who had the greatest difficulty adjusting to the expanded and reoriented family networks.

The View From Hyderabad

REPORTING THE DIASPORA: COMMUNICATION NODES

Hyderabad's Urdu newspapers were the chief trackers of the Hyderabadi diaspora. The editors of two of these papers, *Siyasat* and *Rehnuma-i-Deccan*, traveled outside India, whereas the editor of *Munsif* did not.[1] Abid Ali Khan, editor of *Siyasat*, was particularly interested in reporting the activities of emigrant Hyderabadis[2] and was himself a popular speaker at events abroad. *Siyasat* actively sought subscribers from the many places Hyderabadis were working and settling around the world, concentrating on the Gulf states, the UK and Europe, and the United States. In 1991, its circulation was said to be 41,000.

Newspaper stories highlighted Hyderabadi and Urdu association meetings abroad and profiled cities where Hyderabadis were settling in large numbers. Readers in Hyderabad learned about Hyderabadi culture in London, Hyderabadi Ganga/Jamna culture (the mingling of the Ganga and Jamna rivers) in Florida, and about American suburbs, particularly the growing Asian presence in Napierville, Skokie, and Oakbrook, Illinois.[3] Occasional profiles featured the few Hyderabadis living in places like Paris or Frankfurt.[4] One article, "The Place of Non-Mulkis in the Progress of the United States," asserted that students securing second- and third-class passes in Indian schools could easily get A grades in America.[5] Interviews with notable overseas Hyderabadis on visits "home" reported their nostalgic feelings and joyful reunions with relatives and friends.

Siyasat's editor, Abid Ali Khan, learned about his readers abroad from his newspaper's reports and his own trips. Despite having had four heart attacks, he traveled to Saudi Arabia, Kuwait, and the UK for Hyderabad's 400th birthday celebrations in 1990, celebrations organized by Hyderabad associations in those places.[6] He noted that the uneducated and the technically and professionally educated people were all doing very well in the Gulf states ("They were overworked, that is, working hard"), but they could not buy Gulf property and invested their earnings back in Hyderabad. In the UK, most emigrants had taken British nationality, and those in the United States, Germany, France, and Canada also were leaving India permanently, selling their property in Hyderabad and buying property abroad. The Urdu literary world, expanded well beyond India and Pakistan, continued to perpetuate visions of old Hyderabad through writers who traveled, speaking and reciting in many sites. Ali Khan was unsure about the numbers of *Siyasat*'s overseas subscribers, as people passed the paper around and also photocopied it, but he planned to publish commemorative books on Hyderabadi culture and history aimed at the diasporic market.

Ironically, Abid Ali Khan noted that Hyderabad's 400th birthday had not yet been celebrated in Hyderabad itself. As I interviewed him in 1991, he was being interviewed by reporters for the *Deccan Chronicle*, Hyderabad's leading English language newspaper, about why nothing had been done so far in Hyderabad. The local Golconda Society[7] was trying to arrange a celebration, and the Andhra Pradesh government was half-heartedly helping;[8] the British Council sponsored a conference but it was limited to a small, chiefly academic, audience.[9]

Writing in English about old Hyderabad has become a popular genre. However, one heard that "outsiders have the only pens writing about Hyderabad" and the perception was that most of these authors were not "real Hyderabadis," mulkis. Despite this frequent complaint, not many "real Hyderabadis" were writing about Hyderabad. The optimism of some Hyderabadis just after 1948 that the Hyderabadi synthesis could be a model for independent India, given Nehru's reported enthusiasm for it,[10] soon faded. The reality was that invoking the old state brought feelings of failure and perhaps served no useful purpose for anyone living in the new context of Andhra Pradesh.

In the 1980s, as Hyderabad associations sprang up abroad, the Hyderabad Deccan Society was started in Hyderabad. This society tried to serve as a communications center and model for the associations abroad. Founded in 1983 and registered in 1989 with the Andhra Pradesh government, it celebrated the cultural synthesis of old Hyderabad. Prince Muffakham Jah, patron of many overseas associations and often resident in Hyderabad, was its patron. The members, with no requirement to have been born in Hyderabad, numbered about sixty. New members were recommended by a membership committee and admitted by an executive committee.[11] The association saw itself not as a nostalgic body but a future-oriented one, trying to help Hyderabadis coming back for spouses, property, or jobs. It occasionally put on cultural events such as displays of Hyderabadi costumes, mushairas, and talks.

EXPERIENCING THE DIASPORA: CLASS, OCCUPATION,
RELIGION, AND GENDER

What has it meant to those left at home to have relatives and friends moving out of Hyderabad and India in such numbers, probably permanently? Ancestral roots, properties, and positions inherited from the days of the Nizams and even earlier were being discarded by young emigrants as they carved out positions and acquired properties in new places, looking hopefully to the future. The ruptures within families were deeply felt by parents and grandparents who still drew inspiration from the past achievements of family members.[12] Most people in Hyderabad had firsthand stories of the impact of emigration on their own relatives and close friends. Those who could afford it traveled to see their children and grandchildren in faraway places and experience diasporic differences for themselves.

The family accounts that follow are organized by differences of class, occupation, religion, and gender, yet they reveal striking similarities. In all these narratives, the fact of the diaspora has reoriented people's thinking about the past and future. Some families, ignoring changes hard for them to accept, saw Hyderabad, the center of the diaspora, as an empty place. Others testified to stressful interactions between the old culture and the new one evolving in the city. Certainly the narratives show the declining relevance of the term mulki and the coexistence of several meanings of Hyderabadi.

Class and occupational rankings and qualifications in the city changed over the course of the twentieth century, but in most family accounts 1948 and 1956 were major turning points. After 1948, members of some Hyderabad families joined an India-wide elite. Some joined the Indian Administrative Service (the IAS, successor to the British Indian Civil Service or ICS and, in Hyderabad, to the Hyderabad Civil Service or HCS). Hyderabadi Hindus from the districts assumed important positions in the new regime, as did incoming migrants from the former Madras Presidency's Telugu-speaking districts. The latter saw themselves as new Hyderabadis but not mulkis in the old sense. Some members of Hyderabad's traditional urban elite families did well; others experienced downward mobility. Hyderabadi Muslims of all classes perceived themselves especially disadvantaged in modern India, yet many Muslim families from lower-middle- and working-class backgrounds have benefited from working and settling abroad. Women in post-1948 Hyderabad as in the diaspora have experienced both opportunities and constraints in public and domestic arenas.

Hyderabadis in the all-India Elite. Some Hyderabadis elevated to all-India positions were already mentioned in chapter 2, chiefly those who moved away from the city. Other Hyderabadi men in military and judicial service served at the national level but returned to Hyderabad. Chief Marshal I. H. Lateef (descended from Sir Akbar Hydari, prime minister of Hyderabad in the late 1930s) and his wife Bilkees (a Bilgrami, daughter of Nawab Ali Yavar Jung) were posted all over the world during his air force career. The Lateefs lived in the United States for several years from 1960 and in many other countries; she purchased kitchen equipment for their Delhi home in Paris. They considered retiring in Delhi but settled in Hyderabad in Banjara Hills. The Lateefs' two sons had worked in the Gulf with her brother, but both boys were in New York and were expected to return to Hyderabad. Their daughter and her Sikh husband had lived in Kathmandu but were in Bombay in 1993. The Lateefs and their children valued Hyderabadi culture and likened it to the cosmopolitanism that they saw accompanying globalization.[13]

Two Hyderabadis became Supreme Court justices of India. Justice Pingle Jagan Mohan Reddy's distinguished career began with his study of law in Cambridge, UK, in 1928. From a landed gentry family in Telingana, Reddy became Chief Justice of AP, a member of India's Supreme Court, and vice-chancellor of Osmania University.[14] One of his sons was in Chicago, married to a non-Hyderabadi and with a daughter at Indiana University. The son had property in Hyderabad, but Reddy was sure he would not come back.[15] Reddy spoke fondly of Hyderabad's past, when he had thought and written in Urdu, and said "I'm a blue blood Hyderabadi, my wife and I, six or seven generations now, longer than many." However, he disapproved of any project valorizing Hyderabadi culture, saying it had become "an impediment, irrelevant to today's voteocracy, to the Hindu/Muslim divisions now being emphasized." He derided the Mandal Commission reservations of educational and service places for lower castes and tribes[16] as against merit and the work ethic; he cited the politicians' setting of a holiday to commemorate the Prophet Muhammad's birthday as an example of the voteocracy. According to him, while Muslim clerics all over India announced that the Prophet's birthday fell on a Sunday, politicians voted Saturday the holiday so that they could win Muslim votes by getting them another day off work. The second Supreme Court justice was Sardar Ali Khan, who studied law in London in 1952–1953 and said that being Hyderabadi was a passport to acceptance in the UK. He viewed old Hyderabad as a city of love, one appreciated by Nehru and by his daughter Indira Gandhi. Acknowledging that things had changed, Khan still saw

Hyderabad as a bridge city, its Telugu and Urdu languages bringing north and south together.

Hyderabadis in the Indian Administrative Service.   The IAS, India's best and brightest, recruited most of its members by competitive examination. People joked about the four "castes" of the IAS: the Brahmans, "competition-walas" who got in by exam; the Kshatriyas, the army commissioned officers who moved in after distinguished careers; the Vaisyas, business executives especially recruited from the private sector; and finally the Sudras, those promoted from the lower service ranks.[17] IAS members trained in batches and one's classmates continued to be crucial points of reference. Sent to administer all of India's states, IAS men and women had some choice in their placement. These IAS families, whether Hindu, Muslim, or Christian, mulki or non-mulki, had many children and young relatives abroad.

Some Hyderabadis transferred from the HCS into the IAS after the Police Action and others successfully entered the IAS after that. Some IAS men from other parts of India also became Hyderabadis, in their own view at least, assigned to duty in Andhra Pradesh and growing to love Hyderabad city and its culture. This administrative elite was well placed to secure the futures of its children in India and in Hyderabad, yet reservations for the "backward classes" in government service had affected the chances of even these members of the "forward classes," pushing young people into independent professions. This class was also well placed to send its children abroad for study, so it had been hit as hard by the emigration of its children as any other class.

An IAS man and his wife, the Umapathis, whose daughter and son-in-law were in the United States, told me that their children were not "Hyderabadis overseas," as they would be coming back. But that outcome seemed problematic. The son-in-law had studied in France, then worked in Thailand, Israel, and the United States. To return to India, he needed a job that would use his highly specialized talents and training in the solar energy field. The daughter and her husband had bought a house in Texas but were building one in Hyderabad too. The daughter, with the double burden of working and caring for the two small children (only the older one spoke Telugu well),[18] wanted to come back, her parents said, and they talked about the many cousins in Hyderabad with whom the children could play. As these parents described their daughter's visits home and their visits to her in America, the strains of the separation were evident.[19]

Umapathi's transition, that of a Hindu in the HCS moving into the IAS, was relatively smooth, and other Hindus from distinguished families in Hyderabad did well under the new regime. The son and grandson of Raja

Sham Raj, the last Rae Rayan Maharashtrian Brahman *daftardar* (revenue collector for half the Nizam's former state), were cases in point. The son served in Delhi after 1948 as secretary general of the Rajya Sabha (the upper house in India's parliament) and the grandson, Bhale Rao, joined the IAS and remained in Hyderabad.[20] Several Mathur Kayasths from the other *daftardar* noble family, the Malwalas, also obtained high government positions.

Continuity initially marked the family trajectory of B. N. Raman, a Brahman whose ancestral village was near Madras and Karnataka. Raman graduated from Nizam College in 1948 just before the Police Action and wanted to continue his family's tradition of service: his uncle, a superintendent of engineering, and his father, a medical officer, were both in the Nizam's service, the latter doing pioneering medical work in rural areas. Raman was schooled in Karimnagar District to the sixth standard and then in Hyderabad city. As Hyderabad fell to India, Raman did well in three sets of competitive exams: the Hyderabad Civil Service, the Indian Foreign Service, and the Reserve State Bank. He ended up in the IAS.[21] Like his father, he worked in the districts. His memories of the educational, health, and medical services of his father's time and his own were vivid.[22] He spoke with appreciation of Hyderabad's cosmopolitan culture,[23] yet the next generation was settling abroad. Many of the children of Raman and his three brothers and four sisters were in Canada, the United States, and Bahrain, where they were members of Karnatak associations and Hyderabad associations. Raman's own two sons worked in computer and medical careers in the United States. The older son had married a woman of his own choice; Raman's wife spent time in the United States cooking for the younger, unmarried son. Raman spoke proudly of his daughter-in-law's social service work with the mentally retarded in a school near Sacramento, California, as proudly as he spoke of the two colleges he had established in Nizamabad as district collector and of his younger son's ambition to come home and work as a doctor in rural or tribal areas. In the fast-changing family landscape, Raman valued old Hyderabad's traditions of service and cultural tolerance but saw their applicability elsewhere.

A. Krishnaswamy Ayyangar, retired IAS officer, came from a family that had furnished distinguished lawyers and administrators to the Nizams for seven generations. Ayyangar served all over India but considered himself a Hyderabadi, although the family history stemmed from Madras, and his wife, from there, did not count herself a Hyderabadi.[24] Their three children had settled in the United States, and almost every day one of them phoned or wrote asking the parents to "come over." The old couple lived in a large house built for an extended family on a main road in Begampet, the

Ayyangar name prominently displayed on a gatepost so that people seeing it could just drop in. The daughter went abroad first, as an exchange student from Osmania University in 1961, and although the Ayyangars were South Indian Brahmans, she married a Punjabi from a Vaisya caste whom she met in Minnesota. Her father traveled to attend her marriage.[25] The two boys went later, the elder to college in Illinois on financial aid in 1973; after working back in India, he was sent by his company to Texas where he switched to a Houston computer firm. The younger son went in 1975 to study astrophysics. He and his wife settled in Washington, D.C., where he was a physicist with NASA. The Ayyangars had visited their children twice, once for a year and once for four months, but they did not want to move to the United States although they faced difficulties in Hyderabad. He had become forgetful and she, despite her lack of schooling in English, had to take care of all the paperwork and property matters. They found it increasingly hard to get servants and they were afraid to rent portions of the house to Andhras, whom they both considered scheming and likely not to vacate when asked. At least they had the house and friends who visit them; he wanted to be in the house "until the last day."[26]

Another IAS man, B. P. R. Vithal, and his wife came from families formerly in Rajahmundry, in the Telugu-speaking districts of the Madras Presidency. Both their fathers, however, had moved to Hyderabad and Vithal's father had been professor of economics in Nizam College. Vithal entered Nizam College in 1942 but left to join the Quit India Movement in Bombay. He shifted to Madras Christian College, graduated in 1949, and took the IAS exams.[27] The Vithals' elder son was in Delhi, while their younger son was in Canada but was becoming a U.S. citizen (he went to the United States in 1981–1982 with others from the noted Indian Institute of Technology in Madras). None of the grandchildren were Hyderabadis, the Vithals said; even the ones from Delhi were typical Punjabis, conversant with Hindi and not Urdu.

The Vithals considered themselves Hyderabadis, strongly shaped by Hyderabadi culture. "But that culture is no longer here," he said, "and we have yet to meet an Andhra who came here after 1956 who'll say he or she is a Hyderabadi." Vithal stated that his own relatives from Andhra, whom he had not previously met, were coming and reclaiming him; his Andhra roots had come to Hyderabad and were taking over. He saw "the erosion of my mulki self."[28] The Vithal son just taking U.S. citizenship called his father often, going through an identity crisis. "Am I letting you down, Dad? Here you are in India's Finance Commission and I'm settling here." But his father told him that citizenship was a civil concept and being Indian was a cultural concept, so he could still be himself.[29]

The transitions to the IAS of young Hyderabadi Hindus beginning their careers just before or after 1948 went well, but that was not necessarily the case for Hyderabadi Muslims. Mehdi Ali, whose career suffered after 1948, started out in the HCS in 1941. Two of his four brothers were also in the HCS (the only Hyderabad family with three sons in the HCS), but after 1948, his four brothers all lost their jobs; two were charged and briefly jailed by the Indian Army. Ali continued in government service, but whereas before 1948 he had opposed the growing influence of the Razakars and found his career blocked because of that, after 1948 he was not immediately taken into the IAS because of a suspected affinity with Pakistan. His own subordinates became his bosses. His promotion to district collector finally took place in 1949 because of Pandit Nehru's opposition to discrimination against Muslims in Hyderabad, but Ali was taken into the IAS only in 1972.[30] Ali saw 1948–1956, when Hyderabadi Hindus took over, as the worst period for Muslims in Hyderabad. After the 1956 advent of Andhra Pradesh, Ali served in Mysore and educated his children chiefly in Karnataka. Three of his four children were abroad, in Chicago, Toronto, and Saudi Arabia.[31] He lived alone in his house, a recent widower. His daughter in Hyderabad stopped daily to see him, and a granddaughter was arriving from Canada to study medicine in Hyderabad and be his companion.

In contrast, Hasanuddin Ahmed had a successful career in the IAS despite his family's close association with the old Hyderabad regime (his father, Deen Yar Jung, was chief of the Hyderabad city police at the Police Action in 1948).[32] The handsome old ancestral home was in the old city near Dar us Shifa.[33] Ahmed demurred at giving too much importance to Hyderabadi culture, as he favored a world culture in which the best features of all cultures would mingle. However, he recounted an early incident between Andhras and Hyderabadis. He said the Andhras used to be barefoot, and in 1956 when Hyderabadis saw them coming without shoes to a sports event at Nizam College, they threw their *chappals* (sandals) at them, shouting "Here's a present for you." He likened the situation to the Arab conquest of Iran: Iran was a superior culture and the Arabs were backward, so the Iranis boasted of their culture even when conquered.[34]

Ahmed had many relatives abroad in the UK and the United States, and on visits to them he helped found Amir Khusro societies. He saw Amir Khusro as a cosmopolitan figure, offering an identity better able to bring people together than that of a Hyderabadi or even a Muslim identity. (Amir Khusro, 1253–1325, was a poet in Persian and Hindustani and a musician in Delhi under seven kings of the Delhi Sultanate; he was born in India and his father was of Turkish origin. A Sufi mystic and founder of Hindustani classical music and *qawwali* music, he symbolized cultural pluralism.) "Why bother about being a Hyderabadi; that sets one apart. Just offer elements of Hyderabadi culture, perhaps *lochmi*, the minced meat pastry, perhaps *pan*, elements that will win people over and become part of world culture. Forget the sherwani/*biryani* talk; emphasize sincerity and courtesy; those are universal values," he said.

Another group of IAS men was that of the outsiders or non-mulkis brought to Hyderabad by IAS service. Dr. Vasant Bawa and Narendra Luther were originally from the Punjab and both have become closely identified with Hyderabad. Dr. Bawa, with a Ph.D. from Tulane University, has published several scholarly books about Hyderabad, during and after his IAS career. From a predominantly Christian family, Bawa served as head of the Andhra Pradesh Archives twice and also as head of the Hyderabad Urban Development Authority (HUDA), positions that helped him master local history. Luther began his career writing in Urdu, not English, and he too has authored books about Hyderabad. Both have close relatives abroad.

Hyderabadis from the Districts: The Newly Empowered.   A group of chiefly Hindu mulkis originally from the Hyderabad districts retained or gained power in 1948. These men and women had struggled for more power within Hyderabad and, not achieving that, worked for its incorporation into India. Many of them had been socialized into the old Hyderabadi culture but were ambivalent about it or hostile to it. Their standing, however, was not necessarily enhanced, and may have been threatened, by the creation of Andhra Pradesh in 1956.[35]

One "freedom fighter" empowered after 1948 was Gopalrao Ekbote, from the Marathi-speaking districts. From Nagpur, he had become a lawyer in Aurangabad and moved to Hyderabad city in 1932, where he became a staunch leader of Maharashtrian groups and Hindi-promoting activities. He was very active in the library movement, the development of libraries in the vernaculars, Telugu, Marathi, and Kannada. This movement was tolerated by the Nizam as a cultural, not political, one.[36] Ekbote rose to be Chief Justice of Hyderabad. Ekbote's Urdu was excellent. He wrote two articles a year for *Siyasat* about old Hyderabad and admired the last Nizam's poetry.[37] Justice Ekbote and his wife were unusual and fortunate to have most of their children home, with three of the five sons and their families living with them. The other two sons and their families were also in Hyderabad.[38] Only their daughter lived abroad. An independent person and a medical doctor, she went to London alone in 1965 without a job and got one there, along with a husband.[39] The young couple moved to the United States in 1976 when the husband got an offer from Emory University.

Despite her husband's early death from cancer in 1989, the Hedas' daughter stayed in the United States with her daughter, who also wanted to be a doctor. This granddaughter, again unusually, spent all her annual vacations in Hyderabad; she knew Marathi and Hindi well.

Dr. H. C. Heda, a political activist from the Marathi-speaking districts, rose to become an Indian National Congress leader. Heda entered Osmania University in 1930 and graduated in philosophy and law. He participated in the 1938 *satyagraha* demonstration organized by the Hyderabad State Congress and the Arya Samaj. The Nizam developed Hyderabad city as the educational center, Heda said, because Muslims were the majority there. He viewed the Hyderabadi identity as limited to some 500 Muslim and 100 Hindu families; nostalgia for it was useless.[40] His wife, herself a noted social worker and activist, pointed to their own son as a *pucca* (true) mulki Hyderabadi, one who would travel far to see a film in Hyderabadi Urdu—but in the United States, where he was a citizen. The Hedas' only child had settled in the United States, while they remained in Hyderabad. Their two grandsons knew India mostly from their reading of Amar Chitra Katha comic books, and when they came to Hyderabad, as they sometimes did on summer vacation, they generally got sick, July and August being hot and rainy there. The parents went to the United States every two years for three months, to New Jersey.[41]

P. Vaman Rao, Nizam College graduate, journalist for *The Hindu*, publisher of *New Swatantra Times* and executive head of Sirpur Paper Mills, also joined the political movements of the 1930s and 1940s. A Telugu-speaker from a family that was in Telingana "earlier than the Nizam, he came only two hundred years ago," he and his wife had a son who was a travel agent in Secunderabad and a daughter who was a law graduate from Osmania. In 1977 the daughter married a chemical engineer from Madras, settled in Texas, and became a U.S. citizen. She did social work, and she and the children visited every three years: "Their language and accents are American but culturally they are still OK." Mrs. Vaman Rao had visited the United States twice, for six and eleven months; Vaman Rao had been able to go only once, for a month.[42]

From an old Telingana landed gentry family, B. Narsing Rao was a Hyderabadi who absorbed Hyderabadi culture under the Nizam's rule but fought against the suppression of Telugu and the other vernaculars. Like Gopalrao Ekbote, he had been active in the library movement. Rao came from his village to attend Viveka Vardhani School and then, in 1946, Nizam College; he earned an M.A. in political science in 1952.[43] Rao spoke passionately about the challenges to princely rule in the 1940s, the Police Action of 1948 when he was in Nizam College, and his own leadership of the mulki movement in 1951–1952. In 1952, with the general elections, his uncle, B. Ramakrishna Rao, became chief minister of Hyderabad State. But this newly empowered class of Telingana politicians was eclipsed in 1956, with the division of the old state and the creation of Andhra Pradesh. "No other part of India has gone through so many changes," Rao said, discussing the serious identity crises accompanying the political shifts. An astute observer in Hyderabad, the UK, and the United States, Rao understood the nostalgia of those who left, having himself been schooled largely before 1948.[44] But he charged that the Muslim nobility had merely reproduced Mughlai culture and that its members still had not acknowledged the extent to which that culture had suppressed the local languages. Yet Hyderabadi Urdu and the urban culture were still seductive, he said; the children of the Andhras had learned this and had become Hyderabadis in a new and broader sense, one going beyond the old closed society.

Finally, Dr. Dharma Reddy, another newly empowered Hyderabadi from the districts, exemplified in his career the shift from government service to independent professions, a shift that placed professionals above politics to some extent. Reddy caught the last of Hyderabadi culture when he came from Nalgonda district to Chaderghat High School in the city in 1937, studying biology in Urdu-medium Osmania and graduating in 1946. He took up medicine in 1951 and entered government service. In 1974 he became first director of the forensic science laboratory and shifted in this role to the police department. In 1983, when Chief Minister N. T. Rama Rao retired all government servants over the age of fifty-five, Reddy established his own laboratory by Niloufer Hospital and prospered. Reddy's wife was from Warangal District, and his wife's sister's husband was a doctor in Kaiser Permanente HMO in Los Angeles. The Reddys' elder son lived in California too, married to an American woman he met in Occidental College. The Reddys' eldest daughter, married to a Vellama from Hyderabad, was also in Los Angeles, as were five of her husband's seven siblings. The Reddys' younger daughter was in London with her Telugu-speaking Hyderabadi husband; the younger son was in Hyderabad and married to the daughter of the famous orthopedic surgeon, Dr. Ranga Reddy. Dharma Reddy owned valuable land in Hyderabad but was disposing of much of it because his children "will not come here . . . but when they are happy, we are happy."

New Hyderabadis. A whole new set of people calling themselves Hyderabadi—but not mulki—has arisen in the city, newcomers from the Andhra districts of the former Madras Presidency. Both Hindu and Muslim, these men and women also had children and grandchildren abroad, some of whom have started websites grounding their Hyderabadi identity in the capital city of Andhra Pradesh. (Old Hyderabadis have started websites based on their schools, Madras-i-Aliya, St. George's, Public School, and so on.)

Middle-class government servants and professionals flocked to the new capital of Andhra after 1956, many of them quickly claiming to be Hyderabadis and intermarrying with families long established in the Nizam's former state. K. G. Somsunder, a Hindu lawyer, became a Hyderabadi, he said, because he loved the city and its tolerant culture. He went to Nizamabad District with the Reserve Bank of India in 1957–1958 to do rural studies and was amazed to find that the Telingana village records were in Urdu but written in Telugu script. Despite his embrace of the new setting, his daughter and her husband settled in Melbourne, Australia. M. Nizam Mohiuddin, a Muslim from Kurnool who came to Hyderabad in 1956 had also become a Hyderabadi, like his friend, Somsunder. Mohiuddin worked in the educational section of the secretariat, acquired property in Hyderabad, and married his daughters to Hyderabadi men. The in-laws of one daughter were in Hyderabad, so she and her family were sure to settle there after the husband's work in Abu Dhabi was over, but the other daughter and a son had settled in the United States. Retired, Mohiuddin and his wife had made four one-year visits to their children and grandchildren in the United States and were uncertain whether to go there permanently. None of the American grandchildren, in 1991, had been to Hyderabad.[45]

The more elite newcomers to Hyderabad were far less likely to identify as Hyderabadis, seeing themselves as bringing Andhra culture to the city and improving or reforming the culture of Telingana. They too had children abroad. Retired in 1987, Justice P. Rama Rao came to Hyderabad from the Madras High Court in 1956, one of those whose arrival suddenly set back judges in Hyderabad State by jumping ahead of them in seniority. Justice Rao felt that the Telugu Desam government had "claimed Hyderabad for the Andhras and induced people to give up the slang of Telingana, the Urdu in the Telugu, in favor of fluent, good Telugu." He built two houses, first in Hyderguda and then in what he termed a Hindu, South Indian neighborhood in Banjara Hills. He and his wife had five children; four were settled in four different cities in the United States. The eldest son, a doctor and an "old Hyderabadi," according to Rao,[46] went to Chicago in 1977, and the eldest daughter, also a doctor, went in 1980. The second daughter was a lawyer in the United States and the youngest son worked in the computer industry there. The second son was refused a U.S. visa, so he worked in Algeria, went to Paris for an M.B.A., then came home and became a real estate developer. All those abroad were married within their Kamma caste before leaving home. Two said they wanted to stay abroad and two wanted to come back, but all the sisters of the Raos' sons-in-law and daughters-in-law were settled in the United States. The grandchildren abroad were young, aged one to eleven, but all said they wanted to stay in the United States. This was fine with the Raos, who had just visited the United States for four months, spending one month with each child. "We're happy here, they're happy there," they said. Note that they, like other satisfied parents, did have a son in Hyderabad.[47]

The Old Hyderabadi Elite. Families rooted in Hyderabad's history and known for their military men, bankers and businessmen, engineers and doctors, or administrators and educators struggled to find secure places in the new context. Many already had educational experience abroad but had returned to manage ancestral property or hold administrative and professional positions in Hyderabad. Traditional family occupations faded as new occupations claimed higher status. Despite differences of background, members of all these families have become part of the diaspora.

Men in the HCS were not all taken into the IAS. Even those who stood publicly against the Razakars were not easily accepted into the ranks of Indian government service. Fareed Mirza, an HCS *tahsildar* (revenue official) in 1948, protested and resigned on July 15, shortly before the Police Action, because Hindus were being robbed and killed by the Razakars and the government was not protecting them. On August 13, he and six other HCS men courageously published a statement in the Urdu daily *Payam*, saying that Hyderabad should accede to India.[48] The Police Action began on September 13 and Hyderabad surrendered on September 17, but, despite his outspoken pro-India stance, Mirza had no job until May of 1949, when he was reinstated. Later, after promotion to deputy collector but not collector, Mirza resigned. All of Mirza's children except one were abroad, four daughters in Chicago (one a doctor married to a Hyderabadi Hindu), one son in San Francisco, one son in Toronto. The last son, a very religious Muslim, would not live in the West; he lived with his parents in Hyderabad.

Dr. Rahimuddin Kemal joined the HCS in 1945 and continued in government service but ultimately resigned. He and his wife, both from distinguished families, married in 1946, went to London in 1947, and returned in 1948 to a very different Hyderabad. Kemal left the service in 1949 and they returned to the UK[49] but came back again to Hyderabad with their two young sons, planning to send them to Switzerland for education (but both grandmothers opposed this so they went to boarding school in Ootacamund instead). Kemal rejoined government service in 1955 while his wife developed an international school. Their two sons settled abroad, one in the UK and one in the United States; the English son had an American wife and the American son had an English wife.[50] From a Telugu Christian family, Dr. Herbert Butt moved from the HCS into Indian government service. His American wife, Helen, had been a U.S. Foreign Service Officer in Burma who met and married Herbert at the American University in Washington, D.C., while getting her Ph.D. Their joke was that Herbert got his M.Sc. at Penn, his Mrs. at American University, and his Ph.D. from Cornell. Herbert considered himself a Hyderabadi, but Helen was critical of the old culture. When Herbert was in service they lived in the Punjab, and she preferred that more egalitarian frontier culture. Their two children went to the United States in 1981 for higher studies and have stayed outside Hyderabad.[51]

A high-ranking family in old Hyderabad's military circles was that of Khusro Yar Khan and his wife Nafissa (first cousins).[52] Khusro's father was a major general in the Hyderabad Army and his uncle was Bridadier Taufiq, famous polo player and gigolo. Nafissa, a noted beauty, had been married to Prince Basalat Jah of the Nizam's family but, emboldened by the Police Action in 1948, left him and married the man she loved. One of five sisters and four brothers, she had only three sisters and one brother still in India. Khusro's siblings had also scattered.[53] Among their relatives, there were three Muslim-Hindu marriages, and through an earlier Anglo-Indian bride the family was related to the Coxes (in Australia).[54] Khusro and Nafissa planned to join two of their children in Canada but were waiting for a property settlement (and in the meantime lost their immigration status and had to reapply). While they waited, the Canadian grandchildren visited Hyderabad, and even though their families had become more religious abroad, the children did not say "*salam aleikum*" but "Hi."

Bridging the military, financial, and religious arenas in old Hyderabad were the Goswamis or, in Hyderabad, Goswami Rajas, members of Hindu *sanyasi* (ascetic) lineages whose wealthy trading and banking houses were conspicuous in Begum Bazar. In this male world of ascetics tracing their lineage back to the ninth century sage Sankaracharya, there were no women and there was no caste. Boys and young men lived as disciples of the older, traditionally unmarried, *sanyasis* in walled compounds called *maths* (temples).[55] Young Hindu boys from various caste backgrounds came as orphans or were brought by impoverished parents to become disciples. However, some of the boys were the biological sons of the Rajas who often kept women. The head of each math designated his chief *chela* (student) and successor, but the practice was not to appoint one's own son to one's math; instead, men appointed each others' sons in complicated rotations. This

FIGURE 10.1   Dilip Gir's initiation as a Goswami *chela* (disciple). Courtesy of Raja Deen Dayal and Sons with thanks to Dilip and Khurshed Gir, Ramona, Illinois.

system continued in Hyderabad longer than elsewhere because it prospered through connections to the Nizam's court and state finances. The Police Action, therefore, had an impact on the Goswamis.

In figure 10.1, seven-year old Dilip Gir was being confirmed (in 1952) according to tradition as *chela* of his uncle Hanuman Girji and successor to his *math*. Dilip remembered crying as *vibhuti* or ashes were rubbed on his forehead, because, as Hanuman Girji was deceased, the confirmation was

being held on his *samadhi* (gravesite). But the Goswami world was changing rapidly. Dilip's father Dilram Gir had twelve children by a woman from
another Goswami math whom he had garlanded (married informally). He
decided in 1961 to acknowledge his marriage publicly and accept Hindu
law. That meant he could declare his own *math* (inherited not from his real
father but from his guru, a cousin) a joint property and divide it among his
sons.[56] Furthermore, marriages had to be arranged and a "caste" had to be
constituted. Of Dilram Gir's twelve children, eleven lived to marry: two
of the spouses were Goswami, three were Muslim, two were Gujarati, two
were Bengali, one was Rajput, and one was Konkani.

Although Goswami law and practices were changing, Dilip Gir did inherit the *math* and his oldest brother resided there for decades until it became dilapidated. However, Dilip and his Muslim wife, a well-known
doctor, lived in Dubai for years and then moved to Chicago in 1991. Dilip's
surviving sister also lived abroad, like him married to a Muslim.[57] Chandrakant Gir, Dilip's elder brother, stayed in Hyderabad and married Lalitha,
daughter of a leading Rajput doctor in the old city, Dr. Digamber Singh.
Lalitha worked for USIS for twenty years and the couple built a home in
Banjara Hills. The Girs' daughter married into a Madras family with a similar (intercaste) background. The Girs' son was one of those who followed
the popular professor, William Mulder, to Salt Lake City. After his American education and a short unsatisfactory job in Hyderabad, he worked in
Dubai (where other relatives were working), made good money, and came
home to marry (also an intercaste marriage).[58]

The Marwaris, another major Hindu financial community in old Hyderabad, were families of bankers, moneylenders, and jewelers based in the
old city and around the British Residency and the Nizam's adjacent King
Kothi palace. From a leading family of jewelers, Parmanand Sanghi tried
to maintain old Hyderabadi culture by using his wealth to hold families
together across religious and national lines after 1948. Parmanand's early
education was at Madras-i-Aliya by order of the Nizam. His grandfather
and father having died early, he was under the guardianship of the state,
specifically of *Kotwal* Raja Venkat Rama Reddy. He studied only to seventh class in Nizam College but continued to sit with his many friends in
their classes and pay for their snacks at the canteen, starting a lifelong career
as a generous host; people called him Raja. He and his friends visited both
Hindu temples and Muslim mosques together. Parmanand sponsored several intercaste or intercommunity marriages in the city, paying for them,
holding them in his own house, and standing in place of the parents. In
addition to inherited wealth, Parmanand profited from starting a modern
gas station in the city. His wealth allowed him to visit his classmates and

friends around the world: he went to Pakistan twice, to London several times, and to the United States and Canada, often for the weddings of his friends' children.[59]

Gujarati Hindus, another major financial community in old Hyderabad, sent family members into independent professions early in the twentieth century, and these families too were changing occupations and joining the diaspora. Chandu Lal Danghoria, a Gold Medalist in Hyderabad, had gone to Ames, Iowa, in 1922 to study for a master of science in engineering. He became a leading civil engineer in Hyderabad in the 1930s and his son, Dhiraj Danghoria, went in turn to Iowa for an engineering degree. Because their marriage network drew on Ahmedabad and Baroda in Gujarat, the in-laws in this family usually came from outside, although Mr. and Mrs. Danghoria considered themselves Hyderabadis. They had a daughter and son-in-law in South Africa, a daughter and son-in-law in the United States, and a son who lived with them.[60] Both sons-in-law and one daughter were medical doctors, as was Dhiraj's sister, whose nursing home in Hyderabad was located in the joint family compound. The Danghorias had no desire to move overseas but did visit the United States. The American family could afford to visit often, and the American grandchildren ate Gujarati vegetarian food but could not speak Hindustani. Through his sister, who affiliated her pioneering village clinic with the American-funded Mediciti, Danghoria and his wife were well acquainted with SHARE and the work the Hyderabadi doctors in the United States were doing in Hyderabad.

Doctors were admired public figures in old Hyderabad, members of a modernizing profession from the late nineteenth century. They continued to be important in the new Hyderabad and the diaspora. Apollo Hospitals, based in Hyderabad and founded by Dr. Prathap Reddy, was India's largest chain of health care providers in the private sector and the third largest in the world. Dr. Reddy had a lucrative practice in the United States but returned to India when an Indian executive died young because he was unable to get to the states for a coronary bypass in 1979. Reddy has pioneered in many ways, most recently by promoting "health tourism" to bring patients from abroad and provide for their stays, sightseeing, cuisine, and other needs at a fraction of the cost of their treatment in their new homelands.[61] This enterprise, along with Mediciti, dominated the medical landscape in Hyderabad and highlighted its transnational linkages.

Hyderabad's pioneer doctor families by the 1990s often had more members abroad than in Hyderabad. One such family was that of Abdul Azrat Hussain; not a doctor, he owned the A. A. Hussain bookstore at Abid's Circle. This Bohra Muslim family originally resided in the old city, in Hussaini Alam, where the ancestral graveyard and an old Bohra mosque remained.[62] Most men in the family have been medical doctors since the late nineteenth century, starting with Abdul Husain, titled Dr. Nawab Aristo Jah Bahadur, superintendent of the Nizam's medical department and head of Osmania University's medical department. Aristo Jah studied medicine in Hyderabad in Urdu but sent his sons abroad. Aristo Jah had seven sons, five of them doctors, two trained in the UK, two trained in the United States, and the last in Hyderabad. In 1991, A. A. Hussain's extended family numbered some 500, 90 percent of whom lived abroad. One of Aristo Jah's sons went to Pakistan in 1958 but even his children had moved to the United States, as had so many other descendants of the Hyderabad main family. Most were in California and a few were in the UK and Canada. Many women in the family were also doctors. Still in Hyderabad was the noted ophthalmologist Dr. Yousuf Hussain, but he and his wife attended family reunions in the United States rather than in Hyderabad. A. A. Hussain's fourth son, Shoukat, managed the Hyderabad bookstore and did not want to go abroad.[63]

Educators were very important in old Hyderabad, especially the Anglo-Indian teachers employed by the city's elite schools and the nobility. Established in India in the late eighteenth century and long-settled in Hyderabad, one leading Anglo-Indian family was ending its tenure there as the sons and other young relatives of J. W. and Marjory Edwards settled in Australia an elsewhere abroad. Many Edwardses were teachers, in Madras-i-Aliya, St. George's, and as private tutors in leading families. J. W. and Marjory ran the respected Golden Rose School across from the Methodist church. Their sons left in the 1970s, as "educated and capable people don't get rewarded for their work anymore; we were a cosmopolitan lot, but the spirit is gone."[64]

Other families proud of their service to old Hyderabad had become part of the diaspora. Telingana Reddys whose ancestors served the Nizam went abroad as often as did "new Hyderabadi" Reddys. Reddys and Kammas were the two dominant castes in Andhra, rivals in the countryside and the capital. S.N. Reddy, a Telingana man and reportedly the first Indian trained in Scotland Yard, headed the Nizam's personal estate, the Sarf-i-Khas, after the Police Action. His brother was a leading barrister whose daughter married Gopal Reddy, graduate of Lawrence School in Ooti and Engineering College in Madras who prospered as an engineer in Hyderabad. Gopal Reddy's only child, a son, studied in Iowa, worked in Texas, and settled in California; his wife was an Andhra Reddy and they had two children, the elder of whom knew some Telugu. The parents had visited California, and Gopal Reddy repeatedly offered to build a medical diagnostic center on the vacant land next to his Banjara Hills house so that their son could practice his profession in Hyderabad. But the Reddys recognized that the grandsons would have better chances in the United States. How, they said, could they ask them to come back to Hyderabad with its problems of population, poverty, and school admissions? In Hyderabad, these Telingana Reddys said, "money cannot buy places, and certainly merit cannot buy places; today, it takes political clout." The parents did visit the United States, especially Mrs. Reddy, and they tried to teach the boys Telugu. The youngsters came from the United States every two years but got sick and did not appreciate the food.[65]

The high-caste Hindu Kayasths who came to the Deccan with the first Nizam and served at all levels of the administration also sent members abroad in great numbers, including members of the pioneering "doctor" families of Dr. Benkat Chandra, Dr. Rup Karen, and Dr. Raghunandan Raj.[66] Descendants of a Gaur Kayasth family well placed in the estate of the Paigah military noble family, most of the nine children of Onker Pershad lived abroad. One son, Hemansu Roy, maintained a splendid house in the outskirts of the old city to receive his siblings when they visited. Of his schoolmates' children, this "anchor" in Hyderabad estimated, 90 percent were in the United States, and 66 percent of his own peers, his friends, were there as well.[67]

A prominent cluster of families, the Shia Muslim Bilgramis from the village of Bilgram in northern India and Iran and Iraq before that, arrived in Hyderabad in the mid-nineteenth century as non-mulki administrators but soon achieved mulki status. Ancestors also served elsewhere in the Deccan for 400 years, some coming to Hyderabad from Iran by way of Mysore through service with Hyder Ali and Tipu Sultan. Syed Hossain Belgrami founded Hyderabad State's modern educational system in the late nineteenth century, and after that few Bilgramis went out of Hyderabad for education or jobs. Most worked for the Nizam and never thought of leaving the state. After 1948, family members continued to hold high positions in Hyderabad but many moved to other parts of India and abroad.

Raza Ali Khan, a Bilgrami whose mother was a pioneer educator in the city, was previously a polo player and big game hunter. Seeing an opportunity, he wrote and published two books about Hyderabad, using his own and others' collections of old photographs, then took his books abroad to market them to Hyderabadis. In Canada, where he had a brother, and in the UK and United States, Ali Khan was disappointed by the diasporic Hyderabadis. Assured by many that Hyderabadis abroad would be eager to buy, he had taken 200 copies of his book along, but at a big meeting of the Chicago Hyderabad Foundation he sold only seven copies! "But, being Hyderabadis, people asked for them after I packed the copies up again, and after I left the city too," he said.

From the same distinguished Bilgrami family of educators, Rasheed Ali Khan was a poet and writer in Hyderabad. Rasheed's only child, a son, lived in Chicago, where he was partner with a Gujarati Hindu in a convenience store while the daughter-in-law managed a Dunkin Donuts shop, jobs their family status might have prevented them taking in Hyderabad. Rasheed's daughter-in-law's mother was part of the Chicago household and she imparted Hyderabadi culture, yet his three granddaughters were "definitely American." His son taught karate there, as he had done in Hyderabad, and he was a fourth degree black belt; more notably, the two older granddaughters were karate champions, holders of brown belts at the ages of nine and seven. Visiting Chicago for almost three months, Rasheed found that everyone was so busy that, although he was "chief guest," his most frequent companions were the three small girls (not that he minded).

Asif Alikhan, son of Najf Ali Khan, and his wife Fatima Alikhan were also Bilgramis. Ali's engineering degree was from the UK, with follow-up experience in Germany, and he thought the UK pace was similar to that of Hyderabad, "civilized," unlike the fast-paced Germany and, he assumed, the United States. Fatima was a professor of geography at Osmania. Ali had two brothers and a sister settled in Los Angeles, where his sister had gone to marry a St. George's classmate of his and his brothers had gone to study. These siblings and their children would not come back. Another sister of Ali's married a relative with a business in Dubai and that couple ended up in the UK. The once-extensive family properties in Hyderabad have been divided up and sold or rented out by the absent siblings.[68]

The Bilgramis had many, many family members abroad in the UK and the United States and a very few in Pakistan, but they met in Hyderabad every December in Banjara Hills for a gala family reunion in what most still considered the homeland. Cousin marriages used to be the practice among them, but they have "opened up the vistas" and Hindu, English, American, Filipino, Korean American, even Sunni Muslim partners have become part of this extended clan.

Muslim Hyderabadis. Aging parents and grandparents of all backgrounds regretted the fact that their children and grandchildren were settling abroad, but Muslims, more than others, saw going abroad as necessary. Khadiji Mehdi explained, "Our children have gone, our job prospects here are nothing. There is no future here for us. There too, we may be second-class citizens, but here, this [Bilgrami] family even, we are second-class citizens. After Abid Hussain, his generation, there will be no more Muslim leaders, no new leadership is coming up. How can one think of living without the children, but to send them away there must be a big reason."

Employment opportunities were a big reason. Muslims had been 80 percent of the government service employees before 1948, Mehdi Ali told me, but now they were below 10 percent. A. M. Khusro said that Muslims had been 80 percent of government employees and Hindus 20 percent before, whereas the current ratio was 20 percent Muslims and 80 percent Hindus.[69] Asif Alikhan estimated that of his 168 classmates at Nizam College, some 20 percent had settled abroad; of these, most were Muslims and in the United States. Anil De stated that some 70 percent of his Muslim IAS colleagues' children had gone abroad, a higher proportion than among his Hindu colleagues.

Many Muslims still in Hyderabad expressed feelings of loss and dissatisfaction and gave graphic accounts of the changes brought by 1948 and 1956. A composite account went something like this:

> The soft, peace-loving people were taken over, terror created in their minds, in the minds of Muslims, many of them used to the lazy life on fixed incomes of *jagirdars* and Nawabs. More outsiders came in from India (and most business had already been in the hands of Marwaris, Gujaratis, and Punjabis). New land laws were introduced, setting urban land ceilings and challenging *jagirdari* titles. Muslims who could afford it sent their children out for education, first to the UK and then to the United States and elsewhere. (Pakistan was easier and safer at first but people were not as happy there; it was a warrior culture, harsh and aggressive and less tolerant; others were already holding the land, there were language difficulties, and there were so many refugees.) Some Muslims stayed back to hold property or do business in Hyderabad, but now, from 90 percent of the property being held by Muslims, it is down to 10 percent and ceilings are imposed against us. Now, we are strangers in our own town, and politics and commerce and education are all oriented toward vote-getting. Today young Muslims have only petty jobs, running *pan* shops, pulling auto rickshaws, and so on.

Hyderabadi Muslims at all levels of the social hierarchy and in all occupations had experienced disadvantage and discrimination. Javed Akbar, in the restaurant business, reported, "restaurants started by Reddys are patronized by Reddys, but Muslims are a less secure base for restaurants, having less money generally. And if they have money, Muslims employ cooks and stay at home eating old Hyderabadi specialties." Fatima Alikhan, a professor at Osmania, reported that when she walked or talked with any other Muslim professor on the campus, someone was sure to remark, "they are making a Pakistan."

The Hyderabadi Arabs in the old city's Barkas locality, established in Hyderabad since the 1850s, complained of declining power. Brought to serve in the Nizam's and nobles' military units and still Arabic-speaking, they often brought wives from the Gulf and gave their own daughters to Arabs there in marriage. Most Barkas families sent men to the Gulf to work at a wide range of jobs. A Barkas Arab Association, started in 1967 to help people going to the Gulf, still met, led by Yasir Ahmed and a fifteen-member executive board. Those able to take their families along to the Gulf sent their children to the English-medium Indian Embassy schools there, and in Hyderabad too the Arabs preferred English-medium schools. In Hyderabad city, they claimed that the government helped Hindu businessmen but not Muslims, and the police force, with fewer and fewer Muslims, failed to maintain law and order in their locality (especially during communal riots).

An extreme case of Muslim downward mobility and attempts to overcome it was presented by a family in Hyderabad's old city tracing its descent from the Mughal emperors. Based in Aurangabad, Aurangzeb's capital in the Deccan, until the 1950s and still drawing a small pension stemming from 1857 when the British displaced the last Mughal emperor, the family had several men working in the Middle East and a few living in the UK, Canada, and the United States. Family members were convinced that not only did the Indian and Andhra governments favor Hindus when it came to jobs, but even recruiters in the Gulf states and Western consulates giving out visas in India favored Hindus over Muslims. Babur, founder of the Mughal dynasty, had come to India from what is now Uzbekistan, so this family was reaching out to Uzbekistan, asking for support. The Uzbek government sent an envoy to Hyderabad to call on the family and extended an invitation to the 510th anniversary of Babur's birth in Tashkent in the late fall of 1993.[70]

But Uzbekistan was not a beacon of hope to most Hyderabad Muslims, and emigration, the more usual response to Muslim laments, had been increasing. "Before, people went out for education and jobs, now they go for security, running away from problems in India." First a sister went, perhaps through marriage, and she called a brother who called the parents who called the other children after getting green cards or citizenship. A few Hindus told me that Muslims helped family members more, gave more assistance on the receiving end, and their explanations of this ranged from closer family bonds to a stronger push from lack of opportunities in India.

Many Hyderabadi Muslims have been enriched and empowered by the diaspora. Almost any encounter in the old city of Hyderabad, still some 60 percent Muslim, led to a discussion of wider horizons, of far-flung family members and their positive impact on old city life. Visiting a well-known Urdu library established by Abdus Samad Khan (preserved and aided by the University of Chicago), I met Mohammed Shamsher Ali, employed by the government electricity department. His three younger brothers worked in the Gulf and a younger sister lived there with her husband. One brother and his Hyderabadi wife both worked in Dubai and the other siblings were in Riyadh. The salaries helped support those in Hyderabad—a salary of 3,000 riyal a month in Saudi Arabia meant 18,000 rupees a month in Hyderabad, a princely amount. Money sent to Hyderabad was used for property acquisition and improvement, better education for the children, and luxuries like television. Shamsher Ali's wife had three brothers abroad, two in Saudi Arabia, and the other in New York; she also had two sisters with husbands in Saudi Arabia. She had just taken her M.A. in Urdu at Osmania and was planning to do her Ph.D. She and other old city women were no longer just staying at home; they too were investing in education.

Educators from the old city were themselves lured by increased opportunities in the Gulf. Mrs. Jaffari, the Montessori teacher in whose Oxford School for Tiny Tots my two children were enrolled in 1971–1972, gave up her school to join her husband in Dubai, taking her children there in the late 1970s and early 1980s. Her two daughters attended an English-medium Islamic school in Dubai. Returned to Hyderabad, one young woman was doing her exams and the other was working in a kidney center. Their parents wanted to marry them to men working in Sharjah and Germany, but one girl wanted to go to the United States instead, to her cousin in California who did not wear a burqah as their mother did.[71]

The workers in the Gulf had profoundly affected the old city social structure.[72] Uneducated young workers were sending so much money back that they were becoming desirable marriage partners and displacing the established educated class in the old city. Those with new money could afford better housing; rents were rising, creating housing shortages. Trying to maintain their identities in the Gulf, men there turned to Urdu poetry or to more orthodox forms of religion, Professors Sadiq Naqvi and Afzal Sharief told me, challenging the former educated elite and its control of the old city's culture. Some felt they had more freedom to be Muslims in the Gulf, that they fulfilled their potential as Hyderabadi Muslims there, and they brought "orthodoxy" back with them.

The theme of working and getting rewarded for one's work was invoked often by Hyderabadi Muslims to explain why family members were abroad. Most believed that "the chances for Muslims in Hyderabad are not so great now," and they saw their children abroad being well paid for their qualifications and skills. Their children sometimes accepted jobs abroad they would never have taken in Hyderabad. The grandson of a former vice-chancellor of Osmania University worked at Target and as a security guard. Descendants of families long associated with the Nizam's service took work as taxi drivers and department store clerks.[73] Wives very often worked in settings abroad. After the Police Action many women in Hyderabad also worked, but not so often as those abroad.

Some Muslims felt they should stay in Hyderabad to provide leadership to their community. Many Hyderabadi Muslims initially decided not to go to the West but to the Gulf for self-advancement, intending to return to Hyderabad and their community. Bonds formed in the Gulf states continued back in Hyderabad. Rashid Qayyum and Syed V. Javeed, friends but quite dissimilar Gulf returnees, had met in Jiddah in 1969 where there was nothing to do other than praying, so they spent lots of time together, sharing music and poetry. Back in Hyderabad, their views about religion and Hyderabadi culture had diverged, but they agreed that, as sons, they had mothers to support in Hyderabad. Further, the poorer Muslims left in the city needed guidance. "How can everyone run away?" they asked.[74]

Not all Muslims sending children abroad to study or work wanted them to "run away." Professor M. A. Muttalib, head of a Muslim family with a strong educational background, said he saw himself as producing middle-class Muslim supporters of Indian democracy when he had five children (his two brothers had five and six children respectively). A professor of public administration originally from Warangal District, Muttalib was a strong believer in the tolerance of Mughal and Hyderabadi culture. He chose not to go to Pakistan, feeling he could serve better in India. However, most of the children in this extended family now lived abroad and supported democracy and cultural tolerance in the UK, the United States, or Canada. Muttalib's three sons were in the United States; the eldest married a Hyderabadi woman brought up there. Sponsored by this eldest son, the Muttalibs became official immigrants to the United States, as the younger unmarried sons could get visas faster by joining citizen parents. Muttalib's daughters, however, were married to Hyderabadis who worked in the Gulf and would presumably return to Hyderabad. Muttalib and his wife went abroad at least once a year for several months to keep their U.S. immigration status and to be with their children and grandchildren. Muttalib disliked these extended stays of nonactivity, stranded in the suburbs and dependent on his sons, but his wife relished time with her children and grandchildren.[75]

Dramatic instances of Muslim success involved men who did so well abroad that they became powerful back in Hyderabad, using their economic resources to raise their status and that of other Muslims. Hoshdar Khan, whose business empire was in Kuwait, was one example. Another was Khan Lateef Khan, from the old city's Jahanuma Lancers' locality.[76]

This Pathan left Hyderabad at age nineteen with a degree in chemistry and "resentment in his heart," reportedly scrubbing the decks of the ship that took him to the United States. He studied in New Mexico, then earned engineering and M.B.A. degrees in Illinois and Indiana. His was a name to be reckoned with in Chicago, Atlanta, and Hyderabad.[77] In Hyderabad, he dealt in real estate and construction; he also purchased an Urdu newspaper and, in 1993, was chairman of the board of the Muffakham Jah Engineering College.[78] Khan was dedicated to helping Muslims get better educations and jobs and played a major role in "minority politics" in the city. Said to have three wives, one in Chicago, one in Atlanta, and one in Hyderabad, Khan counted some of the city's key Muslim public figures as allies and in-laws. A powerful patron who employed many Hyderabadis in Chicago and Atlanta, on one night alone during the wedding season (when many of his Hyderabadi employees came back to celebrate their children's marriages), Khan had seven weddings to attend in the old city.

Hyderabadi Women.   Before 1948, Hyderabad still presented a fairly conservative environment for women, albeit a very cosmopolitan one at the level of the elite. Both Hindu and Muslim brides who married into Hyderabad from elsewhere had found themselves in a vibrant Mughlai culture, with husbands who wore sherwanis and fez and spoke elegant Urdu.[79] With the Police Action and Hyderabad's incorporation into India, women in Hyderabad gained more freedoms and opportunities. The Indian Army seems to have deliberately brought women into the public sphere. Two local girls, the sisters Lalitha and Sarojini Singh, were picked to be National Anthem Girls and sang at many functions. For the first Flag Day in Hyderabad, the army officers from the north gave out flags and asked students of both sexes to sell them for less than a rupee; the proceeds were presented to General J. N. Chaudhuri. Another symbolic gesture was the ripping out of the purdah compartments in Osmania University classrooms, a feat achieved under the leadership of Hyderabadi vice-chancellor Ali Yavar Jung overnight and without advance notice.

Family support was crucial to women who wanted to take advantage of the new society, women who sought higher education and careers.[80] Dr. Salija Begum, who had studied in London and was reportedly the first Muslim woman doctor in Hyderabad, encouraged her niece Hamida to become an architect, the only woman in the College of Fine Arts and Architecture's first class of thirty students.[81] The numbers of "lady doctors" increased rapidly and several of them established nursing homes specializing in the delivery of babies. The Andhra Mahila Sabha, a progressive

Telugu women's organization from the Andhra districts, founded a major social service and medical center for women in Hyderabad.

"In Hyderabad, not only are men working, every lady here is also working, a big change; all are working for themselves, without relying on ancestral property or joint property," said eighty-year-old Gurucharan Das Saxena. This change was finally reflected in the elite Secunderabad Club when it initiated a membership category for single women and allowed members' daughters as well as sons to remain members in the early 1990s.[82] In all of the city's elite clubs, family-oriented activities mushroomed, although the older male-oriented drinking activities remained.

The expansion of the educational industry in Hyderabad engaged many women entrepreneurs; in fact, women dominated the industry. They started schools—small schools, big schools, pre-nursery schools and accredited schools at higher levels—in their own homes and in new facilities constructed in and beyond the city.[83] Montessori schools may have been the first wave, but the variety and number increased rapidly. Khurshid Shahzaman, a pioneer in Montessori education, was sent by her father to the UK to do Montessori training in 1960. Alone and emerging from strict purdah, she asked her British school principal to accompany her somewhere, as her father had advised, but the man, dumbfounded, told her she had to be independent. She went on to run the first Montessori school in Hyderabad. When her father died in 1976, she tried moving to Pakistan, where her own children and many girlfriends of her youth were settled. But she "could not adjust" and returned: "What are Pakistani relatives compared to friends here?"[84]

The educational industry in Hyderabad was spurred by lower class Muslims working in the Gulf investing in their children's futures. Mrs. Anil De, wife of an IAS man, had run a small neighborhood school since 1975 in Banjara Hills (a preschool, nursery, and lower and upper kindergarten), and she testified to the changes brought about by students whose fathers were working in the Gulf. Fathers with money but little knowledge of English filled out the school forms ("biziness," some wrote for occupation) and left their wives and children in Hyderabad. The wives could not write English and seldom spoke it well, but the children were learning very good English. Most of these "Gulf mothers" wore burqahs with the flaps up. Two other types of Muslim women were in Hyderabad, according to Mrs. De, the old Hyderabadi Muslim elite women who wore saris and never burqahs and the "other mothers from the Gulf, Pakistanis," married to Hyderabadi husbands but originally from Pakistan and based in the Gulf. The "Pakistani" women wore elegant *salvar kamiz* outfits, often with hijab. These three types of Muslim mothers Mrs. De now dealt with in her school, and the first and third were new to her.[85]

Anees Khan, head of the popular and respected Nasr School in Khairatabad, had had similar experiences. Her background was not IAS but Nawabi Hyderabadi, and in her husband's family even the men seldom worked, much less the women. But when her daughter reached nursery school age, she found existing schools unsatisfactory and started a play group in her mother-in-law's garage. There were thirty children in it by the end of the year, and the parents begged Anees to continue the cohort and start another class. Her family supported her;[86] her female in-laws taught for her and her mother-in-law continued to provide space in her home for the school. Anees hired her first two paid teachers in 1965 and, in 1968, decided to get a master's degree so the school could become accredited. Her cousin and his American wife in New Mexico received her in the United States and she completed an M.A. in nine months. The Nasr School had students from all backgrounds, and Anees was offered money by parents working in the Middle East to expand so that more children could be enrolled. Khan found that she had problems with children coming back, not from the Gulf but from the West. She got many girls whose parents were sending them back for Indian exposure and schooling, unhappy children who wanted to return to the UK, United States, or Canada. The girls were revolting against their parents (the mothers usually, who were in Hyderabad with the children) but also presented discipline problems at school.[87]

After 1948, Hyderabadi women moved decisively into the public sphere. Some went into politics—for example, Sarojini Pulla Reddy, a Congress Party leader in municipal politics. Meheroo Jussawalla, from the Chenoy Parsi family, earned her Ph.D. in economics from Osmania and became principal of Women's College and Osmania's first woman dean of the faculty of social sciences shortly before migrating to the United States in 1975.[88] Women from old Hyderabadi families actively sought to preserve aspects of Hyderabad's heritage. Lakshmi Devi Raj, daughter of a doctor prominent before the Police Action, tried to keep the old culture alive by placing an Urdu nameplate on her house and an Urdu license plate on her car. She was on the Tourism Board, the Lepakshi Board (government handicraft emporium), and the Urdu Academy Board. Other leading activists were Lalitha Gir and Anuradha Reddy.[89] In-marrying women like Asha Dua and Bilkiz Alladin, from the Punjab and Bombay, respectively, wrote articles and books about old Hyderabad; Bilkiz was very active in heritage preservation. Women participated actively in groups like the Indian National Trust for Art and Cultural Heritage (INTACH), the Society for Preservation of Environment and Quality of Life (SPEQL), the Historical Society of Hyderabad, Friends of Golconda, and others.

With strides being made by women in Hyderabad, the next step was for women to go abroad for marriage, education, or employment. The architect Hamida Begum fulfilled her ambition to work in Saudi Arabia. With the support of her husband and key in-laws, she traveled there and showed her designs to a sheikh and his American collaborator. The latter took responsibility for employing her; the sheikh asked what salary she wanted and she left it up to him, accepting the "half salary" he then offered. To live and work in Jeddah, she needed the help of a male student of hers and of her own twenty-year-old son, whom she brought, along with her eight-year-old daughter, to live with her (Saudi Arabia rarely allows women unaccompanied by male relatives into the country). She assisted with renovations being undertaken on the Kabah at Mecca, advising the Pakistani contractors doing the work and influencing the relocation of the Zamzam well (source of water for thirsty pilgrims on the hajj). Her two sons later worked in Saudi Arabia.

Thus women as well as property, the two "possessions" held precious and thought to bring the emigrant students and workers back home, both moved abroad. Property could be bought, and women could be taken along or could go on their own, with significant consequences for family dispersal. Jobs, careers, educational and social activities, even marriages, divorces, and remarriages undertaken by Hyderabadi women abroad have had repercussions back in Hyderabad.

Reorientations

VIEWS OF THE DIASPORA

Perhaps predictably, because families of all religions, castes, and classes now have more members abroad than once anticipated, negative views of the diaspora prevailed among those left in Hyderabad. Those Hyderabadis who went to Pakistan were certainly regarded negatively.[90] Muslim families in Hyderabad who had relatives in Pakistan were sometimes quite out of touch with that branch of the family. Most Hyderabadis believed that this set of emigrants had relinquished all claims on the homeland. As P. Vaman Rao said, "They are on a different footing, they went at once and for citizenship there; they have forfeited their right to be Hyderabadis. Those who go to study or work in the United States or wherever, they stay without meaning to." Visits back and forth were subject to national politics and security considerations. Rarely did Indian Hyderabadis journey to Pakistan, and strikingly often, it was old Hindu friends who made the effort.

Pakistanis did revisit Hyderabad occasionally, sometimes with negative impact, and a Hyderabadi visiting Pakistan for a nephew's wedding heard his own brother's children say he was from "the enemy country." Indian Hyderabadis still identified primarily as Hyderabadis, whereas those from Pakistan identified as Pakistanis.

Criticism of emigrants to countries other than Pakistan was usually general rather than specific and applied chiefly to other people's relatives. People resented "denationalized, opportunistic Indians abroad," emigrants who ran down India and claimed that "it's no place for a man to stay." The fashion was for educated Indians abroad to be critical of India and to claim that they were playing a part in building Australia or America or wherever, but homestaying Hyderabadis were skeptical of such claims. They recognized that India, by setting quotas in educational institutions and government service for previously underprivileged castes and classes, had helped push talented higher caste people overseas, but people contended that there were plenty of talented people left in Hyderabad. There might be discrimination in India against higher castes or against Muslims, but residents of Hyderabad happily matched such stories with stories of discrimination against Indians abroad. Anecdotes of prejudice and discrimination against Hyderabadis occurring in the host countries were well known and frequently cited, but such anecdotes did not bring the emigrants back.

When relatives did travel abroad, getting visas often stimulated negative feelings about the country to be visited. Asha Dua, whose son invited her to the United States, found the American consulate interview insulting. "The woman interviewing me was behind a glass with a small circular hole in it, as if we were untouchables. I told her, give the visa or don't give it, I have everything here, a driver, a car, a house, servants, why would I stay there? Only the children have urged me to visit. I'm proud of my country, I'm a good Indian." She got the visa but remained angry, resentful of the country to which her son had gone and its power over family members in India. People compared various visa requirements, and family strategies about marriages often involved careful calculations of where and when to hold the marriage and how long it would take for a couple married in Hyderabad to be reunited in this or that country. People questioned whether a child was being married abroad because the match was good, the parents wanted to retire there, or the parents wanted that child to sponsor others.

Many believed that those abroad secretly longed to return, and no doubt some emigrants did say this, even some from Pakistan. Hyderabadis cited the corrupting influences of the material advantages that kept people from returning. Then there were the corrupting influences of Western culture, and accusations abounded of marriage disruptions because of foreign environments. Yet, even those who experienced downward mobility seemed unable to extricate themselves and return. Some maintained that young men left good opportunities in Hyderabad and ended up working as security guards or baggage handlers in the United States and Canada but were too proud to give up and come back.

Other stories countered the pessimistic views, highlighting children abroad who had achieved far more than the parents in Hyderabad, parents who benefited from their children's money and spent it freely. Some highlighted lower- and middle-class emigrants with such high positions abroad that there was no incentive to return to Hyderabad where one's parents might have been bricklayers, shoemakers, or washermen and where such origins were not forgotten. Chandrakant Gir told of a hardworking tailor who came on his bicycle from Moazzam Jahi Market to the Girs' Banjara Hills home, making frequent trips to measure, try on, and deliver clothes. He often brought his son along, but he and the son always refused to take seats inside the house. The tailor was able to send his son for an M.B.B.S. and to the United States for further medical training. Now a top pediatrician, the son frequently traveled to the UK and the United States; "if he ever came to our home now, he would certainly take a chair." There were also stories of millionaires, men whose careers abroad brought them fame and fortune.

Thinking in Hyderabad, however, was decidedly negative when people discussed whether to live abroad with one's children. Aging parents chose to stay in Hyderabad, often on the basis of past experience as visitors abroad. Khadija Mehdi said she had even been encouraged to immigrate to Canada by a Canadian immigration officer, who told her "you have culture, unlike the Punjabis; we get only the Punjabis." "But," she said, "in the homes of my children, I have no identity; I'm just a glorified servant, and there's no way of getting around. Here, within one mile I have all my family and friends and social work activities, and a car and driver." Stories about parents who had settled abroad and regretted it confirmed other parents' decisions to stay.

HOUSES AND HOUSEHOLDS RECONFIGURED

The lives of people in Hyderabad were affected by the diaspora in many ways. Property in Hyderabad was thought to be a magnet pulling the emigrants back, and family after family mentioned ancestral property or investment in new property as performing this function. But properties, especially homes, had altered in form and function because of the diaspora. Gracious, old-fashioned residences, large enough for joint family living, were being pulled down and new flats constructed, with the parents in one flat and another one or two flats left vacant for the children's holiday visits. Aging couples with no children or servants left to assist them were moving to apartments in multistory buildings, only to find that they could not properly receive their visitors or see them out as the old etiquette demanded.

Having their families stretched across national boundaries produced stress among family members in Hyderabad. Parents with one or more sons still in Hyderabad were most content. The parents with sons settled abroad and daughters married to men working in the Gulf faced difficult decisions, torn between going to reside with their sons (the more culturally acceptable option) or staying alone in Hyderabad near their daughters (whose husbands would more likely return to Hyderabad). Patterns of visiting abroad reflected gender differences, as mothers could and did stay longer with their children while fathers could not stay long or preferred to be back in Hyderabad. Parents who wanted to join their children abroad could be held up by litigation or property settlements in Hyderabad. Sometimes "property settlement" was a euphemism, as they really were waiting for an elderly parent or relative to die so that inheritances could be settled. Since households in the countries overseas and in Hyderabad itself were more likely to be nuclear, visiting parents could be a strain on a young couple abroad, particularly if the marriage had not been parentally arranged and one partner was "not from the community." As marriages became more a matter of private individual decisions, the choices could reflect commitments to old Hyderabadi culture or to the new settings, challenging and reorienting other family members.

Daily life in Hyderabad involved changes in eating and dining habits. New foods were being introduced directly by family members from abroad. (In 1981, before this was common, my daughter and I were startled to be served "vegetarian burritos" in a traditional Gujarati banking family's home by a daughter-in-law visiting from California.) Dinner times were shifted to accommodate TV programs from abroad that could be discussed with relatives settled there. Certain days and times were reserved for taking overseas phone calls: People declined invitations or arrived late because Dolly was calling from Canada, Syed from Melbourne, or Shanta from London at a preset time.

People in Hyderabad became resources for those abroad who called upon them for information or performance of family services. While I was staying at the Gir home, the brother of Lalitha's brother's wife called from Toronto and asked who had authored a particular *ghazal*; he and his wife wanted to present it in a mushaira. The Girs told him to call back in fifteen minutes and telephoned a local poet (Rasheed Ali Khan) for the answer in the meantime.[91] Connections between classmates could be drawn upon as well. One man went abroad, after his mother had supported his education for years, and, heading an academic department, he never came back. When his mother was dying, he called on an old classmate to help. She made hospital arrangements and paid for them, and then, after the woman's death, transported the body in her car from the hospital to the cremation grounds and lit the fire. Later, her friend came back, sold the family property, and returned to Canada.

REMEMBERING AND FORGETTING

Political changes in Hyderabad, combined with economic and social changes brought by India's development and globalization, have altered the opportunity structure for successive generations of families based in Hyderabad. Most family histories started with memories of government service with the Qutb Shahis, Mughals, British, and Nizams. Western-style educators, engineers, and doctors pioneered modern livelihoods not dependent on the state, although in old Hyderabad these professionals were often part of the ruling elite or close to it. Those who worked for political and social change in mid-twentieth century Hyderabad, like those in India's nationalist movement, were often lawyers (more commonly called pleaders, *vakils*, and advocates). Some district-based Hyderabadis gained political power after 1948, especially before 1956, and a few Hyderabadi administrators and politicians rose to the all-India level. Women joined modern professions, particularly as educators and doctors, and they too began to study and work abroad. Still newer professions, in computer science, physics, chemistry, academics, and business, attracted young emigrants. Changing occupational structures in Hyderabad and the world have reoriented families.

Language changes in Hyderabad and abroad strongly influenced what was remembered and what was forgotten. People bemoaned the fact that their own children and especially their grandchildren could no longer speak Urdu (or Telugu or Marathi or Kannada), much less read and write it. In Hyderabad itself, knowledge of Urdu was declining, and of course the change dated from the Police Action. Lalitha Gir, a student at Nizam College during the transition years (1948–1952), had intended to take Urdu with Agha Hyder Hasan, a famed teacher whose ancestors served the Mughal court. During those years, Ali Yavar Jung, Hyderabadi vice-chancellor of Osmania, presided over Nizam College's changeover to Hindi as the new mandatory language. To encourage Hyderabadis to take Hindi and Sanskrit, students taking those languages got 50 percent to 60 percent marks despite poor learning, Lalitha charged. In a Muslim family noted for educational achievements, Khadija Mehdi had to choose Urdu or Sanskrit for her son's second Public School language during her husband's absence, and she chose Urdu. Her husband returned and disapproved: "The children now have to learn Hindi, so Sanskrit would have been better." Even among working-class families in the old city, where Urdu remained the home and street language, Urdu was declining. Those who went to the Middle East were opting for English-medium schools for their children, whether they were the Indian Embassy schools in the Gulf or the private schools in Hyderabad newly accessible to them. Major shifts in linguistic competence opened up new vistas but also erased entire worlds of poetry, jokes, and performance traditions.

   Despite the many changes, the older generations clung to the old friendships, the crosscutting networks that anchored them in Hyderabad city and state. One heard stories. Orthodox Muslim women brought whiskey to Hindu friends who appreciated it. Muslims called Hindu friends in the wee hours of the morning, saying they had to get up and come for a wedding ritual that could not be performed without them. Hindus loyal to their Muslim servants in the old city during times of communal riots and curfews braved the police to take them food and water. People called upon each other or phoned each other on the holidays still mutually observed—Id, Diwali, New Year's Day, and the birthdays of family members. Such stories made little sense to the children of Hyderabadi immigrants in Pakistan or elsewhere and will probably be forgotten. The children's own memories, being constituted in new settings abroad as they entered schools, made friends, and met others in their neighborhoods and workplaces, were orienting them to quite different worlds.

CHAPTER 11

Hyderabadis Abroad: Locating Home

LOCATING HYDERABADIS in their original home and then following them abroad involved careful consideration of seven contexts in addition to Hyderabad and India, contexts that were changing even as individuals and communities were changing. The Hyderabadis acted as agents in reformulating their identities abroad, identities shaped by their locations in both old and new settings, but their actions were constrained or encouraged by nation-states and by differing national constellations of fellow immigrants and citizens. Comparing the new sites and the sending societies—in this case, not only Hyderabad and India but also Pakistan[1]—we have seen the ways in which cities and nations and global forces competed for and shaped the identities of citizens.[2] The voices of the migrants show that they theorized meaningfully about their own movements and that those movements were both materially and ideologically produced. Their voices and further detailing of their backgrounds, networks, and views in endnotes exploded the notion of a "diasporic community" and highlighted differences among the emigrants and their differential reworkings of identities in the new sites.[3]

The particularities of religious, linguistic, residential, educational, occupational, and marriage networks based in Hyderabad strongly influenced the maintenance of social networks and the formation of new configurations of these networks abroad. The wealth of qualitative details revealed sensibilities that attached more importance to the relationships among people as aspects of belonging and attachment than to fixed ancestral places.[4] Family histories were marked by previous passages from one place to another, and despite nostalgia for a very special city and symbols of it like the Char Minar and Hyderabadi cuisine, the emigrants displayed, on the whole, a readiness to adapt to new sites. The categories employed by Hyderabadis in discussions at home and abroad—mulki and non-mulki, muhajir, citizen, first generation—were themselves categories that denoted and accommodated migrations and repositionings. Furthermore, following the Hyderabadis' movements meant viewing globalization, transnationalism, and cosmopolitanism from less familiar standpoints, notably from Hyderabad's Indo-Muslim state, Pakistan, and the Gulf states of the Middle East. Along with familiar economic and political concerns, South Asian sensibilities on the move highlighted cultural concerns about sexuality and marriage, religion and the family, in Western contexts.

This concluding chapter briefly reviews theoretical issues of diaspora, discusses the second generation and international marriage networks, and returns to issues of transnationalism, cosmopolitanism, and globalization. It ends by proposing that Hyderabadis are moving into an "emergent structure of feeling" grounded in the English language and urban North America.

Interrogating Diaspora

To be diasporic in William Safran's sense, the Hyderabadis, first of all, should have been dispersed from the center. There was no forcible expulsion in 1947 or 1948, but certainly Muslims felt the loss of power and status and many left for Pakistan. Feelings of loss or fear could have stimulated disproportionately Muslim emigration from India, and tensions among members of different religions, primarily between Hindus and Muslims, were undeniably rising in the last decades of the twentieth century.[5] The 1992 Babri Masjid crisis loomed large in the accounts of Hyderabadis in most sites, causing some to be disillusioned with India and others to become more fiercely committed to full Muslim participation in a secular state. But many Hindus, Christians, Parsis, and Sikhs emigrated from Hyderabad as well.

Another criterion was that people in diaspora felt unaccepted by the host society. Hyderabad itself was probably the site most transformed over the half century since 1947–1948, so much so that some Hyderabadis felt they were no longer accepted there. Although emigration was not the catalyst for the changes in the city and its hinterland, it certainly has contributed to them. The "not feeling accepted" test could not be fairly applied to the Gulf states, where settlement and citizenship were not options, but Pakistan, after Hyderabad, proved most problematic. The Pakistan promised in 1947 was not the Pakistan of the 1990s. The Hyderabadis who went there were still termed muhajirs, and even their children, who termed themselves Pakistanis, Sindhis, or Lahoris, did not always have their self-perceptions confirmed by their fellow citizens.[6] Some Hyderabadi Muslims and Anglo-Indians envisioned their migrations to Pakistan and the UK, respectively, as "returning home." Not finding themselves welcomed or well accepted, many moved again: Pakistani Hyderabadis went to the UK and elsewhere and Anglo-Indians went to other parts of the former British Empire, to Canada or Australia, and later to the United States as well. The UK might be third in terms of "not feeling accepted, as not only did some Anglo-Indians feel uncomfortable enough to move on, but many older Hyderabadis also expressed a certain disillusionment, disappointed to observe the second generation elsewhere being better accepted. Australia at first welcomed only Britons from India (then called Anglo-Indians) and kept out Asians, but its changing immigration policies made it arguably the most popular destination for Hyderabadi emigrants of all backgrounds in the late 1990s. As Australia became receptive to immigrants (and the famous Hyderabadi cricket team, the Deccan Blues, was reincarnated in Sydney), other nations tightened their immigration policies, making it somewhat harder to migrate to the UK and the United States but not quite so hard to migrate to Canada.

Two further criteria for a diaspora were little in evidence among Hyderabadis abroad: that they should regard the homeland as the true home to which they or their descendants should return, and that they should be committed to the homeland's maintenance or restoration. The few who expressed intentions to return generally did so as individuals or couples considering retirement and not as extended families. No one seriously proposed reinstatement of the former state or members of its ruling family.

When it came to the other two criteria for a diaspora, however—retaining collective memories of the homeland and defining a collective consciousness through a continuing relationship to the homeland—we have rich materials about the remembering and forgetting of Hyderabad by those abroad. Most first-generation Hyderabadi immigrants in countries other than Pakistan retained very positive collective memories of old Hyderabad that were important parts of their consciousness and often of their collective life abroad. Hyderabad has become an integral part of Andhra Pradesh and India, but those Hyderabadis who lived in the Nizam's state and many of their children had a lingering sense of loyalty to a state that they viewed as equal to British India and relatively free from communal tensions. Some Hyderabadis proudly proclaimed Hyderabad's cultural synthesis a model for all of India and pointed to Osmania University's pioneering role in the development of vernacular education for the masses. But the ideas about a Deccani synthesis and Hyderabadi culture were qualified in their time, and they have become harder to maintain in the face of rising

Hindu communalism and the decline of Urdu, a language that does not have a territorial base in India. People agreed and disagreed in complicated ways about the nature of Hyderabad in the past and present, but they were participating in one ongoing conversation, their narratives punctuated by key events all had experienced and employing the same categories when generalizing about those events.[7]

Most self-identified Hyderabadis abroad were first-generation migrants over the age of fifty who claimed some connection with the old Hyderabad State and its cosmopolitan Indo-Muslim culture. They continued to use the term mulki as a meaningful social category even when discussing emigrants. Many still voiced the traditional historical narrative so central to their own family histories, that Hyderabad was a successful plural society, perhaps even a cultural synthesis.[8] As Andrew Shryock wrote about an aspiring historian of the Beduoin tribes in Jordan, "Muhammad is a victim of the *real historical power* of the 'Adwan [his own tribe]. His identity is firmly grounded in the shaykhly era, and the memory of local might—now reduced to a kind of haughty nostalgia—makes new identities hard to imagine in any terms other than loss."[9] Hyderabadis from the former ruling class, and not only in the UK, tended to privilege that version of the past based on hierarchies of both caste and class. Their ways of thinking were akin to what Shryock has called a "genealogical imagination," "a tendency to parse society into discrete, vertical chains of inheritance and transmission, some of them biological, others intellectual, and others still a combination of the two."[10] These Hyderabadis did not appreciate my inclusion of a wide range of informants and conflicting versions of the past. The versions of old Hyderabad produced by some Hindus and Anglo-Indians that emphasized the "Muslim" nature of the elite and, in some cases, gave importance to the British Resident, were strange to them.

Many Hyderabadi emigrants took with them romantic notions of Hyderabadi culture, usually conceptualized by the end of the century as surviving better in the diaspora than in the homeland. However, the exact nature of the Hyderabad that emigrants claimed as their homeland was clearly a matter of contention. Ideas about old Hyderabad varied significantly, depending on one's age and status in the old society but also on one's status in the new location and the national narratives of the new states. Hyderabadi culture was being drawn upon differently, redefined, and sometimes consciously discarded in the new locations. It had at least three uses abroad. First, people celebrated the Hyderabadi culture of the past and talked about the virtues of the old state, its royalty, and its cultural synthesis. This stance was a primarily private and nostalgic one and inspired most of the initial invitational Hyderabad associations abroad. Second, people affirmed an ongoing Hyderabadi cultural synthesis and saw it as not only still meaningful but useful in the public arena, analogous to notions of secular pluralism in some of the new countries. This activist stance also played a role in the rhetoric of many Hyderabad associations, often at slightly later stages of their development as membership expanded. It was used, too, by Hyderabadis working to build multicultural alliances, like political coalitions with other South Asians, religious interfaith efforts, or professional coalitions.

A third stance involved fairly drastic reinterpretations of Hyderabadi culture. The assimilative powers of the new national print cultures, most powerfully the nations of India and Pakistan, pulled the old Hyderabad narrative in different directions. The Pakistani version saw Hyderabad as an Islamic state and the Indian version saw it as a backward, feudal society, interpretations anticipated by political groups within Hyderabad in the 1930s and 1940s. Among emigrants, the most powerful reinterpretations invoked Islam to challenge the dominant narrative of the former state. One version was that Hyderabad was really an Islamic state all along and the cultural synthesis was a myth, a view that could be voiced by Hindus and Muslims alike. Another version was that Hyderabad was a failed Islamic state and that the cultural synthesis, while real, evidenced the Nizam's failure to establish a truly Islamic state. To remember Hyderabad as either a successful or failed Islamic state well served those Hyderabadis who sought to recapture or replace Hyderabad by migrating to Pakistan. To remember it as a failed Islamic state paradoxically inspired some Muslims, minorities in predominantly Christian countries, to say that religious freedom in the West permitted them to be better Muslims abroad, where their religion was not tainted by Hindu practices. These Hyderabadi Muslims stressed Islamic ideals and built alliances with other Muslims in the new settings, distancing themselves from Hyderabadis organizing on the basis of culture or language in the new settings. First-generation immigrants voiced all these stances. Unsurprisingly, the nostalgic and plural society interpretations were held by those best placed in both old and new societies, whereas the interpretation stressing Islam was often held by those less well placed in both. These "Islamic twists" to the Hyderabad narrative also found places in some Hyderabad associations, even, arguably, in the most recent sets of officers in both London and Toronto.

The place of Islam and Muslims in the Hyderabad of the past was the most contentious issue. While not endorsing views of Hyderabad as an Islamic state, the upper classes among the Anglo-Indians and the Hindus oriented themselves to what some termed "the Muslim side" of traditional Hyderabad society. Those in the military and those of high rank in the state administration reflected this most. The schools most important in shaping lasting friendship networks were dominated by the Indo-Muslim or Mughlai culture of the ruling class. Even the Australian Christian principal of St. George's had to know Hyderabadi Urdu and Mughlai culture. The Anglo-Indians in Australia from the lower classes—for example, those who worked for the railway—spoke more often of the British Resident, seeing the shadow of the colonial power behind the Nizam's throne buttressing their position in Hyderabad State. Similarly perhaps, the shadow of an Islamic state behind the Nizam's throne seemed empowering to lower-class Muslims, a shadow emerging into full view overseas and embodied in Muslim organizations and institutions being built by pan-ethnic Muslim populations in the Western sites.

The kinds of national projects being undertaken by the states in which Hyderabadis were settling differed markedly, and these new national narratives powerfully influenced immigrant interpretations of the homeland culture. Pakistan's Punjabi-dominated and increasingly polarized society had no comfortable place for a Hyderabadi identity. British, Canadian, Australian, and United States versions of cultural pluralism could accommodate old Hyderabad as a successful plural society. In the Western countries where many Hyderabadis lived, differing constellations of indigenous and immigrant populations offered opportunities for political alliances and social networks beyond the Hyderabadi emigrant community, including new marriage patterns and religious organizations for some immigrants.

A Hyderabadi emigrant collective consciousness based on relationships with the homeland also involved close relationships with Hyderabadis in other diasporic sites. George Marcus writes, "The sense of the system beyond the particular site of research remains contingent and not assumed," [11] but to a very large extent the larger canvas was in mind, for me and my informants, as we talked about people's movements and memories. This was true even in cases of erasure or repression of memories. Hyderabadi immigrants in each site had a sense of what was going on in other sites and often compared and contrasted experiences. This was least true for those in Pakistan, where the immigrants' own prospects depended to some extent on deliberate erasure of connections to Indian relatives, and those in the UK were somewhat slow to sense the broader ebbs and flows, complacent in their sense of having selected the very best destination. I, the researcher, was part of that wider consciousness, playing the role of "circumstantial activist" by both seeking and conveying information and opinions as I moved from site to site.[12] I was interested in mappings of the diaspora as an intellectual exercise, but emigrants were interested in such mappings for their own strategic purposes or those of their friends and relatives.

The collective activities of the immigrants, the associations they formed or joined and their maintenance of social networks brought from Hyderabad, were important measures of the persistence of the Hyderabadi identity abroad. The absence or presence of the Hyderabad associations seemed correlated with the strength of the first generation's commitment to traditional notions of mulki identity, notions founded in pride of ancestry and closeness to power in the former state. Where such immigrants from Hyderabad were numerous enough, as in the UK and North American cities like Toronto, Chicago, Los Angeles, and Houston, efforts were made to establish associations and maintain a Hyderabadi identity.[13] Where the earliest immigrants were not from the elite or where Hyderabadi identity served no useful purpose, as in Australia and many American settings, or where Hyderabadi identity was a disadvantage, as in Pakistan, Hyderabad associations were not established or were weak. Where multiclass and often multinational groups supported other kinds of associations, like Urdu, Muslim, Indian, or Pakistani associations, these thrived with varying degrees of Hyderabadi participation. Linguistic associations, chiefly Urdu and Telugu ones,[14] attracted Hyderabadi immigrants. Everywhere, spoken Hyderabadi Urdu continued to distinguish Hyderabadis from other speakers of Urdu.[15] In Pakistan, however, it marked a negative ethnic identity.

National policies helped shape decisions, actions, and cultural orientations. Educational institutions and their orientations to government service loomed large in people's memories. The schools in Hyderabad—Madras-i-Aliya, Mahbubiyah, Nizam College, St. George's Grammar School, Public School or Jagirdar's College, Osmania University, and Residency Women's College—that shaped Hyderabad's elite had lasting impacts on networks abroad.[16] Classmates filled both instrumental and expressive roles for emigrants, and the classmate cohorts affected sibling and friendship and marital networks as well. Leading educators were reference figures, from the Reverend Bellingham and Miss Linnell to William Mulder and Peace Corps and Kansas State teachers (and more recent teachers are being memorialized on the current "old boy" websites).

Changes of language in schools spurred emigration in numerous instances. Urdu's place at the top of the administrative, literary, and educational domains in Hyderabad was unchallenged until 1948, even as the regional vernaculars gained importance through expanded secondary education and the library movement in Hyderabad State. Urdu's displacement, at first gradual and by English in elite higher educational institutions, and then abrupt and by Hindi and Telugu as well at all levels of the administrative and educational systems, has had continuing repercussions on Hyderabadis at home and abroad. India's three-language policy spelled doom for Anglo-Indian and Indo-Muslim culture alike, and Anglo-Indians and Muslims adapted or migrated. In Pakistan, even though Urdu became the national language, the dominance of Punjabi-speakers and the rootedness of the regional vernaculars helped reduce muhajir influence. In the Gulf, Urdu and Indo-Muslim culture flourished in the UAE but Arabic and Arabic culture dominated in Kuwait, differentially shaping migrant experiences. Despite the gradual decline of Urdu in India, Urdu literary societies functioned throughout the diaspora and maintained a more truly international set of vital, inclusive first-generation linkages overseas than any other associational activity.

The remembering and forgetting of the homeland was more fluid because Hyderabadi emigrants initially moved without supporting casts, without the servants or members of the older generation who had been crucial to the transmission and maintenance of Hyderabadi culture. The role of servants came up again and again, their presence, absence, or degree of cultural knowledge an indicator of the strength of Hyderabadi culture in any site. There was a growing tendency to bring aging parents to live abroad, especially in Australia, Canada, and the United States. The immigrants in Pakistan were less able to do this, constrained by parental commitments to Hyderabad or by politics. Those in the UK had settled earlier when parents were less mobile and those working in the Gulf were constrained from bringing their parents by legal regimes. In recent decades, emigrants moving as families have eventually resettled their parents abroad, putting the burden of cultural maintenance on women, whether mothers or grandmothers.

In all the overseas sites, Hyderabadi women have experienced family and work relationships in new ways. Women's participation in public life in Hyderabad also increased markedly after 1948, but in a setting where immediate and extended family members and servants helped diffuse responsibilities across a broad support network. Women working in the new contexts bore heavier responsibilities for embodying and transmitting cultural traditions, and, with narrower support bases, inevitably changed traditions even as they contributed to the material prosperity of families. In most sites abroad, Hyderabadi women participated prominently in public life, in linguistic and religious associations and particularly in educational and social welfare activities. James Clifford's point about the gendering of diasporic experience applies well here: Hyderabadi women were concerned with placement not displacement, with dwelling not traveling, and with rearticulation not disarticulation.[17] Their educational and welfare activities involved them with host society policies and institutions at the local level.

Commodity movements, often traced in diasporic studies, most strikingly involved clothing, jewelry, and especially wedding paraphernalia from Hyderabad and Karachi, reflecting degrees of attachment to traditional tastes. Even more crucial, Hyderabadi food remained at the core of identity construction, and this domain was strongly affected by both gender and generation. In Pakistan, the UK, Australia, the United States, Canada, and even the Gulf, potluck dinners brought Hyderabadis together. A crucial marker of mulki status was the love of dishes central to the old Hyderabad cuisine. Women abroad, however, played hostess to guests from many other places besides Hyderabad, so they adjusted recipes and menus. They also had to cater to their own children, who typically were strongly attracted by other cuisines. Thus mothers were charged both with enculturation of their children in Hyderabadi ways and with catering to their changing tastes. Indeed, some of the second-generation Hyderabadis expressed irritation with their elders' insistence on preparing and serving the old favorites.

Another measure of attachment to the homeland was journeying. People traveled often for weddings and sometimes for funerals or property disputes. Hyderabadis abroad took their children back to the homeland for visits (except for those in Pakistan), and the relatives in Hyderabad made changes in their homes, putting in Western-style toilets or adding screens to windows, to make such visits more successful. Yet the visits of children and grandchildren were often somewhat tense, as the visitors fell ill or did not take easily to Hyderabadi food or clothing. We saw the ambivalence of young Chicago Hyderabadis (and their hosts) about the special visits arranged for them to Hyderabad. Young people from all the Western sites tended to voice a generalized appreciation of India or Pakistan rather than a strong preference for Hyderabad.

Journeys were undertaken from Hyderabad to sites abroad as well. Parents visited their children in other countries for months at a time, moving from one household to another and often fulfilling requirements for green cards, permanent residence status, or citizenship as they did so. More distant relatives and friends made shorter visits, sometimes while visiting their own children and sometimes for weddings, medical treatment, or reunions with classmates. Speakers, poets, and musicians traveled for occasions like the 400th anniversary of Hyderabad city, and they could also be prevailed upon for performances when visiting their children or friends.

There was a high level of commitment to weddings, numerous instances of travel from Dubai to Toronto, from Hyderabad to Los Angeles, from Miami to Melbourne, from London to Karachi, and so forth, for the

weddings of the children of friends and relatives. Old childhood friends
and classmates from Hyderabad were, in their later years, bridging religious and national boundaries to attend the weddings of each others' children: Hindu guests were traveling to Pakistan and Pakistani Muslim ones
to Hyderabad, although my impression was that they met more often in
places like New Jersey, making numerous visits to relatives and friends
around the world en route. If the parents of the bride or groom were rich,
they flew guests over from Hyderabad and put them up in hotels; if their
circumstances were more modest, they might settle for holding a reception
back in Hyderabad, sending the newly married couple there to accommodate relatives and friends. These arrangements and journeys were being
made by members of the parental generation, but the weddings were of
members of the second generation abroad.

Generations Abroad

This issue of generational changes in identities, citizenship, and relationships with the homeland is a significant and understudied one, and my
findings emphasize the limitations of the theories about transnationalism,
cosmopolitanism, and globalization when applied to the descendants of
immigrants. I contend that even though some first-generation migrants
could be truly transnational or cosmopolitan, their children rarely could
be so. To complicate matters, many first-generation immigrants, admitting that they were settled permanently abroad, were bringing their aging
parents to the new homelands. The parents and grandparents might think
of the children as South Asian and Hyderabadi, heirs to an identity that was
an extension in space and time of what Akhil Gupta and James Ferguson
call "a prior natural identity rooted in locality and community,"[18] but the
Hyderabadi children being raised abroad did not and could not share that
ancestral world. Not sharing the physical space or sociocultural landscape
nostalgically recalled by their elders, members of the second generation located themselves firmly in the Pakistani, American, Australian, and other
new contexts.

For members of the second generation, there was no question that their
parents' "peculiar allegiances and alienations" (to reintroduce James Clifford's phrase), however remembered, rejected, or reinvented, were no
longer theirs. They rarely called themselves Hyderabadis and defined their
identities and communities quite differently from those of their parents.
Young Anglo-Indians in Australia became Indian not British, youngsters
in the United States became Indian or Pakistani or Asian American, youngsters in Britain became British Asian or British Muslim, and so on. When

visiting Hyderabad, they could be "just tourists." As they matured, the friends, occupations, spouses, and patterns of family life of the young people reflected these diverging personal, ethnic, and national identities.

Members of the second generation abroad claimed new and different identities, but most of them moved cautiously with respect to making their own choices of spouse. Choosing one's own marriage partner was a direct challenge to parental preferences and authority in most cases, and doing so risked losing parental love and support. The young people were more apt to try to make changes in the wedding festivities: inviting more of their own friends and fewer Hyderabadis of their parents' generation, having family members sit together instead of being segregated by gender, letting Pakistani and Punjabi friends dance the *bhangra*.

MARRIAGES

"What's happened to the Mughal princess?" one immigrant asked, trying to frame for me the subject of the marriages of young Hyderabadis abroad. Ram Mohan Roy, a Hyderabadi Hindu in California, told me that, brought up in old Hyderabad in the culture of the Nizam's days before 1948, his boyhood dreams were always of a Mughal princess, an image very familiar from Persian and Urdu poetry and Indo-Muslim miniature paintings. Possibly many young men from Hyderabad hoped to see a Mughal princess when they came to the part of the Hyderabadi Muslim marriage ceremony where, after the *nikah* or official part of the ceremony, the bride and groom sit side by side holding an open Qur'an with a mirror on one page, and, after reading a verse, look in the mirror and see each other. But in the diaspora, the dreams of Hyderabadi young people and the actual brides and grooms they confronted were less easily imagined. Who stood in the place of the Mughal princess or prince for young members of the Hyderabad diaspora communities? Some answers were emerging, ones not conforming to my friend's boyhood fantasy (Roy married a Greek American).

One could discern patterns of spousal preference, by countries and by gender, in what has become a transnational marriage market. The directions of bridegiving indicated a new North American center of the Hyderabadi global networks. Few brides were sent to India or Pakistan from abroad, although some families continued marriages that drew on close relatives wherever they were. A few brides went to Australia but it did not appear to be a magnet for brides from Hyderabad and Karachi. Hyderabadis went to Australia as couples, or Hyderabadi men tended to marry local Australians or New Zealanders, or grooms were brought from Hyderabad, pointing to the good prospects for employment. The UK drew upon Hyderabad and Pakistan for brides and also sent brides to the United States, although the dominant pattern was to arrange marriages between young people of Hyderabadi background in the UK. The United States and Canada attracted both brides and grooms from all other sites, although young men brought up in India or Pakistan were thought far more difficult to "socialize" than young women from anywhere. Young women of Hyderabadi or Karachi background were, however, apprehensive about marrying men brought up in the West.

Settlement patterns within and across nations influenced marriage arrangements. In Pakistan, young men on their own in places other than Karachi tended to marry non-Hyderabadi Pakistanis, whereas members of the large community of Hyderabadis in Karachi preferred to arrange marriages within that community. The earliest students in the UK, the United States, and Canada sometimes married outside their communities, and the Anglo-Indian immigrants in Australia did so as well. The numerous later-arriving professional immigrants in the Western countries tried to maintain the practice of arranged marriages. Matchmaking proceeded through relatives, advertisements, and, sometimes, functions held to bring youth together. Families and communities preferred marriages of various sorts (cousins, regional or national origins), with Muslims either deliberately crossing or maintaining the Pakistan/India boundary depending on family preferences. The notion that extended family membership overcame differences of national socialization was tested often and increasingly found wanting.

Unsuccessful cross-national marriages have inclined people toward matches made within the countries. Marriages arranged with or between expatriates, even between relatives, sometimes "went bad," and one heard of such tragedies in family after family. Usually these stories concerned daughters given in marriage to a man working abroad, especially in the Western countries. Indeed, young girls in Hyderabad talked warily about the need to avoid such marriages. "We are afraid of that, marrying there, a boy from the United States. We don't know if they have somebody there. Our parents may say the boy is OK but we don't know. We have so many friends, one returned to India because of this, and another will divorce but is staying there to not burden her parents. Another friend got engaged to a man who came, then he left and asked her to wait two years before joining him, then to wait another three years, and finally she broke the engagement."[19] Another young woman married into the United States when she was sixteen (saying she was eighteen) but returned after a year before becoming "caught by the many attractions there."[20]

Parents feared love marriages far more than arranged ones, but they knew that when one's children went abroad to study or work, they might make their own choices and marry there. Sometimes young people used study abroad to do just that: at least two couples arranged to study in the same places abroad and married when they got there, one couple in London and another in Pittsburgh. Unable to control the marriages of young people abroad, parents and relatives in Hyderabad invariably expected the worst. They inquired anxiously about the participation of the non-Hyderabadi spouse's family in the wedding and about the spouse's interest in the language, culture, and religion of the Hyderabadi. Sometimes religion and language were in apparent agreement, but sectarian or national origin differences intruded.[21] To the surprise of relatives in Hyderabad, some marriages abroad worked out well. I heard of one American wife "from a good family, the Gustafsons of Minnesota," whose relatives were cosmopolitan enough to satisfy an elite Shia Muslim family from Hyderabad. Another American wife was highly praised by her Punjabi Hindu mother-in-law, who waited eagerly for her visits to Hyderabad. In fact, while generalizations predicted negative outcomes, in most instances families came to terms with the spouses of their children and grandchildren.

In Hyderabad, there was general agreement on the impact of emigration on marriage patterns. Most people thought there was a shortage of "good boys" in Hyderabad because so many middle- and upper-class boys were going abroad, and this meant that more daughters were being sent abroad for marriage. Families in Hyderabad sold property to raise dowries and secure sons-in-law who had good jobs overseas. Certainly it was girls, not boys, who were more often sent away for marriage. Whether because of supply and demand or cultural preferences, boys from Hyderabad were not in demand overseas.

There did seem to be a shortage of marriageable young men in Hyderabad. A Muslim's daughter fell in love with a Sikh and wanted to marry him. When her parents protested, she said, "You didn't go to Karachi, you weren't thinking of us. There are no Muslim boys here for me, none in my class, but this boy is there." In Delhi and Bombay, because Muslims left earlier for Pakistan and also went abroad earlier, the shortage was reputedly worse. Another version of the "shortage theory" claimed that Muslim women in Hyderabad were domineering because they were "marrying down" and bossing husbands whom they outranked, since all the better prospects had moved out two or three decades before.

Marriages reflected parents' political prejudices and orientations to the future. Parents sought spouses for their children in the country where most relatives and friends were settling and where they themselves might want to go later on. Although some Hyderabadi Muslim families were marrying Andhra Muslims, there was a prejudice against Andhras, and Hindu friends maintained that they knew of more instances of young Hyderabadi Hindu women marrying African Americans than Andhra Hindus. Marriages across caste and community boundaries increased, with old Hyderabadis marrying other old Hyderabadis both in the city and in the diaspora. Such instances included not only love marriages but arranged or semi-arranged marriages.

The Gulf connections tempted many more working-class Muslims from the old city to marry their daughters to Gulf Arabs. Many of the Arabs seeking Hyderabadi brides were older and had one or two wives already, facts that brought unwelcome attention to the practice.[22] However, as several people said, "Are there no fifteen-year-old brides here in India, no third wives, no old husbands? Such cases go unnoticed in India but are headlined when done by Muslims. These marriages are better than starving here. When poor Muslims go to the Gulf and do well, it attracts resentment and envy."

For working-class families in Hyderabad, an emigrant offspring's dramatic upward mobility in the diaspora could pose problems for that emigrant's marriage. One instance came from the owners of the Muslim Sari Ghar, a residence-cum-workshop in a crowded locality near the Char Minar where valuable old saris were renovated. This artisan family had many customers among Hyderabad's elite families, and the second son was a very successful immigrant in the United States. A biochemical engineer with a Ph.D. from Cornell, he was settled in Washington, D.C., and wanted a bride from Hyderabad. His mother told me anxiously in Urdu (she and her husband did not speak or read English) that he wanted a literate, educated girl. She was giving out an English language photocopied biodata packet to her customers and seeking their assistance. The family talked of renting a house temporarily in a good locality in order to receive future in-laws in a better setting than the old city workshop, a strategy they were not sure would work.

WEDDINGS

Weddings were major events connecting Hyderabadis in the homeland and abroad. One partner in a marriage might be from Hyderabad, or the weddings of young second-generation Hyderabadis abroad were held wholly or partially back in Hyderabad, or relatives and friends flew here and there around the world to attend weddings.[23] Wedding rituals in Hyderabad almost always showed strong overseas influences, and at weddings, one heard of other marriages in other countries involving the same families and sets of friends. At weddings of all classes, one was sure to encounter people who spoke English well and had relatives in Canada, the United States, the UAE, and so on. Although it was more costly and difficult to hold Hyderabadi weddings outside Hyderabad or Karachi, the balance was tipping toward holding weddings in the countries where the young couples or their families were residing. Hyderabadis were flexible people and, mastering various national regulations about visas for fiancees, spouses, and wedding guests, they were scheduling weddings all over the world.

A South Asian wedding economy had developed by the end of the twentieth century in major North American cities, so that weddings could be carried out in Chicago or Los Angeles or Toronto more or less adequately. In such cities, several famed Hyderabadi cooks, some of them running public restaurants, could be called upon for private parties and weddings, and *pucca* (true) Hyderabadi food was served with great pride. In the UK and Australia in the 1990s, Indian cuisine was more readily available than Hyderabadi cuisine. In Karachi, one wedding dinner featured Chinese food, and in Hyderabad too the food could be eclectic, mixing Hyderabadi and Chinese or other cuisines. Some Hyderabadis overseas were more intent on maintaining traditional food and customs than those at home.

The weddings themselves were important integrative events, in location, content, and audience. Relatives in Hyderabad, with more and more weddings being held abroad, sometimes participated by sending costumes or other items.[24] But weddings were still magnets pulling emigrants back even if only temporarily. Many weddings where both bride and groom were from abroad were held in Hyderabad, for several reasons. Most relatives might still be in Hyderabad, or the family's audience, those it wanted to impress with its success abroad, was still chiefly there. Then, the older generation had more success in maintaining the tradition of five to seven days of ceremonies in Hyderabad, and stories abounded of the young independent women, living in their own apartments in the United States, made to sit meekly for hours in heavy wedding finery in a Hyderabad function hall. Another reason was the availability and cheaper cost of everything needed for a Hyderabadi wedding.

Weddings were being done differently, both in Hyderabad and abroad, although some elements of "a traditional Hyderabadi wedding" survived everywhere. For affluent Muslim families, weddings traditionally lasted six days, successively featuring ceremonies termed *manjher, sanchak, mehndi, nikah, chauthi,* and *valima.* The last days featured festive dinners, the *nikah* hosted by the bride's family and the *valima* by the groom's. Depending on caste and community, other Hyderabadi family weddings also lasted several days. Weddings used to be held in one's own large residence or that of a relative. Then in the 1970s and 1980s they began to be held in "function halls," often former palatial residences, with festive lights, folding chairs, and buffet tables. Most recently, big hotels have been the sites of high-status weddings. In Hyderabad, the successive days of the wedding ceremonies still followed each other, but in the UK and Australia, the two most important, the *nikah* and the *valima*, were held on successive Saturdays. Everywhere, some of the ceremonies were skipped, telescoped, or sparsely attended. Weddings scheduled in five star hotels became much shorter, even in Hyderabad.

A wedding in Pittsburgh and reception in Hyderabad well illustrated the transnational marriage culture and its impact back in the city. Vikar Shaikh Imam and his wife and two young daughters traveled to Pittsburgh for the wedding of his sister's daughter. Although members of the second generation abroad were "not much Hyderabadi," the niece's wedding was a *pucca* Hyderabad one, according to this couple. But the wedding details and photographs showed other influences. Of the 700 guests in Pittsburgh, 500 were South Asian and 200 were American, and there was a four-tier American wedding cake. The bride had studied in the UK, so one "bridesmaid" was from Ireland, and two others were American. In fact, these three, with two other women friends, had given the bride a shower before the wedding, and these five women flanked the bride in many photos of the ceremonies. Seating at the dinner was not segregated by gender, and there were two caterers, one for Hyderabadi and one for American food. The groom and many men did wear sherwanis, a white one for the groom, and the bride wore the traditional *kurti choli* and *khara dupatta* from Hyderabad for the *nikah*. The bride's *valima* outfit was sent by the bride's mother's sister from her home in Lahore, Pakistan, and the flowers were sent from Los Angeles by the groom's brother. Following the Pittsburgh festivities, Mr. and Mrs. Imam took their daughters and the bride and groom back to Hyderabad and hosted a reception for them there.[25]

Finally, parents in Hyderabad could be pulled abroad through the marriages of their children, retiring to a country to which they had never thought of migrating. This happened with Ather Ali Khan and his wife. A distinguished graduate of St. George's, his children have settled in Australia. First the daughter married her cousin there, and many years later the son ended up getting such a good job offer he relocated from the United States. He found a bride in Hyderabad, had the *nikah* in April 1991 by power of attorney and the *valima* in December in Hyderabad, and the couple moved to Sydney. The parents were eager to join their children but have been held up by an ongoing property settlement case in Hyderabad's

High Court; they missed their first immigration acceptance period but still planned to migrate.[26]

Despite the ways in which Hyderabadis abroad remembered and interpreted Hyderabadi culture and history and maintained or recreated Hyderabadi networks through journeys, associational activities, marriages, and weddings, the words *diaspora* and *diasporic* can be used only loosely about the Hyderabadi emigrants (as indeed they are used loosely about many other migrants). Those who were abroad were abroad to stay and they were reorienting themselves and their families to new nations and histories, selectively using the past as they did so.

Transnationalism, Globalization, Cosmopolitanism?

How did Hyderabadi migration experiences relate to the narratives of transnationalism, globalization, and cosmopolitanism? Did Hyderabadis provide a good example of transnationalism? Hyderabadis were certainly moving from their homeland to other societies, linking at least two societies. Most were extending their social fields, their knowledge, and their networks across national frontiers. It may be true that for Hyderabadi emigrants, "their public identities are configured in relationship to more than one nation-state,"[27] but I would argue that the fundamental orientation of Hyderabadis abroad was not a transnational or transmigrant one. Could a vanished cultural world be carried abroad, and if it or significant elements of it were carried or reconstituted abroad, were they circumscribed by religious or family ties? I rely here on the perspective that differentiated transnationals and cosmopolitans by defining the former as people who, while moving, carried cultural worlds that were typically circumscribed by religious or family ties and the latter as people familiar with other cultures and able to move easily across cultural boundaries.

The first and most obvious problem concerns the collapse of the center. If the city or state one claimed as one's homeland no longer existed, could one be a transmigrant? Recall the Hyderabadi, now a citizen of Pakistan, who told me, "there is no Hyderabad; you have seen Andhra Pradesh." He was one of many who thought that the old center had disappeared (or "been disappeared," in the Latin American sense, by the Indians or the Andhras). Many descendants of the old Hyderabadi ruling class in the UK and elsewhere held this conviction. Transnationalism was not what those who went to Pakistan had in mind either, as they repudiated Hyderabad and India and chose a new homeland.

Some Hyderabadis substituted third countries for the homeland in the creative invention of new identities abroad, usually members of the second generation but also members of the first. Recall the families in Melbourne, Australia, trying to organize a Hyderabad association. Many of the parents involved had worked in the Middle East but most of them came from India; nevertheless, emphasizing their religious identity in a context in which Muslim political coalitions were becoming important, many joined the Pakistan rather than the India association. In contrast, their youngsters seemed to identify as Indians. The flexibility exercised here and elsewhere by members of both generations as they formulated personal identities invoked various nations but did not seem adequately captured by the kind of concrete, anchored transnationalism assumed in much of the literature. Even where Hyderabadis were truly immigrants, settling permanently abroad, the romantic aura of the relationships postulated in much of the transnationalism literature seemed lacking as the emigrants struggled to situate themselves with respect to their old and new homelands and with respect to their parents and their children.

The Hyderabadis abroad were not without agency. Processes of withdrawal, adaptation, and shifting commitment highlighted the tensions of their lives, the uneven stretching and bending of loyalties. In Kuwait, with Arab not South Asian culture hegemonic and that Arab culture largely unaware of nuanced historical patterns in South Asia, the Indian-dominated South Asian expatriate population was focused inward, dealing with issues internal to it such as shifting identities within India. In Kuwait, coastal Andhras could more easily claim identity as Hyderabadis and, perhaps in response, Hyderabadi Muslims seemed to be accommodating themselves to a more Islamic world. In the very specific foreign context of Kuwait, expatriates from India and Pakistan were freer to deviate from historical patterns, patterns that were being supported and reinforced in the UAE by greater Arab knowledge of and complicity with those patterns. In the UAE, the higher proportion of South Asians among expatriates and their shared knowledges with the local Arabs helped preserve a South Asian social landscape complete with historically grounded regional identities, including the Hyderabadi identity.

In many, many instances, individuals seized opportunities abroad and used them to personal or family advantage, even in the Gulf where the constraints were severe and the darker view of transnationalism fit better. The relationship of Hyderabadis to the Gulf states was basically a negative one, one of non-belonging. This non-belonging had important, if unintended, consequences for their belonging in their homelands. They did not set out to be transmigrants, in the positive sense of relating significantly to a nation-state beyond their homeland, yet many of the middle-class families among them felt compelled to consider moving elsewhere for the sake of their children. Again, they were really choosing new homelands rather than stretching loyalties across nation-states as transnational migrants.

Those who eventually settled in Western nations were not able to carry with them encapsulated worlds focused on family or religion, though some may have tried to do this. Most families extended across several national boundaries, their attitudes and behaviors influenced by the several societies in which they and their relatives and friends lived, and differences arose among them. Close family relationships or recommendations failed to guarantee successful arranged marriages across national boundaries. Religion did not serve as a protective, bounded arena either, particularly for Muslims who found that their religion involved them in each site with co-believers from many other parts of the world. Hyderabadi Muslims in Australia, the United States, and Canada were actively engaged in creating new configurations of belief and practice in each place and there was no international Islamic network. Even an emphasis on Urdu, the language of the homeland, failed to maintain boundaries as other speakers of the language participated in associations and literary events overseas along with Hyderabadis, challenging their version of the language and broadening their horizons. Cosmopolitanism—familiarity with diverse cultures and the ability to move among them with some degree of ease—characterized most Hyderabadis abroad.

THE IMPORTANCE OF NATION-STATES

Andrew Shryock writes, "Before wandering into the open (and possibly empty) spaces along the postnational frontier, cosmopolitan ethnographers—whose agendas are shaped by borders as well as crossings—will have to confront the constant *re*location of identity that even the most transient attachment to nation-states makes necessary." This sets exactly the right note for Hyderabadis, who, rather than entering zones of allegiance to two nations or of deterritorialization, subjected themselves to "new hegemonies capable of (re)bounding local and translocal identities alike."[28] The new identity politics was determined by the hegemonic structures and cultures of Pakistan, the UK, Australia, the United States, or Canada, the new contexts shaping the everyday lives and evolving identities of the Hyderabadi emigrants. Beyond the immediate locality or city of settlement, it was the nation-state that determined their presentations of self and community and their reorientations of resources and activities.

Hyderabadi networks across national boundaries were strongly shaped by the laws of the nation-states involved. Consider one Hyderabadi wedding that might be labeled transnational. The bride lived in Kuwait, the groom in the United States, and key family members resided in India,

Pakistan, and other sites around the world. In this case, the wedding was held in Dubai in the UAE, where visas and South Asian things could be gotten most easily. But did this event demonstrate loyalty to multiple nations or loyalty to some notion of Hyderabad as a nonterritorial transnation or a deterritorialized nation-state? Rather, it demonstrated cosmopolitanism, the strategic knowledge of legal regimes and resources in various sites applied to the problem of staging an important life cycle event with maximum participation by family and friends.

The Hyderabadi diaspora was worldwide, but citizenship requirements and national symbols or rituals influenced settlement patterns. There were isolated Hyderabadis in Germany, Switzerland, and France, for example, and the very few Hyderabadis who settled in France easily became citizens. Their children born in France, however, were not automatically French citizens, although they could apply after turning eighteen within a certain time period. One husband and wife had taken French citizenship but sent their children to study in the United States; while visiting relatives in Houston, they told me that their children probably would not become French citizens. Indeed, the wife commented on the French national appreciation of wine, an important part of French culture that they, as observant Muslims, could not share and that emphasized their non-belonging to the nation. Germany in the 1990s had many foreigners but no immigrants, yet a few Hyderabadis lived and worked there; it was still an ethnic state that extended the right of return only to those of German blood. Other Hyderabadis lived in Malaysia, Singapore, Korea, and Indonesia, pioneer businessmen moving east not west.

Decisions about becoming citizens abroad required careful consideration, as many migrants had family networks, financial interests, and political commitments spanning two or more nations. Hyderabadis responded to changed immigration laws in the Western countries in the 1960s and 1970s but did not immediately seek citizenship; many thought of themselves as educational or economic migrants. They planned to take their expertise back home when employment opportunities there improved, and many had promised their parents that they would return. There were both emotional and practical reasons for remaining an Indian or Pakistani citizen, such as the right to hold property and bank accounts and the nonnecessity of getting visas to visit. Dual citizenship was possible for some immigrants but not others. Citizenship status did expedite family reunification, as citizens were preferred over permanent residents when it came to bringing relatives, to shifting entire families permanently abroad.

Other factors bearing on citizenship were less personal but nonetheless had strong impacts on immigrant decisionmaking. Although remittances flowed back to relatives and Hyderabadis sometimes responded collectively to needs in the homeland, they also had needs in the new homelands. These related to economic and social discrimination against minorities or immigrants and the need for political representation. Citizens were in a much stronger position than noncitizens to challenge existing laws and practices, mobilize public opinion, and initiate new laws. Then there was the desire to help the Indian or Pakistani homelands by changing other nations' policies toward them, influencing governments to be more pro-India or pro-Pakistan. This kind of influence required funding and voting for political parties in the new nations, so the move everywhere was toward taking citizenship.

In Hyderabad and abroad, legal and social distinctions within national populations proved important and contentious. Legal distinctions like mulki and non-mulki or the less institutionalized "son of the soil" and muhajir in Pakistan rested on strong and widely shared social understandings. Within the Indian nation, the legal quotas increasingly set for educational institutions, government service, and other benefits have not only worked to uplift former untouchables, low castes, and tribals but have changed the parameters of democratic politics and pushed higher caste urban young people into educations and careers abroad. In Australia, race explicitly guided immigration policy at first, giving way to skill, age, and health preferences, details well known to potential immigrants and affecting the timing of migrations. In other countries as well, changing immigration policies and preferences helped determine choices of destination. Once immigrants were established, parents, children, and even some late-arriving grandparents claimed "first generation" status. All of these legal and social categories and contests helped form the evolving cultural worlds of the immigrants.

Social distinctions within the national populations were highly significant too as demographic constellations of fellow citizens and immigrants shaped identity politics within the nations. In Canada, the overwhelming presence of other immigrants in Ontario pushed second-generation Hyderabadis further from their ancestral culture faster than elsewhere, although the Anglo-Indians in Australia were a close second. In the UAE, the great numbers of South Asian expatriates helped preserve a South Asian social landscape complete with Indian-Pakistani tensions. In Kuwait, with Arab not South Asian culture hegemonic and proportionally fewer South Asians, coastal Andhras could more easily appropriate the Hyderabadi identity.

Finally, religious and linguistic distinctions varied across national boundaries. Religion proved quite significant for identity formation in some countries and for some individuals, far more significant in the diaspora than in the homeland. Islam and Muslims were poised to impact UK, Australian, U.S., and Canadian society, but differently. The dominance of Arab immigrants in the Australian Muslim world shaped Islamic activism there, whereas South Asian Muslim rivalry with Arab Muslims in the United States drew Hyderabadis into leadership roles. South Asian Muslims but not Hyderabadis dominated religious activism in the UK, and South Asian Muslims including Hyderabadis participated heavily in religious activism in Canada. Differences of national origin and class explained these outcomes, but generally cosmopolitan patterns of adaptation were produced rather than narrowly transnational ones.

Similar differences and adaptations characterized Urdu literary activities and Hyderabadi roles in them. Punjabi Pakistanis participated prominently in Urdu literary activities in the UK and to some extent in Canada; conversely, Urdu-speakers in the United States were prosperous and numerous enough to support such activities without drawing on Punjabis. Urdu literary activities in Australia overlapped almost completely with Islamic ones; in the UK, the United States, Canada, and the Gulf states, however, these were separate arenas and, in the UK and the United States, usually opposing ones. Everywhere, spoken Hyderabadi Urdu was giving way to the standard or North Indian literary language; it was no longer a marker of national but of subnational and sometimes undesirable identity. A contest between Hyderabadi and North Indian Urdu had occurred at the time of Osmania's founding in the early twentieth century and was no longer relevant in a world setting. One could say that in both religious and linguistic arenas, parochial or particular understandings and regional peculiarities were giving way to increasingly standardized or more generally shared understandings and practices. Interestingly, the religious identities being forged through controversy in diasporic settings engaged both first- and second-generation Hyderabadi immigrants,[29] but the linguistic identity—that is, Urdu and the Indo-Muslim cultural world it represented—seemed limited to the first generation.

The emigrants increasingly recognized the nation-states in which they were settling as fundamentally constitutive of family and community identities. It was hard to sustain dual loyalties and harder still to exercise them. The sharp differences of opinion between Pakistani Hyderabadis and Indian Hyderabadis reflected not only initial self-selective emigration but state educational and political machines that strongly shaped national identities in opposition to each other. These differences were clearly reflected in the, on the whole, mutually antagonistic views of each other of the two groups, views that influenced associational and marital patterns throughout the diaspora.[30]

Emigrants were attentive to international politics: relations between places were continuously shifting with the reorganization of political and economic space in the world system. Not just Hyderabad itself, but India, Pakistan, the UK, Australia, the United States, Canada, and the Gulf states were unstable sites. Hyderabadi culture had become thinner and diffused, challenged and redefined, and not only abroad. There were migrants who thought that the old Hyderabadi culture persisted in its city of origin and that it was still winning followers, creating new Hyderabadis. Most agreed, however, that the "new Hyderabadis" represented a genuinely new cultural synthesis in which Telugu and English created the "structures of feeling" even if Urdu lingered in the streets of the city.

AN EMERGENT STRUCTURE OF FEELING

Was there a sense of globalization, an experience of belonging to an international or cosmopolitan landscape beyond the nation-state? We have seen the pervasiveness of state power and its influence on the lives of the Hyderabadi emigrants, but there was also the power of culture, of shifting structures of feeling. Although state power and the economic forces of globalization strongly affected social and cultural domains, cultural forces powerfully influenced the movements and the meanings given to them of the Hyderabadi emigrants. In this case, a Mughlai or Indo-Muslim culture in decline, and in decline in Pakistan and the UAE as well as India, can be seen giving way to another culture with global reach.

As Nigel Thrift suggested, we are all becoming part of landscapes of speed, light, and power, which he collapses into a new concept of mobility, a change of both style and content. He does not call this globalization, transnationalism, or cosmopolitanism, but "an emergent structure of feeling."[31] I too used "structures of feeling" to set Hyderabad in the context of India's three successive hegemonic cultures, ones based not in linguistic regions but in cities. Early Sanskritic civilization was followed by Indo-Muslim civilization and then British imperial culture in South Asia. Persian, Urdu, and Indo-Muslim civilization lasted longer in Hyderabad than elsewhere in South Asia but have declined there and in the diaspora since the mid-twentieth century.

The phrase, an emergent structure of feeling, best captures the new landscape into which Hyderabadis, like others in the world, were being swept by the end of the twentieth century, the specificity of place giving way to a larger and more homogeneous international public space. This is an English- and urban-based structure of feeling that goes well beyond the old British empire and is centered, like the Hyderabadi diaspora, in North America. Hyderabadis abroad were linking urban communities of the past, present, and future, relating to each other quite directly across national boundaries in new ways. Movies, television, videos, cassettes—visual and aural culture was circulated with minimal or ineffective state control. Through both public and private channels people in and from Hyderabad have become part of a global culture more than ever before.

This was not just an information revolution but the evolution of an increasingly cosmopolitan cultural identity, as Hyderabadis in their home city and elsewhere interacted with what they saw on their screens and read in various media. There was a mobility in their self-concepts and concepts of communities, a sense of belonging that could be both expanded and compartmentalized. In London, Los Angeles, Jeddah, and Kuwait, and in many other places, Hyderabadis stretched their networks beyond Hyderabad and often across several national boundaries. Yet many did carry Hyderabad with them, in their hearts, their food, their festive dress, and their family and community rituals. It was true that Hyderabad's Urdu-based urban culture survived as well or perhaps better in the diaspora than in its homeland. In a sense, it was the postmodern phenomenon: the center had disappeared and existed only in the margins. As we saw, many of those in the first generation living and working abroad felt they had some special responsibility to help preserve the old Hyderabadi culture and community.

Yet that is too nostalgic a view; we must recognize that all Hyderabadis, members of the old community and the newer Andhra-led one, members of the former Hyderabad State and the Indian nation, were being swept into a global community. Travel had greatly increased in volume, for work, education, tourism, and family visiting. Hyderabadis abroad interacted constantly with those at home and cultural influences flowed both ways. Church roofs in Secunderabad were repaired with funds from Anglo-Indians settled in Australia. Muslim children in the rural districts, and not only the old Telingana districts now in Andhra Pradesh but the Nizam's old Marathwara and Karnataka districts now part of two other states, were being educated with funds collected by Muslim Hyderabadis in the West.

There was a very different sense of time and space. In earlier days, people sent letters and photos, then tape cassettes, faxes, e-mails, and videos, and, even more recently, DVDs and digital photos. Photos and videos testified to changing hair and dress styles and to new or reinvented recreations or home furnishings, with the latest Hyderabadi styles in demand in Dallas or Sydney as much as the reverse. With videos, the private could become public, as videos sent from Hyderabad to America were taken by youngsters to school to show classmates what Hyderabadi Hindu or Muslim weddings were like. The reverse was also true: the public could become private, as London's celebration of Hyderabad's 400th anniversary was captured on video and shown in hundreds of homes from Melbourne to Austin to Toronto.

Changes in Hyderabad's telephone system reflected the new global connections among relatives and friends. The new system forced its customers
to choose between only local or both local and long distance capability.
Also, given the frequent failures of the telephone service, people who
could afford it had two or more phones so that when one was not working
they could still be connected. Telephones set new schedules, as one's children's calls from overseas determined when one had to stay at home. Time
took on simultaneous dimensions as time in the locations of the migrating
children determined social schedules back in Hyderabad. Cable TV also
set timings, as dinners were eaten before or after favorite serial dramas
that could be local or foreign. The mobile telephone, much used by Hyderabadi businessmen in the Middle East in the early 1990s and beginning
to be used in India and Pakistan after that, led to direct person-to-person
communication with no time lags. In Thrift's analysis, such individually
directed and constructed flows and networks could hardly be bounded by
states, whereas speed was immediate or greatly increased; time became a
matter of complex multiple references. All of these effects were multiplied
in cities, and Thrift argued that this was a genuinely new mobility or
structure of feeling, not just modernity renamed, and that it could be and
was being experienced even by those with fewer resources. The experiences of the Hyderabadis abroad illustrated this analysis and deepened it by
strengthening the evidence of strong, simultaneous commitments to the
future, to citizenship in the new nations.

In Hyderabad city, the communities of the future were emerging from
the chaotic demolition and construction of the 1980s. The graceful hills
of Banjara were cluttered with servants' quarters, commercial buildings,
and zoning violations of all sorts, like the rest of the city. Jubilee Hills, the
new, wealthier suburb, pulled the new city back toward Golconda Fort and
the magnificent Qutb Shahi tombs. A new commercial elite has become
part of Hyderabad life. Although the German and American cultural and
intellectual centers were gone or in decline, dozens of families of foreigners have accompanied new international firms. An international business
elite was replacing the international cultural elite and its organizations as
fertilizer companies, computer software businesses, and electronics firms
trooped to the city. Ring roads bypassed the crowded older parts of the
city and Mediciti, that huge new medical complex financed by Hyderabadi
doctors in the United States, anchored an expanding suburban area to the
north of Secunderabad.

All over Hyderabad, demographic changes in the city propelled its residents into the communities of the future. The households with servants
and boarders (as district schoolboys came into the city) were replaced by

small households of aging parents or widows living alone as the adult children dispersed across the world's cities, to Riyadh, Kuwait, Melbourne, Toronto, Chicago, and London. Old family residences were pulled down and replaced with flats. Some parents traveled abroad, experiencing for themselves the cities and towns formerly known to them only through their children's letters, tapes, and photos.

Urdu was the link language for old Hyderabadis, but even more than Telugu, English has become the link language of new Hyderabadis. A variety of websites in English represented the city and state and "old boy" school associations. For Muslims everywhere in the Western countries, Islamic activities or social welfare activities based on Muslim congregations and institutions were being carried out with English as the medium of communication. The emerging new "structure of feeling" inherent in the globalization of the English language has gone far beyond the British colonial culture that Hyderabad State once tried to hold at bay.

The old hierarchies of language, class, and culture have become irrelevant. Club life was one of the anchors of the communities of the future, and new and different collectivities were forming. The growing middle class was so eager to join clubs that new ones were founded and waiting lists were long. Some people belonged to three different clubs: the Secunderabad Club with its expansive lawns and Anglicized ambience, the Nizam Club with more constricted facilities but an old Hyderabad ambience and cuisine, and one of the modern, family-oriented clubs dominated by the upwardly mobile or newcomers to the city. Brunch, theme meals, and "multicuisine"—this is, Chinese, Indian, and European food—were popular features.

The club was the first structure to be built in the new "agricultural" developments outside Hyderabad city. People were securing "farms" outside the city, using an "encouragement of agriculture" act to get land and turning to private developers for water and electricity. Friends bought a plot for their son in a subsection of Dream Valley Estates, barren land with fences and signs, dirt roads, and watchmen hired by the development company. Before houses went up, the clubhouse, changing rooms, and swimming pools were ready. This and other clubs—for example, Dollar Hills next door—featured "multicuisine" and three swimming pools, a purdah pool, a big pool, and a children's pool. Some of the old patterns continued: old Hyderabadi Muslim, Kayasth, and other civil service and banking caste families were planning residences and social events together in the Dream Valley setting.

Even the old city of Hyderabad engaged in building communities of the future, although it seemed in some ways more linked to Dubai, Kuwait,

Riyadh, and even Chicago than to new Hyderabad. Its workers were in those global cities, experiencing modernity more than in their homes in Hyderabad. Hospitals and software facilities in the new city did not benefit the old city, which remained isolated and in decline, with far higher numbers of people but lower percentages of wage earners in households and higher levels of reliance on the informal sector and service jobs. Most residents of the old city worked outside of it and when there were communal riots or difficulties with public transportation, they could not get to their jobs. The old city seethed with frustration, despite Gulf workers' investments in housing upgrades, consumer goods, and public celebration of weddings and other rituals.[32] Because the old city was predominantly Muslim and migrants to it came from the former Nizam's state districts, including those now in Karnataka and Maharashtra, it offered a political constituency for Muslim communal politicians. But the horizons of those in the old city also stretched beyond it, as some women attended Urdu colleges in Hyderabad and some children were sent to the best schools in new Hyderabad city.

Locating Home

I quoted James Clifford in the opening chapter, his characterization of people migrating, "changed by their travel but marked by places of origin, by peculiar allegiances and alienations."[33] We have seen much of the "peculiar allegiances and alienations" associated with Hyderabad and also of the changes brought about by travel. We have seen that the Deccani cultural synthesis was not entirely a myth. An urban-based Indo-Muslim culture connected members of the ruling class of Hyderabad State's plural society, and also, to a considerable extent, all mulkis, or former citizens, of that state. Some emigrants tried to maintain and transmit Hyderabadi culture abroad. The Urdu language and one Urdu newspaper, *Siyasat*, were particularly important to emigrants. A young wife taken to Germany after marriage by her professional husband wrote of her loneliness and her reliance on *Siyasat*: "the truth is this, that in a foreign country memories sustain us, whether they are bitter or sweet."[34] The markings of old Hyderabad, however, were remembered, rejected, or reinvented to suit the migrants' new contexts, as their destinations significantly shaped migrant identities.

Abundant details from the interviews evidenced close friendships across religious and linguistic lines that continued to link emigrants and those who stayed at home. The interviews provided eloquent testimony to international journeys, old boy and old girl networks, and some associational

activities that kept people actively in touch with one another. The very
strongest network that many first-generation Hyderabadi emigrants tried
to sustain was that of classmates or schoolmates. "We went to school together," "His sister was in my class," "She and my wife were classmates,"
and variations on these remarks were almost always the first response when
I named people met elsewhere. Being classmates or schoolmates most frequently explained expensive and difficult journeys to attend reunions and
weddings. But the members of the second generation were being schooled
in the new homelands. They were forming friendships with co-learners of
Pakistani, Australian, British, or North American history and culture and
heading for careers in their new nations.

The generational differences emerged clearly in all of the research sites.
Some young people of Hyderabadi background in both Canada and the
United States claimed to be "first generation" because they were the first
generation born or raised abroad. They thought of themselves as very different from their parents, decisively formed by the new context and not by
Hyderabad. Another cohort, that of parents brought to North America,
also contained some members who claimed to be first generation. As they
were older, some parents (especially men with successful careers behind
them) asserted this, even though they were following their children. Their
deliberate attempt to appropriate the term for themselves could be the diasporic English language equivalent of contests over mulki/non-mulki or
muhajir/non-muhajir status in India and Pakistan. Western social scientists
should acknowledge the unsettled nature of these generational categories
in the minds of immigrants.[35] Who was a native and who was a newcomer
was a controversial and socially meaningful issue in all these cases, involving claims to citizenship and national identity. These terms signaled
cultural claims to power in new settings.

The Hyderabadi experiences abroad spoke to the selective shaping of
new national identities, the forgetting of much about Hyderabad but the
mobilization of memories to claim places in new homes abroad. Jonathan
Boyarin, discussing Maurice Halbwachs' seminal 1950 work *On Collective
Memory*, commented that Halbwachs spoke not of fantasies or of people
defining themselves as a collective in the present, but of the invocation of
memories based on family, schoolmates, and village, of the shared reminis-
cences linking given sets of people in the past.[36] Here it was not a village
but a city, a city that symbolized a state and its Indo-Muslim culture, that
was the subject of memory and of research.

While first-generation Hyderabadis abroad drew on memories and networks based on families and localities, schools and schoolmates, in old Hyderabad, such memories and networks were not successfully extended to

the second generation in any of the sites abroad. Jacob Climo also wrote of memory, defining transmitted or "vicarious" memory as "strong, personal identifications with historical collective memories that belong to people other than those who experienced them directly." Vicarious memories, he specified, are passed through strong emotional attachments from generation to generation in groups that share not only a common historical identity but also the process of its redefinition.[37] Talking to members of the second generation, one was struck by the absence of cross-generational vicarious memories. For the descendants of the Hyderabadis abroad, there could not be an absorption and assimilation of a continuing identity, but rather responses to an interruption, a consciousness of difference. At best, the descendants tried to constitute and interrogate their parents' memories, which in any case invoked a range of interpretations and uses of Hyderabadi culture. The powerful new conceptions of citizenship in the new nation-states reoriented memories and shaped the evolving personal and national identities of the young people of Hyderabadi ancestry and even of their parents. Privileging the homeland in relation to a diaspora proved less relevant than careful examination of the changes wrought by state policies and regulations, new demographic configurations, and the identity politics of the new homelands.

The extent of the changes in Hyderabad itself also helped to explain the generational rupture, but the chief reason was that the children of the immigrants identified strongly as citizens of the new nations. Indo-Muslim culture was in sharp decline, yet elements of Hyderabadi culture might continue if they appeared useful to the children's futures—for example, multicultural values in a plural society, respect and courtesy in everyday relations with others, or the winning tastes of foods like *bagara baigan* and Hyderabadi *biryani* as they entered the "multicuisines" of the destination countries. In this study, interrogating transnationalism, globalization, and cosmopolitanism pointed to the continuing importance of nation-states, yet the power of culture was evident. The nation-states in which the Hyderabadi emigrants resided and worked set the parameters for their participation in the new sites, marking members of the first generation and definitively shaping the identities of members of the second and subsequent generations. While constrained and shaped by their sites of settlement, Hyderabadis everywhere simultaneously participated in an emergent structure of feeling that was global and flowed across national boundaries.

Notes

1. Ramusack 2004, 210. The 1857 uprising against the British East India Company led the Crown to take over and proclaim Queen Victoria Empress of India in 1858.

2. Safran 1991. James Clifford and Stanley Tambiah both caution that Safran's criteria constitute an "ideal type" but, like others, continue to use it: Clifford 1997, 248–49; Tambiah 2000, 169.

3. Some think that Indian Muslims, given their concentration in urban areas and the rise of neo-Hindu politics, may be more likely than others to migrate; but others think that, because as a group Muslims are poorer and less educated, they may be less likely to migrate.

4. Hall circa 1996, 129.

5. Hall circa 1996, 131–32; Werbner 1998.

6. Werbner 1998, 5.

7. Schiller, Basch, and Blanc-Szanton 1992, especially the "Introduction" by the same three authors.

8. Schiller, Basch, and Blanc-Szanton 1992, 11.

9. Rouse 1992, 41; Wiltshire 1992, 175.

10. Appadurai 1996, 173–176. In their 1994 book, Basch, Schiller, and Blanc, locating transnationalism as a development in the long-term process of global capitalist penetration, similarly discuss deterritorialized nation-states and global cultural constructions as aspects of transnationalism.

11. Harvey 1990, 427–428. This view is echoed by Gardezi, who states that globalization's neo-colonial agenda has most drastically affected "the ordinary people of post-colonial societies": Gardezi 1997, 116.

12. Ong 1999, 4–6.

13. Werbner 1999, 19–20, drawing on Ulf Hannerz and Jonathan Friedman. Hannerz defines cosmopolitans as "willing to engage with the Other" and transnationals as frequent travelers who carry with them meanings embedded in social networks (1992, 252). Friedman's discussion shows the encapsulation of cosmopolitans as well (1997, 84–85).

14. Rao was a Hyderabadi. Born in Mysore in 1908, he studied in Madras-i-Aliya in Hyderabad from 1915 to 1925, spent a year at Aligarh Muslim University,

continued at Nizam College, Hyderabad, 1927–1929, and studied in France on a scholarship from the Nizam's government, 1929–1931: Parthasarathy 1998, 176.

15. Assisi 1989, 26.

16. Werbner 1998, 7.

17. Fentress and Wickham 1992; Bertaux 1981; Schrager 1983; Yans-McLaughlin 1990.

18. Clifford 1989, 185.

19. Banga 1991, xv. *Mulki* was used elsewhere too, e.g., Bayly 1978.

20. As he moves toward theorizing a South Asian cultural sensibility that contrasts with Western notions of motility, Srivastava (2005) asserts that journeying, moving, going, and coming have been a recurring leitmotif in South Asian life, and that notions of home, ancestral place, and attachment have always been complex.

21. Williams 1961, 41–71 and passim; Williams 1973.

22. Ramanujan 1970, 229.

23. van Buitenen 1966; Basham 1961.

24. Handler 1985, 178–179.

25. Marcus 1995, 106.

26. Marcus 1995, 112–114, proposing that ethnographers become "circumstantial activists."

27. Leonard 1978b; Leonard 1997.

28. I am grateful for Fulbright grants in 1992 and 1993 for work in Pakistan and for a Committee on American Overseas Research Centers grant in 1995–1996 for work in Kuwait, the UAE, and Pakistan. For Hyderabad (1991, 1993, 1994, 1996, 1997), the UK (1991, 1992, 1997, 1999), Australia (1993), Canada (1994, 1997, 2000), Pakistan (again in 1994, 1995, 1999), and the United States (1991–1999), I got small grants from the University of California, Irvine, or funded the trips myself.

29. Hyderabadi Muslim leaders in American Muslim politics led to my interest in Islam and Muslims in America; I held a conference on Muslim identities in North America in 1999 and have been publishing on American Muslims since then. Unable to reinterview so many people in so many places, I can only observe here that after the attacks on the Pentagon and the World Trade Center of September 11, 2001, Hyderabadis in America have become increasingly active, engaging in secular coalitions, progressive Muslim movements, and interfaith endeavors at all levels.

30. See Leonard, Stepick, Vasquez, and Holdaway 2005 for overviews of the new scholarly attention to religion and migration.

31. The latter effort was conducted with Dr. M. A. Muttalib, retired from Osmania University in Hyderabad. We thank the Nizam's Charitable Trust for funds to analyze these questionnaires by computer in Hyderabad; Dr. Muttalib has written up the results. The responses were uneven. We had 168 respondents in Hyderabad among the relatives of emigrants, using some of the Nizam's Trust funds to employ interviewers. In the United States, we had 50 responses from first-generation men, 20 responses from first-generation women, and 20 responses, 10 male and 10 female, from second-generation Hyderabadis.

32. Marcus 1995, 100.

1. Leonard 1971.
2. Lynton and Rajan 1974; Karaka 1975.
3. Leonard 1973.
4. Hall 1992, 275–277; Ferguson and Gupta 1992, 7.
5. See *A Collection of Hyderabadi Limericks* 1994, 111 and 59, for these limericks by Ravi Boothalingam and Fatima Alikhan, respectively. *Channel 6*, a monthly review of events in the city, ran a limerick contest in 1991 and 1992 and published selected submissions.
6. *Parsaun* means day after tomorrow; *sarsaun* refers to a proverb about trying to grow mustard on one's palm (implying undue haste); *Huzoor* is the salutation "sir"; the last line means "Everything will get done, day after tomorrow," with an irregular Deccani twist to the verb. Thanks to Professor C. M. Naim for help with the proverb.
7. The italicized specialities of Deccani cuisine are tamarind-seasoned sauce, minced meat, steamed seasoned rice, potatoes, sour greens, charcoal-steamed kebab, and chicken.
8. *Bagara baigan* is eggplant, *mirch ka salan* is green chilies, both in a thick tamarind sauce. There are several kinds of *pan*, sweet, sour, opium, and Ram Pyari; Hyderabadi ladies traditionally kept the ingredients in a silver *pandan* and prepared individual *pans* for visitors.
9. Leonard 1979 and 1981.
10. Cole 2001 estimated that in 1700 there were seven times as many Persian speakers in India as in Iran.
11. This battle over succession to the caliphate caused the lasting split between Sunnis and Shias in Islam: Shias supported Husain and are a minority of Muslims today, based in Iran and Iraq.
12. See the dissertation by Benjamin Cohen (2002) for details of these Hindu rulers, 1850 to 1949.
13. Leonard 2002a.
14. From 1884 to 1886, government resolutions outlined the recruitment and certification procedures for government employment of mulkis, defined as persons permanently residing in Hyderabad State for fifteen years or continuously serving the government for at least twelve years; they and their lineal descendants to two generations were legally mulkis. Non-mulkis could be appointed only with special permission, pleading special knowledge and experience, and they received a certificate of domicile, or a mulki certificate: Jung 1319 F [1909–1910], 35–37; Government of Hyderabad 1938, 10–12.
15. Leonard 1978a, and chapter 7 of Leonard 1978b.
16. As before, Hyderabad was looking west, following Bombay Presidency rather than the eastern coastal Telugu-speaking districts of the Madras Presidency, where municipal reforms had also come in the nineteenth century: John Leonard 1973, 227–251.
17. Belgrami was one of the first Bilgramis to come to Hyderabad from the northern Indian village of Bilgram, home to famous scholars, but many members

of this Shia clan settled in Hyderabad in the late nineteenth century and became mulkis.

18. The Hyderabad College resulted from the 1880 merger of an English branch of the Dar-ul-Ulum, the City High School begun in 1870, and an English middle school attached to the Civil Engineering College Salar Jung started in 1870.

19. In Aliya, preference went to the sons of "old boys," nobles, the landed gentry, the professions, and government servants; Nizam College was more plebian as it recruited also from the Chadarghat and City High Schools: Jung 1983, 126–127.

20. From 1897 to 1902 all seventeen awardees were Muslims (some allegedly non-mulkis), at least partly because of doubt about whether Hindus were eligible because of an orthodox ban on ocean travel: Government of Hyderabad 1907, 357–358; *The Hindu*, February 15, 1895, in Clippings Collection 1890–1904 in the Andhra Pradesh State Archives.

21. Founded by the Church of England in 1834, this school in the new city of Hyderabad admitted only expatriate children until 1865, when it began admitting Hyderabadis.

22. Also known as Chaderghat School or the Gloria High School, it was founded in 1877 by a Bengali educator working in Hyderabad, Aghornath Chattopadhyya (Sarojini Naidu's father).

23. Sherwani 1966, 237. The British actually learned of Osmania only after the vernacular press in North India announced its sanction by the Nizam: Henson 1974, 61–62.

24. The latter, a Methodist missionary undertaking, became a high school in 1908; in 1911, four Hyderabadi girls appeared for the school-leaving exam. The first Muslim woman graduate in all of India was a Bilgrami from Hyderabad, Tyeba Bilgrami, who took her B.A. from Madras University in 1910 (she was the only daughter of Syed Hossain Belgrami Nawab Imad-ul-Mulk, founder of Hyderabad's modern educational system): Chandraiah 1996, 250.

25. Minault 1998, 206.

26. Pernau 2000 has tables showing the development of the educational system to 1935; in that year, Osmania had 1806 students and Nizam College 300 (366).

27. Such intermarriages across class and origin lines emphasized differential access to administrative positions: Leonard 1978a, 81.

28. Memorandum, Sir Akbar Hydari, Home Secretary in 1917, to the Nizam, Files of the Chief Secretariat, installment 36, list 5, serial number 9, file O1/al, Andhra Pradesh State Archives.

29. V. K. Bawa calls the literary works of Dr. Zore and his followers primary sources: Bawa 1993, 351. Anjuman Taraqqi Urdu, a rival Urdu-promoting organization led by non-mulki Dr. Abdul Huq (in the Translation Bureau and Osmania's Urdu department) founded Urdu Hall and was later linked to the Ittehad ul Muslimeen.

30. Benichou 2000.

31. Leonard 1978a; Pernau 2000; Copland 1988.

32. See Ramusack 2004 for Hyderabad's position vis-à-vis other princely states in early-twentieth-century politics.

33. Elliott 1974; Leonard 1981–1982; Khalidi 1988, especially W. C. Smith's article; Pernau 2000; Copland 1988; Benichou 2000; V. K. Bawa 1993.

34. Some protest this euphemism: Omar Khalidi, a librarian in the Aga Khan Program for Islamic Architecture at MIT and Harvard Library and a historian of Hyderabad, has pointed out that the name should be Operation Polo, the name of the military action, and he has alleged large numbers of casualties. (Omar's father was professor of medieval Deccani history at Osmania and taught me Persian in the 1960s; Omar's siblings were in Hyderabad, Pakistan, and the United States.) In Hyderabad city there were few deaths, although in some districts Muslims were killed (before the Police Action, the Razakars had killed some Hindus). The fall of Hyderabad (in Urdu, *suqut-i-Hyderabad*) remains controversial: Aziz 1993; Razvi circa 2000).

35. Dr. Fatima Alikhan, Geography and Women's Studies at Osmania, first suggested this.

36. Huge crowds thronged the streets mourning his death in 1967: Bawa 1993, xiii–xviii.

37. Das Gupta 1970. The Kannada- and Marathi-speaking districts were added to the states of Karnataka and, eventually, Maharashtra (in 1960), respectively.

38. John and Karen Leonard 1992, 151–175.

39. See Kavita Datla's forthcoming Ph.D. dissertation on Osmania University (University of California, Berkeley, history department); I thank her for the reference for the switch to English: Kamal 1990, 284.

40. Hyderabad's older Urdu-medium Medical College was taken over by Osmania after its founding in 1917 and the Urdu texts were abandoned for English ones. Students had thirteen years of primary and secondary education, including a final year of pre-med training, before joining the four-and-a-half-year M.B.B.S. course, and then they gained their degree and license to practice after a one-year internship. The M.B.B.S. is the equivalent of an American Doctor of Medicine or M.D. degree. Osmania M.B.B.S. holders abroad often train further, in Britain becoming members or fellows of the Royal College of Physicians and the Royal College of Surgeons, or, in the United States, doing residencies in various specialties to attain American Board Certification.

41. Old Hyderabadis were still hesitant to speak critically about the last Nizam's grandsons but are disappointed that the elder one, the successor, who controlled most of the resources, has done so little for Hyderabad. Loyalty to the Nizam called for restraint and courtesy about family members, an attitude not understood by newcomers to the city and state.

42. They included Padmaja Naidu, sister of nationalist leader Sarojini Naidu, governor of Bengal; B. Ramakrishna Rao, governor of Kerala (and Hyderabad's chief minister from 1948 to 1956); Akbar Ali Khan, governor of Uttar Pradesh and then Orissa; Ali Yavar Jung, governor of Maharashtra; and Mehdi Nawaz Jung, governor of Gujarat. The latter two were closely connected with the Bilgramis, that distinguished cluster of Shia families in old Hyderabad.

43. Abid Hussain was ambassador to the United States; Zahir Ahmed was ambassador to Saudi Arabia and served in the UN; A. M. Khusro was ambassador

to Germany and served as chancellor of Aligarh Muslim University. Ali Yavar Jung (the only son of Tyeba Begum, note 24) represented India at the UN, was ambassador to Argentina, Egypt, the United States, and Yugoslavia, and served as vice-chancellor of Osmania (1945–1946 and 1948–1952) and of Aligarh Muslim University (1968–1970).

44. The brothers Rashiduddin Khan and Bashiruddin Khan went to Delhi's Jawaharlal Nehru University and the University of Delhi, respectively; others who settled outside Hyderabad were Sadath Ali Khan, Prime Minister Nehru's parliamentary secretary and later ambassador to Iraq and Turkey, Moazzam Hussein, chief of UNESCO in Libya and then with UNESCO in Paris, and Shiv Shankar, a judge of the AP High Court who defended Indira Gandhi and whom she later appointed India's law minister.

45. Evocative stories are in (Hyderabadi) Anees Jung 1987 and 1990.

46. See *A Collection of Hyderabadi Limericks* 1994, 44, for the limerick by Michael and Lita Menezes.

47. Table 2, p. 96, in Mohammad 1993.

48. See *A Collection of Hyderabadi Limericks*, 1994, 160, for the limerick by Karen Leonard.

49. The British Council in Hyderabad city held a celebration in 1991 and published a commemorative volume in 1993, *Hyderabad-400: Saga of a City*. The government tried to mount a celebration in 1994, but the centerpiece procession from Golconda to the new city could not be held, as a proposed float featuring the last Nizam aroused controversy and the organizers would not hold the procession without some recognition of the Nizam.

50. One thinks of Delhi in 1857, when the Sepoy Mutiny/First War of Independence brought British vengeance down on the city and banished the last Mughal emperor, though these events were far more destructive of life and property than those in Hyderabad in 1948: Gupta 1981. One thinks also of Lucknow in 1856 and 1857, when the British displaced the Nawab of Oudh and annexed his kingdom: Ganju 1980.

51. Leonard 1978b, chapter 15; Duncan and Duncan 1980.

52. Few realize that Andhra is the richest site for early Buddhist *stupas* and *viharas*: Paraasher 1991, 24.

53. The Buddha first sank into the lake and had to be pulled up and reset, an effort taking lots of time and rupees. Muslim friends pointed out that Ganesh statues cluttered up the water annually and now a Buddha had been added. The members of INTACH (Indian National Trust for Art and Cultural Heritage), activists who fiercely defend the Qutb Shahis and the Nizams, cooperate with this attempt to base tourism on the early Buddhist monuments, hoping for reciprocal support for the preservation of the Indo-Muslim heritage. They have barely succeeded in getting government support for preservation of the home and laboratory of Ronald Ross, discoverer of the anopheles mosquito as carrier of malaria in 1897 in Hyderabad.

54. Abul Hasan Tana Shah succeeded his father-in-law in 1674 and lost Golconda to Aurangzeb in 1687; Mahbub Ali Khan's statue stands uneasily at the Secunderabad, not Hyderabad, end of the line; Makhdum Mohiuddin was also a leading Urdu poet.

55. Historic buildings are too infrequently designated for preservation and there is marked antipathy to renovation for tourist purposes of even the most outstanding of them by the government. The history of the Nizams' Hyderabad simply has not been of interest to the A. P. government, although, with the extraordinary interest in the Nizam's spectacular jewelry collection (now Government of India property, it is being shown all over India), the chief minister in 2001, Chandrababu Naidu, began giving more attention to Hyderabad's heritage.

56. Clearly a book like Lynton and Rajan's *Days of the Beloved* overstates the earlier case. But representatives of the older plural society commemorate figures like the Maharajahs Chandu Lal and Kishen Pershad, Salar Jung, and the Nizams themselves. The Andhras commemorate Pandit Viresalingam, social reformer, leader of the widow marriage movement and innovator in Telugu language and journalism from Rajahmundry. There is little shared knowledge. Old Hyderabadis, when they think of social reform or widow marriage, think of the Bengali Ram Mohan Roy or perhaps of the Maharashtrian Mahadev Govind Ranade, while the Andhras know nothing of major Urdu poets and Osmania University teachers who shaped the intellectual landscape for those growing up under the last Nizam.

57. Spodek and Srinivasan 1993, 263; Gupta 1993, 244.

58. Gupta 1993, 246.

59. This was followed by the onset of prohibition and its repercussions—the clubs lost much of their business and began to publicize Sunday family brunches, while most pubs turned into ice cream parlors. The prohibition was lifted again in the late 1990s.

60. An earlier system had eleven years before college and then four years of college, with the intermediate exam at the end of the second year of college. Students in India were thus slightly younger than in the United States, especially medical students, who enter Bachelor of Medicine and Bachelor of Surgery (M.B.B.S.) training after their intermediate course and one year of pre-med courses.

61. Mirza 1976 and 1996.

62. Tillotson 1998 contains many details characteristic of Hyderabad's old city *mohallas*.

63. Papers at a seminar titled Development of Old City: Problems and Prospects in January, 1997, made this point, particularly those by S. P. Shorey, Afzal Mohammed, and Mohamed Akbar Ali Khan. The Society for Preservation of Environment and Quality of Life (SPEQL) and other groups were especially concerned about the Charminar-Ladh Bazar area.

64. Rao 1969; Jagannadham 1969; Elliott 1972, 277.

1. Minocha 1987, 359.
2. An estimated one-fourth of the graduates of Indian medical colleges come to the United States annually: Weiner 1990, 243; Minocha 1987, 364–367.
3. Tololyan 1996.
4. Hall 1987.
5. This is unlike the Indian term for the Sikhs and Hindus who fled from

Pakistan, *sharanarthi* (refugees), a nonprivileging title that was quickly disclaimed: Naim 1993.

6. Wright 1974, 191.

7. Chayya 1995, 34.

8. Wright 1974, 188.

9. Khalidi 1997.

10. Cohn 1996.

11. Kennedy 1993, 142, note 7. This muhajir category did not appear in the 1972 census overview, *Statistical Report of Pakistan*, issued in 1982 by the Population Census Organisation, Government of Pakistan (Islamabad); it was in the earlier district reports, 1975–1978.

12. Wright 1974, 195.

13. The Fifth National Population Housing Census was finally held in late 1998: Weiss 1999.

14. Scholars and others help continue this "underground" definition by using it to update tables of participation in public and corporate service, e.g., Kennedy 1993, 138–139.

15. Kennedy 1993, 138–139; Papanek 1972, 26–27.

16. Percentages and argument from Wright 1974, 190, and Wright 1991; Kennedy 1993, 138–139, for the Punjabis' increased hegemony.

17. Duncan 1988; Lamb 1991.

18. Wright 1991; Verkaaik 1994.

19. Different claims on Karachi have produced urban violence: see Sassen 1996, 219–221.

20. Nawaz Sharif, prime minister from 1997 to the fall of 1999, changed the nation's official holiday from Friday to Sunday but was pressured to make formal teaching of the Qur'an compulsory in public education; the educational system also suffered from other "Islamic initiatives": Candland 2000. Pakistan's banking and financial system was to become interest-free by June, 2001, but this was postponed.

21. Ahsan 1997; Waseem 2001.

22. Omar Khalidi remarked that "the new generation of *muhajirs*" was still demanding Pakistani recognition of muhajir ethnicity in the 1990s and pointed out that Israel enacted the law of return, enabling any Jew to come to Israel, but Pakistan still refused to accept the so-called Biharis displaced by the 1971 Indian-Pakistani-Bangladeshi war: Khalidi 1997; Abdul Latif Bhatti, letter, *India Journal*, February 28, 1997.

23. Kennedy 2000.

24. United Nations Fund for Population, "The State of World Population, 1998—the New Generations," shows Pakistan spending only 1.6 percent of its gross domestic product on education and 1 percent on health, the lowest of the eight countries in South Central Asia (Iran, Bangladesh, Bhutan, Nepal, Sri Lanka, and India, in descending order of percentages). It was 138th on the list of 174 nations in terms of the Human Development Report, also published by the United Nations: *Pakistan Link*, October 24, 1997, and September 11, 1998, 26, 44.

25. Watson 1977, 5.

26. Deakin, Cohen, and McNeal 1970.

27. Uberoi 1964; Beetham 1970; Helwig 1986; Clarke, Peach, and Vertovec 1990; Wallman 1979.

28. Desai 1963; Lyon 1973.

29. Sylhet, after 1971, was in Bangladesh. Anwar 1979; Werbner 1990.

30. Bhachu 1985.

31. Britain continued to curtail immigration. The Asylum and Immigration Bill of 1993 ended the right of appeal when immigration officials refused entry to visitors or prospective students, controls were tightened on students and casual workers in 1994, and immigration rules were tightened for asylum-seekers and workers again in 1996: *India-West*, January 22, 1993, and May 27, 1994, 36; *The Economist*, May 4, 1996, 16. The government's intention was to distinguish economic migrants from political asylum-seekers.

32. Murphy 1987; Werbner and Anwar 1991.

33. Molteno 1987.

34. Castles 1995, 300–301.

35. Modood, Berthoud, Lakey, Nazroo, Smith, Virdee, and Beishon 1997; Ballard 1997. Pre-set categories were White, Black-Caribbean, Black-African, Indian, Pakistani, Bangladeshi, and Chinese: 185–186.

36. Goulbourne 1991, 233–234.

37. Castles 1995, 300.

38. *The Economist*, April 24, 1993, 60; *The Economist*, February 8, 1997, 58–59; Modood, Berthoud, Lakey, Nazroo, Smith, Virdee, and Beishon 1997.

39. Modood, Berthoud, Lakey, Nazroo, Smith, Virdee, and Beishon 1997, 58–59.

40. *India-West*, July 19, 1996, B24.

41. Chambers 1994; Gilroy 1987.

42. Modood 1988 and 1994. The ethnic press elsewhere, e.g., California's *India-West*, October 14, 1988, took immediate notice of this development.

43. Modood 1992; Werbner and Modood 1997.

44. *The Economist*, December 19, 1992, 55.

45. *India-West*, November 1, 1991, 19; *The Economist*, April 24, 1993, 59; *The Times*, June 27, 1994; *The Economist*, February 8, 1997, 58–59.

46. England's school system developed from the early nineteenth century largely because of church (especially Church of England) initiatives, so that church schools now constitute about a third of all schools in the "maintained" sector: Gay 2000, 16–17.

47. *Pakistan Link*, February 24, 1995, 20, for the denials. The three were Bradford's Feversham Girls' School, North London's Islamia School (set up by Yusuf Islam, the former Cat Stevens), and Birmingham's Al Furquan Primary School: *Islamic Horizons*, January/February 2001, 16.

48. In 1996, British Muslims in Batley (Yorkshire) withdrew their children from Religious Education classes, protesting their Christian emphasis: *Pakistan Link*, February 2, 1996, 18.

49. Coward, Hinnells, and Williams 2000, 67.

50. Growth rates from 1985 to 1990 of 22 percent for Sikhs, 17 percent for

Muslims, and 9 percent for Hindus were explained by high birth rates, younger populations, and converts to Islam from young working-class blacks and middle-class whites: *The Economist*, March 13, 1993, 65.

51. *The Economist*, January 26, 1991, 51 (estimating about 800 mosques in Britain and 400,000 Muslims from Pakistan, 100,000 from India, 100,000 from East Africa, and 12,000 from Bangladesh).

52. On British college campuses, at least, the Hizb-ut-Tahrir and other militant pan-Islamic organizations were targeting the youth, using issues like Palestine, Kashmir, Bosnia, and Kosovo to arouse fervor: *India Today*, December 15, 1994, 114–115. To counter such orthodox thrusts, young British Muslim women were lauded for professional success (e.g., *Telegraph Magazine*, May 13, 1996, 32–36) and the British Navy was recruiting Muslim women and seeking advice about incorporating a veil into the military uniform: *Pakistan Link*, January 9, 1998.

53. Modood 1999, referring to the Fourth Survey.

54. Ballard 1994, 29–33.

55. A special issue of *Diaspora* 9:1 (2000), co-edited by Karen Leonard and Pnina Werbner, considers the dialectic between diaspora aesthetics and "real" political mobilization.

56. It is still part of the Commonwealth; Britain's Queen Elizabeth is Australia's nominal head of state and appoints the governor-general as advised by Australia's prime minister.

57. Brewer and Power 1993.

58. Jayaraman 1999, 7.

59. Moore 1986.

60. Lepervanche 1984; Yarwood 1964.

61. The number of Pakistanis, about 2,776 in the 1981 census, increased rapidly in the 1990s: Dean-Oswald 1988, 728.

62. *India-West*, December 15, 1995, B39, citing reports from Australia's Bureau of Immigration, Multicultural and Population Research.

63. Jupp and Kabala 1993, xvii.

64. Inglis 1995, 16–27; also Castles, Cope, Kalantzis, and Morrissey 1988.

65. Vasta and Castles 1996; Gunew 1996, 111–115.

66. *The Economist*, June 26, 1993, 39.

67. *India-West*, June 1, 1995, 29.

68. Rizvi 1996, 40.

69. Cerwonka 1999.

70. *India-West*, July 26, 1996, A39.

71. TAFEs, or Colleges of Technical and Further Education, advertised in India and Pakistan for students, and consultancy firms and university representatives helped students choose colleges and universities in Australia. The *Deccan Chronicle* (arguably Hyderabad's top English language newspaper) had a lead article January 8, 1997, on "Education in Australia."

72. *India-West*, November 17, 1995, A43, for this Melbourne-based Bureau of Immigration, Multicultural and Population Research study released in 1995.

73. Jayaraman 1988, 543.

74. This was from a survey of 121,500 Australian families, reported in *The*

Australian, November 24, 1993. According to the *Sydney Morning Herald*, November 24, 1993, 13, the survey was conducted from March to May in 1992 and covered 34,000 Australians, 88 percent of whom shared a home with another family member related by blood, marriage, fostering, or adoption.

75. For details of the Barred Zone Act of 1917, the National Origins Quota Act of 1924, and the Supreme Court decision declaring Indians to be Caucasians but not "white" and therefore ineligible for U.S. citizenship in 1923 (naturalized citizenship was based on race, and one had to be white or black until the 1940s), see Leonard 1992.

76. Leonard 1997, 70; for 2000, Springer 2001, A1.

77. Leonard 1997, 68–69.

78. Minocha 1987, 350; *India-West*, April 24, 1992.

79. According to the 1990 census, 815,447 were from India and 81,371 from Pakistan: Leonard 1997, 173; Minocha 1987, 350.

80. See Leonard 2003b for discussion of contested figures for Muslims.

81. Leonard 2001.

82. The Immigrant Visa Lottery, or the Green Card Lottery, randomly selects by computer 55,000 persons annually from countries with low percentages of immigration to the United States. This began in 1995, and Pakistanis, Sri Lankans, and Bangladeshis can qualify.

83. In 1994, India sent the fourth-largest group of foreign students to the United States, after Japan, Korea, and China: *India-West*, May 10 1996, B34.

84. Minocha 1987, 361.

85. For 1970–1979, *India-West*, December 24 and 31, 1993, 35. In 1996, Asian Americans had a naturalization rate of 81 percent, as high as immigrants of European ancestry. Asian Americans still had a low percentage of citizens registered to vote (53%, like Latinos, and lower than African Americans at 61% and whites at 69%), but once they registered, they voted at a higher rate, 76 percent, than any other ethnic group: *Los Angeles Times*, March 27, 1996, A18.

86. Leonard 1997, 77–78.

87. *India-West*, October 1, 1993, and April 22, 1994.

88. *India-West*, October 1 and October 8, 1993.

89. *India-West*, February 26, 1993; *India Today*, August 15, 1994, 48l. In 1980, of the approximately 400,000 Indians in the United States, 11 percent of the men and 8 percent of the women were physicians and another 7 percent of the women were nurses (and 17% of the men were engineers, architects, or surveyors: *India-West*, November 27, 1992). Indian engineers were the second-largest foreign-born group of engineers, just behind the Chinese: *India-West*, December 1, 1995: A29. For the business students, Tilak 1996, 48f.

90. Minocha 1987, 362–363.

91. Illegal immigrants and the second generation of Indian Americans continue to bring down some of the high measures.

92. Prashad ca. 2000.

93. Buchignani, Indra, and Srivastiva 1985.

94. Garcia y Griego 1994, 122.

95. "Unwelcome Aliens," 1997, 35. Toronto was enlarged in 1998 as six

298 *Notes to Chapter 3*

municipalities were amalgamated, but the percentage barely changed: "Toronto Enlarged," 1998.

96. Gupta 1995, 60b–c.

97. "Canada Survey" 1999, 3–5.

98. "Less Welcome" 1994; "Canada Imposes Fees" 1995, A 46.

99. Inglis 1995, 26.

100. "Canada Survey" 1999, 12, 14.

101. *The Toronto Star*, October 15, 1992, E1 and E14.

102. Merchants hired a lawyer to challenge this ban on a two-million-dollar-a-year business by playing "cultural and constitutional cards": Bindra 1993, 48j.

103. Dusenbery 1981, 101–119.

104. There were 100,000 Sikhs, 70,000 Muslims, and 60,000 Hindus in Toronto: *The Toronto Star*, October 15, 1992, E14.

105. Grant 1995b, 37.

106. Azmi 1997, 153–166.

107. Grant 1995b, 37.

108. Grant 1995a, 18; also Hussain 2004, 359–379.

109. Azmi 1997, 154–155.

110. "Canada Survey" 1999, 12.

111. For more details, Leonard 2003a.

112. In the eighteenth century, British efforts to protect the trade route to India meant dealing with the maritime empire of the Omani sultanate and the Qawasim tribal confederacy, the latter based in Sharjah and Ras al-Khaimah. Nineteenth-century battles led to the trucial system, with the small polities of the Gulf signing separate treaties or truces with the British government. The process began in 1820 and ended in 1853 with the Perpetual Maritime Truce signed by the present members of the UAE. Zahlan 1989, 5–9. Bahrain signed a treaty in 1861, Kuwait in 1899, and Qatar in 1916.

113. Zahlan 1989, 16. British relationships with Gulf polities were directed by Bombay's provincial government, then after 1873 by the colonial government of India, and after Indian and Pakistani independence in 1947 by the British Foreign Office. A British Political Resident (stationed in southern Iran until 1946 and thereafter in Bahrain) had several subordinate Political Agents posted in several Gulf locations who conducted all foreign relations for the Gulf states.

114. Zahlan 1989, 10–13.

115. The dependency of Gulf states on pearls ranged from 20 percent to 48 percent: Zahlan 1989, 22, 70.

116. Shryock 1997.

117. Since the eighteenth century the Emir of Kuwait has been from the Al-Sabah family. The UAE was formed in 1971 from the seven emirates of Dubai, Abu Dhabi, Sharjah, Umm al-Quwain, Ras al-Khaimah, Ajman, and Fujairah. The president of the federation was the Sheikh of Abu Dhabi, Sheikh Zayed, and the vice-president was the Sheikh of Dubai, Sheikh Maktum.

118. See the chart in Leonard 2003b and Winckler 2005, 43.

119. *Pakistan Link*, September 16, 1994: 20; Gardezi 1991, 190–191.

120. Watt 1991, 10.

121. Most Gulf states did not release statistics about the expatriate workers' origins, but they sometimes used "nationality" categories to produce crime and

other statistics. In the UAE, the categories were UAE, Gulf (GCC), Other Arab, and Asian, and GCC citizens generally entered each others' countries without visas, while other Arabs and Asians needed visas. Those holding residence visas of any GCC state, except menial laborers, were given visas on entry to the UAE, Oman, and Qatar. Britishers got short-term visas upon arrival in the UAE, and Americans are similarly favored in Kuwait, thanks to historical ties between Britain and the emirates and the U.S. role in the Gulf War, respectively.

122. Leonard 2002b; and see Longva 1997, 128–131, for a discussion of gender status and ethnic identities.

123. The favored destinations for Indians were Saudi Arabia, closely followed by Oman and the UAE, and then Kuwait and Bahrain: Mowli 1992, 81, 83. For Pakistanis, the figures were harder to obtain (it was estimated that as many Pakistanis went to the Gulf illegally as legally), but there were more Pakistanis than Indians in Saudi Arabia: Gardezi 1991, 191–192.

124. *Pakistan Link*, February 17, 1995, 42; Mowli 1992, 54, 81, 61.

125. A breakdown of the expatriate population in Kuwait in 1994 compiled from residency permits recorded from Liberation in February of 1991 to January 1, 1994, put Egyptians at 23 percent, Indians at 18 percent, Bangladeshis and Sri Lankans at 10 percent each, and Pakistanis at 8 percent of the total of 889,347: *Kuwait Pocket Guide* 1995, 116. See also *The Economist*, September 20, 1997; Winckler 2005, 43; Kapiszewski 2001, 63, 65.

126. *India Today* gave a smuggling fee of 1.5 to 2 lakh rupees (150,000 to 200,000 rupees, or $4,280 to $5,700), paid to brokers and agencies in India for sea passage to the Gulf countries: February 15, 1997, 39–40. Women agents were recruiting men in both India and Pakistan in the 1990s.

127. The laws governing expatriates in the UAE were slightly more flexible: visitors' visas for tourists were easier to get, and, whereas the age limit of sixty pertained in theory, many older businessmen and major investors were allowed in: *India-West*, January 16, 1996: A38.

128. The fee for parents was 200 Kuwaiti dinar ($690) a year; the dinar has been a very stable currency, 1 KD equaling $3.30. *Kuwait Pocket Guide* 1995, 38.

129. In Dubai, one had to earn 7,000 dirham, about $1,900, per month to sponsor a maid, higher than for a dependent, and the government collected an annual tax equal to her salary, which was not to be less than 400 dirham ($108) per month. Thus one paid about 800 dirham a month or 9,600 dirham ($2,400) a year for a maid. *Pakistan Link*, September 16, 1994: 20. The dirham has been stable at 3.67 to the dollar since 1980.

130. Lewis and Wigen 1997 discuss varying labels.

131. Sharieff 1994.

132. Hall 1988; Keith and Pile 1993.

NOTES FOR CHAPTER 4

1. Recruited in 1935–1936 by Sir Akbar Hydari, Dr. Qureshi wore a suit, not a sherwani and *rumi topi*, in photos of him in Hyderabad. In Pakistan, he placed many of his students in the State Bank of Pakistan. Bushra had an M.A. in management and was a management consultant, with four years (1951–1955) at the University of Wisconsin.

2. The cheapest route from India was by sea and land to Karachi, and Hyderabad, Sind, where some settled, is near there. The train to Lahore was more expensive.

3. Kasim Razvi, leader of Hyderabad's Razakars, played no major role in Pakistan. Razvi was imprisoned in India for "dacoity" (banditry) in 1948, finally released in 1957, and sent to Pakistan. One man labeled him a non-mulki from the north, an outsider who produced a schism in Hyderabad like leaders of the Rashtriya Swayamsevak Sangh (RSS) and the Arya Samaj.

4. One of the few to look at intermarriage in Pakistan, Wright contends that muhajir-Sindhi intermarriages were numerous in the period just after 1947: Wright 1994, 134–135.

5. Khwaja Masihuddin, after earning a degree in electrical engineering from Berkeley (1948–1952), followed his cousin sister (female first cousin), a navy doctor, and her husband, who had obtained his medical degree from Osmania, to Pakistan. He later married Mir Laik Ali's second daughter.

6. Syed Shah Baleequddin and his elder brother migrated after the Police Action. A businessman, Baleequddin added a University of Karachi M.A. in Urdu Literature to his Osmania B.A., and Zia ul Haq appointed him a member of the national assembly.

7. A. A. Jabbar left as a collector from Hyderabad's Civil Service and had to struggle for a place (joining Pakistan's general administrative reserve, he retired as a deputy secretary).

8. Facing a financial crisis in Pakistan, Governor General Ghulam Mohamed flew to Hyderabad and asked the Nizam for help, with Mir Laik Ali; they asked for Rs 10 crores and the Nizam gave 20 crores. Aziz 1993, 68–69, dates the donation between August 14 and September 1 of 1948, while others date it in 1950 or even 1951. See also Khalidi 1998, 25.

9. Like his relative Admiral Ahsan (aide-de-camp to Mountbatten), Commodore Hussain was a graduate of Dufferin Mercantile Marine Training School in Bombay; he had four uncles who ended up in four countries, the UK, the United States, Canada, and Sweden.

10. Dr. Hameedullah, the Nizam's representative to the UN in 1948, was invited by Prime Minister Liaquat Ali Khan to advise on Islamic content for Pakistan's constitution. Disillusioned by the slow pace of the writing and Liaquat Ali Khan's assassination (Aziz Razvi, Karachi, letter of 2000), Hameedullah moved to Paris after 1951 and headed the Sorbonne's Islamic Studies Faculty for some thirty years. At one time he edited Hyderabad's *Islamic Culture* journal and he published scholarly works on the Qur'an and Islam. A lifelong bachelor, he moved in his late nineties to live with nieces and nephews in the United States.

11. Dr. Abdul Majid Siddiqui, head of history and political science at Osmania, died in Pakistan in 1979. His nephew, Abdul Hafeez Siddiqui, taught law at Osmania but left for Pakistan in 1961 to teach at Sind Muslim Law College and Karachi University when his eldest daughter married in Karachi (other children are in London, Dallas, and Jeddah).

12. Zahid Husain, former finance minister of Hyderabad, was the first governor of the State Bank of Pakistan; Ataur Rahman Alvi, a young Osmania graduate

with an economics M.A., became its head cashier and then established his own commercial bank, Standard Bank of Pakistan, which employed many Hyderabadis and thrived under Ayub Khan's martial law regime (it was nationalized in 1971 when Zulfiqar Ali Bhutto came to power): Aziz Razvi, Karachi, letter of 2000.

13. A few months before the Police Action, the Nizam of Hyderabad delegated three men as diplomatic representatives: Mir Nawaz Jung to London, Zain Yar Jung to Delhi, and Nawab Mushtaq Ahmed Khan to Karachi.

14. The government of India dismissed Mushtaq Ahmed Khan, confiscated his household belongings, demanded the return of the money, and threatened to arrest him if he came back to India. He went to India for consultations with the Nizam in May, posing as a Hindu and entering through Bombay, but then he took his wife and children and returned to Pakistan. He would have come anyway, he said, having felt that partition was inevitable; his own three brothers and his wife's two brothers and a sister came, too, as well as his father. He got a Lahore house in compensation for his Hyderabad one. His grandchildren reside in Karachi, Canada, and the United States.

15. Ahmed Khan 1986 reproduces the State Bank of Pakistan's receipt for the money (one crore ninety-nine lakhs fifty thousand, or 19,950,000 rupees): 275–276.

16. Ghulam Mohamed became second governor general of Pakistan following Jinnah's death in 1948; most Hyderabadis did not view him as a non-mulki Hyderabadi because he was contracted from British India as Hyderabad's finance minister for only three years.

17. In the meantime, Mushtaq Ahmed Khan lost his family's Jullundur as well as Hyderabad properties. He became chairman of the Punjab Road Transport Board, then general manager of West Pakistan Road Transport, then started Karachi Road Transport, and was transportation adviser to the minister of communications. Finally given a Gold Medal in 1992 on Independence Day, he termed it a recognition of Hyderabad's contribution to Pakistan.

18. The Nizam's agent general contended (he was in his nineties in the 1990s) that the money's seizure by the Pakistani government and turnover to "certain Hyderabadis" was illegal. The government of Pakistan did not immediately accept India's takeover of Hyderabad and maintained the agent general until 1953; then Mushtaq Ahmed Khan was either forced out by Ghulam Mohamed or relinquished his office and took Pakistani citizenship (but was shown as a diplomat "out of station" until 1967 in official listings). The agency's Clifton property went to Pakistan and the first secretary of the agent general, Qayum Amin Khan, took over as agent. A building, Victoria Chamber No. 1, that Mushtaq Ahmed Khan had purchased for a Karachi branch of the State Bank of Hyderabad was used to support the agent and his staff. The Nizam allowed displaced persons from Hyderabad to occupy the building at a reduced rent (from rupees 3,000 to 1,365 per month, or lower); Pakistan used this income to maintain the office until Q. A. Khan's death, when the office and its documents went to Pakistan's Foreign Office.

19. Three trusts were set up: the Hyderabad Relief and Rehabilitation Trust, the Hyderabad Imdadi Trust, and the Hyderabad Rehabilitation Trust, all in 1950.

Moin Nawaz Jung (who had been Hyderabad's delegate to the UN) was also a trustee. Mohamed Yousuf became the Trust's vice-chair in 1974 and its chair in 1978; the Trust assisted widows, students, and destitute people, most of them Hyderabadis, in the 1990s.

20. Laik Ali 1962, with an excerpt in Khalidi 1988 mentioning that one of his last acts was informing Mushtaq Ahmed Khan in Karachi of the fall of the government of Hyderabad (59).

21. See Khalidi 1994a, 205, for Laik Ali's escape. When purdah ladies were leaving his house in a car, he hid in the trunk and escaped the cursory inspection. Driven to Bombay, he boarded an aircraft and held a press conference upon arrival in Karachi. His descendants live in Islamabad and overseas.

22. Mustafa Anwer's parents went to Lahore without registering with the Hyderabad Trust in Karachi. His father, Syed Jamil Hussain, from Delhi, was in the Hyderabad Civil Service, then went to Pakistan and helped with refugee rehabilitation; his mother, Mohammadi Begum, had stood first in her field at Osmania and gone to Oxford on a Nizam's scholarship in the 1930s. Mustafa had to establish his origins when he joined the Pakistan Army but did not get verification from the Trust; he enlisted Iskander Mirza, whose sons were at Doon School with Mustafa, to testify that he arrived for school on the morning train from Hyderabad to Delhi. See Srivastava 1998 for the significance of train timings and parental access to their boys, the School, and each other: 96–97.

23. Only the ceramics business, leased out to a private industrialist, did well, its profits still going to the Trust. A. A. Jabbar showed me a written complaint against the trustees in 1971 alleging that most endeavors were in a deplorable condition; documents concerning lawsuits were filed in 1958 and 1983 and papers prepared for a 1992 lawsuit, but funds could not be raised: September 7, 1992, Karachi.

24. The Bahadur Yar Jung Academy was founded in 1953. Its principal planner was Ahmed Ali, whose architecture degree was from Osmania; he became a leading town planner with the Karachi Development Authority. Later, the Hyderabad Trust office was moved to the Academy. Dr. Abdullah Hussaini set up the hospital. Aziz Razvi, letter of 2000, Karachi.

25. In 1993, Pakistan had twenty-eight universities. Qadeer studied law in London after 1948 and went to the Sorbonne for his Ph.D., following Dr. Hameedullah's advice; he had to learn French quickly. After his father's death in 1958, he took his mother and brother and joined other relatives in Pakistan, where he became professor of international relations at the University of Karachi. He married a Hyderabadi by proxy, in 1964, and by the 1990s the family base had shifted from Karachi to the United States as children and grandchildren settled there.

26. Qayyum Khan, first chief minister of the Northwest Frontier Province, was a close friend of Hyderabad's Bahadur Yar Jung (both were of Pathan ancestry); Khan recruited several Hyderabadis to the University of Peshawar. Nawab Samad Yar Jung, chief of the Hyderabad Army, was an important Pathan returnee to Pakistan.

27. Mrs. Siddiqi said that most Muslims stayed faithful to Hyderabad; she had not wanted to leave, but she followed with the children and never regretted the

decision to help build Pakistan. Dr. Siddiqi said, "I didn't want to come either; I was caught. But I am glad, there was much I could do here, whereas in Hyderabad it was finished, there was not much I could do."

28. Born in Aurangabad in 1927, she later wrote a history of that city. She tried to represent Aurangabad's Mughal traditions and often mentioned her upbringing there as "a Mughal princess."

29. Kothari 2000. Other Hyderabadis instrumental in developing Radio Pakistan and Pakistan Television were Aziz Razvi, Mirza Zafrul Hasan, Omer Mohajir, Jehan Ara Sayeed, and Virasat Mirza: Aziz Razvi (chief news editor for Radio Pakistan), Karachi, letter of 2000.

30. Also, the Razakars had commandeered the family's big yard for target practice and meetings, a fact known to the Indian government.

31. Among Bajjia's siblings were Sara Naqvi, a BBC producer, and Zehra Nigah, an Urdu poetess, both in London (the latter's husband was at one time adviser to Abu Dhabi's ruler). Her grandfather and father started a business in Pakistan but it failed, and within two years both men died. "In Hyderabad we never stepped out of our house, we never knew how to get money."

32. In 1947, Ahsan was ADC to Mountbatten, who sent a note to Jinnah saying, "Today I'm giving you two things, Pakistan and Lieutenant Ahsan." His nephew, Syed Sabir Parvaiz, found this note odd, either belittling Pakistan or overpraising Ahsan. Ahsan resigned as governor of East Pakistan because of differences with General Yahya Khan.

33. Baig played for Cowdray Park, Prince Philip for Windsor; Prince Philip sent a condolence telegram upon the accidental death of Hesky's grandson in July, 1992. See the *Friday Times*, July 9–15, 24; Khan 1989.

34. Baig's young relatives live in Karachi, Houston, Canada, the UK, and Australia.

35. Mohamed Yousuf chaired the Hyderabad Trust in 1992.

36. Aziz Razvi, Karachi, letter, 2000.

37. Maseeh uz Zaman's mother accompanied them to Pakistan, not wanting to see her new daughter-in-law depart, but did not like it and went back after a year. Not able to regain Indian nationality, in 1962 she returned to Pakistan and died there. Mrs. Maseeh uz Zaman taught in a girls' school, and Maseeh uz Zaman struck out on his own, building a career in ball bearings and then textiles through German and Swiss company affiliations. Their children and grandchildren were in the Middle East and the United States.

38. Masood Ali attended Warangal College with India's prime minister, P. V. Narasimha Rao, and was born in the same village as M. A. Muttalib, once head of Hyderabad's Management Institute and now retired in Los Angeles.

39. Not supposed to leave, Auj used another man's legal permit to cross the border. Ibrahim Jalis, a Hyderabadi journalist and writer who migrated (author of *Do Mulk Ek Kahani* [Two Countries, One Story], Hyderabad, n.d.), tried to help him join *Navayet*, but he ended up at *Nava-i-Waqt* and other papers. He married before migrating. His wife was Hyderabadi, as was his son's wife (a Karachi Hyderabadi; the couple was in Denmark in 1993); the eldest of his daughters was married to a Punjabi.

40. Of Qamar's four sons, three were well settled in Pakistan and the last was doing an M.B.A. in Manila; two boys were married to Punjabis, and he was looking for a Hyderabadi girl for his third son (a visit to Hyderabad had reminded him how good Hyderabadi food was). His family in Hyderabad was "ordinary," and his two brothers and three sisters in Hyderabad were "not doing too well."

41. Zaidi had spent fifteen years in Lahore, fifteen in Karachi, and fifteen in Islamabad; his two sons were studying in the United States at Dartmouth and Harvard. He had never been back to Hyderabad but had written in 1991 to an old friend, Bihari Lal, in Aurangabad, and had hired an Aurangabadi, Venkat Narayan, as a correspondent in Delhi; "Aurangabad connections were still warm and loving."

42. After film companies were nationalized, Mehmood Ali Khan ran a cinema and then the Pakistan Book Corporation, publishing and distributing scholarly books.

43. Two eminent representatives of old families were Ardeshir Cowasjee, an influential English-language columnist in Pakistan and abroad (in California's *The Pakistan Link*, India's *Asian Age*, and Bangladesh's *Observer*), and Bapsi Sidhwa, author of *The Croweaters*, *The Bride*, and *Cracking India* aka *The Ice Candy Man* (made into the film *Earth* by Deepa Mehta). Cowasjee lived in Karachi, while Sidhwa moved to Texas (and wrote *The American Brat*).

44. Cooper had lived with the Panjwani family for decades and was well known in interfaith circles in Lahore.

45. Mrs. Pestonjee, who had attended Nizam College and taught at Keyes High School, had never seen another Hyderabadi in Pakistan, she said (but the Pestonjees directed me to Mehera Cooper). She had three sisters in India, two brothers in Secunderabad, and two brothers in the United States. Jal had played hockey for the Punjab, and his father and grandfather had been great cricket players; their son Cyrus captained a cricket team in Sydney, Australia.

46. Nayyar's second husband had been vice chancellor of Karachi University and ambassador to Jordan; she was a painter who studied in Chelsea, in London. Her brother was a German national, and she had relatives in Dubai, Kuala Lumpur, and the United States.

47. Begum Qizilbash's mother was from the Hyderabad family of Fakhr ul Mulk and her father was from the Lahore Qizilbash landed family; she attended St. George's Grammar School and Women's College, Osmania, and then returned to her father in the Punjab in 1957 at age eighteen and married in 1959. Her three sons studied abroad, at Boston University, Oxford, and Cambridge; the first worked in Europe and the third wanted to live in Pakistan. She and Mrs. Mehera Cooper were in the Women's International Club together; Mushtaq Ahmed Khan wondered if the Begum was now claiming to be a Hyderabadi (he had attended her mother's wedding in Hyderabad long ago).

48. Mrs. Munawar Ali's husband was president of the Pakistan Medical Association in the mid-1950s, and her only son, a doctor trained in the UK and the United States, lived in the states and had married an American.

49. Many times I was told someone was a Hyderabadi who turned out to be a

Lucknavi or other Urdu-speaker, and just as often I was told that an Urdu-speaker was from north India but the person turned out to be a Hyderabadi.

50. The men's 2½-inch collared sherwanis set them apart in the 1950s and 1960s. Omar Khalidi explained that Hyderabadi sherwanis had six or seven buttons, whereas Hindustani ones had only five; the latter were also called *achkans*, but in the Deccan this term was not used. Personal communication, July, 1997.

51. Written in Urdu, *Khwabrau* is translated into English as *Sleepwalkers* (1998), and Paul says, "On a visit to Karachi in the mid-eighties, I found I had come to a wonderland . . . [of people] who cannot live their present except in the past tense" (112–113).

52. This same prioritizing, of religion, then nation, and finally place of origin, was true of other muhajirs as well: Kennedy 1993, 132, 143.

53. Baig migrated in 1951, via British Army service for President Sukarno in Indonesia, where he helped organize the army. He went into business in Pakistan and was active in Rotary International.

54. Estimates of Hyderabadis in Karachi in the 1990s ranged from 20,000 to 550,000, and most clustered in the Hyderabad Colony opposite the Central Jail.

55. Half of the Lahori Hyderabadis had family ties with east Punjab, Surat, or Loharu (a Rajputana princely state). Some were from eminent families; others were self-made men in Pakistan. People took care to inform me about who was or was not a Nawab, a mulki, or "of our class."

56. Drs. Obaidullah Durrani, Ataullah, and Amjad Ali were in engineering; Yusuf Ali Khan was registrar of the university; Rizwana Siddiqui was principal of the home economics college; Shefqat Siddique chaired the HydraCarbon Institute; Mazhar Ali Khan was chair of English (his brother, Rashid Turabi, was the Shia preacher in Karachi); the Rizvis were in math (he) and English (she); Dr. (Mrs.) Margub was in zoology; Abdur Razzak Khan was principal of the law college; Shamsuddin Siddiqui was in Urdu; Hussain Siddiqui was in chemistry.

57. "Being Muslim," Rizwana Siddiqi said, "my father and others went to Hyderabad for education; the Muslims were always attacked in British India, they couldn't compete with Hindus there." She had come at twelve, learned Pushtu quickly (like her brother, Justice Samdani), and married a muhajir from UP. She was principal of the college of home economics, University of Peshawar.

58. His mother had been widowed in 1942 in Hyderabad city and after the eldest son's death in 1949 the family followed a married daughter to Pakistan (she and her husband were in Rawalpindi). Samdani's uncle was Obaidullah Durrani (above).

59. Justice Samdani earned an M.Sc. in math with Professor Raziuddin Siddiqi, whom he knew from Hyderabad, in Peshawar, and earned his LL.M. at Yale in 1970–1971. When I met him, he had been appointed to head a national commission on corruption. His daughters said they had never had strong feelings about being Hyderabadi or about being muhajirs either, since the latter were "the brightest and most qualified people around." One daughter was going to eastern Slovenia, the other had been admitted to college in Denver, Colorado, but wanted to go to Japan. An elder daughter had married a Pakistani-born "Madrasi" and the

couple lived in New Jersey. Justice Samdani told me that when visiting Sydney in 1979, a Dr. Qadri at a party came and hugged him, saying Samdani was his elder brother's classmate in Warangal (later I met Dr. Qadri in Sydney).

60. Paul 1998 also points to the importance of servants as he contrasts Sindhis, Punjabis, and muhajirs in Karachi, especially 71 et passim.

61. Dr. A. A. Qadeer told how his Hindu best friend, Lakshmi Narayan Singh, sobbed at the railway station when Qadeer's brother went to Pakistan, and Singh's mother wept for four days even though she'd never met Qadeer's brother. Singh was captain of the football team, and, a vegetarian, ate *shami kebab* with his Muslim friends (reminding me that our Hindu vegetarian friends had done the same with us, especially when drinking, in Hyderabad in 1964).

62. Public drinking was not legal in Pakistan but many obtained and drank liquor privately.

63. This was the marriage of Laik Ali's second daughter with Khwaja Masihuddin.

64. Women still put on the *kalipot* as part of the ritual, as I witnessed at a September 1992 wedding on the Bahadur Yar Jung Academy grounds (thanks to Hameed Qureshi). One woman, an aging mother brought over from India very recently, called this a *mangalasutra*, the word Hindus use for their marriage necklaces.

65. In Hyderabad, this institution, popularly known as the Aiwan-i-Urdu, was associated with the mulki Hyderabadi Dr. Zore and featured articles promoting Deccani Urdu and Hyderabad's cultural synthesis. The Bahadur Yar Jung Academy president, Professor Khaja Hameeduddin Shahid (a lecturer in Osmania's Urdu department who migrated to Pakistan in 1959), edited and published *Sabras* from his newly established Aiwan-i-Urdu, while Shahid's former student, Mughni Tabassum, edited Hyderabad's *Sabras* in the 1980s.

66. A St. George's Grammar School group apparently survived only a few years in the mid-1970s; no one formed groups for Nizam College or Madras-i-Aliya, but a few thought of forming a University of California group.

67. Aligarh Old Boys Association of Pakistan, founded in Karachi in 1948; established the Aligarh Institute of Technology in 1988; in 1993, when Pakistan allowed the establishment of private universities, it got permission to open the Sir Syed University of Engineering and Technology. "Seven Aligarians Ruled Pakistan," *Pakistan Link* 5:43 (December 8, 1995, II, 1). Mushtaq Ahmed Khan was active in the Aligarh Association.

68. One man suggested that there was no Hyderabad association because of conflicts over the Trust money; another quoted a Hyderabadi proverb, "*Mai mere bacche, baqi sab loche* (I and my children, the rest are bad)," and said Hyderabadis did little for "community."

69. The Princess Durru Shevar and Prince Muffakham Jah were supposed to come, some said, but as the prince was a citizen of India there was some doubt. When I asked him about this, the prince said he did not recognize Partition or the right of either Pakistan or India to give him a visa for Pakistan and would not go in any case.

70. "Osmania University Old Students Association," *Dawn*, November 28, 1992, 7–9. Finally a president, the neurosugeon Dr. Zaki Hasan, and two vice-

presidents, Fasihuddin Ahmad and Shamim Sayeed, were elected without opposition. An Osmania Association had functioned from 1954 to 1969, when a dispute ended it; in the 1990s, those old leaders could be members but not officers. The Association had a plot of land from the Bahadur Yar Jung Academy but had done nothing with it; it planned to build a secondary school and polytechnic. A member went to Hyderabad and asked the vice-chancellor of Osmania University, Mulla Reddy, to be an honorary member and come to the Platinum Jubilee in January, 1994.

71. The earlier society ran from about 1962 to 1964. Mrs. Aziz Ali, Commodore K. M. Hussain's wife's mother, was the oldest "Mahbubiyah girl" in Pakistan: "They trot her out for special functions; you'll only meet the sisters-in-law tomorrow," I was told by Commodore and Mrs. Hussain. The latter was a St. George's girl; her two sisters-in-law were Mahbubiyans. The moving spirit behind the revived society was Shamim Sayeed, who married young but did teacher training (her mother took her son to Hyderabad for a year while she did that) and, with her husband's support, worked as a teacher. She got a Fulbright scholarship to the United States in 1983. Her daughter went to Mt. Holyoke and then married into a Lahore Punjabi family. One son went to MIT and the Sloan School of Management, and he was with Credit Suisse Bank in London.

72. The Center began in 1989, and most students were girls, including a few Hindus. The parents shifted jobs often or returned to their villages, taking the children away. Another problem was that the teachers' pay was low. Karachi was an urban battlefield in 1993 and most of the school's premises had been taken over by the Pakistan Army as a security headquarters in a "cleanup" operation against the MQM. The women were angry at the Hyderabadi men who had persuaded the army to use the Women's Center instead of the main academy premises and they spoke enviously of the good but relatively undeveloped facilities of the Bahadur Yar Jung Academy.

73. They recruited a headmaster from the UK for the boys' college of 600, the first effort. Like the school's founders in India, they believed that previous experience in India was a disqualification, as the school aimed to transform the mores of the country: Srivastava 1998, 40–41.

74. Mirza 1982. Connected to Loharu State and to Hyderabad through his mother, Colonel Mirza was a young Indian Army man in 1947. Opting for Pakistan, he became ADC to Prime Minister Liaqat Ali Khan. Hesky Baig was his regimental commander in Probyn's Horse.

75. Son of Ali El Edroos, Syed Hussein El-Edroos was "just a Pakistani as such, not even muhajir, not like those in Karachi; I've been all around Pakistan, my father was in the army." His grandfather had retired to Bangalore after 1948, advising his son, Ali, to opt for Pakistan. Ali attended Bishop Cotton's School in Bangalore and Doon School in Dehra Dun; once in Pakistan, he married a Pathan. A general in East Pakistan in 1971, Ali's disagreements with his superiors pushed him to Jordan, where he had close friends and died in 1993.

76. Thus wrote a Muslim reporter from India covering the World Cup in Karachi, viewing an Indian/Pakistani cricket match with his Pakistani relatives: Ansari 1996, 94–95.

77. Hesky Baig wrote Mukarram Jah in Perth in 1983, alleging that the Nizam's Trust had been "sadly mishandled." He asked the Nizam to exercise his influence in Pakistan, to lead and unite "a badly fragmented Muslim world." Sent November 28, 1983, on Hegge and Company Ltd. stationery, it drew a reply from a secretary that the Nizam was not in Perth but the letter would be held for his return.

78. Waheeda Naseem went to Aurangabad many times, in 1954, 1956, 1982, 1983, and 1985. She finally got a visa for Hyderabad in 1988 and saw Dr. Mahender Raj Suxena, her old Osmania botany professor, and four classmates, two Hindu and two Muslim.

79. This classical South Indian dance was originally associated with Hindu temples.

80. Auj had kept in touch with Abid Ali Khan, *Siyasat*'s editor, who invited him in 1988 to Hyderabad to receive an Architect of Urdu award, yet his skepticism about India remained profound. How could a Hindu be faithful to a Muslim, he asked, telling me that a Hindu friend's public expression of regret that Auj was leaving was made "so that the government could seize my property."

81. Jabbar's son, Javed Jabbar, had been an important political figure in several administrations, including the administration of General Musharraf.

82. Kunj Behari Lal was one old HCS/IAS friend who came to Karachi; Ahmed Baig and a very ill friend went to meet him, the friend saying, "he has called, he wants to see me, I must go." Some of Ahmed Baig's children lived in Canada and Australia.

83. The Yousufs mentioned recent weddings of the children of Hindu friends in India to which they had been invited and their reciprocal invitations to Pakistan. Raja Parmanand Bhai had accepted and come, and they had gone to his daughter's wedding. Another person told me how, when Parmanand came to Karachi, his old friends had a special car meet him on the tarmac at the airplane door.

84. "[I]f nonnatives were to become natives, then the natives would become nonnatives . . . [yet] there is no other way but to immediately become the natives of the new place": Paul 1998, 48–49.

85. This was one of the twin sons of Aziz ur Rehman, who said, "Because it's poor, that's perhaps why they send their daughters out, but Karachi is a rich place. The Muslims are not doing well in India, they are working in the Middle East. Here in Pakistan there are no people starving." Asked about the people I saw in Pakistan who seemed very poor, he pronounced them Bangladeshis, Afghanis, and people from India working in Pakistan illegally.

86. The Khans lived in New York with their children. He went to Pakistan and worked in the Habib Bank, marrying a Hyderabadi in 1955. His Nizam College degree dated from the college's pre-1948 affiliation to Madras University, but her Nizam College degree came after its affiliation to Osmania, so she was the member of the Osmania Old Boys Association.

87. But he is marrying a Hyderabadi, his mother's sister's daughter, from an anti-dowry family; he mentioned that Punjabi and Sindhi dowries are much more expensive.

88. She had prepared lunch for her father, his friends, and me (her mother was in Dubai with another daughter): Nasir's grandfather had come from Hadramaut, Yemen, to Bombay in 1869 and joined Hyderabad's army; his maternal great-grandfather was from Bahrain and sold horses to Salar Jang I.

89. Pathans were recruited for the Hyderabad Police "because Hyderabadis were somewhat lazy and given to luxurious life; they wanted fresh blood." Khan and a brother went to Hyderabad in 1930 (because older brothers had been in the Khilafat movement, jailed, and barred from returning to the North West Frontier Province and they were given places in Hyderabad by Sir Ross Masood. After taking an Osmania history degree in 1934, Khan joined the central excise service, and he and his brother married Hyderabadis. In 1947 a warrant was issued for his arrest, so he fled to Pakistan, and his family followed; he went into law, his sons into the customs department and the army.

90. The Institute of Policy Studies surveyed 126 students in 8th, 9th, 10th, and A level and O level classes: More than half did not read Urdu writers and less than one-fourth of them said their prayers five times a day. The author said: "One cannot understand the strange correlation between the presence of affluence and the lack of patriotism and respect for one's Islamic value system which the English medium schools are eroding by encouraging their students' emotional and mental fixation on the West." Shakespeare was the most widely read English writer. "Majority of Pakistani Students Prefer to Settle Abroad," *Pakistan Link*, March 21, 1997, 38.

91. Educated at Ohio Wesleyan and with a Ph.D. in international relations and political science from the University of Pennsylvania and now at the Johns Hopkins University School of Advanced International Studies, Shirin was born in Hyderabad in 1944, left for Peshawar in 1950, and has been in the United States since 1959. Her husband was a Pakistani Pathan.

92. Mahmood Mushtaq and his German wife (the German shipbuilder who built Karachi's shipyard was a close friend of his father's, and Mahmood met the daughter while at Cambridge in the UK) lived for years in Karachi. Then an oil executive, he went with Gulf to Singapore and Japan, then became a U.S. citizen and was in Texas with Pennzoil in 1993.

93. Parvaiz worked for IBM, and she taught fifth grade in the Islamabad Grammar School. His parents migrated in 1949 because "Muslims weren't getting jobs"; hers moved in about 1962 and her father worked for the State Bank of Pakistan in Karachi, taking assignments abroad in New York, Baghdad, and Jeddah.

94. The husband of one daughter had been educated in the United States and worked in the Middle East; he recommended a computer company in Irvine, where I work, as one that employed Hyderabadis, and he recalled that Dr. Benkat Chandra, in Hyderabad, India, had been his family's doctor.

95. Azra learned to be a Hyderabadi in London, through the Hyderabadi cultural association there. In Pakistan, she advocated keeping a Hyderabadi identity, because "Pakistan has no sense of nationhood, everyone has that separate identity." She was starting a boutique featuring Hyderabadi fashions.

NOTES FOR CHAPTER 5

1. Ghose 1965, 1–2.

2. See Yazdani 1985, chapter 9. Begum Yazdani's father, Ghulam Yazdani (a non-mulki from Delhi), joined the Hyderabad government's archaeological department in 1914 and later became its head; he received an Order of the British Empire in 1936. Zubaida and her husband moved to the UK in the 1970s after their

retirements (two sons had settled there in the 1960s) and they ran a Hyderabad Urdu School of Languages and Sciences in London.

3. The Anjuman-i-Islam of London, formed in 1888, included Sayyid Ali Imam, later prime minister of Hyderabad from 1919 to 1922: Minault 1998, 192–197. Minault mentions two other non-mulki Hyderabadis who studied in England in the late nineteenth century: Khuda Baksh, chief justice of Hyderabad (1884–1898), and Humayun Mirza, barrister.

4. Students who became prominent in Hyderabad include, in roughly chronological order from the 1880s to about 1930, George Nundy, Edith Boardman, Mohammad Hameed Ullah Khan, Pingle Jagan Mohan Reddy, Ali Nawaz Jung Bahadur, Dr. S. Mallanah, Mehdi Yar Jung Bahadur, Haroon Khan Sherwani, Zain Yar Jung Bahadur, Syed Ali Akbar, Akbar Ali Khan, S. Narayan Reddy, Nizamat Jung Bahadur, Ali Yavar Jung, Barrister Ataur Rahman, and Syed Mohiuddin Qadri Zore.

5. S. A. Saleem compared the coffee house life to life on the left bank of Paris.

6. Zaidi came from the Mehdi Yar Jung family; his sister, Sayeedia Jafferi, was professor of Urdu at Osmania. His father was in the army and the family lived in Dar us Shifa; Zaidi attended Chaderghat High School and College and Osmania. His wife worked for the post office.

7. Zaidi 1984. Lateef was at Madras-i-Aliya, then Nizam College, and he earned a civil engineering degree from Osmania.

8. Majid's father, Tahir Ali Khan Muslim, was educated at Oxford and the Sorbonne; as private secretary to the Prince of Berar, he tutored him and the Princess Durru Shehvar in Urdu. Majid played with Prince Muffakham Jah as a boy and has assisted him with various endeavors.

9. Mustafa, son of Maqsud Jung, was a key man in the Hyderabad Deccan Association.

10. Mandozai's father, Wali Dad Khan, died in 1950, partly from the shock of the Police Action (he had given Dar us Salam, the ancestral home, to the Ittehad ul Muslimin for its headquarters). As a boy, Wajih Dad Khan painted Western subjects and played the violin; he came to Britain because there was no good architectural training in Hyderabad. He arranged for the tasteful cards sold by Britain's Hyderabad Deccan Association.

11. Tanvir 1991. As a college student, Dr. Saxena stood first in science and second in English in the state. In the UK he helped form, and became president of, the Indian Medical Association in Britain and worked with King's College and other hospitals.

12. Princess Durru Shehvar, daughter of the last Caliph in Turkey, married Azam Jah, the last Nizam's elder son, in 1931 (and the Sultan of Turkey's niece, Niloufer, married Moazzam Jah, the younger son). Princess Niloufer lived in Paris, where she died in 1989. Azam and Moazzam Jah have died (and were disinherited). Muffakham Jah, or "the Prince," contributed to, among other endeavors in Hyderabad, a medical school, a hospital, an engineering college, and the Nizam's Museum in Purani Haveli. The older grandson, called by some "the Nizam of Perth," settled in Australia but moved to Turkey in about 1999.

13. Mir Mohsin Ali Khan held leadership positions in, among others, the English Speaking Union, the British Muslim and Christian Society, the British Muslim Islamic Council, UNICEF, Schiller International University, and various Indian and Pakistani associations. Instrumental in earlier London Hyderabad associations, he was not active in recent ones.

14. The earlier definition of Anglo-Indian was a person "of British blood" settled in India; it came to include those of mixed background, the children of Britons and Indians. Hyderabadis gained the right to move to the UK as Commonwealth members after 1948 when they became citizens of both India and the Commonwealth.

15. Born in 1892 in Hyderabad, he celebrated his ninety-ninth birthday in a London nursing home just before I interviewed him in 1991. Dr. Dennis Thompson Prior Gay was the seventh of ten children in a family descended, on one side, from the Chamarettes with the French army in Mysore and, on the other, from an Englishman who went to India in 1717 and became a Madras Army officer. Dennis was named for a respected Anglican priest in Hyderabad, the Reverend Dennis Osborne (later, influenced by him and his St. George's schooling, Dennis Gay became Anglican rather than Catholic). He was named Thompson for his grandmother, daughter of Captain Thompson, and Prior for the English family that housed his father when the latter was sent "home" briefly after the Mutiny of 1857.

16. Gay qualified in medicine in King's College Hospital, Dulwich (1917), and worked in Hampshire. Then he joined the army in World War I and served in Palestine, Egypt, Turkey, and Armenia (where he met Hyderabadi friends in the 18th Lancers, his cousin Captain Claude Green, Colonel George Clark, and Muslim officers too). He married Molly Horton in Hyderabad's St. George's Church in 1925.

17. Gay served with the British Medical Board, examining young men joining the army, but he never practiced in the UK. In 1968, Mukarram Jah (Nizam after his grandfather's death in 1967) brought the Gays to India for a visit, but Dr. Gay found Hyderabad "too changed, awful." The city population had doubled, and there were "people from anywhere, Calcutta people, Gujaratis . . . and no D'Costas, no Clarks . . . the roads were so crowded."

18. Gay kept in touch with the Princess Niloufer, who always met him when she visited from Paris, and with many ex-Hyderabadi friends and relatives in Australia, Canada, the United States, and the UK; friends from long ago had come for his ninety-ninth birthday party in 1991, and others had sent cards from Hyderabad and Poona.

19. Interview; see also Major A. J. Maitland Hudson, "Memories: 1st Hyderabad Imperial Service Lancers" (manuscript donated to the India Office Library).

20. Purdah did mean that few Muslim wives participated.

21. Hudson had crossed a boundary when, at age thirty ("when marriage was advised"), he met and married a "country-born" woman who owned and operated her own hairdressing salon, thus limiting his career prospects. There were two categories, the "England-returned" and the "country-born"—all the families had "wrong" branches of "black or brown" children because women were scarce. These racial and occupational bigotries faded somewhat as intermarriages increased.

22. Hudson was posted to Burma and Aden during the Second World War, from 1940 to 1946, and even before the Police Action he had resigned his commission and was not in Hyderabad at the time it took place. Despite being clearly marked with Hudson's regimental colors, fourteen of their seventeen trousseau chests were lost on the sea voyage home, symbolizing the sense of loss that seemed to mark his life in England.

23. When I phoned Adams, he asked questions about my project, then asserted he was a mulki and invited me for lunch. Jimmy Adams's father's stepdaughter, Joyce, was married to Henry Corfield, who transferred to the British Indian Army in 1947; Henry and Joyce and their children migrated to the UK in 1950 and Jimmy Adams's parents followed in 1954.

24. His father had to turn his fine sporting rifles in at the Fateh Maidan stadium to the Indian Army, which took the particulars and promised to return them but "threw them all in a heap" and later "lost" his father's most valuable rifle.

25. His mother was a Marrett, from a French family of bridge builders and missionaries. When Jimmy visited his grandfather, the Gurkhas guarding the Mint challenged him to carry out a gold bar, but he couldn't even lift one; he also remembered his father going to the Nizam's birthday fetes, "hiring a sherwani and pants and that cap [*dastar*], and taking one gold and one silver coin to drop in baskets to either side of the Nizam as he bowed to him."

26. Most relatives of Jimmy Adams were in Australia or Canada.

27. A member of Bishop Cotton's Old Boys' Society, Jimmy Adams proudly recounted meeting Prince Basalat Jah, from the royal family, at a Jagirdars' College function.

28. Bhachu 1985.

29. He founded the Nottingham Central Library Urdu collection of some 5,000 volumes, and he and his wife taught Urdu there. Moving to Kent about 1972, he founded an Academy of Urdu Studies, and then a promotion took him to London. Habib ca. 1981, 49–57. *Siyasat* publicized the couple's visit to Hyderabad after twenty-eight years abroad: (April 22, 1985). Habib published his own account of this trip, on which he and his wife were accompanied by their daughter and English (Muslim convert) son-in-law. His first stop in Hyderabad was the office of *Siyasat*, his *adab-i-ashram* or literary ashram, where he saw the wife of Dr. Sideshwar Raj Saxena's older brother and recalled the closeness of the two families. Whenever he was at the Saxena home and the call to prayer came, Sideshwar Raj's mother sent a white cloth to him (to kneel on for prayers), and on Ramadan, she sent a special lentils dish to his home for breaking the fast; his sister and mother never observed purdah with this Saxena household or that of Nar Singh Raj Bahadur. He was happy to find that Hyderabad was still the cradle of Urdu: Habib 1985.

30. Amina had attended St. George's Grammar School in Hyderabad with Jack Hudson's son, and a fellow teacher at her London school put her in touch with Hudson. She helped him just after his wife's death (shortly before I arrived, in 1991), bringing a lunch for us when I first met him, and she continued to visit him after he moved to a nursing home. She met her old classmate, Jack's son, once in 1990, but they did not remember each other.

31. Adeel's grandfather went to Hyderabad in 1902 and became deputy director of registration and stamps; his father, after attending Aligarh and studying law in Allahabad, joined his father and became personal secretary to Sir Akbar Hydari, who was finance minister and then prime minister. Adeel's wife and daughters simplified their names, taking Yousuf as their surname.

32. His father was Hyderabad State's former chief justice V. Lakshman Reddy, a Middle Temple barrister of 1915, and his grandfather was Venkata Rama Reddy, Kotwal (commissioner of police) of Hyderabad City.

33. The airline record for lateness was four minutes per 50,000 miles, in a four-year period, and only four pieces of luggage were lost (he contended they had never been booked). Reddy initiated the yellow health book for travelers and sent it to the World Health Organization (WHO), and he color-coded the baggage tags because baggage handlers were illiterate then. Deccan Airways also began the Indian Night Mail service, one-day delivery time. His four years as manager saw the airline expand from two to sixteen Dakotas and from 600 or 800 route miles to over 3,000 route miles. The airline's hub was in Nagpur, where he married his first wife.

34. That same year he divorced his first wife (and she remarried, taking his children to Madras so that they were not Hyderabadis).

35. Veeraswami's had an earlier Hyderabadi history: a member of the Palmer family had owned it as an Indian restaurant but sold it in 1921 to an Italian, who sold it in 1935 to a Mr. Stewart, who made it Indian again and named it Veeraswami's after his cook.

36. They had in mind not only the final betrayal of 1947 (Razvi ca. 2000). The "return of Berar" was still an issue, as some argued that the Berar districts (ceded by the Nizam to the East India Company in 1853 and 1860 to pay the salaries of the Hyderabad Contingent) should have been returned, giving Hyderabad a better chance for independence in 1947. Princess Durru Shehvar's official title was Princess of Berar. One close reader of my 1978 book chastised me for not including Berar within the state boundaries on the map (53).

37. Ahmed ca. 1980–1981; Saxena n.d.

38. I later met Alex Norton in Sydney, Australia.

39. But it was another Londoner, Humayun Yar Khan, member of the same set of friends, who contended he was the only person to read their niece Polly Chenoy's University of Utah thesis on the American feminist writer, Adrienne Rich.

40. Latif Sayeed reincarnated this organization in Hyderabad as the Progressive Society, with Sarojini Naidu, Ali Yavar Jung, Barristers Akbar Ali Khan and Sri Krishna, and others.

41. Baqar Ali Mirza and Dilsukh Ram were named as first and second chairs (with Rahman as third) in Ali Khan 1993, 5. Ataur Rahman became a barrister and member of parliament in England and wrote under the name of Arthur Raymond. Another early immigrant was Leela Velankar, wife of the filmmaker David Lean. Ahmed interview; Ahmed ca. 1980–1981.

42. As Prince Muffakham Jah, its patron from 1974, observed, "Whether it was founded sixty years ago or forty, to us it is all the same, it is 'pursoon'!" (His

use of *parsaun*, as in the limerick in chapter 2, meant time was not important.) Jah 1993, 1.

43. The 1970s reactivation was led by Ahmed Mohiuddin, Sikander Zaman Khan, and Khaja Ahsanuddin, and it was registered (number 2699W) in 1974; the 1976 *Constitution* is with Majid Ali Khan.

44. There were no or few Anglo-Indians either. Dr. Gay, for example, never attended association meetings in London, and his wife and daughter, who had lived in the UK since 1939, were not Hyderabadis, he said. Similarly, Jack Hudson and Jimmy Adams were not involved, although both knew something of the association's activities.

45. The association produced a very successful tie, black with small gold Char Minars on it, in the 1980s. The designer, Aziz Ahmed, asked a friend to bring along a pack of Char Minar cigarettes to London, meaning to use the packet design for the tie. His friend, thinking the indigenously produced cigarettes were too ordinary, brought instead some other imported cigarettes, and Aziz had to ask yet another friend to bring Char Minar cigarettes.

46. Dues were twenty pounds per family per year in 1991, and thirty pounds in 2000; young adults had to join on their own after they became earners.

47. *News and Views* 1990, 2.

48. Leaders in recent years included Sharafat Walajahi, a Pakistani Hyderabadi but one longtime resident in Dubai, Dr. Sideshwar Raj Saxena, Mrs. Arifa Hussain, Aziz Ahmed, Mrs. Tehniat Jilani, Mrs. Kauser Iqbal Khan, and Shuja Shafi, the last providing a liaison to British Muslim activities.

49. Hyderabadis were hesitant to seek a relationship with the prince, and earlier British Hyderabad associations did not try to involve him. Recently, he, his mother, and his wife have been requested to participate, and attendance soared when they did. The prince was one of the first to have a FAX machine in his home (and then e-mail) and served as a central communications point for Hyderabadis around the world.

50. The club brochure credited the Hyderabad Trust, UK (chaired by Prince Muffakham Jah), the Hyderabad Deccan Association in Hyderabad, the Hyderabad Foundation of Chicago, the Indians' Resettlement–Joint Advisory Association Trust (IRJAA, based in the Middle East), and "friends" with taking this initiative, and eleven names with phone numbers were given, as well as four regional officers' addresses.

51. At twenty-five pounds per guest, twenty for members, with a 350-person limit, the association made 2,800 pounds and donated 1,000 pounds to the Princess Durru Shehvar Children's Hospital in Hyderabad, Action Research for the Crippled Child, and Great Ormond Street Hospital for Children, the latter two in the UK. *News and Views* 1990.

52. "Hyderabad Festival" 1990 set the first week of December for the London celebration and reported the full cooperation of the Indian High Commissioner in London, Kuldeep Nayyar.

53. Leaders of the Urdu Majlis in London advised me to meet *Siyasat* editor Abid Ali Khan and the vice-chancellor of Osmania University, Naveenit Rao, an old Osmania classmate of many and a man who "spoke perfect Urdu," when I

went to Hyderabad. This vice-chancellor was not the same one people in Karachi spoke similarly about and wanted to invite to the Osmania Old Boys' Association event (Mulla Reddy).

54. Russell 1982.

55. Habib ca. 1981, 134 a general meeting (April 8, 1978) at Alliance Hall, London, featured Ralph Russell (Urdu professor at the School of Oriental and African Studies), Ghulam Yazdani, Mohammed Abdul Basit, Abbas Zaidi, Anwar Hussain, Syed Masood Ali, Naqi Tanvir, Naseer Akhtar, and others. Abbas Zaidi followed Anwar Hussain as president, and the journal, *Hayat-i-Nau*, was edited by Naqi Tanvir.

56. *Siyasat*, October 29, 1984. He and she were said to be from the first educated household in Hyderabad's Memom brotherhood.

57. Habib ca. 1981, 167. Zehra Nigah's family had migrated to Pakistan in 1948, settling in Karachi; she married in 1958 and traveled with her husband, a Pakistani senior civil servant: *Dawn*, June 12, 2001, discusses her life and poetry (widowed, she was in Pakistan then, but her two sons lived abroad). Hasnuddin Ahmed (brother of London's Aziz Ahmed), from Hyderabad, helped found branches of the Amir Khusro Society in Hyderabad, London, Chicago, and Canada while traveling to see relatives.

58. "An Evening" 1984; Naqvi 1990. By 1990, Urdu Markaz in London had closed (perhaps eclipsed by the Urdu Majlis).

59. "London is a Second Hyderabad" 1985.

60. Mir Yasin Ali Khan presided, Dr. Ziauddin Shakeb spoke, Pakeeza Baig sang Iqbal's poetry, Drs. S. A. Durrani and Amjad from the Iqbal Academy spoke, and Dr. Siddeshwar Raj Saxena inaugurated the *mushaira* with a *ghazal* of his own composition: "Hyderabad Association's Annual *Mushaira*" 1990. Earlier, in July, the Faiz Academy in Britain also held a celebration of Iqbal, in which Hyderabadis were active: Naqvi 1990.

61. When Ghulam Yazdani settled in London, he was on the late-1960s Hyderabad association's twelve-person executive committee. Yazdani became more active in the Urdu Majlis; in 1991, he said, the Majlis managing committee members were all Hyderabadis. Another Majlis leader, Abbas Zaidi, said that all but one were Hyderabadis; the other was from Delhi.

62. Punjabis who had visited Hyderabad and liked it reportedly bought more copies of Raza Alikhan's book, *Hyderabad 400 Years*, than did Hyderabadis when the author brought it to London in 1992 (according to Aziz Ahmed, who managed the sales).

63. Bilu 1989, 162–169. Another Urdu periodical, *Ravi*, was published from Bradford and reproduced news of Hyderabad from *Siyasat*: *Siyasat*, August 23, 1992, reproduced a page of *Ravi* to show this. Two other Urdu dailies were published in Britain in 1990, *Jang* and *Millat*, and there were three other monthlies besides *Ravi*: *Urdu Adab*, *Ujalla*, and *Shafaq*.

64. Akbar had had a Hyderabad government scholarship to the UK before 1948, but the Police Action and the numbers of returning British war veterans taking places in British institutions led to its lapse, so his family financed him.

65. For the Urdu Majlis reception, *Siyasat*, June 10, 1990; for the Hyderabad

Deccan Association function, *Siyasat*, July 15, 1990. Zehra or Zohra Nigah was sister to Karachi's famous TV family drama authoress Bajjia (previous chapter), and the president of the Hyderabad Association then was from Pakistan, Sharafat Walajahi.

66. His son and daughter have both married Britons (the son-in-law is a committed Muslim) and are professional people.

67. He also spoke at Bahadur Yar Jung Academy events in Karachi, where he has in-laws and where I attended his son's wedding in 1992.

68. See Appadurai 1995.

69. "Sports and Hyderabad" 1993, 29.

70. "Festival Match" 1990, 3.

71. Azharuddin was disgraced by the scandals enveloping cricket in the late 1990s.

72. Mir Mohsin Ali Khan, August 28, 1991, London.

73. An extremely perceptive observer of Hyderabadis, Princess Esin married into Hyderabad in about 1975, lived there for five years, and since then has been continuously involved with Hyderabadis abroad.

74. Tellingly, when Hyderabad's leader of the Ittehad ul Muslimeen in Hyderabad, Salahuddin Owaisi, went to London and wanted to speak about Indian Muslim politics, no platform was given to him.

75. Werbner 1991, 127, 140. A similarity is in the broader Punjabi audience for Urdu *mushairas* (124–125).

76. Abbas Zaidi, despite thirty-two years in the UK, remained an Indian citizen in 1991 (he was suing for property in Hyderabad). He had always intended to return to Hyderabad, but he saw such changes there, and such problems of law and order, that he was no longer sure.

77. One Londoner had gone to Pakistan in the late 1950s and returned to visit his sister in Hyderabad only in 1987, not visiting all those years for fear of harming his brother-in-law's career. He visited relatives in Pakistan frequently, but his children had never been to Hyderabad. The Indian brother-in-law, who became a judge, finally visited Pakistan in 1989 after his retirement.

78. Shakeb 1990.

79. Naqvi 1990.

80. This was Professor Syed Sirajuddin, retired English professor from Nizam College, who often stopped in London on his way to visit his children in the United States.

81. Bilu 1989, 162–169.

82. The family had lived in Kent, without others around them, and she did not read Urdu at all. She had many English girlfriends and was the first of them to marry, at age twenty. Most of the Hyderabadi girls like her in the UK married in the UK and were very happy there, and she also knew Hyderabadi girls marrying into the United States and thought most were happy there. Her husband was a doctor and could have emigrated but had property in Hyderabad.

83. I talked to her father in Hyderabad, where he had come to pursue a property dispute, and at a wedding we were both attending he stuck out in the crowd, wearing a Western suit and bare-headed rather than wearing a sherwani and cap.

84. Of thirteen marriages noted in Hyderabad association newsletters from 1994 to 2000, six occurred between brides and grooms from the UK and took place in the UK, whereas five more occurred between brides and grooms from the UK but took place in Hyderabad (two) or in Karachi (three). The final two marriages sent UK brides to U.S. grooms via marriages in Karachi and Jeddah, Saudi Arabia.

85. For example, Adeel Siddiqui, his wife, Nafiz, and younger daughter, Ruhma, believed that one's children, in Britain, should be loved and respected as friends. Ruhma knew little Urdu and felt she was "a bit Hyderabadi"; she later married an Italian who became a Muslim.

NOTES FOR CHAPTER 6

With thanks to Chinua Achebe, whose fine novel of that title came out in 1967.

1. Lyn Edwards, Hyderabad, November 9, 1991. Marjory was the niece of Dr. Gay in London; she was headmistress of St. George's Preparatory School and educational adviser to the Golden Rose School, set up by the Anglican Domiciled European Community of Chaderghat.

2. In 1999, the Australian prime minister drafted the preamble to a new constitution, mentioning "mateship" as a key value in Australian culture.

3. Moore 1988, 549.

4. In the 1981 census, 77 percent of India-born migrants were Christians, and in Western Australia this percentage was almost 90 percent: Jayaraman 1988, 544.

5. See Khalidi 1994 for reprinted parts of Barker 1969.

6. For the Calcutta diocese, see Moore 1988, 548. St. George's in Hyderabad was founded by the British Anglican congregation in Hyderabad for its own children, and in 1920 the Australian and Tasmanian Christian Missionary Society took over the school: Lateefunnisa 1956, 47–48. The Nizam gave land in 1834 for a church, school, and cemetery for the "Protestant Community of Chaderghat," which existed without connection to the Diocese of Madras, funded by the British Resident, the Nizam's prime minister Salar Jung, and members' donations. In 1917 the Australian Mission offered to sponsor the church and school and this was accepted. Edwards ca. 1998, 80–84.

7. I mentioned this quest to my local host, Geoff Oddie, on my arrival in Sydney in 1993, and within two hours I was talking to the Bellinghams in their retirement home. Geoff, a historian of Christianity in India, and the Bellinghams were members of the same church.

8. The point is echoed in Khalidi 1991, 60.

9. In 1956 the Nizam became a private person but continued to receive certain privileges and a privy purse until his death in 1967. Mukarram Jah succeeded his grandfather then, but in 1970 the government of India abolished all princely privileges and privy purses (breaking promises given upon accession of the princely states to India): see the epilogue of Allen and Dwivedi 1984.

10. Mukarram Jah was involved in litigation with the government of India into the 1990s over landed property and the state jewels. An auction of the Nizam's jewels was to be held in 1979 at the Supreme Court in New Delhi, offering some

29 million pounds' worth of the estimated total of 400 million pounds' worth of jewels (London, *Daily Telegraph*, September 20, 1979). But the likely buyers would have taken them out of India, and the government of India claimed the jewels as state property. In 1994, the Supreme Court set a price of $58 million for a 173-piece collection that the government could buy by the end of that year; otherwise, the Nizam's Trust could auction off the jewels. In 1995, the Indian government offered 40 million pounds for the jewels, but the Nizam wanted more: some 800 writs were filed against him by people claiming to be relatives, and 172 more filed for the proceeds of any sale. He had debts in India, Australia, and Switzerland. In Australia, aborigines filed a claim for his sheep ranch (*The Sunday Times*, April 16, 1995). Financial problems forced him to sell his Australian properties. He lived with his fifth wife, a Turkish woman, in Istanbul in 1999 ("The Pauper Prince," *The Australian Magazine*, April 3–4, 1999, 23–26).

   11. Moore 1988, 547, says the term referred to both the British in India and their Indian-born or mixed-race children.

   12. The Nortons, Luschwitzes, Barrets, Fallons, Finglasses, Corfields (and, in Perth, the Nainees, Harpers, Cordiros, Campos, Frosts, Isaacses, Fruvalls, Camerons, De Prazers, Footmans, Hancocks, Herfts, La Touches, McDonalds, Partridges, Balms, Bradys, Curtises, Jameses, Pauls, Rosses, Wiekenses, Williamses, Wateses, and D'Costas) were Catholics, while the Coxes, Oateses, Chamarettes, Hudsons, Greens, Gays, Boardmans, Gardners, Edwardses, Olivers, and Greens were Protestants. There were individual exceptions and Catholic-Protestant marriages, and Krishna and Joan Green Reddy's sons were Hindu.

   13. Government of Hyderabad 1937 listed members of the Cox, Fallon, Chamarette, Edwards, Ross, and Hudson families as army officers and members of the Verghese, Gay, Adams, and Clarke families as medical officers.

   14. Khalidi 1994b, 197.

   15. Alex Norton's siblings scattered: a sister and brother went to the UK, where the latter married a Scotswoman, and a brother went to the United States, where he married an American woman.

   16. Norton got his friend Krishna Reddy, his classmate at St. George's, appointed his successor as aide-de-camp to Chief Minister Vellodi; Krishna Reddy subsequently visited him and Billy Cox in Sydney (after Reddy's elopement with Joan Green, an Australian, in Hyderabad). Krishna and Joan Reddy visited Australia after their sons migrated to Brisbane.

   17. Norton became a millionaire, traveling frequently (but lost it all and had to start again). He recalled his chance meeting in Los Angeles with a filmmaker from Hyderabad, Ahmed Lateef, the son of the principal of Jagirdars' College, who took him home where they talked for hours.

   18. Among his friends was Mukarram Jah, the Nizam's successor, to whom Alex and Henry Luschwitz remained close.

   19. Among the four who went to Pakistan was a Muslim relative of his, to whose mother in Hyderabad Fallon still felt close. Dennis Fallon, like his mother (a Barrett), was Catholic; his father and uncle, George Cox, were Protestants and Freemasons.

   20. Three of Fallon's maternal aunts (Mavis, Mary, and Winifred) migrated

to Perth, and one (Phyllis) to Melbourne. Fallon's wife from Delhi and three children moved with him to Melbourne, where his fourth child was born and where he worked as administrative assistant to the dean of the faculty of medicine at Monash University. He belonged to the Royal United Service Institute of Victoria (a UK-based strategic studies group), the RIMC Old Boys' Association (ROBA, based in India), and the Airborne Forces Association. A sister lived in Assam and a second sister spent her time in Hyderabad, Dubai, and Australia, where she has children. Fallon is mentioned (as a hockey coach) in Moore 1988, 549.

21. Emile's friend, Saif Mirza, went to Pakistan, and he was trying to locate him; they had been classmates at Bishop Cotton's boarding school in Bangalore. Emile was still a British citizen in 1993.

22. Philip and Billy also married Australians; Betty migrated with her Hyderabadi husband.

23. He visited Hyderabad in 1971 and 1978. Ultimately Emile's mother followed her children to Australia in 1980 after their father's death; their father had refused to migrate. During his last days in Hyderabad, George Cox's Muslim and Parsi friends from his Masonic lodge had visited often, sitting on the front verandah. Told that the colonel was sleeping, these friends refused to leave, saying, "That's all right, Mrs. Cox; when he wakes up he might need something."

24. Her husband started as a hospital orderly, but then he joined the Royal Australian Air Force, which took them to Melbourne and Hong Kong, where he died at thirty-nine. Her second husband was a major in the Indian Army in Bangalore, Delhi, and Burma, and they settled in Sydney.

25. For Anglo-Indian life in the railways, see Muller 1994, with its vivid sketch of the impact of independence and language changes on the Burgher railway families in Sri Lanka.

26. As a guest in the home of Chandrakant and Lalitha Gir in Hyderabad, I heard them receive a call from Bruce on New Year's Eve of 1997.

27. Bruce had photos of William Palmer, an 1858 letter of Lucy Palmer, and a darning sock of the Fallons.

28. In Melbourne, Bruce worked for the taxation department, which also had two women from Hyderabad, one of them a hijab-wearer. He teased her about this non-Hyderabadi custom, which she adopted when in Saudi Arabia.

29. Here, the many letters and questionnaires I had sent ahead had raised questions rather than interest. Some of British blood thought I was mistaking them for those of mixed blood and initially did not want to meet me, but in the end their hospitality was outstanding.

30. This was an eight-hour interview with Barney and Heather Devlin, Jean Luschwitz and her daughter Jackie, Kathleen Chamarette, Heather's brother Jerry Howlett and his wife, and Barney and Heather's son Mathew and daughter Leslie, in the middle of which Barney took me to meet Donald and Winifred Schoeffer nearby.

31. Salar Jang sent imported airguns for the boys and dolls for the girls, forgetfully sending dolls even after the girls got too old for them. He had reportedly given the Bowenpalli locality to the Bowen family, related to Kathleen Chama-

rette (her father's sister married Alfred Bowen and despite eighteen children the family died out).

32. Bishop Cotton's School and St. Mary's School in Bangalore, boys' and girls' boarding high schools, had amazing networks, according to Barney Devlin and Joyce Corfield. Joyce said that an "old boys'" network from Bishop Cotton's School functioned in the UK and Australia. Barney cited a visit to Perth by a woman from Singapore with her English husband, and she knew Barney by name from the school. Her husband said he'd never seen anything like it; she just phoned up people, classmates but also people from the school list she didn't even know, who then put them up all over Australia.

33. Barney got off the ship in Perth, terribly seasick and unwilling to travel further; had he known how bad the voyage would be, he said, he'd never have left India. He and David joined the Royal Automobile Club staff, and later Barney developed a clothing manufacturing business.

34. The picture was photocopied from Alikhan 1990, 204.

35. Kathleen had a copy of the certificate of marriage of Andrew Chamarette, of the surveyor general's department, and Katherine Johannes, married at the French Gardens, Hyderabad, October 3, 1820. This Katherine Johannes or Jahans or Johns (the last spelling given in Jack Hudson's genealogy in London) was said to be Armenian, her father a financial adviser to Falaknuma—a palace, however, built only in the late nineteenth century.

36. An Indian Army doctor captured in Malaysia and imprisoned in Papua New Guinea, Dr. Adams died of malaria in 1943; King George V posthumously awarded him the Military Cross.

37. For his aunt, Mrs. Abid Evans, see Khalidi 1999.

38. Ramalu or Bobby Reddy had a mother who was Scots and French—Daphne Oliver, said Heather Devlin.

39. The Urdu sayings included the Mughal Emperor Akbar's advice about the people of the Deccan: *Kanara kapti, Telinga chor, mang Maratha* (Kanarese are cunning, Telugus are thieves, the Marathas are rascals). Barney also told jokes about a well-known figure in the Public Gardens, a man whose son, later, in Philadelphia, tried to explain why his father had generated so much Hyderabadi humor.

40. Supriya Singh and Shahana Ali Khan, both of Melbourne, testified to this.

41. Of these twelve, three had "become unmarried." Uncommon among the first-generation immigrants, divorce was common among the second-, although this euphemism was used.

42. Like his brothers and sisters, Ernest attended Mahbubiyah; then he went away to boarding school (Montfort Boys School, Yercaud, by Salem). When he and his wife went around the world after his retirement, they went to the Greek Islands, the UK, the United States, and Canada. Yet Ernest knew the Hyderabadi Anglo-Indian family relationships well, and he knew where people had ended up, from Canada to the UK, the United States, and even Kuala Lumpur. His cousin Jimmy, whom I had met in London, was expected to visit Australia in 1995.

43. Meanwhile, they brought Jimmy Adams and his family to the UK.

44. Their daughter's Australian mother-in-law accompanied the Corfields to India and loved it. The two women were close; Joyce's son-in-law built a house for

Joyce on the back of her co-mother-in-law's property, and the Australian woman was in the Hyderabadi widows' potluck group.

45. She could think of only one friend's child who had married someone from India.

46. "The British kept law and order, instilled fear. . . . [N]ow it's all a mess, there's no respect for elders," said Donald, and Winifred chimed in, "Those Andhras were so common, the Muslims were very superior."

47. They became citizens quickly and their children (including nieces they raised) were definitely Australian, they said, except the son who went to the UK directly (he stayed with Winifred's sister's son and has remained there). "The children just laugh" when there is talk of Hyderabad and their servants there (Winifred had never set foot in her kitchen). The Schoeffers visited Hyderabad in 1977, staying with friends for almost three months, but they "hated it." Winifred had forgotten her Urdu and could not even speak to her old servants.

48. Norma Oates convened a group for a November 22 interview and lunch. Those present were Norma and her daughters Joy and Gillian, Norma's sister Iris, Kathleen Chamarette again with her daughter Louise, and (briefly) Norma's son Tim, grandson Christian, Gillian's husband Vince and daughter Esra, and an India-born Sikh neighbor.

49. In Government of Hyderabad 1948, B. L. Oates appeared in the Hyderabad Civil Service list; he joined service in 1940–1941, or 1350 Fasli. Of the 131 names in the HCS list (353–355), his was the only English name.

50. The family became born-again Christians in 1959, leaving the Church of England and joining an American Fellowship, the Good News Center. Bryan had headed Gideon's International in India and given out many Bibles. After his death in 1989, Norma's daughters took her not only to Hyderabad but to Israel ("we just love the Jews and pray for them") and the UK. For Norma's seventieth birthday party, her daughters invited sixty people, all of them from Hyderabad except for a few missionary friends.

51. When she was young, they were still trying to be English, and Norma (and all her children) attended St. George's; Norma was then sent to Baldwin Girls High School in Bangalore. Anglo-Indians too had been part of a zenana culture, with boys and girls not mixing, Norma said.

52. After a first-born son, they had four daughters, and then Tim: "*Oates ke makan me beta paida hua*," the *hijras* said, "A son is born in Oates's house," and Bryan said, "Why not, let them come," and he gave them money.

53. Norma said, "We're not Indian, really," and said she had not been an Indian citizen. But she had had an Indian passport. "Oh, did that mean citizenship?" she said. After the lunch, Norma said to her daughter, "I'll sit like a rani and you clear, dear," and everyone discussed the best methods of getting out curry spots.

54. The plight of aging Anglo-Indians in modern India is beautifully illustrated by Jennifer Kendall's fine last film, *36 Chowringhee Lane*, directed by Aparna Sen (1981).

55. Present on November 21, 1993, at the Balm home were Pat and Malvern Balm, their daughter Marian, and their son Jude with his wife Shahnaz and baby Chelsea.

56. The list of Perth donors included people from the Balm, Brady, Cameron, Curtis, D'Costa, De Prazer, Footman, Fruvall, Hancock, Herft, James, La Touche, McDonald, Partridge, Paul, Ross, Wiekens, Williams, Wates, Schoeffer, Barrett, Stewart, and Isaacs families.

57. It was Balm who told me of one local Hyderabadi Muslim, a man who had been president of the Perth branch of the India League and reportedly married to an Anglo-Indian from Bombay. Balm knew him from school sports back home: Maqsud had played for Chaderghat School and Malvern for All Saints. Otherwise, Balm's Muslim friends were in Hyderabad, including the prominent woman who had given me his name. The Balms knew of Anglo-Indians in the Middle East, and four of Malvern's eight siblings were in Canada (two remained in Hyderabad, one had died in India, and one was in Melbourne); these four siblings tried shifting their families to Australia but came in 1989–1990 during a recession, and their children persuaded them to return to Canada.

58. They got papers to come in 1962 but his parents were in their eighties and could not be left in India; they tried again after his father's death, in 1965, but the children were very small, and they were engaged in a protracted court case. They sent their children on ahead, their daughter marrying an Indian Australian in 1985, and Charles's cousin and his wife, Henry and Joyce Corfield of Sydney, visited them in Hyderabad and urged them to migrate.

59. Blossom's mother taught in the Court of Wards (for minor children of members of the nobility and *jagirdars*) and knew all the old elite families; Blossom told stories of domestic disputes and YWCA politics (stories I knew to be true) involving other women leaders in Hyderabad. An alumnus of Mahbubiyah Girls' School and Nizam College, Blossom named numerous classmates in the UK, the United States, Pakistan, and Australia. She mentioned the strict purdah enforced during her school days. She had once been seated on the bus to school so that she could look out the windows if she wished, but she hadn't—the chaperones praised her, saying, "Look, she's not even a Muslim, but she's not peeping, while all of you are peeping."

60. Charles Corfield's mother, Edith Maud Farrell Corfield, inherited the six-acre estate from her brother, Robert Clive Farrell, in 1930; Robert had bought it in 1916 from the Chinoy Family Trust. Nizam Osman Ali Khan suggested the name, Tiger Hall: Corfield 1993, 163.

61. Joe's closest friend back in Secunderabad was a Parsi classmate, whom he missed intensely; Joe had been sent back to sell Tiger Hall but would need to go again.

62. Hanifa Dean-Oswald, Perth, November 23, 1993. See Abdullah 1993 for an account of those early days; also Deen 1995.

63. Jones 1993, 87–104; also the numerous entries for Muslims in Jupp 1988 and Johns and Saeed 2003, 195–216.

64. One-third of the Anjuman Taraqqi Urdu's 150 members were Hyderabadis, and a woman was current editor of the Anjuman's journal.

65. G. Q. Siddiqui applied to the United States and Australia in the late 1960s and chose Australia in 1970 because his wife's sister's husband, after some years in the Middle East, had gone there and liked it. He got a good job in Australia's

department of defense and the family took Australian citizenship in 1975. He had three daughters (one was married to a Pakistani, a second to an Indian) who considered themselves Hyderabadis and had visited there.

66. They had not thought about going to Pakistan themselves, but when they visited her sister there after settling in Australia, they thought Pakistani living standards were higher than Indian but that there was discrimination against muhajirs.

67. These families, of Qutbuddin Siddiqui, Dr. S. Bader Qadri, Mateen Abbas, Dr. Obeidullah Firdausi, and Dr. Secunder Khan, met once a month to eat, talk, and teach the children about Islam. Dr. K. Hemchander Rao added the name of Dr. Mahmood Ali, like Dr. S. Bader Qadri a Pakistan-trained Hyderabadi, who he thought had migrated first of all (and whose niece was a leading scientist in Los Angeles).

68. But there were two other contenders, depending on one's definition of Indian ancestry. Christopher Puplick, whose paternal grandmother was a Finglas from a Hyderabadi Anglo-Indian family, was Liberal Party senator from NSW and then chair of the NSW Anti-Discrimination Board (he was Fahmi Hussain's mentor). Christabel Chamarette, daughter of Arthur and Aileen Oates Chamarette from Hyderabad, was a leader of the Green Party in Perth.

69. The Islamic Council had twenty-four member associations and represented about 190,000 people, only 7 percent to 8 percent of them from India and Pakistan; others were chiefly from Lebanon, Turkey, Egypt, Yugoslavia, Malaysia, and Indonesia.

70. He stood in Auburn for the Liberal Party and lost, but got one-third of the votes. The election was held one month after the Gulf War ended.

71. The dinner to which they invited me turned out to be also their organizing meeting. I met them through the daughter of a Hyderabadi in Karachi, but except for her, the twenty or so people present were from India, including her husband (her father's nephew through both his mother and father).

72. Also present were Shehnaz Ali Khan, Sabiya ul Jabbar, Amjad Hussain, Maqbul Hussain, Samat Makri, Shahid Sayeed, Tahir uddin Meraj and Tahur Meraj, Dr. Amin, Rafi Ahmed, Dr. Majeed Siddiqui, Zahiruddin Ahmed, Abdur Rahman, Qutb Khan, Nazir, Mrs. and Mrs. Mussaffar, Zafar Shah Khan, Zaheer, and Ahmedullah.

73. Many Australian companies worked in the Middle East and Hyderabadis found opportunities there after moving to Australia.

74. One man told me the hijab was a Hyderabadi custom, but, when I disagreed, admitted his wife had begun to wear it during their stay in the Middle East.

75. The Edwardses' relatives included the Luschwitzes, Alex Norton, Ivan Oliver, and others who migrated in the 1950s. The Edwardses' parents were rejected then because of the "white Australia" policy; they were accepted in 1967 but did not go. They followed their sons, in 1977, but went back after three months; Kerry finally brought his father over in 1995, after their mother's death. Kerry Edwards, letter, 1999.

76. Kerry Edwards, letter, 1999.

77. I found this team because in Lahore, Pakistan, I had met the Pestonjees,

two of whose three sons had migrated to Australia. When I called one son in Sydney, he said that his Pakistani cricket team was playing the Deccan Blues that very Sunday at the Masonic Oval Ground on Seven Hills Road, Baulkham Hills. Raja Jayaraman of the University of Western Sydney and his wife drove me to the match, where Cyrus Pestonjee told me that he was "not a Hyderabadi." He then named a Parsi migrant to Australia whose wife had attended school with Raja's wife Mythhili in Hyderabad and whose phone number Mythili had been trying to find.

78. These teams were named for and loosely based on players from a variety of places: Hyderabad (the Deccan Blues), Karnataka, Maharashtra, Bengal, Kerala, and Sri Lanka (the Marions, Tamil-based). Movement from team to team occurred as players fell out with each other—a Deccan Blues man whose father had been a Madrasi Hyderabadi moved to the Karnataka team.

79. While working in Iraq, Cyrus Pestonjee was encouraged by an Australian colleague to try Australia; Dr. Obeidullah Khan had worked in the Middle East; Syed Murtaza Zaroque (of the Fakhr ul Mulk family, with a New Zealander wife) had worked in Bahrain.

80. At the game, I met (in addition to those already named) G. K. Mohan or Bobby (nephew of founder Dr. Harinath), Raj Murthy (Bombay), Khalid Qayyum, Abid Hasan, Asad Ali, Syed Shirazi, Ahsan, and Ashfaq (most of the latter were muhajirs from Pakistan).

81. Mrs. Rao was secretary of the Tamil Association for two years because a neighbor asked her to help when the Sydney Hindu temple was being built. The Raos were from Brahman *zamindari* (landowning) families in Warangal and Karimnagar districts.

82. Dr. Rao had been president of the Overseas Medical Graduates of Australia (OMGA) and of the India League, each time for three years. The OMGA dialogued with the Australian Medical Council on behalf of the 300 doctors from Pakistan and India as well as others of Chinese, Malaysian, European, and South African background. He spoke of declining membership because of a government quota of 10 percent overseas graduates for medical admissions, unlike the United States' unlimited recruitment by merit. The India League was founded in 1945 by a senior Australian as the India Australian Friendship Association; it lapsed and was revived in 1987 only to suffer from conflicts among the leaders. He was trying to amend the India League constitution to make it the umbrella organization for the thirteen or fourteen regional Indian associations in Australia.

83. Dr. Rao's brother's daughter was married to the son of the then prime minister of India, P. V. Narasimha Rao, who visited the Raos' home in Sydney three times.

84. Mrs. Rao noted that Australians assumed they and other immigrants had been poor at home and became rich in Australia, but they were rich in India too. Feeling it would have been rude to tell Australians this, she never mentioned it.

85. I talked to Mrs. Rao before he came home, and later Dr. Rao drove me to the station, so I saw them separately and together.

86. In Hyderabad, a Hindu "uncle" had given me Farha's name. She had gone to St. George's Grammar School, where there had still been Australian teachers.

Despite his excellent qualifications, her husband had trouble getting a good job in Australia, finally securing one through a Sri Lankan he had known in Kathmandu who had migrated earlier.

87. David Weinman, the "gatekeeper" for the Nizam, Mukarram Jah, to whom I had been referred by Alex Norton in Sydney, was looking for a biographer for the eighth Nizam, and I introduced him to Kamala, right there and sufficiently distanced from the intrigues that surrounded Mukarram Jah in Hyderabad. Co-incidentally, both Kamala and David had lived in Malaysia for some years. In David's earlier career as an auction broker in Geneva, the Nizam had been his first client, selling off some of his treasures (two Mughal *muhurs* or coins) from Hyderabad. David said I could meet Mukarram Jah, but I could not change my ticket to stay another day.

88. Kerry Edwards, letter, 1999.

89. Anne D'Costa said she wouldn't mind meeting the Nizam in Australia because, after all, she had gone to his first birthday party in Hyderabad, as her maternal grandfather, Dr. Newton Barrett, had been a physician to the Nizam; she would also have been glad to know of *mushairas*, since her Urdu was still good.

90. Joyce and Charles Westrip; and see Moore 1988.

91. A Yahoo Club site of St. George's Grammar School graduates to bring all SGGS students together was started recently, administered by Kerry Edwards, whose history of St. George's Church and School came out in 2005.

92. Anne D'Costa enthusiastically showed me a book on Mughal cuisine by a Hyderabadi woman settled in Malaysia whose family details she readily related: *Mughal Cuisine*, by Bilquis Jehan Naseruddeen Khan (Kuala Lumpur: Berita Publishing, 1982); she had bought the book on a visit back to Hyderabad.

93. In her novel about Sri Lankan immigrants in Australia, Yasmine Gooneratne criticizes some Sinhalese Buddhists for a similar rigidity: 1993, 87–98.

NOTES FOR CHAPTER 7

1. Roy, named by his father for the famous Bengali social reformer as an expression of sympathy for the nationalist movement developing outside of Hyderabad State, was a Gaur Kayasth from Shahalibanda (see Leonard 1978b). He majored in international relations and U.S. foreign policy and became professor of political science at California State University, Northridge. Four of his brothers and sisters have followed him to the United States. His two children were baptized Greek Orthodox and both married non-Indian Americans.

2. Omar Khalidi, using *Foreign Medical Graduates* (American Medical Association, 1990 [data from 1986]), found that 922 of the 17,991 graduates from India listed were Muslims, 462 of them from Hyderabad, and 10 more from coastal Andhra: Khalidi 1990; for the 4 percent estimate, *India-West*, February 26, 1993.

3. Only 12 percent of highly educated respondents answering a survey I took in 1992 were still in their first U.S. residence; 26 percent had lived in three to five cities in the United States, and 24 percent had lived in three or more countries since leaving Hyderabad. The survey was biased toward doctors and Muslims, distributed chiefly to a list of physicians of South Asian origin and to contacts

of two Muslim Hyderabadis; only 51 of the 465 people to whom it was given responded.

4. The Mulders listed the following (about half of whom stayed in the United States): C. Seshachari, Polly Chenoy, Isaac Sequeira, Feroza Jussawala, Deepak Gir, Raja Ramdass, H. B. Kulkarni, Sohrab Chenoy, Raminder Reddy, Vinod Reddy, Param Bedi, Neila Seshachari, Prasanna Reddy, Indira Neelameggham, Minhaj and Rafia Ghatala, Vishwa and Jhansi Reddy, and Daphne de Rebello: Helen and William Mulder, C. Seshachari, e-mails, September 2004.

5. A Mathur Kayasth (closely related to the Malwala noble family) from Chowk Maidan Khan, Mathur was close to Dr. Zore, editor of the Urdu journal *Sabras*, and had published a poem in the journal; he also knew Laik Ali of the Ittehad ul Muslimeen as a friend, "before everything changed."

6. Forty years later these friends were still in touch, visiting back and forth, seeing each other through divorces, remarriages, and illnesses. Those in the Philadelphia area celebrated Thanksgiving dinner together; the year I came through, V. Krishna Kumar, then a bachelor, cooked for the others.

7. The reference had multiple explanations but basically relied on the fact that many Muslims were settled there. One man joked that the city had become the tomb of many a Hyderabadi's hopes and dreams and that Hyderabadis there could rub shoulders with, not saints, but gangsters like Al Capone. Another said it simply recalled the term for the old city, *balda-i-sharif*, contrasting it with newer parts of Hyderabad.

8. The Pakistani Hyderabadis who ran the more upscale Shalimar Restaurant "had to be re-educated, had to take the rose water out of the *bagara baigan* and *biryani*." The other Hyderabadi restaurant, while more authentic, was "run by Chenchelguda people and was home cooking, no tandoor," one of my hosts in Chicago said.

9. Chicago was the headquarters of at least two major African-American Muslim movements: the Nation of Islam led by Louis Farrakhan and the American Society of Muslims led by W. D. Mohammed. Some 46 percent of Muslims in Chicago were African American, 20 percent were Arab, 19 percent South Asian, 11 percent Turkish, Bosnian, and other Eastern Europeans, and the rest were mixed. For the percentages, see Ansari 2004, 48.

10. Her father had been a deputy commissioner of police (*naib kotwal*) in charge of the Nizam's palaces; there was no family property left in Hyderabad, and only her father's sister-in-law lived there. Her other sisters and her in-laws were in Pakistan. Shakeela's daughters studied Urdu with Professor C. M. Naim at the University of Chicago, part of the second-generation Hyderabadi contingent that persuaded him to accept nonstandard Urdu in his classes. The first daughter married a doctor, and the couple and baby lived with the Hassans; the second was unmarried and practiced law in La Jolla; the third married a Hyderabadi in Chicago.

11. Here she mentioned Dr. Gita Srinivasan, an old classmate living in San Antonio, Texas, with a son married to an American and a daughter married to a Frenchman in San Francisco; she and Gita talked often on the phone.

12. When Michael Wolfe, American convert to Islam, started planning the film *Muhammad: Legacy of a Prophet*, he turned to Dr. Shakeela Hassan to head the fund-

raising efforts. The film was completed just after the September 11, 2001, attack on New York's World Trade Center and has been shown on public television.

13. Hashmy's father had been secretary of the Nizam's Charitable Trust and the family lived in the old city Fateh Darwaza locality (see figure 2.5). Khatija's father, Syed Ali, was an IAS man.

14. Mansoor Ali was the son of two doctors, his father a surgeon educated in London and his mother the first woman doctor in Trinidad, where she had converted to Islam. The couple met in London, where Mansoor was born, then lived in Hyderabad and Trinidad. In Hyderabad, Mansoor's mother practiced at Osmania Hospital and started the queue system, making people wait in line in order of arrival, not status. She started village *dudhkhanas* (milk stations) for babies and was gynecologist to "the best families" (she delivered Khatija, wife of Asif Ali Hashmy, above). Meher's maternal grandfather was *qiladar* (commander of a fort) of Golconda and her paternal grandmother was the daughter of Afsar ul Mulk, top hunter, polo player, and the Nizam's highest-ranking army officer.

15. Meher's mother-in-law told her, "Finish your education; don't depend on men, even on my son." Meher's first school opened in the Faith United Methodist Church and she borrowed money on their first home to start it.

16. Meher went to Pakistan twice and disliked it; she also disliked Islamic fundamentalists in Chicago and advised her daughters to join world organizations rather than the Muslim Student Association. The eldest daughter studied in London and the second in Paris; the third was fifteen in 1991.

17. Dr. Irene Rebello headed the Victoria Zenana Hospital and built her own hospital in the new city. Known for charity work, she received a medal from the pope. Another sister, a surgeon in London, urged Noel to do a documentary on Dr. Rebello. Noel went to St. George's Grammar School, then to boarding school in Ooti.

18. Some who did go back to Hyderabad tried to fulfill their scholarship obligation to work for the state for three years, but the administrative disruption lasted almost a decade after 1948; if no job was offered, the student was free to go back to the United States or to Pakistan.

19. In Donna's visits to both Karachi and Hyderabad, she found that the family's background of wealth and property inhibited ambition and limited education, especially of daughters. A notable exception was Anees Khan, from the Hyderabad branch of the family, who stayed with Donna and K. M. while getting a degree in education and now runs Hyderabad's successful Nasr School.

20. Hussain, from the family of Afsar Jung and Amin Jung, attended St. Joseph's Convent, the Doon School, and Aligarh Muslim University. His mother's grandfather's place was Rahat Manzil, a 165-room mansion in Panjagutta; when family members tried to draw a floor plan in 1948 for a compensation case filed in Pakistan, they were unable to do so.

21. Shafi felt his family in Hyderabad was too nostalgic about the old Hyderabadi culture, like many immigrants in the United States who reproduced the hierarchies of the old state in their new setting. He attended St. John's and Madras-i-Aliya; he "did not favor any culture, having gone through three national anthems in India: "God Save the Queen," the Nizam's anthem, and then India's.

22. Ahmed's brother in San Francisco studied at Fordham and married an American woman; Ahmed's daughter went back to Hyderabad at age two, returned for visits between sixteen and eighteen, and lived with him in 1992.

23. Princess Esin in London had given me Niloufer's phone number as the president of a Hyderabad association and member of an old family; Mrs. Ulla's family home was in Khairatabad, her husband's in Begumpet.

24. Faizi worked with Islamic schools in southern California, as principal of a South Bay Islamic school and author of Islamic textbooks for children. Her mother was from the Nizam's family, and Faizi felt she had escaped marriage into that family; four of her uncles had married daughters of the Nizam. Her older brother studied in the UK on a Nizam's Trust grant, married a Norwegian, and worked for the UN in Geneva; her other brother worked in Saudi Arabia, had a Hyderabadi wife, and cared for their mother there.

25. Junaid Razvi, e-mails, November, 2004.

26. Razvi retired as a successful journalist in Karachi, Habiba taught at the Pakistan American Cultural Center in Karachi. Habiba's father Habib ur-Rahman took a plane to Karachi in 1991 and died shortly after arrival at his daughter's Clifton home.

27. Shehbaz was very close to the descendants of Dr. Bankat Chandra and Badrivishal Pitti. See Safrani 1992.

28. From Asifnagar in the old city, Asad attended Anwar ul Ulum and Nizam College before Osmania; his wife attended St. Anne's Convent and the Residency Women's College. Of 100 medical students from the Osmania 1968 class, fifty were in the United States and the rest in the UK and Hyderabad.

29. Mohan's father, uncles, and brothers went to Presidency College, Madras. From the Vellama caste, he married a Poona Brahmin classmate. In one sense, Mohan said, the true Hyderabadis were Muslims, also a few Kayasths, Maharashtrians, and Telingana Telugus. He had a condo in Hyderabad. "It's a condo city now," he said.

30. His mother taught him to serve water to a guest in a clean glass not filled to the rim, to walk without speaking, and to present it in a certain way; if the server spoke, the water had to be thrown out and the glass refilled in case one's saliva had gotten into it. He had other advice: allow no wrinkles in carpets, sit in one position only during an all-night *qawwali*, sons must take care of aging fathers, mothers must not work when children are young, and so on. He attended City College, Nizam College, and Osmania.

31. His father was Osmania's first Ph.D. in Arabic literature; his mother's side, however, was from Kurnool and spoke Telugu.

32. Anand was from a Telugu-speaking Telingana Kapu family and married Leela, an old city Urdu-speaking Mathur Kayasth, in 1977 (the marriage was arranged through his older brother's wife, a friend of Leela's). Anand and Leela both studied at Osmania, and the United States was enticing to them, as they associated it with movies and cars and environmental engineering. Leela had taught in Hyderabad and taught English as a second language in Davis.

33. Suraiya had offers, and her father and four of her six brothers were in the United States, so she accepted a job at UC Berkeley. She, her husband, two children, and four suitcases moved but intended to return to the UK. Because

the job at Berkeley did not materialize, the family drove to Los Angeles with a brother's Hyderabadi friend, rented an apartment, bought a car, and began again. Her husband worked as an accountant for the city of Los Angeles. Suraiya's uncle, Dr. Mohammed Ali, the first person in her family to go out for education (to the UK) had migrated to Australia. She said most women in Hyderabad in the 1950s were being educated; she had attended church with Christian classmates at Christmas and Diwali events with Hindu classmates. Her loyalty was to Pakistan, not India, and she was active in Muslim religious activities; I heard her speaking about HIV/AIDS at the mosque near USC, admonishing Muslims who thought the disease could not affect them. She was professor of pathology and director of the viral oncology laboratory and AIDS research.

34. When her old classmate Lakshmi Devi Raj came from Hyderabad to Los Angeles to visit her son, Shamim held a *mushaira* for her, but Lakshmi's son did not attend.

35. Shamim was also a licensed marriage and family counselor. Her son was a doctor in the San Fernando Valley, and her daughter, also a doctor, joined a medical practice in San Diego nicknamed the "Catholic Boys." Shamim's brother Dr. Khaja lived in Rancho Palos Verdes and her mother lived in Pakistan near other relatives.

36. Dr. Samee's two brothers practiced medicine in Chicago, and his sister, also a doctor and married to a doctor, moved from Abu Dhabi to the United States in 1991. It was Dr. Samee who first invited me to a Hyderabadi home in southern California after we met at the 1990 Hyderabad association dinner. I followed his leads to Hyderabadi Urdu poets and writers in other countries. Other Hyderabadis in the India coalition included S. M. Shahed and Riyaz Mahdi, both of whom moved to California after their University of Wisconsin student days; Mahdi became a Sufi and changed his name to John Ishvaradas-Abdallah.

37. Sidhu's father was director of the federal Regional Research Laboratories in Hyderabad; Sidhu attended Hyderabad Public School, studied chemical engineering at Osmania, and earned a master's degree in it at Oklahoma State University. After working for Texas Instruments, he started his own company in 1988. Dr. Abdul Ali grew up in the old city and attended Osmania. The author Narendra Luther, former chief justice Pingle Jagan Mohan Reddy, and former vice-chancellor of Osmania and Aligarh Muslim University Syed Hashim Ali all went for bypass surgery in Houston, performed by Dr. Denton Cooley or Dr. Abdul Ali.

38. Dr. Razvi, a geophysicist, immigrated in 1977 and has edited the Houston Hyderabad Association newsletter since 1986. People said that Razvi had so many relatives in Houston he could fill a hall with them for any event; there were many, many Shia Muslim Hyderabadis in Houston (and in Chicago).

39. Sara's brother Zubair Noor ul Haq studied in New Mexico in 1962, earning a master of science at the University of Oregon and working as a geologist in Canada and Oregon before Houston; Sara's sister's family moved to Houston from Chicago in 1976. Only eight of Sara's thirty-two first cousins were still in Hyderabad in 1993: fourteen were in Pakistan, seven were in North America, two were in the Middle East, and one was in France.

40. In Hyderabad, a servant held up his wife's *dupatta* (a long scarf draped across

one's bodice and over the shoulders, hanging down behind) when she used the toilet, Rizvi said (others mentioned this service). Shahnaz justified wearing hijab because in the United States the women were always moving about in public, "on the road, on the road, all the time, with no servants, driving ourselves, that's why one should wear hijab and have two living rooms (one for the men, one for the women)."

41. Some twenty-five of these families were from Hyderabad, India, and another fifty from Pakistan, but the latter were "not called Hyderabadis," the Ahmeds qualified. They wanted to arrange their son's marriage to a Hyderabadi brought up in America (the daughter will not allow an arrangement) and would even consider a Pakistani Hyderabadi, however, for him. The Ahmeds' daughter later married an American who converted to Islam.

42. Javeed, from Warangal, had two brothers and his mother in Chicago and a sister in Indianapolis with her husband, the latter doing graduate work in engineering. Mahjabeen, from Mehdipatnam, had made friends and had learned that she could change herself, she said, in the United States. There were five other Muslim families in their building, two from Hyderabad, two from Delhi, and one from Egypt.

43. Chishti was an administrator at Osmania for thirty-two years and then worked in Saudi Arabia briefly before coming to Chicago. He had many relatives in Pakistan and Hyderabad, his wife had many relatives in Hyderabad, and they visited both countries. Chishti wrote for California's *Pakistan Link* and for *Siyasat*. His elder son was a computer engineer; the second one had a master of science degree, and the daughters were married.

44. Jeff followed his father to St. George's Grammar School and Hyderabad Public School (Feroze had also attended Madras-i-Aliya, All Saints, and Nizam College), then got a one-year scholarship to Perugia, Italy, and proceeded to Dallas for a bachelor of science in physics and then an M.B.A. Jennifer, the second child, married the youngest son of Bollywood's G. P. Sippi and lived in Bangalore but brought her sons to Dallas. Rosalind, the third, married an Anglo-Indian son of a classmate of Laura's brothers in Secunderabad and brought him to Dallas. Lorraine, the fourth, married a Briton, and David, the fifth, married an English Italian woman. Laura's brothers were in Australia and Canada; the one in Secunderabad had died. Feroze had learned of my research from Laura's Australian relatives and wrote to me.

45. In Chicago, for example, there was an Osmania Graduates Association and also a Hyderabadi-dominated Aligarh Association. There was no St. George's Old Boys' association there in 1993 (although Chicago has since hosted St. George's and Madras-i-Aliya reunions) and there was no Mahbubiyah School Old Girls' association. Mahbubiyah alumnus Khatija Hashmy explained that she had no classmates in Chicago, that the school had lost its elite character after about 1955–1956; those who formed the association in Karachi had moved there just after the last few good years, she said.

46. Ali was president, with nine other board members (including Professor K. D. Mathur and two women).

47. The foundation sponsored Harvard professor Ann-Marie Schimmel to

speak on Hyderabadi history, culture, and language at the local American Islamic College in 1985. *The Letter* had an editor and a managing editor and was published for more than fifteen years with only a slight diminution in quality and regularity; it added pages in Urdu in 1990. Five men and a woman were on the first board of trustees.

48. The 1988 annual dinner benefited the Princess Durru Shehvar Charitable Children's Hospital in Hyderabad, and the princess attended along with Prince Muffakham Jah and Princess Esin.

49. Thus I learned of the Hyderabad Association of Iowa (formed in 1986 and kicked off by a gala dinner with Pakistan's ambassador to Burma as chief guest) and the Hyderabad Association of Houston. Houston's *ghazal* evening in 1986 featured a singer, Hanif Noor Mohammed, from Los Angeles. In 1988, new associations in Atlanta, Georgia, and northern California were noted.

50. I spoke at this event on November 23, 1996. Mirza Ahmed Baig, the founding president, said that the association's core participants were "those involved with traditional Hyderabad, not those who were lower class there and not part of the culture; those people are involved with Islamic associations in the United States." The children's dance teacher was from the Hindu Kayasth caste and two of the four girls were also Kayasths. Few Hindus were members; the hundreds of Telugu-speakers in the area were not considered and did not consider themselves to be Hyderabadis.

51. Parvez 2000; Kawaja 2002, 27; Moazzam Siddiqi, e-mail from Washington, D.C., September 24, 2004. Siddiqi came to UC Berkeley in 1965 to study entomology but switched to Near Eastern and South Asian studies; after teaching at Berkeley, the University of Virginia, and Duke, he worked for the Voice of America in various capacities.

52. It was first led by Hasan Raza, then by Mohammad Yacoob, Shakir Malik Khan (whose brother headed the Toronto association), and Dr. Syed Samee.

53. On April 24, 1995, this association convened to see slides of my trip to Uzbekistan with a London Hyderabadi and another friend; afterward, several members advised me to show more slides of Islamic sites and not so many of Aziz drinking vodka.

54. The Nizam donated a much-needed $34,700: Abdul-Rauf ca. 1978, 22, 95.

55. Mateen Cheeda was a graduate student at the University of Minnesota and Ather A. Quader earned a master of science degree in engineering from Oklahoma State and a Ph.D. from the University of Wisconsin. Both were still active, the first in Islamic publishing and the *halal* grocery business and the second in Detroit's South Asian Muslim community (Moazzam Siddiqi, e-mail from Washington, D.C., September 24, 2004).

56. See Leonard 2001. Of the fifty-four participants listed as attending a 1991 conference in Chicago of the North American Conference of Indian Muslims, nineteen were Hyderabadis.

57. Louis Farrakhan's Nation of Islam deviated in significant ways from orthodox Islam, as the Ahmadis were also alleged to do. See Leonard 2003b. African-American Muslim movements led by W. D. Mohammed and others were generally accepted.

58. Amir Ali's father died in 1948, and his mother remarried in 1950–1951; he lived with an uncle and attended City College. Student demonstrations in 1952 led to the killing of students at the Medina Hotel in the old city, and he left for Pakistan and later returned to escort his mother and brother and sisters to Karachi. He brought most of his family to the United States; only three sisters (of seven siblings) were still in Pakistan.

59. Professor Waqar Ahmed Husaini, a Hyderabadi from Cupertino in northern California, was affiliated with this college; an Islamic activist, he contacted me in June of 1993 and criticized "the course on Islam you are teaching" as presenting relativist perspectives on Islam (but the course he described was a colleague's anthropology course comparing Muslims in several countries).

60. The CCIM worked to further the education of Muslims in India, starting with the lower grades to prevent Muslims from falling behind. Farooqui helped found this organization in 1968 after communal riots in Ahmedabad, and at its height it had local centers in Washington, D.C., Houston, New York, Detroit, Cleveland, and Toronto, Canada. Many participants were from Hyderabad, and the CCIM operated from homes, the MCC, and, later, through ISNA.

61. Bilquees missed her high school leaving exam because it conflicted with her wedding. Her next three sisters went to college before their weddings, but she studied Urdu poetry and literature at home. The first three of her six sisters were married in Hyderabad; the five younger of the eight siblings were settled in the Chicago area. When her son married in Hyderabad, her younger daughter had important exams and did not go. The older daughter majored in English at Northwestern and earned a master of science in marketing. The younger son studied accounting and the younger daughter attended Michigan State University.

62. Usama Khalidi went to Germany in 1970 and worked there as a journalist for two years before coming to the United States. He spent two years in Columbia, Missouri, seven years in Wichita, Kansas (where an uncle had settled), two years in Oman in the Peace Corps, and then moved to West Virginia and finally Virginia. His first marriage to an American Jewish woman ended in the 1980s and he married Nayeema, a Hyderabadi Muslim; he worked for the U.S. Internal Revenue Service and she for Sprint. Usama and Nayeema named their first daughter for a Mughal princess, Anjum Ara, Aurangzeb's sister; their two daughters were being taught Hyderabadi culture and how to be good Muslims.

63. The first was Tasneem Siddiqui's 1992 wedding at the Buena Park Hotel, California; the second was Naseem and Tom Erspamer's 1999 wedding, also in southern California.

64. In Los Angeles, the leader of the Urdu Markaz (Urdu Center) was Nayyar Jahan, who traced her roots to Amaravati, Berar (Berar was once part of Hyderabad State but had been under British rule since the 1850s, a situation always contested). She moved to Hyderabad city with her family just before the Police Action, when Muslims from the districts sought sanctuary in the Nizam's capital city. Her path to the United States was via East Pakistan, and she ran the Urdu Markaz in southern California for many years.

65. Muqtedar Khan, a political scientist who studies Islam in America, married a "Brahman-born" daughter of a serving Indian Army general. Urfi, youngest

brother of Usama and Omar Khalidi, married the "Brahman-born" girl next door.

66. One Pakistani Hyderabadi Muslim woman found an American man and waited four years for her parents to give her permission to marry him; in another case, an Indian Hyderabadi Muslim woman waited more than seven years. Both couples lived together and waited patiently, unwilling to hurt the women's parents or provoke major conflicts. One couple married secretly before moving in together and held a public wedding when parental consent was finally obtained. A tragic ending came for another young Hyderabadi Muslim woman whose Asian American boyfriend agreed to convert and went through a public engagement ceremony. But he was an only child, and his parents refused to agree to his marrying until he finished medical school, for which they were paying. This four-year delay was not acceptable to the woman's parents because she had a younger sister whose marriage could not be postponed that long, so the engagement was annulled and the young woman's marriage was arranged to someone else.

67. Originally from Bombay, Bilkiz Alladin married into Hyderabad in 1954. A conservative grandmother thwarted her early educational goals, but once in Hyderabad she wrote plays and books and participated in many local societies.

68. Prince Muffakham Jah had just been to Hyderabad associations in San Jose and Chicago, and he mentioned two in Texas, two in Georgia, and one in Washington, D.C. He suggested that the Association sponsor cooking classes by Abdus Sattar of Mecca Meats.

69. The president of this forum was Amjad Ali Khan in Hyderabad, a Nizam Club stalwart, and it was strongly supported by Hyderabadis in Houston.

70. The group had powerful backing. After meeting with me, Dr. Mohan was lunching with India's ambassador to the United States, Abid Hussain, a Hyderabadi, and Mr. Narasimhan, who had replaced Jagan Mohan Reddy as the second general chair of SHARE; Narasimhan was former governor of the Reserve Bank of India and an executive director of the World Bank.

NOTES FOR CHAPTER 8

1. Rashida Mirza's parents had moved to Karachi after the Police Action, following her father's boss, Laik Ali; her father became chief officer of the Hyderabad Trust. Rashida was related to Captain Massoud Baig in Karachi and Zubair ul Haq in Houston; both she and Kamran, through their great-grandmother, a daughter of the Nawab of Loharu, were related to Colonel Mirza in Lahore.

2. Correia 2001a, 26i.

3. Of Haroon Siddiqui's four siblings, one was in Hyderabad, one was in Karachi (along with his first cousins), and two were in Canada.

4. Her brother, Siddiq Burney, had gone to Canada in 1964, a pioneer in the Burlington area southwest of Toronto, recruited by a Canadian immigration officer in Hyderabad's Ritz Hotel at a time when members of the Hyderabad nobility were still adjusting to the changes after 1948.

5. Correia 2001b, 24f. According to Siddiqui, his ex-brother-in-law, Siddiq Burney, started a Hyderabad Foundation branch in Burlington.

6. Desh's father had gone to a Hindu revivalist Arya Samaj school in Hardwar and then attended a *mushaira* in Aurangabad, where Abdul Huq (of Urdu Hall fame) was vice-chancellor of the university. Haq admired his recitation and hired him as a professor there. The professor then married a woman from Aurangabad (a Khatri, Maharajah Kishen Pershad's caste) and moved to Hyderabad. Desh had a sister in Hyderabad and a younger brother in Philadelphia.

7. Zehra sought support from her brother in Arizona and her stepmother in Houston. Her divorce was almost immediate; his took longer, but they were finally married in Arizona. His family cut him off, and few in Hyderabad would receive the couple. Her ex-husband remarried and started another family; Desh's wife also remarried briefly.

8. Desh and Zehra were my hosts in Toronto, and people reacted with disapproval when I told them where I was staying.

9. He was the son of Amin Jung, related to K. M. Hussein in Sacramento and Ahmed Lateef in Los Angeles. Before leaving India, Ather had gotten his son into St. George's, urging the principal Bellingham to look in the files for the 1898 paper given to Amin Jung's family saying the school would take anyone from that family. In 1898, he said proudly, only 6 percent of the boys were Indian; the rest were Anglo-Indian. Ather stayed in his son's old college rooms.

10. Best known is Ahmad 1964.

11. He went to Madras-i-Aliya, All Saints, then Nizam College. Three of his five brothers were educated in Chicago and one in Texas; all were married to Hyderabadi women, their weddings held in Hyderabad. His father had fifty-four children, eight of them legitimate, he said.

12. Alikhan mentioned Srinivas Reddy and Sudhakar Reddy in Hyderabad, Shafi Babu Khan, Akbar Hassan, and Nowshir Khan in Los Angeles, and Dr. Shakeela Ahmed in Chicago.

13. I had his address from his father, Fareed Mirza, the courageous officer in the Hyderabad Civil Service who criticized the Nizam just before the Police Action, and I had brought along a video about the Police Action featuring an interview with his father for Farooq to copy.

14. One of her sisters, Meeraj, followed Shehnaz to Canada when Farooq's classmate, in Canada, saw her photo and went to Hyderabad to marry her; another sister was Doctor Khurshed, wife of Chandrakant Gir's brother, Dilip Gir, in Chicago.

15. Both Farooq and his father in Hyderabad termed this brother "too religious." The Jamat is an apolitical pietistic Islamic movement based in South Asia.

16. She and her brother were Canadian citizens; he was working in Dubai. She found the younger generation in the UK very similar to that in Canada, although "it has a harder time there," and, visiting the United States, she felt "there was less or no prejudice there."

17. From Hyderabad's old city, the colonel had attended Bishop Cotton's School and gone to the Officer's Training Academy of the British Indian Army in the early 1940s; he served until 1974 (from 1943 to 1951 in Hyderabad's Imperial Service Lancers).

18. The colonel knew Anglo-Indian Hyderabadis, a D'Costa, a Luschwitz, a

Phillips, and a Cox, in Canada, Australia, the United States, and South Africa, respectively; he had met Ali Edroos in Jordan, where Edroos was King Hussein's military adviser, and he fondly recalled Brigadier Taufiq, who had been his polo instructor.

19. Firoz and Parvez Moos, Parsis, were settled in Montreal and attended the reunion. Firoz had been sent from Toronto to Montreal by his business and his Hyderabadi friends in Toronto told him not to go, because it was French-speaking. But they, like the other Hyderabadi residents there, loved the city and relished its beauty, easy pace, and friendly people.

20. Rashida Mirza's cousin was president of the Pakistan Canadian Council in Montreal, for example.

21. Shahid Malik Khan and his brother, Shakir Malik Khan (an early leader of the Los Angeles Hyderabad association), were the sons of Mohammed Abdul Waheed Khan, noted scholar and head of the former state's archaeological department. Shahid held a *mushaira* while I was in Toronto; my hosts and I were invited but did not attend.

22. Prince Muffakham Jah and Princess Esin photocopied their copy of this booklet for me in London. The Hyderabad contact was Raza Alikhan and the Toronto contact for host family accommodation was Nawab Asif Alikhan. Organizers included Naseer Khan, Sadiq Alikhan, Dilras Faizuddin, Sultan Abu Talib, Imtiaz Hussain, and Nayeem Warisi.

23. http://deccanhyderabad.org.

24. Jamal Khan, e-mails from Toronto, February 12 and March 11, 2002.

25. An Id dinner held in March 2001 featured songs, poems, and *qawwalis* at Mississauga's Hyderabadi-owned banquet hall, Monte Bianco. Some funds from that event were donated to victims of the terrible Gujarat earthquake of early 2001. A third event helped with an international Muslims' interfaith conference, with Toronto's police chief as the chief guest. A fourth event in December 2001 celebrated Diwali, Id, and Christmas with attendance from Hindus, Muslims, Christians, Sikhs, Jains, and Parsis.

26. However, the new organization's leaders hosted Pakistani author Shah Baleeqhuddin, whom I interviewed in Karachi, promoting his Urdu book on some 250 outstanding Osmanians of the early period; his book, *Tazkiri-e-Osmanian*, was also advertised and distributed in the United States.

27. Urdu enthusiasts in Los Angeles, Melbourne, and Sydney referred me to this group.

NOTES FOR CHAPTER 9

1. I tried to get a visa for Saudi Arabia, but despite the best efforts of well-placed Hyderabadis there, I failed, since I had no husband (I am a widow) or male blood relative able to accompany me there.

2. I had not seen Mirza since 1984, when he befriended me and my daughter in Secunderabad (he gave her a Beatles tape). A young teenager whose ambition was to be an air conditioner repairman in the Gulf, he kept in touch with us via Christmas cards. I had written ahead to several Hyderabadis, but it was Mirza who

met me at the Kuwait airport. He had tried to line up affordable housing for me, his Hyderabadi doctor in Kuwait encouraging him to approach a big Hyderabadi businessman, but the latter was too busy; Mirza and I found a good hotel.

3. His best friend, Ashok, whose mother taught in the same school as Mirza's mother, had gone to the United States and married a Kenyan Sindhi with British citizenship (the sister of a co-worker), but Ashok had bought a lot in Secunderabad near Mirza; the young men wanted to start businesses in India. A student of Mirza's mother started a business in Brunei, taking workers there, while an older neighbor, an engineer with a German degree, had retired from the Indian Air Force and was working on irrigation projects in Saudi Arabia.

4. It reminded me of the Medina Hotel area in Hyderabad's old city. On August 4, Mirza and I met two other air conditioning repairmen from Secunderabad, one of them a former student of Mirza's mother. We had tea in the Mann-o-Salwa and talked to jewelry shop salesmen from the Purana Pul and Falaknuma areas of the old city, flashily dressed young men of twenty-three and twenty-four who had been in Kuwait two or three years. Hafiz, the restaurant cook, had been there ten years, and before the Invasion the sign had advertised Hyderabadi *biryani*; the sign was down but people still knew. Another feature of the restaurant was the daily appearance there of a "social worker" from Hyderabad, Qadir Naqvi, who counseled people (he did this voluntarily but worked for the education department; he was also a key member of the Hyderabad Muslim Welfare Organization). Outside, we met several drivers, for ministries or Kuwaiti families, men from Yaqutpura and Char Minar in the old city, and one from Khairatabad in the new city. Many worked for the Kuwait Petrol Company and the Transport Corporation.

5. A man from the Indian embassy, when I repeated a story about a maid weeping on the beach because her charges had eluded her supervision, said, "Arab kids are very naughty, very spoiled; they must be watched every second. And maids like to talk—two minutes and the kids will be gone."

6. From Aghapura, Hamad had a diploma in electrical engineering from Government Polytechnic but could not get a job in Hyderabad; his wife was from Husaini Alam. It was her cousin brother Abdul Karim, from Fateh Darwaza in the old city, who was president of the current Hyderabad Association, of which more later. They knew no Hindu Hyderabadis in Kuwait, although he then recollected a Srivastava Kayasth who came into the shop, and my friend Mirza just then brought into the shop Kola Shankar, a Hindu Hyderabadi who was a security guard at the American Embassy in Kuwait.

7. For example, for medical school, an M.B.B.S. program, ten to twelve lakhs (1,000,000 to 1,200,000 rupees) "donation" would be taken, and seats were very competitive. The Muffakham Jah Engineering College did not take donations, but there was no medical school that did not.

8. Two businessmen, Mohammed Hoshdar Khan and Mir Ibrahim Ali Khan, said that Andhra's chief minister N. T. Rama Rao was "not against Muslim culture, although he is pro-Hindu, but that is different. He keeps law and order, a very important element in daily life."

9. Prasad said Hyderabad-style jewelry was not in stock, was not wanted in Kuwait; his brother-in-law, a goldsmith, was also in Kuwait. He did not know of a Hyderabad association but did know of an Andhra one and recommended a

place for South Indian snacks—*idli* and *dosas*. His clerk, Abdur Rahman, had come after tenth class to Kuwait, learned the jewelry business from an Irani, and then brought his three brothers, who were also working in jewelry stores.

10. Khan's cousin had come in 1982, and about a quarter of his family was in Kuwait.

11. The group aided students, religious schools, and a career guidance center back in Hyderabad; it also had an Urdu library in Kuwait. Mrs. Hamad Nazmuddin's cousin brother, Abdul Karim, was president and it met every second Friday after prayers in the mosque where he had an apartment. Abdul Karim worked for Hyundai. The meetings in his apartment were for men only, so we arranged a meeting at a restaurant. Those present included Mohammed Abdul Karim, president of the Hyderabad Muslim Welfare Organization; Mr. Ehtashamuddin, its convenor; M. Nizamuddin Ahmed; Mohammed Habib-al-Deen and son Mohammed Zaneer; Abdul Mateen Khan; and Qadir Naqvi, the "social worker" who sat daily at the Mann-o-Salwa.

12. They asserted that when Andhra was created in 1956 (linguistic states' reorganization), the higher educational standards in British India put Hyderabadis at an immediate disadvantage, a view not shared by those who attended better schools.

13. Zainul Abuddin, Baliya, Bad Shah Khan, and others present had all come in September 1991, some eighty visa-holders at once.

14. Then in Hyderabad for a Bosnia conference, Hoshdar Khan had sponsored not just eighty workers to Kuwait after Liberation but 1000; his staff had spent days doing nothing but filling out visa forms, which a Lebanese *mandouba* (agent) took to Kuwaiti government departments.

15. Akbar had stayed in Kuwait twenty-two days past the Invasion and said that no difficulties had been posed for Indians; he went to his factory daily and visited friends and relatives, although he sent his children to India; he even ignored the 5 P.M. curfew and came home at 7 or 8.

16. This was Prem Singh; Akbar looked up his name in the cricket program, repeating that Khan and the ambassador were great friends.

17. From Narayanguda in the new city, Kola left school after the tenth class. Dressed when I met him in an American-style open shirt, he greeted me by my first name (Mrs. Karen) and exhibited other "American" characteristics. He said the job was good because, while hard, it was only eight hours. For our talk, we could not sit in one air-conditioned sitting room because it was for U.S. citizens only and another, the resource center, had closed early because of a meeting; Kola encouraged me to leave a complaint note about that.

18. From Husaini Alam, the family decided to stay in India in 1948. Famous singers, especially of songs by Iqbal, the father and several of the brothers attended various political functions, including ones with Sarojini Naidu, the Nawab of Chattari, and Jinnah; Aqueel had a photo of himself on Jinnah's lap but threw it down the well when the Police Action came.

19. D. P. Jain, second secretary in the Indian Embassy in Kuwait, gave the number of Indians as 180,000 to 185,000, although not all were registered with the embassy. Everyone agreed that most were from Kerala, and next most from AP. Estimates by Hyderabadis of Hyderabadis ranged from 3,000 to 13,000.

20. Aqueel attended Osmania, then the Indian Institute of Technology, and an air conditioning institute (both in Bombay), then studied in the UK and the Netherlands. Aqueel had two brothers in Hyderabad, one in Toronto, and one in London; he had one sister in Bombay (married to Rizwana's brother) and two in Hyderabad.

21. The Azimuddin's daughter was to marry the son of Rizwana's first cousin in Karachi in a Hyderabad wedding; the groom would work in Kuwait. The couple met when the Azimuddins were evacuated in 1990 to Karachi. Rizwana, from Bombay, said "Still Hyderabadis are the same, old, lazy Nawabi types; I always want to jab them, give them Benzine."

22. Bilgrami's brother had gone to Iraq in 1955; their uncle was Sadath Ali Khan. Bilgrami's wife was from the family associated with the *dargah* (shrine) of Hazrat Abbas in Salar Jung's old city palace, a family that had moved from Iraq 500 years earlier; Bilgrami's family had moved 800 years earlier.

23. From Bilgrami and other businessmen in the Gulf I first heard of Khan Lateef Khan, whom Bilgrami termed "a helpful guy, a multimillionaire from Chicago; I heard many adjectives about him; he's getting into business and politics in Hyderabad, he's close to both princes." Khan, a Sunni, had taken a daughter of Bilgrami's father's uncle as one of his wives (see chapters 10 and 11).

24. He had one Hyderabadi foreman, and named four other Hyderabadis, two Muslims, a Hindu, and a Christian, who were working for him; he named another but his secretary and driver said that fellow was from Madras. Bilgrami sent his car to my hotel for me, and the Goanese Christian driver pointed out his church on the way to Bilgrami's office.

25. Asked by the Kuwaiti resistance to stay on, get equipment from the Iraqis, and give it to the Kuwaitis, Bilgrami had done that, and his was the first company to operate again after Liberation on February 27. His children, in their twenties and unmarried, held good jobs in Kuwait as computer programmers in banks (two daughters) and head of sales in the company (son). The son, driving back with me in the car, identified himself as both Kuwaiti and Hyderabadi.

26. Bilgrami was one of five brothers and four sisters; the other two sisters were in Karachi and Hyderabad; the brothers (three retired from Aramco) were in Madras and Hyderabad. He mentioned Shia fears of the Ittehad ul Muslimeen leader Kazim Razvi in Hyderabad in 1948, but said that in India, after the 1992 Babri Masjid incident, all Muslims were united; such conflict was only in Pakistan. His name was on the list of the Indian Muslim Welfare Association, which he showed me after scratching his name off (he disliked the Indian Embassy's assumption of his membership), and he checked off fifteen of the forty-eight names as Hyderabadis but asked me to have someone else verify this as he was not certain.

27. The other families were those of Hyder Hussain, son of Amin Jung, who had just died in Chicago, and Asad Bhai, who had died young in 1972.

28. When golfing, one met other merchants and businessmen, Bilgrami said, and he often went to Syria and Iran for golfing holidays. He volunteered that his daughters did not necessarily want to marry men brought up in Hyderabad and were looking at prospective husbands' educational and earning levels.

29. Parveen thanked me for the opportunity to eat out with her husband, who usually got home very late after dinner with others. He and she had a number of small disagreements—about his long work hours that kept him from home and family, about Muslim men in her opinion using Islam against women, about her gaining weight (not apparent to me, but perhaps enough to disqualify her from entering Australia), about her going to Dubai (which he admitted was more fun but might tempt her to do too much shopping).

30. Mukarram had graduated with a chemistry degree from Osmania in 1967 and, not satisfied with the job offers he got in Hyderabad, went to the Middle East. He also owned two restaurants: one a contract-meal restaurant for bachelor workers, the other the Indian (changing to Greek) restaurant that Shahid, Parveen, and I had tried to go to a few nights earlier. I had met his sister's husband in Hyderabad, M. Ather Ali Khan, and his sister, wife of Kazim Hussain, in Sydney, Australia.

31. Mukarram's daughter and son-in-law (the latter from Kerala; they met while working in a Kuwait bank) married in a ceremony in Hyderabad attended by Mukarram's Kuwaiti sponsor and his family. The young couple wanted to stay in Kuwait, but he feared they might not have that option. He had spent some thirty years there and considered Kuwait his second home but still did not know if his residency permit would be renewed each year. He had picked Canada over Australia for his children and bought them a house in Toronto, while he himself could only be a house-renter in Kuwait.

32. Mukarram recalled his days sitting in the Orient Hotel with friends whom he now visited in London. He thought it a pity that, in the Gulf, the "money men" like Hoshdar Khan and Khan Lateef Khan were better known than the princes of Hyderabad; he had heard, in Canada and Hyderabad, that Prince Muffakham Jah had not been properly seated at a recent Hyderabad association function in London.

33. Yousufuddin was recommended to me by a non-Hyderabadi staff member in the Indian Embassy who said he was "very mannered, very polished, also conservative; Hyderabad seems a very respectful culture."

34. They had come in 1977 and 1980, respectively. Both would have loved to be in Hyderabad, their motherland, but "the salaries are so much better here, for the same work," and relatives had helped them secure positions.

35. Mr. and Mrs. Hyder had been educated chiefly in Bombay and Bangalore and were cousins, from Malakpet and Secunderabad, respectively. He was an electrical engineer and business manager and had come to Kuwait about 1977. Mrs. Hyder felt the purdah system curtailed Muslim activities in Kuwait, although not so much as in Saudi Arabia. Mehdvi Pathans, they were members of a Mehdvi association that included the big businessman Hoshdar Khan, but they had more non-Hyderabadi and non-Muslim friends than Hyderabadi or Muslim ones and "moved in wider circles." Each had siblings abroad, in New Jersey and Saudi Arabia.

36. From Gosha Mahal, Rahman attended Chaderghat High School and Osmania Medical College; in Kuwait, he was one of some 100 doctors from Hyderabad who belonged to the Embassy Professional Association. His wife was from

Mehdipatnam and there were six doctors in her family, but she just had an intermediate degree. Both felt Islam had "good provisions for women to be mothers"
and she recounted an argument she had had with the Indian Ambassador, Prem
Singh (who loved her cooking and came often for it), about why Muslim men
could have four wives.

37. He attended the Hyderabad Muslim Welfare Association, when he and his
wife were called by Hoshdar Khan; I took this to mean they attended the religious
meetings Hoshdar Khan had been organizing for Hyderabadi Muslims.

38. The same was true for technicians who stayed, "like Mr. Choudhry, who
went out to the border areas, keeping the electricity going, getting black with oil
and soot every day." When the Kuwaitis came back, they gave 500 Kuwaiti dinars
to each Kuwaiti for hardships but nothing to expatriates.

39. From Mallepalli, Khan was schooled in Secunderabad, majored in chemistry, and worked with United Breweries as an alcohol technician in Hyderabad;
his wife was Hoshdar Khan's sister. His elder brother had been a doctor in Saudi
Arabia since about 1975.

40. During the dangerous time of partition in 1947, his father was in the Kan-
pur Institute in north India (which Akbar later attended), and two Hindu friends
brought him all the way back to Hyderabad and left him at his own gate; only
one of them was from Hyderabad. Most of Akbar's own friends had always been
Hindus; he was the only Muslim at his work and "they never made me feel I was
a Muslim." He still has close Hindu friends, one of whom he had brought to Kuwait, but the man had not liked the job and went back. Before he married, Hindu
friends always visited his family at Id and took food, and his family visited them on
Holi and Diwali; they went together to *masjids* and *mandirs*. But "now all these differences have been created and my own children cannot go to Hindu houses."

41. His wife, fooled by my apparently good Urdu on the phone, wanted to
come to the interview, and her children encouraged her; she knew Arabic well
from watching television but her English was less adequate (they got only local
channels). The children, in the United Indian School, spoke only English, even
to each other. She and her husband grew up in Kachiguda (the new city). He was
a registrar in the College of Technological Studies.

42. His grandfather was Turkish and his grandmother (one of five wives) Saudi
Arabian; the grandfather visited Hyderabad, loved it, and stayed to supply *rumi
topis* to the Nizam's army and invest in sugar cane, rice mills, and the transport
business. Tahar, his six brothers, and three sisters grew up in Nizamabad district
and later in Hyderabad by the Nizam's Sugar Factory; Tahar earned a bachelor's
degree in commerce at Osmania, and worked in Iraq, India, and, from 1986, Kuwait. He married in 1990 and brought his bride to Kuwait after Liberation.

43. His parents were from West Godavari, but he was city-bred (Nallakunta,
the new city) and city-educated (Osmania, then Kansas State University); his education was in Urdu. He mentioned other doctors in Kuwait, another Rao whom
he had brought and a Reddy from Nizamabad who was an Urdu-speaker. He knew
Kayasth doctors in Dubai and elsewhere, "fun-loving food-loving people whom
some call half-Muslims." His own father had been employed in the Sarf-i-Khas,
the Nizam's private estate, which "employed qualified people of all religions."

44. He was recruited by a Pakistani Hyderabadi, Dr. Samee Khan, who went from Kuwait to Hyderabad to meet his relatives and recruit people for Kuwait's Ministry of Health. Khan and Rao had Osmania degrees in common, became friends, and Dr. Rao went to Kuwait. Unfortunately, Dr. Samee Khan (near retirement age) had not been called back after the Occupation, but he was happy in Karachi and three of his four sons were settled in the United States, Dr. Rao reported.

45. One of his sons, a mechanical engineer, was in Kuwait with his wife and child. His daughter and his son both had spouses from Godavari district, but his daughter had considered only men migrating to the United States; she married her husband four days after meeting him and was happy. Ten of her medical school classmates were also in the United States.

46. It was so hot the teams did not practice; they simply played every Friday. The Hyderabad team won a major tournament in 1994. Dr. Rao also mentioned a Telugu association, Telugu Kala Samiti, whose members were professionals but mostly from coastal Andhra; he said that the workers from Cuddapah and East and West Godavari, some 20,000 to 30,000 of them, stayed only among themselves.

47. The commemorative brochure was most impressive: *400-Year Anniversary of Hyderabad (Deccan) (1591–1990 A.D.)*, Kuwait: May 18, 1990, sponsored by the Khan group of Companies, or AKhan Co (Assousi & Khan Trading Co.). Hyderabad's *Siyasat* of April 23 and May 27, 1990, gave details; its editor, Abid Ali Khan, and Mohan Lal Nigam, Salahuddin Owaisi, and others from Hyderabad were brought to Kuwait.

48. Yousufuddin's Urdu connections were transnational, as he knew Urdu writers Riaz ul Jabbar in Toronto and Mateen ul Jabbar in Melbourne (brothers whom I met through Dr. Samee Syed of Los Angeles and Majid Baig of Karachi). Another transnational connection surfaced at my lunch with Yousufuddin, when we met the singer Iqbal Qureshi and his wife, visiting from London where they were permanent residents. The Qureshis were taking Canadian citizenship and knew *mushaira* fans in Toronto and also, because Iqbal had once worked with USIS in Hyderabad, Lalitha Gir and Laura Khan, of Hyderabad and Dallas, respectively.

49. When I mentioned that after the Babri Masjid incident Indian officials in London called Indian Muslims there to reassure them, arousing ire on the part of many who thought that unnecessary, this man said, "No, that was good. Nobody here called us; we have taken it very hard; mutual respect is needed."

50. Another tension was between old and new Hyderabadi businessmen in Kuwait, one with religious dimensions as well. Many of the pioneer businessmen were Shias and they distinguished between themselves and Sunnis, and also between ordinary Sunnis and "those with Wahhabi tendencies, those not valuing Shia saints and beliefs."

51. Anees Ali, daughter of old friends Safia and Aziz Masood, and her husband Maqsood Ali helped me in Dubai, energetically connecting me to various Hyderabadis and taking me to El Ain and Abu Dhabi.

52. Abu Dhabi was the dominant partner in the UAE, and that city was the political capital of the federation; it had the largest area, some 26,000 square miles, and the largest oil reserves. Abu Dhabi also had the two greenest, or garden, cities

in the UAE—El Ain, a small city, and Abu Dhabi itself; Dubai came third. Dubai, once a dependency of Abu Dhabi and only 1,500 square miles, was the commercial and tourist capital of the UAE. Abu Dhabi and Dubai pursued complementary strategies for development, with Abu Dhabi improving the efficiency of its oil operations and balancing finances on education, training, and health. Dubai's laissez-faire style of government and economy depended on the private sector, trade. Sharjah, very powerful before 1920, once included the smaller emirates of Ras al-Khaimah and Fujairah.

53. One founder was Mateen Lala, a former student leader at Osmania and one-time manager of Khan Lateef Khan's business in the Gulf. There was an Indian Association, instead, as there was no permission for sub-associations, only national ones.

54. Mrs. Hassan's welcome was warm: when she exited the plane at 11 A.M., the air was like a ball of fire touching her. They mentioned Khammam, a very hot place in the Nizam's dominions, near Cuddapah, and joked that "the fellow sitting in hell wrapped in a blanket had just come from Khammam." Their children first attended Abu Dhabi's Islamia English School and learned Urdu in a British curriculum; then they went to study in India, where he had a house. Mrs. Hassan's three sisters and brother were in the United States. Hassan, also an Urdu broadcaster, praised the great knowledge of Arab scholars and the effects on ordinary Hyderabadis of the Sharjah station Urdu broadcasts about Islam.

55. Most locals were in government firms and most engineering consultants had previously been Lebanese, Egyptian, or Jordanian. Miraj Ali's was the first local firm, in 1981, and he did go to local *majlises* or men's gatherings and weddings. His married daughter was in the United States; his son was doing an M.B.B.S. in India and taking the U.S. medical entrance exam; his other daughter was studying for a bachelor's degree in science in St. Anne's Convent. His wife had brothers in the United States and Canada. Another relative was a doctor in Chicago but found the culture "bad," and, after a "great job" in Saudi Arabia, was returning to Hyderabad.

56. Leaving Chaderghat School, where he was in his first year of intermediate levels, he finished school in Pakistan, married his first cousin in 1954, and brought her to Karachi. His Pakistani career as a photographer took him all over the world.

57. The *Khaleej Times* ranked slightly ahead of the *Gulf News*, and there were Arabic papers for the locals. Censorship occasionally closed papers down for a day or two, although there were no explicit guidelines about what would cause displeasure.

58. The *Times* assigned Bozai to Karachi in 1989 and he found conditions in Pakistan getting worse, reinforcing his decision to work in the Gulf. He recounted all that Hyderabadis and the Nizam had done for Pakistan ("they didn't have a table or chair for their offices, these were bought for them by the Nizam, yet now we are called names by Punjabis, by Pakistanis") and he said, "if one has options, one will move on to a safer place. I love my country, I'm proud to be a Pakistani, but it is not safe for the children." He told of the Rangers militia in Karachi almost arresting his younger son as a terrorist because he was running to his car.

59. His children had only visited, never resided in, Dubai; they had stayed in Pakistan.

60. Bozai's father-in-law, police officer Daud Jung of Begum Bazar, was close to the Prince of Berar, Azam Jah, and to Azam Jah's son, Prince Muffakham Jah. Thirty-two people in Dubai were contributing fees, with three members in Hyderabad who distributed the fees to the schools, not to the students (mostly boys) or their parents directly. They sponsored particular students from class 8 on and monitored their progress and also sponsored people for jobs in Dubai. The group met for luncheons the first Friday of the month and considered its efforts Islamic charity.

61. Two Hyderabadis working for a Dubai business referred me to Ishrati. Mehdi Abbas Razvi was a young Indian nephew of Kuwait's Shahid Ali Mirza who had come to Dubai in 1991; the other, Salim Hashimi, was a Pakistani Hyderabadi who had been there since 1970 and turned out to be related to Anees Ali.

62. Ishrati grew up in Hyderabad's new city in Cheragh Ali Lane and attended St. George's Grammar School (when Mrs. Edwards was principal). Zehra Ishrati also attended St. George's (with Anees Ali) and, like her husband, worked for the *Khaleej Times*. Their eldest daughter was seventeen and was visiting in Houston, but a U.S. education would be too expensive and they meant to send her to college in India.

63. Aijaz had come from Bombay in 1988 and helped his father run an import/export business in Ras al-Khaimah until they lost everything in the war; small businesssmen left, fearing chemical warfare, and afterward, "people did not give credit but demanded cash," so they could not restart. He came back to Dubai, but, with only a ninth-class Urdu-medium education, had become a driver for Sharafat Walajahi.

64. He disavowed the term *Pakistani Hyderabadi*, since "strictly speaking it is not considered proper in Pakistan to openly align with Hyderabad." But "compared to the Hyderabadis, we in Pakistan have a wider view; my son is married to a Punjabi, my daughter did modern history at Oxford, my nieces are in Houston." His son, in Dubai too, had a master's degree in finance from Chicago; his daughter had married a British Hyderabadi and lived in London. The name Walajahi indicated descent from the Nawabs of Arcot in Madras, titled the Wala Jahis. His father finally visited him in Pakistan but only on the promise to be sent back to Hyderabad if he became ill. He became ill and was sent back to die and be buried in the Hyderabad family graveyard. Walajahi's mother and brother then came to him; his brother later joined relatives in Houston and his mother died in Dubai.

65. The modern factory, in Ajman where rents were cheaper than Dubai, employed 175 Sri Lankan women and produced shirts and other articles of clothing. Walajahi thought the UK provided fewer opportunities than the United States for businessmen; he knew of a dozen cases of South Asian heads of large firms in the United States and none in Britain. In the UAE, Britons got special treatment but South Asians also did well.

66. The Walajahis had recently made the five-hour drive to Oman for Sultana to meet a Mahbubiyah classmate not seen for thirty years, a leading gynecologist in Oman.

67. With a direct flight initiated from Sharjah to Hyderabad, he did plan to visit Hyderabad, although he had lost touch with his first cousins there; he would visit relatives in Los Angeles first.

68. These included a daughter of respected mulki L. N. Gupta (she was married to a Lucknavi senior accountant in the Jabil Ali Free Zone) and big businessman Dasarath Reddy. The evening was partly held to explore the idea of having a Hyderabad association in Dubai and was written up in the *Khaleej Times*.

69. Mrs. Zulfiquar, granddaughter of Mushtaq Ahmed in Lahore and daughter of Qutbuddin Aziz of Karachi and with a Pakistani Hyderabadi UK citizen husband, had just moved to Dubai after nine years in Saudi Arabia; she had loved Saudi Arabia and was wearing Saudi earrings, so unusual that they emphasized the sameness of all the other Hyderabadi jewelry sets. Mrs. Wasee Muneem, raised in Dubai save for a few years in Pakistan, was reconnecting with her Arab girlfriends and went to Pakistan only for shopping. The Naeem Qavis, with adult children, were from Karachi, but as a small boy he had attended St. George's Grammar School and been caned by the Reverend Bellingham. He was the son of Dr. Hai, she was the daughter of Colonel Aslam bin Nasir; they had met in Chicago and had U.S. green cards but were citizens of the UK and Pakistan. Their son was to marry a British woman converting to Islam, in wedding rituals in Hyderabad and Dubai.

70. Mehdvi Pathans, she from Malakpet and he from Mehdipatnam, went to Warangal and Osmania Medical Colleges, respectively. His grandfather was a forest officer and a landlord with a coal mine at Asifabad.

71. He had a sister and brother-in-law and a brother and sister-in-law in the UAE; the sister came as a bride in 1979 and taught in the Sharjah Pakistani school. He also had siblings in Hyderabad. His wife had one brother in Hyderabad and three sisters in the United States.

72. Most highly placed was a manager for a company servicing and repairing appliances, Ghulam Ali Sajan Lal, who came to the UAE in 1977. An "environmentally friendly inventor," he had two cousins in the UAE and also mentioned a Captain Johnson in the Dubai police force, a champion billiards player who showed that he was a typical Hyderabadi by "giving abuses very well in Urdu." Sajan Lal hoped to sell the design for a saw to Black and Decker and then move to the United States, where his sister was settled and one of his sons was studying. That son would return to Secunderabad, where the family had property, but Sajan Lal, his wife, and his younger son thought they would be happiest in America.

73. Of some 200 staff in the UAE in Tony's Meena Bazar Cosmos music store, six or seven were from Hyderabad. Tony and Charles brought over Mahesh and knew Arun De Souza (below). Tony and Elizabeth shared a two-bedroom place with a Goanese Catholic family, paying 1,000 dirham a month instead of the 100 Tony had paid to share bachelor quarters. Tony's salary was high; he had a car and UAE driving license and got three or four months "at home" every summer, with a bonus and air tickets back and forth. He planned to return to India, although one friend had gone to Canada. Tony said that many Hyderabadis got student visas to the United States more easily in the UAE than in India and then worked in the states at least part-time; an acquaintance had "even married an Indian immigrant woman."

74. Arun had been promised 10,000 Indian rupees per month in Dubai but was initially offered only 4,000 as cashier in a cafeteria, which he had to accept because he had signed a two-year commitment and was threatened with jail. He met his former squash pupil in the cafeteria, a Hindu who worked for Usha Fans and had a British wife, who put him in touch with another Hindu Secunderabadi. The second man, married to a Dutch KLM air hostess and about to depart for California, recommended Arun for the Melromass job he was leaving, and the first man also pushed Arun for that job while playing squash with the British Melromass owner in a big hotel in Dubai.

75. Saving money as a bachelor in the Gulf was a better way to do it, Arun said, and he had sent his family back in 1992, but the girls had not liked St. Anne's Convent School and missed air conditioning and their daddy, so they had come back. Now he would have to give big donations to re-enroll them in Secunderabad, since he was known to be working in the Gulf. His own education had stopped after the tenth class, but his wife, Alice, had a commerce degree from Osmania.

76. Vinaya thought of changing jobs, because some Hyderabadi cricket team players asked him to join their company, but they were all Muslims at that company—even some Pakistanis were there—and he thought it unwise to join because religious feelings were stronger than at home. He had one close Hyderabadi Muslim friend, Ashi Khan, who came to him (where Ashi lived they were all Pakistanis, so Vinaya could not go there). He and Ashi spoke Hyderabadi Urdu, although both knew Telugu and in fact Ashi knew it better because Ashi was from Tirupati, coastal Andhra, but Ashi was "of course" a Hyderabadi. He felt unable to leave his job chiefly because of the regulations (he could be banned from the UAE for six months for leaving a job, and it would be difficult get another visa and another job); he also felt he would let down the company that had trained him in his first full-time job.

77. Elizabeth Ellis turned out to be a friend of Anees Ali's from St. George's Grammar School (I knew of the Ellises from Laura and Feroze Khan in Texas and the Malvern Balms in Perth). Eugene married a Madras Christian, had a son born in India, became an Australian citizen, and was working in Singapore. The first son, Philip, married a Hyderbadi Hindu who converted to Christianity, and the family was in Australia. The fifth child married a Maharashtrian Hindu who converted; his children were born in the Gulf but the family moved to Texas. Elizabeth was not married, and Joan married a Tamilnadu Christian and was secretary to one of the businessmen I met at the Walajahi dinner party. Only one cousin was left in Hyderabad. Sydney, Australia, was the family's eventual destination. Philip and Eugene were settled there, Joan had applied for immigration, and Ambrose worked for an Australian company. Liz would settle her parents there before moving herself.

78. Liz and her mother visited Hyderabad in 1984, stayed at the Secunderabad Club, and found rats and mosquitos, high rates, and bad service; things had "really gone down."

79. Fred had retired twice already, in India in 1980 and then from a State Bank of India deputation to the emirates in 1987. He did accounts and auditing for a trading company and served as a lay minister in St. Mary's Church. He said there were 50,000 Catholics in Dubai, some 75 percent of them from India and many of

them Keralites, but forty nationalities were represented. Fred was in touch with the Archbishop of Hyderabad and celebrated mass in St. Joseph's when visiting; lay ministers were used because priests were scarce.

80. They told me that Andhra Pradesh Chief Minister N. T. Rama Rao's government had fallen that very day, challenged by his son-in-law Chandrababu Naidu.

81. Thus, when the subject of divorce came up, the practice was said to be occurring in Canada and in Hyderabad, but not in the UAE. Another man gave the same two locations, but not in Pakistan. A third joked that the difficulty of procuring resident visas prevented a man's having multiple wives in Dubai.

82. At Sarosh's college, all the students were locals, and she had preferred her earlier teaching job at the International School where the students came from everywhere.

83. It was increasingly difficult to bring in such maids. Arab officials questioned the preference for older maids from one's own place instead of the young Sri Lankans or Filipinas whom they themselves hired, and they suspected relatives were being disguised as maids.

84. I had no access to them, but Drs. Razia and Ashfaq Khan and Ahmed Hassan estimated they were between 10 percent and 20 percent of the wives of older Arab men in Kuwait and the UAE generally, and much higher, 50 percent to 70 percent, in certain UAE locations. Centers for these wives in the UAE were Ajman, Umm al-Quwain, Khor Fakkan (in Sharjah), and Abu Dhabi.

85. See Leonard 2002 for more details.

86. Gender constraints were most frequently mentioned as drawbacks in the stricter Islamic sites, along with the obnoxious behavior of Kuwaitis in Dubai during the Gulf War. Maqsood Ali told about his business trip to Saudi Arabia, how after three days of seeing not a single woman on the street or in his meetings, he begged to be assured that they existed there; he was taken to a shopping mall where he saw many women in *abayahs.*

87. The Dubai police chief was a Yemeni and the force consisted of locals, Sudanese, Barkas Arabs, Iranis, and Baluchis; in Abu Dhabi as in Kuwait, most of the force were "other Arabs." Junaid Adil's wife Ayesha was related to Humayun Yar Khan in London and, through Khan's marriage, to Chandrakant Gir in Hyderabad. The Adil children were in the United States and Canada.

88. Mirza told of Queen Victoria giving a "chariot" to Oman's ruler, who asked if he could send it on to the Nizam because Oman had no roads.

89. Adil Yar Khan had a shipping company in Dubai but suffered losses during the Gulf War and retired to the UK; Khan Lateef Khan, from the same Mehdvi Pathan community as Hoshdar Khan in Kuwait, had been "not the traditional Hyderabadi gentleman, but powerful" in the UAE; he was even more important in Chicago and Hyderabad.

90. Once, Dilip Gir said (in Hyderabad), Indians in the stadium cheered when the Australian team that had just beaten Pakistan went by, starting a riot. Another time, the winning Indian cricket team was driven to Abu Dhabi for a reception in the Indian embassy, but the bus driver was a Pakistani, and when the players got down he slashed the seats of his own bus and alleged that the Indians had done it.

The Abu Dhabi police took the players out of the embassy to the police station, and, after investigation, released them and apologized to the Indian ambassador.

91. Arif had gone to an Urdu school by Golconda, and his father was a City College graduate and in the education department. His wife Donut was a secretary (she had been Maqsood Ali's secretary), and she and he had a young son and a maid from Hyderabad. They were thinking of going to Australia or elsewhere, not back to Hyderabad. He has four or five cousins in Houston (and he had had a marriage proposal from there); one Houston cousin was going to Saudi Arabia to work, where Arif's younger brother was working.

92. Arif named a Parsi Nizam College man from Secunderabad and others. *Siyasat*, May 5, 1991, reported two events: a condolence meeting for Dr. Raghunandan Raj Saxena, an Osmania professor and writer of Urdu poetry who had just died in Hyderabad, and a prize distribution for the Hyderabad Karom Tournament. *Siyasat*, May 26, 1991, featured a story about a Dubai musical evening sponsored by the Bazm-i-Deccan, Emirates, with photos of Char Minar and the Qutb Shahi tombs behind the stage and an audience of Deccanis plus a few Pakistanis and Gulf Arabs.

93. *Siyasat*, June 9, 1991, reported a performance of Babban Khan's drama *Adrak-i-Panje* (Ginger Fingers); the Hyderabadi actor was a favorite throughout the Gulf, where he made his reputation.

94. This dissolution took place at the house of Shahidullah: *Siyasat*, October 6, 1991.

95. *Siyasat*, June 17, 1990; Mohamed Hussain Arif interview.

96. "His Highness the Nizam's Sona Masoor Rice" was brought as seed from Egypt 400 years ago and controlled by the Nizam for his own use before 1948, Ramachandran asserted, and it did three things: increased intelligence, increased sexual potency (in a whisper), and improved digestion. Asked if he gave the Nizam compensation for use of the name, he replied, "the Nizam is a zero now; he should pay me for the publicity."

97. Ramachandran was famous in Hyderabad, he said, for a program of Naxalite rehabilitation, a "Zero Begging" scheme, a Scooter Taxi program, and a rural employment program; he had also held seminars for pickpockets and established a colony for eighty-two eunuchs (*hijras*). He started a public limited company in Dubai in 1988, the NRI Trading Establishment in 1991, and the Super Market in 1994.

98. His one good Hyderabadi friend, a Hindu senior to him in Hyderabad Public School, lived in Egypt.

99. Vipin became a CPA in Denver, worked in Greece, and wanted to earn a Ph.D. or M.B.A. in economics at an American Ivy League school. He went often to Delhi, where he had a business venture and where his parents had lived. His parents, however, moved to Hyderabad where his father wrote Urdu poetry.

NOTES FOR CHAPTER 10

1. *Munsif* gave less coverage to Hyderabadis abroad but around 2000, *Munsif* was bought by Khan Lateef Khan (from Chicago), and its coverage has increased.

2. Some Hyderabadis abroad urged him to print a back page in English so that young people abroad could read the paper too.

3. Salahuddin 1991; "London Is a Second Hyderabad," 1985; Zainallahuddin, "Chicago's Vicinity," 1991.

4. Hussain 1985 remarked on resident Hyderabadis Masrur Khurshed and Professors Hamiddullah and Abdul Majid. In Nayar 1991, Parvin, wife of Mustafa Kamal (computer engineer working in Germany) and educated to intermediate level in Osmania, spoke of her reliance on *Siyasat* for news of home and her career of writing for it too.

5. Naqvi 1984.

6. Abid Ali Khan would have gone to Muscat save for the Gulf War of 1990–1991. The Kuwaiti function he pronounced best of all, a one-man show (funded and organized by Hoshdar Khan). The Jeddah one was marred by organizational infighting, and the London one had been peculiar in that two consecutive Saturday nights were the only times people could meet. But all the celebrations had featured speakers and poets from Hyderabad.

7. One of several Hyderabadi organizations, it suffered from internal dissension; there was also the Hyderabad Deccan Association, of which more later; INTACH, the Indian National Trust for Art and Cultural Heritage; SPEQL, an environmental organization; Save the Rocks Society; and women's organizations like the University Forum for Women and the YWCA.

8. Government's lack of interest was partially explained by the fact that Chenna Reddy, chief minister in 1990, had gone to the United States for a kidney transplant. Narendra Luther, IAS man, had then been appointed to help the Golconda Society; one version is that when the organizers insisted on honoring the last Nizam as part of the celebrations the government pulled out. Some events were held in 1992.

9. Hosted by the Andhra Pradesh chapter of the Association of British Council Scholars on September 28, 1991, at the Golconda Hotel, this 400th Anniversary Conference produced a publication: Seshan 1993.

10. People said this was in Nehru's *Discovery of India*, but I could not find it.

11. In 1991, the executive committee consisted of Bilkis Alladin, president; Abdul Quayyum, vice-president; Khusro Ali Beg, treasurer; Mrs. Gul Chenoy, secretary; Asim Ali Khan, joint secretary; Dr. Herbert Butt, publicity; Arjuman Ali Khan, membership; Dr. Polly Chenoy, program committee; and Mrs. Orian Scott, Mr. Gobind Das Mukand Das, Habib Ansari, and Abdul Qader.

12. Vatuk 1990 analyzes the cultural construction of family identity by a Nawayati Muslim family that experienced ruptures and reorientations in 1855, when the British refused to recognize a successor to their employer, the Nawab of Arcot, in Madras. Comparable perhaps to the seizure of Hyderabad by India in 1948, this earlier event sent a branch of the Madrasi family to Hyderabad (Hasnuddin Ahmed, below, and Aziz Ahmed in London).

13. Bilkees, who wrote about her French mother (Lateef 1984), was writing books about the women and men of the Deccan and working on social projects in both Delhi and Hyderabad.

14. In his home I met Anees Ali (another, not my friend in Dubai), now

from Austin, Texas, whose foster father, Zahir Ahmed, was Reddy's old friend and India's ambassador to Saudi Arabia. Anees's daughter Fatima, twenty-nine, was also there and when asked if she was a Hyderabadi said, "No, I'm just on holiday here."

15. Reddy had visited the United States but did not enjoy it, although he admired hard work and the dignity of labor. Yet he was ambivalent even about that: he observed that when people went to America, they became such hard workers that they had no time to write, they only telephoned. He told of a man who bathed at night because there was no time in the morning, got up early, fixed a cup of coffee and took it to his car at 7:30 A.M. to drink it when stopped at red lights, and arrived at work at 8 A.M. The Hyderabadi workday typically started at 10 or 11, included long lunch and tea breaks, and ended between 4 and 6; the work week also usually included some time on Saturdays.

16. The Mandal Commission set reservations (27%) in public institutions and service for Scheduled Castes and Tribes in 1980; attempts to implement this from 1990 have been controversial. Reddy's own sons had gone out of India for education, he said, but now people had to go out because of the reservations, preventing those with merit from gaining admission.

17. An IAS man told me there could be a seniority gap of twenty to thirty years between a "Brahman" and a "Sudra" of the same age.

18. They spoke English in the home, but English was also spoken in the parental home that included the son and his wife and two children. Umapathi had traveled abroad, but the family had ancestral property in Hyderabad.

19. Mrs. Umapathi's brother in San Francisco played on a Hyderabadi cricket team, and her sister's son, also there, married a Korean American woman. The Umapathis cited a story they had heard from a Muslim family and took to be typical, of a little granddaughter being brought up alone in the West, surrounded by foreigners whose homes she did not enter and who did not enter her home.

20. Raja Sham Raj, an extremely orthodox Hindu, customarily toasted the Nizam with Ganga water (from the river sacred to Hindus, the Ganges). Most of the family was in Poona or abroad, so the family property in Shahalibanda had been broken up, with only the family temple still held jointly and used annually.

21. His father's family migrated to Hyderabad from Madras in the early twentieth century; his mother, from Bangalore, knew Kannada, Tamil, and English and then learned Telugu, Sanskrit, and Urdu after marrying into Hyderabad. The Hyderabad family home was in Sultan Bazar, and Raman attended Chaderghat Government High School, studying Urdu and Persian.

22. Raman spoke of Major Naidu, Sarojini Naidu's husband and the Nizam's chief medical officer, and his organization of the medical services and the "Walker style" of rural hospitals; about famine, drought, and influenza work in the early twentieth century in conjunction with Catholics, Methodists, and the Madras government; about the French-built *dak* bungalows on the road from Vijayawada to Nandir; and about Meadows Taylor's still-standing residence in Shorapur.

23. Raman stayed in touch with Muslim friends who went to Pakistan, the UK, and the Gulf states. Unsigned Id Mubarak cards sent to him after an Indian/Pakistan conflict by Hamid Ali of Pakistan's Reserve Bank (older brother of India's

table tennis champion who married into Pakistan) and Qayyum of the Pakistani Navy drew the attention of Indian Intelligence.

24. She viewed herself as a Tamil-speaker married into a Madras family in Hyderabad. To her, Hyderabadi meant Muslim: "They alone had the Hyderabadi culture; we are not Hyderabadis in the true sense, although my husband [educated in Madras-i-Aliya and Nizam College] knows Urdu and Muslim culture well. He wore a sherwani, attended Muslim weddings and so on."

25. "The boy's family was respectable and he was a brilliant physicist," they said. Mrs. Ayyangar could not go to the wedding, as her father-in-law was dying and they could not afford it anyway; later she went with her husband to visit the children twice. She went on her own, tragically, to assist her daughter-in-law dying of cancer in a hospice in Texas.

26. None of the children had visited India since leaving. But the Ayyangars thought themselves lucky because many with children abroad were poorer, whereas they at least could afford to visit the United States. And there was always the possibility their bereaved son would remarry, and perhaps "a wife who will want to live in Hyderabad."

27. Vithal's cousin and Nizam College classmate went on a Nizam's scholarship to the University of Wisconsin from 1946 to 1951; later that cousin's son married Vithal's daughter (South Indians, like Muslims, often marry close relatives) and the young couple lived in Hyderabad.

28. As a professor's son, Vithal got a free education at Aliya and Nizam College: "my classmates were from a high class, Muslims and others, but they never rubbed that in; we were simply there with them. It was quite a gracious culture, before." His wife's uncle was an ICS man (with the British), Jaya Rao, a close friend of Ali Yavar Jung, and Rao died young. The only other Hyderabadi in the ICS, Vithal said, may have been a man named Kirmani, who also died young and whose children came back and were given a free education by the Nizam's government.

29. Vithal has been visiting the United States since 1964 and felt comfortable there. "In all honesty, I cannot tell my son there are better opportunities for him in India. Only those with property are coming back, managing it, becoming international in their holdings, and those who fear for their growing daughters. And some doctors were coming back, either to contribute here or to escape from the pressures abroad; the doctors who remained in Hyderabad have often become quite distinguished, treating a great variety of diseases." Supporting Vithal's last point, Dr. Yousuf Husain did 10,000 operations for cataracts from 1991 to 1993, and, decades ago, when in West Virginia doing a three-year residency, he found he had, as a student of Dr. Ramchander in Hyderabad, already done more operations than the American chief of residency.

30. At the end of his career then, he told a governor of Karnataka with whom he worked closely of his setbacks, and that man secured his appointment to the IAS (but without appropriate seniority). Ali does have relatives in Pakistan but has never visited there and wrote only one letter to someone there, a condolence letter. Another injustice involved Ali's nephew, who, trying to follow the family tradition of government service, was temporarily barred by an interview board in India for correcting his date of birth on a form. The young man then went to Pakistan against his father's wishes and appeared before an interview board for the

Pakistan Civil Service, where a senior member from Hyderabad reported that the youth's father had opposed the Razakars and got him rejected. Then the nephew was sent to the UK to do accountancy, but, failing the exam, became so depressed he had to be sent home. Because he had become a Pakistani citizen, it took three governors of Hyderabadi background (Padmaja Naidu of Bengal, Mehdi Nawaz Jung of Gujarat, and B. Ramakrishna Rao of Kerala) writing on his behalf to win him an indefinite stay in India, where he died.

31. When the son in Chicago got U.S. citizenship, Mehdi Ali would get a green card and then sponsor his son in Saudi Arabia to the United States, a faster way than brother sponsoring brother.

32. A branch of this Nawayati Muslim family migrated to Hyderabad from Madras, where it had served the Nawab of Arcot, in the eighteenth century.

33. The home was featured in architectural publications (Slesin and Cliff ca. 1990).

34. In 1993, a friend was also present, and shoes and socks and *chappals* came up again: Ahmed said that he wore *chappals* after 1956 despite his father's objections; his friend, a professor of chemistry, wore shoes and socks for thirty years but one day he wore *chappals*, attracting many student remarks.

35. Some were the "sons-in-law of the state" in Leonard 2002a.

36. He wrote a book in Hindi on the public library system while visiting his daughter's family in the United States for ten months.

37. One article suggested that all the Nizam had needed for independence was a sea outlet and the full support of all his people. Ekbote was one of dozens of people to attribute to the Nizam a remark about Hindus and Muslims being his two eyes (although he thought that the Nizam had favored the Muslims).

38. The sons were an electrical engineer, a civil engineer, a captain in the military and now chief security officer in a corporation, a doctor, and a marketing consultant (the last studied in the United States, at New York University). Like the daughter, one of the sons also made a love marriage, with a Gujarati Jain woman from Hyderabad.

39. The husband was from the same caste and a Hyderabadi and a doctor, but his father had opposed the marriage in Hyderabad, so the couple went to London and married there.

40. Yet Heda told a wonderful story, about when the Shah of Iran came to Delhi in 1954–1955, and Heda asked him when the first newspaper was published in Persian. The Shah gave a name and date, but Heda pulled out of his pocket a journal published in Persian by Raja Rammohan Roy dated earlier! Heda used to speak and write Urdu well and wanted to write his memoirs. He has written one book about the separatist movement for Telingana and another on the Congress Party over the years.

41. The Heda's son Sharad went to Osmania, then to Pilani Engineering College in Rajasthan, then to Stanford in 1963; he married in Hyderabad, by arrangement, a Punjabi woman and got his U.S. citizenship in 1973.

42. One of Vaman Rao's employees, a Christian Telugu-speaker from the Nizam's districts, had a brother in Kansas. Raja Paul's brother John, with his wife and three children, migrated in 1986 with a visa as pastor of a Telugu Baptist Church.

43. His wife was a doctor, he taught political science, and in 1991 he headed his ancestral village *panchayat* (council).

44. Rao had spent time in the 1960s in the UK and in the United States (visiting his daughter, who married a Kannada speaker from old Hyderabadi elite, Srinivas Melkote, professor of mass communications in Bowling Green, Ohio; Rao's sister was also married to a Melkote, in Hyderabad).

45. Omar Khalidi, of the Aga Khan Program in Islamic Architecture at MIT, was Mohiuddin's son-in-law.

46. This son had attended Madras-i-Aliya because Rama Rao, new to Hyderabad, had been influenced by G. N. Reddy, registrar general at the time and from Telingana, to send his son to the same school as Reddy's son. This son therefore became an "old Hyderabadi" and was in partnership in Chicago with a Kayasth doctor from Hyderabad; their son "may even be a member of the Hyderabad association there," they said.

47. Justice Rao joked that in India, the parents do the dating, but in America, the grandchildren will date. Despite their apparent unconcern, he and his wife told some "horror stories" about young Hyderabadis in the United States: a sixteen-year-old girl, married off by her fearful father, ran away and no one knows where she is; a twenty-year-old boy pressed too hard to study committed suicide; a daughter married a black American man.

48. On the night of August 21, *Payam*'s young editor, Shoebullah, was killed, presumably by Razakars. Breaking a long silence, Mirza and others were featured in 1991 in an hour-long television documentary by India's national television station, Doordarshan, on the events of 1948 in Hyderabad.

49. On Kemal's mother's side were Albari Turks who came with the Khiljis and had chiefdoms in the Bahmani kingdom, and on Kemal's father's side he was a direct descendant of the second Caliph of Islam, Umar, and of the Wahhabi leader Hazrat Shah Waliullah. Her family, *zamindars* in Meerut district, United Provinces, took service after 1857 in Lahore and then Allahabad; she has many scholars among her close relatives. Kemal studied at the Dar ul Ulum and Osmania. Kemal accompanied his wife in 1949 for her M.A. in education and then Ph.D. in psychology in the UK. He took a Ph.D. in public law and worked in the Urdu section of the BBC. He now works to establish an Urdu university and an Urdu international newspaper in Hyderabad.

50. Dr. Salimuddin Kamal was professor of philosophy at Penn State in the United States and his younger brother worked in investments in the UK.

51. Helen had many stories about old Hyderabadi pride and anti-Andhra prejudice. She took a job in 1981 as UNESCO literacy program chief technical adviser in Malawi, the high salary making it possible to send the children to the United States. The daughter married an Indian and lived in Australia; the son worked in New York City.

52. Khusro attended Jagirdar's College, Nizam College, and the military academy in Dehra Dun, retiring from his military career in 1968 (he started in the Hyderabad Army, with Jack Hudson as his squadron commander).

53. Of Nafissa's brothers, one in the Royal Air Force opted for Pakistan in 1947, as did a second brother who joined the Pakistan Navy; another, whose wife

was Anglo-Indian, went to the UK; the fourth brother lived in the Nilgiris and had a daughter married to a Hyderabadi doctor in New York. Nafissa's two sisters abroad were in Canada and Pakistan, and some children of Nafissa's three sisters in India were in Canada, the UK, and the Gulf states. Khusro had a brother in London.

54. Khusro's brother in London was married to a Goswami woman doctor, and a brother of that doctor was married to the youngest of Nafissa's five sisters, Farida (a marriage between the men's and women's badminton champions in Hyderabad). A son of Khusro's sister married a Hindu from Orissa whom he met at college. The connection with the Anglo-Indian Cox family (see chapter 6) had been discovered, so when Khusro and Nafissa were visiting Nafissa's sister Femida in Canada, Betty Cox traveled from Melbourne to Canada to meet them. Femida also met Bruce Cox when she visited Australia.

55. These *maths* were both banking establishments and sites of Hindu piety, housing Arab or Afghan military units to guard the riches as well as the *samadhis* or graves of the deceased gurus (Goswamis are buried, not cremated). The aboveground *samadhis* commemorated venerated gurus, but the Goswami *math* heads were termed Rajas in Hyderabad because they were also men of the world, participants in Hyderabad's court culture.

56. Following a strategy advised by lawyers, he arranged for his three eldest sons (who had attained legal age) to file a suit against him, petitioning to make the property joint under Hindu law and then distribute it in nine parts, one to the father and eight to his sons.

57. Dilip Gir's wife was a daughter of Fareed Mirza (above); Jayakumari, a doctor, lived in London and her husband (Humayun Yar Khan, a retired IAS man) was the brother of Khusro Yar Khan (above). Legal disputes hindered the *math*'s sale and redevelopment.

58. This property included several old classic cars (many Rajas and Nawabs in Hyderabad were proud owners of expensive cars, still lovingly tended). Like many young men with similar trajectories, he found it difficult to get an appropriate job in Hyderabad.

59. His wife Shanta was eventually unable to have children, so he took a second wife, with Shanta's permission, from another caste; but in the end Parmanand and Shanta adopted a daughter.

60. In Tampa, Florida, when Mrs. Danghoria visited her daughter, she thought Muslims there were becoming more orthodox. The daughter's excellent Urdu prompted a Pakistani in Tampa to ask her why she did not convert to Islam.

61. For details, Vijayakar 2003, B15, B23. One of Reddy's daughters was married to the son of the Umapathis (above).

62. Mohammed, husband of the third daughter of Aristo Jah, built the Mohammedi Mosque in Red Hills, near A. A. Hussain's residence; it was in litigation in a dispute with the Bohra *moulvi* (cleric) and most of this family had become ordinary Shias, in effect blacklisted by the leader of the Bohra Muslims.

63. After Shoukat Hussain's early death in the late 1990s, his son and a nephew managed the bookstore.

64. After Marjory's death, J. W. did join his sons in Australia.

65. The Reddys knew their son wanted his boys to attend Stanford and the cost astounded them. They had recently learned about a Maharashtrian parent association in Bombay, for parents left behind, professionals who helped each other in their specialties and consoled each other.

66. See Leonard 1978b, 282.

67. Roy's oldest brother, Ram Mohan Roy, had been the first to go, in order to study (chapter 7).

68. Ali and Fatima's elder daughter married and settled in Glasgow, and their younger daughter was studying and working in New York. His Los Angeles relatives had as many American friends as Hyderabadi friends, he said, and he had had many English friends when studying in the UK because he met his Hyderabad teachers in the UK who introduced him around. Also, he said, so many people in the UK knew about the Nizam and Hyderabad. Once, in Hyde Park, an old chap had come up to him and asked if he was a son of Hussein Ali Khan (Ali's uncle), whom the Englishman had known in Hyderabad.

69. In A. M. Khusro's view, educated Muslims were indeed finding few jobs in Hyderabad but were going confidently to the UK, United States, Canada, and elsewhere. But Hyderabadi Muslims abroad were becoming more religious, especially in the United States he thought, because the "aggressiveness" of U.S. culture required a strong identity to withstand it.

70. The seven siblings heading this family had three children each, and when I went to their home in Asmangadh I was introduced to "Mughal Princess X," "Mughal Prince Y," and so on. The Mughal Family Society had sixty-six members in 1993, including children. The younger generation was finding more opportunities in the Gulf, despite deceptive recruiting and employment practices there. One young man, on whom the family had spent 75,000 rupees for his mechanical engineering education, was still unemployed in Hyderabad. Having sent their genealogy to Uzbekistan to validate their claim, they told me, they had no copy to show me. "Uzbek envoy calls on Babur's descendants" 1993 reported that President Islam Karimov sent a personal message to Ziauddin Tucy, head of the Mughal Family Society, who asked for more science and technology seats for Indian students in the Babur University. (As tourists in Tashkent in 1994, a Hyderabadi friend and I met a member of this Uzbek delegation, who showed us photos of my friend's brother and another friend in Hyderabad.)

71. Mrs. Jaffari's grandfather, Abbas Ali Sharif Maulana, had come from Zanzibar, married a Hyderabadi woman, and built the Koh-i-Qayam (a Shia religious shrine) at Bare Imam Pahar south of Hyderabad city. In 1991, Mrs. Jaffari lived on the hereditary property and ran the shrine herself.

72. See Ali 2007.

73. Dr. Waheed Khan's second son, Sayeed, had a medical degree from Warangal but worked at Target and as a security guard as he prepared to pass his U.S. medical exams. Syed Sirajuddin's maternal grandfather was a magistrate and *talukdar* (revenue collector), his paternal grandfather was an *alim* (Islamic scholar) and a magistrate, his father was a deputy director of public instruction, and he himself was a professor of English at Nizam College. But his son, in Detroit to

study electrical engineering, worked as a taxi driver, and when his daughter and her husband lived in Ottawa, Canada, she worked in a department store.

74. One was quite religious and said *salam aleikum* instead of *adab*; the other celebrated old Hyderabadi culture and had a brother, married to an American Jewish woman, who had converted to Judaism. Both socialized with Americans while in the Gulf and generally liked them. Javeed said that "Mohammed was just like an American, straightforward, and against culture, opposed to traditions and rituals not actually allowed in Islam." Javeed was an architect, and Rashid agreed with him that "Andhra clients have money and leave the execution of the job to you but are not courteous and do not properly thank you, whereas old Hyderabadis haggle about money and want to poke their noses into all aspects of the job."

75. Muttalib's wife did her high school, intermediate, M.A., and Ph.D. (in Urdu literature) after her marriage at seventeen. When she went to Aligarh, properly chaperoned, for her degree, she did not touch beef, although many Muslims there ate it. In Hyderabad, middle-class Muslims did not and do not eat beef out of respect for their Hindu friends, Muttalib asserted (I heard this from many others as well).

76. Khan's father died when he was five or six; the father had been one of the Hanafi Risala, Pathans from Danishmandar on the Afghan/Pakistan (then Indian) frontier brought by the Nizam's state and stationed at Nalgonda, defending the Nizam's personal estate. At the Police Action, "in two days we were starving, we left our homes with only our clothes, I and my four brothers and two sisters; my father's name was announced nightly on the radio, telling him to report to the Union government. He did that and narrowly escaped execution, saved only because a local revenue official said he had been a good, honest person who united the majority and minority people. We went to Hyderabad city; he came there and resigned his post and died in five months. My mother died a year later."

77. One older brother of Khan's went to the UK to study accounting and is now in Cleveland, Ohio; another older brother went to Canada and ended up in Chicago in pharmacy; a younger brother was in Chicago too. A sister became a colonel in the army, fought for India in four wars, and retired early to Chicago. The oldest brother stayed in Hyderabad, although he (like Khan) had a U.S. green card; his other sister, whose husband was in the police, died young in Hyderabad. Khan's ventures in the United States included urban real estate, factories manufacturing high speed duplicating machines for audio cassettes and other electronics, and a new product to shield and cool products being shipped such as beer and soft drinks. He moved one factory from Chicago to Japan in 1985 because production there was cheaper and the workers were better.

78. Founded to benefit the minority—that is, Muslims—because only 1 percent or 2 percent of students in government colleges are Muslim, the college had 100 percent minority students, but then a judicial decision opened 50 percent of the seats to merit admissions, reducing the Muslim percentage. The college was contesting this.

79. Remarks came from Mrs. Raza Alikhan, from Bangalore; Dr. Digamber Singh (via her daughter Lalitha Gir), also from Bangalore, who married into

Hyderabad in the 1920s and asked her husband why he was wearing Muslim clothes and speaking a Muslim language); and Mrs. A. K. Ayyangar, from Madras.

80. Sylvia Vatuk's 2004 analysis of the life story of Zakira Ghouse (1921–2003), from a prominent Nawayati Muslim family in Hyderabad, emphasizes how Zakira Ghouse worked within her family and societal culture to achieve her goals and mentions the increase in women's educational and work opportunities in Hyderabad after 1948 (note 6).

81. The niece, Hamida, graduated from Mahbubiyah and Nizam College and then was allowed to proceed to the College of Fine Arts and Architecture, although her two sisters had married at age fourteen. There was still strict purdah, so she was ushered first into a small lady's room with an *ayah* (servant) attending her, and the boys then entered the larger classroom. Although she married after that first year, her in-laws allowed her to continue attending school. She secured a merit scholarship in the second year and supervised the construction of the State Bank of Hyderabad in the two months between her third and fourth year despite opposition because she was a woman. She taught in the Hyderabad architecture department and worked abroad.

82. According to B. V. Hemchander and Dr. Khurshed Adiga, it had, in 1991, some 1,600 permanent members, 450 memberships for members' sons, 500 long-term temporary memberships primarily for military men posted there, and 100 memberships for "single ladies." In 1993 the club decided that daughters could also remain members after marrying and their spouses could become members too (but both would be nonvoting).

83. Competition among schools had intensified, and the better-funded schools relocated to the edges of the city where there was clean air and less urban crowding. Almost all the private schools were English-medium and modeled on schools abroad.

84. Family members were zamindars in Kapurthala State and some who worked in Hyderabad became *jagirdars* there; her father was in the police, and when 1948 came, he alone of the family did not go to Pakistan. Khurshid said she was the only Punjabi Muslim left in Andhra Pradesh. She was married early, at twelve when in sixth class at St. Anne's Convent, because her father had no sons and wanted progeny to inherit his land. After three children, whom her father adopted himself, she became a widow at nineteen and never remarried. Her daughter, married to a Kashmiri in Pakistan, had a daughter married to a doctor in Buffalo, New York.

85. Mrs. De and her husband were Bengali Christians; his father had come to Hyderabad and been secretary of the YMCA. Anil was in the IAS batch with Abid Hussain, later ambassador to the United States. The Des considered themselves Hyderabadis.

86. Another leading school, CHIREC, was founded by a young divorcee returning from an unsuccessful marriage in the United States; her brothers supported her. She remarried and the school was an outstanding one, relocated out near the University of Hyderabad.

87. Anees Khan was a Gold Medalist in history at Osmania. Donna Hussein told her to come live with them and to get typing and driving certificates before coming (Anees got the typing one). She found her American experience trying,

as she saw how cut off from their roots people were and how much time it took to do one's own housework. Her husband, "a finicky Hyderabadi," would want so many things done "just so" that she would be unable to do anything else, she was sure. Anees hoped her two daughters and son would stay in Hyderabad. Although the first daughter had married a man in Canada, the couple had come back; the younger daughter had accompanied her husband to Dubai but the couple, perhaps temporarily, had gone on to Canada. The son and his wife were in Hyderabad.

88. Dr. Jussawalla had spent one year in the United States in 1957 as a U.S.-sponsored lecturer (through the PL480 program). In 1975, recently widowed, she left India because of Prime Minister Indira Gandhi's discouragement of free market economics. Resettled at the East West Center in Honolulu, she published fifteen books and earned awards over the next twenty-five years. Her daughter, Feroza, had preceded her, recruited by William and Helen Mulder to earn an M.A. and Ph.D. in English literature from the University of Utah; Feroza married an American and teaches at the University of New Mexico.

89. Lalitha worked for the USIS in Hyderabad for almost two decades and then headed a government cooperative for women; Anuradha has written about old Hyderabad.

90. Intizar Husain's short story, "A Letter from India," beautifully captures Indian views of Pakistani relatives (translated from Urdu and published in Bhalla in 1994).

91. The caller was Desh Bandhu (his new wife Zehra was related to Rasheed Ali Khan but from the Pakistan branch of the family).

1. Few studies of migration involve more than two receiving societies and few examine the impact of emigration and transnationalism on the sending society, according to Brettell and Hollifield 2000, 13, 18.

2. Holston and Appadurai 1996 argued that cities are challenging and replacing nations as the important space of citizenship. Cities vary, of course, and I would argue that Hyderabad city was far more important in the past as an urban space of citizenship, one located in a lingering Indo-Muslim cultural sphere. However, it is clearly becoming an important node in the operations of globally oriented capital and labor (a topic for another study) and part of an emergent globalized structure of feeling, of which more below.

3. I draw here on Silvey and Lawson 1999, 122–123.

4. Srivastava 2005 proposes a South Asian "very different sensibility of culture" as he theorizes about an ethnography of home, belonging, and attachment, using primarily Hindi literary materials in his essay.

5. Varshney 1997, 1–20.

6. Leonard 2000.

7. Schrager's 1983 discussion of what is social in oral history is still, I think, the most insightful discussion of the richness of what he terms experience narratives (life histories, oral histories, event narratives).

8. Leonard 1973; Sirajuddin 1990; Butt 1990.

9. Shryock 1996, 39. Shryock discusses, here and in his 1997 book, identities based on received versions of particular tribal histories that conflict with other versions and with new, modern assimilative languages of identity circulating in print culture and at the level of the nation-state. Like Shryock, I was collecting oral materials often based on genealogical notions of transmission and authenticity.

10. As Shryock 1995, 5, says, this was not a way of thinking that was purely tribal, but part of "a larger political and historical discourse . . . which owes its legitimacy to voices and identities which are much older . . . [than Hashemite Jordan]."

11. Marcus 1995, 110.

12. For most of the sites, I either made return visits or sent drafts of chapters to informants to obtain comments and updates.

13. Hindu Kayasths abroad conspicuously continued to associate with Hyderabadi Muslim emigrants and help to form Hyderabad associations. This, according to critics, reproduced the old elite partnership that celebrated Mughlai culture and Urdu rather than other vernacular languages in Hyderabad State.

14. Political associations competed for the Telugu-speakers: the Telugu Association of North America was dominated by members of the Kamma caste and the American Telugu Association was dominated by members of the Reddy caste.

15. C. M. Naim, professor of Urdu at the University of Chicago, remarked that the Hyderabadi habit of speaking Urdu when together meant that their children knew only Hyderabadi Urdu; he found that their ignorance of "standard" Urdu was a problem when they attended his classes. But language was the only marker of difference for the second-generation Hyderabadis, he said; they were like other second-generation immigrants from India in all other respects.

16. Antoun 1998 suggested that academics underestimate the importance of their own occupation, of the impact of higher education and the institutions that deliver it, and I agree.

17. Clifford 1997, 258–259.

18. Gupta and Ferguson 1992, 7.

19. Bhavana and Kavita Koratkar reported this. They had an aunt in Australia, three uncles who were doctors in the United States, and cousins in the United States (including a female astrophysicist with NASA).

20. The phrase is Lalitha Gir's.

21. One Hyderabadi Shia Muslim man whose marriage ended in divorce remarried in Canada but to a Hyderabadi Pakistani Sunni woman, dismaying his mother in Hyderabad.

22. Sunder Rajan 2003 discusses the 1991 "rescue" by an air hostess of Ameena, a young Muslim bride, from her sixty-year-old Saudi husband.

23. In one case, the bride and her family were in Hyderabad, but the groom's family wanted to hold the wedding in Ohio, where most of the relatives on both sides resided. The U.S. Immigration and Naturalization Service (INS) had to be persuaded to let the fiancee come in for her wedding (the prospective bride and groom had not met, as was traditional in that Muslim family, whereas INS queries focus on how well couples know each other).

24. In a Los Angeles wedding, jasmine was flown in from the Philippines and

special needles for threading flowers were sent from Hyderabad so that family members in Los Angeles could produce the garlands. The groom was from Pakistan and the bride, born in London, lived in Los Angeles.

25. The wedding should have been in Hyderabad, the Imams felt, but the groom's brothers had visited there so recently that it would have been hard for them to get time off again. They were from the Babu Khan family of Secunderabad, builders of Osmania University, Hyderabad's airport, and the city's sewage system; many members of the family were abroad, in the United States, UK, and the Gulf states.

26. Ather Ali Khan's wife's sister migrated there with her husband in about 1970, and when the Khans' daughter was ready to marry they sent her to Australia to meet her cousin and see the country. She liked him and it and the wedding was held in Hyderabad in 1984. Later, the Khans' son was admitted to a U.S. school to study electrical engineering but could not get a visa, so he started his studies in Australia, secured a U.S. visa there, and switched his studies to Houston. He then got a good job in Houston, trained in Scotland, and accompanied his parents on a visit to Australia, where a shortage of electrical engineers secured him a better job. The elder Khans visited twice and liked it: there were many Hyderabadis and the Australians were friendly. When Ali picked up his grandchild at the school, the others, mostly Australian ladies, all smiled at him. They kept an apartment in Hyderabad, possibly for their final years.

27. Schiller, Basch, and Blanc 1995.

28. Shryock 2000, 58, 38.

29. See Leonard 2006 for a general essay on South Asian religions in the United States.

30. See Powell 1996 for an analysis of English-medium history textbooks in Pakistan and India and their contrasting and conflicting appropriations of the past.

31. See Thrift 1996 for full discussion of the transformations of the last century in sources of power, systems of communication and transportation, and other material determinants of mental and visual perceptions.

32. Sharieff 1994; see also Naidu ca. 1990.

33. Clifford 1989, 185.

34. Nayar 1991.

35. Interestingly, I found the same situation among the children of the Punjabi Mexican couples whom I studied in the 1980s, the same proud assertion that they were the "first generation" of Americans.

36. Boyarin 1994, 23 et passim.

37. Climo 1995, 176.

Bibliography

PRIMARY SOURCES

Cohen, Benjamin. 2002. "Hindu Rulers in a Muslim State: Hyderabad, 1850–1949." Ph.D. dissertation, Department of History, University of Wisconsin.

Datla, Kavita. Forthcoming. "Mobilizing the Vernacular: Urdu, Education, and Osmania University, 1883–1938." Ph.D. dissertation, Department of History, University of California, Berkeley.

Hyderi, Sir Akbar (Home Secretary). 1917. Memorandum to the Nizam, Files of the Chief Secretariat, installment 36, list 5, serial number 9, file O1/al, Andhra Pradesh State Archives.

Lateefunisa, Begum. 1956. "Private Enterprise in Education and the Contribution of Some Famous Private High Schools to the Advancement of Education in the Cities of Hyderabad and Secunderabad," M.A. dissertation, Osmania University.

BOOKS AND ARTICLES

Abdullah, Mena. 1993. *The Time of the Peacock*. New Delhi: Indus.

Abdul-Rauf, Muhammad. ca. 1978. *History of the Islamic Center: From Dream to Reality*. Washington, D.C.: Islamic Center.

Achebe, Chinua. 1967. *Things Fall Apart*. London: Heinemann Educational Press.

Ahmad, Aziz. 1964. *Studies in Islamic Culture in the Indian Environment*. Oxford: Clarendon Press.

Ahmed, Aziz. n.d. [1980–1981?]. "The Char Minar by Charing Cross." *Siyasat*.

Ahmed Khan, Nawab Mushtaq. 1986. *Zawal-i Hyderabad ki Ankahi Dastan* [The Fall of Hyderabad, the Untold Story]. Lahore, Pakistan.

Ahsan, Aitzaz. 1997. *The Indus Saga and the Making of Pakistan*. Karachi: Oxford University Press.

Ali, Syed Faiz. 2007. "'Go West Young Man': The Culture of Migration among Muslims in Hyderabad, India." *Journal of Ethnic and Migration Studies*.

Ali Khan, Majeed. 1993. "Hyderabad Deccan Association." *Festival of Hyderabad London 1993 Souvenir*. London: Hyderabad Association.

Alikhan, Raza. 1990. *Hyderabad 400 Years*. Secunderabad: Zenith Services.

Allen, Charles, and Sharada Dwivedi. 1984. *Lives of the Indian Princes*. London: Century Publishing.

Ansari, Javed M. 1996. "Last Namaaz in Karachi." *India Today*, April 15.

Ansari, Kiran. 2004. "The American Medina." *Islamic Horizons* 33:5.

Antoun, Richard T. 1998. "Transnational Migration for Higher Education: A Comparison of Jordanians in Greece and Pakistan." Paper presented at the American Anthropological Association, Philadelphia, December 3.

Anwar, Muhammad. 1979. *The Myth of Return: Pakistanis in Britain*. London: Heinemann.

Appadurai, Arjun. 1995. "Playing with Modernity: The Decolonization of Indian Cricket." In *Consuming Modernity: Public Culture in a South Asian World*, edited by Carol A. Breckenridge. Minneapolis: University of Minnesota Press.

———. 1996. *Modernity at Large: Cultural Dimensions of Globalization*. Minneapolis: University of Minnesota Press.

Assisi, Frances. 1989. "Overseas Indians." *India-West*, August 18.

Aziz, Qutubuddin. 1993. *The Murder of a State*. Karachi: Islamic Media Corporation.

Azmi, Shaheen. 1997. "Canadian Social Service Provision and the Muslim Community in Metropolitan Toronto." *Journal of Muslim Minority Affairs* 17:1.

Ballard, Roger. 1994. *Desh Pardesh: The South Asian Presence in Britain*. London: Hurst.

———. 1997. "The Construction of a Conceptual Vision: 'Ethnic Groups' and the 1991 UK Census." *Ethnic and Racial Studies* 20:1.

Banga, Indu, ed. 1991. *The City in Indian History: Urban Demography, Society, and Politics*. New Delhi: Manohar.

Barker, Ralph. 1969. *Aviator Extraordinary: The Sydney Cotton Story*. London: Chatto & Windus.

Basch, Linda, Nina Glick Schiller, and Cristina Szanton Blanc. 1994. *Nations Unbound: Transnational Projects, Postcolonial Predicaments, and Deterritorialized Nation-States*. Amsterdam: Overseas Publishers Association.

Basham, A. L. 1961. *The Wonder That Was India: A Survey of the Culture of the Indian Subcontinent before the Coming of the Muslims*. London: Sedgwick and Jackson.

Bawa, V. K. 1993. *The Last Nizam: The Life and Times of Mir Osman Ali Khan*. New Delhi: Penguin Books.

Bayly, C. A. 1978. "Indian Merchants in a 'Traditional' Setting: Benares, 1780–1830." In *The Imperial Impact: Studies in the Economic History of Africa and India*, edited by Clive Dewey and A. G. Hopkins. London: Athlone Press.

Beetham, David. 1970. *Transport and Turbans*. Oxford: Oxford University Press.

Benichou, Lucien. 2000. *From Autocracy to Integration: Political Developments in Hyderabad State (1938–1948)*. Hyderabad: Orient Longman.

Bertaux, Daniel. 1981. "From the Life-History Approach to the Transformation of Sociological Practice." In *Biography and Society*, edited by Daniel Bertaux. Beverly Hills: Sage.

Bhachu, Parminder. ca. 1985. *Twice Migrants: East African Sikh Settlers in Britain*. New York: Tavistock.

Bhalla, Alok, ed. 1994. *Stories about the Partition of India*. Vol. 1. New Delhi: Indus.

Bilu, Jitendar. 1989. "Bicharti Dhuup." *Hayat-i-Nau* (London), May.

Bindra, Satinder. 1993. "Battle for Betel." *India Today*, August 31.

Boyarin, Jonathan. 1994. "Space, Time, and the Politics of Memory." In *Remapping Memory: The Politics of TimeSpace*, edited by Jonathan Boyarin. Minneapolis: University of Minnesota.

Brettell, Caroline B., and James F. Hollifield. 2000. *Migration Theory: Talking across Disciplines*. New York: Routledge.

Brewer, Jeremy, and John Power. 1993. "The Changing Role of the Department of Immigration." In *The Politics of Australian Immigration*, edited by James Jupp and Marie Kabala. Canberra: Australian Government Publishing Service.

Buchignani, Norman, Doreen M. Indra, and Ram Srivastiva. 1985. *Continuous Journey: A Social History of South Asians in Canada*. Toronto: McClelland and Stewart.

Butt, Helen B., ed. 1990. *The Composite Nature of Hyderabadi Culture*. Hyderabad: Intercultural Cooperation Hyderabad Chapter & Osmania University.

Candland, Christopher. 2000. "Liberalization, Education, and Sectarianism: Pakistan in the 1990s." Paper presented at the Association for Asian Studies, San Diego, Calif., March 11.

Castles, Stephen. 1995. "How Nation-States Respond to Immigration and Ethnic Diversity." *New Community* 21:3.

Castles, Stephen, Bill Cope, Mary Kalantzis, and Michael Morrissey. 1988. *Mistaken Identity: Multiculturalism and the Demise of Nationalism in Australia*. Sydney: Pluto Press.

Cerwonka, Allaine. 1999. "Constructed Geographies: Redefining National Identity and Geography in a Shifting International Landscape." *International Politics* 36:3.

Chambers, Iain. 1994. *Migrancy, Culture, Identity*. London: Routledge.

Chandraiah, K. 1996. *Hyderabad 400 Glorious Years*. Hyderabad: Government of Andhra Pradesh.

Chayya, Mayank. 1995. "Cross-Border Marriages Defy Indo-Pak Tensions." *India Abroad*, November 10.

Clarke, Colin, Ceri Peach, and Steven Vertovec, eds. 1990. *South Asians Overseas: Migration and Ethnicity*. Cambridge: Cambridge University Press.

Clifford, James. 1989. "Notes on Theory and Travel." In *Traveling Theory Traveling Theorists*, edited by James Clifford and Vivek Dhareshwar. Santa Cruz: Center for Cultural Studies.

———. 1997. *Routes: Travel and Translation in the Late Twentieth Century*. Cambridge, Mass.: Harvard University Press.

Climo, Jacob. 1995. "Prisoners of Silence: A Vicarious Holocaust Memory." In *The Labyrinth of Memory: Ethnographic Journeys*, edited by Marea C. Teski and Jacob J. Climo. Westport, Conn.: Bergin and Garvey.

Cohn, Bernard S. 1996. *Colonialism and Its Forms of Knowledge: The British in India*. Princeton: Princeton University Press.

Cole, Juan. 2001. "Iranian Culture and South Asia, 1500–1900." In *Iran and the Surrounding World 1500–2000: Interactions in Culture and Cultural Politics*, edited by Nikki Keddie and Rudi Matthee. Seattle: University of Washington Press.

A Collection of Hyderabadi Limericks. 1994. Hyderabad: SAMHITA.

Copland, Ian. 1988. "Communalism in Princely India: The Case of Hyderabad, 1930–1940." *Modern Asian Studies* 22:4.

Corfield, Justin J. 1993. *The Corfields: a History of the Corfields from 1180 to the Present Day.* VIC, Australia: Corfield & Company.

Correia, Eugene. 2001a. "Media Marvel." *India Today,* January 1.

————. 2001b. "Crusade by Ink." *India Today,* September 10.

Coward, Harold, John R. Hinnells, and Raymond Brady Williams. 2000. *The South Asian Religious Diaspora in Britain, Canada, and the United States.* Albany: State University of New York Press.

Das Gupta, Jyotindira. 1970. *Language Conflict and National Development.* Berkeley: University of California Press.

Dawn. 1992. "Osmania University Old Students Association," November 28.

Deakin, Nicholas, with Brian Cohen and Julia McNeal. 1970. *Colour, Citizenship and British Society: Based on the Race Relations Report.* London: Panther Modern Society.

Dean-Oswald, H. 1988. "Pakistanis." In *The Australian People: An Encyclopedia of the Nation, Its People, and Their Origins,* edited by James Jupp. North Ryde, New South Wales: Angus & Robertson.

Deccan Chronicle. 1993. "Uzbek Envoy Calls on Babur's Descendants," October 21.

Deen, Hanifa. 1995. *Caravanserai: Journey among Australian Muslims.* Sydney: Allen & Unwin.

Desai, Rashmi H. 1963. *Indian Immigrants in Britain.* Oxford: Oxford University Press.

Duncan, Emma. 1988. *Breaking the Curfew.* London: Michael Joseph.

Duncan, James S., and Nancy G. Duncan. 1980. "Residential Landscapes and Social Worlds: A Case-Study in Hyderabad, Andhra Pradesh." In *An Exploration of India: Geographical Perspectives on Society and Culture,* edited by David E. Sopher. Ithaca: Cornell University Press.

Dusenbery, Verne A. 1981. "Canadian Ideology and Public Policy: The Impact on Vancouver Sikh Ethnic and Religious Adaptation." *Canadian Ethnic Studies* 13:3.

Dwivedi, Sharada. 1984. *Lives of the Indian Princes.* London: Century Publishing.

The Economist. 1999. "Canada Survey: Welcome to the World," July 24.

Edwards, John Willoughby. n.d. [ca. 1998]. *A Migrant's Tale.* n.p. [Canberra].

Edwards, Kerry. 2005. *Our Joyous Days: Historical Sketches of St. George's Church and Schools Hyderabad Deccan.* Madras: self-published.

Elliott, Carolyn. 1972. "The Problem of Autonomy: The Osmania University Case." In *Education and Politics in India,* edited by Susanne H. Rudolph and Lloyd I. Rudolph. Cambridge: Harvard University Press.

————. 1974. "Decline of a Patrimonial Regime: The Telengana Rebellion in India, 1946–51." *Journal of Asian Studies* 34:1.

Fentress, James, and Chris Wickham. 1992. *Social Memory.* Cambridge: Blackwell.

"Festival Match and Picnic." 1990. *News and Views* (newsletter of the London Hyderabad Association), May, 3.

400-Year Anniversary of Hyderabad (Deccan) (1591–1990 A.D.). 1990. Kuwait: Assousi & Khan Trading Co.

Friedman, Jonathan. 1997. "Global Crises, the Struggle for Cultural Identity and Intellectual Porkbarrelling: Cosmopolitans versus Locals, Ethnics and Nationals in an Era of De-hegemonisation." In *Debating Cultural Hybridity: Multicultural Identities and the Politics of Anti-racism*, edited by Pnina Werbner and Tariq Modood. London: Zed Books.

Ganju, Sarojini. 1980. "The Muslims of Lucknow—1919–1939." In *The City in South Asia*, edited by Kenneth Ballhatchet and John Harrison. London: Curzon Press.

Garcia y Griego, Manuel. 1994. "Canada: Flexibility and Control in Immigration and Refugee Policy." In *Controlling Immigration: A Global Perspective*, edited by Wayne A. Cornelius, Philip L. Martin, and James F. Hollifield. Palo Alto: Stanford University Press.

Gardezi, Hassan N. 1991. "Asian Workers in the Gulf States of the Middle East." *Journal of Contemporary Asia* 21:2.

———. 1997. "Making of the Neo-Colonial State in South Asia: The Pakistan Experience," *Comparative Studies of South Asia, Africa, and the Middle East* 17:2.

Gay, John. 2000. "Church Schools: A Geography Lesson." *Church Times*, February 11.

Ghose, Zulfikar. 1965. *Confessions of a Native-Alien*. London: Routledge and Kegan Paul.

Gilroy, Paul. 1987. *There Ain't No Black in the Union Jack: The Cultural Politics of Race and Nation*. London: Hutchinson.

Gooneratne, Yasmine. 1993. *A Change of Skies*. Maryborough, Victoria: Picador Australia.

Goulbourne, Harry. 1991. *Ethnicity and Nationalism in Post-Imperial Britain*. Cambridge: Cambridge University Press.

Government of Hyderabad. 1907. *Report on the Administration of His Highness the Nizam's Dominions, for the Four Years 1308 to 1312 Fasli [1898–1903]*. Hyderabad: Government of Hyderabad.

———. 1937. *Seniority and Classified Army List of Officers of H.E.H. the Nizam's Regular Forces*. Hyderabad: Government of Hyderabad.

———. 1938. *Regulations relating to Salary, Leave, Pension, and Travelling Allowances*. Hyderabad: Government Press.

———. 1948. *The Classified List of Officers of the Civil Departments of H.E.H. the Nizam's Government*. Hyderabad: Office of the Controller-General of Audit and Accounts.

Government of Pakistan. 1975–78. *Population Census of Pakistan, 1972: District Census Report*. Vols. 1–49. Islamabad: Census Organisation.

———. 1982. *Statistical Report of Pakistan*. Islamabad: Population Census Organisation.

Grant, Noor. 1995a. "A New Islamic Center in Canada." *The Minaret*, November.

———. 1995b. "Muslim Work in Canada." *The Minaret*, July.

Gunew, Sneja. 1996. "Denaturalizing Cultural Nationalisms: Multicultural Readings of 'Australia.'" In *Nation and Narration*, edited by Homi Bhabha. New York: Routledge.

Gupta, Akhil, and James Ferguson. 1992. "Beyond 'Culture': Space, Identity, and the Politics of Difference." *Cultural Anthropology* 7:2.

Gupta, Aruna Mallya. 1995. "Migration Replay." *India Today*, April 15.

Gupta, Narayani. 1981. *Delhi between Two Empires 1803–1931*. Delhi: Oxford University Press.

————. 1993. "Urban Form and Meaning in South Asia: Perspectives from the Modern Era." In *Urban Form and Meaning in South Asia: The Shaping of Cities from Prehistoric to Precolonial Times*, edited by Howard Spodek and Doris Meth Srinivasan. Washington: National Gallery of Art.

Habib, Abdul Qadar. ca. 1981. *Inglistan Me* [In England]. Dartford, Kent: Academy of Urdu Studies.

————. 1985. "Some Days in Hyderabad." *Siyasat*, May 18.

Hall, Stuart. 1987. "Minimal Selves." In *Identity*, edited by Homi Bhabha. London: Institute of Contemporary Arts.

————. 1988. "New Ethnicities." *Black Film British Cinema*. London: Institute of Contemporary Arts.

————. 1992. "The Question of Cultural Identity." In *Modernity and Its Futures*, edited by Stuart Hall, David Held, and Tony McGrew. London: Polity Press, Open University.

————. ca. 1996. "Politics of Identity." In *Culture, Identity, and Politics: Ethnic Minorities in Britain*, edited by Terence Ranger, Yunus Samad, and Ossie Stuart. Brookfield, Vt.: Avebury.

Handler, Richard. 1985. "On Dialogue and Destructive Analysis: Problems in Narrating Nationalism and Ethnicity." *Journal of Anthropological Research* 41:2.

Hannerz, Ulf. 1987. "The World in Creolisation." *Africa* 57:4.

————. 1992. *Cultural Complexity: Studies in the Social Organisation of Meaning*. New York: Columbia University Press.

Harvey, David. 1990. "Between Space and Time: Reflections on the Geographical Imagination." *Annals of the Association of American Geographers* 80: 3.

Helwig, Arthur S. 1986. *Sikhs in England*. 2nd ed. Delhi: Oxford University Press.

Henson, Harlan N. 1974. "Elites, Language Policy and Political Integration in Hyderabad." Ph.D. dissertation, Department of Education, University of Illinois.

The Hindu. Feb. 15, 1895. In the Clippings Collection, 1890–1904 (three newspaper scrapbooks). Hyderabad: Andhra Pradesh State Archives.

Holston, James, and Arjun Appadurai. 1996. "Cities and Citizenship." *Public Culture* 8:2.

Hudson, Major A. J. Maitland. n.d. [1990?] "Memories: 1st Hyderabad Imperial Service Lancers" (manuscript donated to the India Office Library).

Hussain, Amir. 2004. "Muslims in Canada: Opportunities and Challenges." *Studies in Religion/Sciences Religieuses* 33:3–4.

Hussain, Mushtaba. 1985. "Visit to Paris." *Siyasat*, July 28.

"Hyderabad Festival in London." 1990. *Siyasat*, June 10.

Inglis, Christine. 1995. "Multiculturalism, a Policy Response to Diversity." Draft for UNESCO MOST Program, July 11.

Jagannadham, V. 1969. "Telangana—an Essay in Democratic Conflict-Resolution." *Journal of the Society for the Study of State Government* (Banaras Hindu University), July–September.

Jah, Muffakham. 1993. "Patron's Message." *Festival of Hyderabad London 1993 Souvenir.*

Jayaraman, R. 1988. "Indians." In *The Australian People: An Encyclopedia of the Nation, Its People, and Their Origins,* edited by James Jupp. North Ryde, New South Wales: Angus & Robertson.

———. 1999. "Inclusion and Exclusion: An Analysis of the Australian Immigration History and Ethnic Relations." Unpublished paper.

Johns, Anthony H., and Abdullah Saeed. 2003. "Muslims in Australia: The Building of a Community." In *Muslim Minorities in the West: Visible and Invisible,* edited by Yvonne Yazbeck Haddad and Jane I. Smith. New York: Altamira Press.

Jones, Mary Lucille. 1993. "To Rebuild What Was Lost: The Post-War Years and Beyond." In *An Australian Pilgrimage: Muslims in Australia from the Seventeenth Century to the Present,* edited by Mary Lucille Jones. Melbourne: Victoria Press.

Jung, Ali Yavar. 1983. "Hyderabad in Retrospect." In *Ali Yavar Jung: Commemoration Volume,* Abul Kalam Azad Oriental Research Institute. Bombay: Popular Prakashan.

Jung, Anees. 1987. *Unveiling India.* New Delhi: Penguin.

———. 1990. *The Song of India.* New Delhi: Himalayan Books.

Jung, Nawab Aziz. 1319 Fasli [1909–10]. *Khazina-i-Finance va Hisab.* Hyderabad: Government of Hyderabad.

Jupp, James, ed. 1988. *The Australian People: An Encyclopedia of the Nation, Its People, and Their Origins.* North Ryde, New South Wales: Angus & Robertson.

Jupp, James, and Marie Kabala. 1993. *The Politics of Australian Immigration.* Canberra: Australian Government Public Service.

Jussawala, Meheroo, and Feroza. E-mails from Honolulu and New Mexico, respectively, December 2005.

Kamal, Syed Mustafa. 1990. *Hyderabad Mein Urdu Ki Taraqqi.* Hyderabad: Matbu'at Shagufa Publications.

Kapiszewski, Andrzej. 2001. *Nationals and Expatriates: Population and Labour Dilemmas of the Gulf Cooperation Council States.* Ithaca: Garner Publishing.

Karaka, D. F. 1975. *Fabulous Mogul.* Lahore: Progressive Books.

Kawaja, Kaleem. 2002. "Hyderabad in Washington!" *Pakistan Link,* May 10.

Keith, Michael, and Steve Pile, eds. 1993. *Place and the Politics of Identity.* London: Routledge.

Kennedy, Charles H. 1993. "Managing Ethnic Conflict: The Case of Pakistan." *Regional Politics and Policy* 3:1.

———. 2000. "The Superior Courts and Legal Change in Pakistan since 1997." Paper presented at the South Asia conference, University of California, Berkeley, February 19–20.

Khalidi, Omar. 1990. "Indian Muslim Physicians in the United States." *Azan* (New York), May.

———. 1991. *Memoirs of Cyril Jones: People, Society, and Railways in Hyderabad.* Delhi: Manohar.

———. 1994b. *Memoirs of Sidney Cotton.* Hyderabad: Hyderabad Historical Society.

———. 1997. "From Torrent to Trickle: Indian Muslim Migration to Pakistan, 1947–1997." *Bulletin of the Henry Martyn Institute of Islamic Studies* 16 (January–June).

———. 1998. "How Hyderabad Saved Pakistan from Strangulation at Birth." *Islamic Horizons,* November/December.

———. 1999. "Amazing Abid." *Devon and Cornwall Notes and Queries,* spring.

———, ed. 1988. *Hyderabad: After the Fall.* Wichita, Kan.: Hyderabad Historical Society.

———, ed. 1994a. "Memoirs of Gen Ed-Edroos of Hyderabad." *Quarterly Journal of the Pakistan Historical Society* 42, Part II, April 1994.

Khan, Sairah Irshad. 1989. "Days of Wine and Roses." *Newsline,* December.

Kothari, Shuchi. 2000. "From Genre to Zanaana: Urdu Drama Serials and Women in Pakistan." Paper presented at the South Asian Women conference, Los Angeles.

Kuwait Pocket Guide, 1995. 1995. Kuwait: Multimedia Publishing and Distribution.

Laiq Ali, Mir. 1962. *Tragedy of Hyderabad.* Karachi: Pakistan Cooperative Book Society.

Lamb, Christine. 1991. *Waiting for Allah: Pakistan's Struggle for Democracy.* Calcutta: Viking.

Lateef, Bilkees. 1984. *Her India: The Fragrance of Forgotten Years.* New Delhi: Arnold Heinemann.

Leonard, John. 1973. "Urban Government under the Raj: A Case Study of Municipal Administration in Nineteenth-century South India." *Modern Asian Studies* 7:2.

Leonard, John, and Karen Leonard. 1992. "Viresalingam and the Ideology of Social Change in Andhra." In *Religious Controversy in British India: Dialogues in South Asian Languages,* edited by Kenneth Jones. Albany: State University of New York.

Leonard, Karen Isaksen. 1971. "The Hyderabad Political System and Its Participants." *Journal of Asian Studies* 30:3.

———. 1973. "The Deccani Synthesis in Old Hyderabad: An Historiographic Essay." *Journal of the Pakistan Historical Society,* October.

———. 1978a. "Mulki–non-Mulki Conflict in Hyderabad State." In *People, Princes and Paramount Power: Society and Politics in the Indian Princely States,* edited by Robin Jeffrey. Oxford: Oxford University Press.

———. 1978b. *Social History of an Indian Caste: The Kayasths of Hyderabad.* Berkeley: University of California Press.

———. 1979. "The Great Firm Theory of Mughal Decline." *Comparative Studies in Society and History,* April.

———. 1981. "Bankers in Nineteenth Century Hyderabad State Politics." *Modern Asian Studies* 15:2.

———. 1981–1982."Aspects of the Nationalist Movement in the Princely States of India." *Quarterly Review of Historical Studies* 21: 2 & 3.

———. 1992. *Making Ethnic Choices: California's Punjabi Mexican Americans.* Philadelphia: Temple University Press.

————. 1997. *The South Asian Americans.* Westport, Conn.: Greenwood Press.

————. 1999. "Construction of Identity in Diaspora: Emigrants from Hyderabad, India." In *Expanding Landscapes: South Asians in Diaspora,* edited by Carla Petievich. Delhi: Manohar.

————. 2000. "Hyderabadis in Pakistan: Changing Nations." In *Community, Empire, and Migration: South Asians in Diaspora,* edited by Crispin Bates. London: Macmillan.

————. 2001. "South Asian Leadership of American Muslims." In *Muslims in the West: Sojourners to Citizens,* edited by Yvonne Haddad. New York: Oxford University Press.

————. 2002a. "Reassessing Indirect Rule in Hyderabad: Rule, Ruler, or Sons-in-Law of the State?" *Modern Asian Studies* 36:3.

————. 2002b. "South Asian Women in the Gulf: Families and Futures Reconfigured." In *Trans-Status Subjects: Gender in the Globalization of South and Southeast Asia,* edited by Sonita Sarker and Esha De. Durham, N.C.: Duke University Press.

————. 2003a. "Guests in the Gulf: South Asian Expatriates." In *Globalization under Construction: Governmentality, Law, and Identity,* edited by Richard Perry and William Maurer. Minneapolis: University of Minnesota Press.

————. 2003b. *Muslims in the United States: The State of Research.* New York: Russell Sage Foundation.

————. 2006. "South Asian Religions in the US: New Contexts and Configurations." In *New Cosmopolitanisms: South Asians in the United States at the turn of the 21st Century,* edited by Gita Rajan and Shailja Sharma. Palo Alto: Stanford University Press.

Leonard, Karen I., Alex Stepick, Manuel A. Vasquez, and Jennifer Holdaway, eds. 2005. *Immigrant Faiths: Transforming Religious Life in America.* Lanham, Md.: Altamira Press.

Lepervanche, Marie M. 1984. *Indians in a White Australia: An Account of Race, Class and Indian Immigration to Eastern Australia.* Sydney: George Allen & Unwin.

Lewis, Martin W., and Karen E. Wigen. 1997. *The Myth of Continents: A Critique of Metageography.* Berkeley: University of California Press.

Longva, Anh Nga. 1997. *Walls Built on Sand: Migration, Exclusion and Society in Kuwait.* Boulder, Colo.: Westview Press.

Luther, Narendra. 2006. *Hyderabad, a Biography.* New Delhi: Oxford.

Lynton, Harriett Ronkin, and Mohini Rajan. 1974. *Days of the Beloved.* Berkeley: University of California Press.

Lyon, Michael. 1973. "Ethnicity in Britain: The Gujarati tradition." *New Community* 2.

Marcus, George E. 1995. "Ethnography in/of the World System: The Emergence of Multi-Sited Ethnography." *Annual Review of Anthropology* 24.

Minault, Gail. 1998. *Secluded Scholars: Women's Education and Muslim Social Reform in Colonial India.* Delhi: Oxford University Press.

Minocha, Urmilla. 1987. "South Asian Immigrants: Trends and Impacts on the Sending and Receiving Societies." In *Pacific Bridges: The New Immigration from Asia and the Pacific Islands,* edited by James T. Fawcett and Benjamin V. Carino. New York: Center for Migration Studies.

Mirza, Fareed. 1976. *Pre and Police Action Days in the Erstwhile Hyderabad State: What I Saw, Felt and Did.* Hyderabad: Fareed Mirza.

————. 1996. *Police Action in the Erstwhile Hyderabad State.* Hyderabad: Fareed Mirza.

Mirza, Najmuddin. 1982. "Hyderabad Culture under Nizam." *Pakistan Times*, Lahore, November 5.

Modood, Tariq. 1988. "'Black,' Racial Equality and Asian Identity." *New Community* 14:3.

————. 1992. *Not Easy Being British: Colour, Culture and Citizenship.* London: Trentham Books.

————. 1994. "Political Blackness and British Asians." *Sociology* 28:4.

————. 1999. "British Multiculturalism: Some Rival Positions and Thoughts on the Way Forward." Talk presented at Sociology colloquium, UCLA, spring.

————, ed. 1997. *Church, State and Religious Minorities.* London: Policy Studies Institute.

Modood, Tariq, Richard Berthoud, Jane Lakey, James Nazroo, Patten Smith, Satnam Virdee, and Sharon Beishon. 1997. *Ethnic Minorities in Britain: Diversity and Disadvantage.* London: Grantham Books.

Mohammad, Afzal. 1993. "Socio Economic Structure of Hyderabad City." In *Hyderabad-400: Saga of a City*, edited by K. S. S. Seshan. Hyderabad: Association of British Council Scholars.

Molteno, Marion. 1987. *A Language in Common.* London: The Women's Press.

Moore, Gloria Jean. 1986. *The Lotus and the Rose: An Anglo Indian Story.* Melbourne: River Seine Publications.

————. 1988. "Anglo-Indians." In *The Australian People: An Encyclopedia of the Nation, Its People and Their Origins*, edited by James Jupp. Sydney: Angus & Robertson Publishers.

Mowli, V. Chandra. 1992. *Bridging the "Gulf": India's Manpower Migrations to West Asia.* New Delhi: Sterling Publishers.

Muller, Carl. 1994. *Yakada Yaka: The Continuing Saga of Sonnaboy von Bloss and the Burgher Railwaymen of Sri Lanka.* New Delhi: Penguin.

Murphy, Dervla. 1987. *Tales from Two Cities: Travel of Another Sort.* London: John Murray.

Naidu, Ratna. ca. 1990. *Old Cities, New Predicaments: A Study of Hyderabad.* New Delhi: Sage.

Naim, C. M. 1993. "Exile, Displacement, Hijrat—What's in a Name!" *The Toronto South Asian Review* 11:2.

Naqvi, Dr. Sadiq. 1990. "Hyderabadis in Britain, a Conversation with Syed Masud Ali." *Siyasat*, November 25.

Naqvi, Syed Ansari Hussein. 1984. *Siyasat*, August 19.

Nayar, Salahuddin. 1991. "Writer Parvin Kamal in Frankfurt." *Siyasat*, April 8.

News and Views. 1990. "Festival Match and Picnic," May.

Ong, Aihwa. 1999. *Flexible Citizenship: The Cultural Logics of Transnationality.* Durham, N.C.: Duke University Press.

Pakistan Link. 1995. "Seven Aligarians Ruled Pakistan," December 8.

————. 1997. "Majority of Pakistani Students Prefer to Settle Abroad," March 21.

Papanek, Hanna. 1972. "Pakistan's Big Businessman." *Economic Development and Cultural Change* 21.

Parasher, Aloka. 1991. "Social Structure and Economy of Settlements in the Central Deccan (200 B.C.–A.D. 200)." In *The City in Indian History: Urban Demography, Society, and Politics*, edited by Indu Banga. New Delhi: Manohar.

Parthasarathy, R. 1998. "Raja Rao: A Chronology." In *Word as Mantra: The Art of Raja Rao*, edited by Robert L. Hardgrave, Jr. New Delhi: Katha.

Parvez, Kausar. 2000. "Woman Scientist Honored." *Pakistan Link*, November 17.

Paul, Joginder. 1998. *Sleepwalkers*. New Delhi: Katha.

"The Pauper Prince." 1999. *The Australian Magazine* April 3–4.

Pernau, Margrit. 2000. *The Passing of Patrimonialism: Politics and Political Culture in Hyderabad 1911–1948*. Delhi: Manohar.

Powell, Avril. 1996. "Perceptions of the South Asian Past: Ideology, Nationalism and School History Textbooks." In *The Transmission of Knowledge in South Asia: Essays on Education, Religion, History, and Politics*, edited by Nigel Crook. Delhi: Oxford University Press.

Prashad, Vijay. ca. 2000. *The Karma of Brown Folk*. Palo Alto: Stanford University Press.

Ramanujan, A. K. 1970. "Towards an Anthology of City Images." In *Urban India: Society, Space and Image*, edited by Richard G. Fox. Durham, N.C.: Duke University Press.

Ramusack, Barbara N. 2004. "The Indian Princes and Their States" (*The New Cambridge History of India* 3:6). Cambridge: Cambridge University Press.

Rao, K. V. N. 1969. "Separate Telangana State?" *Journal of the Society for the Study of State Government* (Banaras Hindu University), July–September.

Razvi, Aziz. ca. 2000. *Betrayal: A Political Study of British Relations with the Nizams of Hyderabad*. Karachi: South Asia Publications.

Rizvi, Fazal. 1996. "Racism, Reorientation and the Cultural Politics of Asia-Australia Relations." In *The Teeth Are Smiling: The Persistence of Racism in Multicultural Australia*, edited by Ellie Vasta and Stephen Castles. St. Leonards, New South Wales: Allen and Unwin.

Rouse, Roger. 1992. "Making Sense of Settlement: Class Transformation, Cultural Struggle, and Transnationalism among Mexican Migrants in the United States." In *Towards a Transnational Perspective on Migration: Race, Class, Ethnicity, and Nationalism Reconsidered*, edited by Nina Glick Schiller, Linda Basch, and Cristina Blanc-Szanton. New York: New York Academy of Sciences.

Russell, Ralph. 1982. *Urdu in Britain*. Karachi: Golden Block Works.

Safran, William. 1991. "Diasporas in Modern Societies: Myths of Homeland and Return." *Diaspora* 1:1.

Safrani, Shehbaz, ed. 1992. *Golconda and Hyderabad*. Bombay: Marg Publications.

Salahuddin. 1991. "Hyderabad Association in Florida." *Siyasat*, October 13.

Sassen, Saskia. 1996. "Whose City Is It? Globalization and the Formation of New Claims." *Public Culture* 8:2.

Saxena, Dr. Siddeshwar Raj. n.d. [1988?] "Body in London, Heart in Hyderabad." *Siyasat* n.d.

Schiller, Nina Glick, Linda Basch, and Cristina Blanc-Szanton, eds. 1992. *Towards a Transnational Perspective on Migration: Race, Class, Ethnicity, and Nationalism Reconsidered.* New York: New York Academy of Sciences.

———, eds. 1995. "From Immigrant to Transmigrant: Theorizing Transnational Migration." *Anthropological Quarterly* 68:1.

Schrager, Samuel. 1983. "What Is Social in Oral History?" *International Journal of Oral History* 4:2.

Seshan, K. S. S., ed. 1993. *Hyderabad-400: Saga of a City.* Hyderabad: Association of British Council Scholars.

Shakeb, Dr. Ziauddin. 1990. "Indian Immigrants in Britain." *Siyasat*, September 2.

Sharieff, Afzal. 1994. "Socio-Economic Transformation of the Kuwaiti Repatriates—a Case Study of Hyderabad." Ph.D. dissertation, Department of Geography, Osmania University.

Sherwani, H. K. 1966. "The Osmania University, First Phase: The Urdu Medium (1917–1948)." In *Dr. Ghulam Yazdani: Commemoration Volume*, edited by H. K. Sherwani. Hyderabad: Maulana Abul Kalam Azad Oriental Research Institute.

Shryock, Andrew. 1995. "Writing Oral History in Tribal Jordan: Developments on the Margins of Literate Culture." *Anthropology Today* 11.

———. 1996. "Tribes and the Print Trade: Notes from the Margins of Literate Culture in Jordan." *American Anthropologist* 98:1.

———. 1997. *Nationalism and the Genealogical Imagination.* Berkeley: University of California Press.

———. 2000. "Public Culture in Arab Detroit: Creating Arab/American Identities in a Transnational Domain." In *Mass Mediations: New Approaches to Popular Culture in the Middle East and Beyond*, edited by Walter Armbrust. Berkeley: University of California Press.

Silvey, Rachel, and Victoria Lawson. 1999. "Placing the Migrant." *Annals of the Association of American Geographers* 89:1.

Sirajuddin, Syed. 1990. "Deccan-Hyderabadi Culture." Hyderabad, private manuscript.

Siyasat. 1984. "An Evening with Ali Sardar Jaferi in London," December 10.

———. 1985. "London Is a Second Hyderabad," April 22, 1985.

———. 1990. "Hyderabad Festival in London," June 10.

———. 1990. "Hyderabad Association's Annual Mushaira in London," November 24.

Slesin, Suzanne, and Stafford Cliff. ca. 1990. *Indian Style.* New York: C. N. Potter.

Smith, W. C. 1950. "Hyderabad: Muslim Tragedy." *The Middle East Journal* 4:1.

Spodek, Howard, and Doris Meth Srinivasan, eds. 1993. *Urban Form and Meaning in South Asia: The Shaping of Cities from Prehistoric to Precolonial Times.* Washington: National Gallery of Art.

"Sports and Hyderabad." 1993. In *Festival of Hyderabad London 1993.* London: Hyderabad Association.

Springer, Richard. 2001. "Indian Americans Double in Census." *India-West*, May 18.

Srivastava, Sanjay. 1998. *Constructing Post-Colonial India: National Character and the Doon School*. New York: Routledge.

———. 2005. "Ghummakkads, a Woman's Place, and the LTCwalas: Towards a Critical History of 'Home,' 'Belonging,' and 'Attachment.'" *Contributions to Indian Sociology* 39:3.

Sunder Rajan, Rajeswari. 2003. *The Scandal of the State: Women, Law, and Citizenship in postcolonial India*. Durham, N.C.: Duke University Press.

Tambiah, Stanley. 2000. "Transnational Movements, Diaspora, and Multiple Modernities." *Daedalus* 129:1.

Tanvir, Naqi. 1991. "A Distinguished Hyderabadi Doctor in Britain." *Siyasat*, January 13.

Thrift, Nigel. 1996. *Spatial Formations*. London: Sage.

Tilak, Visi R. 1996. "Boom in Business." *India Today*, March 31.

Tillotson, Sarah. 1998. *Indian Mansions: A Social History of the Haveli*. Hyderabad: Orient Longman.

Tololyan, Khachig. 1996. "Rethinking Diaspora(s): Stateless Power in the Transnational Moment." *Diaspora* 5:1.

Uberoi, Narindar. 1964. "Sikh Women in Southall." *Race: The Journal of the Institute of Race Relations* 7:1.

Ugra, Sharda. 2000. "Fallen Hero." *India Today*, October 18.

van Buitenen. J. A. B. 1966. "On the Archaism of the Bhagavata Purana." In *Krishna: Myths, Rites, and Attitudes*, edited by Milton Singer. Honolulu: East-West Center Press.

Varshney, Asutosh. 1997. "Postmodernism, Civic Engagement, and Ethnic Conflict: A Passage to India." *Comparative Politics*, October.

Vasta, Ellie, and Stephen Castles, eds. 1996. *The Teeth Are Smiling: The Persistence of Racism in Multicultural Australia*. New South Wales: Allen and Unwin.

Vatuk, Sylvia. 1990. "The Cultural Construction of Shared Identity: A South Indian Family History." *Social Analysis* 28.

———. 2004. "Hamara Daur-i Hayat: An Indian Muslim Woman Writes Her Life." In *Telling Lives in India: Biography, Autobiography, and Life History*, edited by David Arnold and Stuart Blackburn. Bloomington: Indiana University Press.

Verkaaik, Oskar. 1994. *A People of Migration: Ethnicity, State, and Religion in Karachi*. Amsterdam: VU University Press.

Vijayakar, R. M. 2003. "Apollo Hospitals: 20 Years of Extraordinary Achievement." *India-West*, October 10.

Wallman, Sandra, ed. 1979. *Ethnicity at Work*. London: Macmillan.

Waseem, Mohammad. 2001. "Mohajirs in Pakistan: A Case of Nativization of Migrants." In *Community, Empire, and Migration: South Asians in Diaspora*, edited by Crispin Bates. London: Macmillan.

Watson, James, ed. 1977. *Between Two Cultures: Migrants and Minorities in Britain*. Oxford: Basil Blackwell.

Watt, Michael J. 1991. "Mapping Meaning, Denoting Difference, Imagining Identity: Dialectical Images and Postmodern Geographies." *Geografiska Annaler* 73B.

Weiner, Myron. 1990. "The Indian Presence in America: What Difference Will It Make?" In *Conflicting Images: India and the United States*, edited by Sulochana Raghavan Glazer and Nathan Glazer. New York: Riverdale.

Weiss, Anita M. 1999. "Much Ado about Counting: The Conflict over Holding a Census in Pakistan." *Asian Survey* 34:4.

Werbner, Pnina. 1990. *The Migration Process: Capital, Gifts and Offerings among British Pakistanis.* Oxford: Berg.

———. 1991. "The Fiction of Unity in Ethnic Politics: Aspects of Representation and the State among British Pakistanis." In *Black and Ethnic Leaderships in Britain: the Cultural Dimentions of Political Action,* edited by Tariq Modood and Pnina Werbner. New York: Routledge.

———. 1998. "Exoticising Citizenship: Anthropology and the New Citizenship Debate." *Canberra Anthropology* 21:2.

———. 1999. "Global Pathways, Working Class Cosmopolitans and the Creation of Transnational Ethnic Worlds." *Social Anthropology* 7:1.

Werbner, Pnina, and Muhammad Anwar, eds. 1991. *Black and Ethnic Leaderships in Britain: The Cultural Dimensions of Political Action.* London: Routledge.

Werbner, Pnina, and Tariq Modood, eds. 1997. *Debating Cultural Hybridity: Multi-Cultural Identities and the Politics of Anti-Racism.* London: Zed Books.

Williams, Raymond. 1961. *The Long Revolution.* Westport, Conn.: Greenwood Press.

———. 1973. *The Country and the City.* New York: Oxford University Press.

Wiltshire, Rosina. 1992. "Implications of Transnational Migration for Nationalism: The Caribbean Example." In *Towards a Transnational Perspective on Migration: Race, Class, Ethnicity, and Nationalism Reconsidered,* edited by Nina Glick Schiller, Linda Basch, and Cristina Blanc-Szanton. New York: New York Academy of Sciences.

Winckler, Onn. 2005. *Arab Political Demography.* Vol. 1. Portland: Sussex Academic Press.

Wright, Theodore P., Jr. 1974. "Indian Muslim Refugees in the Politics of Pakistan." *Journal of Commonwealth and Comparative Politics* 12:2.

———. 1991. "Center-Periphery Relations and Ethnic Conflict in Pakistan: Sindhis, Muhajirs, and Punjabis." *Comparative Politics* 233, April.

———. 1994. "Can There Be a Melting Pot in Pakistan? Interprovincial Marriage and National Integration." *Contemporary South Asia* 3:2.

Yans-McLaughlin, Virginia. 1990. "Metaphors of Self in History: Subjectivity, Oral Narrative, and Immigration Studies." In *Immigration Reconsidered: History, Sociology, and Politics,* edited by Virginia Yans-McLaughlin. New York: Oxford University Press.

Yarwood, A. T. 1964. *Asian Migration to Australia: The Background to Exclusion, 1896–1923.* Parkville: Melbourne University Press.

Yazdani, Zubaida Yazdani (with Mary Chrystal). 1985. *The Seventh Nizam: The Fallen Empire.* Zubaida Yazdani: Cambridge University Press.

Zahlan, Rosemarie Said. 1989. *The Making of the Modern Gulf States: Kuwait, Bahrain, Qatar, the United Arab Emirates, and Oman.* London: Unwin Hyman.

Zaidi, Abbas. 1984. "Hyderabadis in London." *Siyasat,* November 18.

Zainallahuddin, Syed. 1991. "Chicago's Vicinity: Asians' Best Living Places." *Siyasat,* October 13.

JOURNALS, NEWSPAPERS, AND WEBSITES CONSULTED
(cited in endnotes by dates, no authors or titles)

Deccan Chronicle (Hyderabad, India)
http://deccanhyderabad.org. (Toronto, Canada)
Hyderabad Cultural Society (Arlington: Hyderabad Cultural Society of North Texas)
India Journal (Santa Fe Springs, California)
India-West (Fremont, California)
Islamic Horizons (Plainfield, Illinois)
Los Angeles Times (Los Angeles, California)
News and Views (London: Hyderabad Deccan Association).
Pakistan Link (Newport Beach, California)
Sydney Morning Herald (Sydney, Australia)
Tahzeeb-e-Deccan (Houston: Hyderabad Cultural Association)
Telegraph Magazine (London, UK)
The Australian (Australia)
The Daily Telegraph (London, UK)
The Economist (London, UK)
The Friday Times (Islamabad, Pakistan)
The Letter (Chicago: Hyderabad Foundation)
The Sunday Times (London, UK)
The Times (London, UK)
The Toronto Star (Toronto, Canada)

AUSTRALIA INTERVIEWS (1993)

Adams, Ernest. Perth, November 21.
Ali Khan, Shahana. Melbourne, November 12.
Balm, Marian. Perth, November 21.
Bangera, Farha. Melbourne, November 15.
Bangera, Farha and Ajit, and guests. Melbourne, November 13.
Bellingham, the Reverend and Mrs. C. E. W. Sydney, November 4.
Chamarette, Kathleen, with Norma Oates et al. Perth, November 22.
Chamarette, Stamford. Melbourne (telephone), November 10.
Corfield, Blossom and Charles, with son Joe Corfield and daughter Christine Wates, Melbourne, November 14.
Corfield, Joyce. Sydney, November 8.
Corfield, Justin. Melbourne, November 13.
Cox, Betty. Melbourne (telephone), November 18.
Cox, Bruce. Melbourne, November 15.
Cox, Emile. Melbourne, November 15.
Cyrus Pestonjee, Sydney, November 7.
D'Costa, Anne and Bernie. Perth, November 19.
Dean-Oswald, Hanifa. Perth, November 23.

Devlin, Barney and Heather, with Jean and Jackie Luschwitz, Kathleen Chamarette, Jerry and Mrs. Howlett, and Mathew and Leslie Devlin. Perth, November 20.
Fallon, Dennis. Melbourne (telephone), November 17.
Hussain, Fahmi. Sydney, November 7.
Hussain, Kazim and Mrs. Sydney, November 7.
Norton, Alex and Christopher. Sydney, November 10.
Oates, Norma, with daughters Joy and Gillian and sister Iris, Kathleen Chamarette and her daughter Louise, and (briefly) Norma's son Tim, grandson Christian, Gillian's husband Vince and daughter Esra, and an India-born Sikh neighbor. Perth, November 22.
Pestonjee, Cyrus and Khurshed. Sydney, November 7.
Qadri, Dr. S. Bader. Sydney, November 6.
Rajah, Kamala. Perth, November 22.
Rao, Dr. and Mrs. K. Hemchander. Sydney, November 9.
Rao, Dr. K. Hemchander. Sydney, November 7.
Schoeffer, Dick. Melbourne (telephone), November 17.
Schoeffer, Donald and Winifred. Perth, November 20.
Siddiqui, G. Q., Sydney (telephone), November 4.
Singh, Supriya. Melbourne, November 10.
ul Jabbar, Dr. Mateen, with Dr. Farhat Ali Khan, Shehnaz Ali Khan, Sabiya ul Jabbar, Amjad Hussain, Maqbul Hussain, Samat Makri, Shahid Sayeed, Tahir uddin Meraj and Tahur Meraj, Dr. Amin, Rafi Ahmed, Dr. Majeed Siddiqui, Zahiruddin Ahmed, Abdur Rahman, Qutb Khan, Nazir, Mrs. and Mrs. Mussaffar, Zafar Shah Khan, Zaheer, and Ahmedullah. Melbourne, November 12.
Weinman, David. Perth, November 22.
Westrip, Joyce and Charles. Mount Washington, November 21.
Zaroque, Syed Murtaza. Sydney, November 7.

CANADA INTERVIEWS (1994 UNLESS INDICATED)

Alikhan, Asif and Mrs., with Desh and Zehra Bandhu. Mississauga, August 1.
Alikhan, Husna. Mississauga, August 1.
Ashraf, Shahbaz. Montreal, July 2–3, 2000.
Asmatullah, Colonel M. Toronto, August 1.
Bandhu, Desh and Zehra. Mississauga, July 29 and 31.
Bandhu, Desh and Zehra, Fareeda and Fawad Baig, Asima and Aijz Ahmed, Kuldip and Mrs. Chohan. Toronto, July 29.
Beig, Sabiha, with her mother. Toronto, July 31.
Hussein, Ather. Toronto, August 1.
Isaacs, Enid. Toronto (telephone), August 3.
Jabbar, Razaul, and Mohammad Abdul Aleem, Abbas Syed, Ahmed Khan, Qazi Syed Abdul Kamal, Laila Kamal. Toronto (telephone), August 3.
Khan, Fehmida. Montreal, July 2, 2000.
Lodhi, Ghulam Mohammed Khan. Toronto, July 30.
Mirza, Farooq and Shehnaz. Toronto, July 30.

Mirza, Rashida, and her mother. Toronto, August 2.
Moos, Firoz and Parvez. Montreal, July 2, 2000.
Qayyum, Kamal Razvi, and Halim Yusuf Siddiqui. Toronto, August 1.
Siddiqui, Haroon. Toronto, August 2.

INDIA INTERVIEWS (HYDERABAD UNLESS SPECIFIED)

Adiga, Dr. Khurshed. Secunderabad, October 15, 1993.
Ahmed, Hasanuddin. October 10 and 16, 1991.
Akbar, Javed. October 14, 1992.
Ali, Mehdi. October 5 and 26, 1993.
Ali, Mohammed Shamsher, and Amatas Salam Aina Siddiqui. October 10, 1991.
Ali Khan, Abid. September 24, 1991.
Ali Khan, Ather and Mrs., with Lalitha Gir. October 5, 1993.
Ali Khan, Justice Sardar. September 28, 1991.
Ali Khan, Rasheed. October 4, 1993.
Ali Khan, Sardar. September 28, 1991.
Alikhan, Asif and Fatima. October 17, 1991; November 10, 1991.
Alikhan, Raza. November 5, 1991.
Alikhan, Asif. October 13, 1993.
Alladin, Bilkiz. October 17, 1991.
Ayyangar, A. Krishnaswamy and Mrs. October 24, 1991.
Bilgrami, Miriam, and Khadija Mehdi. October 21, 1991.
Butt, Dr. Helen. October 31, 1991.
Chenoy, Yadgar and Gul, with Polly Chenoy. November 10, 1991.
De, Anil, and Mrs. October 20, 1991.
De, Mrs. Anil. October 20, 1991.
Dhangoria, Dhiraj and Mrs. October 27, 1993.
Dua, Asha. November 5, 1991.
Edwards, J. W., and Lyn. October 20, 1991.
Ekbote, Gopalrao, with Gurucharan Das Saxena. October 30, 1991.
Gir, Chandrakant. October 9, 1993; January 23, 1997.
Gir, Chandrakant and Lalitha. October 10, 1993; January 8, 1997.
Gir, Dilip. January 3 and 7, 1997.
Gir, Lalitha. September 25, 1991; October 25, 1991.
Hamida Begum, with Lalitha Gir. September 25, 1991.
Heda, Dr. and Mrs. Harish Chandra, with Gurucharan Das. October 30, 1991.
Hemchander. B. V. Secunderabad. November 10, 1991.
Husain, Dr. Yousuf. October 18, 1993.
Hussain, Abdul Azrat, and Shoukat Hussain. October 9, 1991.
Imam, Vikar Shaikh and Mrs. October 28, 1993.
Jaffari, Mrs. Sayeda Suraiya, and daughters. November 2, 1991.
Jah, Prince Muffakham. December, 2003.
Kemal, Dr. and Dr. Rahimuddin. November 6, 1991.
Khan, Anees. October 12, 1993.
Khan, Khusro Yar, with his wife Nafissa, her sisters Shamim and Farida, and Lalitha Gir. October 7, 1993.

Khan, Lateef Khan, with Mehdi Ali and Amjad Ali Khan. October 21, 1993.
Khurso, A. M. Delhi, November 3, 1993.
Koratkar, Bhavana and Kavita. October 3, 1991.
Lateef, I. H. and Bilkees. October 6, 1993.
Luther, Narendra. October 6, 1991.
Mehdi, Khadija, with Miriam Bilgrami. October 21, 1991.
Mirza, Fareed. October 10, 1993.
Mohiuddin, M. Nizam. October 29, 1991.
Muslim, Mohammed and Mrs., with Lalitha Gir. October 25, 1991.
Muttalib, M. A. October 14, 1991.
Naqvi, Dr. Sadiq. November 2, 1991.
Patel, Mumtaz, with Sarojini Singh, Lalitha and Chandrakant Gir, and B. V. Hemchander. Secunderabad, October 17, 1993.
Paul, Raja, with Gurucharan Das Saxena. October 30, 1991.
Qayyum, Rashid, and Syed V. Javeed. October 12, 1993.
Raj, Lakshmi Devi. October 27, 1993.
Raman, B. N. September 26, 1991.
Rao, Bhale, and family, with Lakshmi Devi Raj. October 30, 1993.
Rao, B. Narsing. October 23, 1991.
Rao, Justice and Mrs. P. Rama. November 7, 1991.
Rao, P. Vaman, with Gurucharan Das Saxena. October 30, 1991.
Reddy, Dr. Dharma and Mrs. October 13, 1993.
Reddy, Justice Pingle Jogan Mohan. September 28 or 29, 1991.
Reddy, Mr. and Mrs. Gopal. October 10, 1993.
Roy, Hemansu. November 11, 1991.
Saleem, S. A. 1991, 1992.
Sanghi, Parmanand and Shanta. October 26, 1993.
Saxena, Gurucharan Das. September 23, 1991.
Shahzaman, Khurshid. Secunderabad, October 10, 1993.
Sharief, Afzal. November 11, 1991.
Sirajuddin, Dr. Syed. November 3, 1991.
Somsunder, K. G. October 29, 1991.
Tucy, Ziauddin, and Masihuddin Tucy, October 21 and 22, 1993.
Umapathi, Mr. and Pushpa. September 25, 1991.
Vithal, B.P.R. and Mrs. October 18, 1993.
Yasir Ahmed, with Sheikh Tayab Bazaraf, and other Barkas Arab Association members, Abid, and Ashutosh Varshney. October 23, 1993.
Zaidi, Abbas. October 1 and November 4, 1991.
Zehra, October 1 and 6, 1991.

KUWAIT INTERVIEWS (1995)

Abuddin, Zainul, with Baliya and Bad Shah Khan. August 5.
Affandi, Tahar and Husna, with Mr. and Mrs. Abdur Rauf Qazmi, Fazlur Haq, Mohammed Mukarram Khan, and Anwar Khurshed. August 8.
Ahmed, Khaja Idris. August 2.

Azimuddin, Aqueel and Rizwana. August 2.
Beg, Mirza Shamsher Ali. July 31, August 2, 3, 4, 9.
Bilgrami, Syed M. (with others intermittently present). August 1.
Habib-al-Deen, with Mirza Shamsher Ali Beg. August 9.
Habib-al-Deen and son Mohammed Zaneer, Abdul Mateen Khan, and Qadir Naqvi. August 9.
Hyder, Mr. and Mrs. Taqi, and son Zulfiqar. August 10.
Jain, D. P. August 3.
Karim, Mohammed Abdul, with Mr. Ehtashamuddin; M. Nizamuddin Ahmed, Mohammed Habib-al-Deen and son Mohammed Zaneer, Abdul Mateen Khan, and Qadir Naqvi. August 9.
Khan, Akbar. August 5 and 6.
Khan, Hidayat. August 2.
Khan, Mohammed Hoshdar, with Mir Ibrahim Ali Khan. August 7.
Mirza, Parveen, and daughters. August 5.
Mirza, Shahid Ali and Parveen. August 1.
Mujeebuddin, Abu Turab and Mrs. August 8.
Mukarram, Mujeebulla. August 10.
Nazmuddin, Hamad. July 31; with Mrs. Nazmuddin, August 3 (both with Shamsher Ali Beg).
Prasad, A. G., and Abdur Rahman, August 2.
Qureshi, Iqbal and Mrs. Qureshi. August 3.
Rao, Dr. Naidu Venkat. August 9.
Shankar, Kola. August 5.
Sharfuddin, Dr. and Mrs. K. M. and Syed Masood, with Mirza Shamsher Ali Beg. August 9.
Ur Rahman, Syed Mehmood and Mrs. August 11.
Yousufuddin, Mohamed. August 3.

PAKISTAN INTERVIEWS

Ahmed Khan, Mushtaq. Lahore, August 29, 1992, and September 6, 1993.
Alam, Tami. Lahore, September 5, 1993.
Ali, Dr. and Mrs. Ehsan. Peshawar, September 18, 1993.
Ali, Masood with Abdul Hadi. Lahore, August 31, 1992.
Ali, Mehmood, with Hameed Qureshi and Fatima Suraiya. Karachi, September 8, 1992.
Ali, Mrs. Munawar. Karachi, August 29, 1993.
Ali Khan, Mehmood, with Abdul Hadi. Lahore, August 26, 1992.
Ali Khan, Yusuf and Mrs. Peshawar, September 19, 1993.
Anwer, Brigidier Mustafa. Lahore, September 7, 1993.
Asim, Mahboob Ali. Lahore, September 7, 1993.
Ata-Ullah, Naajish, and Farida Said. Lahore, September 5, 1993.
Auj, Habibullah. Lahore, September 8, 1993.
Baig, Ahmed Faruq, with A. A. Jabbar and Majid Baig. Karachi, September 7, 1992.
Baig, Captain Massoud. Karachi, August 26, 1993.

Baig, Hesky. Karachi, September 2 and 6, 1992.
Baig, Majid. Karachi, August 28, 1993.
Baig, Majid, and Mrs. Sakia Qureshi, Mrs. Rooha and Himayat Syed Haque. Karachi, September 7, 1992.
Baleequddin, Syed Shah. Karachi, September 5, 1992.
Barkatullah, Mrs., and son. Karachi, August 27, 1993.
Bin Ahmed, Lieutenant Colonel Ali. Karachi, September 5, 1992.
Bin Nasir, Major Aslam, with daughter, Colonel Ali, and Colonel Raheem. Karachi, August 30, 1993.
Cooper, Mrs. Mehera, with a Panjwani son. Lahore, August 29, 1992.
El-Edroos, Syed Hussein. Islamabad, September 18, 1995.
Hussain, Commodore and Mrs. K.M. Karachi, September 9, 1992.
Hussein, Azra. Lahore, September 12 and 13, 1995.
Jabbar, A. A. Karachi, September 6 and 7, 1992; August 25, 1993.
Khan, Abdur Razak. Islamabad, September 21, 1993.
Khan, A. R., and son. Karachi, August 28, 1993.
Khan, Mr. and Mrs. M. A. Rashid. Karachi, August 27, 1993.
Masihuddin, Khwaja and Sadia and Humaira. Islamabad, September 22, 1993.
Masihuddin, Mr. and Mrs. Khwaja, and daughter Humaira. Islamabad, September 22, 1993.
Mushtaq, Naseem. Karachi, August 26, 1993.
Naseem, Waheeda. Karachi, September 5, 1992.
Osmani, M. Farooq Ali. Karachi, August 30, 1993.
Parvaiz, Syed Sabir and Mrs. Islamabad, September 22, 1993.
Pestonjee, Jal and Mrs. Lahore, August 26, 1992.
Qadeer, Dr. A. A. Karachi, August 26, 1993.
Qamar, Syed Khan. Islamabad, August 21, 1993.
Qizilbash, Begum Afsar Riza. Lahore, August 26, 1992.
Qureshi, Hameed. Karachi, September 10, 1992.
Rasheed, Nayyer Ehsan. Karachi, August 28, 1993.
Samdani, Justice, and his daughters Batur and Annie. Lahore, September 22, 1993.
Sayeed, Shamim. Karachi, September 12, 1992.
Sayeed, Shamim, and Sultana Basith and Mahbubiyah "old girls'" luncheon, Karachi, September 10, 1992.
Shah, Asadullah. Lahore, September 10, 1993.
Siddiqui, Dr. and Mrs. Abdul Hafeez. Karachi, September 8, 1992.
Siddiqi, Dr. and Mrs. M. Raziuddin. Islamabad, August 22, 1992.
Siddiqui, Rizwana. Peshawar, September 19, 1993.
Suraiya, Fatima. Karachi, September 8, 1992.
Tahrir-Kheli, Shirin. Islamabad, September 16, 1993.
Uddin, Dr. Muneer. Karachi, September 4, 1992.
ur-Rehman, Aziz, and son. Karachi, August 29, 1993.
uz-Zaman, Maseeh and Mrs. Karachi, August 25, 1993.
Waheed, Bushra, and five other Hyderabadi women. Lahore, September 12, 1993.

Waheed, Mrs. Bushra. Lahore, September 7 and 26, 1993.
Yousuf, Mohamed and Mehrukh. Islamabad, September 13, 1992.
Zaidi, Farhad. Islamabad, September 16, 1993.
Zaidi, Farhad and Mrs. and son Ali. Islamabad, September 15, 1993.

UAE INTERVIEWS (1995)

Adil, Junaid and Ayesha (see Ali Ishrati dinner party). Dubai, August 21.
Aijaz. Dubai, August 15.
Ali, Maqsood and Anees. Dubai, August 13, 14, 18.
Ali, Mir Miraj, with Ahmed and Mrs. Hassan, Abu Dhabi, August 24.
Ali, Mir Miraj, with Anees and Maqsood Ali. Dubai, August 18.
Arif, Mohamed Hussain and Donut, with Anees and Maqsood Ali. Dubai, August 26.
Arsalan, Mirza (see Ali Ishrati dinner party). Dubai, August 21.
Bozai, Hasan. Dubai, August 20.
David, Anthony. Dubai, August 15.
De Souza, Arun. Dubai, August 16.
Ellis, Elizabeth, Mavis, and Fred, with Anees Ali. Dubai, August 26.
Hassan, Ahmed and Mrs., with Mir Miraj Ali. Abu Dhabi, August 24.
Ishrati, Ali and Zehra, with Ayesha and Junaid Adil, Sarosh and Moin, and Mirza Arsalan. Dubai, August 21.
Jabbar, Muhammed Abdul, with his brother Mohammed Mahmood and Anees and Maqsood Ali. Sharjah, August 20.
Khan, Drs. Ashfaq and Razia. Dubai, August 19; Umm al-Qawain, August 21.
Ramachandran, Sharjah, August 20.
Rao, Mahesh Jetty Maheshwar. Dubai, August 16.
Razvi, Mehdi Abbas, with Salim Hashimi. Dubai, August 16.
Sajan Lal, Ghulam Ali. Dubai, August 26.
Sarosh, and Moin (see Ali Ishrati dinner party). Dubai, August 21.
Shekhar, Vinaya. Dubai, August 19.
Singh, Vipin. Dubai, August 23.
Walajahi, Sharafat. Dubai, August 15.
Walajahi, Sharafat and Sultana, with M. A. Saleem, Shoukatullah, Surender Singh, Hasan Bozai, Taufiq Baig, Mrs. Zulfiquar, Mrs. Wasee Muneem, and the Naeem Qavis (dinner party). Dubai, August 17.

UK INTERVIEWS

Adams, Jimmy. Croydon, December 14, 1992.
Ahmed, Amina Tahira, with Jack Hudson. London, August 28, 1991.
Ahmed, Aziz. London, August 29, 1991.
Ali Khan, Majid. Harrow, September 4, 1991.
Ali Khan, Mir Mohsin. London, August 28 and September 4, 1991.
Ali Khan, Mustafa. London, August 29 and 30, 1991.
Gay, Dr. Dennis P. London, August 29, 1991.

Hudson, Jack. Golders Green, August 28 and September 2, 1991; Chislehurst, December 17, 1992.
Hyderabadi, Akbar, with Aziz Ahmed. Oxford, September 24, 2002.
Jah, Prince Muffakham. London, December 9, 1992.
Jah, Princess Esin. London, September 1, 1991.
Khan, Humayun Yar. London, September 2, 1991.
Mandozai, Wajih Dad Khan. London, September 4, 1991.
Quraishi, Salim. London, December 9, 1992.
Reddy, V. Keshav. London, August 30, 1991.
Saxena, Dr. Siddeshwar Raj, with Aziz Ahmed. London, August 29, 1991.
Siddiqui, Adeel Yousuf. Wembley, August 31, 1991.
Yazdani, Mr. and Mrs. Ghulam. London, September 2, 1991.
Yazdani, Zubaida, with Yasin Ali Khan, Aziz Ahmed, and Ziaudddin Shakeb. London, September 3, 1991.

U.S. INTERVIEWS

Ahmed, Bashir and Shakila. Arlington, Texas, March 18, 1993.
Ahmed, Irshad. Washington, D.C., November 19, 1995.
Ali, Amir. Chicago, July 11, 1993.
Ali, Dr. Mir Mohiuddin. Washington, D.C. (telephone), February 2, 1992.
Ali, Faizi Akbar. Lomita, California, June 23, 1993.
Ali, Meher. Oakbrook, Illinois, November 25, 1991,
Ali Khan, Zulfiqar. Chicago, July 10, 1993.
Asad, Dr. S. N. Huntington, New York (telephone), January 29, 1992; with C. S. Tibrewal and J. McCully, March 3, 1993.
Babu Khan, Shafi and Calliope. Pacific Palisades, California, November 4, 1992.
Baig. Mirza Ahmed. January 22, 1995, Fremont, California; Hayward, November 23, 1996.
Chishti, Hasan, with Zulfiqar Ali Khan, Dr. Baseer, Shoaib Khan, and Dr. Yusuf Azmi. Chicago, July 10, 1993.
de Souza, Noel. Los Angeles, July 15, 1992.
Farooqui, Bilquees. Chicago, July 13, 1993.
Farooqui, Dr. M. M. Chicago, July 12, 1993.
Farooqui, Dr. M. M., with Dr. Aejaz Hashmi and Dr. Khurshed Khan. Chicago, July 10, 1993.
Farooqui, Zubair. Chicago, July 12, 1993.
Ghafoor, Sara. Houston, Texas, March 22, 1993.
Ghatala, M. Habeeb. Bala Cynwyd, Pennsylvania, December 4 and 6, 1998.
Haq, Dr. Talib-ul. Sacramento (telephone), September 17, 2004.
Hasan, Akbar and Rehana. Los Angeles, July 3, 1992.
Hasan, Suraya. Chicago, July 11, 1993.
Hashmy, Asif Ali and Khatija. Chicago, November 24, 1991; July 12 and 13, 1993.
Hassan, Dr. Shakeela. Chicago, November 24, 1991.

Hussain, Donna and K. M. Sacramento, March 20, 1994.
Ibrahim, Shamim. Torrance, California, July 3, 1993.
Jah, Prince Muffakham. Buena Park, California, October 11, 1992.
Khalidi, Usama and Nayeema. Reston, Virginia, April 5, 1992.
Khan, Laura and Feroze. April 30–May 1, 1995, Dallas, Texas; Los Angeles, December 26–28, 1995.
Khan, Noshir. Malibu, California, June 23, 1993.
Kumar, V. Krishna. Philadelphia, Pennsylvania, December 3, 1998.
Lateef, Ahmed. Sherman Oaks, California, May 4, 1992.
"Mahdi" (pseudonym). (telephone) July, 1993.
Mamida, Anand and Leela. Davis, California, March 20, 1994.
Mathur, Kishen Dayal. Washington, D.C., November 18, 1995.
Mirza, Javeed and Mahjabeen. Brooklyn, New York, March 12, 1993.
Mohan, Dr. Madhu. Washington, D.C., April 5, 1992.
Mushtaq, Mahmood. Houston, Texas, March 22, 1993.
Naim, C. M. Chicago, July 12, 1993.
Rasheed, Suraiya. Los Angeles, June 29, 1993.
Razvi, Aziz and Habiba. San Diego, California, January, 1994.
Razvi, Khalid. Houston, Texas (telephone), July 23, 1995.
Rizvi, Syed and Shahnaz. Missouri City, Texas, April 25, 1995.
Roy, Ram Mohan. Northridge, California, July 10, 1991.
Saeed, Ayesha and Ashfaq. Los Angeles, July 3, 1993.
Safrani, Shehbaz. New York, March 12, 1993.
Samee, Dr. Syed. Fullerton, California, November, 1990.
Syed, Ahsan and Mrs. Palo Alto, California, May 31, 1992.
Ulla, Niloufer. San Jose, California, June 1, 1992.
Ulla, Shahana. San Jose, California, June 1, 1992.

Glossary

adab, adab arz	respects, respects and honor [to you]; common salutation among Hyderabadis
ADC	aide-de-camp; an officer serving as assistant and confidential secretary to a superior officer
Babri Masjid	sixteenth-century mosque in Ayodhya, northern India, connected with Babur, the first Mughal emperor; the political crisis caused by its destruction in 1992 by Hindu fanatics
bagara baigan	eggplant in tamarind sauce, a distinctive Hyderabadi dish
banghra	vigorous line dance from the Punjab region of South Asia
bharata natyam	South Indian classical dance, originally connected with Hindu temples and worship
bindi	red dot on a woman's forehead; beauty spot
biryani	fragrant steamed rice dish, usually made with chicken or mutton
BJP	Bharatiya Janata Party; a Hindu nationalist political party in India
burqah	full body covering for Muslim women in purdah
Char Minar	the Four Minarets, historic building at the heart of Hyderabad's old city
chowki	*chowki* dinner; style of eating seated on the floor around a tablecloth
daftardar	recordkeeper, in the Mughlai Hyderabad administration
Dakhni	correct transliteration of Deccani, or southern, referring to the plateau on which Hyderabad is situated
dal	a lentils dish
dam ka kebab	roasted kebab, usually beef or mutton
dastar	the style of turban associated with the Nizam of Hyderabad and his noblemen
dastarkhan	tablecloth, laid on the floor or lawn
Deccan	the south, as in the Deccan plateau on which Hyderabad is situated
dinar	the currency unit of Kuwait
dirham	the currency unit of the United Arab Emirates

Diwali	the harvest festival or festival of lights; the new moon day ending the fortnight of the month of Karttika, and for some communities also New Year's Day; national holiday in India
diwan	prime minister, in the Mughlai Hyderabad administration
dupatta	long scarf, draped by women over the head or bodice
Dusserah	new moon day the month before Diwali, when ancestors and/or occupational tools are commemorated; national holiday in India
ghair-mulki	non-mulki, foreigner
ghazal	musical renditions of Persian or Urdu poetry
hajj	annual pilgrimage to Mecca, enjoined on all Muslims who can afford it once in a lifetime
halal	permitted by Islam, lawful; for food, the equivalent of kosher among Jews
hijab	head covering, headscarf
hijra	emigration of Muhammad from Mecca to Medina in 622 C.E.; also, the name of the South Asian community of men of all religious backgrounds who have become eunuchs or transgenders, dressing as women and dancing to commemorate the birth of children
Holi	spring festival, usually connected with the god Krishna and involving bonfires and the throwing of colored water on people; national holiday in India
Id	two Islamic festivals: Id al-Adha, the festival of sacrifice on the last day of the annual hajj (often called Bakr Id because goats, bakr, are the usual sacrifice); Id al-Fitra, the festival of the breaking of the annual fast for the month of Ramadan, when Muslims take no food or water from sunup to sundown
imam	Muslim preacher, cleric
jagirdar	holder of *jagirs*, large grants of land; a nobleman in the Mughlai Hyderabad administration
kalipot	black wedding necklace, usually associated with South Indian Hindus
khara dupatta	long scarf worn by Hyderabadi brides over short bodice
khatti	sour, tamarind taste
kotwal	municipal commissioner, city magistrate, and police commissioner, in the Mughlai Hyderabad administration
kurti choli	short bodice; part of the Hyderabadi bridal attire
majlis	mourning session, held by Shia Muslims during the month of Muharram to commemorate the death of Husain (he was the son of the fourth caliph of Islam [the Prophet's son-in-law and cousin Ali]; Husain's death in the battle of Karbala in 680 C.E. initiated the division between Sunnis and Shias in Islam); also, men's social gathering in the UAE
maths	Hindu temple or monastery
M.B.B.S.	Bachelor of Medicine and Bachelor of Surgery; South Asian equivalent of an American M.D.

mirch ka salan	green chilis in a tamarind sauce, a distinctive Hyderabadi dish
MQM	Muhajir Qaumi Movement; political party formed by immigrants from India, based in Karachi, Pakistan
muhajir	one who has performed the *hijra* or migrated; Muslims from India who moved to Pakistan after Partition in 1947
mulki	countryman, native; citizen of Hyderabad State
mushaira	event featuring poetry recitations, usually Persian or Urdu
namaste	salutation, of Sanskritic and therefore Hindu origin; common Indian greeting: slight bow with joined hands pointed upward before the chest
nikah	the signing of the official Islamic marriage certificate, the wedding ceremony hosted by the bride's family; part of Hyderabadi Muslim weddings
pan	betel nut and condiments wrapped in betel leaf
pandan	silver box containing the ingredients for *pan*; accessory of Hyderabadi women
peshkar	deputy prime minister, in the Mughlai Hyderabad administration
purdah	seclusion of women, accomplished through separate seating, separate rooms, or head or body coverings (hijab or burqah)
qawwali	Sufi Muslim devotional singing in Persian, Punjabi, or Urdu
Ramadan	the lunar month of fasting; *see* Id al-Fitra
roti	bread, ranging from English-style white bread to many varieties of Indian bread
RSS	Rashtriya Sevaka Sangam; Hindu fundamentalist political party in India
rukhsati	the consummation of the marriage, the homecoming of the bride, in Hyderabadi Muslim weddings; can be long after the *nikah* ceremony
rumi topi	Turkish cap, fez
rupee	unit of currency in India and Pakistan
salam, salam aleikum	peace, peace be with you; Islamic salutation
salvar kamiz	women's clothing, long overshirt and baggy pants, originally from North India
samasthans	small hereditary kingdoms, recognized and incorporated by the Hyderabad administration
shari'a	Islamic law, general term including several schools of Islamic law
sherwani	long, high-collared men's suit jacket, the Nehru jacket; originally from North India
valima	reception held by the groom's family the night after the *nikah* ceremony and reception held by the bride's family; part of most Hyderabadi weddings
zamindar	major landholder, in the Mughlai Hyderabad administration

Index

parents arriving in, 155, 163–164; connections to Hyderabad, 167–170; context of migration to, 35, 44–48; Hyderabadi associations in, 156–159; identity politics in, 47–48; immigration law of 1965, 137; Islamic activities in, 159–162; latest arrivals in, 153–156; Pakistani Hyderabadis migrating to, 82; post-1965 immigrants in, 144–153; pre-1965 immigrants in, 137–144; research methodology and, 7, 8, 9, 11; second-generation Hyderabadis in, 138, 164–167; Urdu literary activities in, 162–163; waves of immigrants to, 136–137, 170; women's activities in, 163–164; women sent for marriage in, 268
University of Hyderabad, 30, 31, 32
Urdu: in Australia, 124, 125, 126, 129, 132, 133, 322*n*64; in Canada, 173, 175, 177, 179, 180, 181, 183–187; culture associated with, 6–7, 293*n*56; diasporic adaptations of, 225, 263, 264, 275, 278; educational system and, 20, 22, 23, 26, 263, 291*n*40; in Gulf states, 191, 246; Hindustani language and, 26, 51; Hyderabad as stronghold of, 6, 13; of Hyderabadi migrants, 9; Hyderabadi version of, 14, 19, 263, 278, 358*n*15; as Hyderabad state language, 20; in Kuwait, 193, 194, 195, 206, 337*n*11; of muhajirs, 35–36; newspapers publishing in, 224–225, 248 (*see also* Siyasat); Nizam's ruling class and, 13, 18; in Pakistan, 66, 67, 78, 79, 91, 264; in present-day Hyderabad, 28, 30, 246, 250, 255–256; transnational connections of, 341*n*48; in United Arab Emirates, 210, 264; in UK, 86, 90, 96, 97–99, 103–104, 312*n*29; in United States, 147–148, 150–151, 153, 155–160, 162–163, 330*n*47, 332*n*64. *See also* mushairas
Urdu Hall, 290*n*29
Urdu Markaz, 163, 332*n*64
ur-Rahman, Aisha and Habib, 144, 328*n*26

U.S. Agency for International Development (USAID), 137
U.S. Information Service (USIS), 137–138, 151, 152, 155, 239, 357*n*89

Vatuk, Sylvia, 348*n*12, 356*n*80
Vellodi, M. K., 25, 113
Viresalingam, Pandit, 293*n*56

Watt, Michael, 52
weddings, 270–273; cosmopolitanism and, 276; dress for, 162, 204, 265; of Hyderabadis in Canada, 179, 214; of Hyderabadis in Pakistan, 67, 70, 83, 306*n*64; of Hyderabadis in United States, 162, 214; of Kuwait resident in Hyderabad, 339*n*31; second generation's choices for, 267; travel for, 265–266; of UK second generation, 106, 107; of U.S. immigrants in Hyderabad, 160–161, 271. *See also* marriage
Werbner, Pnina, 3, 5, 287*n*13, 296*n*55
West Asia, 54
Williams, Raymond, 6
Wolfe, Michael, 326*n*12
women: Australian Muslim attitudes toward, 127; British Hyderabadis, 108; Canadian Muslims, 183; empowered by earnings abroad, 55; going abroad on their own, 251, 255; in Kuwait, 193, 199, 202, 204, 205, 206; of modernizing Hyderabad, 226, 247, 248–251; as Pakistan immigrants, 61–62, 64–65; in public sphere, 250–251, 264; in United Arab Emirates, 154, 214–216; in United States, 137, 139, 143, 149, 152, 163–164. *See also* gender; hijab
Wright, Theodore P., Jr., 300*n*4

Yemen, 51

Zia ul Haq, 37, 68, 69, 300*n*6
Zore, Mohiuddin Qadri, 23, 290*n*29, 306*n*65, 326*n*5